Physical Activity for Individuals With Mental Retardation

Infancy Through Adulthood

Carl B. Eichstaedt, PhD
Illinois State University

Barry W. Lavay, PhD
California State University, Long Beach

Human Kinetics Books
Champaign, Illinois

Library of Congress Cataloging-in-Publication Data

Eichstaedt, Carl B.
  Physical activity for individuals with mental retardation / Carl
B. Eichstaedt, Barry W. Lavay.
    p. cm.
  ISBN 0-87322-361-6
  1. Physical education for mentally handicapped persons. 2. Mental
    retardation. I. Lavay, Barry Wayne. II. Title.
GV445.E35 1992
796'.0196—dc20   91-42283
                                                              CIP

ISBN: 0-87322-361-6

Photos on pages 1, 69, 145, 255, 321, and 383 courtesy of Special Olympics International.

Photos on pages 3, 259, and 301 courtesy of Carl Eichstaedt.

Photos on pages 35 and 195 by Ken Regan, courtesy of Special Olympics International.

Photo on page 109 courtesy of Bob Fraley.

Photo on page 143 by Mike Hubred, courtesy of Special Olympics International.

Photo on page 173 courtesy of Jim DePaepe.

Photo on page 359 by Rhett Arens, courtesy of Special Olympics International.

Acquisitions Editor: Richard Frey, PhD
Developmental Editor: John Robert King
Managing Editor: Julia Anderson
Assistant Editors: Laura Bofinger, Julie Swadener, Valerie Hall
Copyeditor: Wendy Nelson
Proofreader: Dawn Barker
Indexer: Theresa Schaefer
Production Director: Ernie Noa

Typesetters: Ruby Zimmerman and Kathy Boudreau-Fuoss
Text Design: Keith Blomberg
Text Layout: Tara Welsch, Denise Peters, Denise Lowry
Cover Design: Jack Davis
Cover Photo: Special Olympics International
Interior Art: Gretchen Walters and Tim Offenstein
Printer: Edwards Brothers

Printed in the United States of America

10 9 8 7 6 5 4 3 2 1

Human Kinetics Books
A Division of Human Kinetics Publishers, Inc.
Box 5076, Champaign, IL 61825-5076
1-800-747-4457

Canada Office:
Human Kinetics Publishers, Inc.
P.O. Box 2503, Windsor, ON N8Y 4S2
1-800-465-7301 (in Canada only)

Europe Office:
Human Kinetics Publishers (Europe) Ltd.
P.O. Box IW14
Leeds LS16 6TR
England
0532-781708

Although retarded children may be victims of fate, they will not be the victims of our neglect.

John Fitzgerald Kennedy, 1963

Contents

Preface

Physical Activity for Individuals With Mental Retardation: Infancy Through Adulthood is based on the conviction that physical activity is for everyone! All persons—including those with mental retardation—must have the opportunity to experience the joys and benefits that physical activity can bring. If people with mental retardation are to derive health, social, vocational, and personal benefits from physical activity, it must be integral to their everyday lives. And because participation in physical activity is so much a part of our society, if people with mental retardation are to be accepted and to function in the mainstream of society, movement competency is imperative.

We decided to write this book to provide comprehensive and up-to-date information for students and professionals regarding physical activity for people with mental retardation. Since 1980, extensive changes in methodology and techniques used for individuals with disabilities have evolved from both empirical and experimental practices. Within the area of mental retardation, new terminology has developed and better research has provided a growing knowledge base.

Often in the past, those with mental retardation have simply been left on their own for physical activity or, worse, excluded from it altogether. But it has been demonstrated that, provided enriched movement experiences through quality instruction, persons with mental retardation can learn and benefit from physical activity. However, quality instruction for these individuals cannot occur by chance; it requires

a systematic approach of assessment, program planning, prescription, teaching, and evaluation. This process requires great instructor flexibility in order to meet the unique needs of each individual.

We have included in the book realistic instructional strategies gleaned from adapted/special physical education, traditional physical education, therapeutic recreation, recreation, special education, physical therapy, occupational therapy, kinesiotherapy, and the medical professions. There remains a need to combine and synthesize the many unique and outstanding methods and techniques offered by these various disciplines. We have attempted to remove barriers often erected by professional elitism and to develop a working model that professionals among the different disciplines can use to benefit persons with mental retardation. Although we include many theoretical models, we emphasize basic information that can be used by everyday practitioners. College students, the future professionals, will find innumerable ideas, lists, games, and suggestions. We have worked to provide a state-of-the-art discussion for a variety of readers, both students and professionals, with varied backgrounds and whose goal is to provide a meaningful quality of life for individuals with mental retardation.

Although this book specifically examines persons with mental retardation, with classifications ranging from mild to profound, our premise is that everyone is a person first, and a person with a disability second. Degrees of mental retardation exist along a continuum, with each individual possessing distinct and different abilities. Our focus is on ability rather than disability. Much of the theory and practical application we present can be used with all persons, not just those with mental retardation.

This book offers a life-span approach by examining physical activity programming from infancy to adulthood, and the information provided follows the protocol of Public Law (PL) 94-142, the Education for All Handicapped Children Act of 1975 (currently known as PL 101-476, the Individuals With Disabilities Education Act of 1990). Also, because of the new emphasis placed on infants and preschool children found to be "at risk," specific attention is given to PL 99-457, Part H, the Education of Children with Disabilities Amendments of 1986.

Physical Activity for Individuals With Mental Retardation is divided into three parts and 12 chapters. Part I, "Foundations and Implications of Mental Retardation," introduces the complicated and exciting world of physical activity for people with mental retardation. Its four chapters chart the history and development of education for persons with mental retardation and the legal implications for programming in the 1990s; discuss disabling conditions often found in combination with mental retardation and the related development of movement skills and physical fitness; present assessment procedures for interpreting test data to make appropriate placement and programming decisions; and thoroughly discuss behavior management procedures for successful instruction.

Part II, "Program Development and Implementation," begins with a step-by-step progression from assessment through evaluation, using the Individualized Education Plan (IEP) as the basic format and emphasizing cooperation among all professionals and parents. We discuss the challenge of integrating in activity individuals with mental retardation and those without disabilities, analyzing the issue of least restrictive environment and providing program strategies. We then present options for programming in the areas defined in PL 94-142: physical fitness, fundamental motor skills, aquatics, and dance.

Part III, "Physical Activity for a Life Span," comprehensively addresses physical activities for persons of all ages with mental retardation, from infancy through adulthood, and examines Special Olympics International, the most visible sport organization in the world for persons with mental retardation.

The four appendixes provide information on associations, sign language, normative data for physical and motor fitness, and health-related fitness items that can be modified for persons with mental retardation.

We hope that you will never lose sight of your critical role in the development of those who come under your guidance. Don't underestimate the physical, emotional, social, and cognitive benefits of positive experiences in exciting physical activity programs. No one with mental retardation should be excluded from the opportunity to participate in satisfying and enriching physical activity—and you can help ensure that the doors to activity are opened.

Carl B. Eichstaedt
Barry W. Lavay

Acknowledgments

We wish to acknowledge the following people. Rob King, our developmental editor at Human Kinetics, who had the unique ability to understand our commitment and at the same time allow new blood and creativity to flow into what could have been sterile words and unimaginative phrases. He was a pleasure to work with. To Pat Krebs, of Special Olympics International, who critically reviewed the entire manuscript and also made invaluable contributions to the chapter on Special Olympics. Her insight is greatly appreciated. Finally, we thank Human Kinetics Publishers for believing in us from the beginning and allowing us to develop a very specialized book . . . to guide but not dictate, to suggest but not demand, to organize but not destroy. As publishers go, we rank them with the very best.

My (CBE) professional life has allowed me many accomplishments, and the completion of this book is one of the most rewarding. None of my gains would have been possible without the constant encouragement and dedication of my wife, Donna. She has been a wonderful and exciting force in my life. Thus, to her, I dedicate this book.

I (BL) would like to thank my parents, who have always been supportive of my efforts; Don Brown, who taught me discipline; Carl Eichstaedt, who pushed me in the right direction; Ron French, who in the beginning guided me in my writing; Mick, Keith, and Bruce, who provided the inspiration; and Cherie, for listening. Finally I would like to dedicate this book to my wife, Penny—thanks for helping me keep this all in perspective, Hon.

PART I

Foundations and Implications of Mental Retardation

Part I consists of four chapters. Chapter 1, "Overview of Mental Retardation," begins by defining and clarifying terminology, classifications, and etiologies (causes), and thoroughly discusses the debate over how many individuals have mental retardation. We divide the physical domain, a main focus of this book, into the major areas of physical education, therapeutic recreation, physical therapy, occupational therapy, kinesiotherapy, and athletics; and we discuss the concept of a transdisciplinary approach. Our cursory review of the history of individuals with mental retardation begins with the 19th century and progresses into the 1990s. Included is an in-depth analysis of PL 94-142, the Education for All Handicapped Children Act of 1975 (currently known as PL 101-476, the Individuals With Disabilities Education Act of 1990) and

1

its subsequent amendments, with special reference to physical education, recreation, therapy, and athletics for individuals with mental retardation.

Chapter 2, "Conditions Related to Mental Retardation," explores numerous disabling conditions often found in individuals with mental retardation, including cerebral palsy, seizures, spina bifida, congenital heart defects, visual and hearing impairments, and obesity. We identify safety concerns and give program suggestions.

Chapter 3, "Assessment: The First Step," focuses on the critical role that assessment plays in establishing excellence in physical activity programs for individuals with mental retardation. We discuss current assessment practices and the justification for assessment, including proper referral and screening procedures, all in reference to PL 94-142 and its specific directives. We then discuss proper test selection, interpretation of data, streamlining the assessment process, and the use of standardized or informal test batteries. A survey is provided of standardized assessment instruments that pertain to motor skill development and physical fitness performance.

Chapter 4, "Behavior Management," presents specific techniques, program suggestions, and research dealing with behavior management and behavior modification. Behavior management is thoroughly defined, and readers are given the opportunity to follow the design of a behavior management program for an individual with mental retardation through a series of steps that terminate in final program evaluation. Procedures are discussed for maintaining or strengthening desirable behaviors and reducing or eliminating undesirable behaviors. Strategies are given for guiding individuals with severe or profound mental retardation and for coping and interacting with individuals who are being violent or self-injurious.

CHAPTER 1

Overview of Mental Retardation

PREVIEW   Cory was 12 years old, confused, concerned, and unhappy. He and his parents had just moved from another state, and things were not going well for him. It was the end of Cory's second week at the junior high school and he had no friends, he didn't know a single teacher, he often got lost in the unfamiliar maze of halls and rooms, and worst of all, no one seemed to care. Even the physical education teacher told him, in no uncertain terms, that he would need different gym clothes and that his Chicago Cubs T-shirt would not do.

His classmates were also different from the ones in his other school. He found an uncomfortable mixture of *different* boys and girls—some black, some Oriental, some Hispanic, and even one boy who wore an unusual small round cloth hat that sat snugly on the back of his head (when Cory came to school this morning, a teacher reminded him to take off his Cubs baseball hat and to not wear it inside the building—why was this other boy allowed to wear *his* hat?). Also, in his math class there was a girl in a wheelchair. He didn't know what was wrong with her, but she seemed to be nice and was constantly smiling, not to mention that she had the right answers when the teacher asked questions.

In his 10:00 PE class, he met a boy whose name was Franklin. Franklin *was* different! Cory had heard about kids like him, and there was even a TV program whose star had a condition like Franklin's—it was called Down syndrome. The teenager was friendly, and it appeared that most of the other kids liked him, although there were three or four others who made fun of him behind his back. Franklin had difficulty with some of the skills and games in PE, but the teacher was helpful and encouraging. Yesterday, Cory and Franklin were on a relay team together, and although Franklin couldn't run as fast as the others, he sure seemed to be trying his hardest. Cory wondered why Franklin was so much shorter than the other kids, and why his hands and fingers were so stubby. Franklin wasn't in any of Cory's other classes, and when he asked, someone said Franklin was retarded, which probably meant he couldn't learn like the rest of the students. Cory wished he knew more about Franklin, and the girl in the wheelchair. Did these kids learn differently? Were they able to take regular PE classes, or did they have to be in special groups? What did they do for fun after school? Cory was confused, and it seemed there was no one to answer his questions.

HIGHLIGHT QUESTIONS

- **What is mental retardation, and what causes it?**
- **How many people in our society today have mental retardation, and how severely are they affected?**
- **How has education of those with mental retardation evolved from the 1800s to today?**
- **What areas are contained in the physical domain?**
- **What can professionals contribute to the development of motor skill and physical fitness of individuals with mental retardation?**
- **What is the future of physical activity for those with mental retardation?**

With the approach of the year 2000, numerous groups that focus on individuals with mental retardation are attempting to examine the issues and challenges such persons will face in the coming century. School administrators, teachers, recreation leaders, rehabilitation teams, communities, and the medical profession, to name a few groups, are finding that special planning is essential, but also extremely difficult, particularly in light of the complexity of issues that will face society in the 21st century (Hilton, 1988).

In an attempt to provide new and useful information, we have incorporated physical education, therapy, and recreation, whose foundations demand movement. Meaningful and controlled movement has many interesting components, including strength, endurance, agility, fundamental skills, and coordination. All have a bearing on how movement is used: for example, to protect ourselves, to feed ourselves, to move from place to place, to perform vocational pursuits, and to enjoy leisure activities. In a world of movement, extreme emotional and social complications often arise for an individual who cannot move easily. For those with mental retardation, whose motor skills are often far below average, improved physical and motor skills can help add reward and excitement to their quality of life.

Defining Mental Retardation

Most authorities use the term *mental retardation* in referring to someone who scores below 70 or 75 on a standardized IQ test. Other commonly used synonyms include *handicapped*, *impaired*, or *disabled*. Different "levels," or classifications, of retardation also have dual labels. For example, a youngster with an IQ of 60 could be classified as educable mentally handicapped (EMH) or mildly mentally retarded —both terms are accepted, and they are often used interchangeably. The same is true for *trainable mentally handicapped* (TMH) and *moderately mentally retarded*, terms used for those with IQ scores lower than 50. A local school district may establish different terminology within the constraints of its state's special education unit. For example, a particular district may feel the word *retarded* is negative and stigmatizing and substitute *impaired*, *handicapped*, or *disabled* in its place.

Though we understand the differing opinions on this issue, we have decided to use the term *mental retardation* in this text, following the lead of the majority of experts in the field. We also will favor the phrase "person with mental retardation" because we believe these individuals are persons first, and are persons with mental retardation second.

Mental retardation, as defined by the American Association on Mental Retardation (AAMR) and accepted by most authorities, "refers to significant subaverage general intellectual functioning existing concurrently with deficits in adapted behavior and manifested during the developmental period" (Grossman, 1983, p. 11). More specifically this definition means the following:

- *General intellectual functioning* pertains to the results found by appropriate testing and the use of one or more standardized test batteries developed to measure intellectual quotient (IQ). General intelligence is "reflected in the pervasive manner in which we respond to everyday challenges, the speed with which we learn and the complexity and scope of material we can understand, the curiosity and interest we show in a range of subjects or in one engrossing problem, the intricacy of the problems we can solve" (Spitz, 1988, p. 2).
- *Significantly subaverage* refers to an IQ of 70 or below, although the upper limit is often extended to 75 or more, depending on the reliability of the particular test battery used (Grossman, 1983). See Table 1.1.

Table 1.1 Classifications of Mental Retardation

	Classification source		
Level	AAMR[a] (1983)	DSM-III-R[b] (1987)	ICD-9[c] (1980)
Mild	50-55 to approx. 70	50-70	50-70
Moderate	35-40 to 50-55	25-49	25-49
Severe	20-25 to 35-40	20-34	20-34
Profound	Below 20-25	Below 20	Under 20

Note. From "Classifications of Mental Retardation as a Function of Intellectual Functioning" by J.R. Patton, and E.A. Polloway. In *Exceptional Children and Youth* (5th ed.) (p. 203) by N.G. Haring, and L. McCormick (Eds.), 1990, Columbus, OH: Merrill. Copyright © 1990, 1986, 1982, 1978, 1974 by Merrill Publishing Company. Reprinted with permission of Merrill, an imprint of Macmillan Publishing Company.

[a]AAMR. American Association on Mental Retardation

[b]DSM-III-R. Diagnostic & Statistical Manual of Mental Disorders-Revised

[c]ICD-9. International Classification of Diseases World Health Organization

- *Deficits in adaptive behavior* are seen as outstanding limitations in effectively meeting general standards of maturation, learning, personal dependence, and/or social responsibility for youngsters of similar age and cultural group. Again, these deficits must be determined by clinical assessment and, hopefully, standardized scales. Specific examples and comparisons of adaptive and maladaptive behavior are shown in Table 1.2.
- *Developmental period* is defined as the time between conception and 18 years of age.

Although the definition of mental retardation has been well established, Zigler and Hodapp (1986) believe that it is extremely difficult, if even possible, to arrive at a good working definition.

> Social adaptation is not a well-defined construct; it varies across subcultural groups, changing societal expectations for various age groups, and important life changes for each individual (e.g., losing a job). Since this sort of imprecision may spare some individuals from and subject others to the mental retardation label, it creates a poorly defined clinical entity. It also makes the job of describing the mentally retarded population virtually impossible. (p. 91)

The AAMR is in the process of revising the definition of mental retardation. The proposed definition of mental retardation refers to substantial limitations in certain personal capabilities. It is manifested as significantly subaverage intellectual functioning, existing concurrently with related disabilities in two or more of the following adaptive skill areas: communication, self-care, home living, social skills, community use, self-direction, health and safety, functional academics and work. Mental retardation begins before age 18 but may not always be of lifelong duration.

Table 1.2   Major Areas Assessed by the American Association for Mental Retardation Adaptive Behavior Scale—Public School Version

Area	Measures
Part I	
Physical development	Physical development
Cognitive development	Language
	Number and time concepts
Functional skills	Independent living
	Economic skills
	Vocational skills
Volitional domains	Self-direction
	Responsibility
Socialization	Socialization
Part II	
Social maladaptation	Violent and destructive behaviors
	Antisocial behavior
	Rebellious behavior
	Untrustworthy behavior
Personal maladaptation	Odd mannerisms
	Eccentric habits
	Odd speech patterns
	Self-abusive behavior
	Hyperactive behavior

Note. From *Teaching the Mentally Retarded Student: Curriculum, Methods, and Strategies* (p. 12) by R.L. Luftig, 1987, Boston: Allyn & Bacon. Copyright © 1987 by Allyn & Bacon. Reprinted by permission.

Determining Classification Levels of Mental Retardation

Grossman (1983) lists five critical points to use when determining whether an individual is mentally retarded (see Highlight 1.1).

It may be necessary to classify individuals with mental retardation, but it is difficult to do so accurately, and results are often disputed. Educational, psychological, and developmental theorists can be diametrically opposed in their views on who is mentally retarded and why they are mentally retarded.

HIGHLIGHT 1.1

IN PRACTICE

Procedure for Determining Level of Retardation

1. Recognize that a problem exists (e.g., delay in developmental milestones).
2. Determine that an adaptive behavior deficit exists.
3. Determine measured general intellectual functioning.

4. Make decision about whether or not there is retardation of intellectual functioning.
5. Make decision about level of retardation as indicated by level of measured intellectual functioning.

Note. From *Classification in Mental Retardation* (p. 13) by H.J. Grossman (Ed.), 1983, Washington, DC: American Association on Mental Retardation. Copyright 1983 by American Association on Mental Retardation. Reprinted by permission.

The American Psychiatric Association's IQ ranges are generally consistent with those listed by the AAMR, except for a narrow band at each end of each level, where the psychologist, psychiatrist, or diagnostician may use clinical judgment regarding pertinent information, including scores.

The single most common determinant of cognitive ability is the use of a standardized intelligence test battery. California has totally forbidden the use of IQ test scores, but most states deem them necessary. Zigler and Hodapp (1986) observe:

We must begin with the clear understanding that mental retardation is not a homogeneous entity and that individuals labeled mentally retarded (IQs between 0 and 70) are extremely heterogeneous in regard to the cause of their retardation, their levels of cognitive ability, and the adjustments they make to society. The only common element displayed by all retarded persons (by any definition of mental retardation) is that at some point in their lives they display a level of cognitive functioning below that of the average individual of the same age in our society. (p. 105)

The Implications of Labeling Individuals With Mental Retardation

Although social implications of classification systems are often debated, labeling appears to be necessary. The innate problems are highlighted by Hobbs (1975):

Classification can profoundly affect what happens to a child. It can open doors to services and experiences the child needs to grow in competence, to become a person sure of his worth and appreciative of the worth of others, to live with zest and know joy. On the other hand, classification, or inappropriate classification, or failure to get needed classification—and the consequences that ensue—can blight the life of a child, reducing opportunity, diminishing his competence and self-esteem, alienating him from others, nurturing a meanness of spirit, and making him less a person than he could become. Nothing less than the futures of children is at stake. (p. 1)

A major conflict has arisen over inappropriate labeling and resultant negative placement of students based on standardized IQ tests. Some students are placed into special education classes based solely on IQ scores. Opponents of this process point out both that an overwhelming number of these are minority students, and that all of these students experience the negative social effects of separate placement and the "self-fulfilling prophecy" that if you don't expect much from a child, you won't get much. This problem is more evident with youngsters labeled having mild mental retardation.

The most influential legal case pertaining to inappropriate labeling was the 1979 *Larry P. v. Wilson Riles*. Further appeals in 1984 and 1986 confirmed the 1979 decision. Reschly (1988) describes the current status regarding the *Larry P.* case: "The most recent action [1986] . . . establishes a comprehensive ban on the use of IQ tests with black students for any conceivable purpose. Moreover, school districts are even forbidden from requesting permission to use IQ tests with black students" (p. 286). Although this legal decision is binding in California, other states have chosen to disregard the decision.

Three other major court cases provide a totally different outlook on the use of standardized tests. They have found that instead of causing harm, these tests assure special education services for children with special needs. In the 1980 Illinois case of *PASE v. Hannon*, the use of an IQ test battery was upheld despite the overrepresentation of black children in educable mentally retarded special education classes. The ruling judge determined that IQ tests had few, if any, biases, and that any biases that existed in present-day IQ test batteries were overcome by due process procedures. A second case that produced similar conclusions is the 1985 Georgia case of *Marshall v. Georgia*. It was decided that as long as the state followed the AAMR classifications for mental retardation, the court could not ban overrepresentation of minorities in special education programs or establish rigid cutoff scores for general intellectual ability and adaptive behavior (Reschly, 1988). Similar issues were debated in Florida, 1986 *S-1 v.*

Turlington. The trial judge, after hearing several weeks of testimony, agreed that the plaintiffs had failed to show possible harm to black students classified as mildly mentally retarded (Reschly, 1988).

In these three cases, the lawyers were able to convince the courts that mildly mentally retarded children did not possess biological differences, comprehensive incompetence, and permanent disabilities. Furthermore, the defendants individually proved to their specific court that the overrepresentation of minority students in mildly mentally retarded special education programs was due to poverty or psychosocial disadvantage.

The issues involved in the identification and placement of students with mild mental retardation are somewhat paradoxical and attack the very foundation of special education. On the one hand, placement in a special education class is perceived as harming the student by subjecting her or him to negative social consequences and to a self-fulfilling prophecy of low achievement. On the other hand, the specific characteristics of special education classes are supposed to provide conditions in which these students have their best chance of flourishing and of reaching levels of achievement that would elude them in mainstream classrooms. For educators to be completely effective, they must identify children's educational needs and provide appropriate teaching and learning experiences. Departments of special education in public schools are based on the philosophy that once students are referred, presumably based on specific severe and chronic deficits in social, emotional, or academic achievement, they will be provided classes with considerably smaller student-to-teacher ratios, considerably higher per-pupil expenditures, individualized programs, and teachers who are specially trained to teach youngsters with this disability. The issue is, what constitutes excellence in teaching these students? Few teachers would disagree that smaller class size is critical to enhancing learning. All teachers who have taught youngsters with mental disabilities would agree that these students take longer to learn cognitive skills than do non-retarded children of the same age. The learning process takes even longer for individuals with the most severe brain damage (i.e., severe or profound mental retardation). See Figure 1.1.

Figure 1.1 In most cases, it is difficult, if not impossible, to determine through observation if a child has mental retardation. Photo courtesy C. Eichstaedt.

Etiology of Mental Retardation

There are many causes of mental retardation, and only one fourth of all cases can be attributed to specific anatomical involvement of the brain where brain cells are destroyed or (as in Down syndrome) do not completely develop. This brain dysfunction or underdevelopment results in cognitive deficits. Grossman (1983) stated that "the correlation between intelligence level and biological retardation is very high" (p. 59). Grossman's *Classification in Mental Retardation* (1983) lists 10 general medical etiologies; these are listed in Highlight 1.2.

Most biological brain damage (90%) has prenatal and perinatal causes. The fetal brain is extremely delicate and highly susceptible to destruction. According to Grossman (1983),

it is not surprising that disturbances in fetal growth sometimes cause central nervous system deficits, for this is a period of rapid brain development. The *mature* brain can survive the effects of infections, radiation, trauma, and other noxious agents, but they can be devastating to the *developing* organism. (p. 60)

Regarding the degree of retardation as compared to brain involvement, Hogg and Sebba (1987a) state that "any full account of people with profound retardation and multiple impairment will eventually have to come to terms with the nature and extent of CNS damage" (p. 27).

Due to new research and medical technology, certain causes of mental retardation are better understood today and are slowly being reduced. Metabolic screening of newborn children has produced miraculous results. The negative effects on the brain of phenylketonuria (PKU), galactosemia, and hypothyroidism (formerly called cretinism) are now identified by a practical and cost-effective filter-paper testing process. Moser (1988) explains the future possibilities of this procedure: "Use of the filter-paper specimen technique include DNA analysis of blood to detect inherited diseases, blood testing for congenital infections, and urine testing for congenital tumors" (p. 151). Credit should be given to Dr. Robert Guthrie, who conceived and developed the basic test, which uses only a few drops of blood, to serve as a practical method of screening all newborn babies (Levy, 1988).

Down Syndrome

Down syndrome is caused by a chromosome abnormality in which individuals have 47 chromosomes instead of the usual 46. John Langdon

---

HIGHLIGHT 1.2

IN THEORY

AAMR Etiological Classifications of Mental Retardation

1. Following infection and intoxication (e.g., congenital rubella, syphilis)
2. Following trauma or physical agent (e.g., mechanical injury at birth)
3. With disorders of metabolism or nutrition (e.g., phenylketonuria or PKU, galactosemia)
4. Associated with gross brain disease, postnatal (e.g., neurofibromatosis, intracranial neoplasm)
5. Associated with diseases and conditions resulting from unknown prenatal influence (e.g., hydrocephalus, microcephaly)
6. Associated with chromosomal abnormality (e.g., Down syndrome, Fragile X syndrome)
7. Associated with other perinatal (gestational) conditions (e.g., prematurity)
8. Following psychiatric disorder (e.g., autism)
9. Associated with environmental influences (e.g., cultural-familial retardation)
10. Associated with other conditions

Note. From *Mental Retardation: A Life Cycle Approach* (4th ed.) (pp. 21, 23) by C.J. Drew, D.R. Logan, & M.L. Hardman, 1988, Columbus, OH: Merrill. Copyright 1988 by Merrill. Reprinted by permission.

Down, a British physician, described the clinical features in 1866 and gave the disorder the name "mongolism," a term no longer in use. Down syndrome is one of the leading causes of mental retardation in the world. Its incidence has no relation to race, nationality, religion, or socioeconomic status. Approximately 4,000 infants are born with Down syndrome each year (National Down Syndrome Congress, 1988).

Down syndrome is usually diagnosed by physical examination of newborns and confirmed by chromosome analysis, although a fetus with Down syndrome can be detected through amniocentesis. Approximately 95% of all persons with Down syndrome have *trisomy 21*, an extra copy of chromosome 21, which results from a malfunction during the cell division phase of meiosis. This process is called *nondisjunction* and "takes place prior to conception, during the formation of the sperm or ovum in the parent. The abnormal gamete then joins with the normal gamete at conception to form a fertilized egg with three (a trisomy) of chromosome 21" (Blackman, 1990, p. 108). The risk of chromosome nondisjunction increases with increasing maternal age ("Down Syndrome," 1991). In 20% to 30% of cases of Down syndrome, the extra chromosome is known to originate with the father (National Down Syndrome Congress, 1988).

Translocation, another type of Down syndrome, is found in approximately 4% of all cases. The extra chromosome is attached (translocated) to another chromosome (usually number 14, 15, or 22). Approximately 50% of the time, this type is inherited from a parent who is a "carrier." A third type of Down syndrome is *mosaicism* and occurs in about 1% or 2% of cases. Abnormal separation of the 21st chromosome occurs sometime after conception. All future divisions of the involved cell produce cells with an extra chromosome. Thus, the child has some cells with an extra chromosome and other cells with the normal number of chromosomes.

The extent to which the child has the features of individuals with Down syndrome depends on the percentage of body cells with an extra chromosome 21 (Blackman, 1990).

Common physical and developmental features vary in degree and presence among individuals with Down syndrome. These include upward-slanting eyes, flattened midface, flattened back of the head, smaller nose and ears, decreased muscle tone (hypotonia), hyperflexibility of joints, speckling of the iris (Brushfield spots), extra folds at the inner corners of the eyes (epicanthal folds), a small oral cavity (often resulting in a protruding tongue), short height, short fingers, broad hands with a single palmar crease (simian crease), and a wide gap between the first and second toes (Patton, Payne, & Beirne-Smith, 1990).

Of persons with Down syndrome, 30% to 50% have congenital heart defects, and 8% to 12% have congenital gastrointestinal tract abnormalities. Most of these defects are correctable with surgery (National Down Syndrome Congress, 1988). Additionally, 78% possess hearing impairments (Downs & Balkany, 1988), and myopia (nearsightedness) is prevalent in up to 70% (Niva, 1988).

Atlantoaxial instability (AAI), a condition involving the misalignment of the first and second cervical vertebrae, is found in approximately 12% to 22% of individuals with Down syndrome. Instability at the atlantoaxial joint is more prevalent in girls and women than in men (Collacott, Ellison, Harper, Newland, & Ray-Chaudhurt, 1989). According to Barclay (1988),

> this [AAI] is a movement of one vertebra on another in the upper neck. If movement is marked, then severe injury to the spinal cord can occur, causing cessation of breathing and paralysis. Usually, this only occurs after an accident has occurred and total dislocation occurs. This is extremely difficult to treat successfully, and most of these individuals die. (p. 1)

Special Olympics International requires that all athletes with Down syndrome receive a neck X-ray before participation is allowed, to determine whether AAI is present. Barclay (1988) stresses that this condition is likely to develop after age 15 (especially in males) and that the condition is progressive. Therefore, AAI cannot be effectively screened by a single X-ray at a young age. Barclay (1988) recommends the following:

> 1. Each individual with Down syndrome should have lateral cervical spine X-rays at the age of 4 and then every 3 years thereafter. These X-rays should be in flexion, neutral, and extension position.
> 2. Activities which cause flexion of the neck such as the forward somersault should be avoided. (pp. 1-2)

Most children and teenagers aged 6 to 18 with Down syndrome have both developmental motor delays and low levels of physical fitness performance (Eichstaedt, Wang, Polacek, & Dohrmann, 1991). Appropriate physical activity programs have resulted in significant improvement in motor performance scores (Hanson, 1988). O'Brien (1991), program director of the Illinois Special Olympics, reports positive improvement in physical fitness levels of youngsters, teenagers, and adults with Down syndrome when they take part in organized and ongoing Special Olympics track and field programs.

Early intervention programs for infants and toddlers with Down syndrome have produced excellent results and are credited with progress well beyond what was expected. Payne and Isaacs (1991) observe that "Down syndrome children may take twice as long as normal children to develop early motor skills, although with proper intervention this lag can be reduced or eliminated" (p. 9).

As individuals with Down syndrome grow older, pathological changes in the brain occur that increase the risk of dementia of the Alzheimer type—that is, loss of intellectual functioning. Zigman, Schupf, Lubin, and Silverman (1987) report that "the most significant decline in cognitive skills among individuals with Down syndrome does not appear until individuals reach 60 years of age" (p. 166).

Regarding the life expectancy of individuals with Down syndrome, Coleman (1988) reports that

> studies of the life tables of Down syndrome infants have shown that if a Down syndrome child lives to five years of age, he is only 6 percent less likely than a normal child to live to 40 years of age. Patients tend to die under five years of age for a variety of causes, most often associated with congenital cardiac disease. (p. 15)

Blackman (1990) has found that due to medical and surgical intervention and improved educational opportunities, the prognosis has improved dramatically; many survive beyond the age of 60, and some persons with Down syndrome have lived beyond 90.

All subsequent chapters of this book make specific reference to physical activity programming for individuals with Down syndrome.

Fragile X (Martin-Bell) Syndrome

Recent technological advances have uncovered a new chromosome abnormality termed *fragile X syndrome*. Spitz (1988) believes fragile X syndrome rivals Down syndrome as a major genetic cause of mental retardation. According to Rogers and Simensen (1987), "if . . . a 3% prevalence of mental retardation in the general population is used, [fragile] (X) syndrome may account for up to 10% of all mental retardation" (p. 445). Spitz comments: "The important point is that some afflicted individuals had previously been diagnosed as 'cultural-familial' retarded because the syndrome usually does not produce any gross or obvious physical anoma-

lies, particularly in prepubertal boys'' (p. 15).

Fragile X syndrome is a heterogeneous group of X-linked recessive disorders controlled by one or more genes found on the X chromosome. The condition occurs more in males than in females. The syndrome derives its name from a delicate site on the X chromosome of affected individuals—the tips of the long arm of the chromosome appear "pinched." This problem produces specific characteristics. Blackman (1990) describes the typical features found in this syndrome: "large head; prominent forehead and ears; occasional autisticlike behaviors . . . mental retardation" (p. 262). Additionally, the individual is likely to possess an enlarged jaw. Priest (1985) has found a delay in development, but the youngsters walk, talk, and can function in society. Measurements of their intelligence range from mild to moderate retardation, and the children have no neurological abnormalities. These characteristics are more commonly found in males and are less obvious in females (Grossman & Tarjan, 1987).

Fetal Alcohol Syndrome

Fetal alcohol syndrome (FAS) has been strongly linked to mental retardation. Scott (1988) lists FAS as one of the three most prevalent causes of biological mental retardation. Abel (1984) substantiates that FAS is directly associated with pre- and postnatal growth retardation and mental retardation. Grossman (1983) identifies chronic alcoholism and "binge" drinking by the pregnant woman as a cause of mental retardation and congenital malformations. Alcohol breaks down into a toxic substance that impairs normal growth of embryonic tissue. Most infants with FAS have moderate retardation, droopy eyelids, and heart defects and are small in size (Westling, 1986).

Cytomegalovirus

Cytomegalovirus (CMV, a herpes virus) is an extremely common intrauterine infection and occurs in approximately 1% of all live births throughout the world. The incidence is highest in lower socioeconomic groups, with approximately 36,000 infants with CMV born in the United States each year (Alford, 1988). Ten percent of infected fetuses will develop severe mental retardation. When the virus is transmitted to the fetus, it develops into a devastating infection, involving encephalitis, microcephaly, or hydrocephalus (Grossman, 1983). All three conditions have been known to cause damage to the brain. According to Alford (1988), "Although it has been difficult to define, minimal brain damage with learning and behavior disorders is believed to be a late feature of subclinical congenital CMV infection" (p. 142). Damage to the vestibular mechanism in the inner ear and sensorineural hearing loss also often result.

Premature Birth

Prematurity is defined as weighing less than 5.5 pounds (2500 grams), and/or less than 36 weeks of gestational age (Fenton, 1990). Premature birth has been strongly linked to learning dysfunctions, behavior problems, and mental retardation. Duffy and Als (1988) observe that

> it is well known that continuing advances in medical technology have resulted in greater survival and functional viability of premature human infants. It is not uncommon for premature babies less than a kilogram (2.2 lb) in weight at birth to survive. (p. 179)

The major problem with premature infants is usually respiratory distress syndrome, which in essence decreases the amount of oxygen delivered to the brain and causes permanent damage. Control of ventilation (breathing) is critical in babies less than 28 weeks at birth. At this age, infants have not yet formed alveoli in the lungs, which are necessary for the exchange of oxygen and carbon dioxide (Nyhan,

1988). Anoxia (deficiency of oxygen) in the brain is worsened by the potential for intraventricular and intracerebral hemorrhaging. These problems are likely to produce brain damage.

Hydrocephalus

Hydrocephalus often results in brain damage. In this condition there is blockage of the cerebrospinal fluid pathways, producing an accumulation of fluid within the skull. The fluid is usually under increasing pressure. Characteristics include enlargement of the head (sometimes becoming larger than a basketball), prominence of the forehead, brain atrophy, mental deterioration, and convulsions. Vision may be affected, due to degeneration of the optic nerve. The blockage occurs soon after birth (and in some cases prenatally). The increasing pressure is likely to cause considerable brain damage.

Negative hydrocephalic conditions are controlled through the use of a shunt (tube) that is inserted into the cerebral ventricles of the brain. The shunt allows excessive fluid to drain away from the brain through a plastic tube that flows into one of the heart's upper receiving chambers (atria) or into the stomach. The fluid is then absorbed into the system. Hydrocephalus is occasionally found in children with spina bifida and is the major cause of mental retardation associated with that condition.

Microcephaly

Microcephaly is characterized by a small head that is cone shaped. The head circumference is 13 inches or less in a 6-month-old infant and 16 inches or less in an adult. The brain is smaller and possesses simplified cerebral hemispheres. This condition usually results in severe mental retardation.

Individuals with microchephaly are known to be of small stature, although they tend to have adequate muscular ability. Their disproportionately long arms and legs cause them to walk in an unusual way, "somewhat resembling the gait of a monkey" (Hutt & Gibby, 1979).

How Many Individuals Are Mentally Retarded?

The actual number of individuals classified as mentally retarded is a matter of dispute. Zigler and Hodapp (1986) estimate that the number is somewhere between 2% and 2.5% of the population, which in the United States is approximately 4.6 to 5.75 million people. In the 1989-1990 school year, the actual number of children ages 6 to 21 classified as mentally retarded and provided special educational services was 566,120 students. This figure represents 13.3% of all children classified as having a legal disability, and it is a decrease of 98,304 from 1987-1988 (U.S. Department of Education). This reduction in number should not be misinterpreted, as most of these "lost" students have been reclassified into other areas of special education (e.g., learning disabled). Additionally, over 10,000 children have been declassified in California as a result of court actions declaring mental retardation labeling to be inappropriate. The state of Florida has also declassified 44% of mildly mentally retarded students for the same reason. The percentage of all U.S. schoolchildren with mental retardation being provided special programs during the 1984-1985 school year was approximately 1.8% (Heward & Orlansky, 1988). Illinois reports that 1.64% of its 1988-1989 school-age youngsters were classified as mentally retarded (*Illinois Comprehensive System of Personnel Development*, 1990).

Retardation figures are not consistent across the United States. States' statistics will differ according to their classification system. For example, Illinois' percentages differ from the traditionally accepted estimates: During the 1988-1989 school year, 25,683 Illinois students aged zero through 21 were identified as mentally retarded, with 60% of these labeled as mild, 29% labeled as moderate, and 11% labeled as severe or profound (*Illinois Comprehensive System of Personnel Development*, 1990).

Identifying the adult population is even more difficult. It is particularly difficult to follow those classified as mildly mentally retarded, because few records specifically label adults as retarded (and to do so would disadvantage these individuals when they apply for jobs). Persons labeled as mildly mentally retarded when they were 21 should be assumed to have the same classification as adults. We generally find that most of these adults are quite employable and tend to fit into the mainstream of everyday life. They are generally not noticeably different from the nonretarded, though they hold jobs that do not require reading or math skills beyond a fifth- or sixth-grade level. Thus, society tends to lose track of most teenagers who were once labeled as mildly mentally retarded, and this group constitutes approximately 60% of the entire mentally retarded population (Patton, Payne, and Beirne-Smith, 1990). Taking the many inconsistencies into consideration, we estimate that the number of individuals labeled as mentally retarded is somewhere between 1.5% and 2.5% of the U.S. population.

Mild Mental Retardation

The etiology of mild mental retardation is still under debate. Approximately 15% to 25% of individuals with IQs between 50 and 70 have some degree of brain damage, resulting in lower cognitive potential (Drew, Hardman, & Logan, 1988). Most possess cultural/familial mental retardation (CFMR)—that is, some aspect of nature and/or nurture is identified as the largest "cause" of mental retardation for individuals who have no apparent brain damage. Spitz (1988) describes the difference between cultural and familial causes:

Whereas empiricists [advocates of cultural causation] ignore the role of the central nervous system—believing that thinking is an entirely conscious process that can be imposed by a tutor—rationalists [advocates of familial causation] would counter that training does not affect the most important aspects of thinking; that is, that at present there is no way in which the efficiency of the central nervous system can be upgraded to any meaningful degree beyond the somewhat flexible but still limited restraints set by the individual's genotype [inherited traits]. (p. 24)

At this point, Spitz (1988) leans strongly toward a rationalist perspective:

> Children are no more taught to think than they are taught to walk, although of course thinking is shaped and modified by the environment, within certain limits. Humans (and many other animals) are innately endowed with the capacity to think, which under normal conditions emerges in its various manifestations according to a genetic timetable. Furthermore, excepting the effects of pathologies and catastrophic deprivations, differences in how efficiently people learn and think are largely genetically determined. (p. 2)

Finally, Spitz emphatically asserts that "intellectual potential is inherent in the brain, waiting to be tapped, not *given* by the environment. If it were produced by sensory training, 180 years of effort with retarded persons who have all their senses intact would have shown by now more favorable results" (p. 5).

In defense of the theorists who believe that "cultural" influences control mild mental retardation, Spitz (1988) discusses the concept presented by Feuerstein, Rand, & Hoffman (1979):

> It is Feuerstein's contention that the crucial determinant of cognitive development is the "mediated learning experience"; that is to say, although children can develop intellectually from direct exposure to stimuli, only when a competent, caring person explains the experience (mediates between the ex-

perience and the child) will the child really benefit to the greatest extent possible. Feuerstein considers native intellectual endowment important only in the sense that more poorly endowed individuals require a larger investment of time and greater ingenuity on the part of the mediator than do less well endowed individuals. (p. 17)

The outlook for individuals with mental retardation would be devastatingly bleak if nothing could be done to enhance their potential. Outstanding education and training become essential if society expects each child with a disability to reach the highest levels possible.

Do Children With Mild Mental Retardation Learn Differently?

MacMillan (1988) questions our present "understanding" of how children with retardation learn and how this process differs from that of nonretarded youngsters:

> In light of the dramatic shift in definition of and the resultant change in labeling practices (PL 94-142), particularly regarding minority children functioning in the IQ range of 70-85, we believe that the entire literature base generated on such children when they were "mentally retarded" (1961-1973 or so) may be invalid for today's higher functioning retarded children. In fact, since so many of the investigators sampling in EMR [educable mentally retarded] classes used the higher functioning EMRs most of the time, the literature may today reflect more about low functioning "normal" children than it does about retarded children. (p. 277)

If MacMillan is correct, then teaching methods must be adjusted, because cognitive learning among those presently classified as having mild mental retardation is slower and demands techniques different from those usually used with low-functioning "normal" students. Smaller class sizes are appropriate, and specially trained classroom teachers are a necessity. Being labeled as having mild mental retardation does not mean that the person has a similarly low level of physical fitness or motor performance. Only a comprehensive test battery can determine ability levels. Patton, Payne, and Beirne-Smith (1990) list common characteristics of individuals with mild mental retardation (see Table 1.3).

Educators cannot change genetic makeup or the destructive results of brain damage in children, so they must be intensively involved in

Table 1.3   Behavioral Descriptions for Individuals Labeled as Mildly Mentally Retarded

Level of retardation	Communication skills	Physical dimensions	Social adjustments	Independent functioning	Occupational/ vocational level	Academic performance
Mild	Ability to listen and speak effectively Can carry on an involved conversation May have difficulty understanding some concepts and vocabulary Restricted expressive vocabulary	No major problems	Interactions with others are reasonably acceptable Some social skill deficiencies	Self-supporting	Good potential for competitive employment	Can achieve academic competence and literacy

MR classification	Approximate percentage of total MR population		Age(s) when identification typically occurs	Individual(s) typically first recognizing problems	Individual(s) typically confirming diagnosis of MR	Visibility of person as MR
	Traditional	New				
Mild	70%-75%	60%	6 yr +	Teacher Parent	School psychologist Diagnostic team	Changes with chronological age; tend to be identified upon entry to school and to lose label upon exit from school setting.

Note. From *Mental Retardation* (3rd ed.) (pp. 53, 68) by J.R. Patton, J.S. Payne, and M.B. Beirne-Smith, 1990, Columbus, OH: Merrill. Copyright ©1990 by Merrill Publishing Company. Reprinted with permission of Merrill, an imprint of Macmillan Publishing Company.

providing maximum and appropriate opportunities for children with special physical and motor needs. The physical domain—that is, physical fitness and motor skill—is an extremely important area of education and training for individuals with mental retardation. Specially trained adapted physical education teachers, therapeutic recreation specialists, and therapists are indispensable to special activity programs for individuals with major motor and fitness needs; without these trained specialists, these people are in danger of being relegated to inferior or inappropriate activities.

Moderate Mental Retardation

People classified as moderately mentally retarded (MoMR) or trainably mentally retarded (TMR) (IQs of 35 to 50) comprise up to 32% of all individuals labeled as mentally retarded (Patton, Payne, & Beirne-Smith, 1990). These individuals are more easily identified because of their lower intellectual, physical, and social functioning and their tendency to be more dependent. Their limitations are more pronounced in adulthood than those of higher functioning individuals with mild retardation, and society seems accustomed to providing them with appropriate care, including living and vocational opportunities (see Table 1.4). Most individuals with Down syndrome are found in this group (Pueschel, 1988). People in this group are much less physically fit than people without retardation. In the past, few integrated leisure and recreational activities have been available for this population.

Severe and Profound Mental Retardation

Individuals needing the most help are labeled as having severe (IQ 20 to 35) or profound (IQ 20 and lower) mental retardation. These people are the smallest groups of all individuals with mental retardation and are easily identified by their constant need for support services (see Table 1.5). They comprise approximately 8% of all people with mental retardation, with estimates of 5.5% for those with severe mental retardation and 2.5% for those with profound mental retardation. In most cases, extensive brain damage is the cause of their particular level of dependence. Exciting developments are occurring in the education and rehabilitation of these individuals, whereas only a few years ago their programs were hopelessly mired in providing them with seemingly useless experiences.

Marked differences are usually found between the two groups. For example, individuals with *profound* retardation function at the level of infants and very small children. Their programs may include the development of the skill of *attending*—that is, skills such as focusing the eyes, turning the head, and orienting the body toward an object for a specified amount of time. Patton, Payne, and Beirne-Smith (1990) suggest other learning activities commonly used for those with profound retardation:

> Responding to stimulation, familiar people, and objects by cooing, smiling, relaxing, or moving body parts; . . . social skills of making eye contact or touching another person; motor and verbal imitation; gross and fine motor movements—head control, reaching, grasping, sitting, and protective behaviors; and following simple directions. Teachers try to increase and improve the variety, rate and quality of the adaptive responses the child or adult can make. (p. 319)

Typical learning experiences for persons with *severe* mental retardation include reinforcement of the activities just described, but paced for quicker progress. Their programs should stress self-care, socialization, communication, and physical development. Today, new expectations and appropriate programming are providing positive results for these people, who formerly were considered totally dependent (Bauer & Shea, 1989).

Table 1.4   Behavioral Descriptions for Individuals Labeled as Moderately Mentally Retarded

Level of retardation	Communication skills	Physical dimensions	Social adjustment	Independent functioning	Occupational/ vocational level	Academic performance
Moderate	Can carry on simple conversations Problems in listening and speaking are likely	Some motor and health problems	Can interact with others but may be awkward Friendships possible	Can master self-help skills Typically live in supported settings May require financial support	Can gain employment in competitive or supported settings	Survival and functional skills can be learned

MR classification	Approximate percentage of total MR population		Age(s) when identification typically occurs	Individual(s) typically first recognizing problems	Individual(s) typically confirming diagnosis of MR	Visibility of person as MR
	Traditional	New				
Moderate	20%	32%	1-5 yr	Parents Physician	Physician Diagnostic team	For most part, tend to be recognized as MR throughout their lifetimes

Note. From *Mental Retardation* (3rd ed.) (pp. 53, 68) by J.R. Patton, J.S. Payne, and M.B. Beirne-Smith, 1990, Columbus, OH: Merrill. Copyright © 1990 by Merrill Publishing Company. Reprinted with permission of Merrill, an imprint of Macmillan Publishing Company.

Kirk and Gallagher (1989) make interesting comparisons among mild, moderate, and severe and profound mental retardation (see Table 1.6).

Life expectancy of the nondisabled population is increasing, and this is also true for those with mental retardation. According to Janicki (1988),

the results of increased birth weight, lowered infant mortality rates, effective nutritional and early intervention practices, health maintenance, and community care for all age groups, and notable increases in lon-gevity among older adults, are contributing to a change within the distribution of the mentally retarded population. Furthermore, the increased rate of survival of severely and profoundly retarded infants into childhood and even adolescence has shifted the distribution of the population to include a greater percentage of younger, yet more organically impaired individuals. (p. 303)

The brain cell destruction found in most individuals with moderate, severe, or profound retardation brings with it additional complica-

Table 1.5   Behavioral Descriptions for Individuals Labeled as Severely and Profoundly Mentally Retarded

Level of retardation	Communication skills	Physical dimensions	Social adjustment	Independent functioning	Occupational/ vocational level	Academic performance
Severe	Can understand very simple communication Limited verbal skills May use nonverbal techniques (e.g., gestures, sign language)	Typically have significant motor and health problems	Social interactions may be limited	Need certain amount of assistance with daily activities	Employment possible for some Typically found in sheltered settings but can perform in supported settings	Focus on functional needs Can acquire requisite self-help skills
Profound	Communication skills are very limited, if they exist at all Often communication is through nonverbal sounds No effective speech	Few useful motor skills May be medically fragile	May be nonexistent	Totally dependent	Employment or training not likely	Focus on basic skills such as attending, positioning

MR classification	Approximate percentage of total MR population		Age(s) when identification typically occurs	Individual(s) typically first recognizing problems	Individual(s) typically confirming diagnosis of MR	Visibility of person as MR
	Traditional	New				
Severe/ profound	5%	8%	0–1 yr	Physician	Physician	Maintain MR distinction throughout their lifetimes

Note. From *Mental Retardation* (3rd ed.) (pp. 53, 68) by J.R. Patton, J.S. Payne, and M.B. Beirne-Smith, 1990, Columbus, OH: Merrill. Copyright © 1990 by Merrill Publishing Company. Reprinted with permission of Merrill, an imprint of Macmillan Publishing Company.

tions. For example, seizures requiring medication or surgery are highly probable. Jacobson and Janicki (1983) believe seizures become more prevalent as the degree of retardation increases. Note, however, that people with Down syndrome seldom experience seizures, because their retardation is due not to brain cell destruction but to an underdeveloped brain (Tonelson & Santilli, 1987).

Table 1.6   Comparisons of Levels of Mental Retardation

	Mild	Moderate	Severe and profound
Etiology	Often a combination of unfavorable environmental conditions together with genetic, neurological, and metabolic factors	A wide variety of relatively rare neurological, glandular, or metabolic defects or disorders	
Prevalence	About 10 out of every 1,000 people	About 3 out of every 1,000 people	About 1 out of every 10,000 people
School expectations	Will have difficulty in usual school program; needs special adaptations for appropriate education	Needs major adaptation in educational programs; focus is on self-care or social skills; should learn basic academic and vocational skills	Needs training in self-care skills (feeding, toileting, dressing)
Adult expectations	With special education can make productive adjustment at an unskilled or semi-skilled level	Can make social and economic adaptation in a sheltered workshop or in a routine job under supervision	Is likely to be dependent on others for care

Note. From *Educating Exceptional Children* (6th ed.) (p. 136) by S.A. Kirk & J.J. Gallagher, 1989, Boston: Houghton Mifflin. Copyright © 1989 by Houghton Mifflin. Used with permission.

Education and the Transdisciplinary Approach

The general goals of public school education have been accepted for many years: For example, an education for all children should be concerned with the development of independence, increased opportunities, and socialization (Hogg & Sebba, 1987b), and more specifically, education includes the development of intellectual potential, emotional well-being, social integration, and physical health and wellness. Zigler and Hodapp (1986) give a similar list of goals for persons with mental retardation: health and well-being, formal cognition, academic achievement, and motivation and personality development. All children should have the opportunity to develop these goals to their maximum ability; in our society, anything less would be unacceptable. Yet school administrators tend to ascribe differing degrees of importance to these goals. For example, most principals value intellectual development over health and physical development—observe the lack of importance placed on physical education in the total curriculum. In some school districts, physical education is considered a frill and is offered as seldom as once a week, or not at all. For children with mental retardation, the importance of physical activity in the total educational plan must be seriously reevaluated, because these children's lives are strongly focused on motor skill and physical fitness demands.

Hogg and Sebba (1987a) consider physical activity important and an integral component of education:

We commented on the adaptive value of movement and postural control, an obvious point and one of which we are all aware. Less obviously, however, movement has consequences that reach beyond those that are immediately apparent. It is also clear that voluntary, active movement is important for the development of sensory perception and beyond that for cognition. (p. 83)

They stress that "movement in the environment leads to changes in our relation to objects and people and enables us not only to realize our specific objectives but also results in changing experiences which have important cognitive and perceptual consequences" (p. 74). Zigler and Hodapp (1986) concur: "There is an important, if often overlooked, health component to the optimal functioning of any child, retarded or normally intelligent" (p. 175). Jensen (1980) believes that health factors have more influence on intellectual development than many of the social and cognitive factors that are usually assumed to be most influential.

The importance of education and physical activity for individuals with mental retardation are best summarized by Hogg and Sebba (1987a):

Our view of the nature of development has changed and this change fits well with the more positive attitudes towards the education of people with mental handicaps that have evolved. At the heart of these changes is the view that development occurs through the way in which the individual interacts with his or her social and physical environment. Not only does the environment influence the child, but the child's behavior alters the environment, which in turn further influences the child. The key word here is *interdependence*. The child and the environment mutually affect each other, for better or worse, and each in different ways adapts to the other. (p. 29)

Teachers, leaders, and researchers must become attuned to the immediate needs of those with mental retardation and not be so involved in the traditional contrast of retarded and nonretarded performance (see Figure 1.2). Borkowski and Turner (1988) stress that a better understanding of mental retardation will come when we "examine *development in retarded persons*, per se, with special focus on the use of longitudinal designs. Given the striking variability in performance among retarded individuals, longitudinal analyses permit a more precise assessment of developmental changes, in both laboratory and naturalistic contexts" (p. 262).

Although much emphasis has been placed on integration of the child with mental retardation into classrooms with nondisabled students, school administrators must be more concerned with the learning environment and not only with the social implications that accompany mainstreaming. Gottlieb, Rose, and Lessen (1983) found that youngsters with mental retardation are not well accepted by peers who do not have disabilities. Say these authors, "A considerable amount of research has already indicated that merely placing retarded children in regular classes does not improve the social acceptance of them by nonretarded peers. . . . Retarded children in regular classes who misbehave or cannot conform to the standards of the classroom are apt to be socially rejected, regardless of whether they are labeled as mentally retarded" (p. 197).

Figure 1.2 Most activities are conducive to mainstreaming individuals with mental retardation into traditional physical education programs.

Physical education programs have similar problems with mainstreaming. Traditional physical education teachers have difficulty adapting their activities for students with major differences in ability. This is not to say that traditional physical education teachers should not attempt to modify activities and include disabled youngsters in regular classes, but inappropriate placement will likely cause more harm than benefit. For example, a 12-year-old child functioning at a motor developmental level of a 7-year-old will be extremely difficult to mainstream into a class that is being taught fundamental skills of badminton. Teachers tend to lose their effectiveness when the range of abilities is so great that they cannot focus their efforts.

All students must be placed in environments that help them flourish. In the case of physical fitness and motor development, mainstreaming is not always the best option for students with special needs. The decision whether to mainstream should come after an initial assessment that determines what level of performance the individual has achieved so far. Obviously, the assessment should be completed by someone with the appropriate training. In the case of motor skills and physical fitness for persons with mental retardation, this is most often the adapted/special physical education instructor, who has been trained to assess all children with disabilities, with the possible exception of the child with profound, multihandicapping conditions.

The comparatively new discipline of special education was developed in the late 1940s to provide better teachers, and thus better learning experiences, for children with disabilities. The early leaders of this discipline believed that too many children were failing because of existing educational programs and that traditional teachers were unable to meet the unique needs of youths with disabilities. Gorton (1977) sums up the problem: ''I continually hear teachers complain that children have been precipitously and indiscriminately mainstreamed. The children have been placed back into the very environment in which they failed'' (p. 28).

Regarding placement of students into ideal learning environments, Dr. Robert Leininger, superintendent of the Illinois State Board of Education, suggests that grades K through 3 be discontinued, in favor of grouping these same students by ability. He would eventually like to see all grade levels disappear from Illinois schools as well, allowing students to graduate as soon as they have mastered high school skills. His proposal is backed up with $1.6 million in experimental grants to school districts, which began in the fall of 1991. This unique approach follows the state of Kentucky's lead in establishing nongraded primary classrooms. Says Leininger (1991),

> This is a major change in philosophy for traditional education as we know it. . . . The traditional education program . . . isn't producing the product that we want. . . . The students will be grouped on the basis of where they're at and what abilities they have. Some people would call it the one-room school concept. I'd rather say we're meeting the individual needs of the kids. (p. A8)

The concept of meeting the individual needs of students by placing them in the most appropriate learning environments coincides with the basic principles of PL 94-142. Yet placement of students by ability tends to conflict with the principles of mainstreaming.

Educational ability grouping has been strongly challenged because of its potential to segregate students. The states of Illinois and Kentucky are venturing into uncharted waters and are likely to experience difficult times. Is the pendulum swinging back to the early '60s, when *homogeneous grouping* was the newest educational byword? What will happen to the proponents of the concept of ''regular education initiative'' (who are overwhelmingly pro-mainstreaming)? Chapters 3 and 6 of this textbook further discuss the areas of assessment and mainstreaming in reference to physical activities for individuals with mental retardation.

Education of "the whole person" must include all dimensions of education—not only intellectual development but also the emotional, social, and physical well-being of all students. Thus, few school boards would exclude the component of health and physical development, the critical area of the physical domain.

The Physical Domain

The physical domain is a combination of several areas of concentration, including physical fitness and fundamental motor skill development. Dauer and Pangrazi (1989) argue that the outcomes of a program in the physical domain should include the promotion of physical development and achievement of personal physical fitness goals, and the development of competencies in a wide variety of physical skills, which allows individuals to function effectively in physical activities.

Seaman and DePauw (1989) emphasize that "motor development encompasses (1) development of abilities that are essential to movement; and (2) the acquisition and refinement of motor skills. It is an extensive, lifelong process" (p. 43). Eichstaedt and Kalakian (1987) list, as specific components of the physical domain, muscular strength, muscular endurance, cardiorespiratory endurance, flexibility, balance, agility, speed, coordination (e.g., eye/hand), reaction time, and explosive strength.

Hogg and Sebba (1987b) have found that *all* behavior, whether cognitive or movement oriented, is dependent on movement activity. Obviously, brain damage produces degrees of movement impairment. Hogg and Sebba (1987b) observe that "damage to, or abnormality of, the central nervous system (CNS) resulting in shortcomings in motor activity has wide-ranging consequences for the individual's ability to adapt to the environment and intervention to improve this situation is central to remediation" (p. 184).

Good physical health is extremely important in daily life. We need adequate levels of strength to carry on daily activities, endurance to sustain effort throughout the day, motor coordination for walking and moving activities, eye/hand coordination to complete required tasks at school or work, and so on. Movement competence is crucial! Teachers who develop appropriate educational programs for students with mental retardation must not overlook the value of quality movement activity programs. PL 94-142 mandates physical education as part of the definition of special education. Physical education is a "direct service" and must be addressed *and included* in all individualized education plans. Anything less is not only inadequate for meeting the identified needs of the students, but also a direct violation of federal law. Obviously, all guidelines pertaining to PL 94-142 must be followed—that is, assessment of physical fitness and motor ability; program writing; proper placement suggestions; appropriate teaching; and evaluation.

Physical Education

Some people think of physical education as being loosely structured and consisting of nothing more than free play or a recess period. With good physical education programs, nothing is farther from the truth. Yet even professionals in the field disagree about how best to define physical education. Siedentop (1990) explains:

What does *physical education* mean? How should this field's content be defined? Is it human movement? Is it play? Is it fitness? Is it sport? Is it social development? Is it risk and adventure? Is it general human development? Or is it all these things together? . . . A group of educational models . . . [appear] to fit most clearly under the developmental model that has historically been the most widely adopted model for physical education. In this model, the *activities* themselves are not as important as is *what they are used to accomplish*. This is why this model has always been referred to as *education through the physical*. (pp. 228-229)

PL 94-142 (1975) defines physical education as "the development of: (A) physical and motor fitness; (B) fundamental motor skills and patterns; and (C) skills in aquatics, dance, and individual and group games, and sports (including intramural and lifetime sports)" (p. 42480).

Obviously, the discipline of physical education is broadly based and can contribute greatly to the goals of education. But what is of outstanding importance is the issue of treating the whole person. This can be effectively accomplished only through an approach that intelligently blends the knowledge and methods of many disciplines and interest groups. Professionals can no longer myopically isolate themselves within their fields or make their job survival depend upon the protection of narrow self-interest. If society is to be successful in the education and training of individuals with mental retardation, then a transdisciplinary approach must be initiated. Lavay and French (1985) describe the transdisciplinary approach as ongoing communication between physical educators, regular and special educators, physicians, therapists, and psychologists (see chapter 5).

Therapeutic Recreation

Although the discipline of recreation is based on a philosophical method unique to physical education, it uses the medium of movement to achieve its goals. *Therapeutic recreation* is a subset of the broad field of recreation; its focus is to provide services to individuals with disabilities. Incorporating common elements of past definitions, Austin and Crawford (1991) define therapeutic recreation as "(1) the purposeful nature of the use of recreation/leisure as an intervention, and (2) the personal enhancement of the client as a result of the intervention" (p. 3). That is, recreational activities, including motor skill and physical fitness development, can be instrumental in the therapeutic recreation

leader's plan to improve students' cognitive, emotional, and social abilities.

Therapy

Physical therapists, occupational therapists, and kinesiotherapists, are often called upon to provide developmental and rehabilitation services for individuals with movement disabilities. Therapy programs are specific to each person, and outcomes should allow individuals to progress upward on the developmental scale.

Groups of therapists differ in the training they have received, yet their expertise and the services they provide may overlap. All have training in orthotics and prosthetics (braces and artificial limbs). All have extensive clinical training prior to their certification. Each group tends to use its own assessment and evaluation techniques. All groups use a holistic approach to rehabilitation, that is, concern for the emotional, social, intellectual, and physical well-being of their clients.

The *physical therapist* (RPT) is trained to use movement rehabilitation techniques and the modalities of heat, cold, water, and mechanical manipulation (e.g., ultrasound, muscle stimulation).

The *occupational therapist* (OTR) has extensive training in movement therapy and specializes in helping people adapt to their daily routines in the school, home, vocation, and leisure.

The *kinesiotherapist* (RKT) has basic expertise based on the discipline of physical education, plus considerable training in the rehabilitation sciences, including anatomy, physiology, kinesiology, chemistry, and physics.

Physical education teachers, therapeutic recreation leaders, and therapists can provide a dynamic combination that allows cooperative planning and service delivery. This transdisciplinary teaming is an ideal blending of professionals *whose focus is movement*, and the outcome can be a coordinated and ongoing program whose end result is an individual with improved physical fitness and movement performance.

A Historical Look at Mental Retardation

To better understand the problems facing individuals with mental retardation, it is important to become familiar with the progress made by professionals in the field. History allows us to measure where we were and how far we have progressed.

The education of children classified as having mental retardation has been a major social concern for centuries. Records reveal that in early history, misunderstanding and inhumane treatment were usually the rule. Pre-Christian Greeks and Romans were known to leave disabled youngsters alone in the wilderness to die. Understanding and meeting the needs of this particular population came slowly to our world. It wasn't until the 19th century that mental institutions were established, and even then most of their administrators viewed their role as one of custodial care rather than education of the "defective" people under their care.

An important event in this history occurred in 1798 when three hunters found and captured a preteenage boy in a forest outside of Aveyron, France. The youngster had no social or language skills and was placed in the National Institution of the Deaf and Dumb in Paris. Jean Marc Gaspard Itard (1775-1838), a physician working at the institution, refused to believe the initial diagnosis that the boy was an "incurable idiot," and he set about to prove that this individual could learn. Itard began a comprehensive training program with the boy, now named Victor. He focused his teaching on three areas—the senses, the intellect, and the emotions—using a series of perceptual stimulations and discrimination tasks that required Victor to use his senses. After almost 5 years, Itard concluded his training, declaring it a total failure because it did not reach his original goals. It should be noted that the boy did improve in many areas, including his socialization, and could read and write a few words. It is hypothesized that Victor's "retardation" may have been entirely due to social deprivation and may have had nothing to do with brain damage. History does not make this point clear. The written report of the experiment, *The Wild Boy of Aveyron* (Itard, 1962), is considered a classic and should be read by everyone working in the area of mental retardation.

An early advocate for education and educational reform was Maria Montessori (1870-1952), physician and educator. Her philosophy and methods continue to have a strong following today. Dr. Montessori's initial teaching was with children classified as mentally defective; her original work, and the concepts she developed, were within the context of meeting the educational needs of youngsters who were mentally retarded. She openly spoke on behalf of individuals with mental retardation, and she made strong appeals to the 1889 Italian Education Congress, stressing that persons with mental retardation should be recognized as social human beings with the same rights and needs as others for education and care. Montessori was a great advocate of "muscular education" and believed that without this development many youngsters could not go about their daily routines or accomplish simple living tasks. One of her basic concepts was that through movement, children seek the exercise that helps to organize and coordinate their behavior so that purposeful learning can take place (Gitter, 1971). See Table 1.7.

The first American institution for people with mental retardation was founded in 1848 in Massachusetts by Samuel G. Howe (1801-1876). Although Howe believed this population could learn and should have an organized education, very few others felt this way. Above all, Howe stressed, children needed more than custodial care, whatever their circumstances (Kirk & Gallagher, 1989).

Table 1.7   Individuals Who Made Major Contributions to the Education of Children With Disabilities

Initiator	Dates	Nationality	Major idea
Jean Marc Gaspard Itard	1775-1838	French	Single-subject research can be used to develop training methods for those who are mentally retarded.
Thomas Hopkins Gallaudet	1787-1851	American	Children who are deaf can learn to communicate by spelling and gesturing with their fingers.
Samuel Gridley Howe	1801-1876	American	Children who are handicapped can learn and should have an organized education, not just compassionate care.
Louis Braille	1809-1852	French	Children who are blind can learn through an alternative system of communication based on a code of raised dots.
Edward Seguin	1812-1880	French	Children who are mentally retarded can learn if taught through specific sensory-motor exercises.
Francis Galton	1822-1911	English	Genius tends to run in families, and its origin can be determined.
Alexander Graham Bell	1847-1922	American	Children who are hearing handicapped can learn to speak, and can use their limited hearing if it is amplified.
Alfred Binet	1857-1911	French	Intelligence can be measured, and can be improved through education.
Maria Montessori	1870-1952	Italian	Children can learn at very early ages, using concrete experiences designed around special instructional materials.
Lewis Terman	1877-1956	American	Intelligence tests can be used to identify gifted children, who tend to maintain superiority throughout life.
Anna Freud	1895-1982	Austrian	The techniques of psychoanalysis can be applied to children who have emotional problems.
Alfred Strauss	1897-1957	German	Some children show unique patterns of learning disabilities, probably due to brain injury, that require special training.

Note. From *Educating Exceptional Children* (6th ed.) (p. 40) by S.A. Kirk and J.J. Gallagher, 1989, Boston: Houghton Mifflin. Copyright © 1989 by Houghton Mifflin. Used with permission.

Public school classes for children with mental retardation surfaced at about the turn of the 20th century. But again another lapse of time followed before educators began to demand special programming and the training of teachers for the disabled. The 1950s saw universities develop special education departments whose role was to train special education teachers. School administrators and parents were demanding more specialized teachers to provide more effective teaching and learning experiences for children with disabilities.

The decade of the 1960s is known for federal support for education of all children, including those with special educational needs. In 1965, Public Law 89-750 (the Elementary and Secondary Education Act) authorized grants to states to initiate, expand, and improve educational programs for children with handicapping conditions. The Bureau of Education for the Handicapped was also established in this law. Although PL 89-750 was designed to provide educational opportunities for youngsters with disabilities, many schools circumvented its directives (Eichstaedt & Kalakian, 1987). Institutional services for those classified as mentally retarded peaked in 1967 with over 195,000 individuals living in the nation's public mental retardation institutional facilities (Janicki, 1988). In a good vein, the *Special Olympics* held its first organized competition in Chicago in 1968, with 1,000 athletes competing at Soldier Field; little did we know, then, that today over 1 million athletes with mental retardation would be participating in highly competitive athletic events worldwide.

But this was not enough. The parents of children with disabilities had had enough! Litigation began in earnest. The first major case came in 1971 when the Pennsylvania Association for Retarded Children filed a suit (*PARC v. Commonwealth of Pennsylvania*) on behalf of 13 children with mental retardation. The attorneys for the children cited guarantees in the U.S. Constitution of due process and equal protection under the law. The suit argued that these youngsters' access to public education should be equal to that afforded other children. In a consent agreement, the court ruled in favor of the youths (Haring & McCormick, 1990). This was the beginning of exciting times when parents were demanding action and willing to follow up their demands in court.

The 1970s were the era of specific legislation aimed at improving opportunities for individuals with disabling conditions. With the passage of the Vocational Rehabilitation Act of 1973 (Section 504) and the monumental 1975 PL 94-142 Education for All Handicapped Children Act (now named, as of October 1990, PL 101-476 Individuals With Disabilities Education Act), the rules and regulations were finalized, and the framework of free and appropriate opportunities for individuals with disabilities was established. Strong feelings, expressed by influential people, were surfacing during this time. Joseph A. Califano, Jr., then secretary of health, education, and welfare, was quoted as follows in the *Federal Register* (1977):

Today I am issuing a regulation, pursuant to Section 504 of the Rehabilitation Act of 1973, that will open a new world of equal opportunity for more than 35 million handicapped Americans—the blind, the deaf, persons confined to wheelchairs, the mentally ill or retarded, and those with other handicaps. . . . The 504 Regulation attacks the discrimination, the demeaning practices and the injustices that have afflicted the nation's handicapped citizens. It reflects the recognition of Congress that most handicapped persons can lead proud and productive lives. It will usher in an era of equality for handicapped individuals in which unfair barriers . . . will begin to fall before the force of law. (p. 22682)

The 1980s became the era of child advocacy, normalization, deinstitutionalization, mainstreaming, and intensified litigation (Heland & Orlansky, 1988). Included in this decade's accomplishments was PL 99-457 (Education of the Handicapped Act Amendments of 1986), which strongly encouraged states to develop and implement comprehensive, coordinated, multidisciplinary, interagency programs of early intervention services for infants and toddlers with disabilities. The "encouragement" to the states was and is to gradually increase the amount of federal money awarded when the states agree to identify and serve all children with disabilities between birth and age 2 years. In addition, PL 99-457 continues to support all of the major concepts of PL 94-142. PL 101-476 Individuals With Disabilities Education Act of 1990 gives educators an excellent model to follow for determining specific needs of youngsters with disabilities. The following list from Cowden and Eason (1991) shows the progression of laws since 1975.

- 1975 PL 94-142: The Education for all Handicapped Children Act
- 1983 PL 98-199: Education of the Handicapped Act Amendments of 1983
- 1986 PL 99-457: Education of the Handicapped Act Amendments of 1986
- 1990 PL 101-476: Individuals With Disabilities Education Act (IDEA)

The major components of PL 94-142 have been retained throughout the years. The newest revision (PL 101-476) specifically addresses the needs of preschool children (ages 3-5) with disabilities in Section 619 of Part B, and infants and toddlers (age birth through 2) in Part H. This law's specific guidelines emphasize teaching and accountability, to assure that each child has the appropriate educational process and the opportunity for maximum learning. The 1990s, and the accomplishments of education for the disabled, are yet to be determined. See Table 1.8.

Addressing Mental Retardation in the Future

Schmickel (1988) provides the following analysis regarding the reduction of mental retardation.

> Where is the field today? Each year almost 1,000 people are prevented from having mental retardation by those pioneering studies that were begun 25 years ago. According to statistical predictions, about 70 people do not have mental retardation caused by galactosemia because of screening and diet, 150 people do not have phenylketonuria because of screening and diet, and 700 do not have the severe retardation of cretinism [galactosemia] because of screening and treatment. Untold thousands do not have kernicterus and mental retardation caused by neonatal hyperbilirubinemia. (pp. 19-20)

Baird and Sadovnick (1985) identified the largest single group of individuals with mental retardation as being those of ages 15 through 29. The trend is definitely moving toward a large population of persons with mental retardation who will become middle-aged by the year 2005. The implications are great, and society must begin preparing to allow this population to become contributing members of society rather than dependents.

Several private organizations have been extremely influential in advocacy, program development, and financial support for individuals with mental retardation. These include the Association for Retarded Citizens (ARC); the American Association on Mental Retardation (AAMR); the National Association for Down Syndrome (NADS); the Association for the Severely Handicapped (TASH); and Special Olympics International (SOI). The Council for Exceptional Children (CEC) has a major division that addresses individuals with mental retardation. Other professional organizations include the National Consortium on Physical Education and Recreation for Individuals With Disabilities; the National Therapeutic Recreation Association (NTRA); the National Therapeutic Recreation Society (NTRS); the American Kinesiotherapy Association (AKTA); the American Occupational Therapy Association (AOTA); and the American Physical Therapy Association (APTA). Most of these associations publish excellent journals, often with articles and research dealing with children and adults with mental retardation. The names and addresses of these groups are found in Appendix A.

Summary

Individuals with mental retardation have new opportunities due to advances being made in medicine, rehabilitation, education, physical education, and leisure. The federal government has passed strict laws that provide specific guidelines for education, recreation, and vocational pursuits. PL 94-142 was preceded by a long and difficult history in the education and rehabilitation of those with mental retardation. Today teachers, therapists, recreational leaders, physicians, parents, and community members are learning and using new techniques to provide more and better opportunities for people with

Table 1.8   Important Dates of Federal Legislation Regarding Individuals With Disabilities

Title	Purpose
PL 85-926 (1958)	Provided grants for teaching in the education of handicapped children, related to education of children who are mentally retarded.
PL 88-164, Title III (1963)	Authorized funds for teacher training and for research and demonstration projects in the education of the handicapped.
PL 89-750 (1965)	Elementary and Secondary Education Act. Title III authorized assistance to handicapped children in state-operated and state-supported private day and residential schools.
PL 89-313	Amendments to PL 89-10. Provided grants to state educational agencies for the education of handicapped children in state-supported institutions.
PL 90-170 (1967)	Amendments to PL 88-164. Provided funds for personnel training to care for individuals who are mentally retarded, and the inclusion of individuals with neurological conditions related to mental retardation.
PL 90-247 (1968)	Amendments to PL 89-10. Provided regional resource centers for the improvement of education of children with handicaps.
PL 90-538 (1968)	Handicapped Children's Early Education Assistance Act. Provided grants for the development and implementation of experimental programs in early education for children with handicaps, from birth to age 6.
PL 91-230 (1969)	Amendments to PL 89-10. Title VI consolidated into one act—Education of the Handicapped—the previous enactments relating to handicapped children.
PL 92-424 (1972)	Economic Opportunity Amendments. Required that not less than 10 percent of Head Start enrollment opportunities be available to children with handicaps.
PL 93-380 (1974)	Amended and expanded Education of the Handicapped Act (PL 91-230) in response to right-to-education mandates. Required states to establish goal of providing full educational opportunity for all children with handicaps, from birth to age 21.
PL 94-142 (1975)	Education for All Handicapped Children Act. Required states to provide by September 1, 1978, a free appropriate education for all handicapped children between the ages of 3 and 18.
PL 98-199 (1984)	Amended the Handicapped Children's Early Education Assistance Act (PL 90-538). Provided funds for planning statewide comprehensive services for handicapped children through age 5.
PL 99-457, Part H (1986)	Amended the Education of the Handicapped Act. Mandated comprehensive multidisciplinary services for infants and toddlers (birth through age 2) and their families.

Note. From "Alternative Administrative Strategies for Young Handicapped Children" by S. Behr and J. Gallagher, 1981, *Journal of the Division of Early Childhood*, **2**, pp. 113-122. Copyright by the Journal. Adapted by permission.

mental retardation at all levels—mild, moderate, severe, and profound.

Individuals classified as mentally retarded include approximately 1.5% to 2.5% of the total population, of which most are capable of leading normal lives—that is, to live independently, enjoy leisure pursuits, be meaningfully employed, get married, raise a family, and enjoy life to its fullest.

For those with less ability and a more restricted future, the challenge to professionals is more difficult. Society must make individuals labeled as having moderate, severe, or profound retardation its top priority, because these persons can and will improve significantly if given appropriate programs to meet their immediate and future needs. They can become contributing members of society if given the tools to do so. Transdisciplinary cooperation among professionals is necessary if society is truly to provide exemplary programs. To paraphrase an old saying: "Give me a fish and I will eat today. Teach me to fish and I will care for myself forever."

Controlled and meaningful movement is critical to success in our complicated world. Health and fitness are means to attain both indepen-dence and the opportunity for a life without disease and restricting impairments. Physical activity, including the basic skills of body control and locomotion, is extremely important for everyone, but particularly for individuals with mental retardation. For persons restricted by mental and physical impairments, the world of movement is often difficult and overwhelming. Body control, through the development of strength, endurance, and coordination, is of utmost importance. Motor activity programs must not only be included in, but in some cases be the major focus of, education programs for this population.

DISCUSSIONS AND NEW DIRECTIONS

1. PL 94-142 states that "to the maximum extent possible and when appropriate, handicapped children [should be] educated with children who are nonhandicapped and that . . . removal of the handicapped child from the regular educational environment occurs only when the nature or severity of the handicap [precludes satisfactory integration]" (p. 42497). How does your school district determine "the maximum extent possible," "when appropriate," and "when the nature or severity of the handicap [precludes satisfactory integration]"?

2. Are the systems that are used in your school district valid for determining the variables in question 1? Are they reliable? constantly applied? fair? What weaknesses do the present practices show, and how might these weaknesses be eliminated?

3. Discuss whether reverse mainstreaming places the student-tutor who does not have disabilities in a more or less restrictive environment. To what degree does PL 94-142 apply to students without disabilities? Should units teaching human movement in adapted settings (e.g., wheelchair basketball) be routinely included in regular physical education classes?

4. In the past, there have been communication problems among educational, medical, and therapy professionals (i.e., regular educators, special educators, physical educators, adapted physical educators, physicians, recreation therapists, Special Olympics coaches, physical therapists, occupational therapists, and kinesiotherapists). What can be done to improve working relationships among these groups in regard to programs for individuals with mental retardation?

References

Abel, E.L. (1984). Prenatal effects of alcohol. *Drug and Alcohol Dependence*, **14**, 1-10.

Alford, C.A. (1988). Chronic perinatal infections and mental retardation. In J.F. Kavanagh (Ed.), *Understanding mental retardation* (pp. 137-148). Baltimore: Brooks.

Austin, D.R., & Crawford, M.E. (1991). *Therapeutic recreation: An introduction.* Englewood Cliffs, NJ: Prentice Hall.

Baird, P.A., & Sadovnick, A.D. (1985). Mental retardation in over half-a-million consecutive livebirths: An epidemiological study. *American Journal of Mental Deficiency*, **89**, 323-330.

Barclay, A.M. (1988). Atlantoaxial subluration: A review of research. *Down Syndrome News*, **12**, 1-52.

Bauer, A.M., & Shea, T.M. (1989). *Teaching exceptional students in your classroom.* Boston: Allyn & Bacon.

Blackman, J.A. (1990). *Medical aspects of developmental disabilities in children birth to three* (2nd ed.). Rockville, MD: Aspen.

Borkowski, J.G., & Turner, L.A. (1988). Cognitive development. In J.F. Kavanagh (Ed.), *Understanding mental retardation* (pp. 251-265). Baltimore: Brooks.

Coleman, M. (1988). Medical care of children and adults with Down syndrome. In V. Dmitriev and P.L. Oelwein (Eds.), *Advances in Down syndrome* (pp. 7-18). Seattle: Special Child.

Collacott, R.A., Ellison, D., Harper, W., Newland, C., & Ray-Chaudhurt, K. (1989). Atlanto-occipital instability in Down's syndrome. *Journal of Mental Deficiency Research*, **33**, 499-505.

Cowden, J.E., & Eason, R.L. (1991). Legislative terminology affecting adapted physical education. *Journal of Physical Education, Recreation and Dance*, **62**(2), 34.

Dauer, V.P., & Pangrazi, R.P. (1989). *Dynamic physical education for elementary school children* (9th ed.). New York: Macmillan.

Downs, M.P., & Balkany, T.J. (1988). Otologic problems and hearing impairment in Down syndrome. In V. Dmitriev & P.L. Oelwein (Eds.), *Advances in Down syndrome* (pp. 19-34). Seattle: Special Child.

Down Syndrome (1991). *Encyclopedia Americana*, Vol. 9, p. 320.

Drew, C.J., Hardman, M.L., & Logan, D.R. (1988). *Mental retardation* (4th ed.). Columbus, OH: Merrill.

Duffy, F.H., & Als, H. (1988). Neural plasticity and the effect of a positive supportive hospital environment on premature newborns. In J.F. Kavanagh (Ed.), *Understanding mental retardation* (pp. 179-206). Baltimore: Brooks.

Eichstaedt, C.B., & Kalakian, L.H. (1987). *Developmental/adapted physical education: Making ability count* (2nd ed.). New York: Macmillan.

Eichstaedt, C.B., Wang, P.Y., Polacek, J.J., & Dohrmann, P.F. (1991). *Physical fitness and motor skill levels of individuals with mental retardation: Mild, moderate, and Down syndrome ages 6-21.* Normal, IL: Illinois State University Printing Services.

Federal Register. Rules and regulations— Section 504. Department of Health, Education, and Welfare, Office of Education, **42**(65), 4 May 1977, Section 84.34 Participation of Students, p. 22682.

Fenton, L.J. (1990). Care of the high risk neonate. In R.E. Rakel (Ed.), *Conn's current therapy 1990* (pp. 937-950). Philadelphia: Saunders.

Feuerstein, R., Rand, Y., & Hoffman, M. (1979). *The dynamic assessment of retarded performers: The learning potential assessment device, theory, instruments, and techniques.* Baltimore: University Park Press.

Gitter, L.L. (1971). *The Montessori approach to special education.* Johnstown, PA: Mafex.

Gorton, C.E. (1977). The mainstream—both wide and deep. *Mainstreaming in Health, Physical Education, Recreation, and Dance: Proceedings of National Conference* (p. 28). Denton, TX: Texas Women's University.

Gottlieb, J., Rose, T., & Lessen, E. (1983). Mainstreaming. In K. Kernau, M. Begab, & R. Edgerton (Eds.), *Environments and behavior: The adaptation of mentally retarded persons* (pp. 195-212). Baltimore: University Park Press.

Grossman, H.J. (Ed.) (1983). *Classification in*

mental retardation. Washington, DC: American Association on Mental Deficiency.

Grossman, H.J., & Tarjan, G. (Eds.) (1987). *AMA handbook on mental retardation*. Elwyn, PA: Elwyn Institutes.

Hanson, M.J. (1988). Effects of gross-motor activity on development. In V. Dmitriev & P.L. Oelwein (Eds.), *Advances in Down syndrome* (pp. 167-173). Seattle: Special Child.

Haring, N.G., & McCormick, L. (Eds.) (1990). *Exceptional children and youth* (5th ed.). Columbus, OH: Merrill.

Heward, W.L., & Orlansky, M.D. (1988). *Exceptional children* (3rd ed.). Columbus, OH: Merrill.

Hilton, A. (1988). Mental retardation: Emerging challenges. *Education and Training in Mental Retardation*, **23**, 245-247.

Hobbs, N. (1975). *The futures of children*. San Francisco: Jossey-Bass.

Hogg, J., & Sebba, J. (1987a). *Profound retardation and multiple impairment: Vol. 1. Development and learning*. Rockville, MD: Aspen.

Hogg, J., & Sebba, J. (1987b). *Profound retardation and multiple impairment: Vol. 2. Education and therapy*. Rockville, MD: Aspen.

Hutt, M.L., & Gibby, R.G. (1979). *The mentally retarded child* (4th ed.). Boston: Allyn & Bacon.

Illinois comprehensive system of personnel development. (1989). Springfield: Illinois Department of Special Education.

Itard, J.M.G. (1962). *The wild boy of Aveyron*. (G. Humphrey & M. Humphrey, Eds. and Trans.). New York: Appleton-Century-Crofts. (Originally published 1894)

Jacobson, J.W., & Janicki, M.P. (1983). Observed prevalence of multiple developmental disabilities. *Mental Retardation*, **21**, 87-94.

Janicki, M.P. (1988). The changing nature of the population of individuals with mental retardation. In J.F. Kavanagh (Ed.), *Understanding mental retardation* (pp. 297-309). Baltimore: Brooks.

Jensen, A.R. (1980). *Bias in mental testing*. New York: Free Press.

Kirk, S.A., & Gallagher, J.J. (1989). *Educating exceptional children* (6th ed.). Boston: Houghton Mifflin.

Lavay, B., & French, R. (1985). The special physical educator: Meeting educational goals through a transdisciplinary approach. *American Corrective Therapy Journal*, **39**, 77-81.

Leininger, R. (1991, February 6). Major change. *Pantagraph*, p. A8.

Levy, H.L. (1988). Newborn screening. In J.F. Kavanagh (Ed.), *Understanding mental retardation* (pp. 155-158). Baltimore: Brooks.

MacMillan, D.L. (1988). Issues in mild mental retardation. *Education & Training in Mental Retardation*, **23**, 273-284.

Moser, H.W. (1988). Overview. In J.F. Kavanagh (Ed.), *Understanding mental retardation* (pp. 151-154). Baltimore: Brooks.

National Down Syndrome Congress. (1988). *Facts about Down syndrome*. Park Ridge, IL: Author.

Niva, R.A. (1988). Eye abnormalities and their treatment. In V. Dmitriev & P.L. Oelwein (Eds.), *Advances in Down syndrome* (pp. 45-57). Seattle: Special Child.

Nyhan, W.L. (1988). Research challenges and opportunities in the next quarter century. In J.F. Kavanagh (Ed.), *Understanding mental retardation* (pp. 3-16). Baltimore: Brooks.

O'Brien, K.P. (1991). Personal communication, March 5, 1991.

Patton, J.R., Payne, J.S., & Beirne-Smith, M. (1990). *Mental retardation* (3rd ed.). Columbus, OH: Merrill.

Payne, V.G., & Isaacs, L.D. (1991). *Human motor development* (2nd ed.). Mountain View, CA: Mayfield.

Priest, J.H. (1985). Chromosomal disorders. In

R.B. Conn (Ed.), *Current diagnosis 7* (pp. 1265-1289). Philadelphia: Saunders.

Pueschel, S.M. (1988). *The young person with Down syndrome*. Baltimore: Brooks.

Reschly, D.J. (1988). Assessment issues, placement litigation, and the future of mild mental retardation classification and programming. *Education and Training in Mental Retardation*, **23**, 285-301.

Rogers, R.C., & Simensen, R.J. (1987). Fragile X syndrome: A common etiology of mental retardation. *American Journal of Mental Retardation*, **91**, 445-449.

Schmickel, R.D. (1988). Overview. In J.F. Kavanagh (Ed.), *Understanding mental retardation* (pp. 19-22). Baltimore: Brooks.

Scott, K.G. (1988). Theoretical epidemiology: Environment and lifestyle. In J.F. Kavanagh (Ed.), *Understanding mental retardation* (pp. 23-33). Baltimore: Brooks.

Seaman, J.A., & DePauw, K.P. (1989). *The new adapted physical education: A developmental approach* (2nd ed.). Mountain View, CA: Mayfield.

Siedentop, D. (1990). *Introduction to physical education, fitness, and sport*. Mountain View, CA: Mayfield.

Spitz, H.H. (1988). Mental retardation as a thinking disorder: The rationalist alternative to empiricism. In N.W. Bray (Ed.), *International review of research in mental retardation* (pp. 1-32). New York: Academic Press.

Tonelson, S.W., & Santilli, N. (1987). Detecting and treating seizure disorders in developmentally delayed children. In S.E. Breuning & R.A. Gable (Eds.), *Advances in mental retardation and developmental disabilities: Vol. 3* (pp. 151-177). Greenwich, CT: JAI Press.

U.S. Department of Education. (1991). *"To assure the free appropriate public education of all handicapped children". Education of the Handicapped Act, Section 618*. (13th Annual Report to Congress on the Implementation of the Education of the Handicapped Act). Washington, D.C.: Office of Special Education Programs, U.S. Office of Special Education and Rehabilitative Services.

U.S. Office of Education. Federal Register. (1977). The Individuals with Disabilities Education Act, formerly The Education for All Handicapped Children Act of 1975, Section 94-142, 99-457, 89-750, 42 U.S.C., Section 42480-54579.

Westling, D.L. (1986). *Introduction to mental retardation*. Englewood Cliffs, NJ: Prentice Hall.

Zigler, E., & Hodapp, R.M. (1986). *Understanding mental retardation*. New York: Cambridge University Press.

Zigman, W.B., Schupf, N., Lubin, R.A., & Silverman, W.P. (1987). Preventive regression of adults with Down syndrome. *American Journal of Mental Deficiency*, **92**, 161-168.

CHAPTER 2

Conditions Related to Mental Retardation

PREVIEW   School District 27 has just received records for Paul D., who will be moving into the district in the fall. His records show he is 9 years old and eligible for special education services, as he is labeled as having moderate mental retardation. He has a second disabling condition of spastic cerebral palsy. Additionally, Paul has experienced grand mal seizures, although these have been controlled. The information is turned over for further processing to Mr. Don March, director of special education, who will determine what information is needed to place Paul into the most appropriate learning environments.

Most important are Paul's present levels of ability. Therefore, the teachers who provide direct services (the special education and adapted physical education teachers) must be given a timeline for assessment, program writing, and placement. The school diagnostician might be asked to test the youngster to measure current levels of IQ and social, emotional, and behavioral competency. The adapted physical educator will be asked to give Paul a series of motor and physical fitness tests.

Past medical records will be consulted to determine Paul's state of health. If his last physical examination was more than a year ago, it would be appropriate to ask his parents to have Paul reexamined by a physician before school testing begins. Therapists might also be called upon to evaluate Paul. This is not usually necessary for children with no irregularities, but Paul's combination of moderate mental retardation, spastic cerebral palsy, and seizures might give rise to problems; in particular, if Paul has complications such as abnormal tonic neck reflexes or muscle contractures, it is important to know to what extent they will interfere with normal motor development.

HIGHLIGHT QUESTIONS

- What is cerebral palsy, and what problems does it raise for planning physical activity programs? How does cerebral palsy affect motor performance? What physical activities are suggested for individuals with cerebral palsy?
- What are seizures, and why are they so common in individuals with mental retardation? Are there different types of seizures? What should be done if a seizure occurs? Can medications control seizures? Are any physical activities contraindicated for individuals who sometimes have seizures?
- What is spina bifida and what is its etiology? What causes mental retardation in children who have spina bifida? What types of physical impairments are common in children who have spina bifida? Are there special physical activities for children with spina bifida?
- Which congenital heart defects are commonly found in children with mental retardation? What physical activity restrictions can be expected for individuals with congenital heart defects?
- Are visual and hearing impairments common in individuals with mental retardation? How does visual impairment or hearing impairment affect the motor learning of individuals with mental retardation? Which physical activities are recommended for individuals with visual impairment? with hearing impairment?
- How does obesity affect individuals with mental retardation? Which physical activities are suggested for obese individuals with mental retardation? How can individuals with mental retardation be motivated to lose weight?

Circumstances such as Paul D.'s are commonly faced by administrators, teachers, and therapists who deal with individuals with disabilities. The IEP team must be knowledgeable about disabling conditions associated with mental retardation so that the transdisciplinary approach can be best implemented. Problems commonly associated with mental retardation that are addressed in this chapter are cerebral palsy, seizures and seizure medications, spina bifida, congenital heart defects, visual and hearing impairments, and obesity.

Cerebral Palsy

Cerebral palsy (CP) is often described as a chronic, nonprogressive neurological injury, resulting from brain injury during the early developmental stages (prenatal, perinatal, and early postnatal). The term literally means brain (cerebral) paralysis (palsy). Bleck (1982) describes CP:

> The nonprogressive nature of cerebral palsy serves as an important criterion in diagnosis. For example, a brain tumor is not cerebral palsy; rather, its effects lead to a permanent and nonprogressive movement disorder of the limbs that becomes cerebral palsy. The same holds true of skull fractures and brain hemorrhages; only the late effects of such injuries to the brain, and the resultant movement disorder, would be termed cerebral palsy. The majority of children afflicted, however, do not acquire the condition from such late childhood injuries; rather, their disorder is caused by one of a variety of diseases and disturbances occurring during pregnancy or at the time of birth. (p. 59)

The lack of voluntary motor control is a major concern for professionals whose role is to improve motor performance. Healy (1990) explains CP as a disorder of muscle control or coordination that may be associated with lower intelligence, seizures, or visual impairment; regarding retardation, Healy estimates 60% to 70% of all persons having CP also possess some degree of mental retardation. Nelson and Ellenberg (1986) found that 41% of children with CP scored below 70 on a standardized IQ test. Therefore, at least 40%, and up to 70%, of those with CP also possess some degree of mental retardation. Jacobson and Janicki (1983) have shown that the prevalence of cerebral palsy is greater when the retardation is severe or profound (IQ less than 35).

Regarding correlation between motor performance and intelligence, Heward and Orlansky (1988) observe that "it is also important to bear in mind that no clear relationship exists between the degree of motor impairment and the degree of intellectual impairment (if any) in children with cerebral palsy. A student may experience severe developmental delays, whereas a student with severe motor impairments may be intellectually gifted" (p. 337).

Youngsters with CP find their problems further complicated when they are restricted by orthotic devices (braces) or confined to wheelchairs. Bleck (1982) estimates that about 80% of all children with cerebral palsy are capable of learning to develop some method of locomotion, though many will need to use wheelchairs, braces, or other assistive devices. Physical development then revolves around the child's movement capabilities. Some activity programs resemble pure therapy, with improvement of existing physical conditions as the main focus. A colorful playroom or gym can have an extremely powerful and positive impact on these children. These areas can be quite motivational, establishing a genuine "set to learn," this environmental stimulation making the children more receptive. Therefore, the fun and excitement of physical education and recreation must always be among the major outcomes of the total educational program.

Etiology of Cerebral Palsy

Cerebral palsy has exactly the same causes as mental retardation (see chapter 1); anything that can cause damage to the brain can produce the physical effects of cerebral palsy. So it is not surprising that a significant number of individuals with CP also have some degree of mental retardation (Westling, 1986).

Nelson and Ellenberg (1986) concluded that cerebral palsy in infants is most directly associated with four major causes: (a) mental retardation of the mother, (b) premature birth of 32 weeks or less, (c) low birth weight, and (d) a delay of 5 min or more after birth before the baby's first cry. To avoid misinterpreting (a), we must remember that cerebral palsy is a direct result of brain damage and *cannot be inherited*. The role of retardation in this case is that if a woman who has mental retardation does not have the intellectual ability to assure herself good prenatal care, she is at greater risk for an irregular pregnancy involving brain damage to the fetus. The other three causes are also conditions in which brain damage is likely to occur.

Classifications of Cerebral Palsy

Approximately 97% of all cases of CP fall under the three major types (Kirk & Gallagher, 1989): spastic (60% to 65%), athetoid (''dyskinesia,'' 25%), and ataxic (7%). Minor types of CP include tremor, rigidity, and hypotonia. Kirk and Gallagher do not include a general classification which incorporates two or more types in the same individual. Healy (1990) has found that 30% will exhibit characteristics of two types, although one may be more pronounced than the other. Healy uses the word *mixed* to describe the dual classification.

Youngsters are also grouped by affected body parts. For example, the classification *spastic quadriplegic* indicates that all four limbs are involved (with spastic movement characteristics). Other groups include *monoplegia, paraplegia, diplegia, triplegia, quadriplegia*, and *hemiplegia*. Table 2.1 lists the body parts involved in these CP classifications.

Spastic Cerebral Palsy

Spastic cerebral palsy comprises 60% to 65% of all CP cases. Spasticity is characterized by hard and jerky movements that result from poor muscle control. When the arms are involved, the individual has difficulty grasping, releasing, and catching objects. When the legs are affected, standing, walking, and running are impaired. Fast, quick, precise movements are difficult be-

Table 2.1   Labels Used With Cerebral Palsy Classifications to Describe Body Parts Involved

Label	Body part involved
Monoplegia	One limb (rare)
Paraplegia	Legs only
Diplegia	Trunk and all limbs, with the legs more than the arms
Triplegia	Three limbs (rare)
Quadriplegia	All limbs, head, and trunk
Hemiplegia	One side of body (e.g., right arm and right leg)

cause the antagonist muscles cannot relax at the proper times. This is true for all muscle groups involved. Eichstaedt and Kalakian (1987) explain this process:

Spasticity is characterized by presence of an increased *stretch reflex*, the principle diagnostic sign. The stretch reflex is a tendency of the muscle to contract when stretched rapidly; the reflex does not occur when the muscle is stretched slowly. . . . In cerebral palsy, when force is applied to stretch the spastic muscle, there is an increased resistance to the movement, but at a certain point, a rapid release occurs and the body part 'flys' in an uncontrollable manner. This is similar to the action of a pocket knife upon opening: there is a tension on the blade, but at a certain point, it springs open. Children with spastic cerebral palsy can hold a limb in either extreme extension or extreme flexion, but they cannot regulate muscle contraction sufficiently to control movements between these extremes. (p. 409)

Because they encounter so much difficulty when they try to move, these youngsters tend to restrict their actions. Also, parents and teachers are prone to give too much assistance. These children benefit more when they are asked and expected to perform movements on their own. Instructors must allow adequate time and not be impatient when working with them.

Spasticity has a very detrimental effect on certain muscle groups and often results in *muscle contractures*. When little or no movement occurs in muscle over an extended period of time, the tendons shorten and continually pull until the joint becomes almost closed and in some cases frozen in an immovable position. An example of this is a tightly closed fist with the fingers wrapped snugly around the thumb. Walking and running is often complicated by tight and contracted leg muscles that produce the characteristic *scissors gait* (see Figure 2.1). For all muscle contractures, the ever present dominance of flexion, internal rotation, and adduction must be overcome. That is, the muscles should be *slowly* stretched (elongated) to reduce negative effects. This assistive action is usually performed by the therapist or teacher and should never be done in a ballistic (fast) or

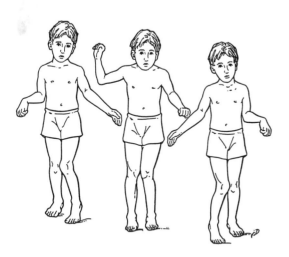

Figure 2.1 Scissors gait is commonly found in children with spastic cerebral palsy.

Note. From *Developmental/Adapted Physical Education: Making Ability Count* (2nd ed.) (p. 410) by C.B. Eichstaedt and L.H. Kalakian, 1987, New York: Macmillan. Copyright 1987 by Macmillan Publishers. Reprinted by permission.

"bouncy" movement. The normal path for range of motion should be followed. It is also beneficial to strengthen the extensors, external rotators, and abductors. Opening the hands and improving the skill of releasing objects can be very helpful to a child attempting to play games involving small objects such as blocks, pegs, marbles, checkers, or balls. Finnie's (1975) book includes excellent descriptions and diagrams for proper handling, positioning, and moving techniques for individuals with spastic and athetoid tendencies. The book is highly recommended and should be in the library of every adapted physical educator, therapeutic recreation leader, or special education teacher.

Healy (1990) suggests that as many as 50% of all youngsters with spastic cerebral palsy will have eye muscle imbalance. Refractive errors (near- or farsightedness) are almost as common. Thus, visual tracking may be difficult for those with visual impairments, and catching and striking games should be modified. For example, in a game of badminton, a balloon could be used in place of the traditional birdie.

Athetoid or Dyskinetic Cerebral Palsy

Athetosis comprises approximately 25% of all cases of cerebral palsy. Healy (1990) suggests that the word *dyskinesia* more accurately describes this type of CP: "Dyskinesia is a term describing the unwanted, involuntary movements of cerebral palsy. These include slow writhing movements, particularly of the wrist and fingers (athetosis), which may be accompanied by more abrupt and jerky movements (choreoathetosis). Another form of dyskinesia comprises slow, rhythmic movements involving the trunk or an entire extremity (dystonia)" (p. 59). Says Bleck (1982), who uses the old term *athetosis* but identifies "worm-like" movements as the major characteristic: "Movements are, at times, rotary (rotation and twisting of the limbs), dystonic (distorted positioning of the limbs, neck, or trunk, that is held for a few seconds, then released), flailing (limbs thrashing about), or chorea 'the dance' (spontaneous jerking motions, usually of the fingers or toes)'' (p. 64).

People with athetosis commonly have little control of their lips, tongue, and throat muscles, which makes speech extremely difficult for them and often causes drooling. This inability to speak clearly, compounded by drooling, tends to give others the impression that these youngsters are severely mentally retarded; but many children with athetosis have average or above average intellectual capabilities. Communication is one of the major obstacles for these children, and it is common for them to use language or conversation boards. The board is placed across the arms of the wheelchair and displays pictures, letters, words, numbers, and phrases. The child points to the appropriate words with a finger or hand or a pointer attached to a headband. Newer, computerized equipment allows more advanced methods of communication. The role of the physical educator or therapeutic recreation specialist is to improve eye/hand coordination, thus helping the students to control their hand and arm movements. Pressing keys or pointing can be major objectives, and students' success can be increased through drills that stress motor control. A most effective approach is to use games that create interest and challenges while developing skill through fun-oriented activities.

Ataxia

Ataxia involves having difficulty with balance and walking with a pronounced lurching and stumbling gait. The condition stems from damage to the cerebellum and is usually not associated with mental retardation. Static and dynamic balance activities that stress sitting, standing, and walking are useful. Individuals with ataxia can develop upper body strength by doing weight training exercises while sitting down. They can improve their cardiorespiratory endurance by using hand ergometers.

General Activity Suggestions

Ambulation is often difficult and deviant for individuals with cerebral palsy, and it requires a great deal of energy. This problem is compounded as children grow and their body weight increases, changing their center of gravity. This ongoing process may cause individuals to tire more easily as they grow older.

Major activities must be directed toward improving voluntary motor control. Daily stretching is essential for individuals with contractures. Limbs that are not exercised may lose their usefulness altogether (Patton, Payne, & Beirne-Smith, 1990). The time needed for stretching varies, depending on the number of severely involved joints, and could constitute most of the activity period. We should remember that children respond better when the activities are fun and somewhat challenging. Games that use releasing skills, and movements that emphasize extension, external rotation, and abduction, are described in Highlight 2.1.

Generally speaking, individuals with spastic CP are static and need to increase their mobility. Movement should be done in straight planes of flexion and extension, and movement should be assisted through handling and not by vocal directions. Youngsters with athetoid CP, on the other hand, are usually hypermobile and need stability. These children need midline activities because they tend to be asymmetrical and have poor head control. An upright weight-bearing position usually adds stability and control.

The child's *body positioning* is important during any attempt to increase positive pressure against the negative action of contractured muscles. Propping the child up with bolsters and wedges allows the child to be involved in play activities but still reduces the overpowering consequences of flexion, internal rotation, and adduction.

Orthotic devices (braces) are often needed to restrict unwanted movement or to hold fingers, hands, wrists, arms, legs, or the body in desirable positions. These implements should be

IN PRACTICE

Games and Activities to Improve Eye-Hand Coordination and Object Release

Dropping and Releasing Skills

Clothespin Drop. Place a large coffee can on the floor at the side of the wheelchair. The child drops clothespins into the can. Equipment: 1 2-lb coffee can, 5 clothespins

Slippery Coins. Place a glass inside a bucket filled with water. The child drops coins into the glass. Equipment: 1 bucket; 1 large drinking glass; 20 coins, metal washers, or slugs

Pushing and Sliding Skills

Miniature Shuffleboard. The child slides small disks or checkers into a tape target on the floor or a table. Equipment: 10 checkers or disks, tape target

Slip and Slide. Place a large box or wastebasket on the floor at the end of a table. Slide disks or checkers along the table so they fall off into the receptacle. Equipment: 20 disks or checkers, 1 large box or wastebasket

Ball-Rolling Skills

Ball in the Cave. The child rolls tennis balls from an 8-foot baseline at 3 holes cut in the bottom edge of a cardboard box. Equipment: 3 tennis balls, cardboard box with 3 holes cut out

Bowling. Use any ball the child can handle; use a ramp for rolling the ball if needed. Set up plastic or wooden pins. Equipment: ball, 10 pins

Ball-Bouncing Skills

Cupcake Bounce. The child bounces Ping-Pong balls into a cupcake pan or egg carton from 5 feet away. Equipment: Cupcake pan or egg carton, 6 Ping-Pong balls

Volleyball Bounce. The child bounces a volleyball into a wastebasket from 6 feet away. Equipment: 1 wastebasket, 2 volleyballs

Michael Jordan Special. The child bounces a basketball or large rubber ball into an upright box or large garbage can 8 feet away. Equipment: 1 box or large garbage can, ball

Underhand Throwing Skills

Folger Special. Set 5 coffee cans on the floor in an irregular order. The child throws beanbags or small foam balls into the cans. Equipment: 5 coffee cans, 10 beanbags or small foam balls

Chair Toss. The child throws rings at the legs of an upturned chair. Equipment: 1 chair; 10 rings made of rope, plastic, or wire

HIGHLIGHT 2.1 CONTINUED

Horseshoe Pitch. The child pitches 3 rubber or cardboard horseshoes at a 12-inch stake 8 feet away. Equipment: 1 or 2 stakes, 7 horseshoes

Tossing and Flipping Skills

Paper Plate Flip. The child sails paper plates into a large box 15 feet away (closer if needed). Equipment: 5 paper plates, 1 large box

Throw the Discus. The child sails paper plates for distance. Equipment: 5 paper plates

The Dealer's Wild. The child flips playing cards into a box set at an angle on its edge facing the child. Equipment: 1 deck of playing cards, 1 box

Ring the Bottle. The child tosses rubber jar rings onto soft-drink bottles. Equipment: 6 large pop bottles, 12 jar rings

Bottle Cap Pitch. The child pitches bottle caps onto a small pie plate that is floating in a washtub filled with water. Equipment: Bottle caps, washtub, small pie plate

removed when specific range of motion activities are being conducted, including some games. For instance, during a game that calls for catching a foam ball, the instructor should remove the arm support brace that the youngster wears to restrict elbow bending.

Wheelchairs are used to facilitate locomotion. For individuals who would be able to walk only with extensive use of leg braces and arm crutches, the wheelchair is a more desirable method of travel, and for them, motor skill development, physical fitness improvement, athletic competition, and leisure-time activities should be provided that are done from the wheelchair. Winnick and Short (1991) found that for individuals between 10 and 17 years of age with both cerebral palsy and mild mental retardation, the development of grip strength is directly proportional to age. That is, the older the subject, the greater the grip strength. Thus, it can be assumed that hand strength is likely to improve in these individuals as they move through their teenage years, if they are provided with appropriate physical activities.

Wheelchair athletic associations have been formed to provide opportunities for competition. Since 1960, international events for individuals in wheelchairs have been held annually at Stoke Mandeville, England, and every fourth year in the city hosting the Olympic Games. These events, designated in 1960 as the Paralympics, became the Olympics for the Disabled in 1980 (Winnick, 1990). The Special Olympics organization has included specific events for competitors in wheelchairs, including even those with the most severe complications. Local, state, and regional competition is common and may include activities such as obstacle courses, speed-racing events, endurance races (for both time and distance), and modified wheelchair basketball, badminton, and shuffleboard. Many other activities can be modified by changing the equipment, floor layout, and rules.

An example of such a competitive event is the wheelchair slalom:

WHEELCHAIR SLALOM

Distance:
30 yards

Participants:
Individuals who travel forward by the use of their hands, and those who travel backward by the use of their feet

Equipment needed:
- A straight, flat stretch of hard, smooth surface (wooden surfaces are not recommended)
- Catchers (one for each lane)
- 5 safety cones, placed in 5-yard intervals, which the participant must zigzag around
- Tape to mark start, finish, and lane widths
- Stopwatches (one for each competitor)

Special considerations:
- Participants may travel the course either forward or backward
- Participants may compete one against another or against the clock

Seizures and Convulsive Disorders

The same injuries and diseases that cause mental retardation are likely to cause seizures. Seizures are induced by an overload of electrical impulses in the brain. Because the brain's working ability has been impaired, the central nervous system attempts to protect the individual from this excessive electrical surge by generating a seizure. Wolraich (1990c) describes the problem: "Normally, minute electrical impulses travel along specific nerve pathways in a controlled fashion and at appropriate times. A seizure occurs when bursts of unorganized electrical impulses interfere with this normal brain functioning. Electrical bursts of different types or in different locations of the brain result in different kinds of seizures" (p. 251).

Classifications of Seizures

Seizures are divided into two major groups, *partial* and *generalized*. Generalized seizures are the largest group and include grand mal, petit (pet'-tee') mal, and akinetic seizures. Vining's (1989) classification of seizures is given in Table 2.2.

Epstein, Polloway, Patton, and Foley (1989) believe that seizures are much more common among individuals who have retardation than among those who do not. Teachers and other workers must be aware of what is likely to cause a seizure for each child and what to do during a seizure. Also, because most seizure-prone individuals take medication, it is beneficial to be aware of potential side effects of these medications (Hallahan & Kauffman, 1988).

Generalized Tonic-Clonic (Grand Mal) Seizures

Grand mal, or generalized tonic-clonic, seizures are the most violent of seizures and comprise approximately 60% of all convulsive disorders (Blackman, 1990c). During a grand mal seizure the individual loses consciousness and falls, and the generalized tonic action of the limb and axial muscles makes the body stiffen. The legs usually extend, and the arms partially flex (this tonic phase usually lasts less than a minute). The clonic phase follows immediately with jerking movements in all four limbs for about 1 to 4 minutes. During the recovery period (of about 1 minute), there is little movement, and the individual appears more relaxed. Consciousness is then regained, and if the seizure is comparatively minor, the person will act unaffected. But if the person seems confused, uncooperative, or sleepy for several minutes prior to full recovery, she or he should be closely supervised.

Most serious injuries during grand mal seizures occur when the person falls to the ground and hits his or her head on a hard surface or, when on the ground, violently bangs the head during the thrashing contractions of the clonic (jerking) phase. Knowing when a seizure is going to happen can help prevent injury. Some individuals will "feel" a seizure coming on and can tell the teacher, "I don't feel good" or "I

Table 2.2   Seizure Classifications

International classification	"Old terms"
Partial seizures	Focal or local seizures
Simple partial seizures (Consciousness not impaired)	Focal motor seizures
With motor symptoms	Jacksonian seizures
With somatosensory or special sensory symptoms	Focal sensory seizures
With autonomic symptoms	
With psychic symptoms	
Complex partial seizures (with impairment of consciousness)	Psychomotor seizures
Simple partial onset	Temporal lobe seizures
With impairment of consciousness at onset	
Partial seizures that secondarily generalize	
Generalized seizures (convulsive or nonconvulsive)	
Absence seizures	Petit mal seizures
Absence	
Atypical	
Myoclonic seizures	Minor motor seizures
Clonic seizures	Grand mal seizures
Tonic seizures	Grand mal seizures
Tonic-clonic seizures	Grand mal seizures
Atonic seizures (astatic)	Akinetic, drop attacks

Note. From "Epilepsy in Infants and Children" by E.P.G. Vinning. In *Conn's 1989 Current Therapy* (p. 792) by R.E. Rakel (Ed.), 1989, Philadelphia: Saunders. Reprinted by permission of W.B. Saunders.

know it's coming.'' This warning is called an *aura*. Keep in mind that many youngsters who are mentally retarded and experiencing seizures will be functioning with comparatively low mental capacities and may not recognize the warning signs. For those children it is essential that teachers and other workers be able to recognize the characteristics typical for *each child*. For example, you are working with Barbara, who begins to utter unusual, gurgling sounds. This mannerism is consistent with Barbara's past seizures and occurs only before her attacks. You should attempt to place Barbara on the floor so that she does not injure herself by falling. Do not attempt to put anything in her mouth, but turn her head to the side to allow saliva to trickle out. Finally, cradle her head in your hands to protect her from banging it against the floor.

The thrashing portion of a seizure usually lasts anywhere from several seconds to several min-

utes. Once the seizure begins, nothing can be done to prevent it, and no attempt should be made to stop the child's movements. "The major concern is to keep the child from injuring himself. . . . The child should be eased to the floor, furniture and other objects pushed away from him. . . . Someone should remain with the child until the seizure ends, and then allow him to rest" (Patton et al., 1990, p. 224).

If a seizure lasts more than 4 minutes, it should be considered severe, and the instructor should alert the appropriate school personnel for assistance (e.g., school nurse, principal). If the child awakes and then passes into another seizure (see *status epilepticus* later in this section), she or he may need additional care, and it is appropriate to call for outside assistance such as an emergency medical team (EMT).

Medical personnel tell us that it is the fall that causes the injury and not the injury that causes

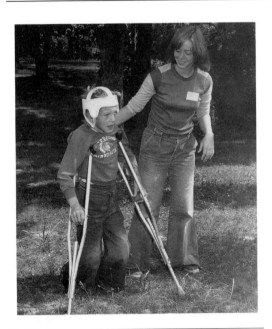

Figure 2.2 A helmet helps protect individuals from head injuries if they fall. Photo courtesy of J. Polacek, Illinois State University, Normal, Illinois.

the seizure. A blow to the head will *not* cause a seizure, and head trauma due to falling is no more likely to cause convulsions in these individuals than in persons without disabilities (Eichstaedt & Kalakian, 1987). Individuals who have grand mal seizures are often encouraged to wear protective head devices, with padded chin straps, that reduce the chance of head injury (see Figure 2.2).

"Photosensitive" seizures are extremely rare, and too much attention has been given to this minor problem. At one time, seizures were thought to be caused by flickering fluorescent ceiling lights, rolling television pictures, light reflecting off wavy swimming pool water, and so forth. If a child has this rare problem, the medical record should list photosensitivity as a cause. It is totally unwarranted to overprotect these individuals or exclude them from most activities lest they have a seizure during them; they will only become outcasts from their peers. Teachers and leaders must protect against unnecessary activity restrictions.

Generalized Absence (Petit Mal) Seizures

Petit mal, or generalized absence, seizures are found almost exclusively in children and adolescents. Onset occurs after age 2-1/2 and rarely occurs for the first time after age 20 (Berg, 1987). Therefore, infants born with brain damage seldom experience petit mal seizures (Browne, 1989). When an attack occurs, individuals stop what they are doing and experience a temporary loss of consciousness without falling or having convulsions. The seizures last for only a few seconds but may occur many times during the day. When consciousness is regained, the person remembers nothing about the seizure. Individuals have been accused of daydreaming when in reality they were having petit mal seizures. Medication is capable of controlling over 80% of all petit mal seizures.

Atonic (Akinetic or Drop) Seizures

Akinetic seizures are often seen in children with mental retardation, and they persist into adulthood. The attacks occur without warning, are extremely short, and are characterized by a sudden fall. The person momentarily loses consciousness and is not able to keep from falling to the floor. In *drop seizures*, a sudden weakness of the legs forces the child to fall to his or her knees, but the child does not lose consciousness. The youngster usually falls forward, and sharp blows to the head or chin are likely. These children should wear protective headgear (Haring & McCormick, 1990). Of all seizures, akinetic or drop seizures are often the most difficult to control through medication, thus activities and areas of play for these children should be carefully assessed.

Status Epilepticus

Status epilepticus is most often associated with tonic-clonic (grand mal) seizures that last for more than 30 minutes or with a series of seizures in which one immediately follows another (Vining, 1989). Extended and recurring seizures have been the most common causes of death associated with seizures. Individuals with extensive brain damage and poor control through medication are the most likely to experience status epilepticus. Emergency medical treatment is definitely indicated.

Medications That Control Seizures

Seizures usually occur when an individual has failed to take prescribed medication. Medications are the most common method of controlling seizures, and only after extensive trial and error and failure to control do alternative methods (such as brain surgery) become considerations. Anticonvulsants, which limit the spread of abnormal electrical discharges in the brain, are neither sedatives nor tranquilizers. The long-range goal of anticonvulsants is to completely eliminate seizures without negative side effects. Eichstaedt and Kalakian (1987) observe that "in general, the amount of medication prescribed is based on a rough estimate of the condition's severity and the possibility of complete seizure control. In the drug management of seizures, children generally have a better prognosis than adults" (p. 392). Table 2.3 lists commonly used anticonvulsant medications and their more common side effects.

The process for prescribing anticonvulsant medications is to select and administer an appropriate drug for the specific type of seizure and continue its use until control is achieved or

Table 2.3   Anticonvulsant Medications and Their Side Effects for Children

Drug	Indications	Usual dosage schedule	Side effects
Carbamazepine[a] (Tetretol)	F[b], C, G	bid-qid	Headache, drowsiness, dizziness, diplopia, blood dyscrasia, hepatotoxicity, arrhythmia
Clonazepam (Klonopin)	M, A	bid-qid	Drowsiness, ataxia, secretions, hypotonia, behavioral problems
Ethosuximide (Zarontin)	A (? C, M)	bid	GI distress, rash, drowsiness, dizziness, SLE, blood dyscrasia
Phenobarbital	F, C, G, S	qd-bid	Drowsiness, rash, ataxia, behavioral and cognitive problems
Phenytoin (Dilantin)	F, C, G, S	qd-bid	Drowsiness, gum hyperplasia, rash, anemia, ataxia, hirsutism, folate deficiency, teratogenicity
Primidone (Mysoline)	F, C, G	bid-qid	Drowsiness, dizziness, rash, anemia, ataxia, diplopia
Valproate (Depakene, Depakote)	F, C, G, M, A	bid-qid	GI distress, hepatitis, alopecia, drowsiness, ataxia, tremors, pancreatitis, thrombocytopenia

Note. From "Epilepsy in Infants and Children" by E.P.G. Vinning. In *Conn's 1989 Current Therapy* (p. 793) by R.E. Rakel (Ed.), 1989, Philadelphia: Saunders. Adapted and used by permission of W.B. Saunders.

[a]Safety and efficacy for use in children have not been established.

[b]Abbreviations: F = focal (partial-simple); G = generalized (tonic-clonic); C = partial-complex; A = absence; M = minor motor (akinetic, atonic, myoclonic); S = status; qd = every day; bid = twice daily; qid = 4 times daily; GI = gastrointestinal.

toxic side effects become evident. When the appropriate dosage has been established, taking the medication on schedule is critical. For youngsters whose mental capacity is limited, this becomes the responsibility of the teacher or leader. Even the slightest deviation or delay can result in a seizure. Grossman and Tarjan (1987) warn that "many severely and profoundly retarded persons have epilepsy [seizures], and their resulting problems—often severe and complex—reflect considerable disturbance of brain function. Management of these seizures often is more difficult than that of typical seizures in nonretarded persons. Close neurologic monitoring and medical follow-up are essential" (p. 81).

Physicians must balance seizure control against negative side effects in the trial-and-error process of finding the best medication for the individual. Negative side effects listed by Vinning (1989) include detrimental effects on physical appearance, motor coordination, learning, and behavior. She observes that "frequently, the physician will have to rely on more than his or her own observation of the patient, and it may be necessary to carefully question both parents and school personnel regarding any changes they may perceive in the child" (p. 794). The most common drugs, which tend to cause loss of motor coordination, include phenobarbital, phenytoin (Dilantin), primidone (Mysoline), and valproate (Depakene/Depakote). The periods of unusual awkwardness often experienced by individuals taking these medications could be negative effects of the medications and have little to do with the children's true levels of ability. Motor assessment should be delayed during these "down times."

General Activity Suggestions

When planning movement activities for children prone to seizures, instructors should ask themselves these questions: What are the consequences to the youngster if suddenly she or he stops in midaction? Will the child fall from the balance beam? If the child is in the pool, will he or she go underwater? Might the child get hit in the face with the thrown ball? The activity dictates the potential for accident. It is always extremely important to determine whether the child's seizures are under control. If they are, the child should be allowed to participate in *all* motor activities, for there is little danger of a seizure occurring.

Spina Bifida (Myelomeningocele)

Spina bifida is the major cause of paralysis in children, and the most serious type is *myelomeningocele* (Kirk & Gallagher, 1989; Wolraich, 1990b). This condition is characterized by the spinal cord (and its covering, the meninges) protruding outside the vertebral column and becoming encased in a tough, sac-like growth. The sac looks and feels like a small, skin-colored cauliflower (see Figure 2.3). This problem occurs when the rear part of one of the vertebrae has failed to close during the prenatal period; the severe impairment of the spinal cord usually leaves the individual with some degree of paraplegia (involvement or paralysis of the legs). Many youngsters will need orthotic devices (braces), canes, or wheelchairs. Approximately 80% of children with myelomeningocele attain some ability to walk, the remaining 20% will use wheelchairs (see Table 2.4). As with cerebral palsy, ambulation is often difficult for individuals with spina bifida, which causes them to expend more energy. This problem is compounded as they grow and their body weight increases—a process that causes these individuals to tire more easily as they grow older. Minor types of spina bifida include occulta and meningocele, but these are much less severe and do not involve damage to the spinal cord.

Hydrocephalus

In approximately 80% of babies with myelomeningocele, the cerebrospinal fluid is prevented

Table 2.4 Relationship Between Location of Spina Bifida, Loss of Muscle Control, and Type of Ambulation

Approximate location of vertebral defect	Point below which control is lost	Prognosis for ambulation	Equipment used for ambulation
12th thoracic	Trunk	Nonambulatory	Wheelchair, standing brace
1st lumbar	Pelvis	Exercise ambulation	Wheelchair, long leg braces, and crutches
3rd lumbar	Hip	Household ambulation	Long leg braces and crutches
5th lumbar	Knee	Community ambulation	Short leg braces and crutches

Note. From "Relationship Between Location of Spina Bifida, Loss of Muscle Control, and Type of Ambulation" by D. Brunt. In *Adapted Physical Education and Recreation* (3rd ed.) (p. 515) by C. Sherrill, 1986, Dubuque, IA: W.C. Brown. Adapted and used with permission of W.C. Brown Publishers.

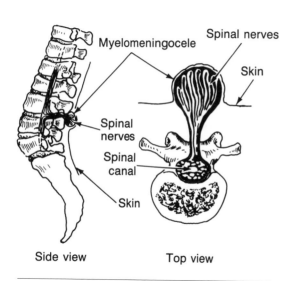

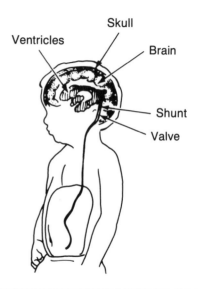

Figure 2.3 Myelomeningocele.
Note. Adapted from Eichstaedt and Kalakian (1987, p. 358).

Figure 2.4 Ventriculopertoneal shunt leading from the ventricles of the brain to the abdominal cavity.
Note. From *Medical Aspects of Developmental Disabilities in Children Birth to Three* (2nd ed.) (p. 178) by J.A. Blackman, 1990, Rockville, MD: Aspen. Copyright © 1990 by Aspen Publishers, Inc. Reprinted by permission.

from circulating around the brain and spinal cord, and excessive fluid buildup occurs (Wolraich, 1990a). The term *hydrocephalus* (water on the brain) is given to this condition. Without proper drainage, the increased pressure can cause brain damage resulting in mental retardation. Bleck and Nagel (1982) estimate

that 11% of children with hydrocephalus will possess an IQ below 80. Also, it is at this time that the head can become permanently enlarged. If a shunt (drain) is inserted into the skull soon enough, brain damage and enlargement can be prevented. Figure 2.4 shows a ventriculoperitoneal shunt. The drainage tube is inserted just under the skin and down into the abdominal cavity. A one-way valve lets the spinal fluid flow away from the brain. A less common shunt (ventriculoatrial) drains the fluid into the right atrium of the heart.

Brunt (1984) found that, in addition to the potential for mental retardation, myelomeningocele (MM) hydrocephalic youngsters perform significantly lower in simple and sequenced motor tasks than myelomeningocele non-hydrocephalic subjects. In his study, he concludes that "known involvement of the cerebellum and brain stem in MM children with hydrocephalus could affect primary motor skills and . . . therefore be the underlying cause of observed coordination problems" (p. 66).

General Activity Suggestions

For children in wheelchairs, motor activities should include the development of upper body strength. Wheelchair push-ups are very beneficial, as are hand- and grip-strengthening exercises. Flexed arm hanging and pull-ups on a low chinning bar are also recommended. Physical fitness can be improved by establishing a progressive overload program of manual wheelchair activities. Begin by having the youngsters propel their chairs to the end of the gym and back. Use a stopwatch to time the trips. Record how long it takes to complete the round-trip, and use this time for developing a baseline of performance. Repeat the drill in the next day or two. Also time how long each child takes to wheel once around the gym. With this drill you can add more laps, thereby increasing cardiorespiratory endurance. In the slalom-course drill, the individuals zigzag their chairs through a line of five cones or chairs set out at 6-foot intervals. These drills, if used regularly, should increase upper body strength, cardiorespiratory endurance, and wheelchair agility.

Nothing can be done to strengthen legs that are completely paralyzed. However, for youngsters who are ambulatory, leg strengthening should be included in the developmental program along with static and dynamic balance activities.

Eye/hand coordination activities should also be included, because well-defined manipulative skills are critical for these individuals. Brunt (1984) suggests that physical educators assess fine motor abilities and include appropriate skills and drills in the childrens' individualized educational plans (IEPs).

Congenital Heart Defects

Congenital heart defects (CHD) can be found in infants of whom brain damage occurred during the prenatal period. CHD more commonly occurs with severe and profound mental retardation.

In CHD the normal anatomy and pathways for blood flow in the newborn's defective heart are altered in ways that place an extra burden on the tiny heart. With the development of cardiopulmonary bypass techniques for open heart surgery in babies, along with the deep hypothermia process, surgical procedures for repair of congenital heart defects among neonates and infants have advanced tremendously. According to Rao (1989), "Almost every congenital heart defect can be 'corrected,' and the few that cannot be completely repaired can be effectively palliated [given relief]" (p. 212).

Of all individuals with mental retardation, children with Down syndrome are the most likely to have congenital heart defects. Blackman (1990a) puts their incidence at approximately 20% to 40%; Patton et al. (1990) have found the incidence to be approximately 33%.

Feit (1988) discusses the role of the physician, regarding heart defects:

The goals of the medical and surgical team of cardiac disease in patients with Down syndrome are to relieve symptoms, improve longevity, and alleviate a secondary handicapping condition. The burden of caring for a chronically ill child is quite different from and additional to the extra difficulties associated with rearing one who is mentally retarded. The application of timely, aggressive therapy should not be postponed or moderated because of the past prejudicial [detrimental] misconceptions about Down syndrome. (p. 35)

Within the population with Down syndrome the most common CHD is a complete atrioventricular canal defect (i.e., an endocardial cushion). In this condition, the heart's four chambers are not distinctly separated, and the valves between the upper chambers (atria) and lower chambers (ventricles) are incompletely formed. There is a large hole in the septal walls between both the atria and the ventricles (Blackman, 1990b). Coleman (1988) believes that complete surgical correction of the endocardial cushion defect should be performed on infants at less than 1 year of age. With other types of congenital heart defects, individual factors need to be considered before a decision is made as to the time for cardiac surgery.

The second most common problem is ventricular septal defect. In this case there is a hole in the wall of the lower chambers, producing "blue baby" symptoms—not enough oxygen is getting to the child's body, because fresh blood is mixing with unoxygenated blood in the heart. An infant with this problem will tire rapidly and not be able to sustain activity. Even active crawling or creeping may greatly tire the baby.

There appears to be a correlation between congenital heart defects and heart murmurs. A heart murmur involves an ineffective valve that allows blood to move backward (regurgitate) instead of being forced on. Feit (1988) believes that "prompt cardiac evaluation, the performance of precise diagnostic studies, and timely early surgical intervention should result in a much brighter outlook for the infant born with Down syndrome and congenital heart disease" (p. 44).

General Activity Suggestions

Exercise and activity for an individual with CHD depend entirely upon the physician's recommendations. The instructor should carefully review the child's medical history to determine whether the defect is still present. For example, look to see if and when surgery was performed. If the child had a successful operation several years ago, his or her heart may now be comparatively normal and the activity program would need no restrictions. However, if the defect is still present, overload activities could cause undue stress. The medical records should describe any contraindications. When the physician's instructions are old or vague, contact the parents to request that their physician update their records on the current cardiac condition of their child. It is strongly recommended that the physician describe what the student *cannot* do, and leave program development to the activity specialist. It is essential that there be close communication among the physician, the parent, and the special/adapted physical educator. Letters describing contraindications (from the physician) and the proposed activity program (from the activity specialist) should be mailed to everyone involved. Alterations in the activity program, including changes reflecting progress that has been made, are to be shared.

Even individuals with the most severe CHD can benefit from activities designed to improve their recreational skills. Games that can be done sitting down are important because they provide a dimension of leisure activity without the discomfort and possible danger that more active pursuits could cause. This sedentary lifestyle must be viewed not as a disability but as an opportunity to develop activities that involve the child with the other students. Games such as table hockey, shuffleboard, and table tennis can effectively increase eye/hand coordination. Hand-strengthening exercises, such as squeezing a tennis ball, are encouraged. Games can be modified to allow children with CHD to participate. For instance, if fast walking is contraindicated for some children and the group activity is indoor floor hockey, these children can wield hockey sticks from wheelchairs while being pushed about by other students.

Gidding (1988), a child cardiac specialist, believes that children with CHD should be discouraged from sedentary behavior and that they should participate to the limits of their tolerance; but he also warns that they should not be forced into competitive activities. He has found that young children (less than 6 years old) self-limit their activities. Dr. Gidding recommends there be *no* physical restrictions for most individuals with atrial septal defects, ventricular septal defects, patent ductus arterious, mild valve murmurs, or irregular heartbeats that go away with exercise. Gidding's progressive approach is encouraging, but programs should allow for individual differences among children. Therefore, it is recommended that all contraindications regarding activity programs be approved by the child's physician.

When activity programs are initiated, the instructor should watch for signs of cardiac stress. These include labored breathing (dyspnea), dizziness, pulse rate above 116, chest pain, or nausea. If any of these occurs, the individual should be stopped and allowed to rest. Then the activity can be modified to a lower level of intensity.

Visual Impairment

Individuals with mental retardation have more vision abnormalities than the population without disabilities. Again, brain damage is the cause of the most severe impairments. Eyeglasses are effective for mild visual impairment, but correction is extremely difficult for severe visual complications.

Developmental Delays

Major motor developmental delays are found in youngsters with mental retardation who are either blind or have limited light perception. Hogg and Sebba (1987) have developed the following conclusions:

The developments in mobility that might follow these [motor] milestones are markedly delayed. The blind child does not elevate his/her body when laid prone, pull to standing, or walk alone at the stage when postural control and neuromuscular development would permit these activities. The consequence is, then, that, without early intervention, the child is immobile and in remaining immobile is denied a whole range of crucial experiences critical to the developing child's attempt to construct a "picture" of the world. And yet most blind children do become mobile and learn that objects beyond their immediate reach can be attained through bodily movement in space. While the sighted child achieves this through coordination of movement in visual space, the blind child has to use sound as a substitute. For the former, creeping, crawling or hitching to get a seen object will occur around 7 months. For the latter, only when he or she learns to localize an object in space on the basis of sound will the blind child move off to obtain the "heard" object. Though there is no such thing as "auditory space," the blind child has had to create a framework comparable to the visual space in which the sighted child develops. (pp. 89-90)

With reference to motor learning and blind children, Adelson and Fraiberg (1976) say that "once reach on sound has been achieved [the blind child] can be lured into motion and can begin to cope with relatively less difficult problems of balance, co-ordination, speed and safety'' (p. 14; quoted by Hogg and Sebba, 1987, p. 90).

Problems are compounded for individuals with both mental retardation and visual impairment, because the natural curiosity found in the nonretarded is less intense, and in the most severe cases, absent. The entire sensory system must be called into play, to have the best opportunities for learning. But visual sensory stimulation is not available to these individuals, and thus the instructor must give them extra attention and must not assume that these children are learning in traditional ways. Repetition is again paramount, and numerous trials and experiences are necessary. Instructors need to use play objects that are highly visible in color (bright, shining, etc.) against opposing backgrounds, large enough to be clearly seen, and sound-emitting (e.g., bells, rattles, buzzers).

Visual Impairment and Down Syndrome

People with Down syndrome are likely to have visual impairments. The most common are eye crossing (strabismus) and refractory error— nearsightedness (myopia) and farsightedness (hyperopia) (Blackman, 1990b). Coleman (1988) has found crossed eyes in approximately 30% of individuals with Down syndrome. Treatment by the physician may include patching one eye or surgical procedures. Niva (1988) warns that ''occasionally, an ophthalmologist's motives are questioned when intervening surgically in a Down syndrome patient with strabismus, since the only benefit may be cosmetic. Not enough consideration, however, has been given to the greater social acceptability of a child with straight eyes. Also, surgery may result in enhanced binocular vision in some patients'' (p. 56). When considering refractory errors, Niva (1988) has found that approximately 73% of persons with Down syndrome will have refractory problems, with two thirds of these being nearsighted. Encouragingly, most of these impairments are correctable by prescription eyeglasses.

Cataracts

Cataracts, the clouding of the normally clear lens of the eye, are commonly found in individuals with mental retardation. According to Niva (1988), ''Usually, progression of lens opacities [cloudy spots] is not significant enough to warrant surgical intervention in these patients. Only in the congenital types is vision significantly enough reduced to indicate surgery'' (p. 55). Over 50% of persons with Down syndrome will have cataracts sometime in their lives.

General Activity Suggestions

If individuals with mild vision impairments are having problems catching, kicking, and striking, there is a good chance that they cannot see the object clearly. Lerner, Mardell-Czudnowski, and Goldenberg (1987) list symptoms that might indicate visual difficulties: ''frequent rubbing of eyes; sensitivity to light; tears produced by close work; difficulty playing games requiring judgment of distance; headache; nausea or dizziness; squinting; crusty, watery, or red eyes; eyes turning inward or outward; difficulty keeping a place when reading; covering one eye to see an object; double vision; turning or tilting head to one side; and excessive blinking behavior'' (p. 41). For a child who does not wear glasses or has not had an eye exam lately, it may be appropriate to suggest to the parents that they have a visual examination for their child.

It is important to remember that physical activity and physical fitness do not depend entirely on vision. Program planners should include activities that develop muscular strength, cardiorespiratory endurance, and overall body coordination, as well as skills that will enable the individual to pursue more exciting leisure and recreational opportunities. Instructors should consider strength programs using traditional pieces of equipment (e.g., Nautilus); cardiorespiratory programs, including aerobic dance, swimming, walking, jogging, and stationary bicycling (exercycle), stair-climbing machines; and activities that promote coordination, such as trampoline, bowling, and social, square, and folk dancing. The "buddy system" will be necessary for many of these activities, but the outcomes are innumerable. The improvement of physical fitness should increase the individual's potential for finding and keeping a job, as well as her or his pleasure in daily life.

Athletic competition is available through state and national competitions. Two of the more popular sports are Beep Baseball and Goal Ball. Traditional individual and team sports are also available, including golf and skiing. The level of competition is high, and participants are highly conditioned and trained. More information is available from the groups listed in Appendix A.

Hearing Impairment

Children with hearing impairments face an extremely difficult world, because so much of learning depends on being able to hear. An individual who has both mental retardation and a hearing impairment is likely to experience more difficulty in cognitive ventures than one who has only mental retardation. Westling (1986) reports that 24% of persons with mild or moderate mental retardation, and 44% of those with severe or profound mental retardation, possess some degree of hearing impairment.

Etiology of Hearing Impairment

The typical etiologies of mental retardation (cytomegalovirus, herpes, syphilis, rubella, toxoplasmosis, prematurity, meningitis) also cause hearing impairment. Different degrees of hearing loss (from a minor reduction to total deafness) produce different problems. Newborns with intact auditory systems are able to respond to auditory stimuli, but for those who have brain damage, the potential for hearing loss is more pronounced. Hearing assessment by the neonatal staff, particularly the audiologist, has become

routine for babies with major birth complications, and highly sophisticated medical equipment is available to measure infant hearing. Kahn (1990) suggests that "the most common technique for children under six months of age is observing their response (e.g., cessation of sucking, widening of the eyes, blinking, quieting, or turning of the head) to sounds of controlled intensities and frequencies" (p. 170). But infant assessments are not always performed on the less severely involved. There is a great need for early identification of hearing loss in infants who are minimally brain damaged, because many will have moderate hearing losses. If months or even years pass before this problem is diagnosed, valuable learning delays will have already occurred. This problem is further complicated when the baby is also mentally retarded. Kahn (1990) continues: "Hearing impairment may be overlooked in children with developmental disabilities, or the behavior is thought to be related to mental retardation or cerebral palsy rather than hearing impairment" (p. 170). It appears that whenever brain damage is even remotely suspected, a thorough hearing evaluation should be conducted on the newborn.

Structural Deformities

Among the extensive problems encountered by individuals with Down syndrome are structural deformities that directly cause hearing impairment. The hearing problems begin in the neonatal period, and by 3 years of age, from 60% to 80% have evidence of hearing loss (Coleman, 1988). According to Coleman, "Probably, the most significant problem in infancy and early childhood of a Down syndrome patient is that of ear infections and their sequelae [complications]. Studies of the ear in Down syndrome children have disclosed an increased incidence in abnormalities in many patients in a variety of anatomical locations" (p. 11).

According to Lerner et al. (1987), a child above the age of 2 may have difficulty in hearing if she or he

1. does not respond to sound;
2. does not talk or even attempt to talk;
3. uses indistinct speech;
4. is usually attentive to facial expressions and lip movements;
5. is unduly sensitive to movement and visual cues;
6. has a perpetual cold or runny nose, frequent earaches, or is a mouth breather;
7. has recently recovered from scarlet fever, measles, meningitis, or from a severe head injury;
8. needs much repetition before demonstrating understanding;
9. is unusually active, running about and touching things;
10. does not respond to being called in a normal voice when out of sight;
11. requires many activities and visual cues before responding;
12. uses voice that has a nonmelodious quality;
13. does not moderate own voice and either talks too loudly or too softly. (pp. 36-37)

Conductive Hearing Loss

Conductive hearing loss is characterized by damage to the outer and middle ear, preventing sound from being transmitted to the inner ear. Deformities of the bones of the ear due to prenatal causes or postnatal disease (e.g., otitis media) result in hearing impairment. Conductive hearing loss is usually treated through medication, surgery, or the use of hearing aids.

Otitis Media

Otitis media is an inflammatory disease of the middle ear and is common in infancy and childhood. Ages 6 months up to approximately 7 years is the period of the highest risk for otitis media, with the peak incidence occurring in the 1-year-old population (Gulya & Wilson, 1989).

The danger of otitis media is highlighted in this comment by Downs and Balkany (1988): "If recurrent otitis media results in language deficits in otherwise normal children, it is reasonable to expect that children with other problems, including mental retardation, might be even more affected by the condition" (p. 21). Coleman (1988) has found that approximately 60% of children with Down syndrome will have had otitis media in early childhood. She describes the potential dangers:

> It has been reported that any child with chronic or severe otitis media (even if he or she is an otherwise normal individual) may manifest some delay in speech and language development, have auditory processing deficits, disturbances in auditory and visual integration, and is more likely to have reading disorders and even poor spelling skills. The middle ear infusions which are so common in Down syndrome children may be one important factor in the language delay in these children which in the past has been attributed solely to their "retardation." (p. 12)

Coleman adds: "When indicated, tympanic membrane tubes, or (if necessary) hearing aids, should be used in young children with Down syndrome" (p. 13).

Tympanic Membrane Tubes

Some youngsters will have tubes inserted into their ears to drain unwanted fluid. The eardrum tube insertion process (tympanostomy) is suggested if individuals have two or more episodes of acute otitis media in less than 3 months (Gulya & Wilson, 1989). Custom-fitted ear plugs are also recommended, along with medication to control the infection. If eardrop medication is being used, the child will likely have plugs or cotton in the ears to retain the fluid. Care should be taken so the youngster does not get the cotton wet, because the inside of the ear will have to be dried and new drops inserted. Thus, swimming or showering at school is usually not appropriate. When youngsters are having bouts of otitis media, the instructor could expect that they will feel weakness and discomfort and may not want to participate in activities that involve extensive running and jumping. Also, overload activities to increase strength or endurance should be avoided. Mild walking and sit-down games are encouraged. When the child should return to active participation is best determined by consultation with the physician.

Hearing Aids

Today even infants are able to profit from the use of hearing aids. Grossman and Tarjan (1987) believe that children with mental retardation can benefit from properly fitted hearing aids. Kahn (1990) describes a typical hearing aid (see Figure 2.5):

> A hearing aid basically is a miniature, wearable, public address system with a microphone to pick up the sound; an amplifier to increase the sound intensity; and a loudspeaker to deliver the amplified sound to the ear. The hearing aid is coupled to the ear with a custom-made earmold. The two most commonly used with infants and children are body-style hearing aids and behind-the-ear hearing aids. Unfortunately, a hearing aid cannot correct hearing the same way that eyeglasses usually correct vision. While the hearing aid increases sound intensity, it does not clarify the sound perceived by the impaired inner ear. Furthermore, the hearing aid amplifies all sound, including undesirable noises. It is important, therefore, to have realistic expectations of amplification. While improvement is highly significant, hearing is still far from normal. (pp. 171-172)

Most hearing loss in children with Down syndrome is conductive, so hearing aids should be relatively common—but they are not. In a study by Downs and Balkany (1988), 78% of subjects

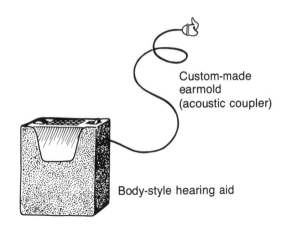

Custom-made earmold (acoustic coupler)

Body-style hearing aid

Behind-the-ear hearing aid

Figure 2.5   Two types of hearing aids.
Note. From *Medical Aspects of Developmental Disabilities in Children Birth to Three* (2nd ed.) (p. 172) by J.A. Blackman, 1990, Rockville, MD: Aspen. Copyright © 1990 by Aspen Publishers, Inc. Reprinted by permission.

with Down syndrome (N = 107) were reported to have some degree of hearing impairment (greater than 15 decibels of loss). The authors also reported, in reviewing four other studies, that 67% to 77% of Down syndrome subjects possessed marked hearing impairments. Conductive hearing loss was the most prevalent type. But the authors found little use of hearing aids:

> Our population had hearing losses in one or both ears at levels greater than 15 dB; 54 percent of the population had conductive hearing losses; 16 percent, sensorineural; and 8 percent, mixed losses. Sixty-five percent . . . had significant levels of hearing loss in both ears. . . . Of this 65 percent, only 16 percent had been given hearing aids—none of them at an early age. This reflects the customary neglect of hearing problems of Down syndrome individuals. (p. 26)

Sensorineural Hearing Loss

Sensorineural (SN) hearing loss involves impairment of the nerve pathways between the inner ear and the brain—specifically, damage of the microscopic sensory hairs in the inner ear (cochlea) or damage to the nerves (cochlear or auditory) that lead away from the inner ear to the brain. Sensorineural hearing loss is rarely surgically or medically curable and is almost always permanent.

For individuals with profound SN hearing loss (including the deaf/blind), *vibrotactile* devices are now being used. They change sound stimuli into vibratory stimuli, providing alternative sensory information about the auditory environment (Kahn, 1990). The vibrator is usually worn on the sternum or wrist.

Obviously, children who are deaf or have severe or profound hearing impairment will need manual communication in the form of signing and fingerspelling. Youngsters with mental retardation classifications below mild will have major problems with spelling, and most of them will use only signing.

There is, of course, a strong correlation between hearing impairment and speech problems. Many individuals with hearing impairments will be difficult to understand because their speech will be poor, and with them, signing is an important avenue of communication. Therefore, these persons and their teachers and leaders should become at least minimally proficient in manual communication. With a little practice, professionals working with individuals who are hearing impaired can learn to ''get by'' quite well with signing and fingerspelling in a physical education or recreational setting. Examples of common signs used in these settings can be found in Appendix B.

General Activity Suggestions

The incidence of hearing impairment in individuals with mental retardation has been substantiated, but hearing impairment is not an excuse for muscle weakness or poor cardiorespiratory endurance. Below average eye/hand coordination skills or uncoordinated movement may be present, but overall physical fitness programs usually have extremely rewarding results. It is beneficial, during instruction, to (a) speak slowly and distinctly, (b) face the students and be sure the student with the hearing impairment is close enough to clearly see your mouth, and (c) use physical demonstration and guidance, being sure to keep verbal instruction to a minimum.

Obesity

Obesity is a major problem for at least one third of the population without disabilities. Evidence exists that the incidence of obesity among children and adults with mental retardation is even higher (Fernhall & Tymeson, 1987; Fox, Hartney, Rotatori, & Kurpiers, 1985; Kelly, Rimmer, & Ness, 1986).

Obesity is particularly a problem for children and teenagers classified as having mild mental retardation and those with Down syndrome (Eichstaedt, Wang, Polacek, & Dohrmann, 1991) (see Tables 2.5 and 2.6). Individuals with moderate mental retardation tend to be of average or below-average weight, whereas children and teenagers with mild mental retardation or Down syndrome are markedly heavier. For example, note the figures for 11-year-old females in Table 2.5.

Heights are quite similar for individuals without disabilities and individuals with mild or moderate mental retardation, whereas children with Down syndrome are more than 5 inches shorter. There are also major differences in weight. Individuals with moderate mental retardation are the lightest group, children without disabilities are approximately 5 pounds heavier, and children with mild mental retardation and Down syndrome are heavier by 11 and 12 pounds, respectively.

Eichstaedt et al. (1991) analyzed skinfold data from 4,464 individuals with mild retardation, moderate retardation, and Down syndrome. The

Table 2.5   Female Height (in Inches) and Weight (in Pounds) for Individuals Nondisabled, Mildly MR, Moderately MR, and With Down Syndrome, Ages 6-18

Age	Nondisabled[a]		Mild MR		Moderate MR		Down syndrome	
	Ht (in)	Wt (lb)	Ht	Wt	Ht	Wt	Ht	Wt
6	44.00	42.00	44.33	41.00	44.50	42.50	44.23	52.15
7	46.50	48.50	46.20	46.40	46.71	48.43	45.12	60.67
8	49.00	55.00	48.20	47.40	49.50	53.33	45.60	69.00
9	51.00	61.00	53.43	70.43	53.71	60.71	48.67	70.25
10	53.50	69.00	55.10	76.20	54.91	64.47	48.50	77.00
11	55.50	76.00	56.86	87.43	56.50	71.12	50.17	88.33
12	57.50	84.00	58.43	98.43	57.83	83.00	52.50	102.00
13	60.50	99.00	60.33	104.67	58.95	92.21	54.00	124.50
14	63.50	114.50	61.92	115.75	60.33	101.08	55.21	132.67
15	64.00	119.00	61.36	130.09	60.91	112.30	56.00	138.25
16	64.50	121.50	61.00	134.33	60.86	121.10	56.50	148.20
17	65.00	125.00	62.75	144.63	61.35	129.94	56.91	153.18
18	65.50	128.00	62.62	140.88	62.55	120.55	56.89	159.44

Note. From *Physical Fitness and Motor Skill Levels of Individuals With Mental Retardation: Mild, Moderate, and Down Syndrome, Ages 6-21* by C.B. Eichstaedt, P.Y. Wang, J.J. Polacek, & P.F. Dohrmann, 1991, Normal, IL: Illinois State University Printing Services. Copyright 1991 by C.B. Eichstaedt et al. Reprinted by permission.

[a]Norms for the nondisabled are from *Nutrition for Fitness and Sports* (pp. 56-57) by M.H. Williams, 1983, Dubuque, IA: W.C. Brown. Adapted and used by permission of W.C. Brown Publishers.

ages sampled were 6 through 18. The skinfold sites measured included the triceps, the subscapular, and the calf. The authors found significant differences between groups, and as expected, the population with Down syndrome had the highest measures of excessive adipose tissue (fat cells). Measures for the group with mild mental retardation were also significantly higher than for the subjects with moderate retardation. See Tables 2.7 and 2.8.

This evidence indicates a major problem of overweight and obesity of children and adolescents with Down syndrome *and* mild mental retardation, across all age groups from 6 through 18. Drastic measures must be initiated immediately with any child exhibiting overweight tendencies. IEPs should contain annual goals to reduce excess adipose tissue. Physical educators must be directly involved in this process of assessment, program writing, and teaching.

Complications arise when individuals have adipose tissue more than 20% above ideal levels. The most noted adult problems include shorter life expectancy, due to heart attacks, strokes, and high blood pressure, and a predisposition for diabetes. Allsen, Harrison, and Vance (1980) put it rather dramatically: ''Obesity is a major health hazard. If all deaths from cancer could be eliminated, two years would be added to a person's life span. If all the deaths related to obesity could be eliminated, it is estimated that the life span would increase seven years'' (pp. 1-2).

Skinfold measurement is a comparatively accurate method of assessing percentage of adipose tissue (percent body fat). Pate, Slentz, and Katz (1989) believe that skinfold measures are important and should be used in all health-related physical fitness test batteries. Teachers and leaders should heed the warning signs of an individual beginning to ''get fat.'' When percent body

Table 2.6   Male Height (in Inches) and Weight (in Pounds) for Individuals Nondisabled, Mildly MR, Moderately MR, and With Down Syndrome, Ages 6-18

| Age | Nondisabled[a] | | Mild MR | | Moderate MR | | Down syndrome | |
	Ht (in)	Wt (lb)	Ht	Wt	Ht	Wt	Ht	Wt
6	44.00	44.00	45.67	50.00	45.00	47.40	45.00	47.12
7	47.00	50.00	48.70	58.90	48.27	53.45	45.33	62.50
8	49.00	55.00	48.44	61.78	49.05	55.30	45.40	68.40
9	52.00	62.50	52.22	68.18	52.54	60.58	48.86	76.57
10	53.50	68.50	54.50	72.71	53.55	69.40	51.33	85.15
11	56.00	77.00	56.50	79.25	55.38	74.36	54.10	98.22
12	57.50	83.00	59.00	97.31	57.12	88.42	55.25	107.43
13	59.50	91.00	64.25	124.13	61.35	105.47	56.10	120.60
14	63.00	108.00	64.35	134.88	62.70	117.15	58.05	139.25
15	65.50	122.50	65.88	138.18	64.69	128.41	60.17	146.86
16	66.50	131.00	65.73	140.00	66.40	142.35	59.86	147.71
17	67.50	138.50	66.71	149.71	65.91	144.19	61.17	152.03
18	68.00	143.00	68.50	157.63	66.80	146.73	59.12	161.88

Note. From *Physical Fitness and Motor Skill Levels of Individuals With Mental Retardation: Mild, Moderate, and Down Syndrome, Ages 6-21* by C.B. Eichstaedt, P.Y. Wang, J.J. Polacek, & P.F. Dohrmann, 1991, Normal, IL: Illinois State University Printing Services. Copyright 1991 by C.B. Eichstaedt et al. Reprinted by permission.

[a]Norms for the nondisabled are from *Nutrition for Fitness and Sports* (pp. 56-57) by M.H. Williams, 1983, Dubuque, IA: W.C. Brown. Adapted and used by permission of W.C. Brown Publishers.

fat is more than 10% above the ideal, an individual is considered overweight. When the excess reaches 20% above ideal, the person is classified as obese.

Kelly and Rimmer (1987) express doubt that professionals working with adults with mental retardation have the training and skill to accurately administer skinfold tests. They recommend combining four less difficult measures, including waist and forearm circumference, height, and weight. Raw scores are put into a formula to determine percent body fat. The Kelly and Rimmer regression equation is found in Table 2.9.

Obesity is detrimental to daily life. For example, obese persons usually are limited to certain occupations, not by a lack of intellectual ability or by personality, but by the physical inability to perform the required work skills. Job placement and retention were studied in a 3-year project with individuals with moderate and severe mental retardation (Wehman et al., 1982); the researchers concluded that the subjects with obesity lacked sufficient strength and endurance to perform adequately in competitive jobs.

Not only are physical constraints ever-present for persons with obesity and mental retardation, but the social and emotional problems can become barriers to their attempts to be happy, healthy, and successful citizens. Although this is illegal today, jobs are still being covertly denied on the basis of appearance, including obesity.

Individuals who are obese commonly select sedentary activities for their leisure time and avoid fitness and conditioning activities. The reasons may include feelings such as "I can't do it . . . it is uncomfortable . . . I don't feel

Table 2.7   Female Skinfold Measures (mm) for Individuals With Mild MR, Moderate MR, and Down Syndrome; Including Tricep, Subscapular, Calf, and Sums of the Three Scores

Ages	Level of Retardation	Tricep*	Subscapular	Calf	Sums
6-9	Mild	15.23	9.86	15.50	40.59
	Moderate	15.67	13.77	11.61	41.05
	Down	17.89	14.33	20.00	52.22
10-13	Mild	18.68	14.74	21.17	54.59
	Moderate	16.83	15.36	16.94	49.13
	Down	22.12	18.88	20.00	61.00
14-17	Mild	23.06	19.85	22.90	65.81
	Moderate	19.75	17.70	20.81	58.26
	Down	23.79	25.21	23.84	72.84
18-20	Mild	23.77	24.31	20.85	68.92
	Moderate	22.47	22.05	20.91	65.43
	Down	25.22	26.30	22.15	73.67

Note. From *Physical Fitness and Motor Skill Levels of Individuals With Mental Retardation: Mild, Moderate, and Down Syndrome, Ages 6-21* by C.B. Eichstaedt, P.Y. Wang, J.J. Polacek, & P.F. Dohrmann, 1991, Normal, IL: Illinois State University Printing Services. Copyright 1991 by C.B. Eichstaedt et al. Reprinted by permission.

*Scores are measured in millimeters (mm).

good when doing this activity.'' This attitude promotes avoidance. For the person with mental retardation, these feelings are usually immediate and more open. These individuals tend to stop exercising because of discomfort and may simply slow down, or stop, or sit down, or lie down. This lack of cooperation has been consistently cited by physical education teachers as a major hurdle in working with individuals who are mentally retarded (Eichstaedt & Kalakian, 1987). Even usually successful motivational techniques fail to stimulate them. The more severe the mental retardation, the more this is a problem. Concepts and techniques for motivating individuals with mental retardation are thoroughly discussed in chapter 4.

Negative emotions about their appearance (feeling they look bad, bulging, sloppy) may also lead these individuals to avoid activities such as tennis, swimming, and skiing. Neat little tennis outfits just don't look good on obese people. Teenagers and adults with mild mental retardation are usually very aware of their appearance. For those who do not comprehend the negative social implications of obesity, teachers and leaders must provide social integration training to guide these individuals toward socially acceptable body weight.

The physical, emotional, and social pressures suggest that obesity may sometimes totally control the obese individual's life. Where this is true, there is good reason to expect that if obesity is reduced, many problems will also be reduced.

Weight Reduction

Grossman and Tarjan (1987) believe that obesity is controllable and weight reduction is possible: ''Prevention of obesity in retarded children often is overlooked. Obesity can result from lack of physical activity, improper diet, or both. Some parents become overindulgent with their children and may disregard the need for good nutrition. Many parents of teenagers who are obese

Table 2.8   Male Skinfold Measures (mm) for Individuals With Mild MR, Moderate MR, and Down Syndrome; Including Tricep, Subscapular, Calf, and Sums of the Three Scores

Ages	Level of Retardation	Tricep*	Subscapular	Calf	Sums
6-9	Mild	17.06	12.17	17.95	47.18
	Moderate	11.83	10.40	10.30	32.53
	Down	16.71	14.96	16.58	48.25
10-13	Mild	17.91	13.94	17.10	48.95
	Moderate	14.38	12.78	12.98	40.14
	Down	17.45	17.26	16.71	51.42
14-17	Mild	16.67	15.98	16.09	48.74
	Moderate	13.76	13.92	13.72	41.40
	Down	16.77	17.71	14.97	49.45
18-20	Mild	17.10	18.15	18.90	54.15
	Moderate	13.42	14.22	13.26	40.90
	Down	16.20	20.35	18.68	55.23

Note. From *Physical Fitness and Motor Skill Levels of Individuals With Mental Retardation: Mild, Moderate, and Down Syndrome, Ages 6-21* by C.B. Eichstaedt, P.Y. Wang, J.J. Polacek, & P.F. Dohrmann, 1991, Normal, IL: Illinois State University Printing Services. Copyright 1991 by C.B. Eichstaedt et al. Reprinted by permission.

*Scores are measured in millimeters (mm).

and retarded find it difficult to place them on reducing diets. Counseling parents about proper nutrition and emphasizing the importance of physical activity may help prevent obesity later in life'' (p. 80). When discussing increased weight gain of children with Down syndrome, Pueschel (1988) notes that ''another factor that could account for the increased weight gain is the child's reduced physical activity, since the less exercise performed the less calories are being burned. . . . Once a child is overweight, a vicious circle may develop, as the overweight youngster will be less active, will perhaps watch more television, engage in snacking, and become more obese'' (p. 31).

Children should not be allowed to become fat or stay fat. Teachers and leaders must recognize the negative aspects of obesity and continually encourage parents to seek medical help for their youngsters. Here is an analogy: If a teacher becomes aware that a student is squinting excessively when attempting to read from the chalk-

board, she or he would make sure that the parents are notified of this potential visual problem (and is likely to follow up if nothing is done). The rationale includes the fact that children who cannot see well may not learn to their capacity. For the same reasons, teachers and leaders have a responsibility not to ignore obesity—because it will not go away. Parents must be alerted to the problems. Teachers and leaders can help by encouraging the youngsters with positive statements and motivational devices, such as charts, stars, and colorful stickers for pounds lost. However, although this secondary role of giving information and encouragement is very important, the primary role of instructors is to provide daily physical activities that are positive, interesting, and fun. This is another reason why parents should be spurred to help their children practice weight control.

Reducing food intake is essential for weight loss. Individuals may need to go on diets, and

Table 2.9   Kelly and Rimmer Regression Equation

% Fat = 13.545 + .48691649 (waist circum.) − .52662145 (forearm circum.) − .15504013 (height cm) + .077079958 (weight kg)

Practical calculation procedures

Metric measurements

A. Constant   = 13.545
B.   .487   × Waist circumference (cm)   =
C.   −.527   × Forearm circumference (cm) =   −
D.   −.155   × Height (cm)   =   −
E.   .077   × Weight (kg)   =

Estimated % fat (sum products of steps A-E) =

Imperial measurements

A. Constant   = 13.545
B.   1.237   × Waist circumference (in)   =
C. −1.339   × Forearm circumference (in) =   −
D. − .349   × Height (in)   =   −
E.   .035   × Weight (lb)   =

Estimated % fat (sum products of steps A-E) =

Note. From "A Practical Method for Estimating Percent Body Fat of Adult Mentally Retarded Males" by L.E. Kelly and J.H. Rimmer, 1987, *Adapted Physical Activity Quarterly*, **4**, p. 122. Copyright 1987 by Human Kinetics Publishers. Reprinted by permission.

all diets must be written *only* by physicians. Teachers and leaders are not qualified to diagnose the nutritional needs of students and clients.

Assessment and Measurement

Assessment and measurement of existing levels of cardiovascular fitness are necessary when attempting to determine whether individuals are overweight or obese and whether weight control programs are effective. The reliability of some tests being used with this population is in question. Cressler, Lavay, and Giese (1988), using adults labeled mentally retarded ($N = 17$; age $M = 35$ yr; IQ $M = 54$), suggest that the most effective tests to determine cardiovascular efficiency are (a) the Canadian Step Test, (b) the Balke Ware Treadmill Test, and (c) the Cooper 12-Minute Walk/Run Test. The Canadian Step Test includes ascending and descending two 8-inch steps to an established cadence. The Balke Ware Treadmill Test involves using an expensive piece of laboratory equipment and is not usually available to most schools and communities. Finally, the Cooper 12-Minute Walk/Run Test is the least effective of the three listed but still holds a reliability score of .81.

Jansma, Decker, Ersing, McCubbin, and Combs (1988) discussed the outcomes of their 3-year program with adults labeled as severely mentally retarded ($N = 114$). They used an assessment battery which included the test items of the 300-yard walk/run, grip strength, modified sit-ups, modified bench press, and modified sit-and-reach. The researchers believe these test items correspond to functional everyday skills including endurance and strength to perform physical tasks with the least amount of tiring, grip strength when manipulating objects and tools, upper body strength for lifting and carrying, and maintenance of flexibility and range of motion.

Physical Activities for Weight Loss

In reference to the positive effects of physical activity on obesity, Bray (1989) notes that "obese patients should be encouraged to increase their physical activity for two reasons. First, it consumes calories. Second, and more important, exercise increases glucose [blood sugar] utilization" (p. 517). It has been demonstrated that physical fitness can be improved for persons with mental retardation through specific exercise programs (McConaughy & Salzberg, 1988; Melnick, 1987; Tomporowski & Ellis, 1985; Tomporowski & Jameson, 1985). A review of research regarding cardiovascular (C/V) fitness and individuals with mental retardation was completed by Seidl, Reid, and Montgomery

(1987). They concluded that "the data suggest that cardiovascular systems of mentally retarded persons are responsive to exercise regimens" (p. 106). To effectively improve levels of physical fitness, individuals must participate in C/V programs that safely overload the heart and lungs. Also, these programs must be sustained for a minimal workout of not less than 12 minutes of constant movement a day and not less than every other day (Eichstaedt & Kalakian, 1987). Programs vary in length, but they should continue for *at least* 12 weeks. For more information on physical fitness program implementation, see chapter 7.

The preceding suggestion appears simple, but Nienhuis (1989) uncovered some disturbing information. He compared the progress made by boys and girls with mild mental retardation between the ages of 10 and 12 on five selected test items (flexed arm hang, sit-ups, shuttle run, standing long jump, 50-yard dash) over a 10-year period (1980-1989, $N = 262$). He concluded

> The levels of physical fitness for this age group have neither increased or decreased over this time. . . . The results indicated that teachers' perspectives on physical fitness programming may have to be intensified. If improvement is possible teachers need to place special emphasis on individual improvement. Lessons must provide practice time and adequate concentration on skill and technique. Furthermore, original games and activities need to be implemented which incorporate physical fitness. (pp. 44-45)

Nienhuis's observations might imply that there is a desperate need to evaluate and possibly upgrade present physical education and Special Olympic programs. Given the number of years since the (1975) implementation of PL 94-142, in which physical education was required for *all* children and adolescents labeled as having mental retardation, educators and recreation leaders should be witnessing a much larger increase in physical fitness performance for these groups.

Teachers and leaders are most challenged by children labeled as having severe or profound mental retardation. Adults with mental retardation must also hold a high priority. As Caouette and Reid (1985) observe, "If left to themselves, those who are severely retarded do not generally engage in purposeful activity or play; rather, their behaviors are repetitive and stereotypic or they remain essentially inactive" (p. 296).

Individuals with mental retardation may not be able to, or want to, participate in overload activities. Even jogging for a short distance will be difficult for them. Remember though, *any* extra physical movement is more beneficial than no activity. Even simple bending, stretching, and reaching on a daily basis are helpful. Daily walks are also necessary, as is bending down and picking up objects or getting in and out of chairs. Fifteen to 30 minutes a day of prescribed movement should be required of everyone. Consultation with physicians is strongly recommended before beginning any exercise program with adults with severe or profound retardation.

For individuals with both profound mental retardation and multidisabling conditions, Mulholland and McNeill (1989) offer interesting conclusions from their study of two institutionalized males, ages 10 and 7, with IQs less than 19. They determined that heart rate responses were indeed increased when gross and fine motor actions were attempted. Their major finding was the presence of a fatigue factor in the subjects during selected motor activities. The researchers hypothesize that this could be a problem for other similar individuals when they attempt *to learn* motor skills—that fatigue interferes with the learning process. Thus, gross motor activities, in their simplest form and done on a daily basis, could minimally increase cardiovascular efficiency. This conclusion can serve as fertile ground for future studies with individuals labeled as having profound mental retardation and multiple disabilities.

Stainback, Stainback, Wehman, and Spangiers (1983) found that adults labeled as having profound mental retardation were able to *learn* selected exercises and were able to generalize these experiences into a group physical fitness program. The participants took part in 15-minute sessions 5 days per week. The three individuals reached criterion within 31, 39, and 55 sessions, respectively (three exercises, two times, on 2 consecutive days, on verbal cue and model). These findings indicate that physical fitness activities can be learned by individuals of the lowest function.

Tomporowski and Jameson (1985) demonstrated that adults with severe and profound mental retardation ($N = 19$, IQ $M = 23$) can improve in levels of physical fitness by performing circuit-training programs consisting of treadmill walking, stationary bicycling, rowing, and calisthenics. The subjects exercised for 60 minutes every 3rd day for 18 weeks. A second group of 19 subjects (IQ $M = 25.05$) were given an 18-week jogging program, running progressive distances of 0.5, 1, and 1.5 miles each day. The general exercise program used in both studies did produce significant improvements in physical fitness. Tomporowski and Ellis (1985) conducted a 7-month study of institutionalized adults with severe and profound mental retardation ($N = 86$, IQ $Ex = 21.04$, $Con = 24.20$). The program included jogging, running, dance-aerobics, and circuit training. The experimental group improved significantly (t (18) = 4.91, $p < .001$) over the control group in C/V efficiency.

Pitetti, Jackson, Stubbs, Campbell, and Battar (1989) conducted a comprehensive study to determine the existing levels of physical fitness of adult Special Olympics participants. The 23 Olympians (Age $M = 23.6$ yr, IQ $M = 65$) took part in approximately 13 months of Special Olympics training and competition. The activities included bowling, volleyball, basketball, indoor tennis, softball, track and field, swimming, gymnastics, and cycling. The routine included workouts two times per week, with competition on the weekends. The researchers found that the Special Olympians did *not improve* their levels of physical fitness and believe this was caused by a lack of *intensity* of the activities. That is, each activity must comprise specific components that overload the cardiovascular system to beneficial levels. It is hypothesized that positive physical fitness changes might occur if the program were conducted more days per week, with more cardiovascular overloading during each workout, excluding activities that normally are not cardiovascular endurance sports (e.g., bowling, volleyball, softball, gymnastics). See chapter 12 for more information on this subject.

Schurrer, Weltman, and Brammell (1985) followed five adults with mental retardation (Age $M = 25.2$ yr), in an intermediate-care facility, through a 23-week walk/jog program. They found only a slight reduction in weight but a large improvement in $\dot{V}O_2$max (a positive sign of C/V improvement). The participants also showed an increased interest in their social activities during the study, and they decreased in number of sick days, increased work earnings, and showed less destructive and aggressive behavior.

Behavior Modification

Weight reduction is difficult to maintain because the individuals' negative lifestyles must also be changed. After a period of time, the "reducers" tend to resume their old bad eating habits and poor activity routines. Instructors must understand the problem and know how to help these persons successfully modify their behavior.

Bray (1989) offers a general suggestion for changing behavior:

The basic principles of behavioral approaches to obesity can be summarized under "the ABCs of eating." The "A" stands for antecedent. Eating is often a response to events in the environment.

These antecedent events may then serve to trigger eating. The "B" stands for the behavior of eating itself. This includes, among other things, the place, rate, and frequency with which an individual eats. Limiting the act of eating to one area with a single small plate and place setting may help to provide control over eating. Finally, the "C" in these ABCs is the consequence of the eating. The feelings an individual has about eating patterns can be altered, and rewards for changing eating patterns can be instituted. Behavioral programs for treatment of obesity provide elements for long-term changes that can increase success rates. (p. 517)

A comprehensive program of weight reduction will include many professionals working in a transdisciplinary approach that must also include the parents. Teachers and leaders must guide the development of new lifestyles for individuals who are both mentally retarded and obese.

Summary

Individuals with mental retardation often also have a second or third disabling condition. Whenever brain damage occurs, there is a likelihood for other problems to develop, such as cerebral palsy and seizures. There may also be impairments of the sensory systems of sight and hearing, ranging from mild (requiring eyeglasses and hearing aids) to severe and permanent (requiring surgery or manual communication). In some children with spina bifida, the hydrocephalic complications within the brain could leave these youngsters both mentally and physically disabled. All children with mental retardation are susceptible to overweight and obesity, but those with mild retardation or Down syndrome tend to be heavier than both individuals without disabilities and individuals with severe or profound retardation. Problems of weight control have reached epidemic proportions in all groups in the population, and radical steps must be taken to assure a healthier population.

Activity programs are to be developed that insure appropriate duration and intensity for learning or fitness to occur. Health-related fitness, including strength, cardiovascular efficiency, and flexibility, must be improved. Opportunities for better employment and the pursuit of stimulating leisure-time activities will be easier to attain if the individual's health is at a positive level.

The combination of two or more major disabilities presents unique and greater challenges to teachers and leaders. The multiple complications require a better understanding of each disabling component for efficient program development and implementation. Professionals need to combine information and expertise and open all avenues of communication. The physical educator, classroom teacher, therapeutic recreation leader, occupational and physical therapists, kinesiotherapist, physician, and parents must combine efforts. An exciting quality of life can be provided for individuals with multidisabilities, but an effective transdisciplinary team is needed to help them reach goals society once believed impossible for them.

DISCUSSIONS AND NEW DIRECTIONS

1. What are the unique challenges confronting the professional when planning physical activity programs for individuals with multidisabling conditions? Include responses relating to cerebral palsy, seizures, spina bifida, congenital heart defects, visual impairments, hearing impairments, and obesity.

2. Describe the role each professional on the transdisciplinary team would play in the development of a physical activity program for an individual who has a multidisabling condition including mental retardation (IQ 40), spastic quadriplegic cerebral palsy, and generalized tonic-clonic (grand mal) seizures.

3. Develop a physical activity program for a 12-year-old girl who has Down syndrome, severe hearing impairment, and severe visual impairment. Include activities that stress the physical fitness components of muscular strength and cardiovascular endurance. Describe the problems that must be accounted for, for each of the disabling conditions listed above. For example, what problems arise when planning a walking/running program for an individual with severe visual impairments? Follow this line of thinking throughout the problem.

4. Discuss the implications of developing a physical fitness program for a 35-year-old adult with moderate mental retardation who is also obese. The person is generally uncooperative and tends not to like physical activity. Make suggestions that may lead to positive results.

5. You have been given $350 to purchase equipment for your physical activity program. Survey companies who specialize in equipment for individuals with multidisabling conditions. Within your budget, select (and justify) your purchases.

References

Adelson, E., & Fraiberg, S. (1976). Sensory deficit and motor development in infants blind from birth. In J. Hogg & J. Sebba (Eds.), *Profound retardation and multiple impairment* (Vol. 1, p. 90). Rockville, MD: Aspen.

Allsen, P.E., Harrison, J.M., and Vance, B. (1980). *Fitness for life* (2nd ed.). Dubuque, IA: Brown.

Berg, R.A. (1987). Epilepsy. In C.R. Reynolds & L. Mann (Eds.), *Encyclopedia of special education* (Vol. 3). New York: Wiley.

Blackman, J.A. (1990a). Down syndrome. In J.A. Blackman (Ed.), *Medical aspects of developmental disabilities in children birth to three* (2nd ed., pp. 107-111). Rockville, MD: Aspen.

Blackman, J.A. (1990b). Congenital heart defects. In J.A. Blackman (Ed.), *Medical aspects of developmental disabilities in children birth to three* (2nd ed., pp. 81-87). Rockville, MD: Aspen.

Blackman, J.A. (1990c). *Medical aspects of developmental disabilities in children birth to three* (2nd ed.). Rockville, MD: Aspen.

Bleck, E.E. (1982). Cerebral palsy. In E.E. Bleck & D.A. Nagel (Eds.), *Physically handicapped children: A medical atlas for teachers* (2nd ed., pp. 59-132). New York: Grune & Stratton.

Bleck, E.E., & Nagel, D.A. (Eds.) (1982). *Physically handicapped children: A medical atlas for teachers* (2nd ed.). New York: Grune & Stratton.

Bray, G.A. (1989). Obesity. In R.E. Rakel (Ed.), *Conn's 1989 current therapy* (pp. 510-518). Philadelphia: Saunders.

Browne, T.R. (1989). Epilepsy in adolescents and adults. In R.E. Rakel (Ed.), *Conn's 1989 current therapy* (pp. 781-792). Philadelphia: Saunders.

Brunt, D. (1984). Apraxic tendencies in children with meningomyelocele. *Adapted Physical Activity Quarterly*, **1**, 61-67.

Brunt, D. (1986). Relationship between location of spina bifida, loss of muscle control, and type of ambulation. In C. Sherrill, *Adapted physical education and recreation* (3rd ed., p. 515). Dubuque, IA: Brown.

Caouette, M., & Reid, G. (1985). Increasing the work output of severely retarded adults on a bicycle ergometer. *Education and Training of the Mentally Retarded, 20,* 296-304.

Coleman, M. (1988). Medical care of children and adults with Down syndrome. In V. Dmitriev & P.L. Oelwein (Eds.), *Advances in Down syndrome* (pp. 7-18). Seattle: Special Child.

Cressler, M., Lavay, B., & Giese, M. (1988). The reliability of four measures of cardiovascular fitness with mentally retarded adults. *Adapted Physical Activity Quarterly, 5,* 285-292.

Downs, M.P., & Balkany, T.J. (1988). Otologic problems and hearing impairment in Down syndrome. In V. Dmitriev & P.L. Oelwein (Eds.), *Advances in Down syndrome* (pp. 19-34). Seattle: Special Child.

Eichstaedt, C.B., & Kalakian, L.H. (1987). *Developmental/adapted physical education: Making ability count* (2nd ed.). New York: Macmillan.

Eichstaedt, C.B., Wang, P.Y., Polacek, J.J., & Dohrmann, P.F. (1991). *Physical fitness and motor skill levels of individuals with mental retardation: Mild, moderate, and individuals with Down syndrome, ages 6-21.* Normal: Illinois State University Printing Services.

Epstein, M.H., Polloway, E.A., Patton, J.R., & Foley, R. (1989). Mild retardation: Student characteristics and services. *Education and Training in Mental Retardation, 24,* 7-16.

Feit, T.S. (1988). Aspects of cardiac disease in Down syndrome. In V. Dmitriev & P.L. Oelwein (Eds.), *Advances in Down syndrome* (pp. 35-44). Seattle: Special Child.

Fernhall, B., & Tymeson, G. (1987). Graded exercise testing of mentally retarded adults: A study of physiability. *Archives of Physical and Medical Rehabilitation, 68,* 363-365.

Finnie, N.R. (1975). *Handling the young cerebral palsied child at home* (2nd ed.). New York: Dutton.

Fox, E.L., Hartney, C.W., Rotatori, A.F., & Kurpiers, E.M. (1985). Incidence of obesity among retarded children. *Education and Training of the Mentally Retarded, 20,* 175-181.

Gidding, S. (1988, May). Stress testing and adapted physical education. In R. Gavin (Chair), *Cardiac kids in the schools.* Symposium conducted at the meeting of the Children's Heart Services, Maywood, IL.

Grossman, H.J., & Tarjan, G. (Eds.) (1987). *AMA handbook on mental retardation.* Chicago: American Medical Association.

Gulya, A.J., & Wilson, W.R. (1989). Otitis media. In R.E. Rakel (Ed.), *Conn's 1989 current therapy* (pp. 148-150). Philadelphia: Saunders.

Hallahan, D.P., & Kauffman, J.M. (1988). *Exceptional children: Introduction to special education* (4th ed.). Englewood Cliffs, NJ: Prentice Hall.

Haring, N.G., & McCormick, L. (1990). *Exceptional children and youth: An introduction to special education* (5th ed.). Columbus, OH: Merrill.

Healy, A. (1990). Cerebral palsy. In J.A. Blackman (Ed.), *Medical aspects of developmental disabilities in children birth to three* (pp. 59-66). Rockville, MD: Aspen.

Heward, W.L., & Orlansky, M.D. (1988). *Exceptional children* (3rd ed.). Columbus, OH: Merrill.

Hogg, J., & Sebba, J. (1987). *Profound retardation and multiple impairment* (Vol. 1). Rockville, MD: Aspen.

Jacobson, J.W., & Janicki, M.P. (1983). Observed prevalence of multiple developmental disabilities. *Mental Retardation, 21,* 87-94.

Jansma, P., Decker, J., Ersing, W., McCubbin, J., & Combs, S. (1988). A fitness assessment system for individuals with severe mental retardation. *Adapted Physical Activity Quarterly*, **5**, 223-232.

Kahn, G. (1990). Hearing impairment. In J.A. Blackman (Ed.), *Medical aspects of developmental disabilities in children birth to three* (pp. 167-174). Rockville, MD: Aspen.

Kelly, L.E., & Rimmer, J.H. (1987). A practical method for estimating percent body fat of adult mentally retarded males. *Adapted Physical Activity Quarterly*, **4**, 117-125.

Kelly, L.E., Rimmer, J.H., & Ness, R.A. (1986). Obesity levels of institutionalized mentally retarded adults. *Adapted Physical Activity Quarterly*, **3**, 167-176.

Kirk, S.A., & Gallagher, J.J. (1989). *Educating exceptional children* (6th ed.). Boston: Houghton Mifflin.

Lerner, J., Mardell-Czudnowski, C., & Goldenberg, D. (1987). *Special education for the early childhood years* (2nd ed.). Englewood Cliffs, NJ: Prentice Hall.

McConaughy, E.K., & Salzberg, C.L. (1988). Physical fitness of mentally retarded individuals. *International Review of Research in Mental Retardation*, **15**, 227-258.

Melnick, A.W. (1987). *An investigation of the effects of a cardiorespiratory fitness program on the body fat and weight of male Down syndrome adolescents*. Unpublished master's thesis, Illinois State University, Normal, IL.

Mulholland, R., Jr., & McNeill, A.W. (1989). Heart rate of profoundly retarded, multiply handicapped children during closed-skill fine motor and open-skill gross motor activities. *Adapted Physical Activity Quarterly*, **6**, 68-78.

Nelson, C.M., & Ellenberg, J.H. (1986). Antecedents of cerebral palsy: Multivariate analysis of risk. *New England Journal of Medicine*, **315**, 81-86.

Nienhuis, K.M. (1989). *A comparative analysis of the physical fitness levels of mildly mentally retarded students*. Unpublished master's thesis, Illinois State University, Normal.

Niva, R.A. (1988). Eye abnormalities and their treatment. In V. Dmitriev & P.L. Oelwein (Eds.), *Advances in Down syndrome* (pp. 45-57). Seattle: Special Child.

Pate, R.R., Slentz, A.C., & Katz, D.P. (1989). Relationship between skinfold thickness and performance of health related fitness test items. *Research Quarterly*, **60**, 183-189.

Patton, J.R., Payne, J.S., & Beirne-Smith, M. (1990). *Mental retardation* (3rd ed.). Columbus, OH: Merrill.

Pitetti, K.H., Jackson, J.A., Stubbs, N.B., Campbell, K.D., & Battar, S.B. (1989). Fitness levels of adult Special Olympic participants. *Adapted Physical Activity Quarterly*, **6**, 354-370.

Pueschel, S.M. (Ed.) (1988). *The young person with Down syndrome*. Baltimore: Brooks.

Rao, P.S. (1989). Congenital heart disease. In R.E. Rankel (Ed.), *Conn's 1989 current therapy* (pp. 201-213). Philadelphia: Saunders.

Schurrer, R., Weltman, A., & Brammell, H. (1985). Effects of physical training on cardiovascular fitness and behavior patterns of mentally retarded adults. *American Journal of Mental Deficiency*, **90**, 167-169.

Seidl, C., Reid, G., & Montgomery, D.L. (1987). A critique of cardiovascular fitness testing with mentally retarded persons. *Adapted Physical Activity Quarterly*, **4**, 106-116.

Stainback, S., Stainback, W., Wehman, P., & Spangiers, L. (1983). Acquisition and generalization of physical fitness exercises in three profoundly retarded adults. *The Association for the Severely Handicapped Journal*, **8**, 47-55.

Tomporowski, P.D., & Ellis, N.R. (1985). The effects of exercise on the health, intelligence, and adaptive behavior of institutionalized severely and profoundly mentally retarded adults: A systematic replication.

Applied Research in Mental Retardation, **6**, 465-473.

Tomporowski, P.D., & Jameson, L.D. (1985). Effects of a physical fitness training program on the exercise behavior of institutionalized mentally retarded adults. *Adapted Physical Activity Quarterly*, **2**, 197-205.

U.S. Office of Education. Federal Register. The Individuals With Disabilities Education Act, formerly The Education for All Handicapped Children Act of 1975, Section 94-142, 99-457, 89-750, 42 U.S.C., Section 42480-54579, (1977).

Vining, E.P.G. (1989). Epilepsy in infants and children. In R.E. Rakel (Ed.), *1989 Conn's current therapy* (pp. 792-796). Philadelphia: Saunders.

Wehman, P., Hill, M., Goodall, P., Cleveland, P., Brooke, V., & Pentecost, J.H., Jr. (1982). Job placement and follow-up of moderately and severely handicapped individuals after three years. *Journal of the Association for the Severely Handicapped*, **7**, 5-16.

Westling, D.L. (1986). *Introduction to mental retardation*. Englewood Cliffs, NJ: Prentice Hall.

Winnick, J.P. (Ed.) (1990). *Adapted physical education and sport*. Champaign, IL: Human Kinetics.

Winnick, J.P., & Short, F.X. (1991). A comparison of the physical fitness of nonretarded and mildly mentally retarded adolescents with cerebral palsy. *Adapted Physical Activity Quarterly*, **8**, 43-56.

Wolraich, M.L. (1990a). Hydrocephalus. In J.A. Blackman (Ed.), *Medical aspects of developmental disabilities in children birth to three* (2nd ed., pp. 175-179). Rockville, MD: Aspen.

Wolraich, M.L. (1990b). Myelomeningocele. In J.A. Blackman (Ed.), *Medical aspects of developmental disabilities in children birth to three* (2nd ed., pp. 197-204). Rockville, MD: Aspen.

Wolraich, M.L. (1990c). Seizure disorders. In J.A. Blackman (Ed.), *Medical aspects of developmental disabilities in children birth to three* (2nd ed., pp. 251-257). Rockville, MD: Aspen.

CHAPTER 3

Assessment: The First Step

PREVIEW   Toward the end of the individualized education plan (IEP) meeting, the parents in attendance remarked, "You have spent a considerable amount of time showing us a number of test scores outlining our daughter's progress in the classroom. However, no one on the committee has discussed our daughter's placement in physical education. Why is this? We would like to know what tests the committee used to determine our daughter's placement. Should our daughter be placed in regular physical education, adapted physical education, or both?" The committee sat in silence. They had no test scores to share with the parents. What they did not tell the parents was that the committee assumed that since their daughter had mild mental retardation she should be automatically placed in an adapted physical education class.

HIGHLIGHT QUESTIONS

- **What is assessment, and how is it different from testing?**
- **Why is it important to assess persons with mental retardation?**
- **Are there any issues and problems specific to the assessment of persons with mental retardation?**
- **What competencies are needed for professionals to assess persons with mental retardation?**
- **What factors must be considered to assure proper test selection?**
- **Why are referral and screening procedures needed to assure success during the assessment process?**
- **Are there any standardized tests to measure the physical performance of persons with mental retardation?**

Too often professionals who follow proper test guidelines and procedures mandated by the law to determine criteria for eligibility in special education neglect them when testing the student with a disability in the physical domain. The law, however, is clear: Physical education is a direct service, and professionals testing in this area must adhere to the legal guidelines regardless of scheduling, facility, and monetary constraints. This chapter discusses these factors and other testing and assessment guidelines that professionals should follow when providing physical activity to persons with mental retardation.

What Is Assessment?

Although the terms *testing* and *assessment* are often used interchangeably, a distinct difference does exist. *Testing* is defined as a technique to collect data using specific tools and procedures, such as systematic observation (Seaman & DePauw, 1989). An example of testing would be administering a basketball skills test to Special Olympics athletes.

But testing alone is useless to the individual or the program if scores simply are collected and nothing is done with the results. *Assessment* involves interpreting test results. In the Special Olympics example, the basketball test scores

must be interpreted for the coach to make certain team decisions that vary depending on individual needs. Using test scores, the coach can begin to determine which athlete is the best dribbler, shooter, passer, or rebounder.

Ulrich (1985a) defines assessment as "the collection and interpretation of relevant student information to aid in making nondiscriminatory educational decisions. It should be a continuous process and involve a variety of formal and informal strategies. Various assessment techniques provide valuable information for individualizing the decision-making process" (p. 3). Let's elaborate a bit on the components of this definition:

1. *Collecting test data.* An example would be administering a physical fitness test to a group of youngsters with mental retardation and recording the test data.
2. *Interpreting test data in order to make nondiscriminatory decisions.* Such decisions might include a particular student's placement in regular versus special/adapted physical education, what to include in an individualized program of physical activity such as a written IEP, or whether a program is effective or needs to be modified.
3. *Ongoing assessment.* Continual evaluation is needed to determine in good time whether progress is occurring and, if not,

what changes need to be implemented. Assessment cannot be limited to a pretest and a posttest.

4. *Variety of strategies.* Standardized tests can be supplemented by informal assessment (for example, observing a group of preschool children with mental retardation during a play session).

Assessment is the important first step in successful placement and program problem-solving. An instructor's program development and modifications, teaching, and evaluation must all be based on accurate and effective assessment. Without it, subsequent program planning will fail. Figure 3.1 outlines the necessary steps for effective instructional program implementation in which assessment is an integral part.

This definition of assessment will serve as a guide and will follow the reader throughout the chapter. Upon completion of this chapter the reader will understand the assessment process and be able to make proper placement and

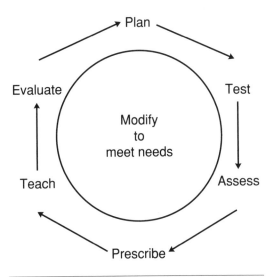

Figure 3.1 Instructional program implementation. In order for each person to reach his or her full potential, effective teaching must be based on following a systematic program of instruction. *Note.* Modified from Wessel and Kelley (1986, p. 37).

programming decisions and effectively evaluate assessment instruments.

Current Practices, Issues, and Problems in Assessment

To determine current assessment practices of professionals who provide physical education to the handicapped, Ulrich (1985a) administered a 28-item questionnaire to 251 professionals from all regions of the country. These findings are important because they begin to show what is taking place in physical education assessment as well as future trends and critical needs. Here is a summary of the findings:

1. The purpose most often cited by professionals for conducting assessment was instructional programming. Therefore, future test development must consider test instruments that can serve a variety of uses for professionals.

2. The primary method of assessment reported was informal observation through teacher-made tests. Therefore, test givers must work to enhance their ability to critically observe movement and understand test development.

3. The pretest-posttest method was used by 29% of the respondents. As noted earlier, testing must be continual, so this method is inadequate.

4. An alarming 69% of the 251 respondents who used standardized tests revealed they had received little or no training regarding proper test administration. This indicates that more scholarship and research as well as proper preservice and inservice training need to be conducted in this area.

5. The respondents made it clear they desired assessment instruments that were practical and easy to interpret. Large caseloads, time constraints, and a lack of proper training made it difficult to administer most standardized assessment instruments. In

general, many felt that the benefits did not warrant the time spent testing.

General Problems of Testing Persons With Disabilities

In 1976, Lewko reported that over 250 motor-based assessment instruments existed but that most were teacher-made, not standardized. This leaves professionals faced with the dilemma of locating proper standardized assessment tools that meet the unique needs of persons with mental retardation. Baumgartner and Horvat (1988) discuss a number of the problems in testing persons with disabilities, including that (a) teacher-made tests are questionable because they lack validity and reliability; (b) professionals are not adequately trained to observe movement deviations; (c) few norms are available on individuals with disabilities; (d) heterogeneity exists among certain disability groups, such as between persons with mild and persons with severe mental retardation; and (e) it is difficult to mass-test persons with limited mental ability, because they usually cannot help with testing (e.g., count the number of laps completed on a running test).

Specific Problems of Testing Persons With Mental Retardation

Persons with mental retardation present unique testing problems. With this in mind, Lavay (1988) suggested a number of test considerations specific to this population:

1. Because they have limited mental ability and a short attention span, this population has difficulty understanding and following complicated test directions.
2. Many of these persons, because of their limited mental ability, are not intrinsically motivated and therefore lack motivation to try their best (see chapter 4 for behavior management strategies that can increase motivation).

3. Inexperience with being tested may make these persons feel extremely uncomfortable around test equipment. Professionals must conduct orientation sessions and have a sufficient number of practice trials to allow these persons to feel comfortable during testing.
4. Tests appropriate to the general population are often used indiscriminately with this population regardless of whether they can comprehend test directions. Highlight 3.1 suggests ways to measure the cardiovascular endurance of persons with mental retardation.

Assessment of Severe and Profound Mental Retardation

The law has increased the number of individuals with severe and profound mental retardation and multiple handicaps that are to be deinstitutionalized and receive physical activity services. Professionals must develop physical activity programs to aid these individuals' total development. Proper assessment procedures are critical to effective program development. But accurate test data for follow-up programs for this special group has only recently emerged (Jansma, 1981).

Guidelines for Testing

Testing persons with severe and profound mental retardation and multiple handicaps presents specific challenges. Areas to be considered in testing include reflexes, muscle tone, posture/body alignment, ambulation, and gait pattern (Rotari, Schwenn, & Fox, 1985). Following are specific guidelines for testing this unique group (Jansma, 1981; Jansma, 1988; Sherrill, 1983):

1. A few of the assessment instruments specifically for use with this population are listed at the end of this chapter. An excellent review of 14 selected tests that measure the psychomotor needs of persons

HIGHLIGHT 3.1

Cardiovascular Fitness Testing for Persons With Mental Retardation

To date, few investigations outline assessment procedures that are valid, reliable, and administratively feasible for persons with mental retardation (MR). It cannot be assumed that assessment instruments and protocols established with the general population can be used successfully with this particular population. A unique set of factors must be considered, such as limited mental ability, motivation, and past experience. This leaves professionals (e.g., adapted/special physical education instructors) faced with the dilemma of choosing effective test modifications to administer tests of cardiovascular fitness. The study described here addresses that problem.

The Study

The purpose of the study was to determine the test-retest reliability of four submaximum oxygen uptake test protocols in predicting the cardiovascular fitness of adults with MR. Also investigated was the administrative feasibility of using these protocols with this particular population. The subjects were employed in a sheltered workshop setting (N=17, Age=35 years, IQ=54). The tests were administered over eight sessions with test-retest reliability scores determined by administering each protocol separately and one week apart.

Results

An intraclass correlation coefficient revealed the following scores: Modified PWC Cycle Ergometry R=.64; Balke Ware Treadmill R=.93; Canadian Step Test R=.95; Cooper 12-Minute Walk/Run R=.81.

Teaching Implications

To successfully measure the cardiovascular fit-

ness of persons with MR, professionals must not only consider a number of factors unique to this population but be able to make proper test modifications.

In general:

- Persons with MR may be apprehensive attempting a new testing procedure or using a certain piece of equipment. Initially professionals must conduct orientation sessions and have a sufficient number of practices before beginning actual testing. Every effort must be made to familiarize and accommodate these persons and make them feel secure during a particular testing procedure.

More specifically:

- Running tests (i.e., Cooper 12-Minute Walk/Run), although field tested and quite reliable with the general population, present problems with this population. Running with an all-out effort is a unique and abstract concept for many of these persons, as they may display difficulty coping with breathlessness and fatigue, staying motivated, and having to maintain a proper pace. These persons may require the use of a running partner (e.g., a peer tutor) who assists with pacing.
- Some research with this population has shown the treadmill to be a reliable fitness test instrument because it can move at a predetermined speed and minimize periods of acceleration and deceleration. However, one serious problem is expense, making this piece of equipment virtually inaccessible for most public schools.

HIGHLIGHT 3.1 CONTINUED

- The bicycle ergometer, although it is somewhat less expensive, presents the problem of maintaining a proper cadence. Necessary modifications may include the use of a metronome or prerecorded cassette tape, physical prompts, and/or visual cues on the speedometer.
- The step test presents a similar problem of maintaining a proper cadence. Modifications similar to those mentioned previously may be necessary. In addition a partner can step with the subject while giving physical prompts. Regression equations with modifications have been developed that are based on the actual steps completed rather than the desired stepping cadence for the test protocol. With proper modifications the step test can be a desirable test protocol for persons with MR, as it does not require expensive equipment and space.

- Most importantly, additional research is needed so that professionals will be able to conduct effective cardiovascular fitness testing, which will enhance program application, which in turn will allow for healthy lifestyle changes in persons with MR.

For complete details, see

Lavay, B., Giese, M., Bussen, M., & Dart, S. (1987). Comparison of three measures of predictor $\dot{V}O_2$ maximum test protocols of adults with mental retardation: A pilot study. *Mental Retardation, 25*, 39-42.

Cressler, M., Lavay, B., & Giese, M. (1988). The reliability of cardiovascular fitness with mentally retarded adults. *Adapted Physical Activity Quarterly, 5*, 235-242.

Note. From ''Cardiovascular Fitness Testing For Adults With Mental Retardation'' by B. Lavay, 1988, *Palaestra*, **5**(1), p. 12. Reprinted by permission of Challenge Publications, Ltd.

with severe handicaps can be found in Jansma (1981).

2. Because this population is heterogeneous in nature and experiences small changes over time, the professional must be well versed in such techniques as task analysis and the collection of baseline data to conduct ongoing testing.

3. The professional must have a sound knowledge of primitive reflexes, automatic postural reactions, and functional skills (see chapters 8 and 9).

4. The professional must be aware of medical or health problems and behavioral problems such as short attention span or sensory deficits.

5. Understanding individuals with severe handicaps can be complex. Therefore, professionals who provide services in the area of special/adapted physical education, physical therapy, and occupational therapy must be willing to share information. Parents and other professionals who have extensive exposure to the individual are excellent sources of information.

In addition, Jansma (1990) has identified seven elements professionals should consider during test selection for this population:

1. Observation based. Decisions can be made by observing the individual perform the test items on a daily basis.

2. Curriculum imbedded. Data gathered is an ongoing and continuous process and part of the instructional phase of the program. Simply stated, testing is teaching and teaching is testing.
3. Developmental low. Test items must be selected that meet the developmental needs of the person being tested, such as the area of reflex and rudimentary movements.
4. Socially valid. The test items are specifically important for the person being tested, as agreed upon by the persons who live and work with the individual.
5. Functional and possessing everyday relevance. For example, rather than test the individual for balance by having her or him walk on a balance beam, have the individual step on and off a curb along a sidewalk or walk up the side of a hill.
6. Stressing skill maintenance. After the skill is learned it is periodically checked to determine if it can still be properly performed.
7. Stressing skill generalization. The individual can successfully perform the skill in various settings and around different persons.

With so many issues and problems regarding the assessment process, some might wonder whether it is worth the effort to assess persons with mental retardation. The next section outlines why this process is so critical.

Justification and Importance of the Assessment Process

The following statement regarding the importance of the assessment process is taken from the state of Louisiana's *Competency Testing for Adapted Physical Education Manual* (Louisiana Department of Education, 1984).

Assessment is one of the most important

aspects of the total educational program, for without it an appropriate program of instructional activities can not be developed. The information obtained through this process will assist in determining whether a student would be unable to profit from the regular physical education program and therefore should be placed in an adapted physical education class. (p. 1)

The assessment process is important for a variety of reasons: placement, programming, evaluation, motivation, determining program effectiveness, and communication. Each of these factors will be separately examined, but it must be kept in mind that these factors are all closely related.

Criteria for Eligibility and Placement

The passage of Public Law 94-142 was designed to assure that each child receives appropriate services in the least restrictive environment (U.S. Office of Education, 1977). Appropriate services are contingent upon proper assessment. In the chapter 3 Preview, the committee could not comment on how the daughter's PE placement was determined, because they had not developed systematic nondiscriminatory procedures for making this decision. Such procedures would include administering a battery of test items to determine the individual's present level of performance and to place her in the environment where she could best function. Therefore, establishing proper eligibility criteria for placement is critical.

The actual eligibility criteria for persons with special needs to receive physical activity services are too often overlooked and not given the systematic attention they require. Loovis (1986) cautions that placement decisions for students with disabilities are mired in political and attitudinal bias that has stymied the effective implementation of physical activity programs for persons with special needs.

With these concerns in mind, the professional assigned to provide physical activity programs to persons with mental retardation must develop guidelines to assure proper placement. Here are factors to consider:

1. Placement decisions should never be based on one test score alone. Rather the tester must utilize various standardized assessment instruments consisting of a battery of subtest items that are valid and reliable.
2. The test must be administered by a qualified instructor with expertise in administering tests in the physical domain.
3. Criteria for eligibility can be best developed by using test results in the form of percentiles, stanines, or developmental age scores. For example, most schools or agencies have established an eligibility criterion that is −1.0 or −1.5 standard deviations below the mean (Ulrich, 1985b). Other professionals advocate eligibility criteria scores below the 25th percentile on standardized norm-referenced tests (Eichstaedt & Kalakian, 1987).
4. In special circumstances, more than test results may be necessary to make the proper placement decision. For example, the person who scores high on a motor skill test but displays emotional and social deficiencies might be severely limited by being placed in a mainstreamed program of physical activity.
5. In the public schools, by law, placement must be formally reviewed at least once a year (Sherrill, 1986).
6. Most importantly, a systematic plan that meets the needs of the particular program must be developed, with clearly established guidelines for eligibility.

Group and Individualized Programming

Proper assessment procedures will allow the instructor to determine the individual's present level of performance. Based on test scores, a program can be designed that best suits the person's deficiencies as well as strengths. Only when the instructor understands the individual or group tested can an educational program with annual goals and short-term behavioral objectives be developed that is tailored to the individual or group. Specific strategies for devising annual goals and short-term behavioral objectives are discussed in chapter 5.

Evaluation

Assessment does not stop once the program is developed. The instructor must determine whether the program is effective and the person or group is effectively progressing toward program goals and objectives. One evaluation method is to use a class checklist to determine which students can properly perform fundamental locomotor skills. For students who cannot perform these skills, the instructor will need to modify teaching strategies to effectively meet their needs. This is why assessment should be ongoing and is critical to proper teaching.

Motivation

Because persons with mental retardation, given their limited mental ability, may not be intrinsically motivated to perform to the best of their ability, methods must be found to increase their motivation. For higher functioning persons with mental retardation, showing test scores in the form of charts or graphs may prove motivational because they display the individual's progress in a visually perceptible manner. This may provide the added incentive necessary to improve physical performance. When test scores are used for motivation, they should always be presented in a positive and nonthreatening manner to encourage individuals to improve and try their best. For example, posting the test scores of students who perform poorly on a skills test may prove discouraging.

Program Effectiveness

Test scores and student profiles can effectively demonstrate to school board members, administrators, parents, and other professionals that certain individuals or groups are making progress. These scores can help to justify the important efforts the physical activity program is making toward contributing to the person's total development. Test score improvement can also serve as an incentive to the instructor. Too often, little daily progress is noted in persons with mental retardation, especially those with severe disabilities. However, by charting test scores over time, the instructor can begin to observe individual, group, and program progress.

Communication

Test score results can be developed into a student profile that can be effectively communicated to parents and other professionals (see Figure 3.2). For example, a physical fitness bar graph can visually demonstrate to parents their son's or daughter's fitness score performance in relation to the rest of the students in class.

Figure 3.2 Communication between instructor and parent regarding test score results is important. Photo courtesy of Bob Fraley.

It is important for parents to remember to not always compare their child's performance to others. Each child is unique.

Public Law 94-142 (PL 101-476) and the Assessment Process

Another important justification for the assessment process is that PL 94-142 (now revised as PL 101-476, Individuals With Disabilities Education Act, 1990) mandates certain guarantees, for both children identified as disabled and their parents, regarding the assessment process and guidelines for assessment procedures, including these:

1. The test shall be administered in the child's native language and preferred mode of communication. For example, picture instructions or a demonstration would be given to an individual with mental retardation who is nonverbal or cannot read.

2. The test shall be administered by trained personnel who are capable of conforming to the test guidelines and instructions. Therefore, only competent personnel who have backgrounds of testing in the physical domain (e.g., motor skill tests) should administer tests in this area.

3. Tests should never be selected that place the individual at an unfair disadvantage due to his or her impairment. The test must be selected and administered so as to best reflect the individual's performance level. The law is clear that the test selected must be validated for the specific purpose it is being used for. As mentioned previously, many standardized tests are developed with the general population in mind and do not take into account the unique mental and physical needs of persons with mental retardation. Therefore, using those tests would place this specific group at an unfair disadvantage. For example, it would

be unfair to expect a child who is blind to pick blocks off the floor while performing the shuttle run.

4. No single procedure, test, or test item can be used as the sole criterion to determine a student's educational placement or program of instruction. Rather, multifaceted testing must be administered utilizing a battery of test items. For example, the instructor cannot determine an individual's overall physical fitness level by using only one fitness item, such as flexibility.

5. The test selected must be validated for the specific purpose it is used for. For example, a Special Olympics volleyball skills test would not be a valid measure for determining a person's overall physical fitness level.

6. The assessment must be conducted by a multidisciplinary team of professionals with at least one expert in the student's suspected disability. The assessment process should include input from a number of professionals, such as the special education classroom teacher, the special/adapted physical education specialist, the regular physical education teacher, the school nurse, the occupational therapist, and the physical therapist. These professionals must remain focused and work together to effectively meet the needs of the person being tested.

Seaman (1988) believes that the combination of mandates in the law and the paucity of adequate assessment instruments present numerous challenges to professionals who provide physical activity to all persons, including those with mental retardation. Therefore, the remaining sections of this chapter focus on the methods and strategies that professionals and students preparing to teach in this area can use to effectively meet the assessment needs of persons with mental retardation.

Competencies Necessary for Observing and Identifying Movement

The survey by Ulrich (1985a) revealed that the primary assessment method used by the professionals studied was informal assessment, for which the ability to observe movement is critical. However, to properly observe movement, the instructor must possess a sound understanding of the components that make up physical education. Physical education as mandated in PL 94-142 is defined as the development of "physical and motor fitness, fundamental motor skills and patterns, and skills in aquatics, dance and individual and group games and sport (including intramurals and lifetime sports)"(p. 42480). For examples of component parts of physical education by this definition, see Figure 3.3. Knowledge of the component parts to the movement elements that make up physical education enables the instructor to make sound decisions regarding proper test selection. For example, a tester with a thorough understanding of the components of physical fitness would never select a test consisting of only one test item. Proper physical fitness measurement consists of a number of factors such as muscular strength and endurance, flexibility, cardiovascular endurance, and percent body fat, and test selection and administration must be based on this fact.

Observational Techniques

According to Seaman and DePauw (1989), certain competencies are necessary for proper observational strategies during testing. These techniques include an understanding of

- developmental milestones,
- proper movement,
- movement deviations,

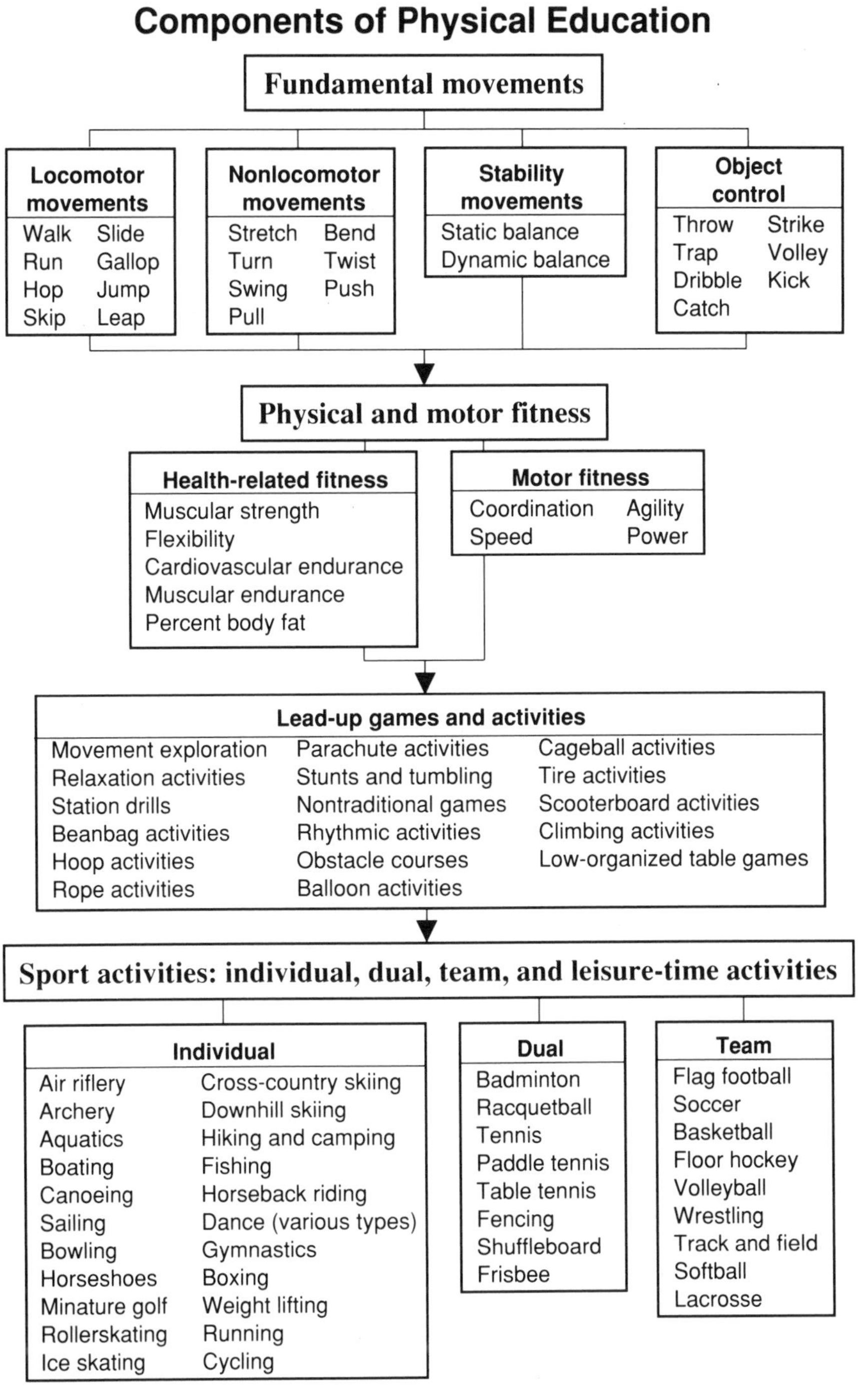

Components of Physical Education

Fundamental movements

Locomotor movements	Nonlocomotor movements	Stability movements	Object control
Walk Slide Run Gallop Hop Jump Skip Leap	Stretch Bend Turn Twist Swing Push Pull	Static balance Dynamic balance	Throw Strike Trap Volley Dribble Kick Catch

Physical and motor fitness

Health-related fitness	Motor fitness
Muscular strength Flexibility Cardiovascular endurance Muscular endurance Percent body fat	Coordination Agility Speed Power

Lead-up games and activities

Movement exploration	Parachute activities	Cageball activities
Relaxation activities	Stunts and tumbling	Tire activities
Station drills	Nontraditional games	Scooterboard activities
Beanbag activities	Rhythmic activities	Climbing activities
Hoop activities	Obstacle courses	Low-organized table games
Rope activities	Balloon activities	

Sport activities: individual, dual, team, and leisure-time activities

Individual		Dual	Team
Air riflery	Cross-country skiing	Badminton	Flag football
Archery	Downhill skiing	Racquetball	Soccer
Aquatics	Hiking and camping	Tennis	Basketball
Boating	Fishing	Paddle tennis	Floor hockey
Canoeing	Horseback riding	Table tennis	Volleyball
Sailing	Dance (various types)	Fencing	Wrestling
Bowling	Gymnastics	Shuffleboard	Track and field
Horseshoes	Boxing	Frisbee	Softball
Minature golf	Weight lifting		Lacrosse
Rollerskating	Running		
Ice skating	Cycling		

Figure 3.3 Knowledge of the component parts of movement will enable the instructor to make sound decisions regarding proper test selection.

- movement description in behavioral terms, and
- interpretation of variables.

Developmental Milestones

The observer must possess a sound knowledge of growth and developmental milestones and must know the ages at which children perform certain movement skills such as running, jumping, skipping, throwing, and catching. She or he must also realize that not all children display a mature skipping pattern at age 7, that developmental rates vary among children. Research indicates, for example, that children with mild mental retardation may lag behind their disabled counterparts by 2 to 4 years (Holland, 1987). Detailed descriptions of appropriate movement programming considerations for persons with mental retardation from birth to adulthood are found throughout this book.

Knowledge of Proper Movement

To successfully identify deviations in movement performance, one must have an understanding of proper movement and an appreciation for the quality or process of movement (see Figure 3.4). In general, children without disabilities display mature fundamental skill performance by the age of 7 or 8 years (Dauer & Pangrazi, 1989), so when observing such a child throw a ball, the instructor must look for such movement components as proper arm swing, trunk rotation, stepping with opposition, and follow-through.

Movement Deviations

Once the observer has mastered an understanding of and ability to observe correct performance, he or she may find it easier to identify movement deviations. This ability is especially important when teaching persons with mental retardation who display a variety of developmental delays and deviations. Seaman and DePauw (1989) have identified three types of movement deviations: omission, substitution, and addition. In omission the person may leave out a certain component part of the skill, such

Figure 3.4 Knowledge of proper skill performance is vital to the assessment process. Photo courtesy of Special Olympics International.

as the follow-through, while throwing a softball. In substitution the individual may replace one or more parts of the normal movement pattern with a less efficient movement. For example, when performing the standing long jump, the individual may swing the legs vigorously to compensate for not obtaining proper upward thrust with the arms. Finally, addition is simply adding an unnecessary movement to the skill, such as swinging the arms vigorously from side to side while running.

Movement Description in Behavioral Terms

Too often untrained observers describe a person's movement deviations in terms such as *clumsy*, *awkward*, *poor*, and *funny looking*. These labels are too imprecise to properly identify a movement deficiency. Movement deviations must be described in behavioral terms that are observable and definable (see Table 3.1), such as ''The individual is not properly rotating the trunk when throwing the ball.'' When a problem occurs, the observer must ask what the person is doing wrong and where the devi-

Table 3.1   Fundamental Movement Skills and Deviations

Common errors	Teaching keys and key sequences
Throwing	
Front facing target	Turn side to target
Throwing side facing target	Keep throwing arm level
Lower throwing arm than shoulder	Step on opposite foot/weight transfer
No step and weight transfer	Rotate the hips and trunk
Stepping with foot on the same side as throwing	Snap the wrist
No rotation of trunk and hips	Follow through to target
No wrist snap	
Abrupt stopping of throwing motion	
Catching	
Legs and hips straight	Bend at the hips and knees
Closing eyes, turning head	Watch the ball
Not in line with the ball, therefore teaching to side	Get in line with the ball
Trapping ball against body or on arms	Extend arms to the ball
Missing the catch because it bounces off a body part	Bend the elbows slightly
Awkward straight arm movement	Absorb the force of the ball
No movement on contact of ball	
Striking	
Poor or no contact	Watch the ball
Facing flight of oncoming ball	Turn side to target
Stepping on same foot as striking arm	Get in line with the ball
No step/weight transfer	Step on the opposite foot
Deflection of the ball in a direction other than would be expected by movement of hand	Hit through the center of gravity
	Rotate the hips and trunk
Weak or less forceful swing	Follow through to target
Abrupt stopping of hand	
Kicking/instep kick	
Missing the ball	Watch the ball
Reaching to kick the ball forward/behind	Body alignment with ball
Approaching ball straight on	Turn your side to target
Kicking with toe	Weight transfer
Backward movement	Rotate hips and trunk
Kicking ball in a direction other than follow through	Kick through center of gravity
Abrupt end to kicking movement	Follow through to target

Note. From "Motor Development and Skill Analysis" by Mielke and Morrison, 1985, *Journal of Physical Education, Recreation and Dance*, **56**, p. 50. The journal is a publication of the American Alliance for Health, Physical Education, Recreation and Dance, 1900 Association Drive, Reston, VA 22091. Reprinted by permission.

ation is. For further discussion and examples of citing movement in behavioral terms (terms that denote actions that are measurable and observable), see chapters 4 and 5.

Interpretation of Observations

Perhaps the most difficult step the observer faces is making sense of all of the acquired movement information and determining links among all of the observed movement deviations. For example, when observing a preschool-age child with moderate mental retardation kick a ball, the tester may attempt to establish a common link between the observed deviations of strength, balance, and eye/foot coordination.

In summary, the novice observer must realize that the necessary competencies for properly observing movement will come only with practice and experience. A good observer must

1. observe the movement several times in an area that is not distracting;
2. position herself or himself at carefully selected angles;
3. observe the total movement as well as the important component parts;
4. while looking for deviations, first consider the proper sequential order of the correct movement;
5. initially be more concerned with the quality (process) of the movement than with the quantity (product) of the movement (Brown, 1982);
6. consider the individual, the skill, and the environment alone and collectively; and most importantly,
7. throughout the entire process, always exhibit flexibility and patience.

Assuring Proper Referral and Screening Procedures

Referral and screening procedures are an important part of the assessment process. The assessment process is supposed to assure proper student placement in the least restrictive environment, but Wessel and Kelly (1986) have cautioned that proper decision making regarding student physical education placement is often overlooked or based on administrative convenience or financial constraints. Therefore, to assure proper student placement, it is of paramount importance to implement systematic and consistent referral guidelines. Proper referral

guidelines are also important for the following reasons:

- They help prevent inappropriate referrals.
- Observing specific problems and concerns noted on the referral form provides the professional administering the test initial direction and decision making regarding test selection.
- Precise identification of problems and deviations noted beforehand saves test time that can be used more effectively during programming. (Lavay & Hall, 1987)

Referral Forms

Persons who may make referral requests for student testing include the classroom teacher, school nurse, speech pathologist, physical therapist, occupational therapist, and parents of the child. However, the regular physical education teacher is the ideal person to initiate a referral request. It is this person who is most likely to observe the child exhibit movement difficulties.

Figure 3.5 shows a referral request form that has been used effectively by the Albuquerque public school system. Referral request forms should include the following information (Lavay & Hall, 1987):

1. Demographic data regarding the student being referred, such as name, birthdate, and grade.
2. The person making the referral and the reasons for the request.
3. Observations noted by the person making the referral regarding the nature of the child's movement difficulty.
4. A section outlining movement difficulties that can be easily noted on the form by untrained or busy personnel who make the request.

Including this information will make the form easy to fill out. The referral form generally should take no longer than 10 to 15 minutes to complete.

Referral for Evaluation in Special Physical Education

Student name _____   Classroom teacher _____

Birth date _____   P.E. teacher _____

Grade/program level _____   Parents' name _____

School _____   Phone number _____

Contact person for student evaluation _____

Please give a brief description of the student in the following areas:

1. Significant medical history that may cause physical limitation: _____

_____

2. Vision or hearing deficits/concerns: _____

_____

3. Movement limitations: _____

_____

4. Behavioral concerns: _____

_____

Avoid making a referral if the student displays difficulties in the following areas:
    . . . irregular spacing in printing activities
    . . . doesn't color within spaces or lines
    . . . difficulties with writing skills

Referral guidelines: After observing the student moving, the following reasons may be applicable for referring a student for a special physical education evaluation. Please check those areas where you feel difficulties exist.

1.   Fitness

_____ tires easily during activities

_____ unable to reach and stretch easily

_____ exhibits limited range of movement

2.   Motor proficiency

_____ unable to repeat movements that have been demonstrated

_____ difficulty performing fundamental movements such as running, jumping, hopping, skipping, throwing and catching

_____ very slow in starting, stopping, and changing directions

3.   Perceptual motor

_____ can not properly identify body parts

_____ unable to find one's space during movement

_____ unable to judge the flight of an oncoming object

_____ misinterprets auditory directions

*Parts of this referral form are taken from the Albuquerque Special Physical Education Handbook.

Figure 3.5 Referral request form.

Note. From ''Assuring Proper Referral Procedures in Special Physical Education'' by B. Lavay and A.M. Hall, 1987, *Physical Educator*, **44**, p. 369. Reprinted by permission of *The Physical Educator*.

Screenings

In general, once the referral request has been completed, then a screening test can be administered. Werder and Kalakian (1985) define a screening test as the initial identification of a child who appears to be displaying movement difficulties. Screening devices are an important means to confirm or allay suspicions regarding a child's movement difficulties (Eichstaedt & Kalakian, 1987). However, these tests can provide only a rough estimate of the child's movement ability and will serve only as an indicator of whether further testing is necessary. Moreover, although it is important to conduct screenings early, if they are implemented too early, they can prove counterproductive for the child (Pencock-Craven, 1983). For example, the child may not be developmentally ready to perform the movement skills requested on the screening test and may become frustrated. Taylor (1984) cautions that it is extremely important that screening tests have good predictive validity. If they do not, erroneous outcomes may include identifying as at risk a child who does not have a movement difficulty or, even worse, not identifying a movement problem in a child who does indeed exhibit one.

Most screenings are based on a referral request for testing. However, there may also be a predetermined schedule by which every child regardless of condition and ability level is screened. Such screenings are usually called "kindergarten round-up" or "preschool screening." A description of some of the screening instruments that have been effectively used is located at the end of this chapter. Here is a partial list:

- Bruininks-Oseretsky Test of Motor Proficiency (short form) (Bruininks, 1978)
- Denver Developmental Screening Test (Frankenburg & Dodd, 1975)
- Peabody Developmental Motor Scale (1983)
- Preschool Test Battery (Morris, 1981)
- Test of Gross Motor Development (Ulrich, 1985b)

Referral and screening procedures are important because they identify students who are at risk or in need of remediation (Wade & Davis, 1982). It is important to realize that referral and screening procedures alone cannot effectively determine the student's movement problem and proper placement but should be thought of as the preliminary step in the entire assessment process, which should include a referral request and/or screening, proper test selection, administration of a standardized test or tests including a full battery of test items, placement in the least restrictive environment, programming, and reevaluation (see Figure 3.6).

Proper Test Selection

The authors of the manual *Testing for the Impaired, Disabled, and Handicapped* (AAHPER, 1975) make the following statement regarding proper test selection:

> Too many educators in every sphere of every discipline fail to realize that a test is not important—how it is used is all that really counts. It does no good and makes no sense to administer a physical fitness test, perceptual motor scale or developmental profile and then stick it in the drawer until next year or until the test is administered again. (p. 9)

Eichstaedt and Kalakian (1987) have stated that there is no "cookbook" approach for evaluating persons with disabilities. The heterogeneity among persons with mental retardation precludes this. Moreover, no one test can effectively measure all of the dimensions of a well-rounded physical activity program, which would include physical and motor fitness; fundamental motor skills and patterns; and skills in aquatics, dance, and individual, dual, and group games and sport (including lifetime leisure ac-

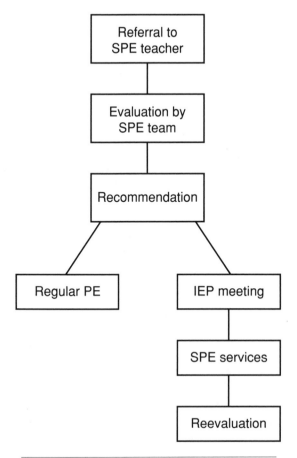

Figure 3.6 Special physical education procedure flowchart.

tivities). A single battery of test items cannot provide the evaluator with a complete profile of the individual's present level of performance in the physical domain. Administering a test of physical fitness to a person with mild mental retardation may allow the tester to better understand that person's physical fitness capabilities but may not allow the tester to determine whether the person displays perceptual motor difficulties. Therefore, the evaluator must remember during test selection that tests are specific and usually measure certain prescribed physical dimensions (e.g., physical fitness, fundamental motor patterns).

The tester's judgment is critical in initial test selection. Before selecting tests, the professional should ask a number of crucial questions. "Why am I testing?" (what is the purpose of the assessment). "Will the test meet the unique needs of the particular individual or group being tested?" (the appropriateness of the assessment instrument selected). "Is the test valid, reliable, and administratively feasible?" (the usefulness of the test selected). These questions deserve a great deal of consideration and must be carefully weighed. Professionals must always keep in mind that tests are implemented to make appropriate placement and programming decisions regarding the individual in question.

General Test Characteristics

Let's take a closer look at the three factors that professionals must weigh carefully during test selection: validity, reliability, and administrative feasibility.

Validity

Validity is defined as the test item measuring what it proports to measure. There are various types of validity, but three types are addressed in this section: content validity, construct validity, and face validity.

Content validity is the degree to which a sample of items on a particular test are representative of the domain or content (Safrit, 1986). For example, a test battery identified as measuring physical fitness must have a representative sample of fitness items (see Figure 3.7). A test battery consisting of only one or two fitness items, such as flexibility and strength, would not be a true overall indicator of physical fitness.

Construct validity is the degree to which a test measures an attribute or trait that cannot be directly measured (Safrit, 1986). In tests of the physical domain the construct is embedded in motor proficiency. Most experts agree that motor behavior consists of four stages: reflexes and reactions; fundamental gross motor patterns and

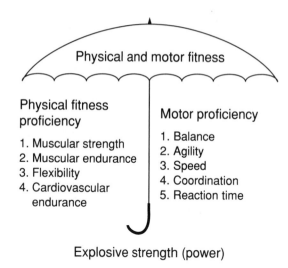

Figure 3.7 Physical and motor fitness.
Note. From *Developmental/Adapted Physical Education* (p. 59) by C. Eichstaedt, and L. Kalakian, 1987, New York: Macmillan. Copyright © 1987 by Macmillan Publishing Company. Reprinted by permission.

skills; lead-up games and skills; and individual, group, and leisure sport skills including dance and aquatics (Ulrich, 1985b). Given the nature of construct validity, test items must be carefully selected. For example, Werder and Kalakian (1985) have questioned whether the 50-yard dash truly measures an individual's speed or reaction time. This question certainly merits consideration when testing persons with mental retardation. The authors offer the solution of using a flying start to minimize the effects of reaction time and explosive leg strength on the student's elapsed time in the 50-yard dash; this procedure has been effectively used to measure running speed and agility with the Bruininks-Oseretsky Test of Motor Proficiency.

Face validity is defined and described by Johnson and Nelson (1986) as follows.

A test has face validity if it appears to measure the ability in question. . . . A test that calls for a student to walk along a narrow board or beam is obviously a test of dynamic balance. . . . While face validity does not lend itself to any type of statisti-

cal coefficient, it is a very important concept that unfortunately is too often overlooked by testers in search of highly objective measures. A tester should always be cognizant of face validity since it is of importance from the student's point of view. (p. 60)

Reliability

Reliability is simply the consistency or stability of results—getting similar results under similar conditions. Ulrich (1985b) states that the degree of confidence that an examiner has in the results of the test is a function of reliability. The two most widely accepted forms of reliability are interrater reliability and intrarater reliability. *Interrater reliability* is the percentage of agreement among observers. Experts agree that an acceptable score of interrater reliability is .80 (Safrit, 1986). *Intrarater reliability* is the percentage of agreement among different administrations of the test by the same observer.

Reliability is usually determined through test-retest methods (see Figure 3.8). Objective or product-oriented tests, such as the number of thrown balls that hit a target, demonstrate a greater percentage of tester agreement than subjective or process-oriented tests, such as evaluating an individual's throwing form. Therefore, it is important that testers who administer process-oriented tests possess competencies and experiences in observing movement; this is the reason for developing expertise in observing movement competencies.

A number of factors can affect test validity and reliability, especially for persons with mental retardation. These factors include the gender and age of the person administering the test, rap-

$$\frac{\text{Tester agreement}}{\text{Tester agreement + disagreement}} \times 100 = \% \text{ agreement}$$

Figure 3.8 Calculation of interrater reliability scores. Interrater reliability is used to determine the percentage of agreement among observers. Experts agree that an acceptable score of agreement is 80%.

port between examiner and participant, presence or absence of others such as peers during test administration (Bowman & Dunn, 1982), the mood or motivational level of the participant, whether the participant is on medication or displays a short attention span, proper warm-up sessions, the equipment and the environment in which the test is administered, and the number of test trials performed. Each of these factors can individually or collectively affect test validity and reliability. To obtain the participant's best performance and true test results, the tester must be aware of these factors and control for them.

Administrative Feasibility

Administrative feasibility is defined as the practicality and usefulness of administering a test. Considerations include the amount of test time necessary and the monetary and personnel cost involved. Equipment, time, and personnel should be kept to a minimum when possible. For example, the best procedure for measuring a person's percent body fat is by hydrostatic weighing. This is administered in a laboratory setting with an underwater weighing tank. Testers working in the public schools and desiring to determine a student's percent body fat would not have access to this type of equipment. Therefore, a simpler, less expensive, and more practical method would be to use skinfold calipers.

Considerations Specific to Persons With Mental Retardation

Few published standardized tests discriminate among the broad range of abilities of persons with mental retardation. When selecting tests for this population, professionals must realize that most of the tests are developed and standardized for the general population.

Test development is usually based on the following assumptions.

1. The administrator of the test is familiar with and has experience administering the

test items. *However, persons with mental retardation may lack the necessary experiences and training to adequately perform the skills necessary to complete the test.*

2. The person being tested understands the concept of performing to the best of his or her ability. *But this population may lack the necessary motivation as well as be so limited in their mental ability that they cannot comprehend the concept of "doing your best."*

3. Test directions are followed specifically. *But certain test directions may be too difficult for this population to comprehend and consequently to perform. However, if the tester makes the necessary modifications, the validity of the test will be affected.*

All of these assumptions can affect test validity and reliability, and the tester must decide whether these test assumptions can be made for the persons with mental retardation who are being tested. Ultimately the tester must use her or his professional judgment and may need to make modifications to get true test results for the person being assessed. Hopefully, this will give a better indication of the person's true performance. These are also important considerations when constructing teacher-made tests, which are discussed later in this chapter.

In summary, the test administrator must carefully weigh all three factors—validity, reliability, and administrative feasibility. No one test is perfect; each has limitations. Most importantly, during test administration, professionals must strive to control these factors and do the best they can to secure the individual's best performance.

Streamlining the Assessment Process

Time is a critical factor to consider when providing programs of physical activity to persons with mental retardation. For example, professionals do not want to spend their entire programming time engaged only in testing. Therefore, test time must be planned wisely with consideration given to a number of key factors including identifying the test, getting to know the individual, preparation of the environment and individual, and streamlining recording procedures.

Test Identification

Because there is no cookbook approach to testing and no one test can adequately measure all of the dimensions of a well-rounded program of physical activity, professionals must select assessment instruments based on the parameters they wish to test and the unique needs of the individual or group. This requires them to be aware of a great variety of assessment instruments available for persons with mental retardation. (See, at the end of this chapter, the annotated bibliography of standardized assessment instruments that can be used with this population.)

Locating tests that meet both the unique needs of the particular population served and specific program needs will not be easy. Professionals must closely review test manuals, examining the test for validity, reliability, and administrative feasibility. Once the test has been selected, the tester must study the test manual, reviewing all directions and equipment needs (Petray, Blazer, Lavay, & Leeds, 1989).

Learning About the Individual

The tester can secure background information about the person being tested before ever meeting the individual. Securing proper background knowledge also assists the tester in proper test selection (Seaman & DePauw, 1989).

Medical records help familiarize the tester with any medication the person may be taking that may adversely affect the individual's performance. The tester must also be aware of any health problems this individual may have, such

as cardiac problems, seizures, or diabetes. It would be contraindicated, for example, for a person with a heart problem to engage in a strenuous test of cardiovascular endurance such as the Cooper 12-Minute Walk/Run.

School files may include the student's achievement tests and individualized educational plan (IEP) and other valuable information. Information of this nature can provide a general idea of the person's present level of performance.

Parents are an excellent source of information and too often are overlooked. They can provide valuable insight into such case history information as the ages at which their child reached certain developmental milestones.

Various professionals, such as the physical therapist, the occupational therapist, the school nurse, the classroom teacher, and the school counselor, can supply the tester with valuable insight regarding the individual to be tested.

Preparing the Environment and the Individual

It is important for the professional to determine whether the test environment is adequate for the movement needs of the person to be tested. For example, too low a ceiling may alter the person's throwing form, while too much environmental stimuli may prove distracting for some individuals and consequently alter test results. Werder and Kalakian (1985) discuss a number of critical factors to consider when preparing the test environment. The authors suggest that testers develop an environmental checklist that considers ceiling height, lighting, temperature and ventilation, noise level, distractions, floor surface, windows, breakable items, and safety.

Before testing, the instructor must review the test manual to determine specific equipment needs and the design of equipment, stations, and markings (see Figure 3.9). The instructor must be careful that markings accurately reflect the measurements specified in the test manual (see Figure 3.10). Reviewing the test manual helps

Figure 3.9 Reading and reviewing the test manual beforehand will help the tester streamline testing. Photo courtesy of Bob Fraley.

Figure 3.10 A professional must make every effort to be sure markings accurately reflect specified measurements. Photo courtesy of Bob Fraley.

assure that test directions are understood and efficiently carried out without wasting valuable test time.

Persons with mental retardation may be apprehensive about being tested, so every effort must be made to create a positive testing atmosphere. This can be accomplished by establishing a noncompetitive atmosphere that accommodates and respects the needs of each individual, making

each person feel as secure and comfortable as possible before testing begins (Petray et al., 1989). Werder and Kalakian (1985) offer the following suggestions for preparing the person for testing.

1. Be friendly and nonthreatening toward the individual. If possible, ask this person questions of interest and things you would like to know about the individual. During this time, determine the individual's preferred style of communication.
2. Explain to the individual as simply as possible the purpose of the meeting and what is going to be happening during this time.
3. Allow the individual to ask any questions he or she wants to ask.
4. Consider the physical needs of the individual, such as allowing for a drink of water or use of the restroom. Be sure all shoelaces are properly tied.
5. Become familiar with the individual. This may require observing the individual engaged in physical activity over a period of time. For example, consider any unique behavior problems that may alter test scores. If possible, determine any types of reinforcement that may motivate the individual to better attend to the task, in order to obtain true test scores.

Most importantly, preparing the environment and student beforehand not only streamlines the assessment process but establishes a comfortable rapport and relaxed test atmosphere. An environment that reduces test anxiety allows the individual to put forth her or his best effort and assists the tester in obtaining accurate test scores.

Streamlining Data Recording

Streamlining data recording during the assessment process can be a real art! The tester must simultaneously administer the test, keep the individual active, observe the individual's movement response, and record the response quickly and accurately. Here are some suggestions for streamlining recording response procedures:

1. Study the scoring procedure and record form beforehand. You will be required to make quick spot decisions and must therefore know what to observe (Werder & Kalakian, 1985).
2. Record the responses on a clipboard and have all other necessary materials, such as the scoresheet and a pencil, ready (see Figure 3.11).
3. Score the response quickly but, most importantly, accurately. If you are not sure about the response, have the person take another trial. However, keep in mind that with some test items, such as an endurance run, this will not be feasible.
4. To ease data recording, have as much of the response as possible on paper beforehand. For example, develop a checklist or task analysis (see Figure 3.12).
5. When recording only a score or checking off a test item, keep in mind any necessary additional comments. If necessary a

few notes can be quickly jotted down in the margins of the scoring response form. These should be indications of any problems or trends you have observed. Later, once testing has been completed, these notes can be expanded upon.
6. The assessment process can be videotaped so you can analyze the movements later. One advantage of this is that the movements can be played back as many times as needed to decide the score.

In summary, assessment should be ongoing and part of the instructional phase whenever possible. Careful consideration of these preplanning factors, such as selecting the test, getting to know the individual, preparing the environment and individual, and studying the recording procedures, will assist in streamlining the assessment process. Time saved can be better spent in providing program instruction.

Standardized Published Tests

Standardized testing involves the formal evaluation of a movement response to a standard set of test items. All individuals are administered the same test items under a uniform set of directions. More specifically, this is a data-gathering technique that uses specific assessment tools or procedures to systematically observe the individual or group, usually during a specific time allotment and following printed, preplanned sets of procedures (Seaman & DePauw, 1989). An annotated list of widely accepted standardized tests that can be administered to persons with mental retardation is located at the end of this chapter.

Two common forms of standardized testing procedures are norm-referenced and criterion-referenced tests. To make appropriate testing decisions for placement and programming, it is important that the professional providing physical activity to persons with mental retardation have an understanding of both kinds of tests.

Figure 3.11 Having the test scoresheet on a clipboard will help the tester streamline testing. Photo courtesy of Bob Fraley.

Student name _____   Date of test _____

Date of birth _____   Examiner _____

Sex _____

Check where correct pattern or deviation(s) is occurring:

Pattern	Deviation
Combines a step with a hop ( )	Extraneous arm movement ( )
Alternates feet ( )	Heavy and flat-footed ( )
Maintains balance ( )	Shuffles with no elevation ( )
Leg and arm opposition ( )	Stiff arms and legs ( )
Rhythmic movement ( )	Does not use arms ( )
Skips various directions ( )	Uses only arms ( )

Comments:

Figure 3.12 Fundamental movement pattern check list for skipping.

Norm-Referenced Tests

Norm-referenced tests measure an individual's performance in relation to the performance of a representative peer group. The representative group is composed of individuals with specifically defined characteristics for which the test is defined, such as age, gender, or specific disability (for example, all 13-year-old girls with mild mental retardation). Norms are constructed by statistical analysis of the raw scores (data) on a large sample of individuals. Based on this analysis, performance standards (norms) are constructed (Seaman & DePauw, 1989). The raw scores are now given meaning and can be used to determine an individual's rank-order in relation to peers or persons with similar characteristics (see Table 3.2). For example, norm-referenced data can help an instructor determine how fast a child can run or how far the child can throw a ball compared to other children of the same age with similar characteristics.

Ulrich (1985b) cautions that if normative data are to detect individual differences, it is critical that test scores adequately represent the population to which the individual's results are compared. This is not always the case, espe-

cially for persons with mental retardation, as tests and norms developed for the population without disabilities are used indiscriminately with this group. However, test norms developed for the population without disabilities would be appropriate to use for persons with mental retardation when the instructor needs to determine proper placement—for example, to determine whether or not a child can properly be mainstreamed.

Advantages

There are many advantages to administering norm-referenced tests. Test scores are usually easy to collect and do not require a great deal of tester experience. Data are collected in the form of a product score, such as the number of seconds it takes to run the 50-yard dash or the number of sit-ups completed in 1 minute. Another advantage, suggested by Werder and Kalakian (1985), is that decisions regarding an individual's overall ability on a particular test can be more easily made, because subtests carry uniform characteristics across items. For example, a student who scores between the 5th and 25th percentile on the subtest items run,

Table 3.2   Physical Fitness Percentile Table of Sit-Ups for 8-Year-Old Males With Mild Mental Retardation

Number of sit-ups (60 s)	Percentile
02	05
04	10
08	15
09	20
10	25
12	30
15	35
16	40
17	45
18	50
20	55
22	60
24	65
27	70
31	75
37	80
41	85
49	90
59	95

Note. From *Physical Fitness and Motor Skills of the Mentally Retarded: Mild, Moderate and Individuals with Down Syndrome, Ages 6 to 21* by C.B. Eichstaedt, P.Y. Wang, J.J. Polacek, P.F. Dohrmann, 1990, Normal, IL: Illinois State University Printing Services. Reprinted by permission of C.B. Eichstaedt.

jump, gallop, slide, and skip would be considered a "poor" performer in locomotor skills.

Proper program placement decisions can be made because the individual's test can be compared to those of peers. For example, a score of 25% or below on a norm-referenced test is a strong indication that a student should be placed in a special/adapted physical education class. Perhaps most importantly, normative data are easy for other professionals and parents to understand. A norm-referenced test allows professionals to easily communicate to parents how their son or daughter performed in relation to classmates.

Disadvantages

As stated earlier in this chapter, one grave problem facing professionals who provide physical activity to this population is the lack of normative data comprised of large sample sizes with regard to the variety of classification systems (mild, moderate, severe, and profound) for persons with mental retardation. Many norm-referenced tests used in the past have become outdated (Johnson & Londeree, 1976) or are no longer available (AAHPER, 1976). Too often professionals are faced with the dilemma of using "norms" developed on other groups, such as the nondisabled population, with persons who have mental retardation. For this reason, Appendix C provides the reader with up-to-date normative tables of various motor and health-related fitness components specific to various age groups and classifications for persons with mental retardation.

Another consideration regarding norm-referenced tests is that the test-item selection is based on the items that produce the greatest diversity of scores. For this reason, items often used and emphasized in the program curriculum may not be included during test construction. Consequently, this type of test provides little assistance during programming and IEP development. King and Summa-Aufsesser (1988) caution that too often norm-referenced tests bear little resemblance to what will be taught in the program. And they cannot easily be changed, because many norm-referenced tests are difficult to modify and lack flexibility.

Criterion-Referenced Tests

Criterion-referenced tests compare an individual's performance to a predetermined criterion or standard of performance for a specific behavior (Safrit, 1986). In the most common type of criterion-referenced test, performance is measured based on the mastery of learning a particular task or components of the task usually outlined in the program curriculum. The focus is on what the learner can and cannot do rather

I CAN

Class performance score sheet
Performance objective: Overhand throw

SCORING

Assessment
× = Achieved
O = Not achieved

Reassessment:
⊗ = Achieved
∅ = Not achieved

Focal points	Std.
1 a Overhand motion; b Ball release	10 ft distance, 2/3 times
2 a Eyes on target; b Overhand motion	20 ft target at 15 ft, 2/3 times
3 a Arm exten./side orient.; b Weight transfer; c Hip and spine rotation; d Follow through; e Smooth integration	2/3 times
4 Angle of release 45°	age/sex norm., 2/3 times
5 Accuracy	8 ft target at 50 ft, 2/3 times
Primary responses°	

Primary Responses
N Nonattending
NR No response
UR Unrelated response
O Other (specify in comments)

	1		2		3					4	5	Primary responses°	
Name	a	b	a	b	a	b	c	d	e				Comments
1. *John J.*	⊗	×	⊗	⊗	∅	⊗	⊗	∅	∅	∅	∅		*Throws side arm*
2. *Katie*	×	×	×	×	⊗	⊗	⊗	×	∅	∅	∅		
3. *Susan*	×	×	×	×	×	×	×	×	×	×	∅		*Practice accuracy*
4. *Mark*	×	×	×	×	∅	×	∅	⊗	∅	∅	∅		*Faces target*
5. *John S.*	×	×	×	×	×	×	×	×	∅	∅	∅		*Follow through inconsistent*
6. *Scott*	⊗	×	∅	⊗	∅	∅	∅	∅	∅	∅	∅		*Throws underhand*
7. *Judy*	×	×	∅	×	∅	∅	∅	∅	∅	∅	∅		*Doesn't look at target*
8. *Cindy*	×	×	×	×	⊗	×	⊗	×	∅	∅	∅		*Faces target*
9. *Kirk*	×	×	×	×	×	×	×	×	∅	∅	∅		*Jerky*
10. *Joanie*	×	×	×	×	×	⊗	⊗	×	∅	∅	∅		
11. *Larry*	×	×	×	×	⊗	×	×	×	∅	∅	∅		*Arm bent*
12. *Chuck*	×	×	⊗	⊗	∅	⊗	∅	∅	∅	∅	∅		*Throws underhand or side arm unless assisted*
13. *Linda*	×	×	×	×	×	×	×	×	⊗	⊗	∅		*Nearly mature*
14. *Sherry*	×	×	×	×	⊗	×	⊗	×	⊗	∅	∅		*Inconsistent beginning position*
15. *Gary*	×	×	×	×	×	×	×	×	⊗	⊗	⊗		*Nearly mature*

Figure 3.13 Criterion-referenced test item.

Note. From *Planning Individualized Education Programs in Special Education* (p. 44) by J.A. Wessell, 1977, Austin, TX: PRO-ED. Reprinted with permission of PRO-ED, Inc.

than on comparing the learner's performance to others' (King & Summa-Aufsesser, 1988). The I CAN model (Wessel, 1976) is an example of a widely accepted criterion-referenced test used for persons with mental retardation (see Figure 3.13).

Advantages

Criterion-referenced tests are easy to interpret and quite flexible for professionals experienced in delivering programs of physical activity and observing quality of movement. Proper test-item selection is based on instructional goals and objectives that the tester believes are important to the learner. Test construction consists of a task analysis approach to a particular skill written in behavioral terms. This is important because it allows the tester to focus on the causative elements of poor performance. The results of a well-constructed criterion-referenced test provide the tester with a profile of the individual's present level of performance (King & Summa-Aufsesser, 1988). Another advantage is that it allows the instructor to individualize and design test items based on the needs of the person or group, which is an important feature, given the heterogeneity among persons with mental retardation.

Disadvantages

One drawback to criterion-referenced testing is that comparisons among individuals tested are usually not possible. Perhaps the greatest drawback is that experienced testers are required to administer the protocol, so it is necessary to secure professionals who are aware of the movement needs of the individual as well as experienced in observing the quality or process of movement. Without experienced testers, the reliability of these tests will always be questioned, and for this reason the proper training of professionals in this area is of paramount importance. Perhaps this is the reason that to date minimal research has been conducted examining criterion-referenced evaluation procedures for persons with mental retardation. In one of the few investigations conducted in this area, Holland (1987) determined that young children with mild mental retardation assessed using criterion-referenced techniques displayed inferior scores on seven fundamental skills when compared to their peers without disabilities. Another concern is that many criterion-referenced tests are not statistically standardized and have only regional usage. However, in recent years more standardized criterion-referenced tests are beginning to emerge, such as I CAN, Data-Based Gymnasium, and the Test of Gross Motor Development. Information on all three of these tests can be found at the end of this chapter.

Both norm-referenced and criterion-referenced evaluation procedures provide the evaluator with valuable information regarding the individual being tested. Each type of test has advantages as well as limitations compared with the other. These factors must be weighed carefully in regard to the context in which the test will be used. Norm-referenced tests offer product-oriented scores the tester can use when comparing the individual to other persons with similar characteristics, which is an important consideration for developing annual goals or making such placement decisions as whether a youngster with mild mental retardation can be successfully mainstreamed into a regular physical education class. In contrast, criterion-referenced tests are process oriented, allowing the tester to observe the individual's quality of movement. This is an advantage for making individualized programming decisions and writing the IEP. Table 3.3 presents a summary of the advantages and disadvantages of norm-referenced and criterion-referenced tests.

Informal Tests

In general, informal tests focus on the individual's natural movement responses in relation to the environment (Werder & Kalakian, 1985). For persons with severe or profound mental retardation or multiple handicaps, informal tests may be the only means by which professionals can determine the individual's present level of movement performance. According to Ulrich (1986), informal tests usually take two forms: teacher observation or teacher-made tests. Werder and Kalakian's (1985) examples of teacher-made tests include

- task analysis, the breaking down of a skill into subtasks;
- checklists or rating scales;
- interviews or questionnaires; and
- progress reports.

Figures 3.14 and 3.15 are examples of teacher-made tests.

Informal or teacher-made tests have some unique advantages. They are usually constructed

Table 3.3 Advantages and Disadvantages of Norm-Referenced and Criterion-Referenced Tests

Test type	Advantages	Disadvantages
Norm-referenced (product-oriented)	• Easy to interpret, as measurements are simple • Little tester experience required • Usually statistically standardized • Comparisons can be made across peers • Easy for parents to understand • Used primarily with groups	• Dependent on the nature of the items and normative sample • There are few norms specific to persons with mental retardation • Lacks flexibility and difficult to modify • Provides little IEP or programming assistance
Criterion-referenced (process-oriented)	• Direct implications for instruction • Flexible and easy to modify items • Individualized to meet persons' needs • Provides individual profile • Used primarily with individuals	• Comparisons between peers is difficult • Requires experienced tester • Not all are statistically standardized

Nonlocomotor movements	Locomotor movements	Object control
_____ Stretch	_____ Walk	_____ Throw
_____ Turn	_____ Run	_____ Trap
_____ Swing	_____ Hop	_____ Dribble
_____ Pull	_____ Skip	_____ Catch
_____ Dodge	_____ Slide	_____ Strike
_____ Bend	_____ Gallop	_____ Volley
_____ Twist	_____ Jump	_____ Kick
_____ Push	_____ Leap	
_____ Pivot		
_____ Lift		

Key:

(0) Cannot perform
(1) Needs physical guidance
(2) Performs at an elementary level
(3) Performs at a mature level

Figure 3.14 Fundamental skills checklist.

in a manner that is relevant to the professional's program or style of teaching. Similarly, they can be designed to be appropriate to needs and characteristics specific to the individual's skill level and style of learning (e.g., developing a volleyball skills test for a high-school-age student with moderate mental retardation who has limited mobility).

___ Hands held correctly on implement with the dominant hand on top

___ Feet shoulder-width apart and knees slightly bent

___ Rotation of the hips and trunk upon execution

___ Coordinates arms, trunk, and legs upon contact of the object

___ Makes contact with the object squarely

___ Follows through with the implement and rotates the wrist

___ Can successfully contact the ball off a batting tee

___ Can successfully contact a slowly tossed ball

___ Can successfully contact a thrown ball from __ ft away

Key:

(0) Cannot perform
(+) Can perform with physical guidance
(*) Can perform with verbal instruction or demonstration

Figure 3.15 Striking pattern task analysis.

There are some disadvantages of teacher-made tests (Werder and Kalakian, 1985):

- They may be time consuming to construct and administer.
- Validity and reliability are questionable.
- Test results may not be useful in determining the individual's performance when compared to that of peers.

Guidelines for Construction

Many of these problems can be eliminated by following Ulrich's (1986) five-step procedure for developing teacher-made tests:

1. Identify the individual's movements of interest or need.
2. Develop movement objectives in behavioral terms. Each skill must be observ-able and include a behavior, condition, and criterion.
3. Develop a specific measurement system.
4. Establish the validity of the test.
5. Evaluate the reliability of the test.

During test design, the professional must ask, "What do I want to find out about the individual being tested?" The tester must consider not only the individual's physical characteristics, but also this person's cognitive and social needs.

Interpretation of Test Data: Putting It All Together

Making sense of test results is perhaps the biggest challenge facing the evaluator. Test results are of no use unless they can be interpreted and communicated effectively to others. The interpretation of test data is important in making a variety of sound and nonbiased decisions regarding the individual being tested, because the individual's programmatic needs in the area of physical activity cannot be adequately met unless the instructor has a thorough understanding of the person's present level of performance. Werder and Kalakian (1985) label this process as translating assessment results into programmatic action. For professionals to meet this challenge and make effective decisions, the following factors must be considered:

- Preparation of the test data
- Interpretation of the test data
- Reporting and communicating the test data to others

Preparing the Data

During the administration of the test, the data are collected in a number of different forms. In general, test data results depend primarily on the type of test administered. For example, standardized test scores may consist of data in raw scores, percentiles, stanines, and standard scores. The results of informal testing may take the form of behavioral observation tallies (Werder & Kalakian, 1985). Regardless of the type of test administered, the professional who has performed a thorough job of testing will have an abundance of test data and information available regarding the individual.

All information should be organized and converted onto one fact or summary sheet. This will prove helpful in interpreting test-data information during future analysis. Only the most relevant data should be chosen and presented. Care must be taken that numbers and other information are not misinterpreted when the data is transferred onto the fact sheet. The following are examples of the information that should be prepared and presented on this summary fact sheet (Werder & Kalakian, 1985):

1. Demographic data, including the individual's name, birthdate, placement/condition, height, and weight; name of the test; administrator; and date of test administration.
2. Background information from parents, physician, therapists, teacher, and caseworker concerning the individual, including information regarding health impairments or medication the individual is presently taking.
3. Observational data including notes taken by the tester during the testing session regarding the individual's mood, particular behaviors demonstrated, and so on.
4. Test data are the raw scores that are tallied and summarized for future analysis. For example, the individual's raw scores obtained on a standardized norm-referenced test should be converted to percentiles. For further information regarding percentiles, stanines, standard scores, and so forth, see Safrit (1990).

Interpreting the Data

Once the test data have been gathered and or-ganized onto a summary sheet, the next step is to make sense of the information in order to make programmatic decisions. A most important step is to develop an individual test profile. During this phase the tester should be considered a detective using clues (the test data) to solve a mystery. The following are some suggestions for effectively interpreting test data (Seaman & DePauw, 1989; Werder & Kalakian, 1985):

1. *Examine problem areas.* This is valuable in detecting trends such as the individual's strengths and weaknesses. The tester must closely examine various test results to determine if an interrelationship among test items exists. Certain test items may or may not be related to movement deficiencies. For example, a lack of strength may be the underlying factor in a poor performance by a young boy with moderate mental retardation on such test items as sit-ups, vertical jump, and hopping as well as static balance on the nondominant foot.

2. *Cluster commonalities.* Once the demands of each test area have been analyzed, these items or areas should be ordered and grouped to better detect patterns or trends. Although some test items may reveal no relationship, others may demonstrate a trend, and these test scores can be grouped by commonalities among deficits. This grouping allows the individual's test profile to begin to take shape. Pie graphs are one method for grouping and detecting commonalities among test scores.

3. *Severity of discrepancies.* The tester must be able to determine the severity of discrepancy in the individual's performance when compared to peers. This is one of the advantages to norm-referenced tests, as test scores can be compared to the scores of persons with similar characteristics. For example, test score results could reveal the individual to be above average, average, or below average in movement performance. Detection of discrepancies with criterion-referenced test scores is much more difficult.

However, it could be determined whether the individual mastered the criteria of certain test items. In addition, the tester must realize that poor performance may also be attributed to the individual's specific disability. For example, some persons with Down syndrome can be expected to display some difficulty in performing certain balance skills.

4. *Specific physical activity needs.* When studying test results, the tester must try to determine how many movement deficits the individual may have. Obviously, an individual who displays a number of movement difficulties as compared to another person who exhibits only a few deficits may need a more intense program with a greater number of modifications. For example, the high-school-age female with mild mental retardation who exhibits adequate physical skills but poor social skills and maladaptive behavior may prove difficult to mainstream into a community-based recreation program. For another example, see Highlight 3.2, which presents test score information for a 10-year-old boy with mild mental retardation.

Reporting the Data

Because test results are of no use unless they can be effectively interpreted and communicated to others, as when writing reports or discussing findings during an IEP meeting, test scores must be organized and reported in a manner that is easy for others to understand. Therefore, it is important to consider the following strategies when reporting test data.

Above all, instructors must realize they are the experts in this area and must always conduct themselves professionally. Reports of the information should begin with an overview of the assessment instruments administered, including a brief background of the test used, what

---

HIGHLIGHT 3.2

IN PRACTICE

Test Score Information to Interpret Placement

Name: Bruce
Chronological Age: 10 years
Sex: Male

School/placement: Special day class
Disability: Mild MR
Height: 53'' (15%) Weight: 98 pounds (85%)

Bruce's physical fitness score as measured by the Health-Related Fitness Test (AAHPERD, 1980) revealed that he was below the 25th percentile in cardiovascular endurance and abdominal strength, whereas his body composition was measured at the 25th percentile and his flexibility was measured at the 45th percentile.

Bruce can perform locomotor skills such as running, jumping, galloping, and sliding at age-group norms as determined by the Test of Gross Motor Development (Ulrich, 1985). Object control skills such as throwing, catching, and striking are very difficult for him to perform, and Bruce is 3 to 4 years below age-group norms in these areas of fundamental movement. His skills in the area of balance were tested at age-group norms.

Bruce seems to get along well with the other students and is, according to his classroom teacher, willing to try new activities. During testing he expressed an interest in learning to play the game of basketball, which he saw played on TV.

Based on this information, what is the most appropriate placement for Bruce?

it measures, and why it was selected for this particular individual. Werder and Kalakian (1985) believe that technical jargon should be minimized when reporting the findings. Terms that are unique to the physical activity profession should be explained so that everyone attending the meeting can understand them. For example, terms such as *cardiovascular endurance*, *fundamental motor skills*, and *bilateral coordination* should be defined as simply and clearly as possible, and examples should be provided. This is especially important when parents are attending the meeting.

The report should always begin by mentioning the positive attributes of the individual who was tested. For example, the tester could explain to the parents that their child was most cooperative and willing to attempt all test items no matter how difficult. During this meeting areas of strength as well as needs or deficiencies should be reported and discussed. The results should be presented in terms of a range of scores. Reporting that a child scored a 24 on a throwing test will have little meaning to anyone who does not know the range and meaning of the scale. Therefore, it is important that test scores be reported descriptively and explained (Werder & Kalakian, 1985). For example, explaining that an individual who scores in the 10th percentile on a physical fitness test item would be considered in the "poor" category, whereas a score in the 50th percentile would place that same individual in the "average" category.

A visual presentation of the test results should also be provided. Charts and graphs allow the tester to better interpret test scores and present this material in a clear and concise manner that is easy for all to follow and understand (see Figure 3.16). It is also most important to be objective when reporting results. Seaman and DePauw (1989) caution that the tester should never speculate beyond the data collected. Interpretations should never be reported that cannot be justified with test score results.

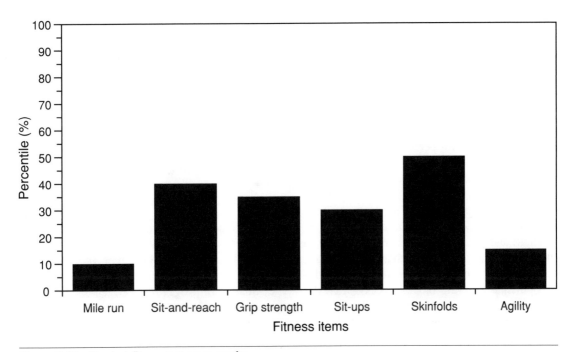

Figure 3.16 Physical fitness test score results.

Finally, program recommendations should be summarized based on the individual's strengths and needs. During the meeting it is critical for team members to listen to one another before summary statements and program recommendations are made. Collectively, team members can provide added insight regarding the individual being tested. They must all communicate well, sharing information in order to meet the unique needs of each individual as effectively as possible.

Some Final Thoughts

Up to this point we have implicitly advocated that you develop a philosophy of assessment, one in which the individual being tested is never made to fit the test, but rather the test is selected to meet the unique needs of the person. Again we emphasize that no cookbook approach to testing will work! Numerous factors must be carefully considered for each case. However, it is also true that the tester must begin somewhere.

It has been our experience that when one is in doubt about testing persons with mental retardation, a good place to begin is to examine the area of physical fitness. Performing poorly in physical fitness can be an underlying cause of many of the other movement difficulties this population encounters. Poor cardiovascular endurance means the individual will lack the stamina necessary for performing many physical activities. For example, a lack of strength may be the reason why a child performs poorly on such items as the vertical jump, hopping on either foot, and performing a stork stand on the nondominant foot. A combination of poor strength and poor endurance can contribute to the child's minimum performance on all fundamental locomotor skills, which are the developmental building blocks necessary to the performance of more advanced skills. It is important to remember that although the selection of physical fitness test items or modifications of items will vary based on a particular person's

needs, the basic underlying principles of physical fitness will not. Appendix D presents adaptations to a number of health-related physical fitness test items that can be successfully performed by this population.

Summary

Assessment is different from testing insofar as testing is merely collecting data using a specific tool and following specific procedures, whereas assessment is the collection and interpretation of information specific to the individual to assist in making nondiscriminatory decisions. It is this interpretation of the data that is vital to the decision-making process and distinguishes assessment from testing. Without properly executed assessment procedures, effective subsequent program planning will fail.

There are a number of problematic issues regarding testing persons with disabilities, including individuals with mental retardation. Some of the concerns specific to persons with mental retardation are these (Baumgartner & Horvat, 1988; Lavay, 1988):

- There is a lack of norm-referenced tests with normative data specific to this population.
- Persons with mental retardation are a heterogeneous group.
- It is difficult to conduct mass testing.
- Limited mental ability and short attention span lead to a lack of test motivation.
- Persons with mental retardation will probably have few past test experiences.

Given so many issues and concerns, the assessment of persons with mental retardation is certainly a challenge. However, this process is critical to proper placement, programming, evaluation of program effectiveness, and communication. Still another reason for taking on the challenge is that PL 94-142 mandates that professionals adhere to proper assessment procedures and guidelines when testing children attending the public schools and identified as having a disability.

It should be obvious by now that effectively addressing the needs of persons with mental retardation cannot be left to chance. Therefore, professionals must be trained in a number of areas related to assessment procedures, including:

- Competencies necessary for observing and identifying movement needs
- Administration of proper referral and screening procedures
- Proper test selection, including an understanding of general test characteristics
- Procedures for streamlining the assessment process

- An awareness and understanding of a variety of standardized tests
- The ability to develop teacher-made tests for persons with unique needs, such as those who have severe handicaps
- Criteria for eligibility and proper placement decisions
- The interpretation of test data in order to effectively report findings

To assure that the individual's assessment needs are effectively met, professionals must carefully consider these items collectively and in a systematic manner.

DISCUSSIONS AND NEW DIRECTIONS

1. Does your school district have a policy statement regarding criteria for eligibility for and placement in the least restrictive environment? Is it based on sound assessment procedures and guidelines? How valid is this policy statement for children with mental retardation attending the school district? Have problems been encountered with the present guidelines, and how may these problems be eliminated or the guidelines streamlined to be more efficient and assure proper placement for each child?

2. Discuss the advantages, disadvantages, similarities, and differences between norm-referenced and criterion-referenced tests. Does each kind have a place in the assessment process for persons with mental retardation?

3. Discuss the various standardized assessment instruments that have been developed to measure the physical abilities of persons with mental retardation. For each instrument, discuss such general test-selection issues as validity, reliability, and administrative feasibility. Discuss the following more specific issues of each instrument: rationale for test-item selection, testing guidelines, test adaptations and modifications, and scoring procedures.

SURVEY OF STANDARDIZED ASSESSMENT INSTRUMENTS

This is a brief list of textbooks and articles that include surveys of standardized assessment in-

struments in the physical domain for persons with special needs.

Folio, M.R. (1986). *Physical education programming for exceptional learners.* Rockville, MD: Aspen.

Jansma, P. (Ed.) (1988). *The psychomotor domain and the seriously handicapped* (3rd ed.). Lantham, MD: University Press of America.

Miles, B.H., Nierengarden, M.E., & Nearing, R.J. (1988). A review of the eleven most often cited assessment instruments used in adapted physical education. *Clinical Kinesiology*, **42**, 33-41.

Seaman, J.A., & DePauw, K.P. (1989). *The new adapted physical education: A developmental approach.* Palo Alto, CA: Mayfield.

Sherrill, C. (1986). *Adapted physical education and recreation: A multidisciplinary approach.* Dubuque, IA: Brown.

Werder, J.A., & Kalakian, L.H. (1985). *Assessment in adapted physical education.* Minneapolis, MN: Burgess.

Standardized Tests for Persons With Mental Retardation

The following is an annotated list of suggested standardized assessment instruments used specifically to measure the physical abilities of persons with moderate to severe and profound mental retardation. Each entry gives the title, an address, and a brief description of the assessment instrument. The list is divided into the following categories:

- Physical fitness
- Motor ability
- Sport skill guides

Physical Fitness

Alabama Special Olympics Fitness Battery (Roswal, Floyd, Roswal, Jessup, Pass, Klecka, Montelione, Vaccaro & Dunleavy, 1985): G. Roswell, Jacksonville State University, Department of Physical Education, Jacksonville, AL 36265.
*The test manual includes normative physical fitness data based on a sample of 2,084 Alabama Special Olympians, ages 8 to 68 years. Twelve commonly used physical fit-*ness items (except cardiovascular endurance) were measured, and norm-referenced tables by sex and age group are included.*

Kansas Adapted/Special Physical Education Test Manual (Johnson & Lavay, 1988): Janet Wilson, Specialist in Physical Education, Kansas State Department of Education, 120 E. 10th St., Topeka, KS 66612.
Included in this manual is Good's Health Related Physical Fitness Test/Kansas Revision. The test procedures were originally developed, and have been used, by Pat Good (Special/Adapted Physical Education Specialist for Students With Mental Retardation, Howe School, 1800 Oakwood Blvd., Dearborn, MI 48124) since 1981 and were revised and field-tested in 1988 by a group of Kansas certified adapted physical education specialists. The health-related fitness test items included in this test are sit-ups, sit-and-reach, isometric push-ups and a bench press, and aerobic movement. The aerobic movement is a unique method of assessing cardiovascular endurance. The individuals ambulate in any fashion possible (e.g., briskly walking, running, propelling themselves in wheelchairs) while maintaining a pulse rate from 140 to 180 beats per minute for 12 minutes after a 6-minute warm-up. The individual's pulse rate is monitored every 3 minutes during testing. A more detailed description and the rationale and adaptations for each test item appear in Appendix D.

Motor Fitness Test Manual for the Mildly Mentally Retarded (Johnson & Londeree, 1976): American Alliance for Health, Physical Education, Recreation and Dance, 1900 Association Dr., Reston, VA 22091.
This test measures 13 items of motor fitness for persons with moderate mental retardation. Only a few of the fitness test items in the battery measure health-related fitness. The normative data was established in the early 1970s with this specific population and the age groups of 6 to 20 years.

Physical Fitness and Motor Skill Levels of the Mentally Retarded: Mild, Moderate, and in Individuals with Down Syndrome, Ages 6-21 Years (Eichstaedt, Wang, Polacek, & Dohrmann, 1990): Illinois State University Printing Service, Normal, IL.

The test includes a battery of 14 items that measure the physical fitness and motor performance of persons with mental retardation from 6 to 21 years of age. Norms were established by testing over 4,000 persons with mental retardation from Illinois schools and agencies. This is one of the few norm-referenced tests to develop normative data with separate categories of mental retardation. See Appendix C for a list of this normative data under the different fitness and motor performance items and categories of mental retardation.

The Project Transition Assessment System (Jansma, Decker, Ersing, McCubbin, & Combs, 1988): Dr. Paul Jansma, The Ohio State University, Department of Physical Education, 343 Larkin Hall, Columbus, OH 43210.

This assessment system includes both qualitative and quantitative measures of the following physical fitness items: sit-ups, bench press, sit-and-reach, grip strength, and 300-yard run/walk. All fitness items were determined to have functional value for individuals with mental retardation, including adults and persons with severe mental retardation. It should be noted that the measure of cardiovascular endurance is questionable. The system includes a unique qualitative format of scoring by measuring such factors as task completion, level of necessary prompting, and reinforcement strategies.

Motor Ability

Brigance Diagnostic Inventory of Early Development (Brigance, 1978): Curriculum Associates, Inc., 5 Esquire Rd., North Bilerica, MA, 01862.

This inventory was designed to assess individuals whose developmental levels range from birth to 7 years. It evaluates a wide range of curriculum areas; of particular interest to professionals providing physical activity are the following: preambulatory motor skills and behaviors, gross motor skills and behaviors, and fine motor skills and behaviors. The inventory is criterion-referenced, sequenced, and quite comprehensive. A unique feature of the assessment instrument is that all test items are written in a behavioral format, enabling the professional to design student long-range goals and short-term objectives.

Bruininks-Oseretsky Test of Motor Proficiency (Bruininks, 1978): American Guidance Service, Circle Pine, MN 55014.

This test measures the overall motor proficiency of children 4.5 to 14.5 years of age. Although standardized with children without disabilities, it can be used to compare the motor ability of children with moderate to mild mental retardation to their nondisabled peers. This test consists of a long form that includes 49 items as well as a short form made up of 14 items that evaluate the areas of gross and fine motor ability.

Data-Based Gymnasium (Dunn, Moorehouse, & Fredericks, 1986): PRO-ED Publishers, 5341 Industrial Oaks Blvd., Austin, TX 78735.

This program is a data-based curriculum approach to providing individualized instruction for students with severe disabilities. Specific to assessment are strategies for collecting baseline data on skills from the game, exercise, and leisure sport curriculum to determine the student's present level of performance and provide individualized programming. The game, exercise, and sport curriculum, which is separate from the textbook, includes detailed task analyses of a wide range of various skills.

I CAN (Wessel, 1976): PRO-ED Publishers, 5341 Industrial Oaks Blvd., Austin, TX 78735.

This program is a diagnostic/prescriptive achievement-based curriculum with materials designed to meet the needs of a wide range of students from preprimary through secondary school. Many of the materials, especially the task analyses of various skills, are useful in the assessment of persons with mental retardation. Professionals who provide physical activity to persons with severe handicaps will find the following material helpful:

Wessell, J., Green, G., Knowlton, K., & Lessard, E. (1981). *I CAN adaptation manual: Teaching physical education to severely handicapped individuals—Preprimary through adulthood.* Michigan State University Instructional Media Center/Marketing Division, East Lansing, MI 48824.

Ohio State University Scale of Intra-Gross Motor Assessment (Loovis & Ersing, 1979): College Town Press, P.O. Box 669, Bloomington, IN 47402.

This is a criterion-referenced test that measures 11 basic movement skills in young children and is applicable to students with moderate to severe mental retardation. A four-point rating scale is used for each of the 11 movement skills: walk, stair climb, run, throw, catch, jump, hop, skip, strike, kick, and ladder climb. The test is accompanied by a performance-based curriculum guide.

Test of Gross Motor Development (Ulrich, 1986): PRO-ED Publishers, 5341 Industrial Oaks Blvd., Austin, TX 78735.

This test measures 12 fundamental motor skills in the areas of locomotion and object control in children of the ages of 3 to 10 years. These test items include run, gallop, hop, leap, skip, slide, two-hand strike, stationary bounce, catch, kick, and throw. Test results can be interpreted by means of both criterion-referenced and norm-referenced standards. Although the test is standardized with children without disabilities, it can be used to compare the fundamental motor-skill development of children with moderate to mild mental retardation to their nondisabled peers.

Sport Skill Guides

Special Olympics Inc. Sport Skill Instructional Program Manuals (Special Olympics Inc.), 1350 New York Avenue NW, Suite 500, Washington, DC 20005.

An individual sport skill guide is available for each of the 22 sports that Special Olympics offers to persons with mental retardation. This includes a Motor Activities Training Program (MATP) for persons with severe handicaps. Each manual includes a section specific to assessment, designed to determine the individual's present level of performance. The test examines the completion of specific fundamental sport skills while moving along a continuum from beginner, to rookie, to winner and including various skill levels. For more information on the Special Olympic sport skill guides, see Figure 3.17 and chapter 12.

Instructions

The Sports Skills Assessment is designed to determine the student's present level of functioning within a specific skill or sport and to determine the student's progress through training.

In administering the test, observe each student as he/she performs each test item. Score the student accordingly by checking the box located to the left of the task performed. If there is any question as to the student's competence in a particular skill, require the student to perform the task 3 out of 5 times.

After scoring each student, add up the total number of boxes and indicate the student's present level of ability (i.e., Beginner, Rookie, Winner). If the student is performing at a higher level than measured in the Skills Assessment—Level I, re-evaluate the student utilizing Skills Assessment—Level II.

Skills assessment—level I

Scoring level—indicates the student's level of achievement

0-10	Beginner
11-20	Rookie
21-30	Winner

Test Item #1   Dribbling skills

☐ Makes an attempt to dribble or bounce ball
☐ Bounces ball with two hands
☐ Bounces ball in any direction with one hand
☐ Dribbles ball with control from a stationary position
☐ Dribbles and controls ball while moving forward

Test Item #2   Catching skills

☐ Makes an attempt to catch a ball
☐ Catches a ball at chest level from 3 meters away
☐ Catches a ball at chest level from 5-7 meters away
☐ Catches a bounce pass.
☐ Catches a ball while walking forward

Test Item #3   Passing skills

☐ Makes an attempt to throw or pass ball
☐ Passes ball in any direction at least 5 meters
☐ Passes ball in intended direction to a target
☐ Passes ball to a stationary teammate
☐ Executes a bounce pass to stationary teammate

Test Item #4   Shooting skills

☐ Shoots ball towards basket
☐ Hits a part of the backboard or rim when shooting
☐ Makes 3 out of 5 baskets from a 1 meter radius
☐ Performs a lay-up

Test Item #5   Rebounding skills

☐ Tracks a rebounded ball
☐ Assumes ready position for rebounds
☐ Moves in direction of rebounded ball
☐ Catches rebounded ball on bounce

Test Item #6   Defensive play

☐ Makes an attempt to guard an opponent
☐ Demonstrates correct defensive stance
☐ Maintains proper distance staying with opponent
☐ Blocks/stops a pass between two players

Test Item #7   Knowledge of game

☐ Stops when the whistle blows
☐ Knows when the ball is in or out of boundaries
☐ Participates a little; recognizes teammates and opponents
☐ Recognizes teammates and opponents' goal areas
☐ Knows how to start game with jump ball

_____ Total score

Figure 3.17 Basketball sport skills assessment—Level 1.

Note. From *Special Olympics Sport Skills Program Guide for Basketball* (p. 10) by Special Olympics International, 1988, Washington, DC: Author. Copyright © 1988 by Special Olympics International. Reprinted with permission.

References

American Alliance of Health, Physical Education and Recreation (AAHPER). (1975). *Testing for the impaired, disabled, and handicapped.* Washington, DC: Author.

American Alliance of Health, Physical Education and Recreation (AAHPER). (1976). *Special fitness test for the mildly mentally retarded.* Washington, DC: Author.

Baumgartner, T.A., & Horvat, M.A. (1988). Problems in measuring the physical and motor performance of the handicapped. *Journal of Physical Education, Recreation and Dance*, **59**(1), 48-52.

Bowman, R., & Dunn, J. (1982). Effects of peer presence on psychomotor measures with EMR children. *Exceptional Children*, **48**, 449-451.

Brown, E.W. (1982). Visual evaluation techniques for skill analysis. *Journal of Physical Education, Recreation and Dance*, **53**(1), 21-26, 29.

Dauer, V.P., & Pangrazi, R.P. (1989). *Dynamic physical education for elementary school children.* New York: Macmillan.

Eichstaedt, C.B., & Kalakian, L.H. (1987). *Developmental/adapted physical education: Making ability count.* New York: Macmillan.

Frankenburg, W.K., & Dodd, J.B. (1975). *Denver developmental screening test.* (Available from Publishing Foundation Inc., East 51 Ave. & Lincoln St., Denver, CO 80216)

Holland, B.V. (1987). Fundamental motor skill performance of nonhandicapped and educable mentally impaired students. *Education and Training in Mental Retardation*, **22**, 197-204.

Jansma, P. (1981). Psychomotor domain tests for the severely and profoundly handicapped. *Journal of the Association for the Severely Handicapped*, **5**, 368-381.

Jansma, P. (1988). Teacher training in adapted physical education for the severely and profoundly handicapped student. In C. Sherrill (Ed.), *Leadership training in adapted physical education* (pp. 423-438). Champaign, IL: Human Kinetics.

Jansma, P. (1990, March). *Adapted physical activity for persons with serious handicaps.* Paper presented at the Distinguished Visiting Scholarship Lecture, California State University, Long Beach.

Johnson, B.L., & Nelson, J.K. (1986). *Practical measurement for evaluation in physical education.* Edina, MN: Burgess.

Johnson, L., & Londeree, B. (1976). *Motor fitness test manual for the mildly mentally retarded.* Reston, VA: American Alliance for Health, Physical Education, Recreation and Dance.

King, H.A., & Summa-Aufsesser, K. (1988). Criterion-referenced testing: An ongoing process. *Journal of Physical Education, Recreation and Dance*, **59**(1), 58-63.

Lavay, B. (1988). Cardiovascular fitness testing for adults with mental retardation (research application). *Palaestra: The forum of sport, physical education, and recreation for the disabled*, **5**, 12.

Lavay, B., & Hall, A.M. (1987). Assuring proper referral procedures in special physical education. *Physical Educator*, **44**, 25-27.

Lewko, J. (1976). Current practices in evaluating motor behaviors of disabled children. *American Journal of Occupational Therapy*, **30**, 413-419.

Loovis, E.M. (1986). Placement of handicapped students: The perceptual dilemma. *Adapted Physical Activity Quarterly*. **3**, 193-198.

Louisiana Department of Education. (1984). *Competency testing for adapted physical education.* Baton Rouge: Office of Special Education Services.

Morris, A. (1981). *Preschool test battery.* Tucson: Department of Physical Education, University of Arizona.

Peabody developmental motor scale. (1983). Nashville: George Peabody College.

Pencock-Craven, A. (1983). Screening tests. In Connecticut State Board of Education, *A guide to program development in special physical education* (pp. 55-57). Hartford: Connecticut Department of Education.

Petray, C., Blazer, S., Lavay, B., & Leeds, M. (1989). Fitting in fitness: Designing the fitness environment. *Journal of Physical Education, Recreation and Dance*, **60**(1), 35-38.

Rotari, A.F., Schwenn, J.O., & Fox, R.A. (1985). *Assessing severely and profoundly handicapped individuals*. Springfield IL: Charles C Thomas.

Safrit, M.J. (1990). *Introduction to measurement in physical education and exercise science* (2nd ed.). St. Louis: Time Mirror Mosby.

Seaman, J. (1988). The challenge. *Journal of Physical Education, Recreation and Dance*, **59**(1), 32-33.

Seaman, J.A., and DePauw, K.P. (1989). *The new adapted physical education: A developmental approach*. Palo Alto, CA: Mayfield.

Sherrill, C. (1983). Pedagogy in the psychomotor domain for the severely handicapped. In R.L. Eason, T.L. Smith, & F. Caron. (Eds.), *Adapted physical activity: From theory to application*. Champaign, IL: Human Kinetics.

Sherrill, C. (1986). *Adapted physical education and recreation: A multidisciplinary approach*. Dubuque, IA: Brown.

Taylor, R.L. (1984). *Assessment of exceptional students: Educational and psychological procedures*. Englewood Cliffs, NJ: Prentice Hall.

Ulrich, D. (1985a). *Current assessment practices in adapted physical education: Implications for future training and research activities*. Unpublished manuscript, Indiana University, Department of Physical Education, Bloomington.

Ulrich, D. (1985b). *Test of gross motor development*. Austin, TX: PRO-ED.

Ulrich, D. (1986, October). Assessment and programming of gross motor skill patterns. *Proceedings of the 14th National Conference on Physical Activity for the Exceptional Individual*, 253-254.

U.S. Office of Education. Federal Register. The Individuals With Disabilities Education Act, formerly The Education for All Handicapped Children Act of 1975, Section 94-142, 99-457, 89-750, 42 U.S.C., Section 42480-54579, (1977).

Wade, M.G., & Davis, W.E. (1982). Motor skill development in young children: Current views on assessment and programming. In L.G. Katz, Ed.), *Current topics in childhood education* (Vol. 4, pp. 55-70). Norwood, NJ: Ablex.

Werder, J.A., & Kalakian, L.H. (1985). *Assessment in adapted physical education*. Minneapolis: Burgess.

Wessell, J. (1976). *I CAN fundamental skills test*. Austin, TX: PRO-ED.

Wessell, J.A., & Kelly, L. (1986). *Achievement based curriculum development in physical education*. Philadelphia: Lea & Febiger.

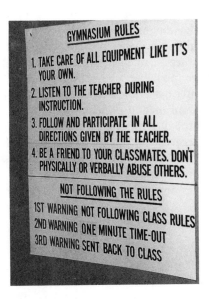

Behavior Management

Jeff is a 14-year-old boy with Down syndrome who is enrolled in a self-contained adapted physical education class. Jeff has a number of the physical impairments that often accompany Down syndrome, including obesity, congenital heart defects, hypotonicity, and poor muscle coordination. These impairments may be part of the reason why Jeff seems not to enjoy participating in the physical fitness exercises and activities that make up the first 15 minutes of daily adapted PE class.

During the annual individualized education plan (IEP) conference on Jeff, the adapted PE teacher notes that Jeff enjoys shooting baskets on the playground at recess but resists participating in the PE class fitness routines. Jeff's parents mention that Jeff admires his older brother John and enjoys the time they spend together playing basketball. This year John is a freshman in college and comes home only on weekends. The teacher asks Jeff's parents for their assistance in developing a program in which a family member shoots baskets with Jeff on weekends only if Jeff participates in the PE fitness routines.

HIGHLIGHT QUESTIONS

- Why are some professionals reluctant to use behavior management strategies in their programs of physical activity instruction?
- What steps and procedures should professionals consider when developing a behavior management plan?
- What types of systems are available to professionals administering positive reinforcement to persons with mental retardation?
- What are modeling, prompting, shaping, and chaining?
- Do effective behavior management strategies exist for persons with severe or profound mental retardation?
- What is the difference between negative reinforcement and punishment?
- What literature and research are available regarding the administration of behavior management programs in physical activity settings specific for persons with mental retardation?

The illustration of Jeff in the chapter 4 Preview is a realistic one. Professionals providing physical activity to persons with mental retardation would agree that learning requires effective instructional strategies that reduce behavior problems and motivate the student to perform to optimum potential. There are no easy solutions for remediating behavior and learning problems, and this is especially true of persons with mental retardation, whose decreased intelligence compounds their difficulties in learning. For example, it is unlikely that Jeff can understand the long-term health benefits derived from participating in a daily physical fitness program.

What Is Behavior Management?

For more than 25 years, systematic programs of behavior management have been successfully incorporated into a variety of settings for persons with mental retardation to elicit optimum performance (Gardner, 1978; Kazdin, 1980). However, practitioners providing programs of physical activity to this population have been hesitant to accept these procedures to promote learning (Loovis, 1980; Presbie & Brown, 1977; Wehman, 1977).

Lack of training in proper administration of behavior management procedures is often cited as a reason for reluctance to incorporate these strategies into physical activity programs. For example, many professionals (e.g., physical educators, occupational therapists, and physical therapists) graduate with sound training in the muscular system, range of motion, and programming activities but with little knowledge of how to properly shape student behavior (Roice, 1978); the ones who have studied behavioral principles often have not had the opportunity to put them to practice. This lack of training may cause misunderstandings, including the following, about behavior management procedures:

- Misinterpretations of behavior management terminology
- The belief that these techniques are dehumanizing
- The belief that applying reinforcement is merely bribery, which in turn leads to the

assumption that once the behavior is reinforced, the student will perform the desired behavior only for a reward

- The assumption that administering reinforcers will become financially too expensive (Lavay, 1985)

We will try to lay these misunderstandings to rest, in order to present behavior management in a positive light and show its program effectiveness.

When practitioners don't understand the terminology, they often use terms incorrectly and treat very different terms and program practices as if they were interchangeable. This of course will tend to confuse individuals administering the program. There is quite a bit of special terminology in the literature. Consider, for instance, this short passage from Repp (1983):

There are a large number of names for systems that use principles of learning in applied settings. Some of these are "Skinnerism, behavioral technology, operant conditioning, behavior modification, behavior training, contingency management, programmed instruction, accountability, performance-based instruction, and competency-based instruction"; one may readily add to this list, precision teaching, behavior therapy and applied behavior analysis. (p. 37)

In this text we use the term *behavior management*. Dunn and French (1982) define this term as follows:

Behavior management encompasses all of the strategies that the physical educator utilizes to develop effective and appropriate student behavior. . . . Presently, the most effective behavior management strategy used in the school setting is behavior modification. The purpose of this specific strategy is to elicit a behavior. . . . Respondent and operant conditioning are two basic

forms of behavior modification. . . . Operant conditioning involves the use of consequences that increase the probability that a behavior will be strengthened, maintained, or weakened. (p. 45)

Too often while participating in physical activity, persons with mental retardation exhibit immature response patterns or utilize inappropriate behaviors in social settings. French (1985) and Wehman (1977) have suggested that perhaps the most significant advance in the educational training of persons with mental retardation has been increased use of operant conditioning principles. For practitioners who provide physical activity to this population to become proficient in operant conditioning, it is of paramount importance that they have a sound background in behavior management terminology and principles. Highlight 4.1 lists basic behavior management terminology and definitions.

Many professionals believe that it is dehumanizing and mechanistic to use behavior management practices. Too often these practices are associated with laboratory research conducted by animal psychologists. However, this chapter shows how behavior management strategies can be used with persons with mental retardation in a positive and humanistic manner. Almost all professionals would agree that individuals with mental retardation will not learn without an organized and well-taught physical activity program. Therefore, professionals must constantly seek effective programming strategies. Behavior management involves exact, systematic observation and measurement (Wehman, 1977). In addition, when its principles are systematically applied in a positive way, they allow the instructor not only to effectively work with this population but to communicate with other professionals such as administrators, classroom teachers, and parents.

Reinforcement does not have to mean bribery. Kazdin (1980) suggests a definite difference between bribery and reinforcement: *Bribery* is the

Behavior Management Terminology

Behavior—Any action by an individual that is observable and measurable and has a beginning and an end (White & Haring, 1980).

Behavior management—An umbrella term for strategies for developing effective and appropriate behavior in an individual. Examples of these strategies are behavior modification, Premack principle, reality therapy, transactional analysis, and relaxation techniques (Dunn & French, 1982).

Chaining—The sequencing of a series of already learned behaviors in a fixed order to achieve a more complex terminal response (French & Jansma, 1978). In **backward chaining**, the last behavior of the terminal response is presented first.

Contingency—A relationship between the target behavior (the response) and the events (consequences) that follow that particular behavior. Sometimes events that precede the behavior (antecedent) are specified by a contingency (Kazdin, 1980).

Extinction—The process of eliminating or reducing a conditioned response by not administering any form of reinforcement.

Fading—The gradual removal of a cue, prompt, or reinforcer.

Feedback—A verbal or physical response given immediately after the individual responds to a cue (Dunn, Moorehouse, & Fredericks, 1986).

Group contingency—The presentation of a highly desired reinforcer (e.g., reward) to a group of individuals based on the behavior (e.g., target behavior) of one person or of the group as a whole. For example, in

the **Good Behavior Game**, the entire group may earn points toward a predetermined reward (Vogler & French, 1983).

Modeling—Performing a behavior, usually as a demonstration, such that another individual, by observing the behavior, can learn to perform the behavior.

Operant conditioning—The use of a consequence to increase the probability that a behavior will be strengthened, maintained, or weakened (Dunn & French, 1982).

Physical activity reinforcement—A procedure in which the individual's structured time to choose among various preferred physical activities is contingent upon the individual meeting a predetermined criterion of behavior (Lavay, 1984).

Premack principle—The principle that a behavior more preferred by the individual can be used as a reinforcer of a behavior less preferred by that individual. A high-probability behavior can reinforce a low-probability behavior.

Prompt—A cue or stimulus, usually in the form of physical guidance to initiate a proper movement, that is intended to occasion a response of performing that behavior.

Punishment—The presentation of an adversive event or removal of a positive event contingent upon a response, decreasing the probability of that response (Kazdin, 1980).

Reinforcement—**Positive reinforcement** is the practice of following a response (behavior) with a favorable consequence in order to increase the frequency of that response (behavior) (Kazdin, 1980). **Negative rein-**

HIGHLIGHT 4.1 CONTINUED

forcement is the removal of an aversive event as a consequence of a behavior in order to increase the frequency of that behavior (Henderson & French, 1989).

Reinforcement event menu—A list of highly desirable reinforcement items that is displayed for individuals to observe. These items can be earned by meeting a predetermined criterion of behavior.

Response cost—The withdrawal of a positive reinforcer as a consequence of the occurrence of an undesirable behavior. Examples include fines and loss of privileges.

Shaping—Reinforcing small steps or approximations of the desired behavior.

Satiation—The elimination of the effectiveness of a reinforcer on a behavior, caused by excessive application of the reinforcer.

Time-out—The removal of an individual from a reinforcing environment for a period of time, contingent upon the individual's performance of an inappropriate behavior and in an attempt to decrease that particular behavior (French, Lavay, & Henderson, 1985). A **contingent observation time-out** combines modeling and time-out procedures; the individual is removed from the group but is left near enough to observe peers demonstrating appropriate behavior.

Token economy reinforcement—Tokens, checkmarks, points, or chips earned for fulfilling a predetermined criterion of behavior are later exchanged for items that are reinforcing and of value to the individual.

---

illegal use of gifts to corrupt an individual's conduct, whereas *reinforcement* is designed to change a behavior so learning can occur. Properly administered reinforcers are an accepted part of everyday life. In fact, how many professionals would continue their jobs if they were not paid?

Some professionals fear that once reinforcement is administered, the individual will perform the desired behavior only for a reward or that the desired behavior change will last only for the duration of that particular program. The termination of a reinforcement program does not necessarily mean extinction of the new behavior: "Changing an individual's behavior sometimes produces noticeable changes in how others in the person's environment respond to him. Even when extrinsic reinforcers are withdrawn, the reactions of others to the person whose behavior was changed may maintain the recently acquired behavior" (Kazdin, 1980, p. 58).

Finally, reinforcers need not be expensive to be effective. Reinforcers such as edibles, toys, and money can be costly, but there are other reinforcement alternatives. Much of the equipment in the classroom or playground can be readily used as no-cost tangible reinforcers, and intangible reinforcers (such as praise) are almost limitless (Lavay, 1984; McKenzie, 1979).

Designing the Behavior Management Program

In the 1980s, systematic behavior management programs began to be conducted for persons with mental retardation. These programs have been conducted across different age groups, such as preschool children (Kirby & Holburn, 1986; Watkinson & Wall, 1982), school-age children (Bishop & French, 1982; Halle, Silverman, & Regan, 1983; Lavay & French, 1986), and adults (Allen & Iwata, 1980; Hussey, Maurer, & Schofield, 1976); and also across various settings, such as physical education (Huber, 1973), physical fitness (Bennett, Eisenman, French, Henderson, Shultz, 1989; Tomporowski & Ellis, 1984), leisure recreation (Hsu & Dunn, 1984; Rickard & Dinhoff, 1974; Wehman, 1977), and physical therapy (Horner, 1971). These studies and others have not only demonstrated enhanced physical performance but have helped motivate individuals with mental retardation to successfully participate.

It is not by accident that these programs have successfully enhanced the learners' physical performance and behavior. Before designing and conducting such programs, professionals must consider a number of important factors, such as

1. the individual,
2. the instructor,
3. the learning environment,
4. how to define the desired behavior to be changed,
5. how to analyze the behavior,
6. how to systematically implement the actual management plan, and
7. how to evaluate the program to determine its effectiveness regarding the individual's behavior (see Figure 4.1).

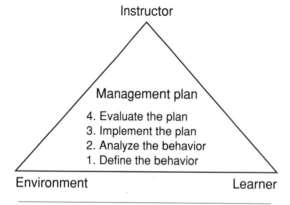

Figure 4.1 The behavior management plan.

The Individual

The most important factor in the overall behavior management plan is the individual whom the program is meant to teach new behaviors. But oddly enough the learner is often overlooked by the instructor during the actual program design. The management program will not be effective if it is not tailored to meet the unique needs of the individual learner and based on her or his present level of performance. For example, understanding the individual is important for choosing effective reinforcers; each individual has likes and dislikes, and what may prove reinforcing to one person may not be to another.

When the total individual is considered—his or her social, emotional, cognitive, and physical abilities and needs—management plans can be developed that not only control behavior but elicit optimum physical performance. Given the limited intelligence levels of persons with mental retardation, it is particularly important to design a program appropriate to the individual's cognitive ability. A program that is too sophisticated will not meet the individual's needs and consequently will not bring about much positive change in behavior.

The Instructor

The instructor is the designer and manager of the program. Behavior management programs are based on the premise that any definable behavior can be controlled and learned (Kazdin, 1980). Patton, Payne, and Beirne-Smith (1990) believe that learning is a most complex process for individuals with mental retardation. However, the instructor can control the environment and other factors that affect learning to make the experience more efficient and successful. It is most important, and also difficult, to foster successful program experiences for these persons—who, generally, have failed so often that they are reluctant to attempt new activities and expect to fail. All too often they have dropped thrown balls, fallen down while running, or been picked last for teams; so games, sports, and other physical activities tend to be threats of misery and embarrassment for them, rather than promises of fun and camaraderie.

To overcome this "failure set," Patton, Payne, and Beirne-Smith (1990) believe persons with mental retardation must experience success rather than merely be told they are successful; so the practitioner must promote successful experiences for the individual to reach the desired learning outcomes. For example, when an introductory recreational activity is based on a movement skill the child previously successfully performed, that initial success helps motivate him or her to attempt new and perhaps more difficult tasks. Most importantly, it helps foster in the learner a trust for the instructor. This feeling of trust is important when the individual is attempting new skills and activities in class and is of paramount importance to the successful implementation of the management plan.

The Environment

Instructors who properly plan the environment in advance promote successful movement experiences and deter potential behavior problems. If the environment is unmanageable, it will be unteachable! Dauer and Pangrazi (1989) sum up this phenomenon by saying that teachers who fail to plan, plan to fail. French, Lavay, and Henderson (1985) suggest the following preventative management techniques instructors should consider when designing the environment and planning the specifics of the program.

1. *Withitness*. Students misbehave less and attend more to the task at hand when the instructor is "tuned in" to what is going on in class—for example, by keeping all youngsters in sight during an activity on the playground.

2. *Movement management*. The instructor must structure activities so they move smoothly and momentum is maintained from activity to activity. For example, moving in a circle or line during a kicking drill can be a complex concept for youngsters with mental retardation. However, the momentum of the drill can be maintained by using cones or flags to tangibly reinforce the shape and location of the circle or line the youngster must follow (see Figure 4.2).

3. *Class structure*. When persons with mental retardation are given activities with minimal

Figure 4.2 Hoops can be used to structure the environment. Photo courtesy of Bob Fraley.

structure or left unattended, behavior problems emerge and little learning occurs. Learning time is important, and the instructor must use it wisely and efficiently. In particular, activities must be structured so that all individuals are actively involved and know they will be held accountable for performing the required skills and activities.

4. *Teacher enthusiasm.* Enthusiasm is contagious, and a good instructor is enthusiastic about the subject being taught. This enthusiasm helps promote positive experiences, a most important instructional consideration. For example, the instructor can participate with the class in activity.

5. *Teacher competence.* Students need to feel that their instructor is competent, or they will lose interest in listening and participating. One thing that helps the instructor look competent in the eyes of the class is to enter activity sessions with a plan. Projecting competence also helps build trust and respect between the learner and instructor.

6. *Self-sufficiency.* The instructor should have control of the group and not continually go to an outside authority, such as a supervisor, for help. For example, managing discipline problems immediately and within the context of the setting where they occur is helpful.

7. *Control of the physical environment.* Many factors, such as extreme temperatures, improper lighting, inappropriate space, and poor equipment preparation can lead to behavior problems. For example, when playground balls are left in a bag in the middle of the gym floor, the children will fight over them. Instead, the balls should be carefully distributed in a manner that allows each child an equal opportunity to secure one. This also helps foster positive social interaction among participants.

8. *Interest boosting.* The instructor should take an active interest in all students and treat them as individuals (see Figure 4.3). This personalized approach is especially important for

Figure 4.3 The instructor should take time to learn the interests of each child. Photo courtesy of Special Olympics International.

individuals with mental retardation. They need to have positive experiences if they are to develop the confidence and self-esteem necessary to successfully participate in physical activity. For example, the instructor should choose movement themes that are of interest to the students being taught.

9. *Teacher proximity.* Staying close to the students can help control disruptive behavior and keep students on task. A good instructor will be viewed by students as a source of protection, strength, and identification. For example, the instructor, rather than yelling at the students who are disruptive, may stand next to them.

10. *Classroom rules.* There must be rules, they must be clear, and each person should know what behaviors are acceptable and unacceptable as well as the consequences for not following the rules. The rules should be developed at the very beginning of the program and kept simple so that persons with mental retardation can easily understand them. For example, pictures can be substituted for written rules and posted where everyone can see them (Lavay, 1984). Rules should be kept to five or six, because more than that can confuse this popula-

tion. Rules should be positive and flexibly designed to cover as many different topic areas as possible. Figure 4.4 is an example of rules that may be used in a special/adapted physical education or recreational program for students with mental retardation. Remember that a clear set of simple, positive rules will decrease misbehavior and enhance physical performance when students know what behaviors are expected and the consequences for not following the rules.

Gymnasium rules

1. Take care of all equipment as if it were your own.
2. Listen to the teacher during instruction.
3. Follow and participate in all directions or rules given by the teacher.
4. Be a friend to your classmates.

Consequences of not following the rules

1. You will be given a warning.
2. You will be given a second warning and a 1-minute time-out.
3. You will be sent back to class.

Figure 4.4 Clear and simple, positive rules for a special/adapted physical education or recreational program.

11. *Signal interference.* The instructor should develop clearly identifiable positive attention signals. For example, when the instructor's hand is raised, all students know it is time to be quiet and listen to the instructions. In this approach the teacher does not need to yell to receive individual attention. Obviously, these signals will be effective only if they are administered consistently and with consequences for not following them.

12. *Creating a learning environment.* Most importantly, individuals with mental retardation must find the provided activities to be within their capabilities. They will want to participate in a program that is designed for them to experience success, motivation, and consequently fun. For example, to improve the upper body

strength of young children with mental retardation, have them propel a scooter board with their arms.

Behavior Identification

To increase, maintain, or weaken a behavior, it must first be identified. This behavior is known as the *target behavior*. A target behavior must be a particular event that is observable and measurable and has a beginning and an end (White & Haring, 1980). The instructor must not only carefully examine the target behavior, but must understand what should be changed in the behavior. For example, it is of no use to merely state, ''Mary is bad and a problem.'' The ''bad'' aspect of Mary's behavior must be explicitly identified, and it must be identified in such a way that it has an observable beginning and end.

For example, after a few days of carefully observing Mary, the instructor realizes that her problem occurs on the playground and more specifically when her peers are sliding down the small playground slide. More specifically still, Mary stands at the end of the slide and grabs her classmates when they reach the end of the slide. The instructor has now determined an exact description of the behavior problem as something specific that can actually be identified. It must be remembered that only when Mary's behavior problem has been correctly identified can it be measured and consequently changed.

Recording Behavior

The individual may exhibit a number of behaviors that need to be changed. At first the instructor should attend to only one or two of the most prevailing of these behaviors. Often, alleviating or controlling one behavior problem helps diminish others.

In the preceding example of Mary's inappropriate behavior on the playground it was not by accident that the instructor was able to pinpoint the actual behavior problem. Direct observation procedures enabled the instructor to identify that Mary's problem was related to grabbing classmates as they traveled down the playground slide. There are many methods for observing and recording behavior. The three major methods of recording continuous behavior, according to Repp (1983), are duration recording, event recording, and interval recording (see Highlight 4.2).

To determine Mary's behavior, the instructor used an event recording system, recording the number of times she grabbed other students during a predetermined period of time. Mary's problem has been carefully identified, recorded, and measured. A systematic intervention program can now be implemented to deter Mary's behavior problem of grabbing other students on the slide (see Table 4.1).

Program Implementation

Only when the actual behavior the instructor desires to strengthen, maintain, or decrease has been recorded, analyzed, and determined can the actual intervention program be introduced. Pinpointing the target behavior provides the management program with direction. The instructor's next step is to emphasize the consequences that follow the target behavior. For a consequence to have any meaning, it must be dependent, or *contingent*, upon the occurrence of that target behavior. Most management plans developed for persons with mental retardation are based on the principle that there is a contingent relationship between the target behavior and the events that follow the behavior (the consequences) (Kazdin, 1980). Later in this chapter we will provide examples of a variety

---

HIGHLIGHT 4.2   **IN THEORY**

Recording Procedures for Determining Continuous Behavior

Event Recording:

Recording the number of times the behavior (event) occurs during a predetermined period of time—for example, the number of sit-ups a child completes during an exercise period.

Duration Recording:

Recording the duration of a behavior during a predetermined period of time—for example, the duration of time a child displays off-task behavior while engaged in a swim program.

Interval Recording:

According to French (1985), in this procedure the recorder divides the observation period into small intervals of time, usually in seconds. The recorder then marks whether the target behavior did or did not occur during each interval. A percentage is usually determined by dividing the number of intervals in which the behavior occurred by the total number of intervals, then multiplying by 100. This procedure is used to record behaviors that occur quite frequently.

Table 4.1   Event Recording Procedures

Day	Monday Day 1	Tuesday Day 2	Wednesday Day 3	Thursday Day 4	Friday Day 5
No. of times event occurs	★ ★ ★	★ ★ ★ ★ ★	★ ★ ★	★ ★ ★ ★	★ ★ ★
Total	3	5	3	4	3

Behavior total:	During a 5-day period = 18 for an average per day = 3.6
Target behavior:	Mary's grabbing behavior when other children are on the playground slide
Recording procedure:	Event recording procedure
Period of time:	Mary's recess 10:00 to 10:20 a.m. each day

of contingency management programs that effectively pair the behavior with the consequence.

The program administrator must be very patient and realize that behavior changes will not occur immediately. Many management plans fail because they are not given ample time to work. One factor that takes time to work out is that initially the students may attempt to manipulate the instructor and the new program. Therefore, the instructor must always display consistency in pairing the consequence with the desired behavior change.

In the previous example of Mary's behavior on the playground, once the instructor recorded Mary's grabbing behavior and spoke with her, it was determined that she was grabbing her classmates because she felt they were ignoring her and not giving her a turn on the playground slide. The instructor developed a plan of providing Mary with an additional 5 minutes of time after recess to play on the slide (reinforcement) if she properly played on the playground equipment without grabbing her classmates (the target behavior) during the recess period. It was no accident that Mary's inappropriate behavior stopped completely after a week, as she enjoyed the additional time on the slide,

finding it quite reinforcing. Many youngsters with mental retardation may not yet have adequately developed behaviors that foster appropriate social interaction among peers and must therefore be taught them.

In another example of effectively using a contingency management program, the instructor allows only individuals who meet the specific criterion of performing all warm-up exercises (target behavior) during a fitness program to be reinforced with a 5-minute session of play on a minitrampoline (consequence). It is critical that the instructor apply the reinforcement system consistently, rewarding only the students who perform the prescribed warm-ups.

In both examples the management plans are simple but effective. Programs are effective only when the management plan is systematically administered through a consistent and direct approach that is understandable to the students. Whenever possible the management program should be administered positively.

Program Evaluation

Once the management plan has been put into action, the program must be evaluated periodically to determine whether the management plan or intervention is working and contributing to the target behavior change. The "A-B-C analysis" (antecedent-behavior-consequence) is a simple evaluation procedure that can be easily implemented by the instructor (French & Jansma, 1978). For example, the recreation leader may say, "Line up and be quiet for swimming [antecedent]. The first child to be in her or his designated area on the pool deck and quiet [behavior] will be first to get in the water [consequence]." In this example, the reward of being first to get in the water to swim motivates the children to line up in their designated areas and be quiet. Obviously the consequence has a positive effect in shaping the desired behavior.

There are many more sophisticated designs for evaluating behavior changes among individuals with mental retardation. For discussions and examples of these designs, see Paul Bishop, "Application of Basic Time Series Designs in Physical Education," in French and Lavay, *Behavior Management Techniques for Physical Educators and Recreators* and Paul Wehman, *Helping the Mentally Retarded Acquire Play Skills: A Behavioral Approach*.

Procedures to Maintain or Strengthen Behavior

Most behavior management programs used for persons with mental retardation are based on the principles of operant conditioning, which involve the systematic application of consequences to strengthen, maintain, or weaken a behavior. Advocates of these programs believe that any behavior can be changed as long as it can be defined and observed. The management procedures and programs introduced in this section not only have effectively controlled behavior problems but have enhanced the physical performance of this particular population.

When designing such programs, the instructor must always remember the importance of individualizing the management system to meet the unique needs of each learner. It cannot be assumed that a management system that worked effectively with one person or group will work effectively with another, especially given the varied levels of intelligence and skill in persons with mental retardation.

Whenever possible, the management program must be administered in a positive manner. Individuals in such a program should never be made to run laps or exercise as punishment (French, et al., 1985). Physical activity should not be equated with punishment. The long-term goal of professionals providing programs of physical activity to persons with mental retardation is to turn these individuals on to the numerous benefits of a healthy and physically active lifestyle.

Positive Reinforcement

Positive reinforcement is based on the principle that a response (behavior) will increase in frequency when it is followed by a favorable consequence (Kazdin, 1980). Positive reinforcement systems have been effectively applied in physical activity settings for individuals with mental retardation using the following methods (see Table 4.2):

- Nonverbal
- Verbal
- Tangible
- Physical activity
- Token economy systems of reinforcement
- Group contingencies

Before any type of reinforcement program is administered, the reinforcer preference of the individual must be given careful consideration. Bishop and French (1982) note that the nature of the reinforcer can have a strong influence on student behavior. The instructor must never assume that each individual in the program will prefer the same reinforcer. For example, one

Table 4.2   Positive Reinforcement Systems

Type	Definition	Advantages	Disadvantages	Population
Nonverbal	Social reinforcement through gesture, contact, and facial expression	• Inexpensive • Immediate • Creates positive atmosphere	• Cannot easily be specific to behavior • May be insufficient to change behavior	All levels, but cognitive ability must be considered
Verbal	Social reinforcement through spoken words or exclamation	• Inexpensive • Immediate • Can be specific to behavior	• Often overused • Often nonspecific • May not be understood by students with severe conditions	Moderate level and higher
Tangible	Reinforcement through provision of primary or secondary needs through edibles, toys, decals, etc.	• Highly motivating • Used for persons with more severe conditions	• Can be expensive • Can lead to dependence upon reinforcer	All levels but should never use reinforcers that are not age-appropriate
Physical activity	Use of physical activity natural to the setting to reinforce the desired behavior	• Readily available reinforcers (i.e., games, equipment) • Inexpensive • Progress toward goals • Improves physical well-being	• Can lead to dependence upon reinforcer • Difficult for students with more severe conditions to understand	All levels, made simple for severe and profound
Token economy	Tokens, checkmarks, or points earned for meeting a predetermined criterion of behavior and later exchanged for a reward	• Individualized menu of items can be offered • Incorporated into program when immediate reinforcement is not possible	• Reinforcement not immediate • Can be expensive • Can lead to dependence	Moderate level and greater
Group contingency	Administration of a highly desired reinforcer to a group or individual, based on the behavior of one person or the group	• Some students respond better to peer pressure • Can be made into a game	• Reinforcement not immediate • Difficult for some students to understand • Peers may place undue pressure on one child	Moderate level and greater

child may be willing to perform sit-ups for a sticker, whereas another child may prefer to play on a swing set as a reward.

Reinforcer preference can be determined by observing the student, talking with the student's classroom teacher or parents (who usually know the student best), or when possible, simply asking the student. For example, Bishop and French (1982) used an "indirect questioning" procedure described by Mercer and Snell (1977) to determine the preferred sensory reinforcers of boys with severe mental retardation. The investigators interviewed the classroom teachers to determine what foods and other sensory reinforcers each particular child enjoyed best.

Nonverbal and Verbal Reinforcement

Positive *nonverbal reinforcement* can take many forms, such as a smile, an approving nod, a "high five," or an arm around the shoulder. Positive *verbal reinforcement* is an approving statement made by the instructor regarding the individual's behavior or actual performance. A mere enthusiastic "Good job!" to a person with mental retardation may only cause confusion—too often he or she will not understand what the reinforcement is for. Verbal reinforcement must include clear, specific reference to the behavior that is being reinforced.

Initially, verbal reinforcement may need to be administered immediately after the individual performs the desired behavior. When praising persons with mental retardation, it is also important to consider the individual's level of language comprehension. The instructor may need to use action-oriented, single-meaning words and limit sentences to two or three words. Highlight 4.3 presents examples of positive verbal statements that can be used in a physical activity setting; the instructor must remember that the phrases chosen must be appropriate to the student's level of comprehension.

Every effort must be made to administer these social reinforcers (nonverbal and verbal) positively. In other words, "catch the person being good." However, this is not simple.

White (1975) recorded the natural rates of teacher approval and disapproval in the classroom. The rates of teacher verbal approval dropped markedly after the second grade; in every grade thereafter, the rate of teacher verbal disapproval exceeded the rate of teacher verbal approval. Thomas,

---

| *HIGHLIGHT 4.3* | IN PRACTICE |

Positive Verbal Reinforcement

Nice swimming!
Good jumping!
I like the way you did your exercises!
Great running, you are getting faster!
Excellent, your squad is the first lined up!
Keep practicing, your forward roll is getting better!
Thank you for helping me pick up all the equipment!
You are really working hard on that kick!

Congratulations! You didn't miss a single turn!
It's great when you share with others!

It is important for the instructor to realize that if positive verbal reinforcement statements for persons with mental retardation are to be effective, the individual's comprehension level must be carefully considered.

Presland, Grant, and Glynn (1978) examined the natural rates of teacher verbal approval and disapproval in 10 seventh-grade classrooms. The majority of the teachers displayed individual approval rates. Jones and Jones (1981) reported a study conducted by Fredericks of first grade teachers in which it was found that only 9 of 17 teachers had reinforcement rates over 50%. Seven were above 70%. These data were correlated with children's liking of school. Baseline data indicated that more than 90% of the first-graders liked school during the first 2 weeks of the school year. Returning in February and surveying the same children, the experimenters found that 90% of the children whose teachers achieved 70% verbal approval still liked school. Children in classrooms where verbal disapproval exceeded verbal approval generally disliked school; in fact 100% of them disliked school in those classrooms where verbal disapproval was 60% or higher. (Dunn & Fredericks, 1985, pp. 342-343)

Tangible Reinforcement

Persons with mental retardation often require a more powerful form of reinforcement than an approving statement. Roice (1978) stated that *primary reinforcers* satisfy a biological need (e.g., food when a person is hungry, or a drink when a person is thirsty). Primary reinforcers are not learned; they exist in each person from birth. For example, in a study conducted by Bishop and French (1982) with youngsters with severe mental retardation, orange juice delivered in a squirt bottle served as a primary reinforcer in increasing the on-task behavior of one particular child performing certain physical tasks.

Secondary reinforcers are reinforcers that an individual learns or is conditioned to respond to. Repp (1983) claims that most reinforcers in fact are conditioned, because their reinforcing properties depend upon a history of pairing with stimuli that is reinforcing. In a study conducted by Caouette and Reid (1985), visual stimuli (flashing lights) and auditory stimuli (music) were used with six institutionalized male adults with severe mental retardation to increase their work output while riding a stationary bicycle. Whether the reinforcement is primary or secondary doesn't really matter. What is important is that the item has a reinforcing property for that particular person.

Tangible reinforcement can consist of just about anything material, including toys, decals, and ribbons. In a 1968 study by Sechrest, eight youngsters with moderate to severe mental retardation pedaled on a stationary bicycle to earn different reinforcement items. The bicycle was constructed to provide the following reinforcements on a predetermined schedule: (a) a small plastic trinket, (b) a small piece of candy, or (c) a series of slides projected on a screen. Results of the study clearly indicate that the youngsters performed more pedal revolutions during the reinforcement period than during the time when no reinforcement was provided.

Physical Activity Reinforcement

Physical activity reinforcement is a procedure in which the individual's being given a structured time in which to choose among various preferred physical activities is contingent on the individual meeting a predetermined criterion of behavior (Lavay, 1984). In other words, physical activity that is natural to the setting in the form of equipment and games (see Figure 4.5) usually adds no extra cost to the program budget and reinforces the desired behavior. This form of reinforcement is a viable and important alternative, because certain individuals may not respond to social reinforcers such as smiles or verbal praise, and tangible reinforcers such as food, toys, and money can become quite expensive. Perhaps the most important benefit of this system of reinforcement is that it not only serves as a reward but has the potential to improve individual and group physical performance levels. Progress toward the goals and

Figure 4.5 Many children find the opportunity to shoot baskets reinforcing. Photo courtesy of Bob Fraley.

objectives written on a child's individualized education plan could be met using activities that are simultaneously serving as reinforcements. Obviously, swimming in a pool, playing on a scooterboard, and horseback riding are more likely to enhance motor performance and well-being than being rewarded with candy or a toy (Lavay, 1984).

Allen and Iwata (1980) reported an increase in the number of minutes institutionalized adults with mental retardation participated in an exercise program when game participation was used as a reinforcer. See Table 4.3 for examples of studies that have used various reinforcement systems for persons with mental

retardation across different classifications and settings.

Token Economy Systems

The immediate administration of reinforcing items to the individual is not always practical in some physical activity settings, such as the gymnasium, swimming pool, or playground. For these situations a *token economy system* can be devised in which checkmarks, points, chips, or tokens can be earned and later exchanged for the desired reinforcer, contingent on the performance of the target behavior (Lavay, 1984; McKenzie, 1979). It is important to note that in a token economy system the administration of the reinforcement is not immediate. For this reason, a token economy system usually is not effective with persons who have severe or profound mental retardation. In a study conducted by Campbell (1972), a group of institutionalized boys with mild and moderate mental retardation earned points for successfully performing certain exercises. They could later exchange these points for various tangible reinforcers in the form of prizes. In another study, by Huber (1973), a token economy system was effectively implemented with 11 school-age youngsters with mild mental retardation. These youngsters could exchange points earned Monday through Thursday in order to participate in an additional physical education class on Friday.

It is important that the rules and guidelines for the token economy exchange system be made clear and understandable for each person. A reinforcement event menu can stimulate individual interest, serving as a reinforcer by providing continuous feedback regarding the rewards being offered (Moon & Renzaglia, 1982). The menu should be posted with pictures for those unable to read. This helps make the reinforcement items understandable and consequently motivational to this particular population.

Lavay (1986) compared the use of a tangible reinforcement exchange system to a physical ac-

Table 4.3   Studies Comparing Various Reinforcement Conditions

Study	Subjects	Reinforcer	Independent variable	Dependent variable	Results
Allen & Iwata (1980)	10 institutionalized adults with mental retardation, 20-56 yr	Participation in games	Premack principle	5 different exercises	Games reinforced exercise
Bishop & French (1982)	6 boys with severe mental retardation, 6-12 yr	Food Sensory stimuli	1. Social praise 2. Social praise + primary reinforcement 3. Social praise + sensory reinforcement	Various physical tasks	Significant increase in attentional behavior
Huber (1973)	11 students with educable mental retardation, 7-11 yr	Additional PE class	Token economy system	Appropriate behavior and motor tasks	Token economy improved behavior
Lavay (1984)	28 males with trainable mental retardation, 12-21 yr	Tangible and physical activity reinforcement	1. Tangible reinforcement 2. Physical activity 3. No reinforcement	3 physical fitness tasks	No significant difference
Leme (1981)	18 institutionalized individuals with severe and profound mental retardation, 12-22 yr	Edible reinforcers	1. Social praise 2. Social praise + tangible reinforcement	Physical fitness test	Social praise + tangible reinforcement increased sit-ups
Shack (1978)	5 boys with trainable mental retardation, 14-17 yr	Token and social reinforcers	1. Instruction 2. Social reinforcement 3. Token reinforcement 4. Social + token	Beanbag and ring toss	Social + tangible reinforcement of best motor response

tivity reinforcement exchange system to determine the effect each had on the physical fitness performance of high-school-age students with moderate mental retardation. No significant difference between the two groups was found, although both groups at the end of the 8-week period improved their performance in two out of the three fitness items. It was also noted by the teachers of the program that the point reinforcement exchange system could be easily incorporated into the school's adapted physical education program. Highlight 4.4 shows example event menus for the two kinds of reinforcement used in this study.

Group Contingencies

A *group contingency* is the presentation of a highly desired reinforcer to a group of individuals based on the behavior of one person or the group as a whole (Vogler & French, 1983). If one person or the group is constantly ruining the entire group's chances of earning a reinforcement, then a separate management program may be needed for the problem individual or group. Obviously, group contingencies are a more sophisticated system of reinforcement and may not be effective for all persons with mental retardation. Group contingencies can be ad-

---

HIGHLIGHT 4.4   **IN PRACTICE**

Tangible Reinforcement Menu

Items	*Point value*
Decal (sport figure)	4
Ribbon (high school)	7
Certificate (sport figure)	10
Button (school mascot)	13

Rules

1. The students may purchase the prizes commensurate with their point totals earned through their performance in the physical task program each week.
2. The students may spend their points any way they wish (e.g., one item for total points, or two items of lesser value). However, points earned on a particular week must be spent that week and cannot be carried over to the next.

Physical Activity Reinforcement Menu

Items

Dancing to music (on a radio or record player)
Bowling (using plastic pins on the gymnasium floor)
Riding a stationary bicycle
Playing table games

Rules

1. Students earn 1 minute of time to engage in the above physical activities for each point earned during performance in the physical task program each week.
2. Students may shift back and forth among the physical activities during their earned amount of physical activity time.
3. Students may accumulate at most 30 minutes of time during each particular week.

ministered in the form of Good Behavior Games. This approach can take many forms. For example, a scoreboard can be used in a Good Behavior Game with a class of higher functioning individuals with mental retardation. The teacher explains to the group, "Each time the horn on the scoreboard blows and everyone in the group is playing on a piece of equipment [on task], then one point will be put on the scoreboard." Each point earned can be traded in for 1 minute of a physical activity (reinforcement) that the group has chosen beforehand as a reward. If an individual is not acting appropriately or on task when the horn blows, then the group is not rewarded with a point.

Reinforcement Schedules

Critical to the success of any reinforcement program, whether the rewards are social or tangible or physical activity, is the application or scheduling of the reinforcement toward the target behavior. The schedule should be determined primarily by the recipients' stage of learning. In general, the following three types of reinforcement schedules are used most often (see Figure 4.6).

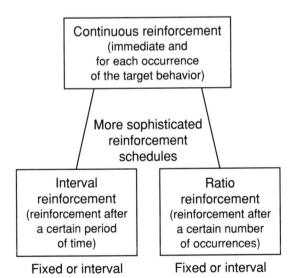

Figure 4.6 Reinforcement schedules.

1. *Continuous reinforcement*. On a continuous reinforcement schedule, the individual is reinforced immediately and each time she or he performs the target behavior. During the initial stages of the individual's learning of the behavior, the reinforcement must be administered continuously and frequently. But eventually, excessive application of the reinforcement may eliminate the effectiveness of the reinforcer. This is known as *satiation*. Once the behavior has been successfully established, it can be maintained with a more sophisticated schedule of reinforcement (see numbers 2 and 3 below).

2. *Ratio reinforcement*. In a ratio reinforcement system, the individual is rewarded for a number of performances of the target behavior. The schedule can be fixed at a set number or variable with the number changing each time. An example of a fixed-ratio schedule of reinforcement is to reward an individual with 5 minutes of physical activity reinforcement for every 10 sit-ups successfully completed.

3. *Interval reinforcement*. On an interval reinforcement schedule, the individual is rewarded over a period of time for performance of the target behavior. Once again, the schedule can be fixed over a predetermined period of time or variable with the time constantly changing. An example of a fixed-interval schedule of reinforcement is to reward the individual with one point or token toward a desired reinforcement for every 5 minutes the individual is on task (e.g., swimming laps in the pool). An example of a variable-interval schedule of reinforcement is to reinforce a person for every 1, 3, or 4 minutes of on-task behavior in the swimming pool.

Other Procedures

So far we have discussed only the use of reinforcing consequences to maintain or strengthen behaviors. Other positive procedures such as modeling, prompting, shaping, and chaining have been found to be quite effective in teaching physical activity to individuals with mental retardation (Dunn, Moorehouse, & Fredericks, 1986; Watkinson & Wall, 1982). In general these procedures are used to teach new behaviors, and they are important strategies in effective program planning for persons with mental retardation.

Modeling

In the *modeling* technique, the individual learns a specific behavior by observing another person perform (model) the target behavior. The person chosen to demonstrate the behavior could be an instructor, a parent, a sibling, or a peer. The effectiveness of modeling as a teaching tool underlies the importance of normalization, mainstreaming, and peer tutor programs for persons with mental retardation. When this population is involved in these programs, they have abundant opportunities to observe appropriate behavior and correct skill performance. For example, in an investigation conducted by DePaepe (1985), the use of a peer tutor program significantly increased the time on task of youngsters with mental retardation during the performance of various balancing activities when compared to comparable youngsters with mental retardation participating in a self-contained adapted physical education class or a regular mainstreamed class.

French et al. (1985) offer the following two examples of effective modeling procedures used to foster positive behavior changes: (a) The physical education teacher or recreation leader who dresses in appropriate attire for physical activity and actively participates in all activities is serving as a positive role model to the class or group. (b) The instructor who praises an individual or a group for following directions is attempting to get the other individuals to model the on-task behavior of the person or group being praised; most importantly, the instructor has recognized the individuals who are acting appropriately rather than reinforcing those who are not. Whenever possible, inappropriate

behavior should be ignored and appropriate behavior should be reinforced.

Prompting

For modeling to be effective, the learner must be able to imitate the behavior being modeled. For individuals having difficulty responding to the modeling procedures, *prompting* procedures may be added. In this procedure a cue or stimulus (prompt) is given by the instructor to occasion a response of the desired behavior by the individual. Prompting may take many forms, including verbal instruction and demonstration, but persons with mental retardation often do not respond to verbal instruction or comply with demonstrations (Wehman, 1977). In these cases physical prompts should be initiated. For example, in teaching a group of youngsters with mild mental retardation to throw a ball, the instructor may need to gently touch one child on the arm to initiate the throw, and a physical prompt at the leg or trunk may be necessary with another child. Visual (environmental) prompts can also be effective. For example, to teach this group proper stepping form while throwing a ball, the instructor could have the children practice stepping with opposition into a hula hoop or taped circle while throwing a ball.

Students who do not respond to a physical prompt may require physical guidance. For example, in teaching a child to strike a ball off a batting tee, the instructor may need to physically guide the child's arms and shoulders. Figure 4.7 shows an instructor using physical guidance with a student.

Dunn et al. (1986) advocate that practitioners use the following teaching model for persons with severe mental retardation:

1. Keep verbal instruction of the task to be learned at a minimum.
2. Demonstrate to the individual the task to be learned.
3. Physically guide the individual through the task.

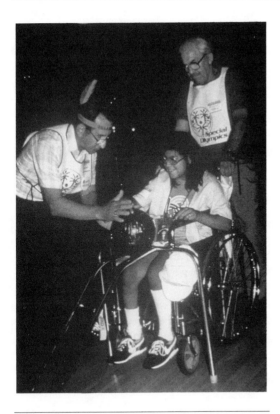

Figure 4.7 Physical guidance can be used to help a person perform a skill. Photo courtesy of Ken Regan.

Instructional prompts should be provided along a continuum depending on the needs of the learner. Here is an example of this teaching model: The instructor says, "Nicole, kick the ball." If Nicole doesn't kick the ball or does so incorrectly, the instructor says, "No, let me show you" and demonstrates. If Nicole still cannot kick the ball, then the instructor says, "No, let me help you" and physically assists Nicole through the task. The instructor then repeats the teaching model procedures.

Shaping

Effective *shaping* of a behavior is accomplished by reinforcing small steps or approximations of the desired target behavior. This procedure is most appropriate when the learner has not quite reached the criterion level of the behavior desired by the instructor but is beginning to approximate the behavior. For example, to effectively teach a youngster with moderate mental retardation to strike a ball off a batting tee, the components of the skill are task analyzed (see Highlight 4.5). *Task analysis* is the procedure of breaking down a skill or task into smaller parts. Using task analysis, the instructor can reinforce each successive approximation of the skill until the behavior is successfully performed.

Chaining

Chaining is sequencing a series of already learned behaviors in a fixed order to achieve a more complex behavioral performance (French & Jansma, 1978). French and Jansma point out that shaping and chaining procedures are different and should not be confused. Shaping ties small approximations together in a forward direction to reach the desired target behavior; chaining links new or already learned responses in either a forward or a backward direction. In a backward chaining procedure the last behavior of the terminal response is taught first. According to Wehman (1977), one advantage of using a backward chaining procedure is that each response in the chain can serve as reinforcement toward performing the next response.

Here is an example of using a forward chaining procedure to successfully teach a youngster with mental retardation to kick a ball a distance of 5 feet and inside a 2-foot-by-4-foot target. First, the youngster must be able to use the proper mechanics to kick a ball. Then he or she learns to kick the ball the 5-foot distance to reach the target area. Finally, the ball must successfully strike inside the 2-foot-by-4-foot target. Once all three behaviors are learned, they can be linked together (chained) to successfully produce the required terminal response (behavior). It is important to remember that some changes in this procedure may be required to suit the

HIGHLIGHT 4.5   **IN PRACTICE**

Task Analysis

Desired or target behavior: The child will demonstrate a mature two-hand striking pattern by hitting a foam ball with a wiffle-ball bat successfully off a batting tee 9 out of 10 times. (Other types of balls and striking implements may be substituted for the bat and ball in accordance with the individual's skill level).

Steps (Task analysis of the desired or target behavior)

1. Demonstrates familiarity with the equipment that will be used to perform the striking pattern.
2. Both hands are held correctly on the bat, with the dominant hand on top.
3. Visually attends to the object (ball) that will be used to perform the striking pattern. (Use brightly colored balls.)
4. Is in proper position in relation to the batting tee. (If necessary, a physical cue such as foot steps taped on the floor can be used.)
5. Brings the bat 2 inches back from the batting tee and strikes the foam ball in a horizontal plane.
6. Brings the bat 1 foot back from the batting tee and strikes the ball in a horizontal plane.
7. Brings the bat back to shoulder height with both elbows flexed and strikes the object in a horizontal plane.
8. Develops proper contact and follow-through upon contacting the ball.

Once the process of the task is mastered the instructor can have the individual increase the striking velocity. (However, do not increase the swinging velocity at the expense of sacrificing control of the striking pattern.)

If an individual is displaying difficulty moving from one step to the next, then the task analysis may need to be altered or broken down to smaller steps. Dunn et al. (1986) define this procedure as branching. For example, the child accomplishes the following:

1. Brings the implement back to shoulder height with both elbows flexed and strikes the object in a horizontal plane
2. Properly grips the bat and brings it back to shoulder height with both elbows flexed
3. Stands with feet shoulder-width apart and knees comfortably flexed
4. Turns body slightly to the side
5. Turns the head and eyes toward the object on the batting tee
6. Positions weight on the back foot
7. Begins the horizontal swing with a lateral step forward on the front foot
8. Begins to extend the arms forward toward the object on the tee
9. Rotates the hips in the direction of the object
10. Shifts weight to the front foot upon contacting the object

needs of the individual, such as starting with a shorter distance for the kick, perhaps 3 feet.

Hsu and Dunn (1984) compare forward and reverse chaining methods to teach a modified four-step approach to bowling to 30 adults with moderate mental retardation. The subjects were randomly assigned to either a forward chaining or a reverse chaining group. Results demonstrated that the 15 subjects in the reverse chaining group required significantly fewer trials and physical assists to properly learn the bowling task than did the 15 subjects taught with the forward chaining procedure. The authors state that the success of the reverse chaining group might be due to the subjects' first completing the last task—releasing the ball and watching it roll toward the pins. The authors found that this task proved to be quite reinforcing, helping to motivate the group to participate.

Here is the task analysis of the modified four-step forward chaining bowling approach used by the investigators:

1. From a standing position, the subject raises the ball to chest-high position and steps forward with the right foot.
2. The subject steps with the left foot forward and pushes the ball forward.
3. The subject steps with the right foot forward and swings the ball backward.
4. The subject steps with the left foot forward, swings the ball forward, and releases the ball in the direction of the pins.

Strategies for Individuals With Severe or Profound Mental Retardation

Individuals with severe or profound mental retardation often require powerful reinforcement procedures to successfully perform a target behavior. One effective strategy advocated by French (1985) to enhance the performance of certain physical skills of persons with severe and profound mental retardation is the use of puppets.

> We have noticed at one of the laboratory sites used by the special physical education graduate students at Texas Woman's University that some students who are seriously disabled will be attentive to colorful hand puppets and perform motor skills at a faster rate when interacting with the puppet as opposed to the teacher. The teacher talks to the student "through" the puppet. For example, one severely physically and mentally involved student would take 2 minutes to crawl down a 6 foot mat using verbal praise and candy from the teacher. Verbal reinforcement followed by a kiss from the student's favorite puppet decreased her crawling time to 32 seconds! (p. 110)

Another approach that has met with recent success in motivating children with profound mental retardation is the use of an electrical response device that emits sensory reinforcers (French, Folsom-Meeks, Cook, & Smith, 1987). A mercury switch is attached by velcro to a custom-designed headcap for each individual. When the person's head is elevated to the desired position or specific head-control task to be learned, the mercury switch completes the electrical circuit and activates a tape recorder to play music or moves the individual's favorite toy (see Figure 4.8). The investigators have found that this type of reinforcement can be effective with individuals possessing a cognitive level of only 4 to 5 months. Their paper gives detailed instructional guidelines for designing various mercury switch devices.

Overall, the use of electrical response devices as a reinforcement technique for persons with severe and profound mental retardation looks quite promising. For example, in a study cited by French (1985), two students increased the time they held their heads in a proper position by over 200% with the electrical response

Figure 4.8 Mercury switch device. A single sponge switch is used to activate music from the tape player.

Note. From ''The Use of Electrical Pressure Switches to Improve the Physical Fitness Levels of Profoundly Mentally Retarded Children'' by R. French, and L.M. Silliman, October 1988, *The 17th National Conference on Physical Activity for the Exceptional Individual*, Oakland, CA. Reprinted by permission of Ron French.

device. The music from the tape recorder was found to be much more reinforcing and effective with the two students than verbal reinforcement or the sugar-coated cereal the investigators had previously used.

Stereotypic and Self-Injurious Behavior

Many individuals with severe or profound mental retardation may exhibit socially unacceptable behaviors that are potentially dangerous to themselves and others. Snell (1987) lists common examples of self-injurious behavior (SIB) as hitting one's head or banging it on objects, biting various parts of the body, pulling hair, scratching, and poking eyes. Head banging, hand biting, and eye poking are the most common. Favell, McGimsey, and Schell (1982) identify several other less common examples of SIB: repeated vomiting, rumination (vomiting and swallowing vomitus), pica (eating inedible objects), and coprophagia (eating feces). Gorman-Smith and Matson (1985) add less injurious stereotypic behaviors such as mouthing (putting fingers and

hands in the mouth), body rocking, head movements (moving the head back and forth), wall patting, and object manipulations. Self-injurious behavior is estimated to exist in approximately 5% to 15% of the population with severe and profound mental retardation (Favell et al., 1982).

MacLean and Baumeister's (1982) description of two such youngsters helps to illustrate examples of this condition.

> Subject A (CA = 42 months) was severely delayed (developmental level = 3 months) and had several congenital disorders including growth deficiency, hydrocephalus, and partial blindness. The child had two behavioral stereotypes. One form was the rotation of the child's hand and wrist in front of his face. The other was leg kicking. Subject B (CA = 34 months) was severely delayed (developmental level = 5 months) and had several congenital disorders including cataracts, heart defect, unusual facies among other physical abnormalities, and growth deficiency. . . . This child exhibited several prominent behavioral stereotypes, including head rolling, leg kicking, and two forms of hand movements. One form of hand movement consisted of a back-and-forth motion of the arm. The other involved placing the back of his hand against his nose. (p. 232)

McClure, Moss, McPeters, and Kirkpatrick (1986) developed a training device for decreasing negative behaviors and reinforcing positive behaviors of a 9-year-old boy with profound mental retardation who was constantly finger sucking (hand mouthing). This behavior is not uncommon in infants without disabilities or individuals with profound retardation, but if it continues beyond the infant stage, it is considered undesirable because the prolonged contact of the hand and mouth often produces health problems such as salivary dermatitis, lesions, and bad breath. Further negative effects occur because this particular behavior is incompatible with many forms of developmental training and social interaction.

The boy was able to turn on either a cassette recorder that played children's music or a vibrator touching the back of his head. Significant results were observed by using this strategy, and reduction of hand and finger sucking was accomplished. In reference to this study, the researchers state: "Of particular interest is that this form of treatment was primarily conducted in the absence of a trainer and was inexpensive. Furthermore, it provided the subject with a rare opportunity to control his environment voluntarily" (p. 219).

Morreau (1988) concurs with this procedure and believes that use of a hand-held vibrator can significantly reduce undesirable stereotypic behaviors.

MacLean and Baumeister (1982) describe the potential reduction of stereotyped behavior of four youngsters with profound disabilities through the use of vestibular stimulation. Believing that semicircular canal stimulation can positively affect abnormal stereotypic behavior, they rotated the children in a motor-driven chair at a velocity of about 17 rpm for 10 minutes daily over a 2-week period. Over the course of the study all children showed positive motor or reflex changes. Additionally, some evidence was obtained linking changes in stereotypic behaviors to the vestibular stimulation. Among their conclusions the authors offer a unique hypothesis that should be considered: "Stereotyped behavior may be a sign of an immature central nervous system. As maturation ensues for normal children the stereotyped behaviors disappear. On the other hand, the maturational sequence begins later, proceeds at a slower rate, and may never be complete for developmentally disabled children. The result could be prolonged exhibition of stereotyped movements" (p. 244).

Gorman-Smith and Matson (1985) conducted an intense review of treatment research for self-injurious and stereotyped behaviors, making statistical comparisons, using a meta-analytic approach, of the relative effects across treatment studies. They reviewed studies referenced in *Psychological Abstracts* between 1976 and 1983. The description of specific treatments used for reduction of stereotyped behavior is found in Highlight 4.6 (Gorman-Smith & Matson, 1985).

Reduction of unwanted behaviors and improvement appears to be most successful when differential reinforcement of other behaviors (DRO), lemon juice therapy, time-out, air splints, and DRO plus overcorrection were used. "It is of interest that the three procedures with the greatest use, overcorrection, physical restraint and facial screening, show a smaller effect size to standard deviation than with some of the less frequently used procedures. The fact that these methods are used more in experimental studies suggests that many professionals see the potential utility of these methods" (Gorman-Smith & Matson, 1985, p. 302).

Treatments for self-injurious and stereotypic behaviors merit special attention and should be preferred to aversive and punishment procedures, which are discussed in the next section. Procedures should begin with positive reinforcement and move to using aversive techniques only as a last resort.

Procedures to Reduce or Eliminate Behavior

This section discusses procedures to reduce or eliminate a behavior, usually one that is inappropriate and is deterring the individual from learning. Henderson and French (1989) point out that because of ordinary connotations of the word *negative*, negative reinforcement and punishment are often confused. But they are not the same. *Negative reinforcement* is the removal of an aversive event as a consequence of a behavior in order to increase the behavior. An example is the child who begins to cooperate with classmates during a game and therefore is no longer made to collect and put equipment away.

Description of Treatments of Stereotyped Behavior

Air splints—Placement of air bags, typically used as a temporary cast on an arm or a leg, as a means of physical restraint.

DRO—Reinforcing an individual for not exhibiting a stereotyped behavior during a prearranged interval of time.

Facial screening—Placing a bib or some other cloth over the eyes for a brief period of time (e.g., 1 minute), contingent on the emission of stereotyped behavior.

Icing—Placing an ice bag on the face or arm for a few seconds, contingent on the appearance of a stereotyped behavior.

Lemon juice—Squirting lemon juice in the mouth, contingent on the occurrence of a stereotyped behavior such as biting or ruminating.

Overcorrection—A work and effort procedure that consists of two components—restitution and positive practice. Restitution involves improving an environment to a condition vastly superior to its previous condition (e.g., cleaning up a mess and then other parts of a room). Positive practice consists of practicing new, alternative appropriate behaviors many times (e.g., a child who had a toileting accident would be required to practice walking to and sitting on the potty 10 times, after an accident).

Physical restraint—Preventing, through either holding or mechanical means, self-hitting, kicking, etc.

Self-monitoring—Counting one's own stereotyped responses.

Shock—Contingently shocking a person for stereotyped behavior. Typically the electrodes are an inch or so apart on an arm or leg.

Time-out—Removal of the person from reinforcement.

Vibratory stimulation—A form of sensory reinforcement given if the target response does not occur for a specified period of time.

Water mist—Procedure similar to lemon juice treatment.

Note. From ''A Review of Treatment Research for Self-Injurious and Stereotyped Responding'' by D. Gorman-Smith and J.L. Matson, 1985, *Journal of Mental Deficiency Research*, **29**, pp. 295-308. Reprinted by permission of Blackwell Scientific Publications.

Punishment is defined as the presentation of an aversive event or the removal of a positive event contingent upon a response decreasing the probability of that response (Kazdin, 1980).

Punishment

In general, punishment doesn't build a strong positive working relationship between the program administrator and the learner. Before administering any punishment procedure, professionals should carefully consider the following factors (French, Lavay, & Henderson, 1985; Sulzar-Azaroff & Mayers, 1977; Wehman, 1977).

1. This procedure may only suppress the inappropriate behavior instead of extinguish

it. In the absence of this procedure the behavior may recur at an even higher rate.

2. This procedure may elicit a number of emotional reactions—such as fear, escape, avoidance, anxiety, anger, hostility, depression, and lower self-esteem—from the person receiving the punishment.

3. The person receiving the punishment may learn to model the aggression displayed by the punishing agent, in this case the administrator of the program.

4. These emotional reactions may cause the person to withdraw or become aggressive toward the administrator of the program.

5. This procedure may negatively affect the person's ability to concentrate on the task or on learning meaningful activities.

This section examines four types of procedures to reduce or eliminate a behavior: extinction, discussion/self-talk, response cost, and time-outs. These procedures are presented in the order of less severe to more severe. Too often, practitioners administer these procedures to persons with mental retardation out of desperation or because at first they get quick results in altering inappropriate behavior. These methods should be administered carefully and only after more positive procedures have been systematically applied.

Extinction

Extinction is a process for eliminating or reducing a conditioned response by not administering any form of reinforcement. The inappropriate behavior is eliminated by removing the reinforcement that maintains or increases the behavior. Ignoring the inappropriate behavior of one individual (extinction) and praising the appropriate behavior of another individual (reinforcement) is an example of how this procedure can be administered to reduce the inappropriate behavior.

According to Wehman (1977), a major problem with this procedure is properly identifying

the reinforcer that is maintaining or increasing the undesirable behavior. For example, the recreational leader who verbally reprimands a person with mental retardation for displaying inappropriate behavior such as talking out of turn during a group outing may be actually reinforcing that person by providing the special attention they are seeking; this person may continue to talk out of turn, seeking to receive the additional reinforcing attention from the recreational leader.

Extinction procedures can usually be successful with minor behavior problems and over a short period of time. Such minor problems may be self-indulgent behaviors, such as crying or pouting, or noncompliant behaviors such as saying no when asked to perform a task (Dunn et al., 1986). Once the inappropriate behavior stops, appropriate behavior should be reinforced by the instructor. However, more sophisticated management plans are necessary when inappropriate behaviors extend over a long period of time and are more serious in nature.

Discussion/Self-Talk

In the *discussion/self-talk* procedure the instructor verbally interacts with the learner (in a positive manner) regarding the particular behavior the instructor would like to see reduced. Obviously, this must be done carefully with individuals with mental retardation, as the dialogue must be at a level the learner can comprehend.

Because all individuals in the program need to be aware of what is acceptable and unacceptable behavior, the rules and the consequences for not adhering to the rules must be made clear and stated in a way that everyone involved can understand. For example, someone who has been acting inappropriately can be taken aside, and the rule that was broken can be carefully explained to her or him. During this discussion the target behavior should be clearly identified. Hellison (1985) advocates the use of a self-talk procedure in which the learner is made to repeat the rule to the practitioner. This helps identify any misunderstanding between the instructor and learner regarding the desired behavior.

The instructor must be positive and unemotional in this discussion. The learner should never be reprimanded in front of peers, but rather he or she should be taken aside and spoken to calmly. The instructor must realize that the problem is the inappropriate or undesired behavior and not the individual. These strategies help foster positive communication between the instructor and the learner. For the instructor, this may mean finding time to have a discussion with the person who is acting inappropriately. When participants have emotional outbursts, the instructor must always remember to act rather than react. In other words, the instructor must take time to think about what she or he will be saying to the child and not simply react to the child's behavior. In addition, the instructor must also be careful to avoid giving the learner angry looks. No matter how severe the problem, it is important for the instructor to remain calm, but firm, and not get into a heated argument with the learner. For example, the instructor can use deep breathing techniques while calmly speaking to an upset adult.

Hellison (1985) offers the following procedural guidelines for promoting positive discussion between the instructor and the learner:

1. Identify the individual's behavior and the program rules.
2. Listen to the individual's response.
3. Provide a transition from the individual's response to a plan that will change the behavior.
4. Help the individual develop the plan.
5. Be sure the individual carries out the plan.
6. If the behavior continues and the first plan is not effective, implement a new plan.

Response Cost

A *response-cost procedure*, also known as *negative reinforcement*, is the withdrawal of a posi-

tive reinforcer (something desirable) as a consequence of the occurrence of an undesirable behavior, to decrease that undesired behavior. Put simply, it is taking away something that is reinforcing to that person (e.g., rescinding a previously earned privilege) or administering a fine (e.g., taking away tokens) to get the individual to quit acting inappropriately. For instance, the child who does not wait his or her turn in line loses the privilege of choosing a piece of equipment to play with during the last 5 minutes of PE class. Note that for response-cost procedures to be effective the withdrawal of the privilege or reinforcement must be significant to the particular person.

Smith (1981) advocates the application of these procedures because they do not require individuals to leave the learning environment, and the consequences of individuals' actions approximate real-life situations. Response cost is most commonly used in token economy systems (discussed earlier in this chapter), in which an individual loses a token or point toward a desired reinforcer for displaying inappropriate behavior. For example, the last 15 minutes of a recreation period may be set aside to practice "Special Olympics basketball"; however, those who do not participate in the outdoor playground obstacle course will have this privilege taken away.

Time-Outs

Time-out procedures are most controversial and require careful planning to be effectively administered. A *time-out* is the removal of an individual for a period of time from a reinforcing environment, contingent upon an inappropriate behavior and as an attempt to decrease that behavior (French et al., 1985). Aggressive behavior, such as cursing, screaming, physically abusing oneself or another person, or destroying property, warrants the immediate application of this procedure (Dunn et al., 1986). If time-out procedures are to be effective, the environment in which the individual is placed during the time-out must be carefully considered and cannot be reinforcing. For example, if Steve is placed in time-out and can still joke and chat with his peers, then in actuality he is being reinforced for his inappropriate behavior. A discrepancy must exist between the time-in and time-out environment (Harris, 1985).

A time-out can take many forms, ranging in severity along a continuum from most to least severe (Brantner & Doherty, 1983):

1. Isolation
2. Exclusion
3. Contingent observation
4. Removal of reinforcing stimulus conditions
5. Ignoring

Ignoring (extinction) and the removal of a reinforcing stimulus condition (response cost) have been discussed earlier in this chapter.

A *contingent observation time-out* can be a most effective procedure if the individual being timed out enjoys physical activity. In this procedure the individual is removed from the reinforcing environment and the group, but remains close enough to observe the group demonstrating appropriate behavior. The individual who enjoys physical activity will desire to rejoin the group. The person in time-out is also being provided with the opportunity to observe others' modeling of appropriate behavior while the activity session continues. In an *exclusion time-out*, the individual is excluded from the area of reinforcement without being removed from the entire setting. For example, the individual sits in the gymnasium bleachers with her or his back to the group as they engage in activity. Finally, in an *isolation time-out*, the person is totally removed from the reinforcing environment. For example, the PE teacher arranges with the classroom teacher that students who continue to remain disruptive after a contingent observation time-out will be sent back to the classroom. The following time-out procedure has been effectively used in an adapted PE setting

for students with mild and moderate mental retardation.

> *A student not cooperating in physical education class will be given one warning. On a student's second warning, there will be a 1-minute time-out. On the third warning, the student will be sent back to class.*

Obviously, if the individual doesn't enjoy physical activity, time-out procedures will be ineffective because the individual will be given an opportunity to escape from a disliked environment (French et al., 1985). According to Harris (1985), a time-out is a complicated intervention procedure that involves far more than simply removing a person from ongoing activities and returning him or her after a predetermined period of time. Although there has been little research on time-outs, Harris suggests that the following parameters be carefully considered before time-out procedures are initiated in any program.

1. *Verbal reason.* There is little research on whether a brief explanation facilitates or hinders the effectiveness of time-out procedures.
2. *Warning.* There is no research available to determine whether a verbal warning should be given before time-out procedures are implemented.
3. *Instructional versus physical administration.* Whether a person is instructed to go to the time-out or physically guided, there often depends on the degree of inappropriateness of the behavior; however, there is little research to determine the best procedure.
4. *Location or type.* The five types of time-out procedures previously mentioned all have demonstrated effectiveness in application. However, the type of time-out chosen should be based on the individual person and should not depend solely on the severity of the problem.

5. *Duration*. Determining the optimal duration or period of a time-out is difficult. Durations ranging from a few seconds up to 3 hours have been found to be effective. Contrasting long and short time-outs also has not been thoroughly researched.

6. *Time-out schedule*. Little information is available regarding the effectiveness of continual versus intermittent time-out scheduling.

7. *Time-out stimulus*. No studies exist to determine whether a signal indicating the onset or termination of time-out is effective or ineffective.

8. *Release from time-out*. Releasing the person from time-out because the duration time is up may present additional problems. For example, it is not a good practice to release an individual who is still upset and acting inappropriately in time-out.

9. *Schedule of reinforcement*. The research is unclear as to the effect time-out procedures have on individuals and whether the reinforcements are abundant when the individual is placed back in time-in.

10. *Group contingencies and group placement*. Little is known regarding the effect time-out placement can have on an entire group based on the behavior of one individual.

Summary

In the past, practitioners providing physical activity to persons with mental retardation have been reluctant to incorporate systematic behavior management procedures. A lack of proper training by professionals in the application of behavior management systems has led to misconceptions regarding the application of these methods. However, recent studies conducted with persons with mental retardation within different classification levels and across various physical activity settings have not only demonstrated improved physical performance among this population but have helped to motivate these persons to successfully participate in a variety of physical activity programs. In fact, Wehman (1977) suggests that perhaps the most significant advance in educational training for persons with mental retardation may be practitioners' increased acceptance of the principles of operant conditioning.

For professionals to effectively implement a successful behavior management plan, a number of factors must be carefully considered. This chapter examined these factors:

- The individual
- The instructor or administrator of the program
- The environment
- The desired behavior
- Recording the behavior
- Systematic program implementation
- Program evaluation to determine its effectiveness on the learner's behavior

All of these factors are important and related to the successful design of an effective management plan to promote an individual behavior change in order for learning to occur.

Most behavior management programs used for this population are based on the principles of operant conditioning, which involves the systematic application of consequences to maintain, strengthen, or weaken behaviors. Whenever possible the management plan must be administered to the learner in a positive manner. A variety of positive management systems and procedures as well as examples were discussed in this chapter, including the following:

- The application of various reinforcement systems in the form of social, tangible, and physical activity reinforcers
- Token economy exchange systems
- Modeling
- Prompting

- Shaping
- Chaining
- Puppets
- Electrical response devices

Also presented in this chapter were procedures to reduce or eliminate inappropriate behavior. These procedures included punishment, extinction, discussion/self-talk, response cost, and time-outs. Professionals using these methods must carefully consider the long-term ramifications of these procedures, which generally do not help build a positive rapport and working relationship between the administrator of the program and the learner.

If you would like more information on this subject, see the textbook edited by French and Lavay, *Behavior Management Techniques for Physical Educators and Recreators* (1990), which is a collection of 36 previously published and unpublished writings carefully selected by the editors after a critical survey of over 200 works in the area of behavior management and physical activity literature. The editors chose readings on behavior management that addressed justification and importance, critical analysis, research designs, general techniques and strategies, and techniques applied to specific populations, including 10 articles on mental retardation.

DISCUSSIONS AND NEW DIRECTIONS

1. What effects do different reinforcement systems have on the behavior and physical performance of persons with mental retardation? Are certain systems more effective than others? Does program effectiveness depend on the age, gender, or classification level of the person with mental retardation?

2. What role will advanced technology play in the development of behavior management programs in physical activity settings for persons with severe and profound mental retardation?

3. What role if any should punishment play in educational settings to reduce inappropriate behavior for persons with mental retardation? What procedures, policies, or restrictions should apply?

References

Allen, L.A. & Iwata, B.A. (1980). Reinforcing exercise maintenance: Using existing high-rate activities. *Behavior Modification*, **4**, 337-354.

Bennett, F., Eisenman, P., French, R., Henderson, H., & Shultz, B. (1989). The effects of a token economy on exercise behavior of individuals with Down Syndrome. *Adapted Physical Activity Quarterly*, **6**, 230-246.

Bishop, P. (1990). Basic time series designs. In R. French & B. Lavay (Eds.), *Behavior management techniques for physical educators and recreators*. Kearney, NE: Educational Systems.

Bishop, P., & French, R. (1982). Effects of reinforcers on attending behavior of severely handicapped boys in physical education. *Journal for Special Educators*, **18**, 48-58.

Branter, J.P., & Doherty, M.A. (1983). A review of timeout: A conceptual and methodological analysis. In S. Axelrod & J. Apshe (Eds.), *The effects of punishment on human behavior*. New York: Academic Press.

Campbell, J.M. (1972). Evaluation of contingency managed physical fitness program for mentally retarded boys (Doctoral dissertation, The Pennsylvania State University, 1971). *Dissertation Abstracts International*, **33**, 1042A.

Caouette, M., & Reid, G. (1985). Increasing the work output of severely retarded adults on a bicycle ergometer. *Education and Training of the Mentally Retarded*, **20**, 296-304.

Dauer, V.P., & Pangrazi, R.P. (1989). *Dynamic physical education for elementary school children* (9th ed.). New York: Macmillan.

DePaepe, J. (1985). The influence of three least restrictive environments on the content motor-alt and performance of moderately mentally retarded students. *Journal of Teaching in Physical Education*, **5**, 34-41.

Dunn, J.M., & Fredericks, H.D. (1985). The utilization of behavior management in mainstreaming in physical education. *Adapted Physical Activity Quarterly*, **2**, 338-346.

Dunn, J.M., & French, R.W. (1982). Operant conditioning: A tool for special physical educators in the 1980s. *Exceptional Education Quarterly*, **3**, 42-53.

Dunn, J.M., Morehouse, J.W., & Fredericks, H.D. (1986). *Physical education for the severely handicapped: A systematic approach to data-based gymnasium*. Austin, TX: PRO-ED.

Favell, J.E., McGimsey, J.F., & Schell, R.M. (1982). Treatment of self-injury by providing alternate sensory activities. *Analysis and Intervention in Developmental Disabilities*, **2**(3), 83-104.

French, R. (1985). Positive reinforcers: A major ingredient in effective teaching. *Proceedings of the 14th National Conference on Physical Activity for the Exceptional Individual*, 108-114.

French, R., Folsom-Meeks, S., Cook, C., & Smith, D. (1987). The use of electrical response devices to motivate nonambulatory profoundly mentally retarded children. *American Corrective Therapy Journal*, **41**, 64-68.

French, R., & Jansma, P. (1978). *Behavior management*. Unpublished manuscript, University of Utah, Salt Lake City.

French, R., & Lavay, B. (Eds.) (1990). *Behavior management techniques for physical educators and recreators*. Kearney, NE: Educational Systems.

French, R., Lavay, B., & Henderson, H. (1985). Take a lap. *Physical Educator*, **42**, 180-185.

Gardner, W.I. (1978). *Children with learning and behavior problems: A behavior management approach*. Boston: Allyn & Bacon.

Gorman-Smith, D., & Matson, J.L. (1985). A review of treatment research for self-injurious and stereotyped responding. *Journal of Mental Deficiency Research*, **29**, 295-308.

Halle, J.W., Silverman, N.A., & Regan, L. (1983). The effect of a data-based exercise program on physical fitness of retarded children. *Education and Training of the Mentally Retarded*, **18**, 279-288.

Harris, K.R. (1985). Definitional, parametric, and procedural considerations in timeout interventions and research. *Exceptional Children*, **51**, 279-288.

Hellison, D.R. (1985). *Goals and strategies for teaching physical education*. Champaign, IL: Human Kinetics.

Henderson, H., & French, R. (1989). Negative reinforcement or punishment? *Journal of Physical Education, Recreation and Dance*, **60**(5), 4.

Horner, R.D. (1971). Establishing use of crutches by a mentally retarded spina bifida child. *Journal of Applied Behavior Analysis*, **4**, 183-189.

Hsu, P., & Dunn, J.M. (1984). Comparing reverse and forward chaining instructional methods on motor tasks with moderately mentally retarded individuals. *Adapted Physical Activity Quarterly*, **1**, 240-246.

Huber, J.H. (1973). The effects of a token economy program on appropriate behavior and motor task performance of educable mentally retarded children in adapted physical education (Doctoral dissertation, Ohio State University, 1973). *Dissertation Abstracts International*, **34**, 2751A.

Hussey, C., Mauerer, J.E., & Schofield, L.J. (1976). Physical education training for adult retardates in a sheltered workshop setting. *Journal of Clinical Psychology*, **32**, 701-705.

Jones, V., & Jones, L. (1981). *Responsible Classroom Performance*. Boston: Allyn & Bacon.

Kazdin, A.E. (1980). *Behavior modification in applied settings*. Homewood, IL: Dorsey Press.

Kirby, K.C., & Holburn, S.W. (1986). Trained, generalized, and collateral behavior changes of preschool children receiving gross-motor skill training. *Journal of Applied Behavior Analysis*, **19**, 283-288.

Lavay, B. (1984). Physical activity as a reinforcer. *Adapted Physical Activity Quarterly*, **1**, 315-321.

Lavay, B. (1985). Help! Class out of control. *Kansas Association for Health, Physical Education, Recreation and Dance*, **53**(2), 29-31.

Lavay, B., & French, R. (1986). The effect of different reinforcers on the physical performance of trainable mentally handicapped students. *American Corrective Therapy Journal*, **40**, 58-61.

Leme, S.A. (1982). The effect of tangible reinforcement plus social praise versus social praise only on the physical fitness test performance of severely/profoundly retarded institutionalized subjects (Doctoral dissertation, University of Wisconsin, 1981). *Dissertation Abstracts International*, **42**, 3554-3555A.

Loovis, M.E. (1980). Behavior modification: Its application in physical education/motor development with children of special needs. *American Corrective Therapy Journal*, **34**, 19-24.

McClure, J.T., Moss, R.A., McPeters, J.W.,

& Kirkpatrick, M.A. (1986). Reduction of hand mouthing by a boy with profound mental retardation. *Mental Retardation*, **24**, 219-222.

McKenzie, T.L. (1979). Token economy research: A review for the physical educator. *Motor Skills: Theory in Practice*, **3**, 102-114.

MacLean, W.E., Jr., & Baumeister, A.A. (1982). Effects of vestibular stimulation on motor development and stereotypic behavior of developmentally disabled children. *Journal of Abnormal Child Psychology*, **10**, 229-245.

Mercer, C.D., & Snell, M.E. (1977). *Learning theory research in mental retardation: Implications for teaching*. Columbus, OH: Merrill.

Moon, M.S., & Renzgalia, A. (1982). Physical fitness and the mentally retarded: A critical review of the literature. *Journal of Special Education*, **16**, 269-287.

Morreau, L.E. (1988, March 8). Personal communication.

Patton, J.R., Payne, J., & Beirne-Smith, M. (1990). *Mental retardation* (2nd ed.). Columbus, OH: Merrill.

Presbie, R.J., & Brown, P.L. (1977). *Physical education: The behavior modification approach*. Washington, DC: National Education Association.

Repp, A.C. (1983). *Teaching the mentally retarded*. Englewood Cliffs, NJ: Prentice Hall.

Rickard, H.C., & Dinhoff, M. (Eds.) (1974). *Behavior modification in children: Case studies and illustrations from a summer camp*. Tuscaloosa: University of Alabama Press.

Roice, G.R. (1978). It's hard to be a leader when your class is rioting behind you—A behavior management approach to adapted physical education. *The Physical Activities Report*, **434**, 1-5.

Schack, F.K., & Ryan, T. (1978). The effects of varying types of reinforcement on gross motor skill learning and retention in trainable mentally retarded boys. *American Corrective Therapy Journal*, **32**, 135-140.

Sechrest, L. (1968). Exercise an operant response for retarded children. *The Journal of Special Education*, **2**, 311-317.

Smith, D.D. (1981). *Teaching the learning disabled*. Englewood Cliffs, NJ: Prentice Hall.

Snell, M.E. (1987). *Systematic instruction of persons with severe handicaps*. Columbus, OH: Merrill.

Sulzar-Azaroff, B., & Mayer, R.G. (1977). *Applying behavior-analysis procedures with children and youth*. New York: Holt, Rinehart & Winston.

Thomas, J.D., Presland, I.E., Grant, M.D. & Glynn, T.L. (1978). Natural rates of teacher approval and disapproval in grade 7 classrooms. *Journal of Applied Behavior Analysis*, **11**, 91-94.

Tomporowski, P.D., & Ellis, N.R. (1984). Preparing severely and profoundly mentally retarded adults for tests of motor fitness. *Adapted Physical Activity Quarterly*, **1**, 158-163.

U.S. Office of Education. Federal Register. The Individuals With Disabilities Education Act, formerly The Education for All Handicapped Children Act of 1975, Section 94-142, 99-457, 89-750, 42 U.S.C., Section 42480-54579, (1977).

Vogler, E.W., & French, R.W. (1983). The effects of a group contingency strategy on behaviorally disordered students in physical education. *Research Quarterly for Exercise and Sport*, **54**, 273-277.

Watkinson, E.J., & Wall, A.E., (1982). *The PREP play program: Play skill instruction for mentally handicapped children*. Ottawa, Ontario: Canadian Association for Health, Physical Education and Recreation.

Wehman, P. (1977). *Helping the mentally retarded acquire play skills: A behavioral approach*. Springfield, IL: Charles C Thomas.

White, M.A. (1975). Natural rates of teacher approval and disapproval in the classroom. *Journal of Applied Behavior Analysis*, **8**, 367-372.

White, O.R., & Haring, N.G. (1980). *Exceptional teaching*. Columbus, OH: Merrill.

PART II

Program Development and Implementation

This part consists of chapters on program development, mainstreaming, and program implementation. Collectively the three chapters provide the information necessary to effectively develop and implement a program of physical activity for persons with mental retardation.

Chapter 5, "Program Development: Administrative Considerations," examines how the passage of the Individuals With Disabilities Education Act (IDEA) has greatly increased the number of professional services available to persons with mental retardation. For the professional assigned the task of developing a program of physical activity for persons with mental retardation, having such an array of professional services to choose from can be confusing. This chapter discusses legal requirements for such physical activity programs, such as requirements regarding individualized education plans (IEPs), and then provides a guided tour of many of the various professional services available, including those of the special education classroom teacher, paraprofessional or volunteer, regular physical education teacher, special/adapted physical education teacher, therapeutic recreation specialist, occupational therapist, physical therapist, and kinesiotherapist. This chapter also discusses an overview of the transdisciplinary approach, programming for the severely and profoundly retarded, and the role of the parents in providing physical activity training to their child at home.

Chapter 6, "Mainstreaming: Program Considerations," discusses the availability of physical activity placement alternatives in the schools for persons with mental retardation as well as strategies for effectively selecting the setting that best meets the needs of the particular individual. Information is also presented that will assist professionals in effectively meeting the mainstreaming challenge and successfully integrating persons with mental retardation into school and community-based recreational programs with their counterparts who do not have disabilities.

Chapter 7, "Program Implementation: Physical Fitness, Fundamental Motor Skills, Aquatics, and Dance," consists of specific information related to the four main areas listed in the definition of physical education under the Individuals With Disabilities Education Act. This information is necessary to successfully develop and implement a program of physical activity to meet the diverse and varied needs of persons with mental retardation. Each of the four sections includes information on safety considerations, activity selection, skill development and progression, and strategies for motivating the individual or the group. Also included are discussions of the latest research findings and exemplary programs specific to persons with mental retardation.

CHAPTER 5

Program Development: Administrative Considerations

PREVIEW During the past 5 years, special education students with mild learning disabilities have attended the Kennedy Elementary School. These students have adjusted well to school life and in general have been accepted by their peers. However, the principal of the school is concerned because this fall, for the first time, a group of children with moderate and severe mental retardation will be attending the school. Previously the school district had taught these children in a special school. The principal realizes that many of these students have severe disabilities, and she is concerned about how the current staff will react to teaching children with such unique needs. In addition, she is uncertain regarding the type and availability of district services necessary to educate these children. The principal has heard of such services as special/adapted physical education, physical therapy, and occupational therapy but knows little about these programs.

HIGHLIGHT QUESTIONS

- **What is the Individuals With Disabilities Education Act (IDEA), and what educational implications does this law have for children with mental retardation?**
- **What is the difference between direct and related educational services?**
- **Why is an IEP so vital to effective programming for children with mental retardation?**
- **What determines a well-written behavioral objective?**
- **What is the transdisciplinary approach?**
- **What are the roles of the special education classroom teacher, special/adapted physical education teacher, therapeutic recreation specialist, occupational therapist, and physical therapist in the delivery of physical activity services to persons with mental retardation?**
- **What will be the future role of the special/adapted physical education teacher in programming for people with severe and profound mental retardation?**
- **Why is parent involvement important to the child's educational plan and program progress?**

The concerns felt by the principal in the chapter 5 Preview are realistic. They are shared by many administrators and other school personnel and parents, who too often are uncertain about what professional services are available to educate persons with mental retardation and do not clearly understand the similarities and differences among such services as special/adapted physical education, physical therapy, and occupational therapy.

The purpose of this chapter is to navigate the maze of available program services for persons with mental retardation. It is of paramount importance that you understand these services if you are to develop exemplary programs of physical activity to meet the diverse needs of persons with mental retardation.

Providing Physical Activity

If effective programs of physical activity are to be developed, professionals must believe that physical activity is important for everyone. All human beings are created with the natural urge to move (Croce & Lavay, 1985). Too often the benefits of physical activity for persons with mental retardation are ignored. This is unfortunate because movement and physical activity experiences can make important contributions toward each person's total development in the physical, cognitive, and affective (social and emotional) areas of learning (see Figure 5.1).

Benefits of Physical Activity

Research indicates that systematic programs of physical exercise can benefit persons with mental retardation in the areas of physical growth and development, movement proficiency, and overall health, thereby helping them be able to successfully perform the functions required in daily life, such as job-related vocational skills and leisure activities. Cognitive benefits include developing a knowledge of safety-related movement principles and an understanding of the rules

Figure 5.1 Physical activity is beneficial to the total development of all persons. Photo courtesy of Ken Regan.

and strategies of games and sports that enables them to appreciate such activities as a participant or a spectator. In the affective area, successful physical activity experiences build individuals' self-confidence and make them feel better about themselves. Through games and sport, persons with mental retardation can develop worthy use of leisure time and learn to interact with others in a socially acceptable manner. In general, physical activity is a necessary part of improving the overall quality of life for all persons, including those with mental retardation (see Highlight 5.1).

Individuals With Disabilities Education Act

The passage of Public Law 94-142 in 1975, now known as the Individuals With Disabilities Education Act (PL 101-476) has greatly enhanced the quality of educational services for children of all ages with disabilities. Most importantly to professionals who provide physical activity to this population, the curricular area of physical education is cited specifically in the definition of special education:

> The term special education means specifically designed instruction at no cost to the

---

HIGHLIGHT 5.1   **IN THEORY**

Benefits of Physical Education for Persons With Mental Retardation

Physical education has the same important benefits for persons with mental retardation as for persons without disabilities. The following are the major benefits in the three learning domains.

Physical Domain

Physical education makes a unique contribution to this area of learning that no other educational subject can claim.

HIGHLIGHT 5.1 CONTINUED

1. Physical growth and development
2. Motor proficiency in performing physical movement, which enhances the individual's play and vocational skills
3. Physical fitness and overall health to perform the skills required in daily living

Affective Domain

1. An appreciation of games and sports, as participant and spectator
2. Worthy use of leisure time
3. Efficient movement and consequently increased confidence and feelings of self-worth and improved self-concept while involved in movement

4. Improvement of ability to interact through games and sports with others in a socially acceptable manner

Cognitive Domain

1. A knowledge of safety-related movement principles
2. An understanding of rules and strategies involved in various games and sports, enabling the individual to better appreciate the activity whether involved as a participant or as a spectator

---

parents, to meet the unique needs of a handicapped child including classroom instruction, *instruction in physical education* [italics added], home instruction, and instruction in hospitals and institutions. (U.S. Office of Education, 1977, p. 42480)

Recently Public Law 99-457, the amendments to PL 94-142 in 1986, recognized the need to implement special education and related services to persons 0 to 5 years of age, including at-risk infants and toddlers from birth to 3 years and their families. All states were required to provide, by 1991, services to preschool-age children with disabilities ages 3 to 5 years. This gives professionals who provide physical activity the added responsibility to develop early intervention programs specific to the needs of this population (see chapters 8 and 9).

Direct Services

The PL 94-142 definition of special education recognizes physical education as a direct service, and therefore physical education must be provided to students with disabilities, including students with mental retardation. The law mandates that physical education services to these students are not a luxury but a right. The law defines the component areas of physical education as follows (U.S. Office of Education, 1977, p. 42480):

- Physical and motor fitness
- Fundamental motor skills and patterns
- Skills in aquatics, dance, and individual and group games and sport (including intramural and lifetime sports)

Figure 3.3 presents a detailed breakdown of the activities comprised in these component areas. The instructor needs to know the definition of physical education to make sound decisions regarding physical activity assessment and program development and implementation. Therefore, the discussions in this textbook are based throughout on the definition of physical education as mandated by PL 94-142.

Related Services

Related services are defined by the law as "supportive services as are required to assist a handicapped child to benefit from special education" (p. 54579). Related services such as occupational therapy, physical therapy, and recreation services play an important role in meeting the educational needs of many students with mental retardation, especially those with multiple disabilities. For example, a physical therapist would assist a seriously disabled youth with proper wheelchair-fitting techniques. Later in this chapter the roles of such related services as physical therapy, occupational therapy, and therapeutic recreation will be defined and explained. It is important to note that related services are provided only when they are required to assist the student in benefitting from special education services. Related services must never serve as a substitute for physical education (Lavay, 1988a).

Program Development

Proper program development of physical activity services for persons with mental retardation is most complex. The program and the persons involved will not meet with success if the instructor adheres to one set procedure or curriculum guide. Program development must be individualized and based from the start on sound assessment procedures to determine the individual's present level of performance. To review the earlier discussion of assessment procedures, see chapter 3. Figure 3.1 presents a diagram of the necessary steps in systematically providing ongoing instruction: plan, test, assess, prescribe, teach, and evaluate. The present chapter describes primarily the phases of program planning and prescription.

Although the program is systematic, it is not a set technique or a package delineating predetermined activities. Rather it is a philosophy of instruction based on the strong conviction that physical activity is important for everyone. This requires the instructor to have a great deal of flexibility to implement a wide range of instructional strategies and program activities. The program prescription must be tailored to meet the unique needs of each student. Only when the instructor has interpreted each student's strengths and needs (present level of performance) can a program be effectively developed. This process is never easy, especially given the heterogeneity of persons with mental retardation. The remainder of this chapter discusses the roles and responsibilities of various professionals who work to assist each person, regardless of their condition, to reach their true physical activity potential.

Individualized Education Plan (IEP)

Program development must begin with the individual. Thus, the individualized education plan (IEP) is an important departure point in the development of effective program instruction. In fact, the unique needs of students identified as having disabilities including mental retardation, and attending public schools are so great that the law mandates this practice. Public Law 94-142 requires that the written IEP contain the following information:

1. The individual's present level of performance
2. Annual goals
3. Short-term behavioral objectives
4. Projected dates for initiating services and the anticipated duration for achieving these goals
5. Strategies and materials for achieving these goals
6. The specific educational and related services provided the student
7. The extent to which the student will participate in regular education

Seaman and DePauw (1989) believe the IEP should serve as a blueprint to the student's educational services and assist professionals in maintaining a focus on the necessary objectives required to meet each student's individual needs. Highlight 5.2 describes and gives examples of present level of performance, annual goals, and short-term objectives.

IEP Components

Short-Term Behavioral Objectives

The individualized education plan is composed of short-term behavioral objectives, projected dates for initiating services, strategies and

---

HIGHLIGHT 5.2

IN THEORY

IEP Components

Present Level of Performance

The statement of the student's present level of performance provides a clear picture of the student's strengths and needs, based on sound assessment practices. The individual's present level of performance should never be determined based on a single test score; it should always be based on a battery of test score items. This statement assists the instructor in formulating annual goals and short-term objectives. In short, it is a statement indicating what the student can and cannot do. Here is an example statement of a student's present level of performance:

> Steve's fundamental motor skills as measured by the Test of Gross Motor Development are at age-group norms except in the areas of throwing and catching. His physical fitness scores as measured by the Health-Related Physical Fitness Test indicate that he is below the 25th percentile in the areas of cardiovascular endurance, abdominal strength and endurance, and upper body strength, whereas in flexibility he is above the 45th percentile.

Annual Goals

Knowing the student's present level of performance helps the instructor determine annual

goals. These are broad general statements of student outcomes projected over the school year. Annual goals are selected based on the components of physical education, such as physical fitness, fundamental movements, and sport. The statement of Steve's present level of performance demonstrated that physical fitness is an area of deficiency for him. Although these goals should be broad in scope, they must be written in terms specific enough to effectively communicate student learning outcomes. For example, ''Steve will improve in physical fitness'' is too broad for an annual goal statement. Here is a more appropriate annual goal statement: ''Steve will score above the 35th percentile on the strength portion of the test items on the AAHPERD Health-Related Physical Fitness test.''

Public Law 94-142 addresses only the physical domain in the definition of physical education. However, designing annual goals in the other two learning domains (affective and cognitive) may be necessary for students who display deficiencies in these areas. For example, a child with mild mental retardation may demonstrate above-average physical and motor skills but be unable to effectively cooperate with peers. For this child, it would be necessary for the instructor to write an annual goal statement in the affective domain spe-

HIGHLIGHT 5.2 CONTINUED

cifically addressing the student's performance in social skills such as taking turns and sharing equipment with peers.

Short-Term Objectives

Statements of short-term objectives explain how the annual goals will be met. Seaman and DePauw (1989) describe short-term objectives as the stepping stones to achieving annual goals. To be effective, short-term objectives must be written in behavioral terms. This means the objectives are observable and definable. A well-written behavioral objective consists of the following components:

- Performance or behavior
- Condition
- Criterion

In the performance or behavior part of the objective, the student is doing something observable. This is described with action verbs such as *run, jump, strike*, or *swim*. The condition element of the objective states the conditions under which the student will perform the behavior—for example, the condition that the student will run on an outdoor track. The criterion portion of the objective describes the standard the behavior must meet and is stated in terms of either quantity (such as how many times) or quality (such as how well the skill will be performed). Examples of criteria include successfully striking a ball *in 8 out of 10 trials* or completing a mile run *in under 10 minutes*. It is important to remember that for a short-term objective to be effectively communicated on the IEP form, it must contain all three parts—behavior, condition, and criterion. The following is an example of a properly written short-term objective:

Steve will perform 15 sit-ups (behavior) with knees bent and arms across the chest (condition) in 1 minute (criterion).

materials for achieving goals, statements of specific and related services, and the extent students will participate in regular education. Statements of short-term behavioral objectives can be either product oriented (quantitative) or process oriented (qualitative). Table 5.1 presents product- and process-oriented examples of properly written short-term behavioral objectives in the physical, cognitive, and affective learning domains.

Achieving Goals

Projecting dates for initiating services and determining appropriate timelines for effectively meeting student objectives can be most difficult, especially for the beginning instructor. For example, the experienced teacher can use a student that he or she has taught in the past as a point of reference for the student presently being assessed (Seaman & DePauw, 1989). However, the new instructor does not have this luxury. Seaman and DePauw suggest that, to effectively determine program progress, the teacher should locate test norms, preferably norms based on the population of the student in question. Using the example of Steve once again, who is an 8-year-old boy with mild mental retardation, it was determined that he performed 15 sit-ups. Table 3.2 on p. 92 is a percentile table for sit-ups taken from the physical fitness normative data in Appendix C. The percentiles are based on the classification of mild mental retardation. By locating Steve's raw score of 15 in sit-up performance, the teacher can determine that he scored in the 35th percentile when compared to other 8-year-old boys

Table 5.1   Short-Term Objectives

Physical domain	Cognitive domain	Affect domain
The student will successfully throw a foam ball into a 5-foot square target from 10 feet away (product). The student will demonstrate a mature throwing form, as determined by the teacher, 9 out of 10 times (process).	The student will be able to successfully answer 80% of the specific questions orally presented on a basketball rules test (product). The student will be able to assume all of the playing positions, as determined by the teacher, during an entire basketball game (process).	The student will listen to and follow all class rules, as outlined in the physical education class, 100% of the time (product). The student will cooperate with classmates by sharing equipment and taking turns, as determined by the teacher, during two out of the three of the weekly class meetings (process).

with mild mental retardation. The instructor also can determine, from the percentile table, what would be the next realistic achievement score for Steve (see Table 3.2). The next step for the instructor would be to develop a series of objectives set at certain monthly intervals. Using the percentile table for 8-year-old boys with mild mental retardation in sit-up performance allows the instructor to design annual goals for the school year that Steve can realistically meet, such as these:

1. Steve will perform 17 sit-ups with knees bent and arms across the chest in 1 minute by September 1.
2. Steve will perform 19 sit-ups with knees bent and arms across the chest in 1 minute by December 1.
3. Steve will perform 21 sit-ups with knees bent and arms across the chest in 1 minute by February 1.
4. Steve will perform 23 sit-ups with knees bent and arms across the chest in 1 minute by April 1.

By using this progressive procedure of programming for realistic and small interval increases of 2 sit-ups every 3 months, the instructor has

projected that Steve will reach the 60th percentile by April 1.

Goals and short-term behavioral objectives need not always be based on test scores. When possible, goals and objectives should be chosen that will prepare the person to effectively encounter movement difficulties and successfully participate in the mainstream of society. This is the reason why both product- and process-oriented short-term behavioral objectives are provided in Table 5.1.

Strategies and Materials for Achieving Goals

The use of specific materials and strategies is also important in effectively meeting instructional objectives. The example of sit-ups, for instance, requires equipment such as a mat and stopwatch. Strategies that may need to be considered include physical cues such as a touch to aid Steve in staying on task while performing the sit-ups. Another strategy that could be communicated on the IEP is a sequencing of the skill from simple to complex (the task analysis approach, or sequencing of a skill, was discussed in chapter 4). This approach could be effectively communicated on the IEP form, for example, to teach Steve to successfully strike a pitched foam ball with a wiffle-ball bat with 80% accuracy:

1. Steve will successfully strike an 8-inch foam ball off a batting tee with his hand 8 out of 10 times.
2. Steve will successfully strike an 8-inch foam ball off a batting tee with a wiffle-ball bat 8 out of 10 times.
3. Steve will successfully strike an 8-inch foam ball slowly moving on a rope with a wiffle-ball bat 8 out of 10 times.
4. Steve will successfully strike an 8-inch foam ball slowly pitched from 8 feet away with a wiffle-ball bat 8 out of 10 times.
5. Steve will successfully strike an 8-inch foam ball slowly pitched from 12 feet away with a wiffle-ball bat 8 out of 10 times.

Statement of the Specific Educational and Related Services Provided the Student

This is a written statement on the IEP form that explains the type of services the child will receive. For example, the IEP team may determine for a child with mental retardation in a wheelchair that physical therapy services are necessary. Information regarding the various educational services, both direct and related, available to persons with mental retardation is presented later in this chapter.

The Extent to Which the Student Will Participate in Regular Education

The IEP team will base this decision on the unique abilities and needs of the individual. For example, based on Steve's assessment scores his IEP may determine that he can safely and successfully be placed in regular physical education class. Information regarding mainstreaming is presented in chapter 6.

Recent provisions in PL 99-457, were developed to improve the relationship between chil-

dren from birth to 5 years and their families. One item required is an individualized family service plan (IFSP). The IFSP process is similar to the IEP process in that a written statement must be developed based on a multidisciplinary assessment of each infant and toddler's needs. However, unique to the IFSP process is an evaluation of family needs, a required inclusion of families as members of the multidisciplinary team, and an appointment of an individual from the profession as a case manager (Campbell, Bellamy, & Bishop, 1988). The IFSP must be evaluated at least once a year and reviewed every 6 months or more often when necessary.

In summary, only when IEPs are well planned and well written can they effectively guide proper program development for each individual served. A well-written IEP is based on the individual's present level of performance and includes annual goals, short-term behavioral objectives, strategies and materials for achieving these goals, projected dates for initiating services, and the anticipated duration for achieving these goals. Most importantly, the IEP will help the instructor focus on the objectives required to meet each student's individual needs. Figure 5.2 is an example of an IEP form used in a local school district.

Transdisciplinary Approach

As you are beginning to see for yourself, developing effective services for persons with mental retardation can be most complex, especially given the variety and severity of conditions in this population. No single professional can be expected to possess all the knowledge necessary to effectively meet the unique needs of each individual (Dunn, Moorehouse, & Fredericks, 1986; Hart, 1977). This is the rationale behind PL 94-142's requirement that evaluation procedures be conducted by a multidisciplinary team. Effectively planning the child's IEP is contingent on the cooperation and

Pupil: _____   Present meeting date: _____

DOB: _____   Annual review date: _____

                                                 3-year review date: _____

Address _____

Present level of physical performance (based on multidisciplinary assessment)

_____

_____

_____

1. Annual goal

    Short-term objectives

    Projected date: _____   Criterion for evaluation   Materials

    1.

    2.

    3.

2. Annual goal

    Short-term objectives

    Projected date: _____   Criterion for evaluation   Materials

    1.

    2.

    3.

Figure 5.2   Individualized education plan (IEP) of physical education.

input of a variety of professionals throughout the evaluation process (Lavay & French, 1985). Furthermore, the law's requirement that the student be placed in the least restrictive environment (see chapter 6) has greatly broadened the student's educational environment and the scope of services provided (Sears, 1982). So it is important that everyone working with this population be willing to work with other professionals and clearly understand what that involves.

Team Approaches

The team approach is a relatively new concept in education (Seaman & DePauw, 1989). This procedure evolved from a medical model and in the past was limited to evaluation procedures (Hart, 1977). Therefore, many people working in educational settings are still somewhat confused by such terms as *multidisciplinary*, *interdisciplinary*, and *transdisciplinary*. Too often these terms have been used interchangeably (Lavay & French, 1985). To clear up this confusion and make the team approach more understandable, we will start by defining these terms.

1. *Multidisciplinary*. The multidisciplinary approach involves separate evaluations and prescriptions by the different specialists assigned to identify the individual's specific problem (French & Jansma, 1992). Traditionally, separate evaluations are provided by team members to the professional requesting the report, with little if any communication among the professionals involved.

2. *Interdisciplinary*. The interdisciplinary approach is just like the multidisciplinary approach except that each professional who conducts an evaluation meets with the educator requesting the information (French & Jansma, 1992). However, as in the multidisciplinary approach, the professional requesting the evaluation is left to implement the prescribed program suggestions.

3. *Transdisciplinary*. The transdisciplinary approach breaks down traditional boundaries and encourages information sharing and cooperation among team members throughout the implementation of services (Sears, 1982). In this approach all professionals are accountable for their recommendations (e.g., providing teaching services to assure that each student's educational goals are effectively met) (see Figure 5.3).

Professionals Working Together

The transdisciplinary approach is believed to be the most effective approach because all involved team members share information and engage the group in open dialogue. This increased communication assists in assuring a more effective development and delivery of services, which in

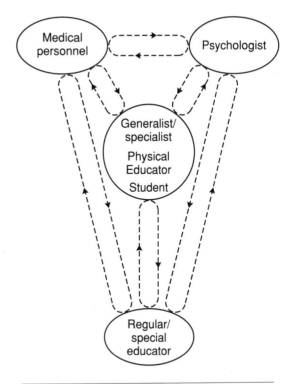

Figure 5.3 Transdisciplinary model (dashes show cooperative relationships between team members). *Note*. From ''The Special Physical Educator: Meeting Educational Goals Through a Transdisciplinary Approach'' by B. Lavay and R. French, 1985, *American Corrective Therapy Journal*, **39**, p. 78. Reprinted with permission of American Corrective Therapy Journal.

turn helps reduce the duplication of services delivered. This approach also renders the implementation of program goals and objectives more consistent and continuous and helps assure that the goals for each individual are effectively met.

A transdisciplinary approach will not come about by accident. Therefore we suggest the following strategies to help professionals effectively work together and communicate to meet program goals (Lavay, 1988b; Lavay & French, 1985; Sherrill, 1986).

1. *Different training backgrounds* and varied philosophies will exist among team members.

For example, the special/adapted physical educator's training has evolved from an educational model, whereas a physical therapist has a medical background. These different professional philosophies and training backgrounds must be communicated and respected if an effective working relationship is to exist.

2. *Professionals must be knowledgeable* about their own job roles as well as those of other team members. This can only occur when professionals stay abreast of the most recent developments and research in their fields as well as in other disciplines. It is important for professionals to read journals, attend conferences and workshops, and keep an open dialogue with other team members.

3. *Preservice training programs* in the various disciplines must make allowances for trainees to work together. For example, students in special physical education should receive coursework or at the very least lectures from professionals in other areas such as special education, therapeutic recreation, physical therapy, and occupational therapy.

4. *Operational procedures* must be designed that allow professionals to effectively work together and share information. For example,

in a school district in New Mexico, a motor evaluation screening procedure to initially identify children with movement difficulties was developed jointly by staff members in special physical education, physical therapy, and occupational therapy.

5. *Effective communication* among staff members of various disciplines will not occur by chance. Time must be set aside and scheduled on a consistent basis. During these scheduled meetings, an agenda should be followed (Figure 5.4).

Team Members

The following professionals may be involved in developing and providing educational services to students with mental retardation.

- Special education classroom teacher
- Paraprofessional or volunteer
- Regular physical education teacher
- Special physical education teacher
- Speech-language pathologist
- Guidance counselor
- School psychologist
- School nurse
- Librarian

Figure 5.4 Communication among staff members is vital to effective program development. Photo courtesy of Bob Fraley.

- Social worker
- Recreation specialist
- Occupational therapist
- Physical therapist
- Art teacher
- Art therapist
- Music teacher
- Music therapist

The basic intent of any program is the total development of the individual. A coordinated effort by all involved professionals is required if effective learning outcomes for each individual are to occur. Moreover, it is important for these professionals to be knowledgeable about their own job roles as well as those of other team members. This section discusses the various job roles of professionals who are responsible for, or will be involved in providing, physical activity services to persons with mental retardation. In addition, Highlight 5.3 presents a list of professional organizations and journals for each of these professional services.

Special Education Classroom Teacher

This professional is perhaps the most vital member of the team. Seaman and DePauw (1989) concur by stating that persons providing physical activity can receive a great deal of information from this professional, because the special education classroom teacher often spends 3 to 6 hours a day with the student in contrast to at best the 30 to 60 minutes spent by instructors assigned to provide physical activity. For example, the special education classroom teacher can provide the physical educator with information about the student's means of communication, appropriate learning styles, effective reinforcers, and cognitive learning level.

In many school districts, providing physical activity to persons with mental retardation is left as the sole responsibility of the special education classroom teacher. This is unfortunate, because often this professional has received little if any training in this area. Moreover, PL 94-142 recognizes the importance of physical education

being provided to students with special needs by a professional trained in this area.

> Special education as set forth in the committee bill includes instruction in physical education, which is provided as a matter of course to all handicapped children enrolled in the public schools. The committee is concerned that although these services are available and required for all children in our schools, they are often viewed as a luxury for handicapped children. (p. 42489)

This mandate is clear. Every effort must be made to provide physical activity to children with special needs by a professional trained in physical education. Eichstaedt and Kalakian (1987) support this view by offering the following analogy: Although almost everyone can learn to drive a car without the assistance of a trained professional, safety and meaningful learning experiences are left to chance by that method.

Reinforced physical activity or movement experiences in the classroom setting (Lavay & Sayers-Lavay, 1988) requires communication and cooperation among the involved professionals. Lavay and Sayers-Lavay (1988) provide examples of various classroom activities that can result from the collaborative efforts of the special education teacher and special/adapted physical education teacher, including pantomime, role playing, movement flashcards, body letters and numbers, word relays, letter and number grids, activity cards, and relaxation techniques (see Highlight 5.4).

Paraprofessionals and Volunteers

Regarding paraprofessionals and volunteers, teachers can often be heard to say, ''I really do not have the time to train them to assist in the program in the way I would like, and they are more trouble than they are worth'' (Dunn et al., 1986). These concerns may be especially true in physical activity settings, where paraprofessionals and volunteers may be reluctant to as-

| HIGHLIGHT 5.3 | IN THEORY |

Professional Organizations

Profession: Occupational therapy
Organization: The American Occupational Therapy Association Inc., 1383 Picard Dr.,
                   P.O. Box 1725, Rockville, MD 20850
Journal(s):   *American Journal of Occupational Therapy*

Profession: Adapted/special physical education
Organizations:

                   Adapted Physical Activity Council (APAC), the American Alliance for Health,
                   Physical Education, Recreation and Dance, 1900 Association Dr., Reston,
                   VA 22091

                   National Consortium on Physical Education and Recreation for Individuals
                   with Disabilities, Dr. Bill Vogler, Arizona State University, Tempe, AZ 85287.
Journal(s):   *Journal of Physical Education, Recreation and Dance*

                   Adapted Physical Activity Journal

                   *Palaestra: The Forum of Sport, Physical Education, and Recreation for the
                   Disabled*

Profession: Physical therapy
Organization: American Physical Therapy Association, 111 N. Fairfax St., Alexandria, VA
                   22314
Journal(s):   *Physical Therapy*

                   Clinical Management

Profession: Therapeutic recreation
Organization: The National Therapeutic Recreation Society (a branch of the National Rec-
                   reation and Park Association), 3101 Park Center Dr., 12th Floor, Alexan-
                   dria, VA 22302
Journal(s):   *Therapeutic Recreation Journal*

                   Journal of Leisurability

Profession: Special education
Organization: The Council for Exceptional Children, Division of Mental Retardation, 1920
                   Association Dr., Reston, VA 22091
Journal(s):   *Exceptional Children*

                   Teaching Exceptional Children

                   Education and Training in Mental Retardation

Profession: Special education
Organization: American Association of Mental Retardation, 1719 Kalorama Rd., NW,
                   Washington, DC 20009
Journal(s):   *Mental Retardation*

Classroom Activity Card

Activity Card: Hula Hoop

Description: The following is a list of activities that can be performed with hula hoops.

Individual Activities

1. Place various parts of the body into or on the hoop.
2. Lay the hoop flat on the floor and jump in various ways, in and out or around the hoop. Various locomotor movements such as hopping and skipping can be substituted for jumping.
3. Roll the hoop as far as it will go.
4. Twirl the hoop and catch it before it falls.
5. Throw the hoop into the air and catch it.
6. Roll the hoop, giving it reverse spin so that it will return.
7. Throw objects into the hoop while it is lying on the floor.

8. Use the hoop as a jump rope.
9. Rotate the hoop on various body parts— hips, neck, arms, wrist, legs, etc.

Teaching Hints

1. Students enjoy using various colored hoops.
2. Give students time to experiment on their own.
3. Younger students will require smaller hoops for better control.

Skill Concepts Reinforced

1. Body awareness
2. Locomotor movements
3. Object control, eye/hand coordination
4. Physical fitness

Note. From "Incorporating Movement Activities in the Special Education Classroom" by B. Lavay and P. Sayers-Lavay. In *Adapted Physical Education: A Resource Manual* (pp. 223-228) by P.Bishop (Ed.), 1988, Kearney, NE: Educational Systems, Inc. Reprinted by permission of Educational Systems Associates, Inc.

sist because they feel inadequate for providing movement and physical activity experiences to students. However, with proper training paraprofessionals and volunteers can play a vital role in providing physical activity programming to students with disabilities (Vogler, French, & Bishop, 1989).

This assistance is especially important when teaching children with severe disabilities that require a one-to-one teacher/student ratio. Dunn and associates have used paraprofessionals and

volunteers with much success in their Data-Based Gymnasium program of physical education for youngsters who have severe disabilities. These authors offer simple guidelines for professionals to consider in order to effectively train paraprofessionals and volunteers (Dunn et al., 1986):

1. Take time to train paraprofessionals and volunteers by explaining and demonstrating their role in the program. During this

time, behavior modification principles specific to operating in the gymnasium should be discussed and developed.

2. Provide paraprofessionals and volunteers with teaching tasks that are compatible with their abilities and levels of training. (This requires that the teacher become knowledgeable regarding each paraprofessional's or volunteer's strong points.)

3. Establish a system of feedback for each paraprofessional's or volunteer's teaching performance. Periodically observe to determine the appropriateness of their interaction skills, ability to present materials, and reinforcement procedures with the students.

4. Establish a simple means of communication with paraprofessionals and volunteers. There is little time during the teaching day to sit down and communicate effectively, so it is important to develop some type of communication system, such as an individual clipboard that includes all of the students' vital information.

5. Maintain a flexible system of scheduling paraprofessionals and volunteers. Their schedules should be posted so that they know their assignments (e.g., which student, curricular area, or learning station).

Figure 5.5 is an example of a "Volunteer Observation Form" used in the Data-Based Gymnasium program. This form is used to observe volunteers and provide them with feedback regarding their ability to deliver physical activity services to children with severe handicapping conditions.

Regular Physical Education Teacher

With the passage of PL 94-142 more and more students identified as having disabilities including those with mild mental retardation, are receiving physical education services in the mainstream. Regular PE teachers must be prepared to effectively meet the needs of this group.

This professional's job role is discussed in detail in chapter 6.

Special/Adapted Physical Education Teacher

The law mandates physical education as a direct service to all students identified as having disabilities, including those with mental retardation. This alone makes the educational role of the special/adapted PE teacher most important. Special/adapted physical education is movement based, designed to allow each person to reach her or his full potential while developing a positive attitude toward, and a lifetime interest in, physical activity (see Figure 5.6).

The term *special/adapted physical education* is used in this textbook. Many professionals believe the term *adapted physical education* is limiting in defining the role of the professional trained to deliver physical education services to persons with disabilities, including persons with mental retardation. These professionals believe *special physical education* is a more appropriate term because it is not limited to the one area (adapted) but includes as well the components of corrective and developmental physical education (Lavay & French, 1985). A definition and example for each component of special physical education follows.

- *Adapted physical education.* This part of the program has the same goals and objectives as the traditional PE program but makes modifications and "adapts" when necessary to effectively meet the needs of the individual. For example, if a child with Down syndrome is exhibiting difficulty striking a pitched ball, the instructor may substitute different equipment by using a batting tee and a larger bat.

- *Corrective physical education.* This part of the program designs appropriate exercises and activities to rehabilitate deficiencies in a person's body alignment and mechanics. For example, an instructor, with the

Volunteer: _____   Date: _____

Student: _____   Program: _____

Observer: _____   Cue (verbal): _____

Time: _____ to _____   Cue (nonverbal): _____

Correction procedure: _____

Criterion: _____

Behavior (phase/step): _____

Reinforcers: _____

Student hand preference: _____

	Yes	No
1. Volunteer has correct materials	☐	☐
2. Materials, volunteer, and data sheet in best position for presentation	☐	☐
3. Student in correct position	☐	☐
4. Student's hearing aid is checked for correct setting before session begins	☐	☐

Cues					Consequences													Data	
					Positive reinforcers							Correction procedures & punishers						Recorded	
Appropriate	No cue	Weak	Change wording	Repeated	Appropriate	No reinforcer	Fail to pair	Weak	Delayed (2 s)	Inappropriate	Appropriate	No correction/ punisher	Delayed	Inappropriate	No	Cue	Help	Reinforcer	Correct	Incorrect

Cues:
Appropriate
Total
_____ equals
_____ %

Consequences:
Appropriate
Total
_____ equals
_____ %

Data:
Correct
Total
_____ equals
_____ %

Positive feedback:

1.

2.

3.

Recommendations for improvement:

1.

2.

3.

Figure 5.5 Volunteer observation form.

Note. From *Physical Education for the Severely Handicapped: A Systematic Approach to Data-Based Gymnasium* (p. 103) by J.M. Dunn, J.W. Moorehouse, and H.D. Fredericks, 1986, Austin, TX: PRO-ED. Reprinted by permission of PRO-ED, Inc.

Figure 5.6 The primary role of the special/adapted physical education teacher is to provide movement-based experiences for children with special needs. Photo courtesy of Bob Fraley.

physician's knowledge, may develop an individualized exercise program to assist in the remediation of functional scoliosis in a child who has severe mental retardation.

• *Developmental physical education.* This part of the program emphasizes the development of fundamental motor patterns and the components of physical fitness for students who are below the desired levels for their age-group peers. For example, an instructor may design movement experiences that reinforce fundamental locomotor and object-control skills for preschool-age children with mild mental retardation. Improvement in this area may assist these individuals to be successfully mainstreamed into a regular physical education program (see Highlight 5.5).

The role of the specialist in special/adapted physical education is changing and will continue to change. During the next decade the specialist's role will expand in a variety of ways. The specialist will primarily provide direct instructional services to those with more severe disabilities and to the preschool-age population. The concept of all students with a particular disability being taught in one particular school (e.g., all children with moderate and severe mental retardation attending a segregated school) is being, and will continue to be, phased out. Students with severe disabilities will attend the school located in their neighborhood. Therefore, the itinerant specialist, no longer assigned to one school, will be the norm—traveling among, and providing services to, a number of schools. Consequently, this specialist's job role will become more complex, incorporating multiple functions such as consulting, team teaching, and providing inservice workshops (see Figure 5.7). The specialist will need expertise in providing services to a variety of students with special needs, including students with mild to profound mental retardation. The delivery of physical education to students with mild disabilities will become primarily the responsibility of the regular physical education teacher. The specialist will provide support services by serving as a consultant or by team teaching with this professional. More information on mainstreaming is presented in chapter 6.

Therapeutic Recreation Specialist

PL 94-142 includes lifetime sport (leisure) in the definition of physical education and recognizes therapeutic recreation as a related service, provided when necessary, to assist students to reach prescribed educational goals. The primary concern of the therapeutic recreation specialist is to provide leisure services to individuals with disabilities (Howe-Murphy & Charboneau, 1987). These services can be offered to persons with mental retardation in a number of different settings such as schools, special camps, community recreation and park departments,

HIGHLIGHT 5.5

IN THEORY

Special Physical Education

Special physical education is a division of PE designed to meet the needs of individuals with movement difficulties. The intent of the special physical education program is to assist in the total development of the individual. The program is motor based, designed to enable each person to reach her or his full potential while developing a positive attitude and lifetime interests in physical activity.

The Components of Special Physical Education

Special physical education consists of three component parts—adapted, corrective, and developmental. Appropriate program-component emphasis is determined by evaluation and student need.

Adapted Physical Education—Adapted physical education has the same goals and objectives as the regular PE program but makes modifications and "adapts" when necessary to effectively meet the needs of the individual.

Corrective Physical Education—Corrective physical education involves designing appropriate exercises and activities to rehabilitate deficiencies in a person's body alignment and mechanics.

Developmental Physical Education—Developmental physical education emphasizes the development of fundamental motor patterns and the components of physical fitness for students who are below the desired level for their age-group peers.

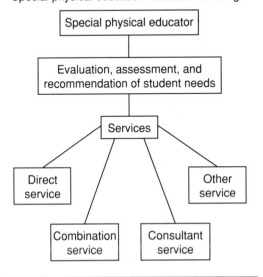

Special physical education instructional design

Figure 5.7 Special physical education service delivery model.

sheltered workshops, group homes, hospitals, and nursing homes.

The National Therapeutic Recreation Society, established in 1966, adopted a position statement in 1982 that defines the purpose, role, and services of therapeutic recreation as

> . . . facilitat[ing] the development, maintenance, and expression of an appropriate leisure lifestyle for individuals with physical, mental, emotional, and social limitations. Accordingly the purpose is accomplished through the provision of professional programs and services which assist the client in eliminating barriers to leisure, developing leisure skills and attitudes, and optimizing leisure involvement. . . . Three specific areas of professional services are employed to provide the comprehensive leisure ability approach toward enabling appropriate leisure lifestyles: therapy, leisure

education, and recreation participation. While these three areas of service have unique purposes in relation to client need, they each employ similar delivery processes using assessment or identification of client need, development of a related program strategy, and monitoring and evaluating client outcomes. (Shivers & Fait, 1985, pp. 330-331)

Although Winslow (1989) believes this position statement has provided specialists in the profession with a proper direction, he also feels that a more uniform and universally accepted defintion is necessary. For this reason the therapeutic recreation section of the California Park and Recreation Society has recently adopted a definition it believes clearly communicates the purpose of the profession to various target audiences: "Therapeutic recreation is a helping profession which promotes wellness and improves the quality of life through leisure" (p. 11). Winslow feels that the unique element in defining therapeutic recreation is the term *leisure*. "Leisure is the vehicle by which therapeutic recreation professionals deliver their services from those of other helping professions. No other helping profession utilizes the leisure concept to achieve [its] goal" (p. 12).

Leisure services can assist in the total growth of persons with mental retardation in a variety of ways. These individuals have an abundance of free time. Through structured leisure activities, this specialist can assist in developing appropriate and constructive use of their leisure time. For example, rather than spend their free time sitting idly in front of the television, a group of adults with mental retardation living in a group home can become involved in such leisure pursuits as participating in a community-based bowling league. Leisure activities can serve as a vehicle to move individuals with mental retardation toward normalization and integration, helping them lead more normal, independent, and functional lives in the community. The

specialist can develop community-based recreational programs to help integrate these persons into the mainstream of society. This involvement will in turn give these individuals the opportunity to receive positive visual exposure and, it is to be hoped, acceptance into the community. Finally, persons with mental retardation should have an abundance of recreational activities for the simple reason that they are enjoyable and fun and allow all involved to feel good about themselves while deriving pleasure and feelings of self-worth. Sherrill (1986) believes that without such leisure competencies, most persons lead entirely passive lives and are unable to maintain physical and mental health.

Occupational Therapist

PL 94-142 recognizes occupational therapy as a related service that is required when it is determined by the IEP team that it will aid the individual in more effectively meeting educational goals. The occupational therapy program is designed to assist individuals in minimizing disabilities by obtaining maximum independence. This specialist provides services to individuals whose abilities to cope with tasks of daily living are impaired, and certainly many persons with mental retardation fit this category. Occupational therapy is based on the belief that the quality of daily living over the life span can be improved for all persons through meaningful activities that include self-care, work, and leisure (Abbott, Franciscus, & Weeks, 1988). To qualify as a registered occupational therapist (OTR) or registered as a certified occupational therapist assistant (COTA), a person must graduate from an accredited or approved occupational therapy educational program and successfully complete a national certification examination developed by the American Occupational Therapy Association Certification Board.

Although this specialist still provides services primarily within a medical model, recently a new direction has emerged with an emphasis on health rather than illness and on the prevention of dysfunction and the maintenance of function. Health care delivery services have been established in medical, community, and educational settings. Professionals working in occupational therapy are primarily concerned with the component of performance necessary to maintain the individual's self-care, work, and leisure activities. According to Abbott et al. (1988), three of the major components provided by these professionals are "(a) motor functioning (range of motion, muscle strength, tone, functional use, gross and fine motor skills); (b) sensory integrative functioning (body integration, body scheme, posture, visual-spatial awareness, sensorimotor integration, reflex and sensory development); (c) cognitive functioning (verbal and written communication, concentration, problem solving, time management, conceptualization, integration of learning)" (p. 4-5). Highlight 5.6 presents two examples of an occupational therapist working in the public schools and assisting a person with mental retardation to more effectively meet educational goals.

Physical Therapist

PL 94-142 also recognizes physical therapy as a related service that is required when there is an identified need for it. A physical therapist provides services to students on a one-to-one basis and primarily on a medical setting. Before passage of PL 94-142, only 5% of all physical therapists were working in the public schools; today this number has doubled to 10%. To secure a license as a physical therapist (RPT) or physical therapist assistant (ARPT), a person must graduate from an accredited professional program and successfully complete a licensure examination developed by the American Physical Therapy Association Certification Board.

The physical therapy program is designed to provide the identification, prevention, remediation, and rehabilitation of acute or prolonged movement dysfunction in the individual. Treatment is by physical means, evaluating patients and treating through physical therapeutic measures as opposed to medicines, surgery, or radiation

---

| HIGHLIGHT 5.6 | **IN THEORY** |

Role of the Occupational Therapist

An occupational therapist may be involved in working with a young child with Down syndrome, who is enrolled in an early intervention program and is slow to develop, by assisting in the development of the muscle tone and movement patterns necessary for this child to perform with minimal assistance such daily living skills as sitting, walking, dressing, eating, and manipulating play equipment. Another important job function of the occupational therapist is recommending or making adaptations to special equipment. For example, after evaluating a teenage boy with moderate mental retardation and spastic cerebral palsy, this specialist might design a special fitted chair that enables the child to feel more comfortable while performing classroom activities. The student can now perform desk activities without increased distractibility, because his muscles will not tighten, become fatigued, or cause additional spasms.

(American Physical Therapy Association, 1986). Physical therapy programs are based on a belief in maximizing functional independence and the quality of daily living through the therapeutic application of exercise. The following are most of the services recognized by the American Physical Therapy Association (1986):

- Evaluation and assessment, with special emphasis on the function of the musculoskeletal, neuromuscular, respiratory, and vascular systems
- Assessment and training in locomotion that includes the use of orthotic, prosthetic, and assistive devices
- Assessment and interpretation of measurements to determine pathophysiological, pathokinesiological, and developmental deficits as they relate to physical dysfunction or pain resulting from disease, injury, or other health impairments
- Development and implementation of therapeutic intervention techniques that focus on locomotion, posture, flexibility, endurance, cardiovascular function, balance, coordination, joint mobility, pain, and functional abilities in daily life
- Application of modalities including, but not limited to, cold, heat, air, light, sound, water, mobilization, massage, bronchopulmonary hygiene, and therapeutic exercise with or without assistive devices

Montgomery (1981) provides the following example of a physical therapist employed in the public schools. This therapist is assisting a school-age boy with mental retardation who displays the gait pattern of a normal 10- to 12-month-old child. This child may walk with his legs abducted in a wide base and his arms extended and spread out to protect himself from falling. To meet this child's educational goal of walking, this specialist must stress the process of ambulation, assisting the child to maintain proper head control, trunk rotation within the body axis, development of righting reactions,

and setting his hands free for support. The physical therapist might place the boy upright and assist him, during ambulation, manually or with a walker, parallel bars, or other devices.

Parental Involvement

Too often in the maze of available services offered to the child, the positive contribution parents can make is forgotten! However, for some time now parental involvement has been advocated and successfully implemented in the area of special education, although this concept is fairly new to physical education (Folsom-Meeks, 1984). Parent involvement, or home-based activity training, is simply defined as parents and/or siblings providing physical activity to the children outside of the school physical education setting. Parents' active involvement in their child's physical activity program is important for a variety of reasons. PL 94-142 advocates parent involvement in students' individualized educational plans. Parents have a right to know about, as well as to get involved in, their child's educational program, including the area of physical education. Instructing children with special needs can be complex, and professionals must realize that parents can serve as a valuable resource. Parents spend the greatest amount of time with the child and in all likelihood understand her or his needs best. For example, parents can be helpful in providing vital case-history information such as when the child did or did not meet certain developmental milestones. Many youngsters, especially those with severe disabilities have special needs that require intense and extra program instruction (Dunn et al., 1986). Too often, adequate instruction cannot be accomplished in one or two periods a week of physical education instruction. Required is the extra effort and support a home-based activity program can provide. Still another justification for parent programs is that parents' involvement can serve as a valuable public relations tool. Parents who become educated about the positive benefits a quality program of physical activity can provide toward their child's total educational growth are more likely to become valuable advocates of the program.

Parental Involvement Programs

In physical education, homework in the form of instructional packages has been used as a supportive technique. French (1979) and Bishop and Horvat (1984) provide examples of various assignments that can be provided to parents to expand the child's physical education program of instruction. Figure 5.8 is an example of a home-based activity assignment.

Other parent programs that have successfully offered physical activity to children with special needs include these three:

- *Data-Based Gymnasium* (Dunn et al., 1986). Parents have been trained to administer this

Name _____   Date _____

	Exercises	S	M	T	W	T	F	S
	 1. Trunk twisters							
	 2. Toe touchers							
	 3. Mountain climbers							
	 4. Balance right foot, balance left foot							
	 5. Sitting stretch, touch toes while sitting							
	 6. Sit-ups							

Figure 5.8 The daily half dozen is an example of a homework assignment consisting of exercises designed for younger students to complete each day under their parents' supervision.

systematic and behavioral program of physical education to children with severe disabilities.

- *Let's Play to Grow* (Joseph P. Kennedy, Jr., Foundation, 1978). First implemented in 1977, this program provides parents with guidelines and materials necessary to involve youngsters with mental retardation in various play and leisure activities. Let's Play to Grow clubs were initiated as a network to enable volunteers and families of youngsters with mental retardation to come together to share leisure time and serve as a support group.
- *Sensory-Motor Experiences for the Home* (Seaman & DePauw, 1979). This is a manual designed to provide parents with information regarding sensory motor activities that can be done with their children. Also included is information for developing homemade equipment.

To date, little empirical research in home-based physical activity programs has been conducted, but in general, studies involving parents in home-based activity programs have demonstrated favorable gains in children's physical fitness and motor ability. For example, a parent-delivered home-based behavioral program implementing contingency contracts and parent-determined rewards was employed to improve the fitness levels of children identified as unfit. Results demonstrated that the program was effective in increasing the children's health-related physical fitness scores and physical activity levels (Taggert, Taggert, & Siedentop, 1986). In a study initiated by Bishop and Donnelly (1987), parent-delivered home-based physical activity was implemented with 11 obese children to determine the influence of the program on the children's physical activity levels, body composition, and cardiovascular endurance. The program proved to be an effective strategy in obesity management, as 9 of the 11 children increased their activity levels. In general, this area of research has been virtually unexplored regarding the parents of children with mental retardation. However, research by Dunn and associates (1986) demonstrated through a coordinated home/school program called the Lunch Box Data System that the acquisition time of motor skills for children identified as having severe disabilities doubled when compared to students who received school instruction alone.

Developing a Parent Program

Folsom-Meeks (1984) offers professionals the following general guidelines for developing a parent- or home-based physical activity program.

1. Initially, communicate with parents regarding the rationale for developing such a program. This initial dialogue can be accomplished at IEP meetings, parent-teacher conferences, and parent advocacy meetings and by written notes or phone conversations.
2. Conduct individual parent-teacher meetings to explain the intent of the program. At this time, skills can be chosen with the development of long-term goals and short-term objectives in mind. Parents should be involved in the selection of these goals. This is also a good time to explore with the parents strategies for motivating the child to participate in the program.
3. Next, parents should be trained to implement the program. This training should include such procedures as teaching and recording skills and implementing reinforcement systems. For example, chapter 4 of this text describes strategies for effectively administering positive reinforcers.
4. Throughout the administration of the program, the lines of communication must be kept open among all involved parties.

Follow-up phone calls, home visits, notes, and so forth allow effective communication between the professional and the parents.

5. Group meetings may prove motivational and serve as a support group for parents to share mutual issues and concerns.

Providing physical activity to children with mental retardation, especially those who with severe disabilities requires a collective effort by all involved. By developing and implementing a home-based activity program, professionals and parents can begin to take steps to assure that these children are given the amount of training necessary to foster the positive benefits of physical activity.

Programming for Individuals With Severe or Profound Mental Retardation

It is often difficult for professionals to determine what physical activity services are available and whether they are effective for persons with severe and profound mental retardation. In addition, Dunn and associates (1986) have cautioned that developing individualized programs of physical activity is usually easier for mildly disabled students than it is for students with more severe conditions, such as severe mental retardation or multiple disabilities. With the mandate of PL 94-142 and the trend toward deinstitutionalization, more severely disabled individuals are being, and will continue in the future to be, placed in the mainstream of society. Therefore, it is of paramount importance that professionals be adequately trained and prepared to serve this population to meet their unique needs.

Professionals who deliver physical activity services must have the following instructional program competencies (Jansma, 1988):

1. A thorough understanding of normal and abnormal processes of growth and development (e.g., reflexes and rudimentary movements).

2. Ability to effectively work in a team approach. The more severe the condition, the more likely a team of specialists will work with the child. The specialist providing physical activity to the student must take an active and major role on the team.

3. Knowledge of specific psychomotor assessment tools to use with this population. Chapter 3 of this textbook provides the reader with information regarding specific assessment instruments to use with this particular population. Professionals must also understand strategies for collecting ongoing student information such as applied behavior analysis. Individuals with severe disabilities are a very heterogeneous group and may require individualized teacher-constructed assessment instruments.

4. Ability to task-analyze skills.

5. Ability to plan programs that incorporate functional skills and to teach skills that help this population perform as independently as possible in the school, home, and community.

6. Ability to develop activities that are age-appropriate (see chapter 7). Activities must never be insulting, given a participant's age—for example, adults with severe mental retardation being instructed to play such games as Duck Duck Goose.

7. Knowledge of behavior management techniques that not only control inappropriate behavior but are used to motivate this population to reach their full movement potential.

8. Ability to use with this population techniques that may rarely be employed with other groups, such as proper lifting, carrying, and positioning.

9. Awareness of unique safety considerations, such as the wearing of helmets by students who have frequent seizures.
10. Ability to utilize and adapt equipment such as bolsters and standing platforms.
11. Awareness of pedagogical models specific to this population, such as Data-Based gymnasium, I CAN, and Project Transition (see chapter 3).

Summary

Developing programs of physical activity for persons with mental retardation can be quite complex. This chapter describes the various types of professional physical activity services available to persons with mental retardation. Professionals who provide these services must work closely together to ensure that the program promotes the individual's total development and enhances her or his quality of life. When they are systematically developed and prescribed, physical activity programs can make important contributions to physical growth and development, movement proficiency, overall health, vocational skills, worthy use of leisure time, and socially acceptable interaction with others.

Since the passage of PL 94-142 of 1975, the quality of physical activity services provided to persons identified as mentally retarded has been greatly enhanced. The law mandates that physical education is a direct service and must be provided to all students identified as having disabilities. Related services such as occupational therapy, physical therapy, and therapeutic recreation are available to students only when they are necessary for reaching prescribed educational goals. The law also mandates that each child shall receive a well-written individualized education plan (IEP) that includes the following information.

1. A statement of the individual's present level of performance
2. A statement of annual goals
3. A list of short-term behavioral objectives
4. Projected dates for initiating services and the anticipated time required for achieving these goals
5. Strategies and materials for achieving these goals
6. A statement of the specific educational and related services that will be provided to the student
7. The extent to which the student will participate in regular education

Because providing effective services to persons with mental retardation, especially those with severe and profound disabilities can be very complicated, no one professional should be expected to have all the knowledge necessary to effectively meet the unique needs of each individual. Various professionals who provide services to persons with mental retardation must work closely while maintaining an open dialogue and sharing information. One way this can occur is if professionals are knowledgeable of their own job roles as well as those of other team members, all of whom may be singly or collectively responsible for providing physical activity services to persons with mental retardation and therefore need to work together in a transdisciplinary approach.

It is also important to develop a parent- or home-based activity training program. Including parents is a fairly new concept in physical education, but many children with severe disabilities have special needs that require intense and extra program instruction that parents can help provide. Finally this chapter discussed strategies and professional competencies necessary for delivering physical activity services to persons with severe conditions such as severe mental retardation with secondary conditions.

DISCUSSIONS AND NEW DIRECTIONS

1. What effects will future changes in legislation have on the competencies necessary for professionals to provide physical activity to persons with mental retardation? Will these changes expand each professional's job role and make it more complex? To effectively meet these future challenges, how should prospective students in university training programs (e.g., special/adapted physical education, occupational therapy, physical therapy, therapeutic recreation) be trained?

2. Given the variety of professionals involved in the transdisciplinary model approach, is it realistic to assume that this is the most effective method to deliver student services? If so, what steps must be taken to assure the success of this model? If not, what alternative models are available?

3. Can home-based physical activity programs be effectively implemented to children with mental retardation to enhance their physical fitness and motor performance? What type of training will be necessary for the parents of the children? What type of instructional packages should be developed to support parents in their implementation efforts?

References

Abbott, M., Franciscus, M., & Weeks, Z.R. (1988). *Opportunities in occupational therapy careers.* Lincolnwood IL: National Textbook.

American Physical Therapy Association. (1986). *Definition and guidelines.* Alexandria, VA: Author.

Bishop, P., & Donnelly, J.E. (1987). Home based activity program for obese children. *American Corrective Therapy Journal*, **41**, 12-19.

Bishop, P., & Horvat, M.A. (1984). Effects of home instruction on the physical and motor performance of a clumsy child. *American Corrective Therapy Journal*, **38**, 6-10.

Campbell, P.H., Bellamy, G.T., & Bishop, K.K. (1988). Statewide intervention systems: An overview of the new federal program for infants and toddlers with handicaps. *Journal of Special Education*, **22**, 25-40.

Croce, R., & Lavay, B. (1985). Now more than ever: Physical education for the elementary school-aged child. *Physical Educator*, **42**, 52-58.

Dunn, J.M., Moorehouse, J.W., & Fredericks, H.D. (1986). *Physical education for the severely handicapped: A systematic approach to data-based gymnasium.* Austin, TX: PRO-ED.

Eichstaedt, C.B., & Kalakian, L.H. (1987). *Developmental/adapted physical education: Making ability count.* New York: Macmillan.

Folsom-Meeks, S.L. (1984). Parents: The forgotten teacher's aid in adapted physical education. *Adapted Physical Activity*, **1**, 275-281.

French, R. (1979). The use of homework as a supportive technique in physical education. *Physical Educators*, **36**, 84-88.

French, R.W., & Jansma, P. (1992). *Special physical education.* Columbus, OH: Merrill.

Hart, V. (1977). The use of many disciplines with the severely and profoundly handicapped. In Sontag, E., Smith, J., & Certo, N. (Eds.), *Educational programming for the severely and profoundly handicapped.* Reston, VA: Division of Mental Retardation, Council for Exceptional Children.

Howe-Murphy, R., & Charboneau, B.G. (1987). *Therapeutic recreation intervention: An ecological perspective.* Englewood Cliffs, NJ: Prentice Hall.

Jansma, P. (1988). Teacher training in adapted physical education for the severely and profoundly handicapped student. In C. Sherrill (Ed.), *Leadership training in adapted physical education* (pp. 423-438). Champaign, IL: Human Kinetics.

Joseph P. Kennedy, Jr., Foundation. (1978). *Let's play-to-grow.* Washington, DC: Author.

Lavay, B. (1988a). Clarity of misconceptions regarding the implementation of adapted/special physical education as determined by PL 94-142. *Kansas Association of Health, Physical Education, Recreation and Dance Journal,* **56**(2), 15-16.

Lavay, B. (1988b). The special physical educator: Communicating effectively in a team approach. In P. Bishop (Ed.), *Adapted physical education: A resource manual* (pp. 34-40). Kearney, NE: Educational System.

Lavay, B., & French, R. (1985). The special physical educator: Meeting education goals through a transdisciplinary approach. *American Corrective Therapy Journal,* **39**, 77-81.

Lavay, B., & Sayers-Lavay, P. (1988). Incorporating movement activities in the special education classroom. In P. Bishop (Ed.), *Adapted physical education: A resource manual* (pp. 223-228). Kearney, NE: Educational System.

Montgomery, P.C. (1981). Assessment and treatment of the child with mental retardation: Guidelines for physical therapists. *Physical Therapy,* **61**, 1265-1271.

Seaman, J.A., & DePauw, K.P. (1979). *Sensory motor experiences for the home.* Los Angeles: Trident Shop.

Seaman, J.A., & DePauw, K.P. (1989). *The new adapted physical education: A developmental approach.* Palo Alto, CA: Mayfield.

Sears, C.J. (1982). The transdisciplinary approach: A process for the compliance with Public Law 94-142. *Journal of the Association for the severely Handicapped,* **6**, 22-29.

Sherrill, C. (1986). *Adapted physical education and recreation: A multidisciplinary approach.* Dubuque, IA: Brown.

Shivers, J.S., & Fait, H.F. (1985). *Special recreational services therapeutic and adapted.* Philadelphia: Lea & Febiger.

Taggert A.C., Taggert, J., & Siedentop, D. (1984). Effects of home-based activity programs: A study with low fitness elementary school children. *Behavior Modification,* **10**, 487-507.

U.S. Office of Education. Federal Register. The Individuals With Disabilities Education Act, formerly The Education for All Handicapped Children Act of 1975, Section 94-142, 99-457, 89-750, 42 U.S.C., Section 42480-54579, (1977).

Vogler, E.W., French R., & Bishop, P. (1989). Paraprofessionals: Implications for adapted physical education. *Physical Educator,* **46**, 69-76.

Winslow, R.M. (1989). Therapeutic recreation: Promoting wellness through leisure. *California Association for Health, Physical Education, Recreation and Dance Journal,* **51**(6), 11-12.

CHAPTER 6

Mainstreaming: Program Considerations

PREVIEW   Penny, who is 13 years old and has mild mental retardation, has been assigned for the first time to a seventh-grade regular physical education class.
The first 6 weeks of the class have been difficult for both Penny and the regular
physical education instructor. With each passing week the instructor has become more and more frustrated, as Penny seems confused when directions
are given and stands around during class activities. Even more frustrating
to the instructor is the fact that for the past 2 weeks a few of the students
have begun to tease Penny because she moves slowly and awkwardly. The
instructor feels he has not been adequately trained to handle this situation.
This problem is further compounded by the fact that the instructor is uncertain where to turn for answers to the following questions and concerns. Is
this the right physical education class for Penny? If Penny is going to spend
the remainder of the school year in this class, how can she become more

involved with class activities? How can Penny receive the individual attention she needs without the rest of the students in class being neglected? Finally, during group activities, how can the entire class get along and participate with Penny?

HIGHLIGHT QUESTIONS

- **Why are mainstreaming experiences important for persons with mental retardation?**
- **Is there a difference between mainstreaming and placing a student in the least restrictive environment?**
- **What physical education placement alternatives are available to children with mental retardation attending the public schools?**
- **What preprogramming strategies should professionals consider to assure all involved a successful mainstreaming experience?**
- **Once the child with mental retardation has been mainstreamed into a regular physical education class, what specific strategies are available to assist professionals?**
- **Are various teaching styles available to meet the unique movement needs and ability levels of children with mental retardation?**
- **What factors should be considered when integrating persons with mental retardation into community-based leisure programs?**

Many professionals have the questions and share the concerns of the regular physical educator in the chapter 6 Preview. Successful mainstreaming will not come about by chance. Mainstreaming is a very complicated process that has often been misunderstood and abused. In too many situations ineffective mainstreaming has turned regular PE classes into mere dumping grounds for persons with mental retardation (Lavay, 1987). Unfortunately, children are often mainstreamed for all the wrong reasons: to save time, facilities, personnel, and money. Sadly, this often leaves students with mental retardation standing on the sidelines of the gymnasium or keeping score instead of participating in games. However, when mainstreaming is administered properly, it has many benefits for both students without disabilities and students with mental retardation. This chapter focuses on mainstreaming in terms of benefits, terminology, placement alternatives, preprogram-

ming considerations, and specific strategies that can make this a positive experience for all involved. Mainstreaming for persons with mental retardation also extends to extracurricular activities such as community-based activities and Special Olympics, which are discussed in chapters 10 and 12.

Benefits of Mainstreaming

When mainstreaming is properly planned and carefully administered, it has positive benefits for everyone involved, including these outlined by Lavay (1987):

1. Research demonstrates generally that many students with mild mental retardation perform more like their peers without disabilities in physical activity than in other academic areas. Effective teaching

strategies specific to physical activity (which are discussed later in this chapter) can be used to promote positive mainstreaming experiences.

2. Many (although not all) persons with mental retardation are motivated to perform better in the presence of their peers without disabilities than in the presence of the instructor. These persons may relate to, be more motivated by, and consequently perform better for someone their own age.

3. Students without disabilities, by displaying appropriate movement and social skills, can serve as effective role models for persons with mental retardation, who might seldom witness such skilled performances in anyone their own age if they are always grouped only with other persons who also have mental retardation.

4. By enabling them to interact socially with individuals who do not have disabilities, mainstreaming gives persons with mental retardation abundant opportunities to adjust to "real life" situations that accord with the principles of normalization. Dunn and Fait (1989) believe this process of normalization can help persons with mental retardation lead more normal and productive lives.

5. By working closely with this population, persons without disabilities learn to respect rather than pity persons with mental retardation, which in turn affords persons with mental retardation opportunities to reach their full potential while making positive and productive contributions to society. For example, in a study by Hamilton and Anderson (1983), the attitudes of nondisabled university students toward persons with disabilities were significantly improved through participation in mainstreamed leisure activites such as wheelchair basketball and 10-pin bowling.

A great deal of research has investigated the advantages and disadvantages of mainstreaming in the classroom (Hallahan & Kauffman, 1982), but little of it focuses on the area of physical activity (Dunn & Craft, 1985; Watkinson & Titus, 1985). Research specific to the effects of mainstreaming on the motor performance of persons with mental retardation is extremely limited. In an account of a field-based research study, Rarick and colleagues found positive motor performance gains in children with moderate mental retardation who participated in a mainstreamed physical education program. These positive gains occurred without adversely affecting the learning outcomes of the nondisabled peers in the class (Rarick & Beuter, 1985).

The Least Restrictive Environment Versus Mainstreaming

The intent of the Individuals With Disabilities Education Act was to place students 3 to 21 years of age identified as having disabilities in least restrictive environments. The *least restrictive environment* is defined as the setting in which the individual can most adequately function. This placement must be based on the person's present level of performance and needs as outlined on the individualized educational plan (see chapter 5). However, there is widespread confusion over the difference between placement in least restrictive environments and mainstreaming. Nowhere does the law refer to mainstreaming. Public Law 94-142 clearly states that

> to the maximum extent possible and when appropriate, handicapped children, . . . are educated with children who are nonhandicapped and that special classes, separate schooling or other removal of handicapped children from the regular educational environment occurs only when the nature or severity of the handicap is such that education in regular classes with the use of supplementary aids and services cannot be achieved satisfactorily. (p. 42497)

The key to this statement is the words *when appropriate*. It is not always appropriate for a child with mental retardation to be mainstreamed (Lavay & DePaepe, 1987). In fact, for a child with severe mental retardation, the regular class setting may be the *most* restrictive environment, for the child will be unable to function well in an environment where his or her needs cannot be met. An alternative placement such as special/adapted physical education must be provided. Ironically, too many schools do not have placement alternatives available for youngsters with disabilities. Mainstreaming has become dictated by financial constraints and administrative convenience.

Placement Alternatives and Criteria

For children with mental retardation, mainstreaming must be viewed never as an automatic placement option but rather as one of a number of available placement alternatives. A continuum of services must be made available. Morreau and Eichstaedt (1983) suggest the following placement alternatives:

1. Adapted physical education program with modified activities
2. Adapted physical education program with regular class activities
3. Regular physical education program with a part-time adapted class
4. Regular physical education program with adapted activities
5. Regular physical education program

Figure 6.1 presents an example of a physical education least-restrictive-environment flowchart that has been used in a large school district in the Southwest. A variety of placement alternatives are included, ranging from full-time placement in a special physical education class to placement in a regular physical education program without any assistance.

Placement alternatives must be based on sound assessment practices to determine the individual's present level of performance. Only when the individual's needs are determined can the proper placement alternative be selected. Each person's individual needs must be appropriately matched with existing placement options. The placement alternatives offered must be capable of modification to successfully meet each individual's unique needs. For example, a child with mild mental retardation might be placed in a full-time special physical education program early in the school year but be provided there, by the special/adapted physical education instructor, with selected activities to prepare the child for a transition to the regular physical education setting. When the child's present level of performance is adequate for regular PE activities, this child may be ready to be mainstreamed. However, assuring mainstreaming success is not simple, and more factors must be taken into account. The next two sections of this chapter discuss specific preprogramming and teaching considerations to assist in this mainstreaming process.

Preprogramming Considerations

Lavay and DePaepe (1987) believe that the key to successful mainstreaming is proper planning and program preparation by all involved professionals—which requires that all professionals involved must effectively cooperate and communicate with one another. Lavay and DePaepe offer a variety of preplanning strategies that must be carefully considered before the student actually enters the mainstream setting. It is important to realize that different settings (e.g., a physical education program, an after-school recreation program) involve different circumstances and therefore require different strategies.

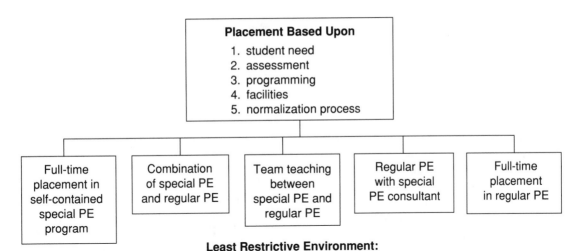

Placement Based Upon

1. student need
2. assessment
3. programming
4. facilities
5. normalization process

| Full-time placement in self-contained special PE program | Combination of special PE and regular PE | Team teaching between special PE and regular PE | Regular PE with special PE consultant | Full-time placement in regular PE |

Least Restrictive Environment:

a. It is not a place but rather a philosophy.
b. The educational direct and related services for children with handicaps are effectively met.
c. This type of child has a wide range of abilities.
d. This continuum of services may be constantly changing, based on a number of different factors: student needs, programming, facilities, and the normalization process.
e. PL 94-142 states that to the maximum extent possible and when appropriate, the child with handicaps should be educated with the nonhandicapped students.
f. The least restrictive environment is not always mainstreaming!

Figure 6.1   Least restrictive environment flowchart.

Regular Physical Education Teacher

Recent research has demonstrated that if mainstreaming is to be a positive experience for all involved, the attitude of the regular physical education teacher toward the individual to be mainstreamed may be the most critical factors (Aloia, Knutson, Minner, & Von Seggern, 1980; Rizzo, 1984). Legislation can be passed to make facilities and programs accessible to persons with mental retardation, but laws cannot legislate positive attitude changes (Price, 1986). However, a favorable attitude toward the person being mainstreamed will carry over not only to the person being mainstreamed, but to the other persons involved in the program.

Many regular physical educators feel inadequately prepared to effectively provide physical activity to persons with special needs. Lavay and DePaepe (1987) have cautioned that the fear of the unknown can cause more strain for these professionals than the actual process of mainstreaming persons with mental retardation into their programs. However, it is true that most regular physical educators do not receive adequate preservice or inservice training in specific teaching techniques and modifications necessary to effectively meet the needs of students with a wide range of ability levels. It is critical that university preservice course work and teacher inservice programs include instruction by professionals with expertise in this area. PE professionals need to be confident and have a positive attitude toward providing physical activity services for all persons, including those with mental retardation (Lavay & Pizarro, 1987). Later in this chapter we will describe specific mainstreaming program strategies that have been successful in applied settings.

Special Physical Education Teacher

It is paramount that the special physical education teacher work closely and in cooperation with the regular physical educator, for the special PE professional is an important link between the person being mainstreamed and the regular PE teacher. The special physical education teacher should assess the person to be mainstreamed, determining strengths and needs. Based on this assessment a student profile for mainstreaming can be developed (see Highlight 6.1). The successful profile provides the teacher or the administrator of the program with vital information regarding the person to be mainstreamed and helps ensure a positive mainstreaming experience. For example, during a typical school day the regular physical educator teaches a great number of students. The teacher could use the profile to determine that the student with mental retardation who is to be mainstreamed has poor physical fitness and locomotor skills but adequate object control skills and social skills. This knowledge helps the instructor, because program modifications can begin based on this profile, and initial programming can focus on providing activities geared to the student's strengths.

The special physical education instructor who teaches students in a self-contained setting must provide these students with activities that prepare them for a smooth transition into the mainstreamed environment at a later date. For example, peer acceptance is often predicated on proper game and sport skills performance. Therefore, to prepare the student for the mainstreaming experience the special physical education teacher must teach to the areas of physical fitness and motor performance that are the building blocks to adequate performance in games and sport (see chapter 7). It is also important to teach social skills, as this will help the children being mainstreamed to be better accepted by their peers in the new environment.

Scheduling Facilities and Programs

Too often mainstreaming is based on administrative issues, such as facility availability and scheduling convenience, rather than what is best for the student being mainstreamed. For all professionals involved to be cooperative and flexible is the key to resolving these scheduling and facility conflicts. An effective strategy to help avoid these problems and that has met with success in certain school districts is the use of the Regular Physical Education Class Profile for Mainstreaming (see Highlight 6.2). This profile is effective because it allows the regular physical educator's input into the mainstreaming process by briefly citing the type of program offered, the support personnel needed, and the most advantageous class periods for mainstreaming.

Mainstream Classes

It cannot be assumed that everyone in the mainstream setting will automatically accept and, more importantly, socially interact with the person to be mainstreamed. It is one thing to place a child with Down syndrome into a community recreation program, and quite another for this child to be accepted and chosen for play by the other children in the group. Mizen and Linton (1983) offer the following excellent strategies for preparing the nondisabled group or class for the arrival of the mainstreamed person.

1. Do not ignore individual differences; rather, these differences should be respected. Students should be made to realize that even though each person is unique, there are many similarities among us. All persons are different and alike.

2. Students should be encouraged to ask questions about various disabilities. For example, a few days before a student with Down syndrome who is to be mainstreamed arrives in class, the teacher can conduct a lesson and discuss with the class why some people have this condition. This

HIGHLIGHT 6.1	IN PRACTICE

Student Profile for Physical Education Mainstreaming Consideration

*To be answered by the special physical education instructor or classroom teacher and to be given to the regular PE teacher.

Student name:

Grade level:

Age:

School:

Contact teacher:

Health factor considerations (vision, hearing, medication, and/or other health impairments):

Briefly describe the student's present level of functioning (attach all student motor assessment and IEP information):
1. Fundamental movement ability
2. Physical fitness
3. Cognitive ability
4. Social and self-management skills
5. Behavior

List any teaching styles and behavior management techniques that may work effectively with this student:

Briefly list the desired student outcome(s) from the mainstreaming experience:

Student's class schedule and most appropriate period(s) for mainstreaming to occur (reasons why):

Note. From ''The Harbinger Helper: Why Mainstreaming in Physical Education Doesn't Always Work'' by B. Lavay and J. DePaepe, 1987, *Journal of Physical Education, Recreation and Dance,* **58**(7), pp. 98-103. The journal is a publication of the American Alliance for Health, Physical Education, Recreation and Dance, 1900 Association Drive, Reston, VA 22091. Reprinted by permission.

would also be an excellent time to conduct a class discussion regarding why people tease one another. With young children, class discussions can include such storybook characters as Tom Thumb.

3. A class session can be conducted in which students can learn and experience ''firsthand'' various disabilities. One such activity is to partner students, with one partner blindfolded and the other partner

---

HIGHLIGHT 6.2   **IN PRACTICE**

Regular Physical Education Class Profile for Mainstreaming

Name of student to be mainstreamed:

Regular physical education teacher:

Teacher schedule:

1. Briefly list the general physical education expectations of your students in the following areas.
   a. Motor ability (fundamental movements, physical fitness, sport-related skills):
   b. Social skills (ability to interact):
   c. Behavior (class rules):
   d. Cognitive ability (understanding game rules):

2. What type of support do you feel is needed to effectively facilitate the mainstreaming process with this student?
   a. Facilities and equipment
   b. Personnel:
      Consultation from specialist:
      Team teaching with specialist:
      Paraprofessional or aide:
      Peer tutor:

3. What period of the day or particular class do you feel would be most appropriate for the student to be mainstreamed? (State reasons)

Note. From ''The Harbinger Helper: Why Mainstreaming in Physical Education Doesn't Always Work'' by B. Lavay and J. DePaepe, 1987, *Journal of Physical Education, Recreation and Dance*, **58**(7), pp. 98-103. The journal is a publication of the American Alliance for Health, Physical Education, Recreation and Dance, 1900 Association Drive, Reston, VA 22091. Reprinted by permission.

---

helping her or him negotiate an obstacle course. Another activity is to have students practice throwing and catching a ball with their nondominant hand. After these activities the teacher can conduct a discussion and encourage class members to share their thoughts and experiences.

4. Another strategy that has been effective in a number of districts and recreational programs is to develop a handicap awareness day (Danaher, 1983). For example, a Saturday morning recreational program can be designed in which parents and children (with and without disabilities) participate side by side in various nontraditional games and recreational activities. Persons without disabilities learn about persons with disabilities when they participate with them.

The Mainstreamed Student

Ironically, students to be mainstreamed are often overlooked or not informed about their placement into the mainstream setting. Some students with mental retardation may be reluctant to join the regular physical education or recreational setting, especially if they have experienced failure in such settings in the past. Many of these students feel safe, secure, and protected within the confines of the small, self-contained group setting of special PE classes. The regular physical education teacher must realize that for some students with mental retardation, dropping a thrown ball, or falling while running, in front of peers can be absolutely devastating. The following instructional considerations can assist you in providing the mainstreamed student with a more productive and positive experience (Lavay, 1986; Mizen & Linton, 1983).

1. Be sensitive to the feelings of all the students involved in the program. Practices such as playing elimination games, choosing teams, and posting test scores usually result in embarrassment for students with low motor ability. Alternatives are to design games that include all participants, choose teams or squads beforehand, and post the most improved test scores.

2. With proper assessment the instructor can determine individual strengths and needs. Initially provide for positive experiences by teaching to the mainstreamed individual's strengths. Many persons with mental retardation have failed so often that they are reluctant to participate or try new activities. But participation in an atmosphere that promotes success will help the person build self-esteem and gain confidence.

3. Provide instruction that is tangible and concrete rather than abstract. For example, line the boundaries of an outdoor soccer field with cones and flags. It may be necessary to keep verbal instruction to a minimum and provide more demonstration and physical guidance.

4. Have some alternate activities prepared, because the attention span of these persons may be short.

5. When the mainstreamed student or group fails, it may be because the instructor is not using effective alternative activities or game modifications. Highlight 6.3 presents a variety of suggestions for effective-

ly modifying activities, games, and sport.

6. Allow the mainstreamed student or group time to adjust to the new setting. For example, show children the locations of all facilities, such as locker room, water fountain, and equipment.

7. Perhaps most importantly, do not become frustrated by the mainstreamed student's lack of skill learning or progress. Remember to be patient and have a positive attitude.

Specific Environmental Programming Strategies

How the environment is organized is critical to the success of mainstreaming. The instructor's work should consist mostly of preplanning and organizing the environment and instructional materials. The environment must be designed to be flexible and, most importantly, responsive to the individual's needs (see Figure 6.2). Sherrill (1986) has stated that individualization does not mean simply teaching on a one-to-one basis, but includes modifying the environment and adopting pedagogical approaches that are necessary to effectively meet each individual's needs.

Often the integration of students into a mainstream setting affects group dynamics, interpersonal relationships, and teacher instruction. There is no set formula for effective mainstreaming, but success is based on the instructor's having a strong conviction that each individual is unique and should be afforded the opportunity to reach her or his full potential. Therefore this section reviews a variety of teaching strategies and environments that have been effective in fostering positive mainstreaming experiences.

Teaching Styles

Every individual, especially those with mental retardation, has a wide array of movement abilities and needs. Therefore, the instructor must

HIGHLIGHT 6.3   **IN PRACTICE**

Strategies for Modifying Activities, Games, and Sport

The following is a general list of activity, game, and/or sport modifications that may assist in providing the mainstreamed student with a more productive and positive experience.

1. Design the environment to fit individual needs
   a. Lower the net in a volleyball game.
   b. Reduce the size of the playing field.
   c. Make boundaries more tangible (e.g., use cones, flags).

2. Modify and adapt equipment
   a. Use large, brightly colored foam balls.
   b. Use a batting tee rather than a pitcher.
   c. Use lighter and larger equipment.

3. Reduce the time limit of play
   a. Use frequent rest periods.
   b. Reduce the number of minutes played in a period.

4. Develop feedback and reinforcement techniques

   a. Insert buzzers or bells on goals to reinforce the concept of scoring.
   b. Reinforce children who display teamwork and share during play.

5. Specific playing positions require certain skills
   a. Rotate positions, giving each child an opportunity to learn and practice various skills.

6. Modify degrees of moving objects and mobility
   a. Have objects (e.g., balls) move slowly.
   b. Reduce the size of the playing area.
   c. Increase the number of children participating on a team.

8. Insure some form of success
   a. Avoid elimination games.
   b. Stress self-competition rather than team competition.

Figure 6.2 Modifications of equipment can help to facilitate successful mainstreaming experiences. Photo courtesy of Bob Fraley.

be able to use a variety of teaching styles. A teacher who lacks such flexibility and uses only one teaching style through the entire instructional session or curriculum unit is teaching to only a few student abilities and shortchanging the many students in class whose abilities, strengths, and weaknesses lie elsewhere. The continuum of teaching styles available to physical educators ranges from the command style, which is quite structured and teacher-centered, to the divergent movement style, in which the student assumes most of the responsibility for learning (Mossten, 1981). Table 6.1 briefly describes the six teaching styles elucidated by Mosston (1981) and their advantages and disadvantages.

Experts agree that ultimately the instructor should strive for maximum use of the divergent

Table 6.1   Teaching Styles

Style	Advantages	Disadvantages
Command: Each student performs to the same instruction at the same pace.	Effective with large groups and when instructional time is limited.	Doesn't meet individual student needs or foster creativity.
Task: The student is provided a single task or series of tasks to perform. Usually in the form of task cards.	Frees the instructor to move around the teaching area and assist students who require individual instruction.	Requires a great deal of teacher preparation, and some students can avoid becoming involved.
Reciprocal: One student serves as the performer while the other evaluates and records that student's performance.	More student involvement and immediate feedback by working in pairs or groups.	The evaluator may provide incorrect feedback or be overcritical.
Individual: Program is individualized based on each student's performance. Student works at own rate. (IEP)	Based on student need.	Requires a great deal of teacher preparation, and some students will not perform or evaluate their performance on their own.
Guided Discovery: The instructor provides the student with a series of steps or questions (sequentially) leading to the specific goal.	The student is involved in the process of problem solving.	This process can be time consuming and difficult with learners of limited mental ability.
Divergent: A single problem may have a variety of solutions and must only meet the instructor's criteria.	Provides the student with the opportunity to discover and try out ideas focused on a particular problem.	Difficult to implement with learners of limited mental ability.

Note. This table describes selected examples of teaching styles developed by Mosston (1981).

movement exploration approach to teaching, in which each student is responsible for his or her own learning. However, not everyone with special needs learns best from this approach initially, especially not those with limited mental ability such as persons with mental retardation, who need a structured learning environment (see Figure 6.3). Gaveron (1989) believes the instructor must match teaching style and materials with the learner's dominant learning modality. For example, visual learners need to be shown through demonstration how to perform a skill, whereas verbal learners need detailed explanations of a skill.

Learning Stations

The learning station strategy is very flexible and varies with the number of students, their ability levels, and the type of activities offered (Hirst & Shelly, 1989; Sherrill, 1986). Most commonly, students all rotate in the same direction from station to station, working on a different skill at each station. The stations can focus on a theme (see Figure 6.4); for example, for a physical fitness theme, each station would reinforce a component of fitness (see Figure 6.5). It is important that the instructor, when designing learning stations, considers the movement and fitness demands of each station; three consecutive stations that tax the cardiovascular system, for instance, may be too demanding for many persons with mental retardation. Fitness stations must also be progressive and self-paced. (For a detailed discussion of physical fitness training and progression, review chapter 7.)

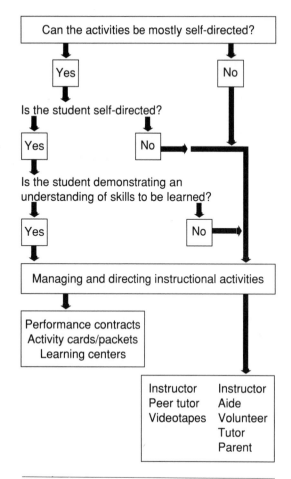

Figure 6.3   Self-direction flowchart.
Note. From *Achievement-Based Curriculum Development in Physical Education* (p. 221) by J.A. Wessell and L.E. Kelly, 1986, Philadelphia: Lea & Febiger. Copyright 1986 by Lea & Febiger. Reprinted by permission.

Task Cards/Learning Packages

Task cards or learning packages present the student with directions to perform a skill. The directions on the cards should be modified appropriately for the students' movement and reading ability levels. Picture cards can be used for students unable to read (see Figure 6.6). Here are a few of the ways task cards can be used in class: (a) picked up and performed when students first enter class; (b) placed randomly around the gymnasium floor, with the students spending 1 minute performing the activity on each card, then choosing another; (c) used as a reinforcer the last few minutes of class for students who successfully complete their lessons; and (d) posted on the gymnasium walls and used in a stations approach. For students who cannot complete the assignment alone and have difficulty following directions, peer tutors can provide assistance.

Peer Tutor Programs

In peer tutor programs, students without disabilities serve as aides or "buddies" to assist the students with mental retardation. This strategy is very beneficial: The students with mental retardation get the one-on-one instruction that is often required for them to successfully complete tasks; the students without disabilities learn acceptance toward persons with mental retardation; and from an administrative standpoint, these programs are a cost-effective means of providing additional support services to teachers (Webster, 1987). In the peer tutor model, a great variety of persons can be tutors, including peers, cross-age peers (older children), or senior citizens, and other persons with mental retardation, when possible. A peer tutor program can be combined with task cards and learning stations. In general, this program is very similar to Mosston's reciprocal teaching model, in which the partner (peer) serves as an observer, corrector, and reinforcer to the student performing the activity (Mosston, 1981).

Peer tutor programs have become fairly common in the public schools in recent years, but little empirical research has been done on the social or performance outcomes for persons with mental retardation (Watkinson & Titus, 1985). The few studies conducted with students who have mental retardation seem quite promising. DePaepe (1985) found a peer tutor program to significantly increase the time students with moderate mental retardation practiced a balance skill when compared to two other placement alternatives. In a study conducted by Webster

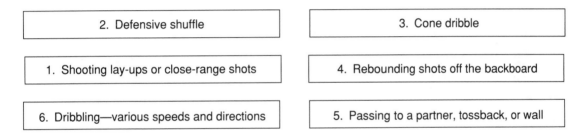

Figure 6.4 Basketball fundamental skill learning stations. The students will spend 5 minutes at each station and rotate in a clockwise manner around the basketball court.

(1987), a peer tutor program of three students with moderate and severe mental retardation, enrolled in either elementary, middle school, or high school settings, significantly increased the amount of time they appropriately participated in such activities as skill practice, game, scrimmage/routines, and fitness. Another interesting finding in the Webster study was that no difference was determined between untrained and trained peer tutors with respect to the time the mainstreamed students with mental retardation were actively engaged in the prescribed skill. To date, the best known and most widely used model of peer teaching is the PEOPEL (physical education opportunity program for exceptional learners) program (Long, Irmer, Burkett, Glassnapp, & Odenkirk, 1980). This model provides field-tested information for properly training high-school-age students to become peer tutors.

When implementing a peer tutor program, the instructor must also consider the needs of the students (peers) without disabilities. They should not spend the entire time serving as a peer tutor but must also receive teacher instruction. Often in these programs, students serve as peers during their free periods or if they have completed school assignments from another class. Participation as a peer tutor should be treated as an honor and an educational experience. In some schools, peer tutors can earn credit or satisfy service requirements toward graduation (Long et al., 1980). Before they start serving as peers, these students should be instructed about their teaching responsibilities. Figure 6.7 shows a system for grading peer tutors that has been effectively implemented in a high school setting.

Reverse Mainstreaming

Reverse mainstreaming is similar to the peer tutor program in that the student without disabilities assists the student with mental retardation. The major difference is that in this program the student without disabilities goes to the special

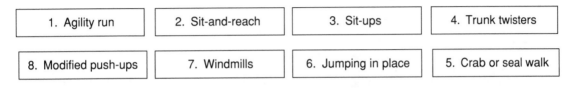

Figure 6.5 Physical fitness learning stations. Students spend 30 seconds at each station, then rotate clockwise. Ten seconds are added each week, per station; by the end of the month students spend 1 minute at each station. Initially give students a 30-second rest when they rotate between stations; then encourage them to run slowly when they rotate with only a 15-second transition period between stations.

Figure 6.6 Picture task card.

Note. Copyright 1979 by Carl B. Eichstaedt. Reprinted by permission.

education setting, which for many students with mental retardation is less threatening than a mainstreamed environment. Highlight 6.4 provides examples of practices in team teaching and reverse mainstreaming that have been successful in a large urban high school setting.

Davis, Woolley, and French (1987) propose a variation of reverse mainstreaming, advocating the active participation of nondisabled persons in sports such as wheelchair basketball or beep baseball in both regular physical education classes and community recreation pro-

Student name:

Class period:

Date:

Each student will be graded and receive a maximum of 4 points in each of the following areas:

1. Ability to help peer: 1 2 3 4

2. Enthusiasm: 1 2 3 4

3. Class participation: 1 2 3 4

4. Cooperation with others: 1 2 3 4

Total grade: (A) 12-11   (B) 10-9   (C) 8-7

Figure 6.7 Peer tutor grading system.

grams. Simulating disabilities in such a sport unit would ready these students for the students with mental retardation who will be mainstreamed into the program at a later date. Most importantly, this program strategy gives instructor and students a start at developing sensitivity to the feelings and needs of persons with mental retardation.

Game Intervention

The concept of game intervention goes by many names—"game analysis" (Morris & Stiehl, 1989), "creative games" (Riley, 1975), "cooperative" or "new games" (Flugelman, 1976; Orlick, 1982), and so on. The heart of this approach is to accommodate all participants by designing new game rules that are inclusive rather than exclusive. The professionals working in this area (including also Arbogast & Lavay, 1987; Gabbard & Miller, 1987) have questioned the benefits of traditional games and have designed nontraditional games and game principles that avoid the drawbacks of traditional games, and they share the belief that games and sport are not sacred and can be changed to meet the unique needs of the group or individual.

The game intervention approach has been found to be an effective strategy in integrating children with mental retardation into games or sport with nondisabled peers. For example, in a study conducted by Marlowe (1979), a game analysis approach was used to increase the social acceptance of a 10-year-old boy with moderate mental retardation by his nondisabled classmates. As determined by a sociometric rating scale, before using game intervention, this boy was the least accepted child in the class. During game sessions, classmates were introduced to training in game analysis procedures. Games were adapted and designed by the investigator to stress the importance of meeting the needs of each individual as well as allowing the children to share in the decision making of the game structure. Results indicated that the game analysis intervention not only was effective in promoting positive gains in the boy's social acceptance with classmates, but increased the time the child was actually participating in the game.

Initially the idea of examining and changing games and sport may be new to the instructor and therefore difficult to initiate. Arbogast and Lavay (1987) suggest that professionals carefully consider the following details when striving to accommodate students of different ability levels in a game or sport.

1. The physical fitness and movement demands of the game or sport. Playing scooterboard floor hockey rather than traditional floor hockey would help neutralize the superior strength and speed of certain students. In a tag game, slower students can be allowed to run while faster students must select a different means of locomotion, such as a hop or gallop.

2. The purpose and skill complexity required for successful performance in the game or sport. For example, certain students may have limited cognitive abilities and movement experience, and therefore it may be necessary to reduce information-processing demands by introducing simple lead-up

Practices in Team Teaching and Reverse Mainstreaming

The following are examples of successful mainstreaming practices in a physical education program at a large urban high school. The physical education department consisted of eight regular full-time physical education teachers who taught at the school all day and an itinerant special physical education teacher who taught at the school for one period a day. All teachers followed a department curriculum and taught a different activity in a different teaching station, rotating to another activity approximately every 4 weeks. Activities varied from soccer, flag football, and volleyball to gymnastics, aerobic dance and others. The special physical education program was designed to be similar to the regular physical education program in order to facilitate mainstreaming.

Team Teaching

1. The students with mental retardation were brought into the regular physical education class, which offered a variety of activities such as aerobic dance, soccer, volleyball, archery, and table tennis. Each student with mental retardation was assigned a peer tutor or "buddy" from the regular class, who served as an aide. The regular physical education teacher and the special physical edu-

cation teacher shared teaching responsibilities.

2. The regular and special physical education classes were combined and then divided into squads of equal ability with 10 to 12 students to a squad. Two squads played soccer with the regular physical education teacher, and the third squad participated in such nontraditional activities as crab soccer and scooterboard hockey. The squads rotated between the two activities.

Reverse Mainstreaming

1. Students in the regular physical education class were selected by their teacher to be peer tutors and help assigned special education students enrolled in the self-contained special physical education class. During this class the peer tutors received a grade that counted toward their grade in the regular physical education class. At the beginning of class the regular education students were briefed by the special physical education instructor regarding the lesson to be taught for that particular period. The classes were always followed by a discussion between the peer tutors and the special physical education instructor.

games (see chapter 7 for a discussion of information processing and skill performance). The game or sport should be designed so that it neither frustrates the low-skilled achiever nor bores the highly skilled performer.

3. The environmental and equipment demands of the game or sport. Skill learn-

ing can be facilitated by using equipment that is appropriate in size and weight for the individual. Consider facility modifications such as reducing the size of the court or playing field in order to reduce the physical intensity of the activity for less physically fit individuals, a strategy discussed earlier in detail in Highlight 6.3.

4. The cognitive and social demands of the game or sport. For example, some students, especially those with limited mental ability, will find rules and strategies quite complex and abstract. Therefore, provide tangible examples, such as highlighting obscure boundaries with cones or flags. Foster positive social experiences by avoiding or changing elimination-type games. For example, change the traditional approach to musical chairs by playing musical hoops instead—when a hoop is taken away, groups of children must cooperate and work together to successfully fit inside the remaining hoops.

Highlight 6.5 presents an example of how these procedures can be implemented to develop a nontraditional game. To become skilled at game intervention, the instructor must be imaginative, creative, and willing to take risks.

Integrating Community Recreation

Everybody, including people with mental retardation, has the right to leisure experiences in the community. Recreational community-based programs are an excellent opportunity for persons with mental retardation to function in and socially interact with mainstream society. The following general strategies for integrating individuals with disabilities into community recreation programs are based on the experiences of two Oregon agencies (Halberg, Earle, & Turpel, 1985).

1. Developing an integration plan requires formulating a philosophy and realistically appraising available resources.
2. The agency must make a commitment to provide all available resources and take time to orient staff members. Planning at the initial stages will be time well spent, because it will help reduce potential problems that may be encountered during the day-to-day administration of the program.
3. The program must focus on the unique needs of each individual. If the program staff is small, the agency must come up with creative solutions to training volunteers.
4. Communication among all involved parties is critical. Staff members are more positive and committed when the professional staff is available for consultation.
5. The specialized staff must be careful to not overcommit themselves. For example, an overzealous staff member might not listen to a participant enrolled in the program. The participant has not only the right to accept leisure experiences, but also the right to reject these experiences. Ultimately all adults participating in the program must be treated with dignity and respect in an age-appropriate manner.

There are no easy answers whether persons with mental retardation should be placed in a segregated program or in an integrated program of recreation. Shivers and Fait (1985) believe that recreational specialists must base this decision on a number of factors, such as availability of staff, support services, skill level of the participant, and perhaps most importantly, which program provides the better leisure educational experience for that particular person. For example, an adult with mild mental retardation might feel more comfortable starting in a segregated program and later changing to an integrated program. Anyone who is going to be mainstreamed must be thoroughly prepared for the experience. Stein (1985) best summarizes the importance of integrating persons who have disabilities including those with mental retardation, into community-based recreational programs:

When all people in the community want mainstreaming to happen, it can be done. But the attitudinal barriers must come tumbling

HIGHLIGHT 6.5

IN PRACTICE

Putting It All Together

The game "Softball, Volleyball, and Basketball" is played on a traditional softball diamond in the gymnasium. The batter strikes a ball into the field using a volleyball serve. The fielder must pass a foam ball to a teammate of the opposite gender before it is thrown to the catcher at home plate (which is located by the basket) who must make a successful basket before the runner circles the bases and returns home. If the batter/runner scores before the basket is made by the catcher, a point is awarded. However, a basket made before the runner scores is an out. The number of outs is determined by the instructor or class. All players must run/walk in place until the batter makes contact and the play ends. After each batter, the fielders rotate positions to assure that there is a new catcher each time and that one particular student does not dominate the game.

A. Movement and fitness demands
   1. Students of low physical ability may walk in place when they become fatigued.
   2. Lighter balls can assure that less physically fit students meet with success when throwing the ball.
   3. More relay passes before throwing to home plate can be required when one batter/runner is significantly slower than another.

B. Skill complexity
   1. The ball can be hit off a batting tee.
   2. Use a larger ball to decrease skill complexity, and use a smaller ball to increase skill complexity.
   3. The teacher can cue to initial fielder as to the most appropriate teammate to pass to, assuring a good relay to the catcher. The catcher with low shooting skills may be required only to hit the basket rim to make an out.

C. Environmental considerations
   1. The distance between bases can be modified commensurate with the age group or ability level of the students.
   2. Various kinds and sizes of balls can be made available.
   3. To assure better contrast for striking and fielding, balls should be brightly colored and the gymnasium should be well lighted.

D. Social considerations
   1. The initial fielder must pass the ball to a fielder of the opposite gender.
   2. After each play, all fielders rotate a position.
   3. When changing from offense to defense, each player must shake hands with a player from the other team.

Note. From "Combining Students of Different Abilities in Games and Sport" by G. Arbogast and B. Lavay, 1987, *Physical Educator*, **44**, pp. 255-260. Adapted by permission of *The Physical Educator*.

down. All facilities must become accessible, and every program must accommodate all who desire to participate. Only after we have accomplished this across our nation will individuals with handicapping conditions be integrated into the mainstream of society. (p. 52)

Meeting the Mainstreaming Challenge

By now it should be quite clear that mainstreaming is a most challenging and complex process requiring a total commitment by all involved. It is also extremely important, because of the many benefits for all involved. However, Lavay and DePaepe (1987) have cautioned that too much emphasis has been placed on the concept and not enough on the process. When mainstreaming fails, all involved must ask themselves why. Mizen and Linton (1983) perhaps offer professionals the best single solution for programming in the mainstream: "By the very nature of their program physical education teachers are constantly reminded that teaching children with handicaps in a mainstreaming program can be frustrating and disappointing. The time has come to meet the challenge" (p. 63). For additional readings on this subject, see the bibliography in DePaepe and Lavay (1985); also see Hutchison (1983) for a review of the research that has been conducted in the recreation integration literature.

Summary

Many people don't understand the difference between least restrictive environment and mainstreaming. Mainstreaming is simply the integration of persons with mental retardation or other disabilities into the regular educational setting with their nondisabled peers. The least restrictive environment is the setting in which the individual can most adequately function.

Proper placement must be based on the person's individual needs and present level of performance. A continuum of services must be made available, ranging from placement in a special/adapted physical education program with modified activities to participation in a regular physical education program. Mainstreaming should be viewed as only one available placement alternative!

In many settings mainstreaming has become ineffective and frustrating for all involved, because regular classrooms have been used as dumping grounds to save time, facilities, personnel, and money. If mainstreaming is to be effective, important preplanning factors must be carefully considered by the regular physical education teacher, the special physical education teacher, the special education classroom teacher, and other involved professionals, who, along with the mainstreamed class and the student to be mainstreamed, must keep an open dialogue while developing a positive attitude toward the experience. The scheduling of facilities, the organization of the environment, and the type of pedagogical program strategies and materials offered must also be carefully considered. Examples of pedagogical strategies include varied teaching styles; learning stations; task cards/ learning packages; peer tutor, reverse mainstreaming, and team teaching programs; and the creative implementation of game intervention strategies.

Strategies for integrating individuals with mental retardation into community-based recreation programs most begin with the question of whether the person with mental retardation will be better off starting in a segregated program rather than an integrated program of recreation. There are many relevant factors, but ultimately all adults participating in the program must be treated with dignity and respect.

Finally, successfully integrating persons with mental retardation with persons who do not have disabilities will never be easy and requires a great deal of effort from all involved. However, when mainstreaming is done properly and sensitively, it has many benefits, including these:

- Research demonstrates that many persons with mild mental retardation may perform more like their nondisabled peers in the area of physical activity than in other academic areas.
- Many (though not all) persons with mental retardation may be motivated to perform better in the presence of their nondisabled peers than in the presence of the instructor, as these persons may relate to, be more motivated by, and consequently perform better for someone their own age.

- Students without disabilities, by displaying appropriate movement and social skills, can serve as effective role models for students with mental retardation.
- This process allows the person with mental retardation to interact with nondisabled individuals in a socially acceptable manner, which provides them with the opportunity to adjust to "real life" situations that adhere to the principles of normalization.
- By working closely with this population, nondisabled individuals learn to respect rather than pity people with mental retardation.

DISCUSSIONS AND NEW DIRECTIONS

1. The Individuals With Disabilities Education Act states that "to the maximum extent possible and when appropriate, children with a disability, . . . are educated with children who are nondisabled and that . . . removal of children with a disability from the regular educational environment occurs only when the nature of severity of the disability is such that education in regular classes with the use of supplementary aids and services cannot be achieved satisfactorily" (p. 42497). How does your school district define the following: "maximum extent possible," "when appropriate," and "when the nature of severity of the disability is such that education in regular classes with the use of supplementary aids and services cannot be achieved satisfactorily."
2. Are physical education placement alternative guidelines developed in your school system for the variables listed in question 1 valid? Are they reliable and consistently applied throughout the school district to all children? What problems have been encountered with the present guidelines, and how might they be eliminated or streamlined to be more efficient?
3. In recent years, peer tutor programs have met with much acceptance in the public schools. However, little empirical research exists regarding the social or performance outcomes of these programs for persons with mental retardation (Watkinson & Titus, 1985). Are peer tutor programs more effective than other types of mainstreaming alternatives such as reverse mainstreaming? Are performance outcomes with peer tutors contingent on the use of trained versus untrained tutors? What considerations should be given to the age of the tutors or the classification level of the persons with mental retardation being mainstreamed?

References

Aloia, G., Knutson, R., Minner, S.J., & Von Seggern, M. (1980). Physical education teacher's initial perceptions of handicapped children. *Mental Retardation*, **18**, 85-87.

Arbogast, G., & Lavay, B. (1987). Combining students of different abilities. *Physical Educator*, **44**, 255-260.

Danaher, P.M. (1983). Handicap awareness program. *Journal of Physical Education, Recreation and Dance*, **54**(3), 67-68.

Davis, R., Woolley, Y., & French, R. (1987). Reverse mainstreaming. *Physical Educator*, **44**, 247-249.

DePaepe, J.L. (1985). The influence of three least restrictive environments on the content motor-ALT and performance of moderately mentally retarded students. *Journal of Teaching Physical Education*, **5**, 34-41.

DePaepe, J., & Lavay, B. (1985). A bibliography of mainstreaming in physical education. *Physical Educator*, **42**, 41-45.

Dunn, J.M., & Craft, D.H. (1985). Mainstreaming theory into practice. *Adapted Physical Activity Quarterly*, **2**, 273-276.

Dunn, J.M., & Fait, H.F. (1989). *Special physical education: Adapted, individualized, developmental*. Philadelphia: W.B. Saunders.

Flugelman, A. (1976). *The new games book: Play hard, play fair, nobody hurt*. Garden City, NY: Dolphin Books.

Gabbard, C., & Miller, G. (1987). Intermediate school game curriculum: A balance of the traditional and contemporary. *Journal of Physical Education, Recreation and Dance*, **58**(7), 66-71.

Gaveron, S. (1989). Surviving the least restrictive alternative. *Strategies*, **2**(3), 5-6, 28.

Halberg, K.J., Earle, P., & Turpel, L.T. (1985). Implementing recreation integration: Specific issues and practical solutions. *Journal of Physical Education, Recreation and Dance*, **55**(5), 29-31.

Hallahan, D.P., & Kauffman, J.M. (1982). *Exceptional children: Introduction to special education*. Englewood Cliffs, NJ: Prentice Hall.

Hamilton, E.J., & Anderson, S.C. (1983). Effects of leisure activities on attitudes toward people with disabilities. *Therapeutic Recreation Journal*, **3**, 50-57.

Hirst, C.H., & Shelly, E.Y. (1989). They too should play. *Teaching Exceptional Children*, **21**(4), 26-28.

Hutchison, P. (1983). The status of recreation integration. *Journal of Leisurability*, **10**(3), 26-35.

Lavay, B. (1986). Strategies for effectively integrating the exceptional student into regular physical education. *Kansas Association for Health, Physical Education, Recreation and Dance Journal*, **54**(2), 30, 32.

Lavay, B. (1987). Is mainstreaming in physical education, recreation, and dance working? (Answer to issues section). *Journal of Physical Education, Recreation and Dance*, **58**(9), 14.

Lavay, B., & DePaepe, J. (1987). Why mainstreaming doesn't always work: The harbinger helper. *Journal of Physical Education, Recreation and Dance*, **58**(7), 98-103.

Lavay, B., & Pizarro, D. (1987). The status of adapted/special physical education. *American Corrective Therapy Journal*, **41**, 77-81.

Long, E., Irmer, L., Burkett, L., Glassnapp, G., & Odenkirk, B. (1980). PEOPEL. *Journal of Physical Education and Recreation*, **51**(7), 28-29.

Marlowe, M. (1979). The game intervention: A procedure to increase the peer acceptance and social adjustment of a retarded child. *Education and Training of the Mentally Retarded*, **14**, 262-268.

Mizen, D.W., & Linton, N. (1983). Guess who's coming to P.E.: Six steps to more effective mainstreaming. *Journal of Physical Education, Recreation and Dance*, **54**(8), 63-65.

Morreau, L.E., & Eichstaedt, C.B. (1983). Least restrictive programming and placement in physical education. *American Corrective Therapy Journal*, **37**, 11-17.

Morris, G.S.D., & Stiehl, J. (1989). *Changing kids' games*. Champaign, IL: Human Kinetics.

Mosston, M. (1981). *Teaching physical education*. Columbus, OH: Merrill.

Orlick, T. (1982). *The second cooperative sports and games book*. New York: Pantheon.

Price, R.J. (1986). The status of international activity in recreation, sports, and cultural activities for disabled persons (part 2).

Palaestra: The Forum of Sport, Physical Education, and Recreation for the Disabled, **3**(1), 32-37.

Rarick, G.L., & Beuter, A.C. (1985). The effect of mainstreaming on the motor performance of mentally retarded and nonhandicapped students. *Adapted Physical Activity Quarterly,* **2**, 277-282.

Riley, M. (1975). Games and humanism. *Journal of Physical Education, Recreation and Dance,* **46**, 46-49.

Rizzo, T.L. (1984). Attitudes of physical educators toward teaching handicapped pupils. *Adapted Physical Activity Quarterly,* **1**, 267-274.

Sherrill, C. (1986). *Adapted physical education and recreation: A multidisciplinary approach.* Dubuque, IA: Brown.

Shivers, J.S., & Fait, H.F. (1985). *Special recreational services therapeutic and adapted.* Philadelphia: Lea & Febiger.

Stein, J.U. (1985). Mainstreaming in recreational settings. *Journal of Physical Education, Recreation and Dance,* **55**(5), 25, 52.

Watkinson, E.J., & Titus, J.A. (1985). Integrating the mentally handicapped in physical activity: A review and a discussion. *Canadian Journal for Exceptional Children,* **2**, 48-53.

Webster, G.E. (1987). Influence of peer tutors upon academic learning time—physical education of mentally handicapped students. *Journal of Teaching Physical Education,* **6**, 393-403.

CHAPTER 7

Program Implementation:
Physical Fitness,
Fundamental Motor Skills,
Aquatics, and Dance

PREVIEW Russell is attending a small teachers' college in the Midwest and is studying to be a physical education teacher. One requirement for a degree is the completion of an introductory special physical education course. Course requirements include observing children with mental retardation in a physical activity setting at a nearby elementary school. Each week Russell observes a class of boys and girls of ages 10 to 12 with moderate mental retardation who are engaged in play during their recess period on the school playground. As he observes these children, he wonders why their movement skills in running, jumping, throwing, catching, and balance are awkward and slow. He also notices that they tire quite easily and often stop after only a few seconds of running. In fact, most of the children spend most of their time standing around on the playground despite the encouragement of their special education teacher. In addition, when Russell observes children without disabilities of the same age who are also at play during this recess period, it is obvious that their movement skills are superior to those of the group of children with mental retardation. Each week as Russell observes the group, he asks himself the same question: "Would a quality physical education program improve their movement skills and increase their physical fitness level?"

HIGHLIGHT QUESTIONS

- **What activities comprise a quality program of physical activity for persons with mental retardation?**
- **Why are skills in physical fitness, fundamental movement, aquatics, and dance important for persons with mental retardation?**
- **Why do persons with mental retardation get inferior scores in physical fitness and movement skills when compared to their nondisabled peers?**
- **Do physical fitness and movement deficits increase as the level of mental retardation becomes more severe?**
- **What are the reasons behind persons with mental retardation withdrawing from physical activity and leading a sedentary lifestyle?**
- **What specific teaching strategies exist to assist professionals in providing movement skills to persons with mental retardation?**
- **Are well-designed, progressive, and systematic programs of physical fitness, fundamental movement, aquatics, and dance available for persons with mental retardation?**

Public Law 94-142 (U.S. Office of Education, 1977) specifically cites the curricular area of physical education in the definition of special education and recognizes it as a direct service. The law mandates that the implementation and delivery of quality physical education services is not a luxury, but rather, it is a right of students identified as having disabilities—including mental retardation. Physical education is specifically defined in the law as

- physical and motor fitness,
- fundamental motor skills and patterns, and
- skills in aquatics, dance, and individual and group games and sport (including intramural and lifetime sports). (p. 42480)

This chapter provides the information necessary to successfully implement a quality program of physical activity for persons with mental retardation; in doing so, it closely follows the definition of physical education given in the law. The four major component areas of this discussion are

1. physical fitness,
2. fundamental motor skills,
3. aquatics, and
4. dance.

Later in the text, chapters 8, 9, 10, and 11 discuss program implementation of individual and group games, sport, and leisure activities for preschool and school-age children and adolescents as well as adults with mental retardation. Figure 7.1 is a curriculum model developed by Kelly (1989) that gives an overview of the component areas critical to the successful implementation of a quality physical education program.

PHYSICAL FITNESS

Proper physical fitness practices lead to a healthy lifestyle (Sharkey, 1984). In general, physical stamina and a healthy lifestyle are necessary to meet the vigorous demands of daily living. The benefits of physical fitness are well documented in the literature and are no different for persons with mental retardation than for the general population (McConaughy & Salzberg, 1988; Moon & Renzaglia, 1982).

Benefits of Physical Fitness Programs

Health, social, personal, and vocational benefits can be derived from proper physical fitness practices, and more specifically, developing these healthy fitness practices should be fundamental to this population's lifestyle for a number of reasons.

Resistance From Disease

There is a direct correlation between being physically fit and being resistant to disease. Many persons with mental retardation may be more susceptible to various diseases because they lead a sedentary lifestyle (McConaughy & Salzberg, 1988). Moreover, this population too often lacks the cognitive ability necessary to make self-directed healthy lifestyle choices. Because these

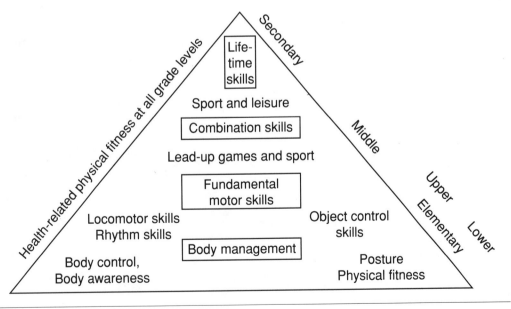

Figure 7.1 Curriculum model.
Note. From "Instructional Time" by L.E. Kelly, 1989, *Journal of Physical Education, Recreation and Dance,* **60**(6), p. 30. The journal is a publication of the American Alliance for Health, Physical Education, Recreation and Dance, 1900 Association Drive, Reston, VA 22091.

choices do not come naturally to them, persons with mental retardation must be taught an appreciation for physical activity and learn to generalize these positive fitness outcomes on their own over an extended period of time, in a variety of settings, and with limited supervision. To date, little research has been conducted in this area, but such research is important if this population is to maintain and generalize sound physical fitness procedures to have a healthy lifestyle (Coleman & Whitman, 1984).

Worthy Use of Leisure Time

Most people with mental retardation have an abundance of free time. It is important to teach them to use this time safely, constructively, and enjoyably rather than sit idly in front of a television set.

Job Productivity

Adhering to sound fitness practices can help this population be competitive in the work force. Most will be employed in manual jobs. Although research is limited, a few studies have demonstrated that engaging in proper physical fitness practices can enhance job productivity (Beasley, 1982) and that adhering to proper physical fitness practices is essential if this population is to qualify, maintain, and compete for employment in the work force (Coleman, Ayoub, & Friedrich, 1976).

Social Interaction

In fitness activities this population can interact with other persons, both with and without disabilities, in a socially acceptable manner and in the mainstream—for example, by participating in proper physical fitness practices alongside their nondisabled peers in health clubs. In addition, the experience these individuals thereby gain in proper social interaction can greatly enhance their employability. A reason that is

often cited for persons with mental retardation being released from their jobs is their inability to get along with co-workers.

Underlying Factors

Experts agree that physical fitness is an underlying factor and necessary to the success of other forms of movement. For example, strength is an underlying factor in successfully performing a balance activity, and cardiovascular endurance is required to meet the demands of such activities as basketball, soccer, and dance. Competencies in the various elements of fitness are necessary if these persons are to successfully perform more advanced skills (see Figure 7.2).

Defining Health-Related Physical Fitness

What constitutes proper physical fitness? In the past, physical fitness testing and training was based primarily on motor performance in such skills as agility, balance, coordination, power, speed, and reaction time. Many individuals, including persons with mental retardation, found

Figure 7.2 All persons can benefit from fitness. Photo courtesy of Ken Regan.

motor fitness skills quite difficult to perform. Today, experts agree that sound physical fitness practices should emphasize the relationship between health and physical activity rather than motor fitness (National Children & Youth Fitness, 1985). *Health-related physical fitness* (HRPF) is the term most widely accepted, and it can be defined by the following components, which measure an individual's current health and potential resistance to disease: cardiovascular endurance, muscular strength, muscular endurance, flexibility, and percent body fat. With slight, if any, modifications, most people with mental retardation are capable of performing adequately in these HRPF components. Highlight 7.1 defines and gives examples for measuring each of these HRPF component items.

Physical Fitness Research

It is well-documented in the literature that persons with mental retardation consistently display inferior physical fitness levels when compared to their nondisabled counterparts (Fernhall, Tymeson, & Webster, 1988; Moon & Renzaglia, 1982). During the past 25 years, investigations have been conducted primarily with children and adolescents; however, recent investigations have begun to examine the physical fitness levels of adults with mental retardation (Lavay, Zody, Solko, & Era, 1990; McCubbin & Jansma, 1987). Studies with adult populations have also revealed inferior fitness levels. In fact, inferior physical fitness levels may be even greater in adult populations, because once they graduate from the public school setting and join the work force, their fitness needs are virtually ignored.

The pioneer work of Rarick, Widdop, and Broadhead (1970) established physical fitness scores for boys and girls ages 8 to 18 with mild mental retardation to be 2 to 4 years behind those of their peers who do not have disabilities. Further work by Rarick and associates revealed that the patterns of developmental progression and performance on specific items of physical fitness for persons with mild mental retardation

---

HIGHLIGHT 7.1   **IN THEORY**

Health-Related Physical Fitness Components

Cardiovascular endurance—Ability to perform numerous repetitions of stress requiring the use of the circulatory and respiratory system. Muscular endurance specific to the heart, lungs, and vascular system. Experts agree the single most important component of HRPF is cardiovascular (aerobic) endurance (e.g., running tests of various distances and durations, such as the mile run/walk or the 12-minute run/walk).

Muscular strength—Ability of the body to exert force. One maximum effort (e.g., bench press, static push-up, pull-ups).

Muscular endurance—Ability to perform work repeatedly against a moderate resistance (e.g., the number of bent-knee sit-ups completed in 60 seconds).

Flexibility—Ability of the joints to move through their full range of motion. Flexibility is joint specific (e.g., sit-and-reach test).

Percent body fat—An individual's degree of body fat as demonstrated by skinfold thickness (measurements may be taken at such sites as the tricep, subscapula, and calf).

were similar to those for peers without disabilities (Rarick, Dobbins, & Broadhead, 1976). Londeree and Johnson (1974) established physical fitness test scores for persons with moderate mental retardation ages 6 to 19 years. These investigators determined the fitness levels of this group to be significantly inferior when compared to those of persons with mild mental retardation as well as nonretarded peers. More recently, the research of Eichstaedt, Wang, Polacek, and Dohrmann (1991) determined the physical fitness levels of males with mental retardation 6 to 20 years of age to be on the average 1 standard deviation below the physical fitness mean score of their nonretarded peers, and females of the same ages displayed fitness scores 1-1/2 standard deviations below the mean when compared to their counterparts without disabilities. Appendix C presents the physical fitness test scores from this study and includes different age groups and classifications (mild, moderate, and Down syndrome) of persons with mental retardation.

Inferior Scores

Investigators agree that persons with mental retardation have inferior fitness scores when compared to peers without disabilities and these scores continue to decrease as the level of retardation becomes more severe. However, research conducted since the late 1960s has demonstrated also that with proper training this population can significantly improve in this area (Lavay, Reid, & Cressler-Chaviz, 1990; Moon & Renzaglia, 1982). What is uncertain and under debate among investigators is why this population receives significantly inferior scores when compared to the general population. Their limited cognitive ability doesn't explain it. Answering this question is vital to assisting professionals to better meet the fitness needs of this group during program implementation and training. Specific factors that need to be considered with this population include

1. a lack of quality fitness instruction,
2. a lack of opportunity to practice fitness, and
3. physical characteristics (e.g., body weight and stature) and medical conditions (e.g., congenital heart disorders).

Prior to PL 94-142 (U.S. Office of Education, 1977) quality instruction in the form of good physical education teaching and athletic coaching were limited or nonexistent for persons with mental retardation. Too often, persons who lacked the expertise and training to provide quality programs of physical fitness (e.g., special education classroom teachers) were made, and in some settings still are, responsible for meeting these persons' fitness needs. For successful programs, it is critical to have qualified personnel who are knowledgeable regarding the following competencies: the components of physical fitness that make for a well-balanced program, the tests available to accurately assess fitness needs specific to the population served (see chapter 3 and Appendixes C and D), and the specific training techniques and motivational strategies necessary to effectively meet the needs of this particular population (see the next section of this chapter, "Training and Program Implementation").

Persons with mental retardation have had little opportunity to participate in proper health-related physical fitness practices. For example, the physical fitness levels of children and youth with mental retardation in the state of Illinois has been under investigation, for the years 1980 to 1990, by Eichstaedt et al. (1991), Polacek, Wang, and Eichstaedt (1985), and Wang and Eichstaedt (1980). A selected comparison of these three studies conducted by Nienhuis (1989) revealed little if any significant difference between the mean scores of 10-, 11-, and 12-year-old males and females with mild mental retardation in the following tests of physical fitness: 50-yard dash, 9-minute run, flexed arm hang, sit-ups in 60 seconds, and standing long jump

Table 7.1   Comparison of 10-Year-Old Males' Physical Fitness Test Results

	1980		1985		1989			
	Number of subjects	Mean score	Number of subjects	Mean score	Number of subjects	Mean score	F-ratio	Significant F-ratio
Flexed arm hang	13	3.10	14	3.89	14	2.45	2.41	.1042
Standing long jump	34	47.79	12	40.75	14	40.29	3.25	.0461*
50-yard dash	33	10.41	10	10.10	13	10.14	0.12	.8879
Shuttle run	15	18.20	12	15.24	14	13.79	1.08	.3488
Modified sit-ups	35	17.00	11	17.45	14	21.50	1.14	.3266

Note. From *A comparison analysis of physical fitness levels of mild mentally retarded students ages 10 to 12 in Illinois*, by K.M. Nienhuis, 1989, unpublished Masters Thesis, Illinois State University, Normal, IL.

*Denotes significant F

(see Table 7.1). One explanation for this lack of change during this period may be the limited opportunities and quality instruction provided to this population to participate in physical fitness practices through structured physical education, athletic competition, and afterschool leisure/recreation programs. These results are especially alarming considering PL 94-142 (U.S. Office of Education, 1977) has been in existence for well over 10 years. To remedy this situation and provide this population with the training opportunities necessary to markedly improve their physical fitness levels, professionals in physical education, athletics, and recreation; classroom teachers; group home leaders; and vocational trainers must cooperate with one another and have a total commitment to developing fitness programs for this population and training themselves and incoming physical activity professionals in the competencies necessary to provide these programs.

Lavay, Reid, and Cressler-Chaviz (1990), discuss the major role physical characteristics and medical conditions play in contributing to this population's inferior fitness levels.

There is a tendency for this population to be shorter in stature than age peers, with this difference increasing with the degree of retardation. . . . Individuals with Down syndrome have usually stunted limbs, whereas their trunks more closely approximate typical expectations. In addition, health specialists are concerned with the prevalence of obesity. . . . When body size differences between mildly mentally retarded and nonretarded children are statistically removed there are fewer motor performance tasks that differentiate between the two groups. . . . It is also important to identify medical conditions. . . . For example, persons with Down syndrome may have congenital heart disorders or respiratory problems. Atlantoaxial instability also occurs in approximately 15% of persons with Down syndrome and thus excessive flexion or extension of the neck is contraindicated. (p. 266)

Exercise and lifestyle are closely related and essential to adhering to sound fitness practices (McConaughy & Salzberg, 1988). Most persons with mental retardation lack the cognitive ability to make self-directed healthy lifestyle choices; for them, the choice to practice daily physical fitness does not come naturally and must be developed. Other factors that have deterred this population from practicing physical fitness—lack of quality instruction, lack of opportunities in recreation and sport, body size, body weight (obesity), and medical considerations—combine to make it all the more difficult for this population to have a commitment to physical fitness. The consequent failure and frustration they experience in physical activity can lead these individuals to not even attempt fitness activities. Therefore, professionals who develop programs of physical fitness training with this group must make every effort to design and implement fitness activities that are safe, fun, motivational, tailored to their needs, and success oriented—programs that persons with mental retardation will want to practice and continue for a lifetime.

Training and Program Implementation

Testing, assessment, and implementation of fitness programs require consideration of many characteristics and needs specific to this population (see chapter 3 and Appendixes C and D). Because of many factors, including their limited intelligence, persons with mental retardation may lack the motivation necessary to complete a fitness program consisting of a series of demanding tasks over an extended period of time. To date, few empirical studies outline well-designed, progressive, and systematic programs of HRPF specific to persons with mental retardation. However, the program guidelines that follow—regarding safety, selection, development, progression, and motivation—have been successfully administered in a training program of HRPF specific to this population (Lavay, Zody, Solko, & Era, 1990).

Safety

The foremost consideration in any fitness program must be the safety and well-being of each participant. The training program must closely adhere to the exercise guidelines outlined by the American College of Sports Medicine (1991). Program administrators and exercise leaders must be aware of medical problems and medications being taken by each participant. Each participant should have recently received a physical and been cleared to exercise by a physician. Throughout the program, exercise pulse rates should be closely monitored. This is important not only from a safety standpoint but also to assist exercise leaders in determining whether participants are exercising within their desired intensity levels. All contraindicated exercises must be avoided (Timmermans & Martin, 1987), such as straight-leg sit-ups, which place a strain on the back.

Persons with Down syndrome have a less developed circulatory system and should be carefully monitored during aerobic exercise. They should also be examined by a physician for atlantoaxial instability (Pueschel, 1988), a condition that can cause greater than normal flexion on the neck and possible damage to vertebrae in the spinal column (see chapter 2). Therefore, instructors should take every precaution to avoid exercises that place a strain on the neck. However, Davidson (1988), a physician, questions this practice of excluding persons with Down syndrome with the potential of atlantoaxial instability from exercise and sport:

> Because approximately 500,000 people in North America have Down syndrome, as many as 100,000 of them could have atlantoaxial instability and thus face potential exclusion from a wide variety of athletic activities. It is important to note that during the past 17 years about 500,000 individuals with Down syndrome have competed in sports events around the world. Not one is known to have suffered serious injury related to atlantoaxial instability while participating in Special Olympics training or competition. (p. 858)

Selection

The activities selected must be fun and enjoyable to each participant. The program administrator must consider the age group and developmental level of the participants. For example, in selecting activities to develop the component of strength, it is appropriate and motivational for a group of young children 5 to 10 years of age with mild or moderate mental retardation to lift toys stuffed with light weights. For a group of adults with mild or moderate mental retardation, the same objective could be met by following a more age-appropriate circuit-training routine on a universal weight machine or free weights. Highlight 7.2 lists various routines and activities administrators of physical fitness programs should consider during program selection.

It is also important during program selection to consider the specificity of exercises. When possible, an HRPF program should be well balanced, providing the participant with benefits in all of the components of HRPF as discussed

| HIGHLIGHT 7.2 | IN PRACTICE |

Physical Fitness Activities/Routines

Dauer and Pangrazi (1989) offer the following suggestions for physical fitness activities and routines that can be adapted for persons with mental retardation of various age groups and ability levels:

Individual or group warm-up exercises/routines. Have individuals exercise various body parts and areas such as legs, trunk, abdomen, arm-shoulder, and head-neck.

Movement exploration. Ask young children to move like various animals, such as a seal or bear. Provide older children with movement challenges such as "Practice putting weight on your hands."

Partner resistance exercises. Various exercises such as an arm curl-up can be performed for 8 to 12 seconds while a partner applies resistance. Partners should be somewhat matched in size and strength. This activity has value in correcting posture and allows persons to socially interact.

Individual exercises or aerobic routines to music. Music adds a fun dimension to this activity. Use commercial records such as "Mousercise," or develop routines individuals can easily follow.

Circuit or station routines. Design each station to provide individuals with a designated fitness task.

Obstacle or challenge courses. These courses can be developed indoors or outdoors using large pieces of equipment for performing such tasks as running, vaulting, climbing, balancing, and hanging.

Astronaut drills. Place children in a circle and have them move clockwise while performing a succession of locomotor movements interspersed with directions to walk or to stop and perform stretching exercises.

Parachute exercises, activities, or routines. A variety of individual and group fitness tasks can be accomplished with a parachute. For example, shaking wiffle balls off of the parachute.

previously in Highlight 7.1. For example, although run/walking is an excellent program selection, its benefits are primarily cardiovascular and will not specifically enhance an individual's flexibility.

Implementation

Program training should consist of warm-up, the fitness program, and cool-down. The actual fitness portion of the program should be primarily aerobic, adhering to the FIT formula: frequency, conducted 3 or 4 times per week; intensity, within 60% to 80% of the individual's target pulse rate, depending on the individual's fitness level; and time, maintaining this intensity level for 18 to 20 minutes. An approximate target pulse rate can be determined by subtracting the individual's age from 220 and then multiplying this number by .60 for a beginner or .80 for an individual who has been involved in a training program. For example, approximately 114 beats per minute would be an appropriate target pulse rate for a 30-year-old adult who is just starting an exercise program.

Circuit training is an excellent way to develop a well-balanced program that reinforces the different concepts of HRPF. In this procedure, each participant spends a prescribed amount of time at a number of exercise stations such as weights, cycle ergometer, and stretching (McCubbin & Jansma, 1987). Figure 6.4 presents an example of a physical fitness circuit program that does not require expensive equipment and can be initiated with different age groups and classifications of persons with mental retardation.

Progression and Motivation

Consideration must be given to the type, number, order, and duration of exercises or exercise bouts provided. The intensity of cardiovascular and muscular systems as well as the recovery time between exercises, must be carefully planned and monitored. Exercise progression must be slow and systematical. Because persons with mental retardation have limited mental ability and inferior fitness levels, the program must be highly structured, progressive in nature, and appropriately paced for each individual. The program should include some form of contingency management reinforcement plan consisting of rewards that are idiosyncratic to each participant. Highlight 7.3 describes program implementation, progression, and motivational methods used in a community-based run/walk program for adults with mental retardation (Lavay, Zody, Solko, and Era, 1990).

In summary, in selection and implementation of HRPF programs, consideration must be given to sound and safe exercise practices as well as the ease of administration. This can be accomplished by not requiring advanced physical skills and elaborate equipment or facilities. Most importantly, if healthy lifestyle changes are to occur in this population, it is simply not enough for these persons to participate in the program a few hours a week. Rather, the program must be based on a total commitment to participants' developing all aspects of a healthy lifestyle—which requires that everyone involved, including administrators, vocational trainers, and group home leaders, be committed to the program. For example, with this population the importance of maintaining a healthy lifestyle must be reinforced in the home living environment (e.g., apartment or group home). Group home leaders can start by being effective role models and exercising alongside their clients. Group home meetings can include discussions regarding the importance of proper nutrition and exercise. For example, a reward system reinforcing the concept of following proper exercise practices and adhering to a healthy lifestyle should be part of each participant's management program.

IN PRACTICE

Community-Based Run/Walk Program for Adults With Mental Retardation

The program was an hour in length and met 3 days a week, adhering to the following format:

Warm-ups. Ten to 15 minutes of slow walking and simple stretching exercises (e.g., trunk twisters); also strengthening exercises such as sit-ups and push-ups for 1 minute. Once participants had learned the warm-up and strengthening exercise routine, each was periodically chosen to lead the group.

Run/walk. Each participant ran or walked for 30 minutes around a 220-yard indoor track at the athletic complex on the university campus in the community.

Cool-down. Ten to 15 minutes of easy walking and slow stretching. Once again, each participant was periodically responsible for leading the group through the cool-down session.

Seven participants ran throughout most of the sessions, and the remaining six primarily walked. Four student assistants (physical education majors) assigned to the program were responsible for monitoring the progress of their specified adults. Each student assistant was assigned to three or four adults and was responsible for monitoring their pulse rates throughout each daily session. The schedule for monitoring pulse rates was as follows: prior to the run/walk phase, 15 minutes into the run/walk session, and 5 minutes following the actual run/walk bout. Each student assistant was also responsible for aiding her or his as-

signed adults in proper overall run/walking, breathing, and pacing techniques. For example, a student assistant would run/walk with one assigned adult for 3 to 4 minutes and then run/walk with another assigned adult.

Throughout the program, each adult was responsible for meeting predetermined run/walk criteria goals. Individual baseline scores were determined by counting the number of laps (8 laps to the mile) each adult ran on the track during the baseline period, which consisted of 18 run/walk sessions. The total distance traveled over the 18 sessions was then averaged to establish each adult's individual baseline score. A program coordinator kept track of each adult's distance traveled during each session. Following the baseline period, criteria goals for each adult were determined on a monthly basis, established in the same manner baseline scores were calculated. The program coordinator at the end of each month would average the number of laps each participant completed over all sessions to establish a new criteria goal. This allowed each individual's running distance to be self-paced and individualized. Points toward rewards were earned by each adult who met his or her individualized criterion goal at the end of the month. Adults who met their goals earned the privilege of selecting an activity of their choice to share with their student assistant (their run/walk partner). For example, adults chose such activities as playing frisbee, golf, going out to dinner, or attending a basketball game. (Lavay et al., 1990)

If physical fitness practices for persons with mental retardation are to advance and effectively meet this population's unique needs, research must continue in this area. With this in mind, Highlight 7.4 suggests future physical fitness research issues specific to this population. In addition, the section on obesity and mental retardation in chapter 11 includes information regarding current research fitness practices to combat the major problem of obesity among persons with mental retardation.

FUNDAMENTAL MOTOR SKILLS AND PATTERNS

According to Gallahue (1989), fundamental motor skills (FMS) for a movement pattern involve the basic elements of that particular movement only, so each movement pattern (e.g., running, jumping, throwing, catching) should first be considered in relative isolation from all others. That is, introducing FMS does not involve combining a variety of complex skills that would

be required to perform, for example, a lay-up shot in basketball. Eventually, when the individual is developmentally ready, these FMS can be linked with others into a variety of movement combinations.

Benefits of Fundamental Motor Skills and Patterns

The importance of FMS development is perhaps best stated by Gallahue (1989): "The development of fundamental movement abilities is basic to the development of all children. A wide variety of movement experiences provide them with a wealth of information on which to base their perceptions of themselves and the world about them" (p. 226). This statement may be even more true of children with mental retardation! Past experience has demonstrated that when these children are left on their own, it is highly unlikely that they will explore their environment through movement or participate in games and sport. Therefore, every effort must

---

HIGHLIGHT 7.4   **IN THEORY**

Future Physical Fitness Research Issues

Personnel training. Professionals required to provide these services are not adequately prepared or trained to meet the unique needs of this population (Moon & Renzaglia, 1982).

Training methods. To date, research has not demonstrated the physical fitness training and motivational methods most appropriate to the varied needs of this population (Moon & Renzaglia, 1982).

Integrated programs. Few programs integrate this population into the mainstream of society with nondisabled peers. For example, few

adults with mental retardation participate in aerobics classes alongside nondisabled peers in privately owned health clubs.

Maintenance programs. Few programs have been developed to provide this population with an appreciation for physical activity to the point of learning to generalize these positive fitness outcomes on their own over an extended period of time with limited supervision (Coleman & Whitman, 1984). For example, few programs teach this population self-recording procedures.

be made by professionals to provide this population with quality instruction and exposure to a wide array of movement experiences.

Although it is true that FMS are specific in nature and uniquely different from health-related physical fitness, the two often directly affect one another. That is, when an individual improves in muscular strength, an improvement is often observed in FMS performance. More specifically, the research of Rarick (1973) regarding factor analysis of movement performance for persons with mental retardation supports this point. Rarick identifies such movement components as strength, speed of movement, agility, balance, coordination, and endurance as affecting FMS performance.

FMS development is an underlying factor critical to the success of more complex movements (see Figure 7.1). Development of these skills provides added insight into other body actions and the foundation to the successful performance of the more complex movements used in aquatics, dance, games, and sport (Wickstom, 1983). Ulrich (1985) concurs: "A child who has developed a high degree of fundamental motor skill proficiency should have an easier time acquiring sport skills than those who experience deficits" (p. 2). For example, if a group of children with moderate mental retardation are to experience success in a Special Olympics soccer game, they must first display command of certain FMS like running, jumping, sliding, kicking, and trapping (Lavay, 1985). If they are unable to perform these FMS, the game could very easily turn into a series of frustrating events and failures that lead to children's reluctance to continue participating. Games and sport should be introduced only after the participants have had quality instruction and fruitful experiences in FMS development.

Games and sport are very much a part of most children's lives and a fixture of our society. If children with mental retardation are to be accepted and function with peers in mainstream school and recreational activities, it is essential

that they have movement competency. Poor movement can lead these children to a vicious cycle of failure and not being accepted or chosen by peers to participate in games and sport, which in turn leads to social isolation and a sedentary lifestyle. Even worse, if they do perform in games and sport with peers, they may experience embarrassment, frustration, and failure, which will also deter these children from the movement practice they so desperately need (see Figure 7.3).

Perhaps the most important benefit of FMS instruction for persons with mental retardation is in the area of functional skills. Competencies in FMS can carry over to the functional skills necessary to perform movements required in everyday living. For example, locomotion is essential to the successful negotiation of one's environment. Proficiency in this area can assist individuals to walk up and down flights of stairs or around objects in their paths. These examples of functional skills would be taken for granted with nondisabled youngsters under the age of 5 years, but many adolescents or even adults with mental retardation may still require proper instruction in this area.

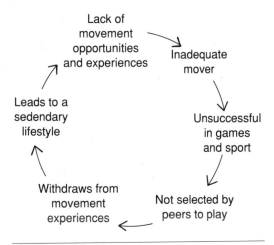

Figure 7.3 Steps leading to movement withdrawal.

Defining Fundamental Motor Skills

FMS include two major movement areas, locomotion and object control. We here present Gallahue's (1989) definitions of these terms. *Locomotion* is moving about in one's environment, traversing from one fixed point in space to another. Examples of locomotor movements include walking, running, jumping, hopping, sliding, leaping, and skipping. To improve one's locomotion skills is to move in these ways more effectively and efficiently. *Object control* movements are characterized by the individual being able to effectively and efficiently give force to, and receive force from, objects. Object control can be further divided into propulsive and absorptive movements. Propulsive movements consist of activities in which the object moves

Table 7.2   Specific Performance Criteria for Locomotor Skills

Skill	Performance criteria	Age[a] 60%	80%
Run	1. Brief period during which both feet are off the ground	3	3
	2. Arms move in opposition to legs, elbows bent	4	5
	3. Foot placement near or on a line (not flat-footed)	3	4
	4. Nonsupport leg bent approximately 90 degrees (close to buttocks)	5	7
Gallop	1. A step forward with the lead foot followed by a step with the trailing foot to a position adjacent to or behind the lead foot	4	5
	2. Brief period during which both feet are off the ground	3	3
	3. Arms bent and lifted to waist level	8	10
	4. Able to lead with the right and left foot	4	5
Hop	1. Foot of nonsupport leg is bent and carried in back of the body	5	6
	2. Nonsupport leg swings in a pendular fashion to produce force	7	8
	3. Arms bent at elbows and swing forward on takeoff	7	10
	4. Able to hop on the right and left foot	4	5
Leap	1. Take off on one foot and land on the opposite foot	6	8
	2. A period during which both feet are off the ground (longer than in running)	7	8
	3. Forward reach with the arm opposite the foot	8	10
Jump	1. Preparatory movement includes flexion of both knees with arms extended behind the head	5	7
	2. Arms extend forcefully forward and upward, reaching full extension above head	9	10
	3. Take off and land on both feet simultaneously	3	3
	4. Arms are brought downward during landing	6	8
Skip	1. A rhythmic repetition of the step-hop on alternate feet	5	6
	2. Foot of nonsupport leg is carried near surface during hop phase	6	7
	3. Arms alternately moving in opposition to legs at about waist level	7	8
Slide	1. Body turns sideways to desired direction of travel	5	7
	2. A step sideways followed by a slide of the trailing foot to next to the lead foot	4	5
	3. A short period during which both feet are off the floor	3	5
	4. Able to slide to the right and to the left	4	7

Note. From *Test of Gross Motor Development* (p. 17) by D. Ulrich, 1985, Austin, TX: PRO-ED. Reprinted with permission of PRO-ED, Inc.

[a]From a standardized sample of 909 nondisabled children ages 3 to 10 years.

away from the individual—as in throwing, striking, and kicking. Absorptive movements involve activities that require the individual to position the body or body parts to effectively stop or deflect an object. Absorptive movements include such skills as catching and trapping.

Tables 7.2 and 7.3, taken from the Test of Gross Motor Development designed by Ulrich (1985), lists the specific performance criteria for each locomotor and object control skill. Each table also lists the age at which 60% and 80% of a standardized sample of 909 nondisabled children 3 to 10 years of age achieved the specific performance criteria for each particular FMS.

This information can serve as a general guideline for instructors as to the approximate ages at which children without disabilities are developmentally ready to perform specific criteria for each FMS. These performance criteria percentages should serve as a general guideline, as most authorities agree that children including the mentally retarded develop FMS at various rates (Rarick, 1973; Wickstrom, 1983).

Quantitative Aspect of FMS

The quantitative or product-oriented aspects of a skill are such factors as how fast a person can

Table 7.3   Specific Performance Criteria for Object Control Skills

Skill	Performance criteria	Age[a] 60%	80%
Two-hand strike	1. Dominant hand grips bat above nondominant hand	3	5
	2. Nondominant side of the body faces the tosser	5	7
	3. Hip and spine rotation	8	9
	4. Weight is transferred by stepping with front foot	8	10
Stationary bounce	1. Contacts ball with one hand at about hip level	7	8
	2. Pushes ball with fingers (not a slap)	6	8
	3. Ball contacts floor in front of (or to the outside of) foot on the side of the hand being used	7	8
Catch	1. Preparation phase where elbows are flexed and hands are in front of the body	4	5
	2. Arms extend in preparation for ball contact	4	6
	3. Ball is caught and controlled by hands only	7	8
	4. Elbows bend to absorb force	7	8
Kick	1. Rapid continuous approach to the ball	4	4
	2. The trunk is inclined backward during ball contact	8	9
	3. Forward swing of the arm opposite the kicking leg	8	9
	4. Follows through by hopping on nonkicking leg	10	NA[b]
Overhand throw	1. A downward arc of the throwing arm initiates the windup	6	7
	2. Rotation of the hip and shoulder to the point where the nondominant side faces an imaginary target	7	8
	3. Weight is transferred by stepping with the foot opposite the throwing hand	6	8
	4. Follows through beyond ball release diagonally across body opposite the throwing arm	8	10

Note. From *Test of Gross Motor Development* (p. 18) by D. Ulrich, 1985. Austin, TX: PRO-ED. Reprinted by permission of PRO-ED, Inc.

[a]From a standardized sample of 909 nondisabled children ages 3 to 10 years.

[b]This performance criterion was not achieved by 80% of the standardized sample at any age from 3 to 10 years.

run or how accurately she or he can hit a target with a thrown ball. In the past, most studies conducted with this population have examined primarily the quantitative aspects of motor skill performance. For example, a study conducted by Rarick and Dobbins (1977) determined that boys with moderate mental retardation displayed lower performance accuracy scores on two throwing tasks when compared to nondisabled boys of a similar chronological age.

Norm-referenced tables, or product-oriented scores, in motor skill performance, including static balance and eye/hand coordination, for males and females (ages 6 to 20) classified as having mild or moderate mental retardation or Down syndrome are located in Appendix C. Although norm-referenced tables for this population are important and can be used to make valuable programming decisions, youngsters with mental retardation should also be judged against the norms of their age peers who do not have disabilities. Information regarding the quantitative aspects of FMS will allow appropriate comparisons and meaningful placement decisions—including placement into traditional physical education or into special/adapted physical education, or what is more desirable, a combination of the two.

Qualitative Aspects of FMS

Only recently have investigators begun to examine the qualitative aspects of FMS performance with this population (DiRocco, Clark, & Phillips, 1987; Ersing, Loovis, & Ryan, 1982; Holland, 1987). Qualitative FMS performance is defined as how well or efficiently an individual moves his or her body while performing a motor skill.

Holland (1987) compared 7 FMS among 89 male and 81 female school-age children who were nonhandicapped (NH) to 87 male and 51 female school-age children with educable mental impairments (EMI). Children ranged in age from 6 to 9 years. Each FMS was divided into

four qualitative components of mature skill level and tested by one of four trained testers. Children were tested individually or in pairs, and were assigned a 2 for each component of the skill demonstrated to criterion and a 1 for each component not met. Results of this study demonstrated that the qualitative fundamental motor skills of the EMI children were significantly lower than those of the NH children.

Why Do Individuals With Mental Retardation Have Deficits in FMS?

Researchers are in agreement that persons with mental retardation display inferior motor performance scores when compared to their nondisabled counterparts. These studies also consistently demonstrate that the more severe the mental retardation, the greater the deficit in motor skill performance (Hayden, 1965; Rarick, 1973). What is unclear, to date, is why this population exhibits inferior FMS. This population's inferior cognitive ability does not adequately explain it. Ersing et al. (1982) state that "in any discussion of factors affecting normal motor development, several are obvious by their frequent reference in the literature. In general these factors include size, physique, rate of maturation, child rearing practices, socioeconomic level and maturation" (p. 65). When one adds to this list poor health, abnormal reflex response, slowness in reaction time, a lack of movement opportunities and experiences, and a lack of quality instruction (Rarick, 1973), it is obvious that a combination of factors must be taken into consideration when trying to explain this population's movement deficiencies.

However, it may be that what's at issue is more than a combination of factors affecting FMS development. DiRocco et al. (1987) believe that persons with mental retardation may develop FMS differently than the nondisabled population:

If mildly mentally retarded persons develop their motor skills in a similar but delayed manner, then their lag behind nonhandicapped individuals may be attributed to a developmental delay. If on the other hand, MMR [mild mental retardation] persons' motor skills develop differently, then it could be argued that their lag in performance was due to qualitative differences in the underlying process of motor skill development. . . . To study the differences and similarities in motor skill development between MMR and NH children, researchers must investigate the process of coordination and control for evidence of developmental delay or qualitative differences. (p. 178-179)

For example, in investigating the developmental sequence of coordination for the propulsive phase of the standing long jump with 39 children with mild mental retardation (MMR) and 90 NH children, ages 4 to 7 years, DiRocco et al. (1987) determined that the patterns of leg and arm coordination were similar, but the distances jumped by the MMR children were 2 to 3 years behind their NH peers. It must be asked why, despite these movement similarities, large differences were evident in the distances jumped by the two groups. The investigators offered some possible explanations for these differences:

Equilibrium may act as a "rate limiter" to full emergence of arm action. . . . If balance were indeed a more slowly developing system, its effect might be anticipated to affect the arm action more than the leg action, since the arms are neurologically linked to the protective equilibrium reactions. . . . Another possibility might lie in the coordination of the two synergies (i.e., the arm and leg action). In jumping not only do the arms and legs need to be coordinated within themselves but they must also be timed together. Poorly coordinated actions

could result in shorter distances jumped, due to decreased takeoff velocity, higher projection angles, or both. . . . Finally the distance-jumped differences may be due to difference in control processes. . . . In the case of jumping, it may well be the MMR children have patterns of coordination similar to those of NH children but are unable to generate the ground reaction forces necessary to project their bodies as far as their NH peers. (p. 188-189)

Davis (1987) believes that to better determine reasons for movement deficiencies in this population, the physiological descriptive level of persons with mental retardation should also be examined. Davis observes that

data seem to suggest that the mentally handicapped subjects can be characterized as having a deficiency in muscle activation. That is, mentally handicapped subjects are unable to generate high levels of muscle activity (compared to their nonhandicapped peers) as measured by the electromyogram (EMG). . . . They appear not to be capable of maintaining constant levels of activity; and there is a marked delay in the onset of muscle activation. Moreover, this muscle activation deficiency appears to be even greater in Down's syndrome subjects than [in] nondistinguished mentally handicapped subjects. We may further speculate that extreme slowness of movement, which so typically characterizes this population, may be an important manifestation of this muscle activation deficiency. (p. 53)

Possible explanations offered by Davis for this muscle activation deficiency among this population include poor muscle tone, differences in muscle fiber, inability to generate high levels of EMG activity, and slow movement speed.

There are still other theories as to why individuals with mental retardation exhibit inferior FMS performance scores when compared to their nondisabled peers. For example, do children with Down syndrome develop FMS differently than other children classified as having mental retardation as well as differently than their nondisabled peers? Although research on this is limited, Parker, Bronks, and Snyder (1986), using cinemagraphic techniques, evaluated the variability of walking-gait development among ten 5-year-old Down syndrome children. They found that when these children's walking patterns were compared to those of Down syndrome adults and nondisabled children and adults, a marked difference existed. At foot contact, the Down syndrome children displayed shorter average step lengths, greater hip and knee flexion, and a more extended ankle position. The investigators suggest that these walking differences among the Down syndrome children may have been due to total body instability.

More research is needed to understand how this population develops FMS and why they display inferior levels of FMS when compared to their peers who do not have disabilities. Evidence indicates that this population has a de-velopmental delay along with other contributing factors including their general body size and physique, poor muscle tone, socioeconomic levels, a lack of movement experiences, and a lack of the opportunities that quality instruction would have provided them. It also appears from the limited research that a lack of muscle control (muscle activation or force generated) and a lack of muscle coordination of various body parts definitely impede movement. The instructor must keep in mind that the overall poor movement performance of the individual cannot be attributed solely to one single factor, but rather a combination of factors must be considered (see Table 7.4).

Program Implementation

Over 20 years of research clearly show that persons with mental retardation can make significant improvement in the area of FMS performance when provided with quality physical activity instruction. Movement deficits exhibited by this population should be considered not as inevitable but rather as a challenge to all

Table 7.4   General Factors Affecting FMS Performance

Prenatal	Childhood factors	Environmental factors
Nutritional and chemical factors of expectant mother	Prematurity	Movement experiences and opportunities
Drug and alcohol use and cigarette smoking of expectant mother	Low birth weight	Quality of instruction
Malnourishment and undernourishment	Young for date	Parent intervention
Heredity	Rate of growth	Adaptability and social and communication skills
Chromosomal-based disorders (e.g., Down syndrome)	Biological or developmental readiness	Attitude toward movement
Medical and health problems	Critical period of learning	
	Body size	
	Physique	
	Muscle tone	
	Illness	
	Neuromuscular process	
	Muscle control (muscle activation or force generated) and coordination	

educators, physical educators, recreation therapists, coaches, and therapists. This section discusses strategies that specifically address the unique needs of these persons and their ability to learn and perform FMS.

Assessment

When specific deficiencies in FMS performance are correctly identified, instruction can be designed to facilitate learning and alleviate movement problems. Thus, assessment of the qualitative aspects of the individual's FMS performance is critical to effective program implementation. For example, when testing her skill in the standing long jump, the instructor determines that a young girl with moderate mental retardation is unable to use her arms to extend forcefully forward and upward while reaching with full extension above her head. Having identified this area of movement deficiency, the instructor can begin instruction in this area by providing the child with a verbal cue (e.g., ''Lift the arms'') or a demonstration of the arm lift or, if necessary, by physically guiding the child's arms to extend forcefully forward and upward while reaching with full extension above the head.

To date, a few assessment instruments specifically address the underlying process of FMS performance with this population. Three such test batteries are the I CAN, the Test of Gross Motor Development (TGMD), and the Ohio State University Scale of Intra-Gross Motor Assessment (SIGMA). For brief descriptions of these tests, see chapter 3. Using the TGMD in an investigation of 40 children (ages 3 to 10 years) with moderate mental retardation, Ulrich (1984) determined the reliability of classification decisions regarding 12 FMS. The TGMD was used to assess 5 children in each age group on 2 separate days. Results of the study indicate that the TGMD is a reliable instrument capable of consistently classifying mastery or nonmastery of FMS performance for children

ages 3 to 10 years with moderate mental retardation.

As reported by Ersing et al. (1982), SIGMA has been effectively used to assess FMS performance in large samples of children with moderate mental retardation ranging from 6 to 15 years of age. The test with this population has been extensively field-tested, and rater reliability coefficients for each of the 11 items has been reported to range from .58 to 1.00 (Loovis, 1989).

Developmental Sequence

As stated earlier, research indicates that this population, with the possible exception of individuals with Down syndrome (Davis, 1987), follows the same developmental sequence as the nondisabled population but at a slower rate. Also, the more pronounced the retardation, the greater the movement deficit. Therefore, instructors must be very patient during program instruction, keeping in mind that these persons require more time and practice opportunities. Instructors must also develop manageable and simple teaching sequence progressions using the practices of task analysis, modeling, prompting, shaping, and chaining (see chapter 4). This developmental/analytical approach will help teachers effectively meet this population's varied entry-level needs.

Because of their developmental delay, children with mild mental retardation cannot be automatically mainstreamed. They should be given the sort of programming that is commonly provided in individualized special/adapted physical education classes. The traditional age-appropriate physical education class is based on the assumption that most of its students are at similar developmental levels and progress at about the same rate. Although physical education teachers would attest that there is a great range of abilities in any one age group, they would agree that most in the age group would be quite similar in performance. The following example shows an inappropriate placement based on disregard for developmental level: Most 10-year-old non-disabled children display a mastery, or mature level, of FMS and by this age are ready to move on to lead-up games and modified sport. However, a 10-year-old child with mild mental retardation is functioning at a motor developmental level of a much younger child in the initial stages of performing a fundamental motor pattern (e.g., a 6-year-old). The traditional fifth-grade physical education program cannot effectively meet the movement needs of a child who is developmentally functioning at the first-grade FMS level. For this child, being mainstreamed into a fifth-grade class produces only failure and frustration. Thus, appropriate placement is critical. Anything less is incompatible with the mandates of PL 94-142 (U.S. Office of Education, 1977), including the mandate to place each child in the least restrictive environment.

Age Appropriateness

Even though instruction must match the developmental level of each individual, the instructor must also keep in mind that learning activities should be developed that are also commensurate with the individual's chronological age. Loovis (1989) argues strongly for the selection and implementation of age-appropriate activities: "It is totally inappropriate to suggest to older, disabled children, adolescents, or adults that they engage in the same movement experiences planned for younger children. This would have the effect of drawing attention to their differences with minimal benefits in terms of skill acquisition and refinement, thereby diminishing the impact and intent of social interaction. What is being suggested is that the differences in fundamental motor skills and pattern and the need to expedite some modification in an existing skill or pattern should be age-related" (p. 151).

For example, adults with moderate mental retardation should never be insulted by being made to play such games as "Duck Duck Goose" or "Drop the Hanky." The focus for adults should be on functional skills and lifetime leisure activities. For more discussion of age-appropriate activities for this adult population, see chapter 11.

Opportunity for Practice

Because this population has developmental delays and movement deficiencies, they need abundant opportunities to practice FMS under quality instruction. The truth is not that "Practice makes perfect" but, rather, that "Perfect practice makes perfect." Persons with mental retardation, when left on their own, either will not practice FMS or may practice them incorrectly, so quality instruction is essential. In addition, because these individuals have short attention spans and tire easily, practice sessions must be short, frequent, and motivational. To keep the participants on task and motivated, the instructor can vary the presentation of task ideas, weave an element of fun into each session, and incorporate the behavior management strategies discussed in chapter 4.

To date, there is little research on the effects of practice opportunities or the retention and transfer of skill learning with this population. Porretta (1988) investigated the effects of contextual interference (random practice) on the immediate transfer and 2-day retention of an underhand beanbag tossing skill conducted on children with mild mental retardation (M IQ = 64). A total of 48 subjects (M = 24, F = 24), with an average chronological age of 10.2 years, were placed into one of three different practice groups (random, blocked, or serial). No significant differences were found among the groups, but subjects in the random practice group performed fewer errors than the other groups during transfer and retention of the throwing skill. Additionally, Poretta concluded:

Another plausible explanation for the lack of significant findings for condition may have been due to an insufficient amount of practice trials to adequately develop distinctive and elaborate memory representations. . . . For example, while this study used 48 acquisition trials, the study by Edwards, Elliot, and Lee (1986), with Down syndrome adolescents used 64 acquisition trials. Therefore an added number of trials or additional practice sessions may well have been necessary in order for subjects with mild mental retardation to develop the memory representations needed to benefit from contextual effects when asked to perform gross motor skills. Too often motor behavior studies utilize only one practice or acquisition session, and only enough trials to obtain change in performance. Whether the change can endure over time remains to be determined in most studies. (pp. 337-338)

Information Processing

Many movement deficiencies exhibited by persons with mental retardation may be due to their limitations in processing information. Brain damage makes it difficult to form adequate perceptions, which are the basis for motor performance and motor learning. This does not mean that there is a deficiency in a particular sensory organ (e.g., the eye or the ear), but rather the perceptual integration and interpretation (which occur in the brain) of the incoming stimuli are faulty (Hutt & Gibby, 1979).

Thomas (1984) believes information processing plays an important role in the development of FMS performance for individuals with mental retardation: "How does cognitive development in MR individuals relate to motor performance? . . . The same system controls all learning and memory, whether cognitive, motor, or affective. A problem in the memory system may affect motor skill acquisition in infinite ways, including less understanding of task variables or verbal instructions, poor motor planning,

slower processing, and inadequate socialization among others. . . . Cognitive development in these children must be understood so that appropriate activities for this special population can be designed" (p. 175).

Moreover, when providing instructions, the instructor must carefully keep in mind how this population processes information. Croce and DePaepe (1989) explain some of the brain's work in information processing with regard to skill execution:

Before skill execution, this central processor must receive information from sensory receptors regarding the environment, body position in space, position of different body parts in relation to each other, and various movement parameters (e.g., force, amplitude, speed, duration, and direction of the movement in question). The central processor generates movement by way of the efferent messages to the body's muscles. As the movement is generated, an "efferent copy" or motor template of the movement is generated. Depending on the task in question, the movement includes kinesthetic feedback, as well as from the visual, auditory, and vestibular systems. Feedback (how the movement was executed) is then matched against the motor template (how the movement was planned). . . . During the initial stages of learning, motor programs are revised frequently in order to match feedback with the motor template. When learning finally occurs, the motor program is well established and can be generated with little need for peripheral feedback. (p. 14)

All information processing models include sensory input, processing or integration of information, motor output, and feedback. Figure 7.4 is the flowchart of a simple information processing model. The relationship of movement performance to the kinesthetic, tactile, visual,

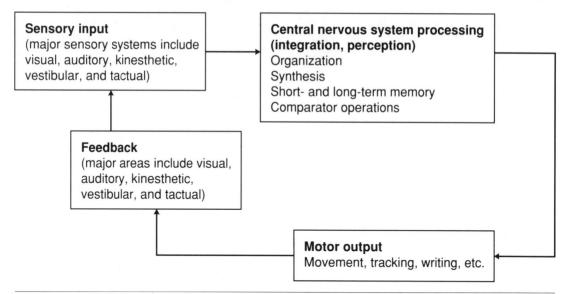

Figure 7.4   Information processing model.

Note. From ''Perceptual-Motor Dimensions'' by J.P. Winnick (ed.), *Adapted Physical Education and Sport* (p. 98), 1990, Champaign IL: Human Kinetics. Copyright 1990 by Joseph P. Winnick. Reprinted by permission.

and auditory sensory systems is discussed in detail in chapter 8.

Deficits in information processing can contribute to this population's difficulty in following and understanding verbal instructions. Phrases such as *run fast, run hard, run as quick as you can,* may confuse these individuals, because they may not be familiar with such abstract terms. Thus, the specific instructions a teacher uses play a vital role in program success. Directions must be clear, concise, consistent, and understandable. They must also be portioned out sparingly and reinforced repeatedly. For example, when introduced to new skills, the participant may tend to forget the ideas and concepts involved and, more importantly, the words that explain the skills. For example, the standing long jump is a highly coordinated task comprising many component movements. The Special Olympics coach who says, ''Swing your arms backward, then forward, then backward; bend your knees; lean forward; swing your arms forward and upward—then jump!'' is providing the participant with too much information. The jumper cannot remember all the

commands. So, even though doing the motions in sequence is necessary for maximum jumping distance, the coach must keep in mind that multiple verbal instructions will confuse the performer. Verbal directions must be kept to a minimum and consistently administered to the learner in simple and commonly understood words.

During the initial stages of teaching a skill, the instructor should vary only one aspect of the introduced task at a time and provide repeated and varied practice trials. Tasks should be introduced in a developmental sequence from simple to complex. Once one part of the task is mastered, another part can be introduced. Eventually all of the tasks can be linked together to form the desired FMS (see chapter 4 on task analysis).

Demonstration

Also vital to program instruction is demonstration. Often when participants observe someone else perform a skill, they seem to comprehend what is to be done and proceed to attempt the task. Participants should also be provided with physical cues they can understand. For example, in the standing long jump, when a child is having difficulty understanding the concept of jumping for distance, one can place a hula hoop on the ground in front of the child and instruct him or her to jump into the hoop. Upon each successful jump, the hoop can be moved farther away to increase the distance. If the student still has difficulty after being given simple and clear verbal directions, a demonstration, and physical cues, the instructor may need to physically guide the child through the various parts of the jumping skill. Highlight 7.5 lists basic principles of teaching fundamental motor skills.

Summary

As we discussed earlier in this chapter, this population lacks the muscle control and coordination of various body parts to master fundamental motor skills (Davis, 1987; DiRocco et al., 1987). But this doesn't mean they can't improve their skills. For instance, the instructor who teaches the standing long jump using a comprehensive program that includes overall strength development (leg strength), coordination (both leg and arm action), and stability and balance (propulsion and landing phase) can assume that the students will make progress.

Hogg and Sebba (1987) believe that certain motor dysfunctions, developmental delays, and incompetence are all linked. Any form of dysfunction will almost certainly slow development and make the successful performance of movement tasks difficult if not impossible. In addition, the cognitive component underlying movement efficiency will be a strong influence on such ability. Brain damage and inherited motor skill ability provide the basic blueprint for existing and future FMS performance. Therefore, professionals will certainly be challenged to provide this population with instruction that will account for movement success and

---

HIGHLIGHT 7.5   **IN PRACTICE**

Principles of Teaching Fundamental Motor Skills

During fundamental motor skill practice, the instructor should

1. consider the physical and cognitive readiness of the performer;
2. provide for positive and successful experience in the early stages of learning, remembering that encouragement and reinforcement are important;
3. develop teaching progressions based on the learner's present level of performance and determine what the learner can and cannot do;
4. analyze skills into simple tasks the learner can perform;
5. provide for overlearning of a skill by

including maximum repetitions of the exact skill;

6. be careful not to rush the learner into the skill in the early stages of learning;
7. practice skills at a speed and force that allow successful, precise performance of the movement;
8. make practice sessions short and frequent during the initial stages of learning and increase practice duration as skill level increases;
9. vary practice to assist in transfer of skills; and
10. provide the learner with both qualitative and quantitative feedback.

Note. Adapted from Croce & DePaepe (1989).

progress. Eichstaedt and Kalakian (1987) believe it is important for the instructor to remember, during program implementation, "that special programming be challenging, but not frustrating. Challenges should be reasonable, and progress will often be measured in inches rather than feet; in seconds rather than minutes. The child should be gently prodded by sincere and regular encouragement with progress, no matter how modest, recognized as an important accomplishment" (p. 91).

AQUATICS

Aquatic programs offer a wide range of activities, including, for many persons with disabilities such as mental retardation, the opportunity and freedom to perform in the water movements that could never be attempted or successfully accomplished on land. Water's buoyancy reduces the gravitational force, so that successful movement requires less muscular effort and efficiency. A person immersed to the neck in water will seem to lose 90% of the weight she or he has on land. Therefore, a person weighing 150 pounds needs to support only 15 pounds of body weight when immersed in water (Horvat & Forbus, 1989). This allows individuals with muscular weakness to maneuver more easily and comfortably in the water. Christie (1985) calls water a great equalizer that lessens the evidence of disability. This newfound success and movement achievement for persons with mental retardation can prove to be fun, rewarding, motivational, and, most importantly, a positive experience.

An appropriate program can be developed and implemented for each person, no matter how severe his or her mental retardation. A well-rounded aquatic program should not only provide this population with instruction in proper safety procedures and correct swimming technique, but include a wide range of activities from shallow-water wading to competitive swimming and diving (which are provided by Special

Olympics), underwater sport, water exercises, aquatic games, boating, sailing, and therapeutic activities (YMCA, 1987). By offering a wide range of activities, the instructor is better able to provide programming appropriate for the wide variety of ability levels in this population. A well-developed aquatics program can foster educational, recreational, therapeutic, and safety benefits for all participants with mental retardation (see Figure 7.5).

Benefits of Aquatic Programs

The water's buoyancy allows many persons with mental retardation, especially those who have severe or multiple disabilities to have positive movement experiences in the water that they could never experience on land (Priest, 1990). These positive opportunities in the water can enhance the students' self-esteem and their acceptance of other forms of physical activity.

Any movement (e.g., physical fitness, fundamental motor skills) taught on land can be modified for successful performance in the water. For example, people who are unable to

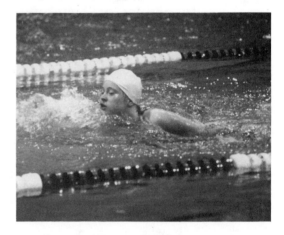

Figure 7.5 Regardless of the severity of mental retardation, an appropriate aquatics program for each person can be implemented. Photo courtesy of Ken Regan.

walk or jog or participate in other forms of exercise because of a weak back or weak ankles, knees, or hips have been found to be able to successfully exercise in the water (Gorman, Brown, Daniel, & Daniel, 1987). In fact, the YMCA (1987) suggests that "gym" programs be reinforced with aquatics programs in order to provide this population with a variety of physical activity experiences and opportunities.

Skills in aquatics can provide this population with the opportunity to pursue a lifelong recreational outlet with family and peers in a socially acceptable manner and in the mainstream of society (Johannsen, 1987). Functional skills such as dressing and grooming can be reinforced in a well-developed aquatics program. Perhaps the most significant benefit is that these individuals can acquire safety skills by learning to properly protect and enjoy themselves while in and near the water (Christie, 1985).

Safety

The first and foremost consideration of any aquatics program must be safety. The instructor must always think safety and seek to instill this concept in all participants. Langendorfer (1986) states that no individual, regardless of age and skill level, can ever be completely safe in the water without supervision. Not only should the safety of each participant be assured, but each individual should be taught safety awareness and skills such as reaching, throwing, and wading assists as well as how to properly wear a personal flotation device (American Red Cross, 1977). Rules must be effectively communicated to everyone involved in the program, including lifeguards, instructors, and participants.

It is important to remember that persons with mental retardation may require a number of unique safety precautions. For example, persons with Down syndrome who have been diagnosed by a physician as having atlantoaxial instability should avoid activities, such as the butter-

fly stroke or diving, that would place a strain on the neck. Because this population is limited in their mental ability, many may not be aware of the water's potential dangers. They may be unable to adequately judge the water depth in the pool and may jump in at any time. For this reason, Eichstaedt and Kalakian (1987) emphasize the importance of developing safety rules that can be understood by all participants. Clear and simple poolside procedures must be established, and the rules must be repeated often and kept consistent. This will structure the environment so that all participants understand what is expected of them and have a feeling of security. These authors advocate poolside procedures in which all participants walk in, sit on the deck, and wait for the command from the instructor before entering the water. Other poolside safety considerations outlined by the American Red Cross (1977) include

- assisting individuals with balance difficulties when they walk on wet decks and ramps;
- using wheelchairs whenever possible, because it is unsafe to carry anyone on the deck, even small children; and
- locking all wheelchairs in place on the deck before taking individuals out of their chairs.

Another important safety consideration is the regulation of water and air temperature. This is especially important for persons with mental retardation who have multiple disabilities. Water that is too cold inhibits movement, especially for persons with severe cerebral palsy; water that is too warm is uncomfortable and can exhaust participants. Eichstaedt and Kalakian (1987) state that authorities are in disagreement over the ideal water temperature and believe it is best to regulate the temperature to accommodate the activity level of the different groups participating in the pool program. In general, youngsters with severe disabilities require higher water temperatures (as much as 96 °F) and shorter periods of activity in the pool. In addition, Campion (1985) suggests that air temperature be slightly lower than water temperature (86 °F to 93 °F) to allow for a gentle cooling of the body.

Campion (1985) also discusses three other factors central to aquatic safety: pool surface, lighting, and noise. Many persons with mental retardation have poor muscle control, balance, vision, and spatial awareness. Therefore, pool and dressing-room floors should have nonslip surfaces. Proper lighting assures that the entire water area and the full depth of the pool are visible, which is especially important during underwater activities, and aids instruction by ensuring that instructors and students are clearly visible to each other at all times. Finally, pools are noisy places with lots of splashing, laughing, and shouting. For persons with mental retardation, this noise can produce anxiety and tension and prove quite disturbing and distracting. Such noise is contraindicated for individuals who have retained the Moro reflex or have an exaggerated startle reflex (see chapter 8 for a discussion of reflexes). Therefore, initial stages of program instruction may need to be in a quiet area of the pool and on a one-to-one basis.

The aquatic program can be particularly hazardous to persons with mental retardation who have a history of seizures (Eichstaedt & Kalakian, 1987). These persons can be involved in swim programs, but administrators must take necessary steps to identify and develop appropriate specific procedures in the locker room, on the pool deck, and in the water. These authors identify the following precautions and procedures instructors should consider when programming for persons with seizures.

1. The type of seizure should be identified. For example, Are the seizures frequent? Are they controlled by medication?

2. In general, persons with infrequent seizures should be allowed to participate if the instructor is aware of the condition and is trained to deal with seizures.

3. Persons with seizures should wear easily identifiable swim caps that distinguish them from the rest of the participants in the pool.

4. A buddy system should be developed, and "buddies" should be instructed beforehand in what to expect when a seizure occurs and who to notify.

5. An individual who is having a seizure should not be removed from the water unless it can be accomplished easily. The water will soothe the individual by absorbing the thrashing movements and presents little danger unless the person is near the side of the pool.

6. In the pool, support the individual face up and out of the water until the seizure passes. Once the seizure is over, the person should rest and not be allowed to return to the water for the remainder of the day.

For more information, see the section on seizures in chapter 2.

Water Orientation

Persons with mental retardation will have a wide range of reactions to the water, ranging from great fear to fearlessness. Campion (1985) suggests that extreme apprehension toward the water can be due to limited comprehension and communication, fear of falling, difficulties with respiration, or inability to create required movements or to control involuntary movements. According to Grosse and McGill (1979), "Many individuals with severe physical impairments have either extremely limited movements or a great deal of extra, unwanted movement due to unpredictable muscle spasms. Nervousness, excitement, fear, or just concentration can increase muscle tension, limit further voluntary movements and increase involuntary actions. Therefore, the primary goal in water adjustment is to make the individual comfortable in the water" (p. 3). If participants are relaxed and comfortable in and around the water, they will have better quality of movement and will enjoy the activity more.

Becoming oriented to the water includes learning techniques in water entry, breath control, and face submersion (American Red Cross, 1977). We will now discuss each of these in detail.

Water Entry

A participant must be adjusted to the water not only physically but also mentally. Horvat and Forbus (1989) believe that pleasurable experiences with water in other contexts prepare children to enter the pool water without undue fear. A great variety of experiences can help children feel comfortable around and in the water, such as sitting or wading in a wading pool or large tub, playing with wet sponges, and being gently doused or splashed with water with a bucket or a toy. These children may need to watch others playing and having fun in the pool before they are ready to get into the pool themselves. Most importantly, they should never be rushed into entering the pool. Let it occur naturally. Their approach may be gradual, starting with sitting with their feet in the water, watching others in the pool. Horvat and Forbus believe that a demonstration by a friend or another child often may prove more helpful than one provided by the instructor.

The "sink or swim" method should never be used with anyone. There is no single solution for helping a person overcome fear of the water, but the American Red Cross (1977) suggests the following:

1. Provide for numerous successful experiences in approaching and entering the water.
2. Let participants bring security props, such as waterproof toys, to the poolside.
3. Explain what will happen as they enter the water and how they may feel once they are in the water.

4. Allow participants the freedom to move in and out of the water without being restricted by the instructor.
5. Most importantly, throughout the entire experience, remain enthusiastic and reassuring toward participants.

Once the child has gained enough confidence to enter the water, the transition from the pool deck to the water must be conducted smoothly and with no hesitation. Campion (1985) suggests using games, such as "Humpty Dumpty"; at the words "had a great fall," the instructor lifts the child quickly and smoothly away from the pool deck and into the water. Once the child is in the water, it is important to begin an activity immediately, as this will help distract the child from any anxiety she or he may have about being in the water. Manual support or flotation devices may be necessary for persons with severe or profound mental retardation. Proper support also helps reduce anxiety in the water, which in turn can make instruction easier.

Once in the water, the individual must be provided with opportunities to adjust to the different characteristics of the water; the water's feel, turbulence, buoyancy, and weight all will affect the person's body balance. For example, the feel of the water is not only the sensation of the water on the skin, but includes the drag effect of the water on the limbs. The participant must also be taught that the water has weight and that it can be used as a force to assist in performing various movements (Campion, 1985). Examples of activities for adjusting to the various properties of the water are provided in Highlight 7.6.

Breath Control

For most aquatic activities, proper breathing techniques are essential. Swallowing a big mouthful of water can be a very frightening experience. Therefore, proper breathing must be not only encouraged but properly taught. Some persons with mental retardation may not be able

Water Adjustment Activities

The following activities will help children adjust to the various properties of the water and are adapted from suggestions offered by the YMCA (1987) and Campion (1985).

- The children wash or gently splash their faces or bodies, using their hands or sponges, buckets, or water toys (water's feel).
- The children play various catch games with the instructor while the child sits with feet in the water at the edge of pool (water's feel).
- Taking a bath by washing various body parts with the hands, a sponge, or a washcloth. This activity can be conducted in the pool or a wading pool (water's feel).
- Pass the Object: Students form a circle

and pass an object, such as a kickboard or sponge ball, around to each other (water's feel).
- Taxi Ride: The instructor provides the child with piggyback ride in the water (water's feel and turbulence).
- Washing Machine: The children place their hands on their hips and swish through the water with torso twists (water's turbulence and buoyancy).
- The instructor holds and gently sways the child in the water pretending he or she is "Rag Doll" or "Seaweed" (water's turbulence).
- The instructor holds the child in the water while playing such games as "Here We Go Round the Mulberry Bush" and "Humpty Dumpty" (water's weight).

---

to correctly form their lips to blow air out; the instructor should teach them, while they are out of the water, to exhale through their nostrils and mouth while humming. The word *Blow* should be the verbal cue used by the instructor when the person's face comes near the water. Blowing is also an important prerequisite skill for proper head control. The blowing action helps to bring the head forward and aids in creating a forward rotation around the center of buoyancy (Campion, 1985). Highlight 7.7 lists activities that can help the child learn to blow properly.

Face Submersion

Children with mental retardation who are newcomers to the aquatic environment will probably be apprehensive about putting their heads under water. Eichstaedt and Kalakian (1987)

suggest that two important concepts the instructor can instill in the learner to overcome this apprehension are that the water will not hurt the eyes and that a mouthful of water can be spit out. Two methods these authors suggest for removing water from the eyes are blinking the eyes several times or wiping one's fingers downward over one's closed eyelids. The following games can help build self-confidence in each participant and alleviate their problems with breath control when their faces are totally submersed.

1. The children place their faces in the water and identify whether the instructor's hand is open or closed in a fist. Next they identify how many fingers the instructor is showing underwater.
2. With their faces underwater, the children determine the number of taps they hear

HIGHLIGHT 7.7

Blowing Activities

The following activities can help the child learn to blow properly; they are adapted from suggestions offered by the YMCA (1987).

- The children blow out pretend "birthday candles" on a cake or blow bubbles with a plastic bubble pipe in the water.
- The children blow "holes" in the water by blowing at the water just above its surface.
- The children blow bubbles in the water with soda straws.
- The children blow table-tennis balls along

the pool gutter or in the water. This activity can be conducted as a relay race, once the children are adept at moving the ball.
- The children blow bubbles in the water, while stretching their arms and holding onto the pool gutter.

Children who still have difficulty with blowing in the water can practice many of these activities while on the pool deck or using whistles and noisemakers.

---

when the instructor taps two metal objects together underwater.
3. The children attempt a jellyfish float or dead man's float.
4. The instructor places a weight (e.g., a lifesaving brick) in a child's hand, and the child sits on the bottom of the pool.
5. The children retrieve objects from the bottom of the shallow end of the pool. Use such objects as a brightly colored plastic clam, a plastic jug filled with sand and wrapped with aluminum foil to add visibility, or a lifesaving brick.

Proper water orientation for persons with mental retardation must be an integral part of any comprehensive aquatic program. To date, little research and few assessment instruments are available to adequately measure water orientation specific to this population. The Water Orientation Checklist—Basic (WOC-B) and the Water Orientation Checklist—Advanced (WOC-A) are two instruments that have been developed to test both traditional aspects (water entry, breath control, face submersion, floating,

and recoveries) and novel aspects (e.g., active buoyancy or being able to move through the water without touching the bottom) of water orientation with various special populations, including preschoolers, children, and youth with mental retardation (Killian, Arena-Ronde, & Bruno, 1987). Interobserver reliability scores of .87 for the WOC-B and .80 for the WOC-A have been determined. Killian et al. reported both instruments to be precise but flexible and able to measure a participant's performance success on a five-choice rating scale (spontaneous, verbal, verbal with demonstration, physical guidance, and objection). The WOC-B and WOC-A are displayed in Highlight 7.8.

Equipment

The proper use of equipment in the aquatic environment is important. It facilitates instruction, provides reinforcement, assists in adjustment to the water, and makes activities and games more enjoyable. Equipment need not be expensive, and can often be modified or homemade. Much

| HIGHLIGHT 7.8 | IN PRACTICE |

Water Orientation Checklist

Directions for the Water Orientation Checklist–Basic (WOC-B): The following 13 items are assessed using a five-choice rating scale. The observer records only successful performances by circling an ''s'' on the appropriate level of the rating scale. Rating-scale choices use the following abbreviations and operational definitions:

Spontaneous (SP): A behavior in which a subject performs 1 of 13 tasks prior to the instructor's verbal directions.

Verbal (VB): The subject performs the specific task after the instructor's verbal directions.

Verbal with demonstration (DMO): The subject performs the specified task after the instructor's verbal directions and visual cues.

Physical guidance (PG): The instructor manipulates the subject's body through the specific task; verbal directions and visual cues accompany manipulation.

Objection (OBJ): The subject is unwilling to attempt the task; the response involves both passive and active objection.

Directions for the Water Orientation Checklist–Advanced (WOC-A): The following 13 items are assessed by recording both successful and unsuccessful performance on each level of the five-choice rating scale. For each item it is possible to record several unsuccessful performances prior to recording a successful performance. The observer records performances by circling one or more abbreviations. The following abbreviations and operational definitions are used:

Successful (s): The subject performs the task as defined.

Unsuccessful (u): The subject demonstrates an overt response in which he or she attempts but fails to perform the specified task.

Passive objection (p): The subject fails to attend to the task, says ''no,'' or shows no overt motor response.

Active objection (a): The subject demonstrates pulling away, running away, tantrum, self-abuse, verbal yells, or screams.

Item		WOC-B		WOC-A	
	1. The instructor holds the subject by the hand as they walk	SP	s	s	u
	to a predetermined location 8 ft from the pool. Instructor	VB	s	s	u
	then releases subject's hand, and subject proceeds toward	DMO	s	s	u
	the pool:	PG	s	s	u
		OBJ	obj	p	a

HIGHLIGHT 7.8 CONTINUED

2. The subject touches the water with either hand or foot:

SP	s	s	u
VB	s	s	u
DMO	s	s	u
PG	s	s	u
OBJ obj		p	a

3. The subject enters the pool by placing both feet in shallow water:

SP	s	s	u
VB	s	s	u
DMO	s	s	u
PG	s	s	u
OBJ obj		p	a

4. The subject remains in the pool throughout the observation:
   a. spontaneously
   b. exits, returns after verbal direction
   c. exits, returns after verbal direction with demonstration
   d. exits, returns with physical guidance
   e. exits and objects to returning to the pool

SP	s	s	u
VB	s	s	u
DMO	s	s	u
PG	s	s	u
OBJ obj		p	a

5. The subject attains a sitting, squatting, or horizontal position (wet up to waist) in the water:

SP	s	s	u
VB	s	s	u
DMO	s	s	u
PG	s	s	u
OBJ obj		p	a

6. The subject blows bubbles (mouth contacts water, and exhalation produces bubbles):

SP	s	s	u
VB	s	s	u
DMO	s	s	u
PG	s	s	u
OBJ obj		p	a

7. The subject submerges entire face (forehead, eyes, nose, mouth, chin in water):

SP	s	s	u
VB	s	s	u
DMO	s	s	u
PG	s	s	u
OBJ obj		p	a

8. The subject performs a back float (ears in water, arms and legs extended, mouth and nose out of water, feet not touching the bottom):

SP	s	s	u
VB	s	s	u
DMO	s	s	u
PG	s	s	u
OBJ obj		p	a

HIGHLIGHT 7.8 CONTINUED

9. The subject performs a back float recovery (attaining a standing position without face submersion):

SP	s	s	u
VB	s	s	u
DMO	s	s	u
PG	s	s	u
OBJ obj		p	a

10. The subject performs a prone float (face submersion, arms and legs extended, feet not touching the bottom):

SP	s	s	u
VB	s	s	u
DMO	s	s	u
PG	s	s	u
OBJ obj		p	a

11. The subject performs a prone float recovery (attaining a standing position without turning over):

SP	s	s	u
VB	s	s	u
DMO	s	s	u
PG	s	s	u
OBJ obj		p	a

12. The subject performs a turnover from back to prone float (without touching the bottom):

SP	s	s	u
VB	s	s	u
DMO	s	s	u
PG	s	s	u
OBJ obj		p	a

13. The subject swims 5 ft (any propulsive movement without touching the bottom):

SP	s	s	u
VB	s	s	u
DMO	s	s	u
PG	s	s	u
OBJ obj		p	a

Note unusual behavior:

_____

_____

_____

Note. From ''Refinement of Two Instruments That Assess Water Orientation in Atypical Swimmers'' by K.J. Killian, S. Arena-Ronde and L. Bruno, 1987, _Adapted Physical Activity Quarterly_, **4**, pp. 25-37. Copyright 1987 by Human Kinetics Publishers. Reprinted by permission.

of the equipment used in the physical education or recreational setting can be improvised for use in the pool. Highlight 7.9 lists a variety of equipment possibilities.

Flotation Devices

Many individuals with mental retardation have poor fitness, balance, head control, and overall motor ability; they require assistive flotation devices to help them maintain correct body position and gain confidence in the water. Many sorts of flotation devices are available, including water wings, inflatable arm supports, rubber tubes, buoyant belts, life jackets, life preservers, inflatable vests, and swimsuits with built-in flotation support. With proper instructional supervision, these devices can serve an important purpose in the aquatic program (American Red Cross, 1977). According to Langendorfer (1986), "Like any teaching method or piece of learning equipment, flotation devices have their place. They should not be substitutes for a good teacher, teaching progression, or parental supervision. On the other hand, they can provide the instructor with an avenue for demonstrating water buoyancy to a fearful young child and a means for the unskilled child to practice arm and leg locomotor movements without submerging" (p. 65). Horvat and Bishop (1981) suggest that by securing a plastic bottle to a life jacket, one can produce a flotation device that will help a child with severe or profound mental retardation maintain head control and assume a comfortable backlying position in the water.

Eichstaedt and Kalakian (1987) suggest that instructors ask the following questions when deciding whether or not to use a flotation device with a student:

| *HIGHLIGHT 7.9* | **IN PRACTICE** |

Aquatic Equipment

Activity Equipment

Floating balls
Balloons
Table-tennis balls
Sponges
Hoops
Ropes
Plastic jugs
Diving rings
Discs
Inflatable toy animals
Inner tubes
Mats
Slides
Squirt guns

Styrofoam blocks
Plastic toys such as boats and buckets
Wading pool
Kickboards
Water saucers
Swim fins
Sound devices

Safety Equipment

Reaching poles
Throwable flotation devices such as ring buoys
Personal flotation devices (PFDs), head supports
Wheelchairs

1. Is the individual capable of standing without assistance?
2. Does the individual display extreme balance difficulties?
3. Does the individual exhibit poor head control, and will the head submerge due to involuntary hypertension?
4. Does the individual display sufficient neck strength?

Program Implementation

Aquatic program instruction should be more than the teaching of swim strokes. For example, Langendorfer, German, and Kral (1988) offer the following description of using a developmental instructional approach during the implementation of an aquatic program for preschool-age children.

> The instructor starts by asking the class members "Who can . . . demonstrate how a whale spouts OR how an otter slides down a bank OR how a porpoise leaps out of the water?" These learning games are accompanied by the inevitable "Watch me! Watch me! I can! I can!" Further imagine this review session is followed by a rousing session of "Rocketship" or "Time machine" as swimmers explore ways to use their limbs to move through the water. These exploration sessions conclude with "Tube Tag" or "Mat Pull." While all this is happening, the instructor is adapting the games and learning experiences to the developmental levels of less experienced class members so they can accomplish these skills at a minimal competency level within each skill. Finally, "Underwater Obstacle Course" concludes the "structured" part of the lesson by combining several previously-learned skills into a problem-solving format. The instructor then devotes individual time to those class members who are having difficulty with a new skill or who

need to be challenged by a more difficult task. (p. 11)

Developmental Individualized Approach

Given the description we just read from Langendorfer and colleagues, swimming ability need not be a prerequisite to aquatic instruction. In fact, Langendorfer (1986) says that "the term 'swimming' should not be limited solely to swimming strokes, but should include any form of intentional aquatic locomotion (i.e., any body movements that purposefully propel the body through the water)" (p. 63). Programs must be developmental in nature if aquatic instruction is to meet the unique needs and wide range of ability levels of persons with mental retardation. This instructional approach is especially important for individuals with severe and profound mental retardation, a population too often neglected in the aquatic setting (Horvat & Bishop, 1981). Instructors not only must be able to develop swim progressions that range from simple to complex, but must also be able to teach these skills.

Because the developmental approach has received little attention in aquatic programs, Langendorfer, Roberts, and Ropka (1987) have developed the Aquatic Readiness Assessment (ARA) instrument to measure the developmental prone swimming locomotion skills of young children 3 to 10 years of age. This instrument can be used with children with or without disabilities (Langendorfer, 1989). As shown in Highlight 7.10, the ARA measures the quality of prone swimming movements while following a task-sequence approach. Very simply, the ARA provides the instructor with a teaching progression for arm and leg action, body position, and combined movement in a prone swimming position.

Perhaps this instrument's greatest strength is its effectiveness for individualizing instruction. For example, using the instrument, the instructor

HIGHLIGHT 7.10

IN PRACTICE

The Aquatic Readiness Assessment Instrument

A. Level of arm action in prone swimming
   1. No arm action
   2. Underarm paddling (short pull only, alternating or bilateral)
   3. Underarm stroking (long pull-push action)
   4. Overarm dropped elbow stroke
   5. Overarm high elbow lift stroke

B. Level of leg action in prone swimming
   1. Prelocomotor (random kicking, effective for movement)
   2. Plantar push (bicycling/running action)
   3a. Bent knee flutter
   b. Asymmetric flutter/trudgeon
   4a. Straight leg flutter
   b. Trudgeon/wedge frog kick

   5. Breaststroke (whip)

C. Level of body action in prone swimming
   1. Vertical suspended position (45 to 90 degrees)
   2. Inclined suspended position (10 to 44 degrees)
   3. Horizontal suspended position (0 to 9 degrees)

D. Level of combined movement in prone swimming
   1. No independent position
   2. Brief dog paddle (6 feet or less)
   3. Extended dog paddle (10 feet or more)
   4. Beginner (human) underarm stroke
   5. Rudimentary overarm strokes
   6. Advanced formal strokes

Note. From ''Aquatic Readiness: A Developmental Test'' by S. Langendorfer, M.S. Roberts and C.R. Ropka, 1988, *National Aquatics Journal*, **3**, pp. 8-12. Reprinted by permission of the Council for National Cooperation in Aquatics.

can determine each participant's present level of prone swimming performance; then instruction for each individual can begin with the next step of the test sequence. Langendorfer (1989) believes that the writing of IEPs integrates naturally with developmentally sequenced assessment instruments such as the ARA, broadening instruction to include a diverse range of skills within the developmental level of each learner. This approach does not limit instruction to the teaching of a few swim strokes, which is all too common in many aquatic programs. Highlight 7.11 presents an example of a hypothetical aquatic IEP for a learner with a disability,

integrated from the ARA and developed by Langendorfer (1989).

Instructional Activities

A well-designed developmental aquatic program can be an integral part of this population's physical activity and movement experiences, although it is important for the instructor to realize that new skills should be introduced at the beginning of the class lesson because this population (especially persons with cerebral palsy) may tire quickly and chill easily (Eichstaedt & Kalakian, 1987). Physical activity and movement instruction provided in the water can reinforce

Aquatic IEP

Child: Susie Swimmer **Age:** 4 yr, 6 mo

Contraindications: Tympanostomy tubes, no deep submersion.
Atlantoaxial instability possible—no diving.

Current Level of Functioning (pretest):
Administered 10/20/88 using Langendorfer's Aquatic Readiness Assessment & Red Cross Infant/Preschool Aquatic Program items.

ARA:
Water entry: Stepped in without assistance (no flight)
Breath control: Brief face submersion (1s)
Leg action: Rudimentary bent knee flutter kick (supported)
Arm action: Pull-push alternating action (supported)
Body position: Inclined 45 degrees

ARC IPAP:
Water adjustment: Child kicks at edge of pool.
Water entry: Child steps to instructor by herself.
Front kick: Child kicks at side in group.
Breath control: Child holds onto support and submerges.
Prone glide: Only with support.
Back float: Only with instructor support.
Unsupported stroking: None evidenced.

Evaluation:
(Posttest): Scheduled for end of lessons. To include same items as pretest (ARA & IPAP).

Immediate Goals (10/25/88):
(1) Increase independence in water to permit movement without instructor's support; (2) longer submersion time (3 to 5 s); (3) water entry advanced to jump with flight; (4) arm action advanced to unsupported pull-push pattern; (5) body position angle to surface reduced to 25 degrees.

Long-Term Goal:
Progress to stroke swimming at ARA Beginner–Advanced Beginner level.

Recommended Activities:
Goal 1: Spidering on wall; pool exploration in water; tunnel travel; walking, jumping, hop onto dock; jump to instructor

Goal 2: Magic candle; ping-pong hurricane; fish talk; ring & poker-chip pickup; finger count; ring-around-rosie

Goal 3: Jump into hula hoop (w/ assistance); jump over stick; jump onto tot dock; jump & turn; jump & touch balloon

Goal 4: Swim with flotation device; handle paddles; feel the fish; toe touching; directed pull practice

Goal 5: Prone glide (assisted); leg pushoff; rocket ship (assisted); porpoise play; prone glide unassisted

Note. This table is reprinted with permission from *Palaestra*, *5*(3), pp. 17-19; 37-40. *Palaestra* is a publication of Challenge Publications, Ltd, P.O. Box 508, Macomb, IL 61455.

and complement physical activity instruction on land. In fact, any activity taught on land can be adapted to the aquatic environment (Horvat & Forbus, 1989; YMCA, 1987). Many of the physical fitness, fundamental skills, and dance/movement activities discussed in other sections of this chapter can be adapted and successfully incorporated as part of the aquatic program. The following activity examples demonstrate how this can be done.

At Weaver School in Akron, Ohio, where a program serves 180 children with mental retardation and multiple disabilities, a mile fitness swim program has been in existence since 1986 (Frieden, 1989). Once a week, swimmers performing an adapted front crawl-stroke complete as many laps as they can in a 25-minute session. Mile lap fitness swim charts are kept to record each student's progress. During the 1987-1988 school year, 16 of the students participating in the program received personal achievement certificates from the President's Council on Physical Fitness and Sports.

Another example of implementing physical fitness activities in the aquatic environment is provided by Gorman et al. (1987), who developed a water exercise program used with older adults that consists of warm-up, cardiovascular, and cool-down exercises. In the warm-up exercise "kickboard press," each participant places her or his hands on the top surface of a kickboard and presses the board underwater until the arms are fully extended. Cardiovascular endurance activities are individually paced walk/jog/march routines in the shallow end of the pool. These exercise routines could easily be adapted to meet the needs of adolescents and adults with mental retardation.

Fundamental locomotor and object control skills can be reinforced in the aquatic environment in a variety of ways. Participants can walk, run, jump, leap, slide, and kick from one side of the shallow end of the pool to the other. A water exercise swim vest attached by a rope to one end of the pool helps the individual remain upright in the water and adds another dimension to performing these fundamental skills. Games such as water basketball and circle dodgeball, played with beach balls, can combine the fun of water sports with instruction in throwing and catching skills.

Various dance and movement factors, such as personal and general space, directionality, and level, can be reinforced in the water. The instructor can pose such questions as "How big [small, wide] can you make yourself in the water?" Level can be taught by having students make themselves high and low in the water. Directionality can be reinforced by having students dog paddle or scull in the water forward or backward or alongside a kickboard. An obstacle course using hula hoops and ropes can enhance such movement concepts as over, under, through, and around. Hirst and Michaelis (1983) describe the activity of water musical hoops: Each child stands in a floating hoop, and when the music stops, he or she must leave that hoop and walk, scull, swim, and so on to another floating hoop.

Special Olympics International (SOI) has developed an instructional program for swimming and diving designed specifically for persons with mental retardation. The guide for this program is divided into two skill progression levels (beginner and advanced) and includes instructional organization, assessment, task analysis, and teaching suggestions. Level one includes activities ranging from water adjustment to floating and kicking. Level two includes various strokes, such as front, back, side, and breast, diving skills, and water safety. Figure 7.6 shows, as an example, the instructional organization necessary for teaching the sidestroke. Chapter 12 provides a detailed discussion of the SOI program guide.

Aquatic Games

Too often games are overlooked in aquatic programs or used as fillers toward the end of a swim lesson. This is unfortunate, because aquatic games that are appropriately designed to meet the developmental needs of each participant can be a fun and exciting method to enhance learning. Langendorfer et al. (1988) define aquatic games as activities with the purpose of enhancing movement experiences in the water and in which all participants are actively involved in and enjoying the experiences. These authors believe that if aquatic games are to assist participants in becoming better movers in the water, instructors must consider the purposes the games serve. Moreover, when designing aquatic games, instructors should strive to create games that

Sidestroke

1.   Demonstrate the correct sidestroke pattern in waist-deep water.

Task analysis

a.   Assume a horizontal position in the water.

b.   Extend left arm out front with palm downward.

c.   Extend right arm backward.

d.   Bend left elbow until arm is directly under the head.

e.   Move the upper arm (starting from the thigh) forward to meet the other arm under the head.

f.   Return arms to original position.

g.   Simultaneously, move left elbow forward and upper arm backward.

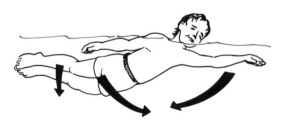

2.   Coordinate the arm and leg movements necessary to perform the sidestroke.

Task analysis

a.   Assume horizontal position on side in the water.

b.   Extend underarm out in front; top arm backward and legs together.

c.   Simultaneously, move both arms to meet each other under the head while flexing knees, hips, and ankles.

d.   Extend and glide.

Figure 7.6 Sidestroke.

Note. From *Special Olympics Sport Skills Program Guide for Swimming & Diving* (p. 33) by Special Olympics International. Copyright © 1988 by Special Olympics International, Inc. Reprinted by permission.

• inspire playfulness, because children are motivated to participate and learn when they are having fun;

• serve as opportunities to practice and improve newly acquired water skills in a variety of settings; and

• reduce fears and distractions for inexperienced or reluctant swimmers.

Langendorfer et al. believe that when appropriately designed aquatic games are introduced as a part of the lesson, participants will be eager to be in the water.

The instructor's selection of aquatic games and learning experiences must be based on each participant's present level of performance and developmental readiness. For example, according to Langendorfer et al. (1988),

> games like "Magic Candle," "Straw Bubble Blowing," or "Whale Spouting" are best used to get the idea of breath control. "Porpoising" and "Fish Talk" are games more suited to stage two children who already have begun breath control activities, but who need to develop consistency in getting and holding the breath. For the child who needs advanced practice in breath control skills, "Water Croquet" and "Charlie Over the Water" are recommended. . . . The child who cannot swim yet may benefit from the "Alligator Swim" or "Spider Swimming." The child who has taken a few strokes of dog paddle will benefit from "Twenty Ways" and from "Rocketship." (p. 13)

Many games and gimmicks reinforce these many aquatic movement concepts (Langendorfer et al., 1988). Table 7.5 provides examples of breath control and breathing games, and Table 7.6 offers examples of arm and leg propulsion games.

Volunteers

For safety and instructional purposes the nature of aquatic activities dictates that the instructor-student ratio be quite small. In fact, students with serious disabilities will require instruction on a one-to-one basis (Horvat & Bishop, 1981). Therefore, it is necessary to train volunteers to assist with the program. Hirst and Michaelis (1983) have had success using members of service organizations such as the Lion's Club and the Junior League as assistants. These organizations not only are capable of providing valuable instructional assistance, but also can serve as important community contacts to enhance the

overall program of physical activity for persons with mental retardation. For information regarding the training of volunteers, paraprofessionals, and parents, see chapter 5.

Horvat and Forbus (1989) have developed an excellent aquatic home-learning program that instructors can use to train parents and volunteers. The skills in the home-learning program are presented in a skill progression and consist of the following components: water adjustment, buoyancy and body adjustment, propulsion and coordination, water safety, water entries, water exercises, and stunts and games. Each skill lists the desired performance objective, procedures to follow, teaching considerations, and game suggestions—which are described in the "Water Exercises, Stunts, and Games" chapter of the manual and reinforce the actual skill being taught. Highlight 7.12 is a reprint from this manual and provides an example of teaching a child to blow bubbles five consecutive times.

DANCE

Too often professionals assigned to provide physical activity to persons with mental retardation have had little or no training in the area of dance and movement. Consequently professionals are hesitant to provide instruction in this area (Roswal, Sherrill, & Roswal, 1988). This is unfortunate, because dance is recognized as an integral component of a well-balanced physical education program, and most importantly, because responding to music through movement is a natural urge for self-expression that should be found and brought out in all persons, including those with mental retardation. The importance of providing dance experiences is described by Schwartz (1989): "Since dance can enrich one's life in so many ways, the experience must be available to everyone. Educators and recreation leaders must adopt a flexible teaching style so their programs respond to the needs of the individuals whom they serve" (p. 49).

Table 7.5   Breath Control and Breathing Games

Game/author	Skill level/prerequisite	Purpose	Description
Magic Candle—Langendorfer & Bruya (in press)	Get the idea, water entry, minimal fear	Learn breath control	Hold finger up as imaginary candle. Challenge child to "blow it out." Move hand rapidly to make the candle disappear. Repeat above and below water surface, and with more than one finger.
Straw Bubble & Blowing—Langendorfer & Bruya (in press)	Get the idea, minimal fear	Learn breath control	Have child blow bubbles out through a drinking straw and suck water in through the straw.
Whale Spout—Langendorfer & Bruya (in press)	Get the idea, minimal fear, water entry	Learn breath control with water in mouth	Challenge child to take water in mouth and spit it into pool gutter. Then have child practice spouting water out of mouth high into the air or at targets.
Porpoising—German (1987)	Practice face submersion	Practice rhythmic breath control	Child jumps high out of water and gets a quick breath before quickly submerging. Have the child repeat and try head-first surface entry.
Fish Talk—German (1987)	Practice face submersion	Practice exhaling; breath control	Child submerges mouth and exhales, making noise like fish or ducks. Have them try to pronounce words underwater and have classmates guess what is said.
Water Croquet—Kral	Adv. practice underwater, swim, breath holding	Improve breath control w/ other skills	Arrange weighted hula hoops. Child swims through as many hoops as possible in one breath. Repeat.
Charlie Over the Water—YMCA (1987)	Adv. practice, breath control, propulsion	Improve intermediate skills	One member is "it," and the others are in a circle around "it." They chant "Charlie over the water; Charlie over the sea; Charlie over the tuna; But he can't catch me." Each swimmer who recovers a ring before being touched is safe.

Note. From "Aquatic Games and Gimmicks for Young Children" by S. Langendorfer, G. German and D. Kral, 1988, *National Aquatic Journal,* **4**(3), pp. 11-14. Reprinted with permission of the Council for National Cooperation in Aquatics.

Benefits of Dance Programs

We all need to feel good about our bodies. Helping people enjoy the pleasures they can experience through movement is perhaps the greatest benefit of dance. Other unique physical, cognitive, social, and emotional benefits may be derived for persons with mental retardation from a dance program that is carefully designed around a series of nonthreatening movement experiences.

Hanson (1979) stated that "dance as a movement is a rigorous activity, requiring little space

Table 7.6   Arm and Leg Propulsion Games

Game/author	Skill level/prerequisite	Purpose	Description
Alligator Swim—Kral	Get the idea, water entry, minimal fear	Getting feet off the bottom	Students place hands on the bottom, gutter, or steps and walk on hands like an alligator; add leg kicking.
Spider Swim—Kral	Get the idea, water entry, minimal fear	Move through water using support of wall	Students hold wall (or gutter) with hands and feet along the wall. Movement can be accompanied by "Eensie Weensie Spider."
Twenty Ways—Canadian Red Cross (1984)	Practice water entry, breath control	Explore ways of moving in the water	Using movement exploration method, ask swimmers to move through the water in different ways. Swimmers should move at their level of skill.
Rocketship—Langendorfer & Bruya (in press)	Practice face submersion, breath control, prone float	Practice a progression of prone propulsion skills	Starting at wall or shallow water, students begin as a group with "count down and blast off." Progression from prone glide, prone kick glide, beginner stroke, and crawl stroke. Repeat with supine skills.
Time Machine—Langendorfer & Bruya (in press)	Adv. practice beginner skills	Lead-ups to front crawl stroke—arms and legs	Using a story format, have swimmers enter "time machine" and learn to swim like a cavedweller (dog paddle), a Roman soldier (human stroke), a knight (sidestroke), and an Olympic athlete (sidestroke).

Note. From "Aquatic Games and Gimmicks for Young Children" by S. Langendorfer, G. German and D. Kral, 1988, *National Aquatic Journal*, **4**(3), pp. 11-14. Reprinted with permission of the Council for National Cooperation in Aquatics.

and equipment'' (p. 42). Physical benefits include enhanced sensory and spatial awareness, physical fitness, and fundamental skills taught in a fun and enjoyable manner (Barton, 1982; Boswell, 1982). Most importantly, this population can develop an understanding of their bodies while gaining movement skill and control as they move through space. Body image is an underlying factor that is necessary to the success of more complex movements and is developed by gaining greater insight into body parts and their actions (Sherrill & Delaney, 1986). Unless they are encouraged or challenged to do more, persons with mental retardation will perform only safe or familiar movements. Through

dance they can expand their movement repertoire and range of quality movements (Riordan, 1980).

Dance provides a unique opportunity to learn to "think on your feet" and remember a sequence of movements while moving. Other cognitive benefits include the development of vocabulary, listening skills, ability to follow directions, attention span, concentration, choice making, and problem solving—as in, for example, waiting for an accompaniment to start without becoming distracted, or concentrating on holding the final position of a dance to demonstrate the ending (Riordan, 1980). Moreover, dance activities provide opportunities to

| *HIGHLIGHT 7.12* | **IN PRACTICE** |

Home-Learning Program

Skill B-3 Accommodation   **Task:** Blow bubbles consecutively

Performance Objective:
To blow bubbles five consecutive times.

Procedure:
Have the child acquire the proper [face in the water] position desired for blowing bubbles and perform the skill five consecutive times.

Teaching Considerations:
If the child is unable to put the entire face in the water, have him or her blow bubbles any way possible. Encourage putting more of the face in the water and blowing bubbles. If the child is still resistant, stand beside the child and perform the skill.

Game Suggestions: 3, 5
Game 3 is "The Little Mermaid Says," which is a variation of "Simon Says."
Game 5 is "Motor Boat Race," in which the child walks across the pool with hands behind the back and chin in the water, blowing short puffs of air at a boat or table-tennis ball.

Note. From *Using the Aquatic Environment for Teaching Handicapped Children* (pp. 34; 74) by M.A. Horvat and W.R. Forbus, 1989, Kearney, NE: Educational Systems Associates, Inc. Reprinted by permission of Educational Systems Associates, Inc.

---

learn such movement concepts as space, direction, speed, shape, time, and flow. For example, a young child with mental retardation can learn the difference between self and general space and anticipate the movements of others while engaged in a group activity.

Socially, dance can provide a vehicle for the worthy use of leisure time by assisting persons with mental retardation to socially interact with others, both with and without disabilities, in the mainstream of society. More specifically, Riordan (1980) believes dance can assist participants to develop such acceptable behaviors as cooperation (e.g., by deciding how to dance with a partner or group), responsibility (e.g., by performing a dance routine that may require supporting another person), and courtesy (e.g., by watching patiently and waiting one's turn while others perform).

Many dance educators believe emotional development is the unique contribution dance can make toward the total physical activity program and each participant. Sherrill and Delaney (1986) observe that through expressive and creative movements, individuals can gain better perspectives about themselves and their own ideas and feelings. Dance provides opportunities to explore, create, discover, and have fun. Feelings of personal self-worth are encouraged and fostered by allowing persons to express their own ideas in movement. This can improve self-expression as well as communication with others. Dance can also be used as a coping mechanism, providing a socially acceptable way to release emotional tension. For example, dance therapists use dance (pantomime) as a substitute for verbal communication with persons who lack or mistrust words to express their feelings.

In recent years dance educators have begun to recognize the benefits of specifically designed dance and movement programs to meet the unique needs of persons with mental retardation. We will describe two such successful programs for this population. The Sunrise Dance Company in Salt Lake City, Utah, has been in existence since the early 1970s, growing from a recreational activity to a performing dance company that has performed before large audiences in many cities throughout the United States. Anne Riordan, the founder of the program and a nationally recognized leader in dance for individuals with disabilities, has seen the program evolve over the years from being therapy to being an art form. Through hard work and practice, Riordan and the performers have discovered and been able to tap the resource of creativity—a resource too often believed to be nonexistent in this population (Riordan, 1980, 1989).

Since 1983, Geraldine Silk, a dance movement therapist, has overseen a dance and movement group for the Morris County Adaptive Recreation Program in Morris Plains, New Jersey. The program consists of approximately 45 individuals with developmental disabilities, ranging in age from 13 to 55 years. Through a variety of dance and movement activities, participants are provided with the opportunity to gain skill, increase fitness, make choices, develop ideas, and strengthen leadership capacity. Most important, Silk believes, is the overall goal of the program—to teach each person the joy of movement (Silk, 1989).

Defining Dance Pedagogy

The scope of this text does not permit a thorough examination of dance therapy. Dance therapy can be implemented only by professionals who are registered with the American Dance Therapy Association (ADTA). These professionals are trained to administer specific treatment modalities and therapeutic intervention used with persons who display mental illness and emotional or behavioral problems. Very often this process of movement is used as an intervention with individuals who have emotional problems that require nonverbal therapy. Treatment emphasis is on rhythmic, expressive movements as a means of establishing initial contact with persons who have lost the capacity to relate effectively with others (Sherrill & Delaney, 1986). For more information on this subject, see Sherrill and Delaney (1986) and Schmais (1976).

According to Roswal et al. (1988), professionals involved in dance pedagogy (for example, special/adapted physical educators, therapeutic recreators) use two types of dance: structured (or data-based) dance and creative dance. These types of dance are sharply contrasting. For a summary comparison of the two dance pedagogies, see Table 7.7.

Structured Dance

Most professionals in special education, physical education, and dance favor a behavioral or structured pedagogy for dance. This pedagogy uses a behavioral, task analysis approach. For example, objectives are met directly, one at a time, through a series of sequential, detailed steps. Professionals justify this type of dance form for persons with mental retardation by saying that these individuals require structure if they are going to learn effectively (Roswal et al., 1988).

Creative Dance

In contrast, creative dance emphasizes movement exploration, with individuals being provided the freedom to choose their own movement responses (see Figure 7.7). Calder (1972) points out that many instructors misinterpret the term *creative dance* to mean free

Table 7.7   Comparison of the Two Dance Pedagogies

Component	Data-structured dance	Creative dance
Student participation	One at a time, taking turns	Simultaneously as a group and continuously during class
Objectives	Are met directly, one at a time, through a series of detailed steps	Are met indirectly, several times, through creative and varied activities
Correct behavior	Only one predetermined correct response	An array of acceptable solutions or behavior choices
Positive reinforcement	Specific to the task and student	General to participation of student and entire class
Learning	Stimulus-response	Guided exploration or problem solving
Success	Built into the teaching methodology as the accomplishment of a series of specific tasks	Built into the philosophy of the value of moving and discovering with confidence and freedom

Note. From "A Comparison of Data-Based and Creative Dance Pedagogies In Teaching Mentally Retarded Youth" by P.M. Roswal, C. Sherrill and G.M. Roswal, 1988, *Adapted Physical Activity Quarterly*, **5**, pp. 212-222. Copyright 1988 by Human Kinetics. Reprinted by permission.

dance, with participants being provided no direction. Creative dance is purposeful and has direction, but the direction is of a sort that allows participants to be spontaneous and experience the joy of dance. For example, objectives are met indirectly, several at a time, through a variety of creative activities. Table 7.8, developed by Roswal et al. (1988), lists creative dance lesson activities in relationship to certain dance skills.

A growing number of specialists believe that individuals with disabilities in general, and more specifically persons with mental retardation, can benefit and learn from creative dance forms (Boswell, 1982, 1989). Advocates of creative dance argue that this form provides unlimited opportunities for creativity and self-expression in each person (Levete, 1982).

According to Roswal et al. (1988), which dance form the instructor chooses should depend on a number of factors, such as the physical and cognitive ability levels of the participants, the teaching style that feels comfortable to both the instructor and the participants, and the instructional goals the instructor wishes to accomplish. For example, some individuals with mental retardation may be unable to effectively cope with the freedom of an unstructured (creative) setting or may not possess the perceptual abilities (e.g., visual, verbal, auditory) required in

Figure 7.7   Dance and movement can help foster creativity and self-expression in each individual with mental retardation. Photo courtesy of Bernhard Wolff.

Table 7.8   Creative Dance Lesson Plans

The following is a list of creative dance lesson plans and their relationship to various dance skills.

Creative dance lesson plans	Stretch and curl, standing	Stretch and curl, lying down	Walk forward and backward	Step to side and together	Move arms forward and backward	Lift arms out and back	Balance on one foot	Jump up and down	Toe touch, standing	Stretch and stand on toes
Follow the leader	X	X	X							
What and where game					X	X			X	
Stop, go, slow				X			X			X
Swimming motions		X	X	X						
Different ways to travel			X	X				X		
High and low		X			X					X
Fours (counting, clapping, moving)			X	X				X		
Body sculptures: choices							X		X	X
Singing games			X	X		X				
Gestures and pantomime					X	X			X	
Creating action word sequences	X						X	X		
Pretending to be a bug and a puppet	X				X	X				
Making shapes—balls and boxes	X	X					X			
Focus, then point or move					X	X			X	
Accent								X	X	X

Note. From "A Comparison of Data-Based and Creative Dance Pedagogies In Teaching Mentally Retarded Youth" by P.M. Roswal, C. Sherrill and G.M. Roswal, 1988, *Adapted Physical Activity Quarterly*, **5**, pp. 212-222. Copyright 1988 by Human Kinetics. Reprinted by permission.

a movement exploration approach. On the other hand, if creative dance forms are not provided, this population will have much less opportunity to explore, create, express, and discover their own movement capabilities. Perhaps even more importantly, their ability to expand their movement repertoire and range of movement choices will be greatly diminished.

Research is quite limited regarding the effective use of dance pedagogies for persons with mental retardation. In an investigation conducted by Roswal et al. (1988), 35 boys and girls, 11 to 16 years of age, with moderate mental retardation, were randomly placed in two dance programs: a data-based dance program based on the work of Dunn, Morehouse, and Dalke (1979) and a creative dance program based primarily on the work of Riordan (Fitt & Riordan, 1980). Eight instructors were trained to implement the programs. Results determined no difference between these two forms of dance pedagogy. The authors found that with a relatively limited amount of training, the teachers were able to effectively implement both forms of dance. The authors concluded that both movement pedagogies can be effective with this population and that the choice of pedagogy should be based on program goals: If the instructor's educational goal is to determine individual progress, then a structured dance form may be best, whereas if the instructor's objective is to promote creativity and expression in the participants, then creative dance may be more applicable.

These findings are similar to those of an investigation by Boswell (1982), who randomly assigned 26 children with mental retardation, ages 8 to 13 years, into two distinct instructional models: adapted dance and movement exploration. Boswell concluded that the two instructional models were similar in their influence on the participants' dynamic balance and rhythmic skills. Silk (1989) concurs with both authors, regarding the question of determining effective dance pedagogies: "Spontaneity and creativity contribute to an individual's sense of self-esteem and personal growth, but structure and predictability are necessary to ensure the individual's comfort" (p. 56).

Program Implementation

In the design and implementation of a dance and movement program for persons with mental retardation, a number of factors must be carefully considered—including the abilities of the instructor or facilitator of the movement experience; the environment, including the use of props and relaxation techniques; and most importantly, which movement elements the participant will bring to the program and which will need to be taught by the instructor.

The Instructor

Many professionals assigned to provide physical activity to persons with mental retardation

have had little or no training in the area of dance and movement, and therefore they feel awkward and reluctant to provide this type of instruction. This is unfortunate, because perhaps the most important characteristic an instructor can bring to the dance program is a positive and enthusiastic attitude toward movement. The instructor must set the stage by being an appropriate role model, dressed properly and visibly enjoying the class and moving with the participants. Hopefully this enthusiastic attitude will carry over to the participants and motivate them to respond to the activity. In general, the instructor's major responsibility is to facilitate movement, stimulating the dancers to explore and expand their full range of movement possibilities. Riordan (1980) suggests that the process is more important than the product and that each participant must be involved in the dance experience for movement's sake. That each person should be accepted for her or his unique movement abilities is perhaps best stated by Boswell (1989):

Indeed, one probably envisions a dancer as a person with a perfect body, with finely tuned technique, who executes turns and leaps throughout the entire stage. Although a well-conditioned body and strong technique are important, I ask you to suspend these traditional views and concentrate on a very different perception of dance. For now consider dance as an ability to move, no matter how small or how simple, using a kind of energy that communicates. (p. 28)

Initially, the instructor who feels awkward teaching dance may compensate by following a detailed lesson plan. But even though this may prove to be a good initial strategy, Fitt and Riordan (1980) believe that this will eventually stifle the performers' creativity. These authors feel that teaching dance to persons with unique needs requires much more than following a detailed lesson plan—that the art of teaching is just as important as the conceptual base—and they offer the following general suggestions to instructors to bring out what they term the "magic" in each performer during the dance and movement program.

1. Know and accept the limitations of your participants without limiting their personal growth. Each person needs encouragement, support, and motivation.

2. There must be a delicate balance between the instructor's acceptance and demands placed on each participant. What the instructor believes is practical or works must be integrated with idealism about what could be. Dance is an art form that uses exploration as a tool to encourage students to explore the dimensions of movement, and students just might discover that their movement capabilities transcend the instructor's assessment of their limitations.

3. The instructor should pose all movement questions and challenges positively. For example, the instructor might say, "It would look great if you could make your arms shake high in the air! Can you make them shake?"

4. Movement demonstrations must be clear and concise, with touch cues or physical guidance provided if necessary to assist participants to feel the movement (see Figure 7.8). A multisensory approach is especially important for persons with mental retardation and will provide this population with a variety of opportunities to follow and comprehend directions. For example, to help a young child learn to move more slowly and under control, have soft music playing in the background while giving directions, and if necessary give gentle touch cues.

5. Finally, the instructor must determine a teaching style that he or she and the participants feel comfortable with, to bring out the magic of movement in each person. (See chapter 6 for an overview of various teaching styles.)

During the initial stages of the program, some persons may be reluctant to participate and may

Figure 7.8 An instructor demonstrates a movement to an individual. Photo courtesy of Bernhard Wolff.

feel uncomfortable with dance and movement. There can be a number of reasons for the reluctance, such as simply being embarrassed to move in front of others or to look at or touch another person, or an inability to handle the concept of expressing their feelings through movement. These individuals should never be forced to participate. Rather, they can begin by observing or participating from the periphery of the group. When working with a shy and reluctant person, Fitt and Riordan (1980) believe, it is important to use smaller space, slower movements, and weaker force. Movement that is slow, gentle, and unthreatening provides the reluctant participant with time to observe the instructor. These authors believe in using verbal directions with a group, but that nonverbal communication is the preferred method of instruction in a one-to-one relationship with a reluctant participant. During instruction this person should be approached from the side so that she or he can see the instructor, but the instructor should avoid eye contact, because it may be perceived by this person as an invasion of personal space and a threat. With time this reluctance may subside, and these persons may start by participating away from the group. Hopefully, the reluctant participant will see the group deriving so much fun and pleasure from the experience that he or she will eventually wish to join the group.

The Environment

The setting plays a major role in facilitating movement. Stinson (1988) believes the environment must be designed for movement to occur naturally. This includes having adequate space and props and equipment that have open-ended and diverse uses. The environment should be multisensory—including interesting things to touch, taste, smell, hear, and see—so that the participant's experiences are multisensory (the cool feeling of rolling one's body in a scarf during a relaxation activity, moving freely to the sharp sound of a beating drum, and so on).

Because the design of the environment will largely dictate the degree of movement, the program may need to begin with a smaller space. Many individuals, especially children with short attention spans, will have difficulty performing in excessive amounts of space. They may feel overwhelmed and wish to run through the entire open setting. During the initial stages of the dance and movement activity in a smaller space, the instructor should introduce the concept of personal space. *Personal space* is defined as the space immediately around one's body. When all participants are staying out of each other's personal space, none of them should be able to touch anyone else. For some children, cues such as a circle of tape or a hula hoop on the floor, with the child standing at its center, can assist with the learning of this concept.

For teaching movement to children with mental retardation, Canner (1975) has found it effective to teach personal space by having the children lie on the floor, forming a circle. She believes that the combination of the children lying supine while in a circle formation allows each child to see each other and form a feeling of unity. Movements can then be observed and

shared by the group. Nonlocomotor movements such as bending, twisting, and swaying can be effectively taught in this setting. Relaxation, another strategy for structuring the environment, will be introduced later in this section.

In contrast, *general space* is all of the space used in the entire room or environment. For reasons of safety and enjoyment, it is important that participants be taught to share general space with the others and to move through the environment without bumping others (that is, without entering anyone else's personal space). Locomotor movements such as the run, jump, hop, and skip can be effectively introduced in this setting.

Props

Props can be used to help structure the environment. Props are also effective in stimulating movement interest, assisting a reluctant participant to attempt to move, promoting individualization, promoting multisensory experiences, creating a fun atmosphere, and serving as extensions of the body (Crain, 1980). Moreover, Schmitz (1989) has found that the special qualities of the materials help to shift participants' attention away from specific movement tasks, allowing more efficient movement to occur. For example, scarves can be used in a variety of ways to teach persons with mental retardation concepts such as lightness, how to extend the arms, and so on, and as a wonderful disguise for mental imagery (Silk, 1989). Highlight 7.13 lists some of the many kinds of props that can be effectively incorporated into a dance and movement program suggested by Miller-Merrill & Horvat (no date) and Sherrill & Delaney (1986).

Relaxation

Relaxation is another effective aid in structuring the environment. There are many relaxation techniques that help reduce tension and anxiety, including music, meditation, biofeedback, yoga, static stretching exercises, imagery, deep body breathing, and muscle relaxation (Rickard, Thrasher, & Elkins, 1984). The type

List of Props for Dance/Movement Program

Scarves and fabric	Stretch jump ropes
Capes and shawls	Leaves and feathers
Soft, stretchable tubular knit fabric	Balloons
Crepe paper streamers	Bells
Ribbons	Poles or tubes
Towels	Yarn balls
Toilet tissue	Parachute
Abstract shapes (rubber or cardboard)	Musical instruments

Note. This list of various props is adapted from work by Miller-Merrill and Horvat (no date) and Sherrill and Delaney (1986).

and level of instruction given in these methods will vary depending on the participants' ages and mental retardation classifications.

Relaxation training provides many benefits (Lavay & Sayers-Lavay, 1988). Persons with mental retardation, just like all other persons, must learn to effectively deal with stress and anxiety. Properly administered relaxation procedures can help this population learn to deal with stress and tension in a positive and socially acceptable manner, conserve energy, and move smoothly and efficiently. These procedures can also help individuals who display hyperactivity to learn to focus on tasks. For example, the instructor can teach the individual or group to stop what they are doing and slip into a relaxation posture on the instructor's signal (a special word or sign), which the instructor can use when she or he senses that an individual or the group is becoming uncontrollable or losing focus. The physical activity environment is not a place for these individuals to "let off steam." Too often, hyperactivity escalates when physical activity is not structured and controlled. Relaxation techniques are also effective closing activities, especially with school-age children who are going to be returning to the classroom (see Figure 7.9).

To date there is little research on relaxation training for persons with mental retardation. In

Figure 7.9 Relaxation techniques are an excellent closing activity. Photo courtesy of Bob Fraley.

an investigation by Rickard et al. (1984), 20 adults labeled as mentally retarded were grouped by IQ ranges of 40 to 54, 55 to 69, 70 to 84, and 85 to 100 and were administered four common forms of relaxation training: muscle/tension relaxation, suggestions of relaxation, controlled breathing, and imagery practice (visualizing situations associated with feelings of relaxation). The authors reported that these techniques were successfully administered to all persons investigated; however, the lowest IQ group (40 to 54) did have some difficulty responding to the relaxation procedures. Results from this study suggest that persons with mental retardation, over a wide intelligence range, are capable of following common instructional strategies used in relaxation training.

Further examples of relaxation procedures and activities that have been successfully used with this population are provided in Highlight 7.14.

Movement Analysis

If dance and movement activities are to be successful and effectively meet individual needs, during the initial stages of the program the instructor must be able to analyze the movement abilities of each participant. This requires analyzing each movement into its simplest form, which in turn includes body part identification, rudimentary movements such as bending and

---

HIGHLIGHT 7.14   **IN PRACTICE**

Relaxation Procedures and Activities

Procedures

The following instructional procedures may be useful in designing relaxation activities.

The environment should be as quiet and free of irrelevant stimuli as possible. For example, close all doors and have the lights dimmed.

Participants should dress in comfortable clothing.

Soft music may assist the participants' ability to relax.

Participants should be lying down in a supine or prone position, if possible. If it does not prove too distracting, participants may choose to lie in the materials or props they have been using, such as soft scarves or parachutes.

When providing instruction, the instructor should speak in clear and graphic terms using a soft and comforting tone of voice.

Activities

Here are general ideas for relaxation activities. Use your imagination, and have your students also dream up some ways to relax.

Deep breathing. Participants are instructed to take slow, deep breaths, inhaling through their noses and exhaling out their mouths. Diaphragmatic breathing is encouraged. Tell younger children to perform "tummy" breathing, having their stomachs move slowly up and down.

Muscle tension/relaxation (Jacobson technique). Participants are instructed to tense and then release specific muscle groups, progressing over time from one group to the next.

Slow stretching exercises. Participants are instructed to slowly stretch various parts of the body and then hold each stretch for 30 to 60 seconds.

Impulse control activities. Participants are instructed to move slowly and under control by pretending to swim in a sea of Jello, walk on the moon, or be a melting ice cream cone on a hot summer day, a floppy rag doll, or thick catsup leaving a bottle.

Fantasy trips. With their eyes closed, participants are instructed to visualize pleasant scenes, such as sitting by a campfire, watching a sunset or snowfall, or walking through a forest with a bubbling brook.

Note. Adapted from Lavay and Sayers-Lavay (1988).

twisting, and fundamental locomotor movements such as running and galloping. Each participant should be afforded the opportunity to explore and learn the movements his or her body is capable of performing. A starting point with this population is body part identification and movement. Initial experiences should include large, free, and isolated movements of the body. Figure 7.10 provides a simple checklist to determine each person's ability to identify and move body parts individually and in combination. Further examples offered by Dauer and Pangrazi (1989) include these body factors: shape (stretch and curl); weight bearing (supporting or receiving the weight of various body parts); execution (unilateral, or one-sided; bilateral, or both sides; and contralateral, or opposite sides); body center orientation (leading with different body parts and body zones such as front, back, side, and lower and upper body).

Next, the instructor should determine each participant's movement repertoire. Figure 7.11 presents a checklist, modified by Crain (1980), for interpreting each person's movement ability in various axial or nonlocomotor movements, such as bending and swinging. Bending, the first example in the figure, demonstrates how this movement could be further broken down into bending the upper and lower body and appendages of the body. Further analyses could be conducted for each of the axial movements listed in the figure. The instructor may also wish to determine each individual's movement ability in fundamental locomotor patterns (see the fundamental skills section of this chapter).

Elements of Movement

It is unlikely that the instructor will be able to plan and implement the program effectively if she or he is unable to analyze basic movement elements and determine each participant's present level of skill performance. Analysis should focus on the movement elements developed by Rudolf Laban (1960). An understanding of these movement elements is essential to

Place a checkmark in the area successfully completed:

Verbal cue: Successfully identifies and moves this part on the teacher's verbal cue.

Physical cue: Successfully identifies and moves this part with a demonstration.

Needs assistance: Unable to complete without assistance.

Body part	Verbal cue	Physical cue	Needs assistance
A. Head			
Forehead	☐	☐	☐
Eyebrows	☐	☐	☐
Eyes	☐	☐	☐
Ears	☐	☐	☐
Cheeks	☐	☐	☐
Mouth	☐	☐	☐
Chin	☐	☐	☐
B. Upper body			
Neck	☐	☐	☐
Shoulders	☐	☐	☐
Stomach	☐	☐	☐
Back	☐	☐	☐
Front	☐	☐	☐
C. Lower body			
Hips	☐	☐	☐
Waist	☐	☐	☐
Seat	☐	☐	☐
Thighs	☐	☐	☐
D. Appendages			
Arms	☐	☐	☐
Elbows	☐	☐	☐
Fingers	☐	☐	☐
Legs	☐	☐	☐
Knees	☐	☐	☐
Feet	☐	☐	☐
Toes	☐	☐	☐
E. Combinations			
Head, waist, and arms	☐	☐	☐
Arms and legs	☐	☐	☐
Head and legs	☐	☐	☐

Figure 7.10 Identification and movement of individual body parts.

Note. Adapted from Crain (1980).

Place a checkmark in the area successfully completed:

Verbal cue: Successfully identifies and moves on the teacher's verbal cue.

Physical cue: Successfully identifies and moves with a demonstration.

Needs assistance: Unable to complete without assistance.

Axial Movements	Verbal cue	Physical cue	Needs assistance
Bend upper body	☐	☐	☐
Bend lower body	☐	☐	☐
Bend appendages			
1. Elbows	☐	☐	☐
2. Knees	☐	☐	☐
3. Toes (rise)	☐	☐	☐
Stretch	☐	☐	☐
Lift	☐	☐	☐
Grasp	☐	☐	☐
Pull	☐	☐	☐
Push	☐	☐	☐
Collapse	☐	☐	☐
Hold a pose	☐	☐	☐
Swing	☐	☐	☐
Sway	☐	☐	☐
Turn	☐	☐	☐
Twist	☐	☐	☐

Figure 7.11   Movement ability repertoire. *Note.* Adapted from Crain (1980).

the overall development and implementation of a well-designed dance and movement program. These elements include space, time, and weight (effort or flow). *Space* can take many forms, such as level, shape, direction or floor pattern, size, space pattern, and torso relationship. *Time* is defined as speed of movement, such as slow, medium, fast, accelerating, and decelerating. The speed of the movement can also be sudden, jerky, smooth, even, and so on. *Weight*, which may also be referred to as effort or flow, is the degree of measurable strength used in a movement. Effort can include such movement exam-

ples as heavy, light, sustained, and abrupt. Movement examples of flow include sustained or free flow and interrupted flow. According to Fitt (1980), "By focusing on the particular combination of time, space and force used in a given skill, the teacher can isolate critical components necessary to perform that skill. In the jump, for example, the extension of the knee, hip, and ankle must be strong (force) and fast (time); to be effective, the space must be relatively small or the jump will go off in all directions simultaneously" (p. 65). Figure 7.12 provides the reader with an outline of these movement elements designed by Boswell and Dart (1984) and adapted from the work of Laban (1960).

Expanding Movement Elements

Perhaps the most important instructional consideration during program implementation is the actual questions or movement problems presented to each participant. The instructor must be careful to pose questions that bring out the movement creativity in each performer. To be effective for persons with mental retardation, questions must be individualized to meet the developmental level and cognitive abilities of each participant. Riordan (1980), an advocate of this individualized creative movement approach, says:

I have found abstract movement experiences carry fewer stereotypes than literal experiences such as be a tree or be a flower. . . . For example, I might begin by asking students to shake their hands. Then the problem might extend to parts of the body, to shake the hands at different levels, to choose a place in space and freeze. . . . I think many beginning teachers have the opposite notion when they begin lessons; thinking that imagery would be more stimulating, they are surprised that students are so responsive to the more abstract ideas. (p. 17)

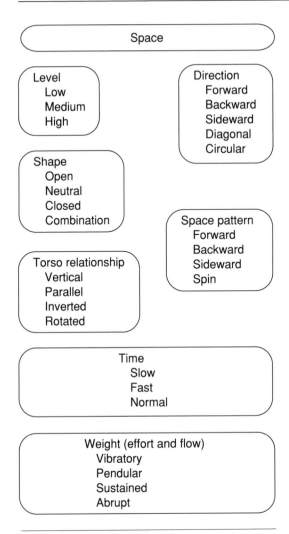

Figure 7.12 Outline of dance/movement elements.
Note. From "Outline of Movement Categories" by B. Boswell and S.K. Dart, 1984, *A Study to Establish a Valid and Reliable Instrument for Analyzing Creative Movement/Dance for Use by Elementary School Physical Educators* by S.K. Dart (Ed.), (p. 63). Unpublished master's thesis, Fort Hays State University, Hays, KS. Reprinted by permission.

Dauer and Pangrazi (1989) provide a five-step progression that, with modifications, can be used by instructors to effectively expand the move-

ment elements, and consequently movement possibilities, for participants with mental retardation.

1. *Define the problem.* What, where, and how is the individual to move? For example, the child is to run (what) in general space (where) changing directions (how).
2. *Increase the variety and depth of the movement factors.* In the previous example, the movement depth could be expanded by posing additional challenges, such as asking each participant to move high and low, and fast and slow, while making themselves big and small. It is this step that will help to expand the movement repertoire in each participant. For persons with mental retardation, demonstration may need to be included with the questions posed.
3. *Develop quality of movement.* Throughout the program the instructor should encourage and bring out the quality of movement in each participant. This can be accomplished by deemphasizing fast movements and praising individuals who move slowly and under control.
4. *Build sequences and combine movements.* When ready, participants can select movements previously practiced and put them together in a sequence. Participants should be encouraged to demonstrate proper transition (flow) from movement to movement.
5. *Move with others.* Eventually participants should be encouraged to cooperate and socially interact with one another in a movement approach. Example of partner activities include imitating various movements, supporting each other's weight, and cooperating together to form shapes or letters.

Through the use of movement questions and the movement elements of space, time, and weight (effort or flow), a great variety of creative movements can emerge. Use your imagination, and have your students use theirs, to develop new combinations. The following statement by Silk (1989) summarizes the importance of incorporating creative movement elements into dance programs for persons with mental retardation:

> The important consideration in doing creative movement with any group is allowing for the spontaneity and creativity which come into play as the group begins to move together. Learn to take the lead from your students, and learn to trust their movement instincts. Be a good observer, and you will find ideas in their improvisations and freedom. Remember that each participant has a unique gift and style of self-expression. Allow space for this expression to happen and your creative movement session will be gifted with a sense of fulfillment and joy. (p. 58)

Summary

Educators cannot change the genetic makeup of persons with mental retardation, so they must be intensively involved in providing maximum and appropriate opportunities geared to meet this population's unique movement needs. The physical domain (physical fitness and motor skills) is an extremely important component of education and training for individuals with mental retardation. The specially trained special/adapted physical education teacher, therapeutic recreation leader, and therapist are indispensable to providing special activity programs for individuals with major movement needs, to en-

sure that these individuals are instructed in appropriate and high-quality activities.

This chapter has provided the information necessary to successfully implement a quality program of physical activity for persons with mental retardation. The information provided closely follows the definition of physical education as identified in the law, specifically examining the following component areas:

- Physical fitness
- Fundamental motor skills
- Aquatics
- Dance

The benefits and definition of each component area were closely examined. Also discussed were the various reasons why persons with mental retardation have inferior fitness scores and movement deficits when compared to their nondisabled peers. More severe levels of retardation are correlated with greater fitness and movement deficits. To date it is still uncertain why this population has significantly inferior scores compared to the general population. More work is needed in this area, because professionals need a better understanding of this question to effectively meet the unique fitness and movement needs of this population.

However, research has demonstrated that with proper training, this population can significantly improve in the areas of physical fitness, fundamental motor skills, aquatics, and dance. This requires the systematic implementation of a number of programming strategies. This chapter discussed important guidelines for program implementation, including safety, activity selection and development, skill progression, and strategies for motivation.

DISCUSSIONS AND NEW DIRECTIONS

1. To date, most fitness programs have been most effective in assisting persons with mental retardation to exercise and make dramatic improvement in this area. However, most of these programs include direct supervision; once this supervision ends, the individual stops exercising and leads

a sedentary lifestyle. What procedures are necessary to assist persons with mental retardation to exercise on their own over an extended period of time and to make healthy lifestyle changes?

2. There are a number of theories as to why persons with mental retardation display inferior movement skills compared to their nondisabled peers. Postulated causes include developmental delays, lack of movement experiences and opportunities due to lack of quality instruction, qualitative differences in the underlying movement process, and a lack of muscle control or activation. Do you agree or disagree with the research that supports each of these theories? In addition, do persons with mental retardation of different classification levels (e.g., moderate mental retardation, Down syndrome) develop skills differently? With this in mind, should different theories apply to different classification levels of mental retardation?

3. An analysis of Laban's (1960) movement elements of space, time, and weight (effort and flow) are essential to the overall development and implementation of dance and movement programs. How can these elements be effectively taught to persons with mental retardation to expand and qualitatively improve their movement repertoires?

REFERENCES

Physical Fitness References

American College of Sports Medicine. (1991). *Guidelines for exercise testing and prescription* (4th ed.) Philadelphia: Lea & Febiger.

Beasley, C.R. (1982). Effects of a jogging program on cardiovascular fitness and work performance of mentally retarded adults. *American Journal of Mental Deficiency, 86,* 609-613.

Coleman, A.E., Ayoub, M.N., & Friedrich, D.W. (1976). Assessment of the physical work capacity of institutionalized mentally retarded males. *American Journal of Mental Deficiency, 80,* 629-635.

Coleman, S.R., & Whitman, T.L. (1984). Developing, generalizing, and maintaining physical fitness in mentally retarded adults: Toward a self-directed program. *Analysis and Intervention in Developmental Disabilities, 4,* 109-127.

Croce, R., & DePaepe, J.A. (1989). Critique of therapeutic intervention programming with reference to an alternative approach based on motor learning theory. *Physical and Occupational Therapy in Pediatrics, 9*(3), 5-33.

Davidson, R.G. (1988). Atlantoaxial instability in individuals with Down syndrome: A fresh look at the evidence. *Pediatrics, 81,* 857-864.

Eichstaedt, C.B., Wang, P.Y., Polacek, J.J., & Dohrmann, P.F. (1991). *Physical fitness and motor skill levels of individuals with mental retardation: Mild, moderate, and individuals with Down syndrome: ages 6 to 21.* Normal: Illinois State University Printing Services.

Fernhall, B., Tymeson, G.T., & Webster, G.E. (1988). Cardiovascular fitness of mentally retarded adults. *Adapted Physical Activity Quarterly, 5,* 12-28.

Kelly, L.E. (1989). Instructional time. *Journal of Physical Education, Recreation and Dance, 60*(6), 29-32.

Lavay, B., Reid, G., & Cressler-Chaviz, M. (1990). Measuring the cardiovascular endurance of persons with mental retardation: A critical review. In K. Pandolf (Ed.), *Exercise science sport review* (pp. 263-290). Baltimore: Williams & Wilkins.

Lavay, B., Zody, J., Solko, C., & Era, K. (1990). The effect of a seven month run/

walk program on the physiological fitness parameters of adults with mental retardation. In G. Doll-Tepper, C. Dahms, B. Doll, & H. von Selzam (Eds.), *Adapted physical activity: An interdisciplinary approach*. Heidelberg: Springer.

Londeree, B.R., & Johnson, L.E. (1974). Motor fitness of TMR vs EMR and normal children. *Medicine Science and Sport*, **6**, 247-252.

McConaughy, E.K., & Salzberg, C.L. (1988). Physical fitness of mentally retarded individuals. In N.W. Bray (Ed.), *International review of research in mental retardation* (pp. 227-258). San Diego: Academic Press.

McCubbin, J.A., & Jansma, P. (1987). The effects of training selected psychomotor skills and the relationship to adaptive behavior. In M.E. Berridge & G.R. Ward (Eds.), *International perspectives on adapted physical activity* (pp. 119-126). Champaign, IL: Human Kinetics.

Moon, M.S., & Renzaglia, A. (1982). Physical fitness and the mentally retarded: A critical review of the literature. *Journal of Special Education*, **16**, 125-132.

National Children and Youth Fitness Study. (1985). *Journal of Physical Education, Recreation and Dance*, **56**(1), 44-90.

Nienhuis, K.M. (1989). *A comparison analysis of physical fitness levels of mild mentally retarded students ages 10 to 12 in Illinois*. Unpublished masters thesis, Illinois State University, Normal.

Polacek, J.J., Wang, P.Y., & Eichstaedt, C.B. (1985). *A study of physical and health related fitness levels of mild, moderate, and Down syndrome students in Illinois*. Normal: Illinois State University Printing Services.

Pueschel, S.M. (1988). *The young person with Down syndrome: Transition from adolescence to adulthood*. Baltimore: Brookes.

Rarick, G.L., Dobbins, D.A., & Broadhead, G.D. (1976). *The motor domain and its correlates in educable mentally handi-*capped children*. Englewood Cliffs, NJ: Prentice Hall.

Rarick, G.L., Widdop, J.H., & Broadhead, G.D. (1970). The physical fitness and motor performance of educable mentally retarded children. *Exceptional Children*, **35**, 509-519.

Sharkey, B. (1984). *Physiology of fitness*. Champaign, IL: Human Kinetics.

Timmermans, H.M., & Martin, M. (1987). Top ten potentially dangerous exercises. *Journal of Physical Education, Recreation and Dance*, **58**(6), 29-31.

Wang, P.Y., & Eichstaedt, C.B. (1980). *A study of physical fitness levels of mentally handicapped children and adolescents in Illinois*. Normal: Illinois State University Printing Services.

Fundamental Motor Skills and Patterns References

Croce, R., & DePaepe, J.A. (1989). Critique of therapeutic intervention programming with reference to an alternative approach based on motor learning theory. *Physical and Occupational Therapy in Pediatrics*, **9**(3), 5-33.

Davis, W.E. (1987). Evidence for muscle activation deficiency in mentally handicapping conditions. In M.E. Berridge & G.R. Ward (Eds.), *International perspectives on adapted physical activity* (pp. 53-64). Champaign, IL: Human Kinetics.

DiRocco, P.J., Clark, J.E., & Phillips, S.J. (1987). Jumping coordination patterns of mildly mentally retarded children. *Adapted Physical Activity Quarterly*, **4**, 178-191.

Edwards, J.M., Elliot, D., and Lee, T.D. (1986). Contextual interference effects during skill acquisition and transfer in Down's syndrome adolescents. *Adapted Physical Activity Quarterly*, **3**, 250-258.

Eichstaedt, C.B., & Kalakian, L.H. (1987). *Developmental/adapted physical education:*

Making ability count. New York: Macmillan.

Ersing, W.F., Loovis, E.M., & Ryan, T.M. (1982). On the nature of motor development in special populations. In J. Winnick (Ed.), Adapted physical education [Special issue, pp. 64-72]. *Exceptional Educational Quarterly*, **3**,(1).

Gallahue, D.L. (1989). *Understanding motor development*. Indianapolis: Benchmark Press.

Hayden, F.J. (1965). *Physical fitness for the mentally retarded*. Toronto: Toronto Association for Retarded Citizens.

Hogg, J., & Sebba, J. (1987). *Profound retardation and multiple impairment. Volume 1: Development and learning*. Rockville, MD: Aspen.

Holland, B.V. (1987). Fundamental motor skill performance of nonhandicapped and educable mentally impaired students. *Education and Training in Mental Retardation*, **22**, 197-204.

Hutt, M.L., & Gibby, R.G. (1979). *The mentally retarded child*. Boston: Allyn & Bacon.

Lavay, B. (1985). Instruction of team sport strategies for the mild/moderate mentally handicapped. *Palaestra*, **2**(1), 10-13.

Loovis, E.M. (1989). Climbing behavior of mentally retarded children: Developmental and environmental issues. *Physical Educator*, **46**(3), 149-153.

Parker, A.W., Bronks, R., & Snyder, C.W. (1986). Walking patterns in Down's syndrome. *Journal of Mental Deficiency Research*, **30**, 317-330.

Porretta, D.L. (1988). Contextual interference effects on the transfer and retention of a gross motor skill by mildly mentally handicapped children. *Adapted Physical Activity Quarterly*, **5**, 332-339.

Rarick, G.L. (1973). Motor performance of mentally retarded children. In G.L. Rarick (Ed.), *Physical activity: Human growth and development* (pp. 225-256). New York: Academic Press.

Rarick, G.L., & Dobbins, D.A. (1977). The performance of intellectually normal and educable mentally retarded boys on tests of throwing accuracy. *Journal of Motor Behavior*, **9**, 23-32.

Thomas, K.T. (1984). Applying knowledge of motor development to mentally retarded children. In J.R. Thomas (Ed.), *Motor development during childhood and adolescence* (pp. 174-183). Minneapolis: Burgess.

Ulrich, D. (1984). The reliability of classification decisions made with the objective-based motor skill assessment instrument. *Adapted Physical Activity Quarterly*, **1**, 52-60.

Ulrich, D. (1985). *Test of gross motor development*. Austin, TX: PRO-ED.

Wickstrom, R. (1983). *Fundamental motor patterns*. Philadelphia: Lea & Febiger.

Aquatics References

American Red Cross. (1977). *Adapted aquatics*. Garden City, NY: Doubleday.

Campion, M.R. (1985). *Hydrotherapy in pediatrics*. Rockville, MD: Aspen.

Christie, I. (1985). Aquatics for the handicapped—a review of literature. *Physical Educator*, **42**(1), 24-33.

Frieden, D. (1989). Weaver mile fitness swim. *Palaestra*, **5**(2), 52-54, 60-62.

Gorman, D.R., Brown, B.S., Daniel, M., & Daniel, C. (1987). Aquatic exercise program for the aged in nursing homes. In M.E. Berridge & G.R. Ward (Eds.), *International perspectives on adapted physical activity* (pp. 291-297). Champaign, IL: Human Kinetics.

Grosse, S.J., & McGill, C.G. (1979). *Independent swimming for children with severe physical impairments. Practical pointers*, Reston, VA: American Alliance for Health, Physical Education, Recreation and Dance.

Hirst, C.C., & Michaelis, E. (1983). *Retarded*

kids need to play. Champaign, IL: Leisure Press.

Horvat, M., & Bishop, P. (1981). Implementing aquatic instruction for severely and profoundly mentally retarded individuals. *Journal of Physical Education*, **78**, 70-71.

Horvat, M.A., & Forbus, W.R. (1989). *Using the aquatic environment for teaching handicapped children*. Kearney, NE: Educational Systems.

Johannsen, S. (1987). A process toward the integration of mentally handicapped students into community learn-to-swim programs. In M.E. Berridge & G.R. Ward (Eds.), *International perspectives on adapted physical activity* (pp. 109-117). Champaign, IL: Human Kinetics.

Killian, K.J., Arena-Ronde, S., & Bruno, L. (1987). Refinement of two instruments that assess water orientation in atypical swimmers. *Adapted Physical Activity Quarterly*, **4**, 25-37.

Langendorfer, S. (1986). Aquatics for the young child: Facts and myths. *Journal of Physical Education, Recreation and Dance*, **57**(9), 61-66.

Langendorfer, S. (1989). Aquatics for young children with handicapping conditions. *Palaestra*, **5**(3), 17-19, 37-40.

Langendorfer, S., German, E., & Kral, D. (1988). Aquatic games and gimmicks for young children. *National Aquatic Journal*, **4**(3), 11-14.

Langendorfer, S., Roberts, M.A., & Ropka, C.R. (1987). Aquatic readiness: A developmental test. *National Aquatic Journal*, **3**(3), 8-12.

Priest, E.L. (1990). Aquatics. In J.P. Winnick (Ed.). *Adapted physical education and sport* (pp. 391-408). Champaign, IL: Human Kinetics.

Special Olympics International (1989). *Special Olympics sport skill program guide for swimming and diving*. 1350 New York Ave., NW, Suite 500, Washington, DC.

YMCA. (1987). *Aquatics for special populations*. Champaign, IL: Human Kinetics.

Dance References

Barton, B. (1982). Aerobic dance for the mentally retarded. *Physical Educator*, **39**, 25-29.

Boswell, B. (1982). Adapted dance for mentally retarded children: An experimental study (Doctoral dissertation, Texas Woman's University). *Dissertation Abstracts International*, **43**/09A, 2925.

Boswell, B. (1989). Dance as a creative expression for the disabled. *Palaestra*, **6**(1), 28-30.

Boswell, B., & Dart, S.K. (1984). Outline of movement categories. In S.K. Dart, *A study to establish a valid and reliable instrument for analyzing creative movement/dance for use by elementary school physical educators* (pp. 63). Unpublished master's thesis, Fort Hays State University, Hays, KS.

Calder, J.E. (1972). Dance for the mentally retarded. *The Slow Learning Child*, **19**, 67-78.

Canner, N. (1975). *And a time to dance*. Boston: Play.

Crain, C.D. (1980). Dance for the handicapped: A mainstreaming approach. In S. Fitt & A. Riordan (Eds.), *Focus on dance IX: Dance for the handicapped* (pp. 1-4). Reston, VA: American Alliance for Health, Physical Education, Recreation and Dance.

Dauer, V.P., & Pangrazi, R.P. (1989). *Dynamic physical education for elementary school children*. New York: Macmillan.

Dunn, J.M., Morehouse, J.W., & Dalke, B. (1979). *Game, exercise, & leisure sport curriculum*. Corvallis: Oregon State University, Department of Physical Education.

Fitt, S. (1980). Simplified movement behavior analysis as a basis for designing dance activities for the handicapped. In S. Fitt & A.

Riordan (Eds.), *Focus on dance IX: Dance for the handicapped* (pp. 65-71). Reston, VA: American Alliance for Health, Physical Education, Recreation and Dance.

Fitt, S., & Riordan, A. (1980). Anne's magic. In S. Fitt & A. Riordan (Eds.), *Focus on dance IX: Dance for the handicapped* (pp. 21-24). Reston, VA: American Alliance for Health, Physical Education, Recreation and Dance.

Hanson, M. (1979). The right of children to experiences in dance/movement/arts. *Journal of Physical Education and Recreation*, **50**(7), 42.

Laban, R. (1960). *The mastery of movement.* London: MacDonald & Evans.

Lavay, B., & Sayers-Lavay, P. (1988). Incorporating movement activities in the classroom. In P. Bishop (Ed.), *Adapted physical education: A comprehensive resource manual* (pp. 223-228). Kearney, NE: Educational Systems.

Levete, G. (1982). *No handicap to dance.* Cambridge, MA: Brookline.

Miller-Merrill, J., & Horvat, M.A. (no date). Dance activities for the handicapped. In M. Horvat (Ed.), *Nevada fitness, games, sport and activities for the handicapped guide* (pp. 123-139). Las Vegas: University of Nevada.

Rickard, H.C., Thrasher, K.A., & Elkins, P.D. (1984). Responses of persons who are mentally retarded to four components of relaxation instruction. *Mental Retardation*, **22**, 248-252.

Riordan, A. (1980). A conceptual framework for teaching dance to the handicapped. In S. Fitt & A. Riordan (Eds.), *Focus on dance IX: Dance for the handicapped* (pp. 13-19). Reston, VA: American Alliance for Health, Physical Education, Recreation and Dance.

Riordan, A. (1989). Sunrise wheels. *Journal of Physical Education, Recreation and Dance*, **60**(9), 62-64.

Roswal, P.M., Sherrill, C., & Roswal, G.M. (1988). A comparison of data based and creative dance pedagogies in teaching mentally retarded youth. *Adapted Physical Activity Quarterly*, **5**, 212-222.

Schmais, C. (1976). What is dance therapy? *Journal of Health, Physical Education and Recreation*, **47**(1), 39.

Schmitz, N.B. (1989). Children with learning disabilities and the dance/movement class. *Journal of Physical Education, Recreation and Dance*, **60**(9), 59-61.

Schwartz, V. (1989). A dance for all people. *Journal of Physical Education, Recreation and Dance*, **60**(9), 49.

Sherrill, C., & Delaney, W. (1986). Dance therapy and adapted dance. In C. Sherrill (Ed.), *Adapted physical education and recreation* (pp. 354-373). Dubuque, IA: Brown.

Silk, G. (1989). Creative movement for people who are developmentally disabled. *Journal of Physical Education, Recreation and Dance*, **60**(9), 56-58.

Stinson, S. (1988). *Dance for young children: Finding the magic in movement.* Reston, VA: American Alliance for Health, Physical Education, Recreation and Dance.

PART III

Physical Activity for a Life Span

The five chapters of Part III emphasize specific physical activities for distinct age groups of individuals with mental retardation. The first four chapters focus on specific age groups, and the fifth chapter is devoted to Special Olympics International.

There is major concern today regarding the effectiveness of early childhood and early intervention programs for infants and toddlers considered "at risk," including those with mental retardation. Chapter 8, "Physical Activity for Infants and Toddlers," looks into the history of such programs and develops a solid rationale for physical activity programs for this age group. A short review of classifications of mental retardation allows the reader to move quickly into motor development of infants and toddlers, exploring the developmental theory of Piaget and the maturational concepts of Gesell. The first 12 months of life are analyzed, beginning with assessment of infants and moving through normal and abnormal muscle tone, primary infant reflexes, and postural reflexes, and concluding with an in-depth look at the vestibular mechanism. General teaching guidelines are presented for the professional who has little background with infants and toddlers. Specific motor activities are suggested, with appropriate developmental milestones serving as constant guides. The discussion progresses through the developmental ages of 3, 6, 9, and 12 months and presents specific developmental activities for each age group.

When the infant becomes a toddler; the fundamental motor skills of balance and walking become paramount, and this chapter presents teaching techniques for these two important areas. Skills and activities are described that can be used with individuals at the developmental levels of 18 and 24 months. Comparisons are made between toddlers with and toddlers without mental retardation to guide the selection of appropriate physical activities.

Chapter 9, ''Physical Activity for Preschoolers,'' is highlighted by an in-depth analysis of the levels of motor development at the developmental ages of 3, 4, and 5 years. Comparisons are made between youngsters with and youngsters without mental retardation. Suggestions and descriptions are included for numerous physical activities for each age group. The fundamental motor skills of running, jumping, hopping, and kicking are described, and activities to improve these skills are included. A final section gives special emphasis to children between the ages of 3 and 5 with Down syndrome.

Chapter 10, ''Physical Activity for School-Age Children and Teenagers,'' establishes guidelines for appropriate progressions in the physical domain for the normal developmental pattern. Height and weight comparisons are made among youngsters and teenagers (ages 6 to 18) with mild mental retardation, moderate retardation, and Down syndrome and those without mental retardation. Motor skill performance is also compared for these groups. The question of placement into *appropriate* physi-

cal activity programs is considered. Specific physical growth and development standards are given for primary-age children, ages 6 through 8 years. Motor learning abilities of youngsters with mental retardation are thoroughly discussed. The fundamental motor skills of galloping, skipping, throwing, catching, and striking are analyzed, and activities to improve these skills are provided. Specific activities that improve general motor performance are included: rope jumping, parachute play, scooter play, and beanbag play.

Chapter 10 continues with motor activities for youngsters with developmental ages of 9 through 12 years and includes a section on physical fitness for the preteenager. The final section is devoted to activities for teenagers, with special emphasis on including individuals with mental retardation in physical education programs. General recommendations are made regarding improving health, developing physical and motor skills to aid in getting and keeping jobs, becoming involved in athletic programs, and leisure activities.

Chapter 11, ''Physical Activity for Adults: Leisure and Lifetime Activities,'' highlights the importance of leisure and recreational play for adults with mental retardation. The role of the therapeutic recreation specialist is described. Several options are presented regarding integration and segregation choices in recreational settings. Techniques are presented for helping adults with mental retardation make choices about leisure-time pursuits. Physical fitness and sport options are included.

The discussion of leisure pursuits for individuals with severe or profound mental retardation includes assessment of leisure needs, teaching and learning recreation skills, and age-appropriate activities.

Chapter 12, ''Special Olympics International: Year-Round Training and Athletic Competition,'' opens with the history, structure, purpose, and philosophy of Special Olympics International. Topics include eligibility and classification for participation in the different sports, sport training, competition divisions, and the role of volunteers. The discussion of the training of athletes with mental retardation covers coaches' training schools, sport skill programs, sports medicine and safety, and coaching and training practices. Research on Special Olympics competition is reviewed, and the physiological benefits and psychosocial outcomes of being a Special Olympian are studied. Finally, future issues are considered, such as Partner Clubs, Unified Sport, School Sports Partnerships, and Outreach.

CHAPTER 8

Physical Activity for Infants and Toddlers

<u>PREVIEW</u>   Marcella is young, just 17 last month, and already a mother. She smiles as she looks down into the crib at Rachel, her beautiful 2-month-old baby girl. Marcella's mind wanders back to her difficult pregnancy and delivery. She hadn't understood what the obstetrician meant when he said that Rachel might have some learning problems. He even used the term *at risk*. But that is in the past, and Marcella is thinking about tomorrow's visit from the social worker, Mrs. Kruzel. The woman phoned her last week and described an early childhood program that was being offered free at the local hospital. This program would give her and the baby an opportunity to do things together that would help Rachel learn better. She didn't completely understand when Mrs. Kruzel talked about "early infant stimulation activities," but they sounded

easy and fun. Also, there would be other mothers and their babies, along with teachers and therapists. As Marcella crawls into her bed, she thinks about tomorrow. Will the teachers be friendly? What do babies need to learn? What will this program be about? What things will they teach us? What does it mean to be a child "at risk"—maybe mentally retarded? Will the activities help Rachel, or will she have problems?

HIGHLIGHT QUESTIONS

- **What are early childhood programs? Who can benefit from them? How would you define a child "at risk"?**
- **Do all infants and toddlers move through the same motor developmental progressions?**
- **What are the motor characteristics of infants and toddlers with mild mental retardation; with moderate mental retardation; with Down syndrome; with severe mental retardation; with profound mental retardation?**
- **What are the major principles regarding motor development of infants and toddlers?**
- **How are infants and toddlers assessed in their motor performance?**
- **How are infant reflexes measured, and how do teachers and therapists use this information?**
- **What general teaching guidelines are most successful for working with infants and toddlers?**
- **Which physical activities are suggested for youngsters under 12 months of age? For toddlers up to 24 months?**

The early childhood years are important for all children, but for the child who deviates from the norm in terms of mental and physical disabilities, the first 2 years are especially crucial. By the time these youngsters reach the age of 3, precious learning time and opportunities for providing essential early intervention experiences may be lost (see Figure 8.1).

Public Law 99-457, the Education of the Handicapped Amendments, was passed on October 8, 1986. This law extended all rights and privileges under PL 94-142 to infants, toddlers, and preschoolers from birth to 5 years and to their families. The infant component of this law (Part H) is voluntary on the part of individual states. It does provide incentive grants to assist

Figure 8.1 Precious time cannot be lost . . . youngsters have to be carefully taught. Photo courtesy of C. Eichstaedt.

states in the development of an interagency council whose purpose is to ensure planned, coordinated services for infants and toddlers aged birth to 2 with disabilities. A unique feature of this law is the recognition of the need for parental involvement in the education of their children.

Under PL 99-457, parents must be given assistance in determining their child's needs and obtaining services (Patton, Payne, & Beirne-Smith, 1990). Parents of these youngsters are to be actively involved in the assessment process and are designated to help develop their own individualized family service plan (IFSP), which describes how family strengths can enhance their child's development (McCormick, 1990; Westling & Koorland, 1988).

Individualized Family Service Plan (IFSP)

Public Law 99-457 specifically identifies the required components of an IFSP. Jordan, Gallagher, Hutinger, and Karnes (1988, pp. 48-49) describe the eight major parts of an IFSP. This list is presented in Highlight 8.1.

"The aim of early intervention programs is to prevent disorders that may arise from pre- or perinatal trauma or impairments and/or remediate the effects of identified disabilities" (Hanson, 1987, p. 6). In spite of a seemingly obvious need to provide early intervention programs for children with mental retardation, many children are not referred to special pro-

---

HIGHLIGHT 8.1

IN THEORY

The Individualized Family Service Plan

According to PL 99-457, the individualized family service plan (IFSP) must contain the following:

1. A statement of the child's present levels of development (cognitive, speech and language, psychosocial, motor, and self-help)
2. A statement of the family's strengths and needs related to enhancing the child's development
3. A statement of major outcomes expected to be achieved for the child and family

4. The criteria, procedures, and timelines for determining progress
5. The specific early intervention services necessary to meet the unique needs of the child and family, including the method, frequency, and intensity of service
6. The projected dates for the initiation of services and expected duration
7. The name of the case manager
8. Procedures for transition from early intervention into the preschool program

Note. From *Early Childhood Special Education: Birth to Three* (pp. 48-49) by J.B. Jordan, J.J. Gallagher, P.L. Hutinger, and M.B. Karnes, 1988, Reston, VA: The Council for Exceptional Children/Division for Early Childhood. Reprinted by permission of the Council for Exceptional Children/Division for Early Childhood.

grams. The "wait and see" and "perhaps the child will outgrow this" attitude are common among physicians and professionals. Filler and Olson (1990) believe that the problem is associated with the inability of current infant screening and assessment devices to predict which youngsters will be delayed at a later age and to determine which children will benefit from particular treatments. Therefore, the decision to specifically identify or label is difficult. By far the most studied and largest group of individuals with developmental disabilities is people with mental retardation. Not too many decades ago, when mental retardation was thought of as a trait fixed at birth, mental subnormality was considered a kind of incurable disease. More recently, psychologists, physicians, and educators working with individuals with mental retardation have come to understand that retardation is relative both to the child's environment and to the time when developmental intervention is begun. Today mental retardation is properly viewed as a symptom, not as a disease. The symptom may change, either because the child's circumstances have changed or because of some improvement in physical status. It is critical that this distinction be kept in mind, for too often mental subnormality is understood, especially by nonprofessionals, as a permanent condition rather than as a current state of affairs.

Hutinger (1988) defines and describes the eligibility of infants and toddlers for special programs:

Section 672 of PL 99-457 defines handicapped infants and toddlers as individuals from birth through 2 who are in need of early intervention services because they (a) are experiencing developmental delays as measured by appropriate diagnostic instruments and procedures in one or more of the following areas: cognitive development, physical development, language development, or self-help skills; or (b) have a diagnosed physical or mental condition that has a high probability of resulting in de-

velopmental delay. The term may also include, at a state's discretion, infants and toddlers who are "at risk" for substantial developmental delays if early intervention services are not provided. However, each state must define the term "developmentally delayed." (p. 37)

History of Early Childhood Programs

During the past 25 years, specific early childhood programs have come into prominence. Legal, social, and scientific factors have provided impetus to develop early intervention programs. Early childhood programs such as the 1964 Project Head Start and the 1972 Brookline Early Education Project (BEEP) have had positive results. School districts were guided by the 1968 federal Children's Early Assistance Act. This legislation encouraged several projects, including the Handicapped Children's Early Education Programs (HCEEP). These projects represent a wide variety of curricular approaches and many different types of disabilities. DeWeerd (1984) reviewed the results of HCEEP projects and found that 55% of the at-risk children were placed in mainstreamed settings and 67% achieved at average to above-average levels when they entered school after their special training. A more detailed account of early childhood projects can be found in Antley and DuBose (1981) and Heward and Orlansky (1988).

Need for Early Motor Stimulation

For young children with mental retardation, common sense dictates that specific programs be given as early in life as possible to ensure that motor development begins and continues toward optimal growth. One of the main reasons for intervening during early childhood is that it can reduce many problems that may become entrenched if they persist into the later years. These programs also provide adapted motor programs for at-risk youngsters, thereby enabling children with mental retardation to develop higher skill levels than would be possible without early intervention. Hanson (1984) states: "Without special, comprehensive intervention, children with known disability and those at high risk for developing problems may not develop early skills and relationships needed in order to lead productive lives" (p. 362).

Shapiro, Palmer, and Capute (1987) have found that gross motor delay is the most common presenting symptom of mental retardation before 18 months of age. They note that "motor development is the developmental focus between 6-15 months. Delay in motor development does not represent cognitive delay, but it does represent aberrant neural development and can be used as a marker of risk. Failure to sit, come to sit, or walk at appropriate times are frequent accompaniments of mental retardation" (p. 216).

Mussen, Conger, and Kagan (1980) developed a series of questions and responses that deal with the importance of early intervention of infants. They ask:

What about those infants who do not have the opportunities for playful intervention? What aspects of caretaking are most important? Does an infant really need much besides a clean dry diaper, a bottle of milk, and a warm place to sleep? In a poorly run, understaffed institution, infants may receive no more than routine care. Seldom are they held, and rarely does anyone talk or play with them. As we would expect, children in such settings are retarded in language, less vocal, less socially acceptable, and less alert to changes around them. (p. 134)

In the early months (before 3 or 4 months), little difference is seen between nondisabled babies raised at home and those raised in an institutional setting. The big change occurs after babies reach 4 months of age. The infants in a poor institutional situation are found to be apathetic and listless, with little responsiveness to careproviders, toys, or other dimensions of their external environment. They seem to have no curiosity about new experiences. For example, all the behaviors that are most likely to be learned as a result of interaction with people (i.e., clinging, crying in distress, reaching for adults for holding and play, and vocalization) are very clearly delayed or absent in the institutionalized youngsters (Hallahan & Kauffman, 1988).

Special note should be made regarding institutional care of infants, children, and adolescents with disabilities. Although heavy criticism has been lodged against institutions, state-operated facilities are now under the guidelines of PL 94-142 and must follow the "letter of the law" regarding the development and educational needs of every person between birth and 21 years. These individuals are to be carefully monitored, and individualized programs must be developed and carried out. Anything less is a violation of federal law. Therefore, today's developmental centers have taken great steps toward providing a rich variety of experiences for all youngsters and adolescents in their care.

Very young children reared in environments that are too quiet and lack daily interaction and movement experiences will fail to develop at a normal rate, because of the lack of variety in stimulation. According to Mussen et al. (1980),

it is the variety that is important, not the absolute level of stimulation. A child in a crowded one-room apartment encounters many sights and sounds simultaneously, while an infant in his own bedroom in a suburban home with a relatively quiet environment is presented with distinctive stimuli. A mother's voice breaking the quiet of the bedroom addressed directly to the infant will be more likely to catch his attention and teach him something than a voice over a television set in a sea of noise. It is the distinctive quality, not simply quantity of stimulation, that is effective in enriching an infant's intellecutal development. (p. 135)

Children with mental retardation are defined as such by their intellectual and adaptive behavior levels. In many instances, however, they will have low levels of motor performance that deviate from the norm.

Infants and Toddlers With Mild Mental Retardation

A large number of youngsters with mild retardation are found to have low levels of intelligence for cultural-familial reasons (i.e., due to environmental or inherited factors). Lerner, Mardell-Czudnowski, and Goldenberg (1987) state that "most authorities agree, today, that one's level of intellectual functioning is not a question of selecting *either* environmental or heredity. . . . there is an interactive relationship between the two factors of environment and heredity. Heredity is a component in one's intellectual capacity, but environmental experiences and educational interventions can significantly raise an individual's intellectual functioning" (pp. 31-32).

Most children with mild retardation are not identified until they enter school. During the preschool years, they will usually not be formally labeled as being retarded, and as Westling (1986) believes, these youngsters (when within their cultural parameters) may indeed function in a most acceptable manner. In fact, Westling further emphasizes that the intellectual level of the child tends to begin at an average IQ level and then decline through the years. He points to the research of Heber, Dever, and Conry (1968), generally referred to as the "Milwaukee Project," which studied children in high-risk environments and concluded that the children under 3 years of age were developmentally average, but older children from the same environmental situations, whose mothers had IQs below 80, were found to have an almost

linear decrease in IQ. The importance of this research tends to emphasize the critical nature of early childhood identification and intervention for preschool-age children with cultural-familial deficits. Although the Milwaukee Project has been criticized by some researchers, the results seem to indicate that early intervention programs may hold the greatest promise for preventing cultural-familial mental retardation (Westling, 1986).

Stedman (1977) compiled the results of 40 longitudinal studies involving high-risk preschoolers and found 13 common conclusions. Of particular importance is the following: "The effects of a stimulating or depriving environment appear to be the most powerful in the early years of childhood when the most rapid growth and development take place. . . . Therefore, home based intervention programs or one-to-one teacher ratio stimulation activities appear to be most appropriate and effective during this period" (p. 2).

Infants and Toddlers With Moderate Mental Retardation

Because moderate retardation is often easier to diagnose than mild retardation, early childhood and preschool programs are relatively common for children classified as having moderate mental retardation. A great deal of emphasis is placed on motor, language, and conceptual development. Additionally, because these children often have multiple disabilities, other professionals (e.g., therapists, psychologists) are frequently involved. MacMillan (1982) has reviewed early childhood programs for youngsters classified as moderately mentally retarded and concludes that "programs like the ones we have described have been successful in preparing established risk children to enter public school programs. Their goal has been not so much to make the children 'normal,' but to optimize their development through early stimulation. . . . The preliminary finding—that these children are capable of higher levels of functioning than previously thought—indicates that early intervention holds some promise for established risk children'' (p. 512).

Infants and Toddlers With Down Syndrome

Hallahan and Kauffman (1988) estimate that approximately 10% of all individuals with moderate and severe cases of mental retardation have Down syndrome. Although the degree of retardation varies widely, most individuals with Down syndrome fall in the moderate range, that is, have IQs between 35 and 55 (Grossman & Tarjan, 1987).

Down syndrome has a unique etiology, and it is not clear whether there are differences between individuals with Down syndrome and others with mental retardation in the cognitive processes used to attain knowledge (Kerr & Blais, 1985). Specifically, the brain of a child with Down syndrome shows no brain-cell destruction (as we would find with other youngsters labeled as moderately mentally retarded), but the brain, brain stem, and cerebellum are smaller and weigh less than in nondisabled children. Therefore, the child with Down syndrome will have less brain-cell mass, which is the major cause of the mental retardation and developmental disabilities.

Birth weight and length of babies with Down syndrome are significantly less than the average for infants without disabilities. Ershow (1986) has found that the average birth weight of males with Down syndrome is 6.6 pounds (nondisabled = 7.5 pounds) and the average birth length is 19.6 inches (nondisabled = 19.9 inches); for females with Down syndrome, average birth weight is 6.09 pounds (nondisabled = 7.4 pounds) and average birth length is 19.13 inches (nondisabled = 19.8 inches).

Share and French (1982) summarize the early growth patterns of young children who have Down syndrome as follows: "During the first

six months of life, motor development of [Down syndrome] infants closely parallels that of normal infants. After the sixth month, differences in development become apparent. By one year of age, the child with Down Syndrome is often four to five months behind a normal one year old'' (p. 2).

Ershow (1986) lists the average weight of 1-year-old males with Down syndrome as 18.56 pounds (nondisabled = 22.2 pounds) and average height as 28.96 inches (nondisabled = 29.60 inches). For females with Down syndrome average weight is 16.1 pounds (nondisabled = 21.5 pounds) and average height is 27.89 inches (nondisabled = 29.2 inches). In her research, Ershow identifies an unusual circumstance that may have had a bearing on her results. She states: "Birthweight [of infants with Down syndrome] was not affected by congenital heart disease, but weight gain during the first year of life was significantly impaired in children with Down syndrome who had congenital heart disease. By seven years, the children with the most severe congenital heart disease had died . . . (of the 13 children with Down syndrome who died, 11 had congenital heart disease)'' (p. 510).

Youngsters who have Down syndrome have a much better prognosis today than was given them prior to the enactment of PL 94-142. Before 1975, a poor prognosis was often given pertaining to marked developmental delays and progressive developmental decline that could be expected in the early years. More recent studies have established that when early intervention is provided, developmental decline is not as great (Hartley, 1986; Kerr & Blais, 1985; Piper, Gosselin, Gendron, & Mazer, 1986; Sharav & Shlomo, 1986; Sloper, Glenn, & Cunningham, 1986).

Preschool programming for children with Down syndrome in the late 1970s resulted in more and more of these youngsters improving their IQ scores into the mildly mentally disabled range. The success of these programs has been substantiated by the work of Rynders, Spiker, and Horrobin (1978).

A major problem has always been that a large proportion of individuals with Down syndrome are very often nonverbal or have low verbal skills. Verbal ability is not essential for learning motor skills; the control of motor skills (i.e., decisions of where, when, how far, and how fast to move) is a cognitive ability. For example, Kerr and Blais (1985) found that subjects with Down syndrome did not respond to directional probability in the same manner as other subjects, with or without retardation, when matched for chronological age or functional age.

Hanson (1987) compares motor milestones of nondisabled children with the progress attained in separate studies of youngsters with Down syndrome (Share & French, 1974; Share & Veale, 1974). See Figure 8.2 for these comparisons.

Infants and Toddlers With Severe or Profound Mental Retardation

Infants and toddlers with severe or profound retardation require extensive help with their daily needs. Their dependence on adults is strongly in evidence. Many have special problems that call for a combined team effort with physical education teachers, special education teachers, pediatricians, therapists, leisure specialists, and parents. According to Dunn, Morehouse, and Fredericks (1986), "Programs must be developed and instruction individualized to help the severely handicapped overcome, to the greatest extent possible, their functional deficits. The expression *severely retarded* communicates clearly that these individuals need and will benefit from physical education programs which are well designed and systematically implemented" (p. 4). Due to the extensive amount of brain damage in these children, the learning of motor skills will be extremely slow, and motor milestones will be delayed. Youngsters classified as having severe retardation (IQ of approximately 20 to 35) will attain higher levels,

and we see more and more of these children placed into programs that previously were exclusively for the moderately retarded. A critical issue seems to be whether the child is ambulatory. Individuals who spend most of the time in a crib or bed tend to be more negatively affected than those who can attain some degree of upright sitting, standing, and ambulation.

Zimmerman (1988) addresses the need of individuals with severe motor disabilities:

Developmentally disabled children cannot successfully be approached in terms of static milestones and measurements. First, severely handicapped children may make important gains and never move up on a milestone chart. . . . Opportunities for learning and fun are multiplied for a child who can sit comfortably and swallow easily, even though scoring 0 on a milestone chart. Second, how a child moves can be as important as what skills are present. In the absence of normal movement components, developmentally disabled children compensate by using abnormal tone and movement patterns in order to achieve their motor goals. Such "milestones" are hardly a true indication of function. They are energy consuming (leaving little endurance or concentration for other activities), are abnormal in appearance (interfering with peer interaction and the development of a positive self-image), and are unable to provide effective stability and mobility at the same time. . . . Motor goals [must be] broken down extensively and sequenced to show the movement components necessary to teach them. (pp. 1-2)

Individuals labeled as *profoundly retarded* (i.e., with an approximate IQ of less than 20) will likely retain many primary reflexes long past the time when these infant reflexes should be integrated into normal responses (see the section on primary infant reflexes). Additionally,

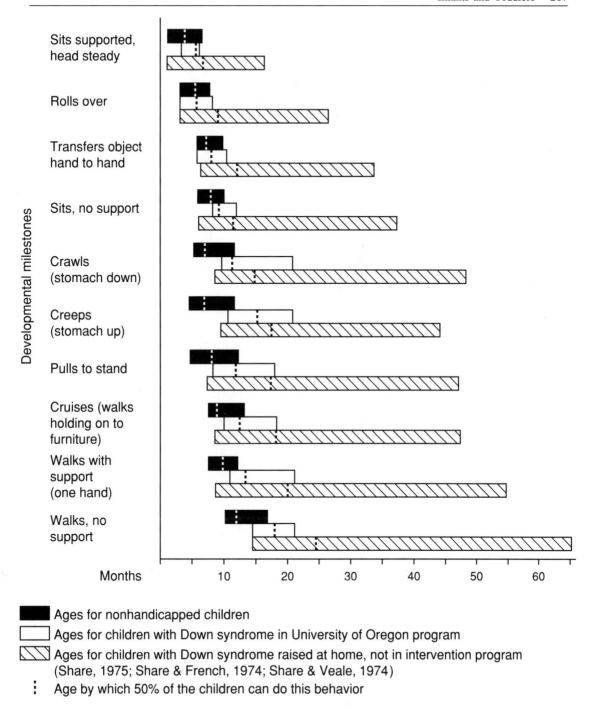

Figure 8.2 Motor milestone comparisons of nonretarded children and children with Down syndrome.
Note. From *Teaching the Infant with Down Syndrome* (2nd ed.) (p. 120) by M.J. Hanson, 1987, Austin, TX: PRO-ED. Reprinted by permission of PRO-ED, Inc.

some children with profound retardation may never develop speech. However, success has been found by teaching them to communicate through sounds, head and eye movements, and hand signing as used with individuals who are hearing impaired. In general, the lower the measured intelligence, the higher the probability that an additional physical anomaly is present. With the more serious physical disabilities, such as cerebral palsy, visual impairment, hearing impairment, or seizures, there often are delays in basic motor functioning. If such a lag exists in a child's motor development, it is likely to hinder adequate functioning in areas involving motor control. Therefore, it is critical to determine such deficiencies early and focus appropriate motor development efforts in this area.

Motor Development Theories

To understand the problems encountered when attempting to develop a comprehensive motor development program for a child with a developmental delay, one must become familiar with normal motor development. Atypical behavior cannot be appreciated without an understanding of "normal" behavior.

Piaget's Developmental Theory

Jean Piaget's early developmental stages span the age range of birth to 2 years, and although these specific stages overlap in development, the general age ranges are quite consistent. There are six major stages considered within the sensorimotor period, that is, from birth to the appearance of language.

- *Stage 1: Infant Primary Reflexes (birth to 6 weeks)*. The infant is dominated by uncontrollable reflexive behavior and simply reacts to external stimuli. The responses are protective in nature. For example, the infant blinks in response to light and softly moving air, makes mouth-sucking actions,

and is startled easily by loud sounds or unexpected movements. Bailey and Wolery (1989) explain: "The primary function of the reflexive stage appears to be simply to 'get the system ready' for learning. The first stage prepares the sensory and motor systems for their roles as response and feedback mechanisms" (p. 251).

- *Stage 2: Primary Circular Reactions (1 to 4 months)*. These first habits are the beginning of primary stable conditionings, that is, relative to the body proper, such as sucking the thumb. The youngster is learning to integrate sensory and motor information and is beginning to interact with the environment. He responds to sounds, watches his hands, and brings them to his mouth.

- *Stage 3: Secondary Circular Reactions (4 to 8 months)*. Coordination of vision and prehension (grasping) are now being used with purpose. The child becomes aware that she has an effect on her environment. She understands that her actions produce desirable results, and she repeats these behaviors again and again to continue the pleasurable actions. Bailey et al. (1989) explain: "They kick in the crib to keep the mobile moving, shake rattles to hear the sound, and swipe at toys to keep them activated" (p. 251).

- *Stage 4: Coordination of Secondary Circular Actions (8 to 12 months)*. During this time the child becomes goal-oriented. He chains actions together to accomplish a desired task. He is able to move his body from a sitting position to crawl to his favorite toy. He reaches for and grasps toys. If when searching for a lost toy, he is unsuccessful, he will not have the ability to continue his search, as it appears he has no alternate method in his approach.

- *Stage 5: Tertiary (3rd) Circular Reactions (12 to 18 months)*. This stage is highlighted by learning new actions through trial and error. She will now pull to her a blanket that has a toy on top of it; or she will use a string to pull, or a stick to reach or grope. She is now able to try a different approach if her first attempt to accomplish a goal was unsuccessful. Say Bailey et al. (1989), ''If the lid does not go on one pot, they try another pot or reach for a different lid and try it. Their actions and thoughts are very flexible and they have many cognitive and motoric alternatives at their disposal'' (p. 252).

- *Stage 6: Combination of New Means through Mental Combinations (18 to 24 months)*. The child now has a sense of understanding problems rather than solving them through trial and error. He can plan and predict what will happen and will be able to make choices regarding his actions.

Many concepts and measures of early childhood development, including assessment instruments, derive from the work of Piaget. Teachers and therapists should be familiar with Piaget's theory, in that it attempts to account for how children come to understand the world through their interaction with it. The first 2 years are referred to as the sensorimotor period. The development of mental representation is closely allied with the emergence of symbolic play and language development. The construction of test batteries of specific aspects of cognitive functioning shows a marked departure from traditional methods of determining intelligence. Attempts are made to establish an overall measure, usually expressed as an intelligence quotient (IQ) or a developmental quotient (DQ). A mental age (MA) equivalent is based on the relation between rate of development as measured by IQ or DQ and the child's actual chronological age (CA).

Gesell's Maturational Concepts

Arnold Gesell's maturational concepts, as described in Bee (1978), apply to all children, with or without mental retardation. Gesell is considered a structural theorist and uses age as an index for establishing developmental stages. In his research, he gathered a large collection of motion pictures showing a wide range of behaviors of children at different ages. Each age was regarded as a separate stage in the child's development. Bergan and Henderson (1979) explain: ''Because Gesell considered behavior genetically predetermined, he treated age as though it caused behavior. For instance, the 2-year-old children he studied were somewhat unruly. Gesell not only documented their unruliness in great detail, but also assumed that they behaved that way *because* they were 2'' (p. 23).

The teaching of motor skills can be enhanced through the use of Gesell's developmental approach. For example, teachers can add developmental behaviors between the entry and exit objectives of a task analysis (Bagnato, Neisworth, & Munson, 1989). The following are examples of Gesell's basic concepts.

The Principle of Directionality

Development is governed by maturation, as opposed to environmental forces, and has a clear directionality. As in the cases of fetal development and motor development, there are two distinct directions: Development proceeds from the head downward (cephalocaudal) and from the trunk outward (proximodistal). For example, the head and trunk develop first, but the arms and hands develop before the feet, because they are closer to the head.

The Principle of Functional Asymmetry

There is a tendency for individuals to develop asymmetrically. This is seen as the development of ''handedness'': Almost everyone has a preferred side, usually the right. We eat with the hand on the preferred side, throw a ball with that hand, and kick with the foot on that same side. Along with this motor asymmetry is an equivalent neural asymmetry. Thus, if you are right-handed, you are left-brained. Additionally, one half of the brain always dominates over the other half.

The Principle of Self-Regulating Fluctuation

Development does not proceed at the same even pace in all areas. Although one system is growing and developing vigorously, another may be dormant, and later the two may reverse activity levels. Bee (1978) provides an excellent example in: "the relationship between motor development and language development. Usually the child doesn't begin talking extensively until after she has learned to walk; the two skills are rarely developed together. Later, after the language system is more firmly established, there are more advances in motor skills" (p. 125). See Figure 8.3.

The Principle of Motor Development

Motor development progresses in from head to foot and from midline out. For example, the baby gains head control before gaining trunk control. Control of the body begins first in a horizontal plane, such as on the back and stomach, and then progresses to vertical positions, such as sitting and standing.

Newborns are incapable of effectively resisting the pull of gravity. Their postures and movements are characterized by flexion, with varying degrees of abduction and adduction, depending on their position. The development of extension in the vertebrae and extremities allows the child to pull up against gravity and move into upright positions. Rotation appears slowly in lying, sitting, standing, and walking and is critical for developing smooth, skilled transition from one position to another.

Motor Development of Infants and Toddlers

Infancy is the period following the first month of life until the baby begins to gain speech and

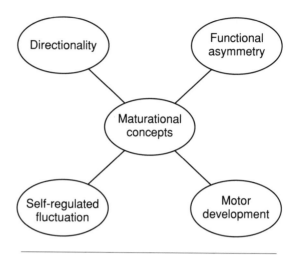

Figure 8.3 Maturational concepts and its subjects.

language, which occurs at about 2 years of age (Cratty, 1986). Average height and weight of nondisabled children from birth through 2 years is given in Table 8.1.

The teacher and leader should remember that motor development will follow a relatively normal course, although lower functioning infants with severe and profound disabilities will progress at a slower rate.

Croce (1987) suggests that learners progress from conscious movement, where there are many responses of extraneous muscle tissue during movement execution and where the skill is crude and poorly coordinated, to an automatic posture, where movement occurs with minimal conscious effort and proceeds in a highly efficient and coordinated manner. To understand the difficulty a child with mental retardation has when attempting to learn a motor skill, one must remember that the ability to remember is the greatest problem a child with mental retardation has. A nondisabled infant's ability to remember improves steadily during the last 4 months of the first year. Mussen et al. (1980) observe that "it is interesting to see the difference that even 3 or 4 months can make in an infant's ability to remember. Infants a year old will hesitate a few seconds before reaching for

Table 8.1   Weight and Height Comparison for Nondisabled Youth—Birth to 2 Years

Girls					Boys			
Weight (lb)		Height (in.)			Weight (lb)		Height (in.)	
50%	Range	50%	Range	Age	50%	Range	50%	Range
7.4	6.2- 8.6	19.8	18.8-20.4	Birth	7.5	6.3- 9.1	19.9	18.9-21.0
9.7	8.0-11.0	21.0	20.2-22.0	1 mo.	10.0	8.5-11.5	21.2	20.2-22.2
11.0	9.5-12.5	22.2	21.5-23.2	2 mo.	11.5	10.0-13.2	22.5	21.5-23.5
12.4	10.7-14.0	23.4	22.4-24.3	3 mo.	12.6	11.1-14.5	23.8	22.8-24.7
13.7	12.0-15.5	24.2	23.2-25.2	4 mo.	14.0	12.5-16.2	24.7	23.7-25.7
14.7	13.0-17.0	25.0	24.0-26.0	5 mo.	15.0	13.7-17.7	25.5	24.5-26.5
16.0	14.1-18.6	25.7	24.0-26.7	6 mo.	16.7	14.8-19.2	26.1	25.2-27.3
19.2	16.6-22.4	27.6	26.4-28.7	9 mo.	20.0	17.8-22.9	28.0	27.0-29.2
21.5	18.4-24.8	29.2	27.8-30.3	12 mo.	22.2	19.6-25.4	29.6	28.5-30.7
24.5	21.1-28.3	31.8	30.2-33.3	18 mo.	25.2	23.3-29.0	32.2	31.0-33.5
27.1	23.5-31.7	34.1	32.3-35.8	24 mo.	27.2	24.7-31.9	34.4	33.1-35.0
31.8	27.6-37.4	37.7	35.6-39.8	36 mo.	32.2	28.7-36.8	37.9	36.3-39.6

Note. From *Child Development* (p. 84) by J.R. Bergan and R.W. Henderson, 1979, Columbus, OH: Merrill. Copyright © 1979 by Bell & Howell Company. Reprinted with permission of Merrill, an imprint of Macmillan Publishing Company.

a new toy after being shown another toy six or seven times in a row, while 6-month-old infants will reach immediately for the new toy. The 1-2 second delay, short but obvious, suggests that older infants remember the first toy and are surprised by the new one'' (p. 101).

Infants and Toddlers With Mental Retardation

Youngsters with mental retardation will show delays in their ability to remember, but in most cases they eventually will attain the same motor milestones as the nondisabled. Exceptions are some children who are profoundly retarded and are "classified" as having a mental age below 6 months of age.

Many young children with mental retardation exhibit poor muscular coordination, lower than that of the nondisabled. In some cases this is due to basic problems in their central nervous systems (e.g., brain damage); in other cases the apparent awkwardness may stem from poor ''motor planning.'' For example, they do not

choose appropriate and efficient ways to perform motor tasks. The incidence of motor ineptitude goes up strikingly when brain damage is more extensive. Efficient learners seem to have different learning styles than ineffective learners. Effective learners are able to organize their thinking processes to facilitate learning. They seem actively involved in the learning process, they have persistence, and they work independently at solving problems and at learning. In contrast, inefficient learners are unconcerned in their approach to learning, waiting for the teacher to take charge and tell them what they should do. That is, they do not know how to go about the task of learning (Lerner, Mardell-Czudnowski, & Goldenberg, 1987).

Well-sequenced and thoughtfully planned motor education programs have been demonstrated to be of substantial help for many of these children (Anderson, Hinjosa, & Strauch, 1987; Jordan et al., 1988; MacWhinney, Cermak, & Fisher, 1987; Palfrey, Walker, Sullivan, & Levine, 1987; Payne & Isaacs, 1991; Sherborne, 1987).

Motor learning, too, is difficult, because these children must experience many more trials than nondisabled children to learn a skill. For example, for a small child who is mentally retarded to attempt to roll from her stomach to her back, she must be encouraged or stimulated to want to roll over. She must be motivated through sensory objects, such as rattles, bells, or voice sounds (see Figure 8.4).

Croce (1987) believes that the major theme of motor information processing is that all movement is the end product of a complex series that begins with sensory input, proceeds to cognition or understanding, and finally results in movement. A fourth dimension of importance is feedback. Feedback, either from the child or from an outside observer (e.g., a physical education teacher), increases the efficiency of learning. The child with a mental disability is likely to have difficulty with any or all phases of the motor learning act. Thus, it is imperative that all phases be overlearned, that is, that extensive repetitions be provided by the teacher to allow the child to (a) receive sensory input (e.g., sounds, sights, touchings), (b) process information (i.e., remember what is heard, seen, touched), (c) make responses to the sensory input (talking, reaching, touching, grasping, releasing), and (d) receive positive reinforce-

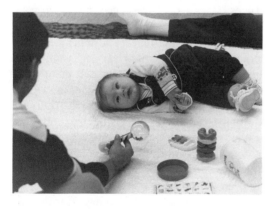

Figure 8.4 Rolling is encouraged by producing interesting sounds. Photo courtesy of C. Eichstaedt.

ment from the teacher (e.g., voice inflection, touching, a food prompt).

Mussen, Conger, and Kagan (1980) caution that too much stimulation, too early, before the child is biologically ready, may accomplish nothing. They refer to the case in which institutionalized infants were placed in an enriched environment and were more irritable and fussy than others who were not moved to richer environments. It appears that the extra stimulation distressed the children. Mussen concludes, "It is possible that the 3-week-old baby, biologically too immature to reach for the brightly colored mobile, may become more upset by the presence of the mobile than if nothing were present" (1980, p. 91).

Motor Development During the First Year

The neonatal period is from birth to approximately 30 days old. During an infant's first year of life, motor development is mostly a matter of biological maturation. However, stimulation and practice can provide meaningful opportunities for growth, and this intervention is especially necessary for babies who have neurological damage or may have developmental delays. Without stimulation, future progressions may be delayed even longer. Motor milestones usually attained in the first 12 months of life are found in Table 8.2 and Figure 8.5.

Assessment of Infants

Assessment of infant IQ is difficult, and this task is left up to the physician or diagnostician. Tjossem (1976) separates "vulnerable" infants into categories that may assist in understanding specific groupings. Infants with *established risks* are defined as "those whose early-appearing aberrant development is related to medical disorders of known etiology bearing well-known expectancies for developmental outcome within specific ranges of developmental delay" (p. 5).

Table 8.2   Motor Milestones in the First Year

Age	Motor behavior	Age	Motor behavior
1 week	Moves head from side to side.	7 months	Sits alone.
1 month	On stomach, turns head from side to permit unobstructed breathing; lifts head up briefly.		Reaches persistently for toys out of reach. Will pick up a second block after securing first.
2 months	On stomach, can raise chest off surface briefly.	8 months	Can get self into sitting position. Stands with help.
	Can raise head erect while held in sitting position, though head bobs up and down.	9 months	Stands holding furniture. May be able to sit down from standing position.
3 months	Will swipe at an object in visual field, but typically misses.		Manipulates and drinks from cup. May crawl upstairs; can turn around.
4 months	Can sit supported with head erect and back unsteady.	10 months	Creeps on hands and knees. Sidesteps along furniture.
	May roll from stomach to side or back.		Walks if both hands are held.
	Can follow object with eyes across visual field.		Responds to simple words and commands (e.g., "Don't touch," "give it to me").
	Can focus eyes on near and far objects.	11 months	Walks when led by one hand.
5 months	Can reach for and grasp object; aim is now good.		Squats and stoops.
	Recognizes familiar objects.	12 months	Stands by flexing knees, pushing self up from squatting position.
6 months	Sits easily in high chair, grasps dangling object.		Sits down smoothly. Crawls up and down stairs.
	Transfers object from one hand to the other.		Cooperates in dressing.

Note. From "Developmental Milestones in the First Year" in *Essentials of Child Development and Personality* (pp. 89-90), by Paul Henry Mussen, John Janeway Conger and Jerome Kagen. Copyright © 1980 by Paul Henry Mussen, John Janeway Conger and Jerome Kagen. Reprinted by permission of HarperCollins Publishers.

The child with Down syndrome is given as an example of a child with an established risk.

A second grouping is that of *biological risk*. Babies at biological risk are defined as "infants presenting a history of prenatal, perinatal, neonatal, and early developmental events suggestive of biological insults to the developing central nervous system and which, either singly or collectively, increase the probability of later appearing aberrant development" (Tjossem, 1976, p. 5). An example would be a child who experienced severe anoxia (lack of oxygen) during the perinatal period (time of birth), with resultant destruction of brain cells.

Regardless of the etiology or severity of the mental retardation, early intervention appears to be highly recommended. Thus, it is desirable to properly identify the motor-delayed child as early as possible.

Standardized Test Batteries

Capute and Shapiro (1985) have determined that gross motor development is the end result of the interaction of neurological processes that mature at different rates, and identification of motor problems should begin by evaluating muscle tone, primitive reflexes, and postural responses. Infants and young children with mental retardation are not always easy to assess. They are sometimes uninterested in what you want them to do, and, as with nonretarded children, they

On tummy

a. Lifts head

b. Head at 45°, support on elbows

c. Prone extension

d. Prone on elbows

f. Reaches out; support on one elbow

g. Support on hands, head at 90°

e. Rolls from stomach to back

h. Pivots in prone position

i. Pulls forward on stomach

On back

a. Turns head

b. Arm and leg movements

c. Hands to mouth

d. Head in midline

e. Reaches for objects at arm's length

f. Feet in air for play

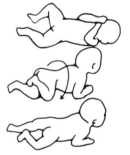

g. Rolls from back to stomach

(Cont.)

Figure 8.5 Motor milestones during the first year.

Note. From *The Carolina Curriculum for Handicapped Infants and Infants at Risk* (pp. 34-35) by N. Johnson-Martin, K.G. Jens, and S.M. Attermeier, 1986, Baltimore: Paul H. Brooks Publishing. Reprinted by permission of Paul H. Brookes Publishing Co.

Upright

a. Head steady when held

b. Trunk steady

On tummy

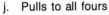

j. Pulls to all fours

k. Rocks on all fours

l. Plays in asymmetrical half-sitting position

m. Creeping on all fours

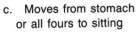

n. Raises one hand high on all fours

Upright

c. Moves from stomach or all fours to sitting

d. Sits alone

e. Pulls from all fours to standing at a support

f. Takes sideways steps at a support

g. Stoops to pick up a toy, holding on to a support

h. Stands alone

i. Walks alone

j. Moves from all fours to standing

Figure 8.5   (Continued)

may resist by crying, throwing toys and materials, or wetting their pants.

Crowe, Deitz, and Bennett (1987) caution that motor assessment of infants using a test battery such as the Bayley Scales of Infant Development (Bayley, 1969) should be taken only as reflective of the infant's performance at the time of testing and not as a prediction of future potential. In this test battery two scales are provided: a mental and a motor form. The motor scale indexes skill at sitting, standing, and walking, along with gross and fine hand manipulation. The battery is standardized to provide scores of current functioning rather than to predict future performance. Berger and Yule (1987) describe the Bayley Scales as follows:

> Very low scores on the Bayley Scales do not indicate poor functioning and a high risk of continuing mental retardation. However, this expectation needs to be modified for infants with Down's Syndrome. . . . What this means is that in general Down's Syndrome children are developmentally delayed, but they show large differences in the rates at which they develop. The earlier such a child is assessed, the more difficult it is to predict . . . later level of functioning. Early assessment is helpful in diagnosis and in describing current functioning; it is less helpful in making prediction. (pp. 23-24)

The Motor Assessment of Infants and the gross motor section of the Peabody Developmental Motor Scales show highly significant correlations among repeated administrations, and thus they are valid, and they are found to be consistent measures of motor ability of infants with Down syndrome. Additionally, the older, more commonly used test batteries such as the Bayley Scales of Motor Development and the Gesell Developmental Schedules are still beneficial in assessing overall milestones; however, for measuring specific motor abilities, the newer assessment tools are recommended (Lydic et al., 1985).

In the research completed by Jordan et al. (1988) regarding assessment of infants between birth and 3, of the 72 instruments used by different agencies, the Bayley Scales of Infant Development were used most frequently.

Normal motor development occurring in the first 12 months of life is dynamic and culminates in the ability to rise to a standing position and to move through space. The work of Bobath and Bobath, cited in Eichstaedt and Kalakian (1987), reinforces the importance of early identification of at-risk infants. The Bobaths have developed a 20-item subjective assessment battery that begins with the infants in a supine position and ends with the infant standing and walking. With practice, this tool is very useful when determining existing levels of infant and toddler gross motor ability.

Regarding specific motor milestones, Gesell (cited in Eckert, 1987, p. 127) has come to the following conclusions:

- In the first quarter (4 to 16 weeks) of the first year an infant gains control of his twelve oculomotor muscles.
- In the second quarter (16 to 28 weeks) she gains command of the muscles that support her head and move her arms. She reaches for things.
- In the third quarter (28 to 40 weeks) he gains command of his trunk and hands. He sits. He grasps, transfers, and manipulates objects.
- In the fourth quarter (40 to 52 weeks) she extends command to her legs and feet; to her forefinger and thumb. She pokes and plucks. She stands upright.

APGAR Scoring System

In the United States, a newborn child will be assessed during his or her first minute of life, and again 5 minutes later. The APGAR Scoring System, developed by Virginia Apgar (Apgar & Beck, 1972) is used to determine the status of newborn babies to identify those who need emergency care. These scores also provide in-

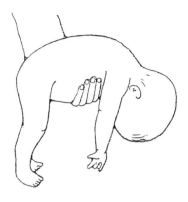

Figure 8.6 The "floppy baby."

formation that is often used to determine if a child is at risk.

Sixty seconds after the baby is born, a delivery room nurse or anesthesiologist rates the baby on five measures, using a scale of 0 to 2. The letters A-P-G-A-R stand for the five measures: Appearance, Pulse, Grimace, Activity, and Respiration.

In appearance (A) the newborn is given a score of 2 if his skin is completely pink; 1 if his body is pink but his arms are bluish; 0 if his entire body is blue. A newborn whose pulse (P), or heart rate, is higher than 100 per minute rates a score of 2; a heart rate less than 100 is scored as a 1; if the pulse is absent, he is scored 0.

A baby who cries vigorously when given a light slap on the soles of her feet is given a score of 2 for her reflex responsiveness; if she grimaces (G) or gives a slight cry, she rates a 1; no response is counted as 0.

A newborn who is making active motions receives a score of 2 for his activity (A) or muscle tone; some movement of arms and legs earns a rating of 1; a limp, motionless infant is counted as 0. Babies with Down syndrome often are born with a limp and hanging appearance and are commonly referred to as "floppy babies" (see Figure 8.6).

The final item involves respiration (R). Strong efforts to breathe, along with vigorous crying,

count 2; slow, irregular breathing, 1; no respiration, 0. A baby whose total score is between 4 and 6 usually needs some immediate assistance to increase her preliminary attempts at breathing and may be given oxygen to assist her respiration. There may also be materials in the throat that must be suctioned out before she can breathe adequately.

An infant with an APGAR score of less than 4 is limp, unresponsive, pale, usually not breathing, and possibly even without a heartbeat. His throat is quickly suctioned to open a clear pathway, and his lungs are artificially inflated as rapidly as possible. He may need help breathing for several minutes, until he is ready to take over for himself.

The APGAR test is repeated with all babies 5 minutes after birth. Both scores are recorded on the child's records. Follow-up studies show that the scores, particularly the second, are strongly predictive of brain damage present at birth (Apgar & Beck, 1972). A score of 6 or more is considered normal.

Normal and Abnormal Muscle Tone

Normal muscle tone can be felt by bending and straightening the arm or leg of a child and feeling the degree of resistance. This amount of resistance will feel the same throughout the child's body. The best way to understand what is meant by "normal" muscle tone is to handle nondisabled babies and feel how their muscles react and how easy it is to move their arms, legs, and heads. Babies with Down syndrome are likely to be extremely loose, whereas children with mental retardation who also have cerebral palsy tend to be on the stiff, rigid, or inflexible side. Most infants with mental retardation will have normal muscle tone unless they have other complicating conditions such as cerebral palsy.

Primary Infant Reflexes

The word *reflex*, when used regarding motor development, refers to a specific movement or posture that occurs when a particular stimulus is given. Several reflexes are present at birth and for this reason are termed primary or primitive reflexes. Their influence gradually diminishes and eventually should no longer influence motor behavior.

Winnick and Short (1985) describe the importance of being able to identify normal reflexes: "If reflexes, when elicited, are uneven in strength, too weak or too strong, or inappropriate at a particular age, neurological dysfunction may be suspected. Various reflexive behaviors are quite predictable and are expected to appear at particular ages and to be inhibited, disappear, or be replaced by higher order reflexes at later ages. Failure of certain reflexes to disappear, be inhibited, or replaced may inhibit the development of voluntary movement" (p. 50).

According to Pyfer (1988),

at least 36 reflexes are crucial to normal motor development. Fourteen of these reflexes appear during the first year of life and eventually enable a child to assume an upright position and begin to move about. If these reflexes do not appear, the child will not be able to lift his or her head, balance on all fours, sit, nor turn the head toward the out stretched hand. After a child becomes mobile, these "primitive" reactions are inhibited and do not reappear unless an individual is traumatized in some way. If the reflexes do appear but fail to be eliminated at the proper time, the child will be slow to walk, will do so in an awkward, clumsy manner. (p. 38)

Zemke (1985) explains that caution must be used when attempting to determine which children still exhibit a primary reflex. She has found that some 3- to 5-year-old children without retardation still possess mild levels of asymmetrical tonic neck reflex, a condition involving unwanted arm and leg movement when the head is turned to the side.

The following primitive reflexes should be understood and recognized by teachers of children with neurological impairments.

Palmar grasp or hand grasp reflex (onset from birth to 3 months)

Stimulus: A finger is stroked across the palm.

Response: The fingers close tightly and remain closed.

Significance: Supports the infant's ability to grasp objects but must fade before objects can be voluntarily released.

Moro reflex or startle reflex (onset from birth to 3 months)

Stimulus: The baby's head is allowed to fall back into teacher's hand.

Response: The arms move suddenly up and back, then are brought forward across the chest; as the reflex fades out, only slight arm movements are apparent.

Significance: The baby cannot use the arms for protection during sudden loss of balance.

Toe grasp or plantar grasp (onset from birth to 12 months)

Stimulus: A slight pressure given over the ball of the foot, or the baby is placed in a standing position.

Response: Toes curl in flexion and stay curled.

Significance: This reflex must fade before the child will have good balance in the standing position.

Asymmetric tonic neck reflex (ATNR, onset from 1 to 4 months)

Stimulus: The head is turned to the side.

Response: The arm and sometimes the leg on the face side (the side to which the head is turned) extend, and the arm and sometimes the leg on the opposite side flex.

Significance: This reflex often assists the baby in reaching out for an object in a back-lying position; but it must fade in order not to induce unwanted arm extension when the head is turned to the side. For example, if children still possess a positive asymmetric tonic neck reflex at the age when they should be rolling over from back to front, the abnormal reflex will cause unwanted arm and leg extension and will inhibit rolling.

Symmetric tonic neck reflex (STNR, onset from 6 to 8 months)

Stimulus: Extension or flexion of the neck.

Response: In a creeping position, with neck extension, the arms tend to extend and the legs to flex; with neck flexion, the arms tend to flex and the legs to extend.

Significance: This reflex provides assistance when learning to creep but must fade because all movements may be affected if they are initiated with head flexion or extension.

Postural Reflexes

Postural reflexes are necessary for normal motor development, and they include body righting, equilibrium, and protective reactions. These begin to appear a few months after birth and continue to develop through the first 5 years of life, although their greatest development takes place in the first 12 to 18 months. These reactions maintain the head in an upright position and ensure alignment of body parts for normal movement. These reflexes persist throughout life, providing an automatic support for voluntary actions. They can be classified, according to their functions, into righting, tilting, and protective-extension reactions.

The *righting reactions* assure the alignment of body parts to each other and the alignment of the body as a whole in space (Johnson-Martin, Jens, & Attermeier, 1986).

Head-righting reflex (onset from 2 to 4 months)

Stimulus: The child is held at the shoulders and tilted forward or sideward.

Response: The child brings the head to an upright position with eyes parallel to the horizon.

Significance: The ability to right the head in space is the first phase of development of postural control. A child with this ability requires less support when being carried and has greater freedom to visually inspect the environment.

Neck-righting reflex (onset from 4 to 6 months)

Stimulus: With the child in the supine position, the teacher turns the child's head to one side.

Response: The child first turns the shoulders, then turns the hips in the same direction.

Significance: This sequence of movements promotes the rolling pattern started when the head turns.

Landau response (onset 4 to 6 months)

Stimulus: While in the prone position, the child is suspended by the chest.

Response: Initially the baby lifts only the head; later, the back and legs extend; the back also arches upward.

Significance: In the prone position, this allows the child to push up on elbows and later push up on hands.

Body-righting reflex (onset 4 to 6 months)

Stimulus: While the child is in the supine position, the teacher bends one of the baby's legs and draws it up and across to the opposite side.

Response: The baby turns shoulders, then head, in the direction of the leg movement, completing a roll onto the stomach.

Significance: This action encourages development of a rolling over pattern.

The *protective extension reactions* are often referred to as parachute reactions, and they consist of automatic movements of the arms or legs to catch oneself after balance has been lost. It is interesting to note that these reactions develop at a time when the baby is learning to sit, stand, and eventually begin the rudimentary stages of walking.

Downward extension reaction (onset 4 to 6 months)

Stimulus: The baby is suspended vertically in the air and then is suddenly lowered toward a supporting surface but without letting the feet actually contact the surface.

Response: The legs extend quickly and move slightly apart; the toes are brought up in preparation for weight bearing.

Forward arm extension reaction (onset 6 to 7 months)

Stimulus: The baby is held horizontally in the air, face down, then moved suddenly toward a supporting surface.

Response: The arms are quickly brought forward, and weight is taken on open hands.

Sideward extension reaction (onset 7 to 8 months)

Stimulus: The baby is placed in a sitting position and is gently but firmly pushed to the side.

Response: The arm, on the side where the baby is pushed, moves quickly to that side, and the weight is taken on an open hand.

Backward extension reaction (onset 9 to 10 months)

Stimulus: In a sitting position, the baby is pushed quickly backward at the shoulder.

Response: On the side where the shoulder is pushed, the arm extends behind the body, and the weight is taken on an open hand.

Johnson-Martin et al. (1986) state that

although there is considerable variety in rate and some variety in order of milestone attainment, infants gain skills in a similar manner. . . . At any given point in development, babies will alternate between using established skills and experimenting with new ones. If left on their own, and not placed in positions that they cannot independently assume, they will generally stay within the limit of their motor ability. Their exploration of movement, then, is continually self-reinforcing. (p. 32)

They continue:

Bear in mind that motor development is not a strictly stepwise process. At any given time a child will have some skills at a proficient level of development and other skills at lower stages of development. The motor program should include a variety of activities in different positions. (p. 37)

What if a child is deprived of stimulation necessary for learning? What if the child has definite neurological signs that indicate mental retardation? Are effects irreversible? Can

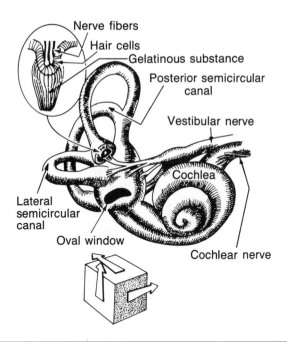

Nerve fibers
Hair cells
Gelatinous substance
Posterior semicircular canal
Vestibular nerve
Cochlea
Lateral semicircular canal
Oval window
Cochlear nerve

Figure 8.7   The superior semicircular canal of the inner ear. The inset shows detail of sensory ending (crista) in the semicircular canal.

Note. From *Developmental/Adapted Physical Education: Making Ability Count* (2nd ed.) (p. 463) by C.B. Eichstaedt and L.H. Kalakian, 1987, New York: Macmillan. Copyright © 1987 by Macmillan Publishing Company. Reprinted by permission of Macmillan Publishing Company.

changes in environment effect changes in development? According to Mussen et al. (1980),

it appears that retardation during the first year or two of life does not necessarily doom the child to permanent incompetence, for with the proper environment, children do have amazing powers of recovery. The secret is to find the proper environment to overcome the initial handicap in these children. . . . Most of the information gathered by psychologists to date does not provide for the popular belief that the experiences of infancy create fixed behavior patterns that persist no matter what environmental circumstances follow. However, neither can we conclude that the experiences of infancy are of no consequence for later childhood. It is encouraging, however, to find that if the conditions that may have caused fearfulness and retardation during infancy are favorably changed during the years 2 to 6, dramatic changes can occur. (pp. 138-139)

Accurate sensory perception of environmental stimuli and integration of sensorimotor information are necessary for neuromotor maturation. Any disruption (as from damage to the brain) of this process of perception and integration may result in a disturbance or delay in normal development.

The Vestibular Mechanism

The role of the vestibular mechanism and its influence on infant development have received much empirical attention (Ottenbacher, 1985). The vestibular mechanism (Figure 8.7), the cerebellum, and the proprioceptors in the muscles, tendons, and joints serve to regulate posture, equilibrium, muscle tone, and the orientation of the head and body in space (Eichstaedt & Kalakian, 1987). The clear neuroanatomical relationship of the vestibular mechanism with other regulators of the sensorimotor functions is well documented (Lydic, Windsor, Short, & Ellis, 1985).

Although results are mixed regarding the effectiveness of vestibular stimulation for infants, it is interesting to note a study by Ottenbacher (1985). He reviewed recent research and listed 18 specific studies containing a total of 44 hypotheses that evaluated the efficacy of vestibular stimulation on at-risk infants and young children with overt developmental delays. He concluded: "An analysis of the results of these tests, using methods of meta-analysis, revealed that subjects receiving vestibular stimulation performed significantly better than members of control or comparison groups who did not receive such stimulation" (p. 119).

Kreutzenberg (1976) suggests that vestibular stimulation provided to infants constitutes a sensory enrichment experience that "accelerated the maturation of synaptic connectivity of some inhibitory circuitry allowing infants to accelerate the inhibition of undesirable reflexes and motor responses. This would create a more stable environment and allow infants to accelerate in motor development" (p. 78).

Children who are mentally retarded (with central nervous system involvement) usually have some degree of developmental delay in the functioning of the vestibular mechanism. Stimulation of the vestibular system is usually desirable, as it allows children with severe retardation to progress as soon as possible through normal developmental stages (Eichstaedt & Kalakian, 1987).

Rotary stimulation of the vestibular system has been used extensively by therapists in their attempts to improve motor skills of children with developmental delays. Lydic, Windsor, Short,

and Ellis (1985) conducted a study with 18 babies with Down syndrome (CA between 4 and 10 months) to compare the effects of vestibular stimulation and a regular sensorimotor intervention program. The study lasted 12 weeks. Children in the treatment group received controlled rotary vestibular stimulation, and the control group received only their regular sensorimotor program. An analysis of variance showed no significant difference in motor development. Lydic and her associates concluded that although there was no significant difference between control and experimental groups, they believe their study demonstrated that infants with the diagnosis of Down syndrome were capable of significant motoric gains during a 12-week period, when specific sensory integration programs are provided. Even though these researchers are optimistic about their findings, the effects of a rotary stimulation program over a straight sensorimotor program for infants with Down syndrome can be questioned. More research in this area is needed.

Similar negative results were found by Thompson and Thelen (1986) when 5-month-old babies without disabilities were given vestibular stimulation for 16 sessions. The researchers determined that the infants' responses to vestibular stimulation varied (including falling asleep and crying). No significant effects on motor performance on the Bayley Scales of Infant Development (Bayley, 1969) were found following vestibular stimulation. Based on these results, these authors encouraged other researchers and therapists to question the effectiveness of vestibular stimulation for all populations.

General Teaching Guidelines

It is important to select motor activities that are appropriate for the children's developmental levels and not their chronological ages. This allows for program development designed to meet existing levels of ability. Norms developed for specific ages could lead to false assumptions. Many youngsters with mental retardation, particularly if they are at the moderate level or lower (IQ less than 50), would have difficulty attaining a 6-month gain in a 6-month period (Johnson-Martin et al., 1986).

Verbal praise and food reinforcers should be used sparingly. As much as possible, let the child experience movement for its own reward. The child's motor performance should be used primarily for play and exploration rather than to gain approval from the teacher.

Motor Activities for the Infant

Anderson et al. (1987) suggest that children's movement is best seen when they are at play and producing natural patterns. When children are absorbed in play, they are not focusing on the motor demands inherent in the activity. Motor analysis is thus accomplished while the infants are showing what they can do.

Play can be used to elicit normal movement and posture patterns by using objects or toys (reaching, throwing, placing; see Figure 8.8) or by positioning (sitting, resting on all fours, high kneeling), thus allowing the instructor the opportunity to observe the actions. Upper extremity stretching, trunk rotation, head and trunk

positioning, appropriate grasp, or a combination of the motor components may be developed by using play activities as stimuli for movement.

Activities should be simple, organized, and limited in scope to allow the instructor to handle the child most effectively (see Figure 8.9). Anderson et al. (1987) suggest that

> less complicated activities with fewer positioning requirements are effective and interfere less with handling. With the young infant (birth to 3 months), the therapist's face and voice can be effective play objects to stimulate visual fixation and tracking, thereby facilitating side-to-side rolling while the child lies supine. (p. 424)

Lerner et al. (1987) list several methods to elicit specific motor responses in infants. Table 8.3 illustrates several of these interesting approaches.

Playful interaction with parents and teachers provides children with a greater variety of meaningful experiences with muscular stimulation, vocalization, and play than the baby could

Figure 8.8 Infants are usually very curious. Instructors should use this inquisitiveness to help stimulate movement. Photo courtesy of C. Eichstaedt.

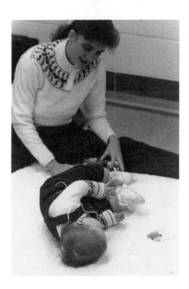

Figure 8.9 Side-to-side rolling is encouraged by the teacher's voice. Photo courtesy of C. Eichstaedt.

Table 8.3   Sequence of Prewalking Gross Motor Behavior and Methods of Stimulation

Motor behavior	Method of stimulating motor behavior

Head and neck control
  Turns head to side
  Raises head from prone position
  Supports head in an upright position
	Stimulate the infant to raise head with the use of a moving light or noise.

Sitting with support
  Sits in a lap with minimal support
  Independently sits with prop (pillow)
  Independently sits in objects with
    reduction of support
	Gradually reduce the need for support and increase the length of time for nonsupport.
	Increasing reduction of support gives the infant new situations to adjust to.

Rolling over Rolls over from back to stomach	Place infant on back and guide roll to left or right.
Raising body Supports the upper body on forearm	Stimulate the infant by placing on stomach and using a noisy toy or colorful object to draw attention.

Sitting without support
  Sits in chair independently
  Sits on the floor independently
	Gradually increase the length of time for nonsupported sitting, and alternate a variety of places for sitting: floor, chair, high chair, swing, and jumper seat.

Precrawling Initiates forward movement, prone	Use a toy or food as an incentive and draw the infant's attention toward it.

Pull to a sitting position
  Pulls to a sitting position, prone
  Requires less adult support in task
	Be an assist and support for the child.
	Support the child in attempts to accomplish the task.

Creeping Locomotes forward on hands and knees	Offer objects to the infant to increase distance accomplished.

Pull to standing position
  Pulls to standing position with support
  Pulls to stand with less physical support
  Uses objects as assists for pull to stand
	Offer infant support to pull to stand from a sitting position and reduce amount of support. Also make objects available for use as supports.

Sidestepping with support Sidesteps around objects while standing	Encourage moving to left and right in moving around objects.

Standing with support
  Stands with minimal adult assistance
  Stands using objects for adult support
  Stands without any support
	Begin with physical support, and then gradually reduce support. First hold with two hands, and reduce to one hand, and then to fingers.

Walking
  Walks with back support
  Walks with front support
  Walks with object support
  Walks with support from side
  Walks without support
  Practices walking skills
	Begin with front and back support of the infant and gradually reduce physical support. Practice the skill with regularity.

Note. From *Special Education for the Early Childhood Years* (2nd ed.) (pp. 173-174) by J. Lerner, C. Mardell-Czudnowski and D. Goldenberg, 1987, Needham Heights, MA: Allyn and Bacon. Copyright 1987. Reprinted by permission of Allyn and Bacon.

get alone. This input stimulates both motor and cognitive growth.

Teaching the Infant

When moving, positioning, or handling infants, it is best to control the baby at the head, shoulders, and hips. Always give the baby the opportunity to perform as much of the movement as possible. This usually involves doing things more slowly, so that the baby is given a chance to think about what is going to be done. Johnson-Martin et al. (1986) give the following example: "When bringing a child from back-lying to sitting, roll the child slowly to the side and give the child time to push up on his or her arm, even if he or she can only do this partially" (p. 38).

Head, Arm, and Leg Control

Infants learn to control head movements through natural curiosity and will purposefully explore the environment. This curiosity may not be as strong in a child who has a mental disability. Nevertheless, this trial-and-error exploration is extremely important. The eventual outcome will allow the child to move more effectually. The following activities are suggested to increase head, arm, and leg control while the baby is in the supine position.

1. Hold the baby's legs at the knee, and bend one leg and then the other. This will encourage back-and-forth kicking of the legs.
2. Encourage movement by stroking the child's arms and legs.
3. Provide rattles and infant toys for the baby to hold and put into the mouth.
4. Hang shiny, bright-colored objects high enough above the baby that the infant can touch and bat them with the arms and legs.
5. Touch and stroke the child's hands and feet and rub them together.
6. Swing the baby gently through space.
7. Lay the baby on her stomach on the floor and put a favorite toy in front of her. Hanson (1987) suggests: "Gradually raise the toy while squeaking it or moving it and encourage the child to watch the toy and lift the head. This activity may be more successful if you place a bolster or rolled blanket under the baby's chest" (p. 93).
8. With the baby lying on his back, hold the baby's hands by putting your thumbs in the baby's hands. Gently pull to a sitting position (see Figure 8.10). It may be necessary to assist the child by supporting him at his shoulders while pulling him to the sitting position.

Babies generally give cues when they are receptive to learning. For example, they will give verbal coos, gaze attentively with their eyes, and move their arms and legs in excited actions. These natural interactions appear to be signals from the baby, saying "I am happy, willing, and eager to learn." Hanson (1987) suggests:

Don't just passively move your baby through exercises. Place the child in the designated situation or position, then give the child a chance to respond. For example, when you are rocking the child from side to side during trunk control exercises, tip

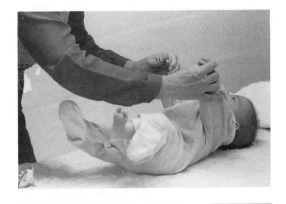

Figure 8.10 By placing her thumbs in the child's hands, the teacher activates the palmar grasp, which allows her to pull the child upward. Photo courtesy of C. Eichstaedt.

the child slightly and wait for the child to right the head and body (bring head and body upright perpendicular to floor), rather than passively rocking the child back and forth. Both you and your baby will have more fun with each other if you take turns responding. (p. 90)

Three-Month-Olds

Lerner et al. (1987) suggest that motor behavior can be improved in infants who have disabilities if specific methods are used to stimulate movement. Highlight 8.2 describes the developmental motor levels that 3-month-old infants without disabilities are able to perform.

When babies reach the developmental level of 4 months, they should be able to visually follow a slow-moving object that is passed in front of them. Also, they should be making "cooing" noises and smiling when they recognize familiar faces. Shapiro et al. (1987) suggest that if a baby does not demonstrate the above actions at 4 months, then referral should be made for more detailed observation and assessment. The implication is that a developmental delay may be present and early intervention programming should be given.

Six-Month-Olds

At the developmental level of 6 months, chil-

HIGHLIGHT 8.2   **IN PRACTICE**

Motor Development Level: 3-Month-Olds

1. Responds differently to hard/soft; warm/cold; rough/smooth
2. Stops movement when noise is heard
3. Visually searches for sound
4. Turns head and looks or reaches for ear-level sound while lying down
5. Visually fixates for 3 seconds
6. Visually tracks object from side to side
7. Visually tracks object from forehead to chest
8. Visually tracks object moving in a circle
9. Gaze lingers where object disappears
10. Shifts visual attention from one object to another
11. Looks for or reaches toward objects in sight that touch body
12. Moves fingers and hand to mouth
13. Moves, shakes, bangs and plays with toys
14. Repeats movement that produces an interesting result

15. Smiles to person talking and gesturing
16. Quiets when hearing a voice
17. Moves arms actively when sees or hears a toy
18. Bats at toy at chest level
19. Looks at hand or toy at side
20. Looks at or plays with toy placed in hands at midline
21. Raises both hands when toy is given, hands partially open
22. Lifts head, freeing nose
23. Lifts head to 45° angle
24. Turns head from side to side in response to visual and/or auditory stimuli while on back
25. Flexes and extends arms and legs
26. Maintains head in midline position while on back
27. Head steady when held in upright position

dren reveal two fundamental sets of movement skills: those involving various ways of moving forward and backward, and those that are leading to upright posture and later to walking.

Crawling and creeping patterns are extremely variable. Some babies only stomach crawl, whereas others bypass crawling altogether. The weight-bearing position of creeping, with its reciprocal arm and leg movements, is acquired during crawling and is an important component of later movement.

For children with Down syndrome, development of creeping is significantly delayed. Share and French (1982) have found that the baby without disabilities creeps by 10 months, whereas the baby with Down syndrome may take 15 months.

Crawling and creeping patterns are encouraged by placing obstacles in front of the child, thus requiring greater awareness and use of the legs. As proficiency is gained, more difficult problems can be presented, such as increasing the height to crawl over and building low bridges to crawl under. Cratty (1986) suggests that such challenges should help young children find out about their movement capacities, through engaging in basic locomotion, and understand their body size, through crawling over, between, into, and under objects of various shapes. Highlight 8.3 lists the motor milestones for the 6-month-old developmental level.

Eckert (1987) suggests the following developmental activities for infants under the developmental age of 6 months.

- Crib mobiles or other toys that are colorful, bright, and interesting, but not potentially harmful, and that can be hung tightly from the crib or playpen. These objects will provide very early visual stimulation and exploration, which also lead to tactual exploration of the toys.
- Rubber or plastic squeeze toys, rattles, soft cuddly animals, and teething toys are beneficial to developing object manipula-

tion, which leads to development of object concepts.
- Plastic buckets, utensils, and discarded junk mail that can be handled without harm often provide visual, auditory, tactual, and kinesthetic input. Care must be taken to ensure that these common household objects will not be potentially dangerous—that is, that there are no pointed ends, parts that can be broken off, small parts that can be swallowed, and so forth.
- Sponges of various shapes for bath play often encourage exploration and a good feeling toward water.
- Music boxes could provide variations in temporal sequencing of auditory input and encourage infants to move rhythmically in response to the music.
- Walkers that support the baby stimulate alternate leg action before the child has developed sufficient balance and strength for standing and walking.

Nine-Month-Olds

Shapiro et al. (1987) suggest that additional assessment of the child (by a physician or therapist) is necessary if the child does not attain the following skills or actions by the 9th month:

- Turns to the sound of a bell or rattle
- Babbles
- Transfers objects from one hand to the other
- Notices a small object about the size of a navy bean pellet
- Plays with paper

Highlight 8.4 lists milestones for the 9-month-old developmental level.

Between the time when children begin to manipulate objects with their hands and the time they learn to walk, there are several months when they have limited opportunities to use their hands, because these are needed for support. Developmental equipment, such as bolsters, incline mats, or thick foam pads, can be used for

Motor Development Level: 6-Month-Olds

1. Allows soft texture to be rubbed on face hands, feet, or body
2. Reacts to tactile stimulation with movement of hands, legs, or facial expression
3. Turns head and looks for source of sound while sitting, for sounds at ear level or shoulder level
4. Continues to look at teacher when teacher's face is covered with a towel
5. Pulls towel away from face
6. Pulls towel from teacher's face
7. Uncovers partially hidden object
8. Looks for or reaches toward objects out of sight
9. Looks for or reaches for objects that fall from view
10. Plays with (e.g., shakes or bangs) toys placed in hand
11. Explores objects and responds to their differences
12. Persists in attempts to obtain something
13. Performs previously learned skill on command
14. Stops activity when name is called
15. Responds to "bye-bye" and "up"
16. Continues a movement if it is imitated by teacher
17. Anticipates frequently occurring events in nursery rhymes
18. Grasps toy in hand (not reflexive grasp)
19. Reaches out and grasps object
20. Uses extended reach and grasp
21. Pulls and scoops small objects (fingers against palm)
22. Plays with feet and toes
23. Glances from one toy to the other when a toy is placed in each hand, or plays alternately with the toys
24. Brings hand together in midline
25. Places both hands on toy at midline
26. Transfers object from hand to hand
27. Extends arms, legs, head, and trunk in prone position
28. Holds weight on elbows when on stomach
29. Rolls from stomach to back
30. Reaches while supported on one elbow
31. Supports on hands with arms extended and head to 90°
32. Turns in prone position
33. Rolls from back to stomach
34. Holds trunk steady when held upright

children to kneel against while playing with toys on the floor.

After children master their bodies in prone, supine, and sitting positions, and all the positions in between, they are ready to use these learned skills to control their bodies in the fully upright position. Upright control begins with kneeling. The child may move into the kneeling position from the creeping or sitting position. Hanson (1984) describes this process: "The infant shifts to one knee, freeing the op-posite leg from weight. This leg is then free to be placed and have weight shifted onto it as the infant comes to a standing position with extended legs. This struggle is soon replaced with a fluid, effortless movement from kneeling to standing" (p. 333).

Twelve-Month-Olds

At the developmental level of 12 months, the child should have easily mastered the following skills:

HIGHLIGHT 8.4

IN PRACTICE

Motor Development Level: 9-Month-Olds

1. Allows hands, feet, or body to be moved over rough-textured materials
2. Explores objects with fingers
3. Plays in water
4. Looks for noisemaker when sound is presented to the side at waist level
5. Watches cover under which toy has disappeared
6. Removes cover from fully hidden toy
7. Head turns and looks back and forth to two different sounds
8. Demonstrates appropriate activities with objects having obviously different properties
9. Crawls over obstacles to get toys
10. Responds to "No"
11. Uses correct gestures to "Up" and "Bye-bye"
12. Raises arms to be picked up
13. Consistently indicates desire to "get down"
14. Points at objects when asked
15. Responds differently to strangers than to familiar people
16. Participates in games
17. Releases one object to take another
18. Grasps, using thumb against index and middle finger
19. Uses pincer grasp (thumb against side of index finger)
20. Uses index finger to poke
21. Uses neat pincer grasp (thumb against tip of index finger)
22. Claps hands on command
23. Pulls forward on stomach
24. Pulls upward to hands and knees
25. Rocks forward and backward in all-fours position
26. Plays with toys in asymmetrical half-sitting, half-side-lying position
27. Creeps on hands and knees
28. Sits alone
29. Pulls to standing position
30. Cruises sideways holding onto support

- Understands "No"
- Plays pat-a-cake and peek-a-boo
- Grasps with opposed thumb and forefinger
- Rings a bell

If the child does not have these skills, developmental delays are present, and additional medical or therapeutic consultation is suggested. See Highlight 8.5 for a list of motor milestones for the 12-month-old developmental level.

"The 12-month-old who acts like a 9-month-old should not be seen as 3 months behind but as developing at a rate that is 75 percent of average. If the child maintains this rate of development, he will be 6 months behind at 2 years"

(Shapiro et al., 1987, p. 217). Hopefully, early intervention motor programs will help children to progress forward and reduce their deficiencies.

Some specific milestones that children with Down syndrome usually attain during the first year are noted by Share and French (1982, p. 87):

- Sits with head erect, but forward and unsteady (3 months)
- Sits with head set forward (5 months)
- On the verge of rolling over (5 months)
- Rolls from back to stomach (7 months)
- Rests weight on hands with chest off floor (7 months)

IN PRACTICE

Motor Development Level: 12-Month-Olds

1. Plays with variety of objects to produce effects
2. Looks to the correct place when toy is hidden in one of two places
3. Searches for toys out of field of vision
4. Imitates activities related to the function of objects
5. Understands "no"
6. Gives objects to others on request
7. Understands "Give to me"
8. Imitates new activities
9. Builds a two-block tower
10. Removes objects from box by reaching into box
11. Puts one or two objects in box
12. Plays with toys in midline; one hand holds the toy, and the other hand manipulates it
13. Creeps on hands and knees
14. Raises one hand high while on hands and knees
15. Sits alone
16. Pulls to standing position
17. Pulls pop beads apart at body midline
18. Crawls upstairs
19. Takes first walking steps
20. Places many objects into box

- Maintains an erect sitting position (11 months)
- Partially turns on stomach (12 months)

Motor Development During the Second Year

With the beginning of the second year, infants are quickly moving into the world of the toddler. The emergence of new skills are the combined effect of physical growth, biological maturation, and perceptual and intellectual learning. Physically, these youngsters are gaining in height and weight. Muscles and bones develop and grow in size, and body proportions change.

Motor development is rapid during this period. By the developmental age of 24 months, youngsters should be fairly well coordinated and can walk, run, and walk up and down stairs alone. Because of their new skills and capabilities, these children usually develop a growing sense of autonomy and competence. Parents and teachers should encourage independence by allowing the children reasonable freedom. For some reason, parents of youngsters who are mentally retarded have tended to be overprotective.

Present-day American infants without retardation gain rapidly in height and weight. By the age of 2, the average girl weighs 27.1 pounds and is 34.1 inches tall; the average boy weighs 27.7 pounds and is 34.4 inches tall. The average child will grow about 5 inches and gain approximately 5 or 6 pounds during the second year.

During this second year children progress from being rather helpless infants, most of whose needs must be taken care of by adults, to toddlers who have begun to achieve some measure of independence and are able to satisfy some of their own needs. A 2-year-old boy who is able to open a toy box where his favorite blocks are kept is physically able to walk, so that he can get to the toy box lid and pull it open, and his brain has developed, through observation and instruction, to the point of biological maturity at which he has the intellectual ability to remember specific details (otherwise he would not be able to remember where the blocks are kept).

For children with mental retardation, the delay in the transition to becoming more independent is directly proportional to the degree of brain damage and environmental learning. In particular, these youngsters will have delays in developing memory. Although their muscular strength, balance, and body coordination may be adequate, their inability to remember leaves these children with less natural curiosity to explore, and their random movement usually appears purposeless and without direction.

The growth of muscle and nerve cells is very important, for these systems are the key to children's coordination and ability to make smooth and precise movements. During the second year, muscles develop and grow, providing a great increase in strength and also accounting for a larger proportion of body weight. The brain is also growing and has increased in size and weight from about 0.75 pounds to 2.2 pounds. The nervous system has developed into a more complex unit and has stored great amounts of information. Although the brain of the child with retardation is also growing, development of the highly sophisticated process of memory is delayed, and learning is slow to follow. Integration and interpretation of information in the brain is slow, and cognitive and motor learning tend to develop at a slower pace.

The development of walking is the most significant milestone of the second year. Similar to earlier motor patterns, walking depends primarily on physical maturation. Practice and repetition in crawling, creeping, and standing play a role, too, in that complete lack of opportunity or stimulation to practice may delay the onset of walking. The child who has brain damage is likely to lack the basic curiosity to explore the environment and thus will not always be self-stimulated to do so. Therefore, teacher and parent intervention are extremely important to ensure that the normal course of physical development continues. That is, exter-

nal stimulation is necessary to ensure neural development, greater muscle strength, and changed body proportions, all of which are prerequisites to walking. DePaepe and Croce (1987) observe:

> Given normal motor control, most children acquire all of their basic subroutines (patterns) by the age of eight. Severely and multiply handicapped children with CNS dysfunction, however, often lack these plans of action, and subsequently must be taught a plan of action through the systematic instruction of subroutines. (p. 158)

Balance

The development of balance is critical for all children, because the ability to control one's center of gravity is necessary for most skilled movement patterns. The acquisition of minimal levels of balance makes possible walking, running, jumping, and their many locomotor variations. Perceptual-motor specialists generally agree that individuals with good balance can focus attention on more important tasks and still keep their balance. These theorists believe that good balance often indicates functional integrity of the nervous system (Eichstaedt & Kalakian, 1987).

Balance comprises three distinct subsets: static balance (e.g., standing on one foot), dynamic balance (e.g., walking on a balance beam), and balance on a moving medium (e.g., walking on a train in motion). Static balance skills should include posturing in standing positions of various kinds, and balancing in relatively stable positions on mats, with the arms, knees, elbows, head, and bottom touching the mat.

Evans (1980) suggests the following drills for development and improvement of static balance:

- Have the child sit on the edge of a small box with feet off the floor; with arms extended to sides or over head.
- Have the child stand sideward on a low balance beam.

- Have the child stand in Romberg position (heel to toe) on a low balance beam.
- Have the child stand with one foot each on little blocks, plastic margarine containers, coffee cans, or books.
- Have the child stand on a rocking board, supported by the teacher holding the hands, and rock back and forth.
- Have the child sit on a rocking board and maintain balance, supported.

Walking

Evans (1980) reminds us, regarding the development of walking skills, that "the broad-based gait characteristic of the very young child is often seen in retarded children . . . who are attempting to learn the skill of walking. Although the arms and legs may be moving alternately, the walk appears stiff and inflexible and almost robot-like" (p. 24).

Most children with mild mental retardation are not delayed in their ability to walk and can use their bodies as well as other children their age. But a small number of children with mild retardation are delayed and at 12 to 18 months are just beginning to use their bodies effectively. Though behind, they fall less often than they did a few months ago, and they are learning the rudimentary skills of running, stopping suddenly, and even changing directions. It can be expected that within the next year they will have mastered the ability to go up and down stairs one step at a time without holding onto the rail.

In contrast, 3- to 5-year-old children classified as moderately mentally handicapped have the locomotor patterns of 18- to 30-month-old nondisabled children. By this time youngsters with moderate mental retardation should be able to walk well, with few falls. They should be able to climb into large chairs and onto the sofa and bed. They will likely be able to walk up stairs with help and creep backward down steps. These youngsters can throw a ball overhand, but it often lands on the ground nearby instead of hitting an intended target. Their running is still stiff and awkward, but they are able to move quite fast.

When teaching individuals classified as having severe or profound mental retardation, teachers will usually find that the children display gross motor skills that initially involve learning to coordinate and overcome primary infant reflexes. As the children progress, they gain control of the head, neck, and torso. Next they begin to bear weight in a standing position, usually by holding on to a parent, teacher, or piece of furniture. They will sit up when propped. Eventually they will be able to sit without support, creep around on the floor, crawl, pull to a standing position, take supported steps, and finally walk.

There is a distinct difference between children labeled as having severe retardation and those labeled as having profound retardation. Those classified as severe make greater progress. Many of these youngsters are being placed into school settings and are making remarkable strides. For example, walking, running, and jumping are now attainable goals for most of them.

Cratty (1974, pp. 122-124) suggests 10 activities to be used in developing walking for children who are mentally retarded.

1. *Walking point to point.* A simple task for a child is to learn to walk from one point to another a few feet away. Teachers may stand 5 to 10 feet apart. One releases the child, and the second intercepts the youngster. Lines could be taped on the floor, or mats or wooden pathways could be used to mark an appropriate pathway at first. Successful efforts should be rewarded. Cratty (1974) notes that "it is, of course, a help to give the child a terminal reward such as a smile from the therapist or some extrinsic award like candy for his success in the endeavor" (p. 123).

2. *Walk, stop, and continue*. The child is told to walk, stop on command, and then continue. This method of pairing words and movement can be accomplished in several ways and may be instrumental in the process by which the youngster first learns the meaning of words, because it is the manner in which children without disabilities begin to learn language.

3. *Walk and return unaided*. Have the child walk to a point, turn around, and come back to you without saying anything to the child. She may be manually guided at first, and she will have to be assisted to turn around and to understand the idea of what is being asked.

4. *Walk with an object*. A toy or beanbag should be put in the child's hand, who again should be asked to walk from point to point, walk to a point and return, or to stop and go while holding the toy. At the same time, he should not release the toy and should not forget that he has it and release it unexpectedly.

5. *Walk and pick up object*. The child is asked to start without a toy, but part way along her walk to pick up the toy and continue to the designated point. At the end of the walk a second teacher or aide may take the toy from the child without requiring that the child release it herself.

6. *Walk, pick up object, and continue to point*. The child is told to walk, pick up a toy, and continue to a point in the same direction without having to turn around. A second teacher or aide may assist the child to release the toy.

7. *Walk, pick up an object, and release it while moving in the same direction*. At this level the child must remember several different things: walk to a point, pick up an object there, continue in the same direction, and release the object at a second point. Cratty (1974) describes the difficulty encountered by a child who is mentally retarded: "This type of task of course becomes increasingly hard when there is more than one object at each destination from which to choose and/or the child must release the object in a controlled manner by putting it into a smaller box each time" (p. 123).

8. *Walk, pick up an object, and return, making a 180-degree turn to the starting point*. In this challenge, the child does not see the final destination she is going to take the toy to as she picks it up. Instead, she must turn around and return to the initial starting point, a task much more difficult than continuing in the same direction.

9. *Walk and search for an unseen object*. Initially, a toy having a high value to the child is shown to the child and placed under a box so the child cannot see it. The child is sent toward the box and must open the box or look under the box to get the toy. Afterward, the child may continue on with the toy in the same direction; later he may be asked to return it to the starting point.

10. *Walk, pick up an unseen object while going around an obstacle, and return to the starting point*. At this level, a small obstacle should be placed between the child and the location of the toy. The child must learn first to push an obstacle out of the way, go to the unseen toy, remove it from the box or from under the box, and return it to the starting point or continue in the same direction.

Cratty (1974) summarizes the above tasks as follows:

Many of these stages may take several months or even longer for a retarded child to learn how to accomplish. Particular difficulty may be encountered when asking such children either to choose one of several objects as they arrive at a starting point or to search for an unseen object and achieve the concept that something exists outside his immediate sensory awareness. . . . The most difficulty will be encountered as the child first is asked to grasp an object, remember he has it, and continue walking in the same direction. (p. 124)

Eighteen-Month-Olds

At the 18-month-old developmental level, the average toddler can hurl a ball, sit alone in a small chair, turn pages in a book (usually two or three pages at a time), walk up and down stairs while holding on to the rail, build a tower of three blocks, and pull a toy wagon. Highlight 8.6 describes motor milestones for the 18-month-old developmental level.

Share and French (1982) list specific motor milestones that the 18-month-old youngster with Down syndrome usually attains:

- Stands and maintains balance briefly when hands are held
- Uses the rail of crib to pull self into a standing position
- Creeps on hands and knees; grasps a small object about the size of a navy bean pellet with finger and thumb in a scissors-type action

When children develop the basic locomotor or other motor responses, ongoing practice helps bring improvement. For example, in walking and stair climbing, coordination improves, unneeded movements are eliminated, and steps become longer, straighter, and more rapid. The youngsters' advances in motor performance seem to be accompanied by a strong desire to explore and experiment. The children seem intent on using newfound skills for the sheer pleasure of doing them. They will repeat and perfect recently acquired motor and manipulative skills.

HIGHLIGHT 8.6 **IN PRACTICE**

Motor Development Level: 18-Month-Olds

1. Uses sounds (e.g., "Bow Wow") in play
2. Plays with other children with some sharing of toys
3. Finds toy after searching under three covers
4. Pulls string to get toy from behind barrier
5. Grasps toy when sitting behind a barrier
6. Moves self around a barrier to get toy
7. Plays alone with a variety of objects and demonstrates their functions
8. Points to or looks at most common objects when they are named
9. Says "Yes" or "No" appropriately when asked
10. Points at or at least indicates two body parts when they are named
11. Plays alone for at least 15 minutes
12. Puts round or square objects in correct holes
13. Makes choices regarding favorite toys
14. Matches objects to pictures
15. Matches colors
16. Imitates building a six-block tower
17. Walks downstairs holding railing
18. Stands on one leg while teacher holds hands
19. Walks backward
20. Squats while playing

Twenty-Four-Month-Olds

The gross and fine motor skills attained by toddlers with Down syndrome at the end of 24 months include creeping up at least one or two stairs; walking around freely while holding on to a rail or with both hands being held; stacking two blocks, one on top of the other; picking up a small object about the size of a navy bean pellet using the thumb and finger; and turning pages in a book, usually two or three at a time (Share & French, 1982). Table 8.4 shows the difference between toddlers with Down syndrome and toddlers without retardation.

Highlight 8.7 describes the 2-year-old motor developmental level.

Summary

One of the first things all infants experience and learn is body movement. They begin with primary reflexes, which eventually fade into controlled movement. Children who are mentally retarded often have motor delays. Youngsters who are not provided meaningful motor experiences are more than likely being deprived of critical opportunities, which will affect all future learning.

Although motor delay is a common presenting symptom of mental retardation, infants and small children with brain damage progress through the same developmental stages as their nondisabled peers. Early intervention and appropriate motor programming tend to increase the chance for optimum development and acquisition of necessary motor skills. Nondisabled children's development of motor skills depends on biological and environmental factors. This is also true for children classified as having mental retardation. As with intelligence and cognitive learning, it is difficult to separate the influences of nature from those of nurture. The fact that many children with mental retardation show improvement in their motor skills with systematic training leads teachers, therapists, physicians, and parents to believe that children's deficits are at least partially due to lack of experience. This information is encouraging, but we must remember that biological influences may be one reason for the delay in motor development, and only with individualized motor programs will these youngsters begin to reach their maximum potentials.

Structured physical education programs, leisure-time opportunities, and in some cases physical therapy, occupational therapy, and kinesiotherapy will be necessary to stimulate the motor systems of infants and toddlers with mental retardation. Teachers must use creative and innovative methods, stimulating environments, and developmental techniques that follow biological motor milestones. Additionally, when children are learning new skills, the instructor must provide repetition in amounts appropriate to the learning capacities of children with mental deficiencies.

Jablow (1982) reflects on her own young daughter as she describes the need for appropriate

Table 8.4   Gross Motor Skills of Down Syndrome and Nondisabled 2-Year-Olds

Motor skill	Age of onset (months)	
	Nondisabled	Down syndrome
Stands and maintains balance briefly, with hands held	8	13
Creeps on hands and knees	10	15
Moves around freely while holding on to a rail or with both hands held	12	21

Note. From *Motor Development of Down Syndrome Children: Birth to Six Years* (pp. 87-91) by J.B. Share and R.W. French, 1982, Sherman Oaks, CA: Available from Jack B. Share. Copyright 1982 by J.B. Share and R.W. French. Reprinted by permission.

HIGHLIGHT 8.7   **IN PRACTICE**

Motor Development Level: 2-Year-Olds

1. Pushes and plays with clay
2. Puts toys away in appropriate places
3. Uses "tools" to deal with spatial problems (extends height with a stool, extends reach with a stick)
4. Solves simple problems without teacher assistance
5. Understands "big"
6. Points or otherwise indicates five body parts
7. Correctly follows three different two-part commands involving one task
8. Correctly follows three different three-part commands
9. "Performs" for others
10. Shares toys with peers
11. Explores different areas of the house
12. Distinguishes between food and nonedible substances
13. Puts round, square, and triangular forms in form box
14. Completes simple puzzles
15. Places square pegs in square holes
16. Puts loose pop beads together
17. Walks upstairs without railing, placing both feet on one step at a time
18. Walks downstairs without railing, placing both feet on one step at a time
19. Walks with one foot on walking board and one foot on floor
20. Stands on one foot without help
21. Walks on line alone, following the general direction
22. Jumps off step with both feet
23. Strings large beads
24. Runs well

motor programming for youngsters with Down syndrome:

I do suggest, by Cara's example, that all retarded children can develop to far greater degrees than previously expected if they are challenged and helped from the very start of their lives. . . . A delayed child needs extra patience and time to learn, to walk downstairs, to button a coat. . . . Three months before she turned five, Cara began to read by phonetically sounding out almost any three- or four-letter word. I mention these facts not to boast about Cara, though I am immensely proud of her, but to emphasize that the myths about the abilities of the retarded are crumbling as more and more retarded children are exposed to early intervention programs. . . . For the child who begins life behind the rest of the pack, those first years are more critical. If those years are full of enriching, stimulating experiences that help the child explore the world, master physical skills and become as self-sufficient and self-confident as possible, then that child will be more of a joy to his or her family and less a burden to society as an adult. (pp. xii-xiii, 195)

DISCUSSIONS AND NEW DIRECTIONS

1. Are early childhood programs for infants and toddlers on the increase, or have these programs decreased in importance?

2. What is the role of the physical education teacher or therapeutic recreation specialist in early childhood programs? Do these professionals have the necessary training to assume leadership roles in infant stimulation programs? What college courses are needed to provide this special expertise?

3. Can a new test battery be developed to evaluate motor performance levels of infants and toddlers?

4. Has motor performance improved significantly in infants and toddlers since the implementation of PL 99-457?

5. Are there major differences among motor programs offered by physical therapists, occupational therapists, kinesiotherapists, adapted physical educators, special educators, and early childhood teachers?

6. Are public school districts actively including infants and toddlers in their programmatic and curricular plans? Are there specific budget lines for these programs? Which professionals are being given the responsibility for program implementation?

References

Anderson, J., Hinjosa, J., & Strauch, C. (1987). Integrating play in neurodevelopmental treatment. *American Journal of Occupational Therapy*, **41**, 421-426.

Antley, T.R., & DuBose, R.F. (1981). *A case for early intervention: Summary of program findings, longitudinal data, and cost effectiveness*. Seattle: Experimental Education Unit.

Apgar, V., & Beck, J. (1972). *Is my baby all right*? New York: Simon & Schuster.

Bagnato, S.J., Neisworth, J.T., & Munson, S.M. (1989). *Linking: Developmental assessment and early intervention* (2nd ed.). Rockville, MD: Aspen.

Bailey, D.B., Jr., & Wolery, M. (1989). *Assessing infants and preschoolers with handicaps*. Columbus, OH: Merrill.

Bayley, N. (1969). *Manual for the Bayley scales of infant development*. New York: Psychological Cooperation.

Bee, H. (1978). *The developing child* (2nd ed.). New York: Harper & Row.

Bergan, J.R., & Henderson, R.W. (1979). *Child development*. Columbus, OH: Merrill.

Berger, M., & Yule, W. (1985). IQ tests and the assessment of mental handicap. In A.D.B. Clarke, A.M. Clarke, & J.M. Berg (Eds.), *Mental deficiency: The changing outlook* (4th ed.). New York: Methuen.

Capute, A.J., & Shapiro, B.K. (1985). The motor quotient. *American Journal of Disabled Children*, **139**, 940-942.

Cratty, B.J. (1974). *Motor activity and the education of retardates* (2nd ed.). Philadelphia: Lea & Febiger.

Cratty, B.J. (1986). *Perceptual and motor development in infants and children* (3rd ed.). Englewood Cliffs, NJ: Prentice Hall.

Croce, R.V. (1987). Motor skill training: A neurological approach. In M.E. Berridge & G.R. Ward (Eds.), *International perspectives on adapted physical activity* (pp. 35-41). Champaign, IL: Human Kinetics.

Crowe, T.K., Deitz, J.C., & Bennett, F.C. (1987). The relationship between the Bayley scales of infant development and preschool gross motor and cognitive performance. *American Journal of Occupational Therapy*, **41**, 374-378.

DePaepe, J., & Croce, R.V. (1987). Neurobehavioral intervention based on pediatric exercise and motor behavior. In L. Bowers, S. Klesius, & B. Price (Eds.), *Proceedings of the CIVITAN–I'M SPECIAL Network International Conference on Physical Education and Sport for Disabled Persons* (pp. 157-160). Tampa, FL: Physical Education

Department, University of South Florida at Tampa.

DeWeerd, J. (1984). Introduction. In D. Assael (Ed.), *Handicapped children's early education program: 1982-83 overview and directory* (pp. vii-xvii). Technical Assistance Development System of Special Education Programs, U.S. Department of Education. Washington, DC: Government Printing Office.

Dunn, J.M., Morehouse, J.W., Jr., & Fredericks, H.D.B. (1986). *Physical education for the severely handicapped*. Austin, TX: PRO-ED.

Eckert, H.M. (1987). *Motor development* (3rd ed.). Indianapolis: Benchmark Press.

Eichstaedt, C.B., & Kalakian, L.H. (1987). *Developmental/adapted physical education: Making ability count* (2nd ed.). New York: Macmillan.

Ershow, A.G. (1986). Growth in black and white children with Down syndrome. *American Journal of Mental Deficiency*, **90**, 507-512.

Evans, J.R. (1980). *They have to be carefully taught: A handbook for parents and teachers of young children with handicapping conditions*. Reston, VA: American Alliance for Health, Physical Education, Recreation and Dance.

Filler, J., & Olson, J. (1990). Early intervention for disabled infants, toddlers, and preschool children. In R. Gaylord-Ross (Ed.), *Issues and research in special education* (Vol. 1, pp. 82-109). New York: Teachers College, Columbia University.

Grossman, H.J., & Tarjan, G. (1987). *AMA handbook on mental retardation*. Chicago: Division of Clinical Science, American Medical Association.

Hallahan, D.P., & Kauffman, J.M. (1988). *Exceptional children* (4th ed.). Englewood Cliffs, NJ: Prentice Hall.

Hanson, M.J. (Ed.) (1984). *Atypical infant development*. Baltimore: University Park Press.

Hanson, M.J. (1987). *Teaching the infant with Down syndrome* (2nd ed.). Austin, TX: PRO-ED.

Hartley, X.Y. (1986). A summary of recent research into the development of children with Down's syndrome. *Journal of Mental Deficiency Research*, **30**, 1-14.

Heber, R., Dever, R.B., & Conry, J. (1968). The influence of environmental and genetic variables on intellectual development. In H.J. Prehm, L.A. Hamerlynck, & J.E. Crosson (Eds.), *Behavioral research in mental retardation*. Eugene, OR: University of Oregon.

Heward, W.L., & Orlansky, M.D. (1988). *Exceptional children* (3rd ed.). Columbus, OH: Merrill.

Huntinger, P.L. (1988). Linking screening, identification, and assessment with curriculum. In J.B. Jordan, J.J. Gallager, P.L. Hutinger, & M.B. Karnes (Eds.), *Early childhood special education: Birth to three* (pp. 29-66). Reston, VA: Council for Exceptional Children/Division for Early Childhood.

Jablow, M.M. (1982). *Cara. Growing with a retarded child*. Philadelphia: Temple University Press.

Johnson-Martin, N., Jens, K.G., & Attermeier, S.M. (1986). *The Carolina curriculum for handicapped infants and infants at risk*. Baltimore: Brooks.

Jordan, J.B., Gallagher, J.J., Hutinger, P.L., & Karnes, M.B. (1988). *Early childhood special education: Birth to three*. Reston, VA: Council for Exceptional Children/Division for Early Childhood.

Kerr, R., & Blais, C. (1985). Motor skill acquisition by individuals with Down syndrome. *American Journal of Mental Deficiency*, **90**, 313-318.

Kreutzenberg, J. (1976). *Effects of vestibular stimulation on the reflex and motor development in normal infants*. Unpublished doctoral dissertation, The Ohio State University, Columbus.

Lerner, J., Mardell-Czudnowski, C., & Goldenberg, D. (1987). *Special education for the early childhood years* (2nd ed.). Englewood Cliffs, NJ: Prentice Hall.

Lydic, J.S., Windsor, M.M., Short, M.A., & Ellis, T.A. (1985). Effects of controlled rotary vestibular stimulation on the motor performance of infants with Down syndrome. *Physical and Occupational Therapy in Pediatrics*, **5**, 93-118.

McCormick, L. (1990). Infant and young children with special needs. In N.G. Haring and L. McCormick (Eds.), *Exceptional children and youth* (5th ed., pp. 77-107). Columbus, OH: Merrill.

MacMillan, D.L. (1982). *Mental retardation in school and society* (2nd ed.). Boston: Little, Brown.

MacWhinney, K., Cermak, S.A., & Fisher, A. (1987). Body part identification in 1- to 4-year-old children. *American Journal of Occupational Therapy*, **41**, 454-459.

Mussen, P.M., Conger, J.J., & Kagan, J. (1980). *Essentials of child development and personality*. New York: Harper & Row.

Ottenbacher, K. (1983). Developmental implications of clinically applied vestibular stimulation. *Physical Therapy*, **63**, 338-342.

Palfrey, J.S., Walker, D.K., Sullivan, M., & Levine, M.D. (1987). Targeted early childhood programming. *American Journal of Disabled Children*, **141**, 55-59.

Patton, J.R., Payne, J.S., & Beirne-Smith, M. (1990). *Mental retardation* (3rd ed.). Columbus, OH: Merrill.

Payne, V.G., & Isaacs, L.D. (1991). *Human motor development: A lifetime approach* (2nd ed.). Mountain View, CA: Mayfield.

Piper, M.C., Gosselin, C., Gendron, M., & Mazer, B. (1986). Developmental profile of Down syndrome infants receiving early intervention. *Child: Care, Health, and Development*, **12**, 183-194.

Pyfer, J.L. (1988). Teachers, don't let your students grow up to be clumsy adults. *Journal of Physical Education, Recreation and Dance*, **59**, 38-42.

Rynders, J.E., Spiker, D., & Horrobin, J.M. (1978). Underestimating the educability of Down's syndrome children: Examination of methodological problems in recent literature. *Journal on Mental Deficiency*, **82**, 440-448.

Shapiro, B.K., Palmer, F.B., & Capute, A.J. (1987). The early detection of mental retardation. *Clinical Pediatrics*, **26**, 215-220.

Sharav, T., & Shlomo, L. (1986). Stimulation of infants with Down syndrome—long term effects. *Mental Retardation*, **24**, 81-86.

Share, J.B., & French, R.W. (1974). Early motor development in Down's syndrome children. *Mental Retardation*, **12**, 23.

Share, J.B., & French, R.W. (1982). *Motor development of Down syndrome children: Birth to six years*. (Available from Jack B. Share, 13546 Riverside Drive, Sherman Oaks, CA 91423.)

Share, J.B., & Veale, A.M. (1974). *Developmental landmarks for children with Down's syndrome (mongolism)*. Dunedin, New Zealand: University of Otago Press.

Sherborne, V. (1987). Movement observation and practice. In M.E. Berridge & G.R. Ward (Eds.), *International perspectives on adapted physical activity* (pp. 3-10). Champaign, IL: Human Kinetics.

Sloper, P., Glenn, M., & Cunningham, C.C. (1986). The effect of intensity of training on sensorimotor development in infants with Down's syndrome. *Journal of Mental Deficiency Research*, **30**, 149-162.

Stedman, D.J. (1977). Early childhood intervention programs. In B.M. Caldwell & D.V. Stedman (Eds.), *Infant education: A guide for helping handicapped children in the first three years*. New York: Walker.

Thompson, D.F., & Thelen, E. (1986). The effects of vestibular stimulation on stereotyped behavior and development in normal infants. *Physical and Occupational Therapy in Pediatrics*, **6**, 57-66.

Tjossem, T.D. (Ed.) (1976). *Intervention strategies for high-risk infants and young children*. Baltimore: University Park Press.

U.S. Office of Education. Federal Register. The Individuals With Disabilities Education Act, formerly the Education for All Handicapped Children Act of 1975, Section 94-142, 99-457, 89-750, 42 U.S.C., Section 42480-54579, (1977).

Westling, D.L. (1986). *Introduction to mental retardation*. Englewood Cliffs, NJ: Prentice Hall.

Westling, D.L., & Koorland, M.A. (1988). *The special educator's handbook*. Boston: Allyn & Bacon.

Winnick, J.P., & Short, F.X. (1985). *Physical fitness testing of the disabled—Project UNIQUE*. Champaign, IL: Human Kinetics.

Zemke, R. (1985). Application of an ATNR rating scale to normal preschool children. *American Journal of Occupational Therapy*, **39**, 178-180.

Zimmerman, J. (1988). *Goals and objectives for developing normal movement patterns*. Rockville, MD: Aspen.

CHAPTER 9

Physical Activity for Preschoolers

PREVIEW   When the two youngsters came as 2-year-olds to the Sunnyside School, no one dreamed they would eventually be admitted to a regular school kindergarten class. Now, at 4-1/2 years old, Louise and Joe are ready. Arrangements for admittance have been made.

The Sunnyside School was one of many preschools in the three-county region that integrated a few hundred children with disabilities into each of their regular programs. The concept behind doing this was based on the assumption that youngsters learn a great deal from other nondisabled children.

Louise had come to Sunnyside by way of a Headstart program and a local developmental center. Her condition was described broadly as a "general failure to thrive." She was thin, withdrawn, and unable to walk or talk, and she failed to respond to all family efforts to toilet train her. The parents were frustrated and impatient with her lack of development.

Joe, a boy with Down syndrome, had been referred by the local association for retarded citizens shortly after his family moved into the community. He was an only child who seemed happy and secure enough but showed signs of developmental delay characteristic of the syndrome.

Each child had a daily 1/2-hour period working on individualized objectives with a resource teacher. Another 20 minutes, given 3 days a week, were spent with the physical therapist. The rest of the time was spent in regular programs, including a daily 30-minute physical education class. Simultaneously, the resource teacher worked with the parents, helping the families to continue working on simple cognitive and motor objectives at home.

At first, Louise responded mainly to the daily individualized program with her resource teacher. According to the teacher, her earliest response was in learning to move. "Louise was helped to crawl up and down stairs. This discovery seemed to please her, and she began to show an eagerness to try other things. Next she stood up, holding a chair and pushing it. Then she used a plastic ball bat to steady herself. After that, she took off! Walking became fun for her, and it opened the way for the next thing we worked on, which was a game of touching other children and letting herself be touched."

Joe's early learning experiences were quite different from Louise's. "Although Joe benefited from our individualized period, he liked being with the rest of the children. In group singing, finger plays, and games, he began to mimic the other children. This kind of 'modeling' was encouraged."

Now at age 4-1/2, the children have mastered toilet training and self-help skills. Both can print their first names. They can recite the alphabet. They understand the simple rules of "Tag" and "Squirrels in the Trees." Both youngsters have no trouble with endurance and now are able to keep up with the others without getting tired. Louise has become a more sociable person. Joe has received a remarkable increase in his attention span and is no longer considered hyperactive.

HIGHLIGHT QUESTIONS

- **Do preschool children with mental retardation, including those with Down syndrome, progress slower in motor skill learning than their nonretarded peers?**
- **What major motor performance differences are found among 3-, 4-, and 5-year-old preschoolers who are nonretarded?**
- **Are preschool-age youngsters with different classifications of mental retardation (mild, moderate, severe, profound) able to improve their levels of physical fitness?**
- **What are the unique motor ability differences found in preschool-age children with Down syndrome?**
- **What physical activity teaching techniques are most successful with preschool children with mental retardation?**
- **Which physical activities will improve motor skills and physical fitness for the developmental level of 3 years? 4 years? 5 years?**

The importance of early childhood motor programming for preschoolers must not be underestimated. Needless to say, critical intervention is necessary for all youngsters regardless of their abilities or disabilities. All children should be involved in movement activities, as movement is fundamental to human life. At this developmental age, they learn also about their relationships to space, make decisions to solve problems, to follow directions, to work with other children, to develop creative ability, and to discover what they are all about. Through movement activities, children are learning and are constantly making decisions, exploring, experimenting, and creating in their world of present and past experiences. Play fascinates preschool children and is an avenue by which all future development can progress. Block (1977) describes the importance of play for the preschool child: "Through play a child learns socialization, direction-following, and the development of motor and language skills. His exposure broadens, and through this comes the opportunity to try new and exciting skills. The child's sense of autonomy is strengthened, and he develops self-confidence through having his efforts positively reinforced. Through movement play, the young child will develop interests and preferences as he matures" (p. 2).

Programs in motor skills and physical fitness for youngsters of developmental ages 3 to 5 years with mental retardation are designed to develop strength and work toward the common goal of making movement more efficient. Strength, balance, and coordination are natural outcomes of *daily* physical activity. An interesting statement by Filler and Olson (1990) stresses the need for daily participation in skill-building activities: "The degree to which one can expect a skill to be maintained over time will depend in large part upon the degree to which it is required by daily activities and produces an immediate and motivating effect. If an array of post-intervention environments demands the performance of a previously learned behavior and provides for intrinsic reward, then maintenance should be evident" (p. 89).

Interaction between the physical education teacher and the classroom teacher is an integral part of all school programming. Motor activity sessions can help children have fun and be happy and feel good about the things they can do and about themselves (self-concept). They can also help them work together (socialization), help teach them to talk so others can understand them, and help them learn new words. For example, they will be learning the names of toys, such as *tricycle*, *wagon*, *rocking horse*, *seesaw*, *barrel*, and *scooterboard*; and they will learn new words that describe their actions (e.g., *pull*, *push*, *dig*, *ride*, *run*, *fast*, *slow*, *up*, *down*, *over*, *under*, *through*, *go*, and *stop*).

The Developmental Age of 3 Years

By the time children reach the developmental age of 3, most of the lingering traces of infancy have disappeared. The "grown-up" little boys and little girls have begun to move, look, talk, think, and act more like children than like babies. The youngsters are now growing at a relatively slower rate than in infancy. The average weight gain is approximately 4 or 5 pounds, and the annual growth will be between 2 and 3 inches.

By the developmental age of 3, the average nondisabled girl is about 37.7 inches tall and weighs about 32 pounds. The average nondisabled boy is about 37.9 inches tall and weighs about 36.4 pounds. Children labeled as having mild mental retardation are very close in height and weight to their nondisabled peers, whereas those with more neurological involvement are smaller in both dimensions. This includes the child with Down syndrome. Physical delays in both height and weight appear closely allied with the lack of movement in children with brain impairment. Teachers, leaders, therapists, and parents have found maximum growth gains when daily structured movement programs are provided (Oelwein, 1988).

Children with moderate, severe, or profound mental retardation are said to have a lower level of biological integrity (Cratty, 1986). Their body size tends to be significantly smaller than that of nondisabled age peers. Early studies by Mosier, Grossman, and Dingman (1965) indicate that the physical stature of children with mental retardation is directly related to intellectual development. In other words, the lower the IQ, the smaller the child. This conclusion is substantiated by Bruininks (1974). Westling (1986) also states that "it is likely that organic sources of brain impairment also affect growth impairment either directly or indirectly. Thus, while organically impaired individuals often have smaller than average bodies, cultural-familial mildly retarded individuals are usually about equal in size to their nonretarded chronological age peers" (p. 155).

Small children with mild and moderate retardation should be focusing on readiness skills—that is, prerequisites for later learning. Hallahan and Kauffman (1988) observe that

preschool classes for mildly mentally retarded children start at a lower level, and the training may take as long as two or three years. Readiness skills include the abilities to:

1. Sit still and attend to the teacher
2. Discriminate auditory and visual stimuli
3. Follow directions
4. Develop language
5. Increase gross- and fine-motor coordination (holding a pencil, cutting with a pair of scissors)
6. Develop self-help skills (tying shoes, buttoning and unbuttoning, zipping and unzipping, toileting)
7. Interact with peers in group situations (pp. 70-71)

Children at the developmental age of 3 seem eager to venture out on their own but still need supervision and protection by teachers and parents when difficulty is experienced. Coopera-

tion and sharing with others are beginning to surface, although these characteristics are still being learned. Taking turns should be stressed. Play with other children is basically parallel; that is, these children choose to be in the company of other children but are still very possessive and tend not to share very well.

Fundamental Motor Skills

Motor skills commonly found at the 3-year-old developmental level include walking on tiptoe, jumping from the bottom stair, standing on one foot, jumping on two feet, riding a tricycle using the pedals, jumping 18 inches, changing feet walking upstairs, and catching a ball using the chest. These skills are usually attainable by 3-year-old youngsters labeled as having mild mental retardation, but for children with more mental retardation, including Down syndrome, the development is delayed as much as 12 to 30 months. Regarding children with Down syndrome, the cause of this delay is described by Woollacott and Shumway-Cook (1986): "The transition from primitive spinally controlled muscle response patterns to more integrated and coordinated movement patterns is delayed and/or absent in Down's syndrome children due to poor myelination of the descending cerebral and brainstem neurons and a reduction in the number of neurons in the higher nervous centers" (p. 45).

Specific comparisons by Share and French (1982) illustrate several differences between nondisabled (ND) youngsters and youngsters with Down syndrome (Ds):

• Walks on tiptoes
    ND = 30 months
    Ds = 48 months

• Jumps up with both feet off floor
    ND = 30 months
    Ds = 54 months

• Jumps from bottom stair
    ND = 36 months
    Ds = 54 months

- Rides tricycle
    ND = 36 months
    Ds = 60 months

Murphy, Callias, and Carr (1985) determined that psychologists and professionals in education now agree that interaction with objects (simple play toys) can contribute to children's early motor and cognitive development. They believe most children who do not have retardation need no encouragement to play with toys. Regarding toys and youngsters with mental retardation, they say: "Those who have visited hospitals for the mentally handicapped are frequently struck by the sight of large numbers of children quite unoccupied by toys. Yet research studies tend to find that, once provided with toys, moderately and severely mentally handicapped children play in a manner approximately appropriate for their mental age" (p. 376). These findings were not totally substantiated in a follow-up study for the individuals labeled as profoundly retarded by Murphy, Carr, and Callias (1986). When using 20 children with profound retardation (CA = 14 years, MA = less than 12 months), these researchers attempted to increase simple toy play by providing the youngsters with specially designed toys, including these: a 3-foot-tall panda bear that produced loud electronic music when its belly was pushed; a car 18 inches long by 7 inches wide, with a seat 9 inches off the floor that vibrated when pressed or sat upon; and a wooden train 11 inches long, 5 inches wide, and 11 inches high that had a light on the front that flashed when the wheels turned (e.g., when the train was pushed or pulled). These researchers concluded that

the kind of toy intervention observed during experimental phase sessions varied from active to investigatory to passive and was partly a function of toy design, the train requiring an active response for stimulus operation (pull or push) while the car required merely hand pressure. None of the children showed any imaginative play with the toys, whether or not the stimuli were available. Few children put the car on the floor, for instance, and none rode on it. (p. 54)

They summarize by mentioning that these responses would be characteristic of nonretarded children of the same chronological age (less than 1 year). Therefore, it can be assumed that more intricate play methods, beyond simple manipulation, will be very difficult for individuals whose mental age is below 12 months. Appropriate motor activities for these youngsters are described in chapter 8.

Most motor activities taught to preschoolers labeled as having mild or moderate mental retardation are the same as those used with nondisabled youngsters. Gabbard (1988) specifically identifies three categories of fundamental movement skills:

1. Nonlocomotor skills—movements executed with little or no movement of a child's base of support, commonly referred to as stability or static balance skills.
2. Locomotor skills—movements that propel the child through space, such as running, jumping, or skipping.
3. Manipulative skills—movements that focus on controlling objects by using the hands or feet.

Thus, programs must include static and dynamic balance skills (balance beam, balance boards, rebound tubes, small trampolines); obstacle course training, self-testing activities, rhythmic activities, ball activities (rolling, bouncing, throwing, catching, kicking); basic low-organized games; and general locomotor skills.

General Activity Suggestions

The following are activity suggestions for developing motor skills for youngsters with developmental skill levels of developmental ages 2 to 5 years.

Places to crawl and creep: over mats, bolsters, hoops, tires, and barrels, and on benches and boards that are on and off the floor (start low, and keep raising the height as children are able to perform at each level); ladders (also make these higher, but start low in the beginning); and under a tunnel made of three rows of adult chairs.

Places to climb: boards, ladders, climbers that can be raised or hooked on tables, boxes, or thick mats

Things to lift: boards, boxes, hollow blocks, suitcases, sand pails, shopping bags, coffee cans

Things to pedal: kiddie cars, tricycles

Things to slide on: plastic mats, movable slides, scooters

Things to rock on: rocking horses, seesaws, rocking boats, balancing boards

Things to push: wheelbarrows, carriages, boxes, large blocks, wagons, bolsters

Things to pull: wagons, ropes attached to walls or objects or ceiling

Things to balance on: bolsters, benches, boards, balance beams, boards set on an angle

Things to throw and catch: beanbags, foam balls, balls of many sizes

Places to run: large areas to run straight, around things, up and down hills; this can also be a place where children can roll, crawl, and get to know their bodies and what they can do with them

Places to jump and tumble: on mats and bolsters, from jumping boards, from boxes, over blocks, on large tractor inner tubes, jumping ropes (see Figure 9.1)

Places to build: large hollow blocks, small solid blocks (these involve lifting, pushing, pulling, and balancing)

Places to swing: swing sets with regular swings, tire swings, rope ladders (swinging helps children get used to heights and is a way for them to see the world differently)

Places to dig: sand, loose dirt, small pebbles

Figure 9.1 Children climbing and jumping.
Note. Adapted from Cratty (1973).

(need rakes, pails, shovels, carts, and wheel-barrows)

Things to punch: pillows, punching bags (this helps children to reach and dodge, and develops strength)

To improve motor skills: jump, hop, and run to the tables, to the wall, through hoops, over pillows, over ropes, and over mats

To improve upper body strength: carry packages, hang laundry, mop, wax, sweep floors, help move furniture, help rake leaves, carry out garbage. Hold a broom handle in both hands parallel to the floor, and let the child practice doing hangs and chin-ups on the handle

The Developmental Age of 4 Years

The growth rate of these youngsters is 2 to 3 inches in height and approximately 4 or 5 pounds in weight between 3 and 4 years of age. Sharing, while playing in small groups, is becoming more consistent with 4-year-old children, although this is still difficult. These youngsters now play in simple, low-organized game settings. Some abstract concepts are still a mystery, such as those found in the games "Squirrels in the Trees" and "Cat and Mouse." They may not understand *why* squirrels need to run to an open tree, or *why* cats chase mice. This will be especially true for children of this age who have mental retardation.

Playing games provides an excellent opportunity to introduce or review words within a 4-year-old's level of understanding, such as *stop*, *go*, *fast*, and *slow*. Youngsters with mental retardation will need to be reminded often regarding verbal commands. Low-organized games should be chosen that stress enthusiastic and energetic running, jumping, starting, stopping, and changing directions.

Fundamental Motor Skills

Running skill has greatly improved over the past year, and most of this is attributed to increased leg-muscle strength, balance, and overall body coordination. When observing their running patterns, one is aware these children can run smoothly, even when changing speeds. They start, turn, and stop quickly. However, these progressions are contingent on whether the children have been allowed and encouraged to play as toddlers and 3-year-olds. For children not provided the opportunity to run and play, or who are discouraged from moving around, as we might find with children with mental retardation, the developmental level will probably be lower. Youngsters with severe and profound limitations may be struggling with much lower developmental levels simply because of their inability to move and explore the environment. Teachers and leaders must provide these children with ample (daily) opportunities for motor experiences. The nervous system cannot develop normally unless meaningful movement experiences are provided.

General Activity Suggestions

Evans (1980) provides excellent activities for teaching running and jumping to young children who have disabling conditions. With specific reference to running she states: "In observing children it is sometimes difficult to distinguish between a run and a walk. Children who are learning to run often perform what is referred to as *fast walking*. The major difference between a walk and a run is that no matter how rapidly one walks, *both feet are never off the ground*. A walk becomes a run when the trailing foot breaks contact with the ground before the lead foot breaks contact with the ground" (p. 28).

The broad-based, almost waddling, gait characteristic of very young nonretarded children is often seen in 3- to 5-year-old children with mental retardation. Although the arms and legs may be moving alternately, the walk appears stiff and inflexible and almost robot-like (see Figure 9.2).

In running, the feet should be pointed straight ahead. Foot placement can be seen when the child runs in a straight line in loose dirt. The foot placement should be parallel to the line. The most common error exhibited by youngsters with mental retardation is placement of the feet in a toes-out position. This is often a major problem with children who have Down syndrome. This flaw reduces leverage, thrust, and therefore speed. If the child is running on a *firm mat* (not on a slippery floor), powdered chalk on the shoe soles will indicate foot placement (Eichstaedt & Kalakian, 1987).

The instructor should also be conscious of arm action. Any arm swing that deviates from a forward-and-backward plane will cause problems and produce an awkward running style. Children who carry their arms at a low level and run using their legs only cannot achieve the necessary forward momentum for controlled and fast running. Youngsters who carry their arms

high but move them across their body also are producing inefficient actions. This arm action is counterproductive to developing forward thrust (Moran & Kalakian, 1977).

Evans (1980, pp. 30-31), when teaching running to children with mental retardation, stresses the following:

- Manipulate the child's arms from behind in a proper flexed position.
- Have the child walk on a spot, bringing the right knee up to touch the opposite hand or elbow.
- Have the child stand and raise or "hug" alternate knees.
- Have the child hold a large ball and bring alternate knees up to touch it.
- Have the child stand facing a wall, with hands against it, and run on the spot with knees lifted high.
- Tell the child to step out of a hoop held at different heights; emphasize lifting the knees.
- Place ropes at different intervals on the floor and have the child walk over them and later run over them; stress use of the knees.
- Hold the child's hand and tell the child to walk fast; then have the child increase speed and encourage the child to run on toes.
- Play tag games.
- The child runs to and slaps the teacher's hands ("Give me five").
- Roll a ball; see if the child can race and beat the ball.
- Use a drum; see if the child can move as fast as the drumbeat.

Other activities should include a wide variety of climbing, balancing, pulling and pushing, and crawling over and under objects.

Helter Skelter is a low-organized game that is suggested when teaching youngsters to run with control and correct form (see Highlight 9.1). Cognitive learning of words and following instructions are associative gains that can be expected.

Figure 9.2 Young children often walk with a stiff, inflexible, almost robot-like pattern.
Note. Adapted from Cratty (1973).

Helter Skelter

Skills
Running, stopping, body control, space awareness

Area
Gym, playground, or playroom

Equipment
None

Formation
Scattered

Directions
Mark the boundaries of the play area so that the children can identify them easily (use plastic jugs, cones, tape, jump ropes, etc., as markers). Walk the youngsters around the area in single file on the boundaries of the play area. Tell them they can run anywhere inside the boundary lines or markers. Explain that they may run as fast as they safely can, attempting to avoid a collision (or ''accident''). A collision includes going outside the boundary lines (colliding with the markers) as well as bumping into anything or anybody. Ask them to run with lips closed, so they can concentrate on running (body control), looking for open spaces to run. When starting, say ''Get ready . . . (pause) . . . Go;'' and ''Red'' or ''Freeze'' can replace *stop*. Be sure to take enough time to explain the new words.

The same rules apply for youngsters in wheelchairs. If someone is pushing them, they must *direct* the pusher with either their arm or their head.

Variations
- Reduce the size of the play area to increase the necessity for special awareness.
- Use different movement skills, such as fast walking, side-sliding, skipping, jumping, leaping, or hopping.
- Change speed and force by using slow and fast signals (e.g., ''Green light,'' ''Yellow light,'' or ''Red light'').

Problems to watch for
- Trouble avoiding collisions or finding the open spaces
- Inability to stop the body with control
- Difficulty controlling the body while running
- Unnecessary yelling or screaming
- Inability to control the body when standing still

The Developmental Age of 5 Years

Block (1977) describes her 5-year-old son: ''He seems to have found himself. He has more self-

motivation and can sort out the real from make-believe. . . . He is stable and fairly reliable. His mother is the center of his world. I found this is where I started *liking* as well as *loving* my child. He has a definite personality that can be dealt with on a more mature level. The questions he asks are interesting, and, although at times tiresome, essential in the development of his mental processes'' (p. 10).

Fundamental Motor Skills

When comparing growth rates with the 3- and 4-year-olds, the 5th year is rather slow. The height gain will be greater than the weight gain. Approximately 20% of these children will be able to skip, hop on one foot 10 or more times, hop a distance of 50 feet in about 11 seconds, and step down large ladders alternating feet with ease. Walking straight on a 2-inch line is somewhat difficult. A tennis ball can be caught while the elbows are at the side of the body, and striking a ball with the hand or a bat is beginning to surface. Striking an object such as a balloon is comparatively easy. Difficulties are experienced when attempting to hit a ball with a bat. Gliner (1985) describes the motor pattern of a 5-year-old:

> When learning a baseball skill such as batting the ball, the naive performer restricts the number of movable joints by immobilizing the legs (which should step into the pitch), the trunk (which should rotate), and perhaps even the elbows, so that only the arms move to contact the ball. Gradually, as the arm swing becomes a coordinative structure (through repetitive actions), the elbow joints become mobilized to form a larger and more efficient coordinative structure to complete the act of batting. The next steps would be to rotate the trunk to the pitch and then to step into the pitch. Eventually, the whole action becomes a single coordinative structure. (p. 31)

Fine and gross muscle control and overall body coordination are improving rapidly at this age, and striking and kicking should be encouraged.

General Activity Suggestions

Hand and finger strength can be increased by having the youngsters form a ''fingertip'' bridge when doing activities such as modified push-ups (while knees are touching the ground) (see Figure 9.3). This finger position may be difficult in the beginning, because most youngsters—particularly girls and boys with Down syndrome—do not have much hand strength. With daily practice, positive results will develop quickly. Say to the youngsters, ''Push up, putting your hands down while holding your weight on your fingertips.'' Also, when teaching the ''squat thrust,'' be sure to remind them to put their arms straight down from their shoulders and make a fingertip bridge with their hands and hold this position when squatting down and thrusting their legs backward.

Arm and upper body strength can be developed with drills, including simple drills such as ''Lie down on your belly and get up very fast.'' This drill, as with all of the following drills, requires the children to push up with their arms in a very fast manner, thus enabling them to get to their feet quickly. Others include: ''Lie down on your belly, roll over to your back, get up

Figure 9.3 Modified push-ups done on the fingertips greatly increases strength. Photo courtesy of C. Eichstaedt.

very fast''; "Lie down on your back, get up very fast''; "Lie down on your back, roll over to your belly, get up very fast.'' Repeating each drill several times in succession will develop both strength *and* endurance, not to mention body-part identification and having to follow sequential commands.

Generalized movement games are encouraged. *Jungle gyms* provide a general "free play" activity that promotes development of hand and arm strength, balance, flexibility, and body coordination. *Relay activities* should be used regularly, as they provide opportunity to develop strength, body coordination, agility, running speed, and static and dynamic balance. Relay "races" encourage participation, cooperation, and teamwork. These relays usually include associative names for which the children simulate or create movements of animals—for example: bear walk, crab walk, seal walk, elephant walk, bunny hop, frog leap, kangaroo jump, lame dog, and snake wiggle. The kids should be encouraged to use the appropriate "voice" or sound of the animal in question. Additional skills that can be used include hopping, jumping, leaping, skipping, galloping, sideward sliding, running, and running backward. The negative aspect of relay races is that the "on-task time" is often poor. For example, suppose the teacher organizes a class of 24 students into 4 lines of 6 students each. If the teacher were to run the relays for 10 minutes, each child would be active for only 100 seconds and would have to sit and wait for 8.5+ minutes. For more on-task time, the teacher could organize the class into 8 lines of 3 students, increasing the active time to 3.5+ minutes, or better yet, 10 lines of 2 students.

Relays for children labeled as having severe or profound mental retardation and in wheelchairs should stress hand and arm control. Thus, grasping, arm extension, and finger extension are emphasized in the relays (Highlight 9.2) suggested by Hirst and Shelley (1989, p. 27).

Jumping

Jumping is defined as taking off from either one or two feet but landing on two feet. Jumping can occur from a stationary position or from a run. Although a jump can be in any direction, most jumping is vertical, straight ahead, or almost straight ahead (Eichstaedt & Kalakian, 1987). The development and improvement of jumping for children with mental retardation involves fairly complicated modifications of walking and running patterns. Because the jump requires elevation of the body off the ground for a longer period than is needed for the run, greater strength is required to provide sufficient force, and more delicate balancing adjustments are necessary to maintain acceptable body position while the child is in the air. Additionally, these forces must be controlled to accommodate the immediate deceleration at landing.

The action necessary for successful jumping results from vigorous extension of the hips and knees and plantar (downward) extension of the feet. The arms assist in lifting the body by swinging upward or forward in the desired direction. When landing, the body should be relaxed. The balls of the feet contact the floor first, and the knees and ankles bend to absorb the landing force. The arms may aid in balancing the body as the legs are straightened and the child returns to a standing position.

There is a significant difference between the jumping performance 4- through 7-year-old children labeled as mildly mentally retarded (MMR) and their nonretarded (NR) peers. DiRocco, Clark, and Phillips (1987) determined that the mean performance of the MMR children was 2 years behind that of their NR counterparts. Close analysis showed the jumping patterns of the subjects to be quite similar, but the performance (distance jumped) was markedly different. These researchers asked, "How is it that the two groups could differ so in their distance-jumped scores while differing so little in their

Relays

Relay
Pin the Kite in the Sky

Equipment	Formation
One paper kite for each child; blue paper sky taped to the wall	Line, with no more than 3 players on a team

Directions
One child holds the paper kite in her hand and is pushed in her wheelchair to the paper sky by a teacher, aide, or another child. The youngster is helped to tape the kite onto the paper sky (give as little help as possible . . . *let the child do the work!*). The child is then pushed back to the starting line to *touch off* the next child. On the second turn, the new child has to retrieve the kite from the sky. The activity becomes a team activity if the total group effort is timed with a stopwatch. The team then attempts to beat their first effort.

Relay
Put on the Hat Relay

Equipment	Formation
One hat for each relay team	Line, with no more than 3 players on a team

Directions
One child wears the team's hat and is pushed to the end line and back to the start. The youngster is helped to take the hat off and put it on the head of the next child.

---

patterns of arm and leg coordination?'' (p. 188). They give two possible explanations for these results: (a) differences in the coordination between arm and leg action, and (b) differences in the control process. Perhaps there is also a difference in leg strength that has not been accounted for.

Evans (1980) suggests the following activities for developing jumping skills when teaching children with mental retardation.

- Assist the child to get the idea of jumping and bounding; hold the child from behind and lift.

- Hold both hands and have the child bend and straighten knees to learn the beginning knee action of jumping.
- Hold both hands and urge the child to jump up and down.
- Use a bouncing tube or minitrampoline; hold the child's hands and ask the child to jump.

When teaching children to jump vertically, arrange on the floor an environmental cue such as a hula hoop or a piece of rope laid in a circle. The child should stand in the circle, jump vertically, and land inside the circle. To stimulate children to jump straight up, suspend a brightly colored ball or toy directly above the circle. Suspend it with elastic to prevent detachment when caught. The height of the object can be adjusted according to each child's vertical jumping ability.

In teaching youngsters to jump forward, place two lengths of rope on the floor, parallel. Again, the distance between the ropes should be adjusted depending on the ability of each child. In jumping across the two ropes, the child can take off using one foot or two. If the takeoff is on one foot, it can be preceded by a walking or running start. Holding the child's hand as she jumps off a low step can also help develop jumping skill. Activities can be made more fun by adding colorful mats (usually made of soft plastic) to use as landing targets and by increasing the number of step risers from which to jump. When jumping from steps above the first riser, the child should jump to the side rather than forward over the lower risers. Also, the landing surface should be a large padded mat.

The children could play the game called ''Bunny Hop'' (although the action is jumping and not hopping). Tell the children that they can jump anywhere within the available area. Tell them that when jumping, they must land on two feet. Remember that children who are mentally retarded may not understand the specific directions you are using, but usually they will imitate the action after you demonstrate the move. Keep verbal instructions to a minimum by using simple commands (instruct *and then demonstrate*):

1. ''*Bend* your knees as you jump.''
2. ''*Swing* your arms back and forth.''
3. ''*Shake* your hands in front of your body.''
4. ''*Push* your hands against your knees.''

Variations could include changing directions (e.g., backward or sideward), speed, and distance. Some children will have difficulty maintaining balance in the initial jumping position, controlling the body in the air, avoiding collisions, following directions when using different body parts, and getting up off the floor. Some may tire very quickly, which indicates that they need more leg strength development.

Hopping

The skill of hopping involves rising and landing on the same foot. The arms and nonhopping leg help in maintaining body balance. The arms are used to lift the body upward and/or forward. Ulrich and Ulrich (1985) found in youngsters of developmental levels from 3 and 5 years that the level of hopping skill is directly related to the existing level of balance skill. There is also a positive correlation between balance and jumping. Hopping is the most demanding of the basic locomotor skills in terms of strength, because it requires that total body weight be carried on one leg. For this reason, hopping is also very demanding in relation to balance, because of the smaller base of support and displacement of the center of gravity.

When teaching hopping, Dauer and Pangrazi (1989) emphasize the following points:

- To increase the height of the hop, the arms must be swung rapidly upward.
- Hopping should be performed on the ball of the foot.
- Small hops should be used in the beginning, with a gradual increase in height and distance.

Kicking

The kicking level seen at the developmental level of 5 years produces a greater backward and forward leg swing, and the child is beginning to use arm opposition. Some children will have developed the mature kicking pattern—that is, to kick *through* the ball. Kicking skills and lead-up kicking games are suggested. ''Popcorn machine'' is fun and allows group participation (See Highlight 9.3).

Eckert (1987) has summarized the general motor developmental levels found at approximately 3 to 5 years of age (see Highlight 9.4).

HIGHLIGHT 9.3

IN PRACTICE

Popcorn Machine

Skills
Kicking, balance

Area
Gym or playroom

Equipment
An empty 1-gallon milk jug (with cap on) for each child

Formation
Scattered

Directions

Describe how popcorn "pops" when it gets hot. Explain that when this game is played, the room will look like the inside of a corn popping machine. Tell the students to spread out and get ready to kick the jugs as hard as they can. Remind the youngsters not to kick directly at other students, as the soft jug may sting if it hits someone at close range. The instructor says: "Get ready . . . (pause) . . . Kick." Continue to kick for a designated time. Begin with 10-second games. Increase up to 15, and then 20 seconds for succeeding games.

Variations

- Play the game with two sides. Each side attempts to kick the jugs into the other team's area. A line divides the two teams. Students cannot go across the dividing line. Signal after 15 seconds to stop the game. Have the students count the number of jugs on their side (this helps counting skills).
- Kick with the other leg. The difference is easily noticed, as the jugs will not be "flying around" as much as before. The use of the opposite leg encourages much-needed balance practice on the nondominant side.
- For children in wheelchairs: (a) Have them wheel their chairs up to their jugs and push them across the line, or (b) have them hit their jugs with plastic sticks as in hockey (someone will have to push them, because they would have trouble wheeling the chair while holding on to the stick).
- Place 8 or 10 chairs on the dividing line. This will produce a barrier and thus a decision-making situation of how to aim and kick around or over the chairs.

Problems to watch for

- Watch for children who are having difficulty when kicking. They will miss the jug often or not kick it very hard. The mature kick involves running up to the jug and kicking without slowing down. The immature kicker slows down and even stops before swinging the leg to kick.
- Youngsters may kick the jug too high above its center, and the jug will not rise or gain much distance.
- Youngsters may contact the jug too far below its center, and the jug will rise too high.
- Some may fail to follow through.

For those still having major kicking problems, consider providing a variety of activities that stress static and dynamic balance. Improvement of balance often improves kicking performance.

HIGHLIGHT 9.4

Summary of General Developmental Characteristics During the Early Childhood Years 3 to 5

1. Large-muscle basic motor skills are acquired rapidly.
2. All skills develop concurrently but at different rates.
3. Amount of variability among individuals increases with increasing age.
4. Strength increases rapidly for both sexes—65% between 3 and 6 years.
5. Limb length increases proportionately more than other body parts.
6. Increased limb length results in greater leverage for speed.
7. Increased coordination and use of leverage allows for maximal application of strength.
8. Increased balance development allows for increased range of movement in executing a skill.
9. Cephalocaudal development of control and coordination (e.g., overhand throw, striking) progresses.
10. Basic concepts of object, space, force, causality, and time develop for conscious control and coordination of movement.
11. Manipulative skills need refinement (e.g., catching balls).
12. Children are very active and have a great deal of energy in short spurts.
13. Increased wakeful periods provide more time for skill development.
14. Attention spans are short.
15. Children are imaginative, imitative, curious.
16. Children are individualistic or egocentric and noisy.
17. Children like rhythm, moving to and/or singing.
18. Some gender differences emerge in performance, particularly in the distance throw.
19. Children begin to judge others on the basis of motoric performance.

Need	Experiences
Vigorous exercise requiring use of large muscles	Running and chasing games; hanging and climbing; large apparatus; stunts (self-testing)
Simple games with short explanation, simple class organization, and quick changes of activities	Hide-and-seek; stunts; simple singing games (Mulberry Bush)
Opportunity to try things and to ''pretend''	Movement exploration using basic skills and small apparatus; creative dance; story plays (animals)
To learn to share and engage in parallel play with others	Small-group work; self-testing activities; exploration of movement
Opportunities to use medium-size objects such as balls	Ball-handling games, beanbags, hoops, wands, etc. Start with larger objects at 2-3 years and work to smaller objects at 5-6 years.

Note. From *Motor Development* (3rd ed.) (p. 232) by H.M. Eckert, 1987, Indianapolis, IN: Benchmark. Copyright 1987 by H.M. Eckert. Reprinted by permission.

Motor Development of Children With Down Syndrome

The purpose of any early preschool program is to develop transitional skills through appropriate and purposeful play with both materials and classmates. Love (1988) states: "The Down Syndrome Early Preschool Program is based on the premise that there is a need for early . . . gross-motor and beginning social skills [that] are developed through careful planning of each day's activities. . . . Its curriculum is based on normal development. Intense educational intervention is used, based on the concept of sequential development" (pp. 121-123).

Share and French (1982) have made comparisons between preschoolers identified as nondisabled and as having Down syndrome regarding expected achievement levels in gross and fine motor skills. Table 9.1 shows developmental progressions and the age of onset between these two groups.

Development of locomotor proficiency often depends on how soon and how well children attain static and dynamic balance. Children with Down syndrome are known to have lower levels of balance ability (Blackman, 1990). A major question arises whether the task of balance is simply delayed in children with Down syndrome or whether there is a true deficit in processing of internal and external sensory information.

In a research review, Woollacott and Shumway-Cook (1986) found the gross motor skills of children with Down syndrome to be constantly below those of nondisabled peers, with poorest performance in the area of static and dynamic balance. These researchers determined that their young subjects with Down syndrome (CA = 5.0 years) were from 18 to 24 months *behind* the control nondisabled youngsters in both static and dynamic balance. Also, they believe that the natural postural responses, which allow individuals to stand without falling, are deficient in individuals with Down syndrome and can cause increased body sway. This condition leads to clumsiness and the potential to fall often. Hypotonia and decreased neuron activity have been identified as reasons for poor motor performance, but Woollacott and Shumway-Cook (1986), along with Davis and Kelso (1982), disagree and believe the problems are related to a combination of slowed onset of response and deficiencies in structural organization. In other words, increased body sway and loss of balance occur because of an external disturbance in stability. Additionally, they believe that these children may demonstrate marked improvement if provided activities that stress organizational processes. Parker, Bronks, and Snyder (1986) found in their study of 10 youngsters, aged 5 years, with Down syndrome, significant differences between the gait patterns of the Down syndrome (Ds) children and those of nondisabled peers. They observed: "These differences are reflected in the retardation [delay] shown in the temporal [time] components of the gait of Ds subjects resulting in smaller average step lengths which are probably a consequence of the shorter limb length in Ds and their increased knee flexion at foot contact. In addition, they exhibited a reduced time of single-limb support which indicates a degree of instability and which would also contribute to the Ds child's inability to increase the length of his step" (pp. 327-328).

Davis (1987) found subjects with Down syndrome to possess an extreme slowness of movement. He believes they have *muscle activation deficiencies* and thus exhibit slower reaction times when compared to other individuals labeled as having mental retardation and obviously their nondisabled peers. This problem could account for the marked differences of locomotor performance (e.g., running, jumping, leaping, hopping) between other youngsters and those with Down syndrome. Davis questions whether there is any correlation between strength development and improvement of motor performance. He suggests that research in this area be conducted to determine if reaction time and motor performance are improved when specific programs of muscular strength are introduced. Strength development, therefore, should be considered as a viable possibility. Certainly, in the

Table 9.1   Fine and Gross Motor Skill Progressions of Children Nonretarded or With Down Syndrome Between 3 and 5 Years of Age

Motor skill	Age in months		Motor skill	Age in months	
	Nonretarded	Down syndrome		Nonretarded	Down syndrome
Fine Motor			Walks downstairs with one hand held	21	36
Turns pages in a book; usually two or three at a time	18	24	Walks on tiptoe after demonstration	30	48
Turns pages of a book one at a time in either direction	24	42	Alternates feet with going upstairs in an adult fashion	42	72+
Holds a crayon with fingers in an adult fashion when drawing	30	42	Seats self in a small chair	18	30
			Throws a ball	18	30
Basic writing and drawing; imitates circular stroke after demonstration	24	54	Throws overhand	48	72
			Squats while playing	21	36
Imitates vertical and horizontal stroke with a crayon	30	60	Kicks a large ball after demonstration	21	36
			Runs well without falling (still not fast)	24	36
Imitates drawing of a cross	36	60	Jumps up with both feet off the floor after demonstration	30	48
Unbuttons coat or shirt	36	72+			
Copies a drawing of a square	54	72+	Jumps from bottom stair, landing erect	36	54
Gross motor			Jumps while running	48	72+
Creeps up at least one or two stairs	15	24	Hops on one foot	54	72+
Walks with only one hand held	13	27	Rides on tricycle using pedals	36	60
Walks a few steps without assistance, starting and stopping	15	30	Skips with one foot forward	48	72+
			Skips, alternating lead foot	60	72+
Walks and seldom falls	18	30			
Walks upstairs with one hand held	18	55			

Note. From *Motor Development of Down Syndrome Children: Birth to Six Years* (pp. 87-91) by J.B. Share and R.W. French, 1982, Sherman Oaks, CA: Available from Jack B. Share. Copyright 1982 by J.B. Share and R. W. French. Adapted by permission.

overall picture, increasing their strength will not be harmful to the children.

Therefore, it would appear that programs of varied balance tasks and strength development should not be delayed but started as soon as possible. Measurable improvement can be expected if specific activities are practiced daily for all youngsters with Down syndrome.

Burns (1988) makes an interesting observation regarding clinicians who tend to shy away from attempting new programs because these "new" activities do not do all things for all people. She believes even small developmental gains may warrant implementation, and says that "frequently, clinicians recognize the advantages of one particular technique or program approach over another for individual children and, subsequently, attempt to find a theoretical framework that will explain their clinical observations. Rather than suggest . . . that clinicians should refrain from using an apparently sucessful program . . . in an attempt to demonstrate validity of therapeutic interventions, it would be counterproductive 'to throw the baby out with the bathwater' " (p. 412).

Activities to develop gross motor objectives must be carefully planned. Oelwein (1988) describes a program specifically designed to provide programs, including gross motor activities for preschool children with Down syndrome:

Programming can be accomplished by leading a small group of children in "follow the leader," so that the child has to walk a board, then climb a ladder, go down a slide, then crawl through a tunnel (the task varies to meet specific objectives of the pupils). This game format ties these activities together and makes them more interesting. Some skills, such as riding a tricycle and balance-beam walking, often require careful programming and one-to-one instruction. Other skills, such as walking up and down stairs, and alternating feet on stairs, are most often taught on the way to and from the classroom, when the pupils have to walk up and down stairs. A programming technique used to teach alternating feet on stairs is to place footprints on the stairs, with the left footprint yellow, the right one, red. Matching bows or flowers (yellow on the left, red on the right) are placed on the pupils' shoes. The pupils then match the colors as they walk up and down stairs. (pp. 147-148)

Motor programs for children with Down syndrome should be similar to those for nonretarded children, with added emphasis on assessment, careful planning of motor programs to meet the objectives gleaned from the assessment, and, finally, the use of evaluation information to determine program modification, continuation, or termination.

Summary

The preschool years are both exciting and challenging for youngsters. The basic skills learned include development in the areas of intelligence, self-concept, socialization, and the physical. Children with mental retardation will experience delays, and the extent of these delays is determined by two major factors: the degree of brain impairment and the amount, intensity, and quality of programming. Professionals providing physical activity to persons with mental retardation cannot change neurological impairment, but they can provide appropriate developmental activities.

As children prepare to move from preschool activities and formal early childhood schooling to regular school programs, educators and parents need to ensure maximum development of the "whole child." General strength development is critical, and with conscientious planning and teaching, a large step can be made to ensure that preschool children with mental retardation will not be left behind in motor skills and physical fitness when it comes time for integration into kindergarten. Obviously, static and dynamic balance activities should be included in the motor program. Efficient running, jumping, and hopping are necessary locomotor skills that all youngsters should take with them into their 6th year.

DISCUSSIONS AND NEW DIRECTIONS

1. In your school, what attempts are being made to develop comprehensive preschool programs for youngsters with mental retardation? Who is responsible for the administration and financial implementation of these programs?

2. Is it feasible to expect that *most* children with mental retardation, when provided with good preschool programs, will be ready for integration into regular kindergarten classes?

3. Will youngsters with severe or profound mental retardation benefit more from an individualized adapted physical education program or from a program that emphasizes traditional physical education?

4. What specific training is *required* for teachers, physical educators, or therapists (KT, PT, and OT) in preschool programs for students with disabilities? Address both specific coursework and fieldwork training for those professionals.

5. If preschool-age children with Down syndrome are given *daily* physical education programs that stress strength and motor skill development, will significant gains be found in the area of general motor ability?

References

Blackman, J.A. (1990). *Medical aspects of developmental disabilities in children birth to three* (2nd ed.). Rockville, MD: Aspen.

Block, S.D. (1977). *Me and I'm great. Physical education for children three through eight*. Minneapolis: Burgess.

Bruininks, R.H. (1974). Physical and motor development of retarded persons. In N.R. Ellis (Ed.), *International Review of Research in Mental Retardation*, **7**, 124-147.

Burns, Y.R. (1988). Sensory integration or the role of sensation in movement. *American Journal on Mental Retardation*, **92**, 412.

Cratty, B.J. (1986). *Perceptual and motor development in infants and children* (3rd ed.). Englewood Cliffs, NJ: Prentice Hall.

Dauer, V.P., & Pangrazi, R.P. (1989). *Dynamic physical education for elementary school children* (9th ed.). New York: Macmillan.

Davis, W.E. (1987). Evidence for muscle activation deficiency in mentally handicapping conditions. In M.E. Berridge & G.R. Ward (Eds.), *International perspectives on adapted physical activity* (pp. 53-64). Champaign, IL: Human Kinetics.

Davis, W.E., & Kelso, J.A. (1982). Analysis of 'invariant characteristics' in motor control of Down's syndrome and normal subjects. *Journal of Motor Development*, **14**, 194-212.

DiRocco, P.J., Clark, J.E., & Phillips, S.J. (1987). Jumping coordination patterns of mildly mentally retarded children. *Adapted Physical Activity Quarterly*, **4**, 178-191.

Dmitriev, V., & Oelwein, P.L. (1988). *Advances in Down syndrome*. Seattle: Special Child.

Eckert, H.M. (1987). *Motor development* (3rd ed.). Indianapolis: Benchmark.

Eichstaedt, C.B., & Kalakian, L.H. (1987). *Developmental/adapted physical education: Making ability count* (2nd ed.). New York: Macmillan.

Evans, J.R. (1980). *They have to be carefully taught: A handbook for parents and teachers of young children with handicapping conditions*. Reston, VA: American Alliance for Health, Physical Education, Recreation and Dance.

Filler, J., & Olson, J. (1990). Early intervention for disabled infants, toddlers, and preschool age children. In R. Gaylord-Ross (Ed.), *Issues and research in special education* (Vol. 1, 82-109). New York: Teachers College Press.

Gabbard, C. (1988). Early childhood physical education. The essential elements. *Journal of Physical Education, Recreation and Dance*, **59**, 65-69.

Gliner, J.A. (1985). Purposeful activity in motor learning theory: An event approach to motor skill acquisition. *Journal of Occupational Therapy*, **59**, 28-34.

Hallahan, D.P., & Kauffman, J.M. (1988). *Exceptional children* (4th ed.). Englewood Cliffs, NJ: Prentice Hall.

Hirst, C.H., & Shelley, E.Y. (1989). They too should play. *Teaching Exceptional Children*, **21**, (26-28).

Love, P. (1988). The early preschool program: The bridge between infancy and childhood. In V. Dmitriev & P.L. Oelwein (Eds.), *Advances in Down syndrome* (pp. 121-130). Seattle: Special Child.

Moran, J.M., & Kalakian, L.H. (1977). *Movement experiences for the mentally retarded or emotionally disturbed* (2nd ed.). Minneapolis: Burgess.

Mosier, H.D., Grossman, H.J., & Dingman, H.F. (1965). Physical growth in mental defectives. *Pediatrics*, **36**(Pt. 2), 465-519.

Murphy, G., Callias, M., & Carr, J. (1985). Increasing simple toy play in profoundly mentally handicapped children. *Journal of Autism and Developmental Disorders*, **15**, 375-388.

Murphy, G., Carr, J., & Callias, M. (1986). Increasing simple toy play in profoundly mentally handicapped children: II. Designing special toys. *Journal of Autism and Developmental Disabilities*, **16**, 45-58.

Oelwein, P.L. (1988). Preschool and kindergarten programs: Strategies for meeting objectives. In V. Dmitriev & P.L. Oelwein (Eds.), *Advances in Down syndrome* (pp. 131-157). Seattle: Special Child.

Parker, A.W., Bronks, R., & Snyder, C.W., Jr. (1986). Walking patterns in Down's syndrome. *Journal of Mental Deficiency Research*, **30**, 317-330.

Share, J.B., & French, R.W. (1982). *Motor development of Down syndrome children: Birth to six years*. (Available from Jack B. Share, 13546 Riverside Drive, Sherman Oaks, CA 91423).

Ulrich, B.D., & Ulrich, D.A. (1985). The role of balancing ability in performance of fundamental motor skill in 3-, 4-, & 5-year-old children. In J.E. Clark & J.H. Humphrey (Eds.), *Motor development—current selected research* (Vol. 1). Princeton, NJ: Princeton Book.

U.S. Office of Education. Federal Register. The Individuals With Disabilities Education Act, formerly The Education for All Handicapped Children Act of 1975, Section 94-142, 99-457, 89-750, 42 U.S.C., Section 42480-54579, (1977).

Westling, D.L. (1986). *Introduction to mental retardation*. Englewood Cliffs, NJ: Prentice Hall.

Woollacott, M.H., & Shumway-Cook, A. (1986). The development of the postural and voluntary motor control systems in Down's syndrome children. In M.G. Wade (Ed.), *Motor skill acquisition of the mentally handicapped. Issues in research and training* (pp. 45-71). Amsterdam: North Holland.

CHAPTER 10

Physical Activity for School-Age Children and Teenagers

PREVIEW Marcus springs into the air and takes a shot. One would never suspect that he has mental retardation. And his contribution to Lincoln High School goes beyond the basketball court.

Marcus, 16, has been labeled as having mild mental retardation since he was 6 years old. But now the label seems inappropriate, because he can handle the pace of interscholastic sophomore basketball.

Two years ago, Marcus nearly did not make the freshman team. Coach Taylor had two positions left and was debating whether or not to cut Marcus. "The last scrimmage, the last day, he looked good—stealing the ball, rebounding, the whole works," said Taylor. "I cut a couple of guys to keep him."

Coaches say he plays aggressively and never looks for any favors. "He never cries or whines about playing time," said Taylor. And coaches say

Marcus's hard work has rubbed off on his teammates. "He's the kind of kid who would give anyone inspiration," said varsity coach Williams. "He gets the most out of what he has." "It blew my mind when I found out he was mentally retarded," said Mr. Graham, Lincoln athletic director. "You can't tell when he plays—there are no blundering mistakes or lapses of memory—he's just a regular contributing member of the team."

Marcus can remember when he first became interested in basketball. He was 7 years old, and his physical education teacher began with easy basketball dribbling and catching games. This led to simple basketball lead-up games. Marcus was encouraged and challenged by his PE teacher: "Try harder . . . bend your knees . . . follow through with your wrist . . . be just like Michael Jordan." Marcus's skill improved, and by the time he was 10 he had won three gold medals in the local Special Olympics competition involving the skills of running, dribbling, and shooting.

Today the coaches at Lincoln High say Marcus has been more than an inspiration to other athletes—he has changed their attitudes about people with mental retardation. Marcus is not content with his accomplishments; his next challenge is to go out for and make the varsity team.

HIGHLIGHT QUESTIONS

- **Are children with mental retardation, between the chronological ages of 6 and 8, developmentally delayed? If so, how far behind their nonretarded peers are they? Do they learn motor skills at different rates than their nonretarded peers? How many of these youngsters are mainstreamed into regular physical education programs?**
- **What standards can be used when developing physical activity programs for individuals with mental retardation? Are there norms available?**
- **Which fundamental motor skills are usually taught to individuals between the developmental ages of 6 and 8?**
- **What physical activities should be emphasized for junior-high-school-age youths with mental retardation? Are these fundamental skills and physical fitness activities different from those taught to their nonretarded peers?**
- **Do physical activity programs for teenagers with mental retardation improve their general health? develop vocational skills? provide for competitive sports? offer leisure-time pursuits?**

Formal education—going to school—is one of the most influential and driving forces an individual will experience. Parents of preschool-age children constantly talk about the time when their youngsters will be going to school. Finally the end of summer comes, and children enter school. In kindergarten a new environment begins to unfold. Kindergarten provides a stepping stone from the security of the family to the outside world. Even though this year-long experience leads to new levels of attainment, it is still considered more a social and play environment than one that stresses the formal goals of education, such as reading, writing, and arithmetic. Passing on to first grade is a landmark accomplishment. Now they are "big boys and girls'' and can look forward to being in school ''all'' day. The school-age years of 6 through 18 have now begun, and this of course is true for youngsters with mental retardation.

Ideally, the school classroom, gymnasium, and playfield become areas of excitement and wonder. These are places of learning where new experiences and creative challenges surface daily and where teachers are opening children's minds and bodies to the excitement of learning. Werder and Bruininks (1990) believe there is a strong association between self-esteem and motor skill ability:

> Being able to run, jump, hop, skip, and play with others is important—not only to one's physical health, but also to emotional and social health. Without these basic motor skills, the child must seek social interaction in other nonphysical ways which limits the young child. In gross motor play, the child expands creativity, develops social skills, enhances physical health, and experiences a positive self-concept. Use of motor skills is the young child's primary means of exploring, learning, and gaining mastery of his or her environment. (p. 3)

As children grow they receive innumerable bits of information, which are constantly being stored in their memory banks. All youngsters will move to, and then through, specific developmental levels and continue to pass on to even higher levels of motor performance. The rate of progress is determined by the integrity of the nervous system and the amount and intensity of stimulation. Because of these variables it is necessary for teachers and recreation leaders to understand general developmental milestones of youngsters regardless of abilities or disabilities.

The Developmental Approach

Effective motor programming should always adhere to developmental milestones. Present levels of performance are the basis for individualized programming. Comparisons between individuals with mental retardation and their nonretarded age-peers are helpful when looking at placement possibilities. (Can Keith be successful and keep up with the other children in his class? Or would it be best to place him in an individualized class where meeting his annual goals can be emphasized?) In addition, when attempting to understand annual goals at meetings, parents are very interested in specific levels of performance. Thus, it might be helpful when talking to parents to describe motor and fitness differences in the form of comparisons. For example, Annie is 9 years old, has moderate mental retardation, and finally is able to skip with control. Most nondisabled children skip somewhere between 7 and 8 years of age. Therefore, compared with nondisabled peers, Annie is 2 to 3 years below average. Compared with other girls labeled as having moderate mental retardation, she is better than average (70th percentile) and seems to be progressing quite well. Both comparisons can be used to describe Annie's present level of performance.

Height and Weight Comparisons

There are interesting differences in height and weight between boys and girls and between persons with mental retardation and their nonretarded peers. (Specific comparisons for ages 6 through 18 can be found in chapter 2, Tables 2.5 and 2.6.) One of the most striking differences is the height at which persons terminate growth. Adolescents with Down syndrome stop growing several years before their nonretarded peers, but when comparing these same groups in weight, there is little, if any, difference. The teenager with Down syndrome often tends to be overweight or obese (Eichstaedt et al., 1991). Obviously, this is a major health problem for teenagers, but just as important are the common negative emotional and social implications. Children's excessive body weight can be controlled, and this should be an ongoing and common goal for all educators, physical educators, recreation leaders, and physicians in their roles on the transdisciplinary team.

Motor Development Comparisons

The years between 5 and 15 have been called by Nash (1963) the great golden decade:

> During this period, the child gains control over his fundamental and accessory muscle groups. He learns to run, climb, dodge, and throw balls. Eventually, these movements are combined into sports and games and lay the basis for manual and muscular skills of later life. A whole set of behavioralistic patterns is laid down in this period.
>
> If there is one lesson which biology and neurology, as well as sociology, teaches, it is that the elementary school years are those in which the most intensive teaching should take place. The younger child has no inhibitions of fear, no worry about failure. He goes on as a dynamic organism four to six hours a day, year after year. This is the period when building of skills should be stressed. This is the golden era for teaching of physical education skills. (p. 171)

Adequate motor performance, such as controlled running, can provide a positive springboard into the mainstream for the child with mental retardation, whereas clumsy, awkward movement may relegate the same child to a world of frustration and unacceptance. There is no question that girls and boys labeled as having mental retardation need to bring with them as many positive characteristics as they can.

Motor development and physical fitness of youngsters and adolescents 6 through 21 with mild mental retardation are significantly below the norms for nonretarded children (Eichstaedt et al., 1991). Specifically, Drew, Logan, and Hardman (1988) reinforce earlier findings of Bruininks that children with mild mental retardation have inferior scores on measures such as

equilibrium, locomotion, and manual dexterity. These motor performance deficits may be more a function of deprivation in practice and learning opportunities than of the mental retardation. Physical fitness—that is, strength, endurance, and power, which are different from motor skill ability—can be significantly improved when fitness exercises are provided in appropriate intensities and durations.

Placement Into Appropriate Physical Activity Programs

The importance of appropriate placement cannot be overemphasized. Gagnon, Tousignant, and Martel (1989) conclude that researchers from various educational fields have consistently observed positive relationships between achievement and the proportion of class time that learners spend actively engaged in learning tasks appropriate to their existing level of ability. The authors also made specific reference to these gains occurring in regular physical education classes.

Proponents of integration continually push for mainstreaming, but Titus and Watkinson (1987) found that youngsters labeled as having moderate mental retardation (CA = 5 to 10 years) *did not profit* from placement into integrated physical activity programs. These researchers were specifically looking for changes in activity participation or social interaction. They concluded: "Activity participation did not appear to be affected by the presence of play vehicles in the environment. Social interaction levels were reduced significantly under this condition" (p. 204). Patton, Payne, and Beirne-Smith (1990) summarize the critical importance of appropriate placement: "In the light of the presumed benefits of having students who are handicapped educated as much as possible with their non-handicapped peers, we still lack a solid research base that supports this idea" (p. 308).

Therefore, one of the first questions to be answered by movement specialists is identification of the most ideal place to learn. But this can only occur after a thorough assessment program has been completed. Instructors and leaders should be able to conduct a comprehensive evaluation of the present levels of motor ability and physical fitness for individuals with mental retardation. Chapter 3 contains specific information on this subject. Developmental milestones, chronological ages, and mental ages must be taken into consideration when developing programs. With these constraints in mind, this chapter discusses motor skill and physical fitness developmental patterns of the nonretarded, with appropriate references to youngsters and teenagers labeled as having mental retardation.

Primary-School-Age Children: 6- to 8-Year-Olds

When children move from the protective confines of kindergarten, new, exciting, and sometimes difficult challenges await. The full-day demands of first grade present situations seldom encountered before. The children will be expected to be more mature, to be more reliable, to sit quietly, and to approach school with a positive desire to learn. They will need more finely developed social skills. At age 6, youngsters have reached a mild plateau and have gone about as far as they can without formal teaching. Linguistically, they have mastered the basics of language and are able to communicate freely. Major locomotor skills, such as walking, running, jumping, and stair climbing, are now easily performed. Cratty (1986) makes an interesting comment:

Often the first year of school is rather sheltered, but by the first and second grades, the 6- and 7-year-old comes face to face with vigorous peers who are either joined in active play or who may elicit fear and withdrawal from active play. . . . In general, virtually all motor performance data obtained between kindergarten and sixth-grade

years reflect upward trends. Plateaus sometimes appear between the sixth and ninth years, and often there tends to be some deceleration in improvement after the ages of 7 and 8. (p. 166)

The 6-year-old is experiencing mass changes in both cognitive functioning and social relationships with peers. As the demands on the youngsters change, these first graders make adaptations quite well. Some are more proficient than others, and it appears that children who have had early childhood education opportunities or preschool classes have an advanced degree of "readiness." Extensive early preschool experiences involving cognitive challenges, peer socialization, and motor skill development are critical for children labeled as having mental retardation, if they are to have a reasonable chance for success in integrated regular classrooms with the nonretarded; too often the intellectual delays and immaturity in motor and adaptive behavior of children who did not get extra help become justification for placing these children into individualized special education classes, thus bypassing the initial opportunity for mainstreaming.

Physical Growth and Development

Generally speaking, during the primary-school-age years, youngsters lose their "baby fat" and begin to develop proportional gains in muscular tissue. This allows for a general increase in arm and leg strength. These youngsters fatigue less easily, but their recovery comes rapidly with just short rest periods. Basic reaction times are slowly improving. The small muscles are finally developing, and along with refined eye/hand coordination, the youngsters begin to show an increased interest in games of kicking, throwing, and catching.

During ages 6 through 8, most children become able to hop skillfully with rhythmical alternation, gallop with skill, and skip with ease and control. They are also able to catch a small ball using their hands only, throw with a mature overhand pattern, and kick with the mature pattern (kicking through the ball). Motor skills continue to develop if appropriate activities are provided. The more complex locomotor skills of galloping and skipping should be included in individual drills and low-organized games. Additionally, catching, throwing, and striking should be included during age 6.

Motor Learning

Youngsters with mental retardation may be behind their nonretarded peers and may have problems learning motor skills. But this disadvantage is not necessary. Thomas (1984) believes that boys and girls with mental retardation (MR) can become motor proficient. She is speaking specifically about general motor learning problems of individuals with mental retardation when she says that

> training studies and other research have manipulated behavior to produce "normal" performance in MR individuals. That is, MR children can perform qualitatively like their chronological-age counterparts when taught or forced to do so. Generalization and transfer are the greatest challenge for remediation. MR individuals can be both cued to attend and forced to rehearse, and exhibit normal retention. With more time (or trials), MR students can reach and maintain mastery. These individuals probably have less experience stored in LTS [long-term storage] than do normal individuals, and have increased difficulty in placing information there. They also have little knowledge about memory and ways to facilitate memory. All of these factors are alterable. (p. 182)

For example, with appropriate teacher feedback, adequate trials, and sufficient practice time, individuals with mental retardation can and will develop long-term memory storage in relation to learning motor skills.

Horgan (1985) determined that spontaneity (e.g., acting without needing to think) in adopting memory skills for the recall of movement cues is essential to understanding memory structure of persons with mental retardation. In his earlier study (1983), Horgan found no differences in instruction of subjects with mental retardation and two instruction groups of subjects without mental retardation. His findings support the idea that people with mental retardation can make improvements in their movement accuracy equal to the improvements made by their nonretarded counterparts. He qualifies his findings by stating that "the retarded *must* be made aware of effective means to assist them in coding, processing, and retaining movement information" (Horgan, 1985, p. 201).

Constant attention must be given to *how* individuals learn. Strategic behaviors and training techniques have been a major concern regarding persons with mental retardation. In a study using 21 subjects classified as mildly mentally retarded (Mean IQ = 59), Del Rey and Stewart (1989) determined that these subjects could enhance their memory and transfer ability when random and sequenced practice schedules were used.

Bouffard (1990) stresses the importance of teaching exact skills when dealing with persons who are mentally retarded. The instructor should teach movement skills by beginning with easy material. The key is sufficient practice, which should lead to mastery and ease of replication. New and more difficult material should be introduced only when the learner is proficient with lower level tasks.

To determine if youngsters are truly learning (i.e., can remember and repeat new motor tasks), a method of recording a child's progress should be used. Specific developmental or progression lists are helpful. In Dunn, Morehouse, and Fredericks's (1986) *Physical Education for the Severely Handicapped*, the *I Can* program developed by Wessel (1976), and the newer project *I CAN—ABC* by Kelly (1989), one can find excellent examples of progression sheets. Figure 10.1 gives an example of a developmental learning sheet, which includes teaching cues and columns for recording progress.

Dunn and Fait (1989) discuss the importance of comprehensive program planning. With reference to individuals labeled as having severe disabilities, they state:

In recent years educators have demonstrated rather convincingly that individuals with severe handicaps can learn if provided an appropriate instructional environment. This means that educational experiences should be structured with the skills to be taught task-analyzed. In addition, the educational approach for severely handicapped students requires precise teaching techniques with appropriate cues and consequences. A system approach, in which data are taken on individual trials, should also be incorporated so that informed decisions can be made about the individual's educational progress. (p. 363)

When planning programs for children, Nichols (1990, p. 161) suggests that the following questions be considered:

- What is the child's present skill level?
- What is the purpose of the skill practice?
- What level of mastery is desired?
- What kinds of activities will move the student from present to desired levels of performance?

Basic Motor Skills

By definition, a motor performance is skilled when a minimum amount of extraneous movement occurs. Newell (1984) uses Guthrie's definition of a *skill* as the ability to bring about a predetermined outcome with maximum certainty and minimum outlay of time and energy. Thus, the development of basic motor skills involves practice and refinement of fundamental movement tasks.

Known causes underlying low motor skill ability can be divided as follows:

- Attitudinal and environmental influences
- Delayed development of the central nervous system
- Minimal neurological dysfunction

Payne and Isaacs (1991) suggest that a low motor skill efficiency can also result if students have inadequate instruction or too few opportunities to practice. In many instances, low motor skill performance cannot be attributed to known causes. For an excellent model of a motor skill development program, see Figure 10.2. Motor program development is thoroughly discussed in chapters 5 and 7.

In very simple terms, basic motor skill learning becomes a matter of selecting appropriate activities, providing a stimulating environment, motivating the learners, selecting and implementing critical teaching cues, and providing an adequate amount of time for learning to occur. The following sections include basic fundamental motor skills most often learned by youngsters at the developmental ages of 6 through 8 and include the skills of galloping, skipping, rope jumping, throwing, catching, and striking. Other activities described use the basic motor skills and include parachute play, scooter play, and beanbag play.

Galloping

Although the locomotor skill of galloping is not used often, it is an activity that helps integrate and coordinate overall body movement. Most nonretarded children can gallop skillfully before age 7. Galloping is a modification of sliding. It involves the same step-close-step pattern but is used in straight forward-backward or diagonal planes. Galloping can be easily taught if the teacher and student face each other and hold hands. Tell the child, "Follow me." Begin slowly to step-close-step forward. As the child moves with the teacher, the tempo can be increased, and as the child's skill improves,

For all skills listed below, cue by saying "Watch me," demonstrate, and then use verbal and/or signed cue listed below.

Skill	Cue	Date	Placement yes/no	Date	Baseline #/total	Date	Posttest #/total	Comments
B. Underhand throw *	"Throw the ball underhand at the target."	10-8 1985	OXO No	10-9 1985	2/7	10-20 1985	7/7	
C. Overhand throw *	"Throw the ball overhand at the target."	10-8 1985	XOX Yes		/7		/7	
D. Underhand strike *	"Hit the ball underhand."	10-8 1985	OO No	10-9 1985	4/7		/7	
E. Overhand strike	"Hit the ball overhand."				/8		/8	
F. Kicking with the toe, preferred foot	"Kick the ball with your toe."				/7		/7	
G. Kicking with the toe, nonpreferred foot	"Kick the ball with your toe using the other foot."				/7		/7	
H. Kicking with the instep, preferred foot	"Kick the ball with your instep."				/7		/7	
I. Kicking with the instep, nonpreferred foot	"Kick the ball with the instep of your other foot."				/7		/7	
J. Kicking with the side of the foot, preferred foot	"Kick the ball with the side of your foot."				/7		/7	
K. Kicking with the side of the foot, nonpreferred foot	"Kick the ball with the side of your other foot."				/7		/7	
L. Trapping or catching a rolled ball	"Stop the ball."				/5		/5	
M. Catching a bouncing ball	"Catch the ball."				/5		/5	
N. Catching a thrown ball	"Catch the ball."				/14		/14	

Figure 10.1 Sample placement form.

Note. From *Physical Education for the Severely Handicapped* (p. 64) by J.M. Dunn, J.W. Morehouse, Jr., and H.D.B. Fredericks, 1986, Austin, TX: PRO-ED. Reprinted by permission of PRO-ED, Inc.

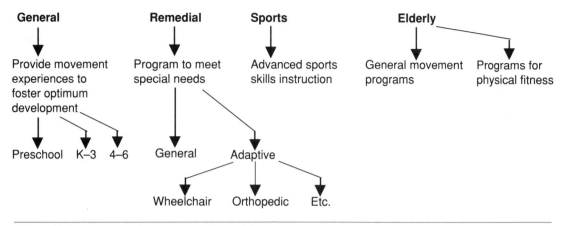

Figure 10.2   Motor development program model.
Note. From *Human Motor Development: A Lifespan Approach* (p. 349) by V.G. Payne and L.D. Isaacs, 1991, Mountain View, CA: Mayfield. Reprinted by permission of Mayfield Publishing Co.

teacher and child can work parallel but need not hold hands. Another way to learn galloping is by walking with a limp. As the child begins limping (by dragging one leg), the tempo is gradually increased. A rapid limp using the step-close-step foot sequence is identical to the gallop (Eichstaedt & Kalakian, 1987). See Highlight 10.1.

The *I CAN* motor development program (Wessel, 1976) has identified specific levels of performance to be used as guides for mastery of motor skills. These suggested criteria were field-tested with individuals labeled as having moderate mental retardation. Throughout this chapter the *I CAN* criteria are listed as minimal levels of performance. Therefore, galloping is judged effective if the youngster can perform the gallop by meeting the following *I CAN* criteria:

1. Given a verbal request and demonstration, can gallop for 50 feet without assistance.
2. Given a verbal request and demonstration, can gallop five times in succession with the right foot leading, and then five times with the left foot leading.

Skipping

Skipping is the most complex of all locomotor skills, as it involves coordinated alternation of the feet. There is a combination of one walking step followed by an immediate hop on the same foot. The pattern is step-hop on one foot and then step-hop on the other foot. Horvat (1990) describes this action: "Skipping occurs at 6 or 7 years from a mature hopping pattern. As hopping proficiency increases, the movement adds a step on one side of the body. With improvement of balance, the step-hop pattern becomes an ingrained movement on the opposite side of the body" (p. 70).

To learn to skip, it is essential to first develop one-foot balancing on both the right and the left leg and then practice hopping in place on one foot. Finally, standing on one foot, the student leans forward and hops straight ahead. These lead-up skills are essential to improving a child's skipping performance.

The coordinated arm swing for skipping is similar to the alternate arm action used in walking and running. Youngsters who have not developed good alternate arm action in walking or running could possibly experience difficulty

HIGHLIGHT 10.1　　　　　　　　　　　　　**IN PRACTICE**

Key Teaching Points for Galloping

Keep one foot in front of the other.

Keep the legs relaxed.

Land lightly.

Use arms to help gain height.

Reverse the lead leg, thus using the nondominant leg.

Teacher's Comments

- "Galloping is: step-together-step."
- "Step forward with this leg [touch one leg]. Now put this leg [touch back leg] behind your front leg. Everyone gallop: step-together-step."
- "Lift your arms and gallop: step-together-step."

Activities to Increase Galloping Skill

- Gallop fast; gallop slow.
- Gallop softly; gallop loudly.
- Gallop high; gallop low.
- Gallop strongly like a *big* powerful horse.

- Gallop lightly like a small, gentle pony.
- Gallop with your arms high; with arms low.
- Gallop in a circle like the letter *O*.
- Gallop in a shape like the letter *C*.
- Gallop in a shape like the letter *L*.
- Gallop in a shape like the letter *W*.
- Gallop in a shape like the first letter of your name.
- Gallop backward.
- Gallop sideways.
- Gallop with a partner.
- Gallop in the shape of a square.
- Gallop in the shape of a triangle.
- Gallop among classmates; don't touch anyone else.
- Gallop and stop on the signal—stop as quickly as you can.
- Gallop as many places as you can, changing directions as you go. Change directions every time you hear a signal.
- Gallop leading with your nondominant foot.

in skipping. This is because arm opposition is necessary to lift the body forward and upward. Poor arm action could also lead to balance difficulties. To produce the desirable springy, joyful, carefree quality in skipping, movements should be done on the balls of the feet (Eichstaedt & Kalakian, 1987).

The teacher should stand in front of the child, holding her hands. Have her step on one foot and immediately hop on the same foot. Have her repeat the same action with the other foot, while standing in place. Assist the child by lifting her up when hopping (see Highlight 10.2).

Wessel (1976) suggests the following performance criterion for skipping:

1. Given a verbal request and demonstration, will skip 50 feet, three times.
2. Given a verbal request and demonstration, will skip zigzagging down and back through four cones placed 10 feet apart.

Rope Jumping

Jumping rope is extremely beneficial, as it develops rhythm, timing, and overall body coordination. Leg and arm strength are improved,

HIGHLIGHT 10.2

Key Teaching Points for Skipping

Emphasize stepping and hopping.

Swing the opposite arm upward and forward to increase height and distance.

Swing the opposite leg forward on each hop.

Lift the front leg for extra height on the hop.

Try to keep an uneven rhythm (Nichols, 1990).

Teacher's Comments

- ''Hop, hop, hop, now with the other foot step, and hop, hop, hop, and now with the other foot step.''
- ''Watch me skip. Step-hop on this foot, and then step-hop the other foot.''
- ''Everyone skip. Step and hop on one foot. Now step and hop on the other foot.''
- ''Move your arms like this as you skip along.''

Activities to Improve Skipping

- Skip fast; then skip slow.

- Skip forward.
- Skip slowly and quickly change to skipping fast.
- Skip softly and lightly.
- Skip with high arm movement.
- Skip with no arm movement.
- Skip with hands held high.
- Skip with hands held low.
- Skip in a small circle; then a large circle.
- Skip in the shape of a square.
- Skip in the shape of a triangle.
- Skip on toes.
- Skip and bounce a ball.
- Skip in a zigzag pattern.
- Skip using only tiny, baby steps.
- Skip using only giant steps.
- Skip with a partner.
- Skip to the beat [instructor uses drum or whistle].
- Skip to the fast music; skip to the slow music.
- Skip, then stop when the instructor signals.

and even cardiorespiratory endurance should benefit. This is an advanced skill and may prove difficult for youngsters who are having difficulty performing basic locomotor skills such as hopping, jumping, and skipping. Therefore, it may be appropriate to concentrate on perfecting these basic skills before moving on to individual rope jumping.

''Jump Rope for Heart'' is an organization developed in 1979 to use rope jumping as a means of developing cardiorespiratory endurance for school-age children and adolescents. In addition to its obvious health benefits, the program is an excellent fund-raiser. The youngsters

obtain pledges based on their number of jumps or time completed. Awards of personal clothing, athletic gear, and certificates of participation are given to the students. Since 1979 over $150 million has been raised. This organization has the enthusiastic endorsement of both the AAHPERD and the American Heart Association.

Lavay and Horvat (1989) describe the benefits of jumping rope for individuals with disabilities and strongly endorse their participation in Jump Rope for Heart activities. They believe that ''most importantly, with slight if any modifications children with special needs can receive the same positive physical, social, and cognitive program benefits as their nonhandicapped peers.'' A descriptive brochure regarding program development, *Jump Rope for Heart—Special Populations Guidelines* (1989), is available from the American Heart Association.

Dauer and Pangrazi (1989) encourage rope jumping and suggest that it should begin in preschool and continue throughout the school years. They provide the following guidelines for determining appropriate jump rope lengths:

The length of the rope will be different for different children. It should be long enough so the ends reach to the child's armpits or slightly higher when the child stands on its center. Preschool children generally use 6-ft ropes, and the primary-level group needs mostly 7-ft ropes, with a few 6-ft and 8-ft lengths. Grades 3-6 needs a mixture of 7-ft and 8-ft ropes. (p. 326)

Lead-Up Activities for Rope Jumping

Rope jumping may be difficult for developmentally delayed youngsters, and the American Heart Association (1989, p. 3) suggests the following lead-up activities for special populations:

- Jumping or stepping over a stationary or slightly swinging rope held at a suitable height
- Swinging a rope overhead and letting it stop on the toes of the shoes before starting the next jump
- Standing next to a jumper (but outside the arc of the rope) and jumping to the same rhythm
- Jumping over a rope swinging slowly back and forth, jumping as many times as possible
- Jumping once over a rope swinging slowly back and forth and then going to the end of the line
- Jumping over a rope lying on the floor, with the rope gradually raised, challenging the child to jump higher
- Jumping side-to-side over a stationary rope (jumping in one place or starting at one end of the rope and jumping back and forth down the length of the rope)

Allow the youngster to listen to the rhythm of the rope as it turns. Have the child say ''jump-bounce'' in rhythm with the turning rope. On the word ''jump,'' the child jumps with both feet together about 3 or 4 inches off the ground; on the word ''bounce,'' he takes a very small bounce in place. Kirchner (1988) suggests that a musical background may help the child keep a steady rhythm. Any folk-dance record, such as ''Shoo Fly'' or ''Pop Goes the Weasel,'' with a 4/4 rhythm works well. See Highlight 10.3.

Parachute Play

Parachute play is an integral part of most elementary school physical education programs. Kirchner (1988) believes that ''without question, this type of activity is one of the most 'fun-type' group experiences for all children—from the highly skilled to the severely handicapped'' (p. 456). Parachute activities are excellent for developing upper body strength, including the fingers, hands, wrists, arms, and shoulders. Cardiorespiratory endurance can be improved if the time for ongoing movement is monitored and small increases are added each new day. Nichols (1990) has found that these activities also involve social development, because cooperation among children is required to complete the games.

Parachutes from 24 to 28 feet in diameter should be used for larger size classes (approximately 30 students), and a 10- to 12-foot-diameter parachute should be used for smaller groups. Some skills will be difficult for the younger children (e.g., 5- and 6-year-olds), and tasks should be selected with this in mind. Also, Dauer and Pangrazi (1989) warn that this younger age group may fatigue easily.

There are several appropriate ways to grip the

Key Teaching Points for Rope Jumping

Students should start without the rope, developing a double- or single-beat jump.

Students should practice over the "long rope," which is swinging back and forth.

Begin with a slow rhythm, giving the student cues such as "ready—jump."

Students should start with the short rope behind the feet.

Activities to Improve Rope Jumping Skill

While turning the short rope:

- Jump on toes of both feet.
- Jump on right foot only.
- Jump on left foot only.
- Jump while spreading feet sideward.
- Jump while placing one foot forward and the other backward.
- Jump and move sideward while jumping.
- Jump and land with legs crossed, then alternate feet.
- Jump, then squat down.
- Turn the rope backward, jump on toes of both feet.
- Jump while moving forward.
- Jump while running forward.
- Jump through an obstacle course made up of rubber cones.
- Jump and toe-tap in back, then hop on one foot and tap other foot in back.
- Jump as many times as you can without missing and record score.
- Jump for 30 seconds, and record number of jumps completed.

---

parachute. The grip can be with either one or two hands, and the palms can face down (overhand) or up (underhand) or be mixed. The grips should be changed to create muscle action in different directions. See Highlight 10.4 for parachute activities.

Scooter Play

Scooters are very popular with all children. They provide opportunities to control a moving object, which can be rewarding and exciting. For the instructor, scooters are a medium to increase balance and strength in arms and legs. The scooter is potentially dangerous, and students must never attempt to stand on them. Also, the youngsters should be taught to be careful not to run over hands and fingers. Establish criteria to allow for goals to be attained (e.g., from a sitting position on a scooter, push back-

ward with the legs for 20 feet; from a prone position on a scooter, pull forward for 20 feet). See Highlight 10.5 for scooter activities, and Figure 10.3 for variations of scooter play.

Beanbag Play

Beanbags are excellent pieces of simple and inexpensive equipment. The bags should be solid colors with varying sizes, shapes, and weights, and made of cloth for easier catching. Kirchner (1988) believes that the wide surface and lack of rebound property help younger children learn to throw and catch. See Highlight 10.6 for beanbag activities.

Throwing

For developmentally delayed girls and boys, the *underhand throw* is an excellent beginning point for learning the overhand throw. The first phase

HIGHLIGHT 10.4   **IN PRACTICE**

Activities With Parachutes

Fruit Basket

This is the beginning and resting position. Youngsters begin with feet shoulder-width apart and arms in a downward position, hands grasping the parachute with an overhand grip. To produce the effect of small waves, the children gently shake the parachute up and down. Large waves can be created by increasing the arm movements.

Variations

- All children hold the chute with the right hand and run in a clockwise rotation.
- Have them change to the left hand and run counterclockwise.
- Change the skill to galloping or sliding.

Balls and Parachutes

On and Off. Place several foam balls in the center. The children attempt to pitch them off by causing big waves.

Variations

- By making small waves, the children attempt to direct the balls into the center hole of the parachute.
- Designate two teams. Each team is given four balls (the teams have different colors) and attempts to get the other team's balls off the chute.

Umbrella

To make an umbrella, the children begin with the parachute on the floor, holding with the overhand grip and kneeling on one knee. The children stand up quickly, pushing their arms above their heads, and then returning their arms to the starting position. A slow count of 1-2-3 is normally used to lift the parachute up to the umbrella position.

Variations

- *Bubble.* Beginning with the chute close to the floor, lift it upward and take two or three steps toward the center, filling the chute with air to form a large bubble. Finally, walk back out to original position.
- *Balloon in the Sky.* Raise the chute as in the bubble, and on a signal let it go so it floats away toward the sky.
- *Mushroom.* Begin in the fruit-basket position. Lift the parachute upward, then quickly take one step in and pull downward, holding the edge of the chute firmly to the ground.
- *In and Out.* Similar to the Mushroom, but this time as the chute starts to descend, the youngsters lie down on their tummies and pull the chute down over their heads with their bodies on the outside.
- *Circus Tent.* From the umbrella position, the children move under, turn around, then kneel down and pull the parachute down to the ground and let it fall around them.
- *Remember Your Name.* Raise the chute up in the air; the teacher calls out the name of a student, who runs to the other side of the parachute.
- *Change Places.* Raise the chute up in the air; the teacher calls the names of two youngsters who change positions.
- *Numbers.* Give each child a number; as the chute is raised, call a number, and that child runs to the other side.
- *Colors.* Raise the chute up in the air; call a color, and any child wearing that color runs to the opposite side.

HIGHLIGHT 10.5

IN PRACTICE

Activities With Scooters

Specific activities could include the following:

- Sit, kneel, or lie down on back or stomach and push or pull with arms and/or legs.
- Move forward, backward, or to the sides.
- Move with control while changing speed from slow to fast.

- Move around, between, and under objects.
- Trace letters and geometric designs on the floor.
- Play tag or "Steal the Bacon" on scooters.

Figure 10.3   Scooter play.

HIGHLIGHT 10.6

IN PRACTICE

Activities With Beanbags

- Throw the bag into the air and catch it with both hands; with the right hand only and then with the left.
- Throw the bag in the air and perform another action before catching it (e.g., clap hands; touch floor).
- Throw beanbags at targets on the floor (e.g., hoops, boxes, baskets).
- Balance the bag on head, ear, nose, elbow, shoulder, leg, foot. Also, put the bag on head and balance on one foot.

Beanbags can be used when youngsters are practicing balance skills and while reviewing identification of body parts. They create a different atmosphere, which may be motivational.

Dauer and Pangrazi (1989, pp. 211-212) suggest two games to play when using beanbags:

- Each child has a beanbag. The children move around the area, tossing the bags upward and catching them as they move. On signal, they drop the bags to the floor and jump (or hop, or leap) over as many as possible. On the next signal, they pick up any convenient bag and resume tossing to themselves.
- Enough beanbags for the whole class are scattered on the floor. The children either run between or jump over the beanbags. When a body part is called out, the children place the body part *on* the nearest beanbag.

---

of underhand throwing occurs quite naturally and involves only arm action with no forward step of either foot. This is usually found in small children and is not a functional teaching step. The second phase includes some follow-through and stepping with the same foot as the throwing arm, and again, should not be taught. Finally, the child swings the throwing arm backward and then steps with the opposite foot forward; as the throwing arm swings forward, the ball is released, and the arm follows through. McClenaghan and Gallahue (1978) suggest that underhand throwing skills should be started by throwing a large playground ball (approximately 8-1/2 inches in diameter). For more of their suggestions, see Highlight 10.7.

The *I CAN* program (Wessel, 1976) lists the following performance criteria as appropriate beginning levels of underhand throwing proficiency:

1. Given a verbal request and a demonstration, throws a 3- to 4-inch ball to a 20-inch-wide target placed 15 feet away, two out of three times.
2. Given a verbal request and a demonstration, throws a 3- to 4-inch ball a distance of at least 20 feet, two out of three times.

When the youngsters have mastered the underhand throw, they should be ready to develop the skill of overhand throwing. By the time children reach age 5 they usually have progressed through the two elementary stages of *overhand throwing*. They should now have moved past phase one (CA = 2-3 years), where only the arm is moving and no body rotation or weight shift is occurring. At about 3.6 to 5 years, there is body rotation and an increase in ball velocity, but still no weight shift. During ages 5 and 6, the throw involves more body ro-

Activities to Improve Underhand Throwing

- Throw with feet wide apart.
- Throw with feet close together.
- Throw with one foot in front of the other.
- Throw from a kneeling position on both knees.
- Throw slowly, then quickly.
- Throw, emphasizing stepping on front foot.

- Throw, emphasizing follow-through.
- Throw with a high arc; then a low arc.
- Throw at a 20-inch wide target on the wall.
- Throw the ball as far as you can.

---

tation and adds a step forward with the same foot as the throwing arm. Finally, at about 6.6 years, the shoulders rotate backward and the weight is transferred to the throwing leg (Dauer & Pangrazi, 1989). Then the nonthrowing foot steps forward as the throwing shoulder moves forward and the elbow leads the throwing arm. The ball is released as the weight is transferred from the back leg to the front leg. A follow-through should occur after the ball is released. The verbal cue is "Step, turn, and throw." See Highlight 10.8 for keys to teaching overhand throwing.

Wessel (1976) suggests the following performance criteria as minimal levels for competence in overhand throwing:

1. Given a verbal request and a demonstration, the child throws a 3-or 4-inch ball to a 20-inch-wide target placed 15 feet away, two out of three times.
2. Given a verbal request and a demonstration, the child throws a 3- or 4-inch ball a distance of at least 46 feet (girls) or 73 feet (boys), two out of three times.

Catching

Catching is considered more difficult than throwing and is usually not perfected until throwing skills are quite well developed. This fundamental movement pattern involves bringing a thrown object under control with the arms and hands. The natural progression of catching begins with children passively waiting for the ball to be placed in their arms, which are held in a cradle position. In the second stage, children hold their arms stiff and in front of their bodies, often turning their heads in fear of being hit in the face. Finally the children hold their arms relaxed and at their sides before attempting to catch the ball with their hands and fingers only.

Catching a rolling ball is the first progression to be practiced. The second is to catch a ball that is first bounced on the ground. Youngsters do well when they bounce a ball and catch it themselves, as the easiest airborne ball to catch is the one you throw yourself. Self-initiation of ball action reduces many uncertainties associated with catching a ball thrown by others. Bouncing and catching lead-up sessions are excellent for beginners and should be practiced daily. During practice sessions, each child should have a ball. It is important not to rush the children into experiences that are too advanced for their development.

Key Teaching Points for Overhand Throwing

Nichols (1990, p. 181) lists six teaching points to consider:

Grip the ball with the fingers.

Turn the opposite side of the body to the target.

Step forward on the foot opposite to the throwing arm.

The elbow leads as the arm moves forward.

Release the ball as the arm extends.

Follow through in the direction of the throw.

It is suggested that youngsters with very small hands grip the ball with three fingers spread on top of the ball and the thumb underneath, instead of the usual two-finger-and-thumb grip. This allows better hand control, thus producing better accuracy and distance.

Activities to Improve Overhand Throwing

- Throw a foam ball while kneeling on both knees.
- Throw a foam ball with the feet wide apart.
- With the hand close to the ear, throw and extend the hand toward a target on the wall.
- Throw the ball as far as you can.
- Throw the ball in a high arc.
- Throw the ball in a low arc.
- Throw hard.
- Throw soft.
- Throw with feet together.
- Throw with feet wide apart.
- Throw while standing on one foot.
- Throw to a partner, aiming for the chest.
- Throw to a partner, aiming for the tummy.
- Throw to a partner, aiming for the knees.
- Throw to a partner, aiming for the nose.

Eichstaedt and Kalakian (1987) discuss potential problems encountered by young children when learning to catch a thrown ball:

A common error in teaching children to catch is throwing the ball too slowly. When learning to catch, many children cue on the thrower, not the ball. Throwing the ball initiates a catching response in the child. If the ball is thrown inordinately slowly, the catching response may occur before the ball has come within reach. . . . The thrower should then adjust the velocity of the ball so it comes within reach at the precise time when the catching response is initiated. (p. 109)

Research by Du Randt (1985) has shown that ball size is critical when youngsters are learning to catch. She found that small balls (tennis-ball size) stimulate a more mature catching response in 6- and 8-year-olds but not in 4-year-olds. She recommends that 6- and 8-year-olds be encouraged to play with small balls as often as possible, but that younger players should not be challenged with the small ball until they are relatively proficient with larger balls. The larger ball provides a more substantial visual stimulus and offers greater surface area for catching. Cratty (1989) has found reasonable success with 5-year-olds attempting to catch an 8-inch diameter ball. He cites little success with 5-year-olds catching a tennis ball. He states: ''Younger children, or delayed youngsters whose developmental age is 6, 7, or lower, should not be expected to engage in ball games in which the balls are much smaller than 8 [inches] in diameter and the balls are to be caught from distances of 20 [feet] to 30 [feet]'' (p. 495). Again, instructors and leaders of boys and girls with mental retardation should remember that developmental motor skill may be somewhat delayed, and these youngsters will benefit most if the skill is practiced daily. See Highlight 10.9 for keys to teaching catching.

Wessel (1976) suggests the following performance criteria as attaining minimal levels of catching:

1. Given a verbal request and demonstration, catches (grasps or traps with hands or arms and chest) an 8-inch ball lofted softly to the middle of the chest from a 6-foot distance, two out of three times.

2. Given a verbal request and demonstration, catches with hands only a 6-inch ball tossed to chest height from 15 feet away, two out of three times. See Highlight 10.10 for catching activities.

Wessel (1976) suggests the following performance criterion for demonstrating the mature catch: Given a verbal request and demonstration, catches a 4- to 6-inch ball thrown at least 20 feet high from a distance of 20 feet, two out of three times.

HIGHLIGHT 10.9   **IN PRACTICE**

Key Teaching Points for Catching

For a low thrown ball, palms face up in the direction of the oncoming ball, with the tips of the little fingers touching.

For a high thrown ball, palms face toward the oncoming ball, with the tips of the thumbs touching.

Fingers are curved and relaxed.

Watch the ball all the way into the hands.

Softly absorb the force of the ball by pulling the hands in toward the body when the ball touches the hands.

Activities to Improve Catching

Have the children use 8-1/2-inch-diameter playground balls for these activities:

- By yourself, bounce and catch with your feet wide apart.
- By yourself, bounce and catch with your feet together.
- By yourself, bounce, clap your hands once, and catch.

- From a partner, catch a rolled ball.
- From a partner, catch a rolled ball to your left.
- From a partner, catch a rolled ball to your right.
- From a partner, catch a bounced ball with your feet wide apart.
- From a partner, catch a bounced ball with your feet together.
- From a partner, catch a high bounced ball.
- From a partner, catch a low bounced ball.
- From a partner, catch an underhand thrown ball.
- From a partner, catch an underhand, high thrown ball.
- From a partner, catch an overhand thrown ball.
- From a partner, catch a ball thrown to your right.
- From a partner, catch a ball thrown to your left.

Activities for Mature Catching

Using a small foam or tennis ball:

- Catch a ball attached to a swinging rope.
- Toss the ball up and catch it yourself.
- Toss the ball up and catch it with one hand.
- Toss the ball up and catch it with your feet wide apart.
- Toss the ball up and catch it with your feet together.
- From a partner, catch with your feet wide apart.

- From a partner, catch with your feet together.
- From a partner, catch a high thrown ball.
- From a partner, catch a ball thrown to your left.
- From a partner, catch a ball thrown to your right.
- From a partner, catch a ball with one hand.

Striking

Striking involves the hand, or some hand-held object such as a bat, racket, or club, hitting an object such as a ball. Underhand and overhand striking is common, but the sidearm pattern is used most in traditional sport skills. The skill of striking requires eye/hand coordination, and keeping the eyes on the ball is important. Thus, tracking skills are necessary. This may be a problem for low-skilled youngsters, so initial experiences are usually most successful if the ball is stationary, bright in color, and large. This reduces the difficulty that visual tracking, spatial awareness, and figure/ground discrimination have for boys and girls with developmental delays. After the children have gained success with the nonmoving ball, it is appropriate for them to begin hitting a moving balloon with the hand. Do not have them progress too quickly to using bats or paddles. Allow them time to develop skill at one level before moving on. See Highlight 10.11 for striking activities.

To practice striking skills, youngsters should be given implements of appropriate size and weight. Small children should not have adult-size equipment; an implement that is too heavy or too big for the user ensures failure. Enlarged

striking surfaces, such as a "fat-headed" plastic bat, should be considered for the developmentally delayed. When students progress to the level of using an implement, they should begin by using a short-handled paddle, such as is used in the game of racquetball. For individuals who have difficulty holding and controlling this racquet, an old pair of panty hose stretched over a wire coat hanger is a fine beginning racquet, particularly for hitting a balloon. See Highlight 10.12.

Wessel (1976) suggests the following performance criteria for striking with a plastic bat:

1. Given a verbal request and demonstration, hits a 12-inch wiffle ball suspended at waist height, two out of three times.
2. Given a verbal request and demonstration, hits a 9-inch wiffle ball pitched between the shoulders and knees, two out of three times.

Older Children: 9- to 12-Year-Olds

During this time period, children experience constant but relatively slow growth. The basic

HIGHLIGHT 10.11

IN PRACTICE

Activities to Improve Beginning Levels of Striking

- With the open palm, strike a balloon that is resting on a batting tee.
- With the open palm, strike a large foam ball that is resting on a batting tee.
- With the open palm, strike a small foam ball that is resting on a batting tee.
- With the open palm, strike a tennis ball that is resting on a batting tee.
- With the fist closed, strike a large playground ball that is resting on a batting tee.
- With the fist closed, strike a small playground ball that is resting on a batting tee.
- Holding a small playground ball, strike a ball for a distance of at least 10 feet.
- Holding a small playground ball, strike a ball at least 30 feet.

The children should then progress to hitting slow-moving objects, again with just their hands. Be aware that the skill of striking must be slowly ingrained, and do not rush the children—let them take enough time for complete learning to take place. The following ac-

tivities should be practiced using only the hands, *before* progressing to the use of a paddle, racquet or bat.

- With your hands, strike a balloon upward—keeping it from hitting the floor.
- With your hands, strike a balloon back and forth with a partner.
- With your hands, strike a swinging foam ball suspended on a string.
- With two hands, dribble a large playground ball.
- With one hand, dribble a small playground ball.
- Drop a large playground ball from waist height and strike it underhand with the palms of both hands.
- With two hands, hit a large playground ball back and forth against a wall.
- Hit a large playground ball back and forth with a partner.
- Hit a small playground ball back and forth with a partner.

---

motor skills have been learned. Eckert (1987) observes:

> Although these years are ones of slow developmental change, it is a time of rapid learning and what may be thought of as growth consolidation, characterized more by perfection and stabilization of previously acquired skills and abilities than by the emergence of new ones. (p. 233)

With reference to preteenagers, Nichols (1990) adds: "Seven- to 12-year-olds are capable of greater body awareness, with increasing ability to analyze their own movements as they progress through elementary years" (p. 22). Regarding youngsters up to the age of 12, Eckert

(1987) describes specific needs and movement experiences that can be developed through specific motor programs (see Highlight 10.13). When teaching individuals with mental retardation, instructors must remember that in general the thinking process and ability to make quick and accurate judgments will be slower than with the nonretarded. Constant practice and review are necessary to ensure that learning will take place. This may include extra physical education periods or motor development classes in community therapeutic recreation programs. Parents should be provided with idea and suggestion sheets that include activities for free-time play. For a review of suggestions for working with parents, see chapter 5.

HIGHLIGHT 10.12   **IN PRACTICE**

Activities to Improve Striking With an Implement

- Using a racquet, hit a balloon into the air.
- Using a racquet, hit a foam ball into the air.
- Using a racquet, hit a balloon back and forth with a partner.

Key Teaching Points for Striking With a Bat

Don't stand too close to the plate.

Hold hands together on the bat handle.

Swing the bat level to the ground.

Choke up the bat for better control (Nichols, 1990).

The ''fat-headed'' plastic bat should then be introduced.

- Using a fat-headed plastic bat, hit a large wiffle ball that is resting on a batting tee.
- Using a fat-headed plastic bat, hit a small wiffle ball that is resting on a batting tee.
- Using a fat-headed plastic bat, hit a small foam ball that is resting on a batting tee.
- Using a fat-headed plastic bat, hit a tennis ball that is resting on a batting tee.

When the children are repeatedly successful, a regular shaped plastic bat (choked up if necessary) should be introduced.

- Hit a large (12-inch) wiffle ball that is resting on a batting tee.
- Hit a small (9-inch) wiffle ball that is resting on a batting tee.
- Hit a small foam ball that is resting on a batting tee.
- Hit a tennis ball that is resting on a batting tee.

Finally, a moving object should be introduced, and again, begin with the short-handled racquet and progress to the fat-headed bat to the regular shaped bat.

- Hit a balloon thrown by the teacher.
- Hit a large foam ball thrown by the teacher.
- Hit a small foam ball thrown by the teacher.
- Hit a large wiffle ball thrown by the teacher.
- Hit a small wiffle ball thrown by the teacher.

Youngsters labeled as having mild or moderate mental retardation or with Down syndrome generally have much lower physical fitness and motor performance than their nonretarded age peers. Eichstaedt et al. (1991) studied the physical fitness and motor skill levels of girls and boys classified as having mild or moderate mental retardation or Down syndrome. The 4,464 Illinois boys and girls, ages 6 through 20, were tested by physical education teachers and Special Olympics coaches. Variables included height, weight, modified sit-ups (for 60 seconds), flexed arm hang, standing long jump, shuttle run, 50-yard dash, 6- or 9-minute run, skinfolds (subscapular, triceps, calf), stork stand, basketball wall bounce (for 15 seconds), and sit-and-reach. The number of individuals within groups is found in Table 10.1.

These researchers found that girls and boys with mild mental retardation are more proficient, although not significant ($p < .05$), in all dimensions of physical fitness and motor ability than individuals with either moderate retardation or Down syndrome. The areas that did show significant difference were height, flexed arm hang, sit-ups, standing long jump, 50-yard dash; stork

HIGHLIGHT 10.13

Summary of General Developmental Characteristics During Late Childhood (Ages 9-12)

Characteristics

1. Relative stability in growth
2. Limbs continue to grow more rapidly in proportion to the rest of the body
3. Some preadolescent changes in the shoulder/hip ratio for the sexes
4. Preadolescent fat spurt for some individuals, particularly males
5. Differential growth rates become more marked at end of period as early maturers begin adolescent growth spurt
6. Balance becomes well developed
7. Basic motor patterns are more refined and adapted to structural differences
8. Better coordination and body control
9. Continued increase in strength and endurance
10. Eye-hand coordination improved; increased proficiency in manipulative skills
11. Increased attention span
12. Sees need to practice skills for improvement, to gain social status and to develop endurance
13. Spirit of adventure high
14. More socially mature; interested in group welfare
15. Intellectually curious
16. Greater interest in proficiency and competitive spirit—hero worship of athletes
17. Some gender differences in performance and some antagonism towards opposite sex

Need	Experiences
Use of skill for specific purposes; opportunity to take part in a wide variety of activities to gain knowledge of proficiencies	Introduction to sport skills; lead-up games; self-testing activities; use of apparatus; drills and self-testing practice situations; low organization games requiring courage
Opportunity for group activities	Team activities; dance composition; folk and square dance
Opportunities to explore; learn mechanical principles; physiology, kinesiology of movement	Self-testing and problem-solving activities related to own skill; creative dance; developmental exercise programs
Ability grouping for some individual activities and team games, particularly those involving strength and endurance components	Self-testing activities; relaxation techniques; developmental exercises and interval training; combatives

Note. From *Motor Development* (3rd ed.) by H.M. Eckert, 1987, Indianapolis, IN: Benchmark. Copyright 1987 by H.M. Eckert. Reprinted by permission.

Table 10.1   Breakdown of Subjects in Eichstaedt, Wang, Polacek, and Dohrmann Study

Ages	Mild	Moderate	Down	Total
Females				
6-9	93	142	71	306
10-13	160	279	114	553
14-17	164	337	174	675
18-20	77	159	178	414
	494	917	537	1,948
Males				
6-9	139	233	118	490
10-13	194	374	194	762
14-17	166	454	184	804
18-20	58	318	84	460
	557	1,379	580	2,516
Subject totals	1,051	2,296	1,117	4,464

Note. From *Physical Fitness and Motor Skill Levels of Individuals with Mental Retardation: Mild, Moderate, and Down Syndrome, Ages 6-21* by C.B. Eichstaedt, P.Y. Wang, J.J. Polacek, & P.F. Dohrmann, 1991, Normal, IL: Illinois State University Printing Services. Copyright 1991 by C.B. Eichstaedt et al. Reprinted by permission.

stand and shuttle run (boys only). Individuals with moderate mental retardation are more proficient than those with Down syndrome but significantly only in stork stand, shuttle run (boys only), and flexed arm hang (boys only). Individuals with Down syndrome are more flexible than the other groups. Percentile scores in the 75th, 50th, and 25th levels for all groups and test items are found in Appendix C.

The implications of the Eichstaedt et al. (1991) study can be better understood when comparisons are made among similar-age peers labeled as mild, moderate, Down syndrome, and nonretarded. Table 10.2 highlights differences of static balance, running speed, running agility, and trunk flexibility for youngsters ages 9 through 12. There are distinct differences among the groups, but these researchers question

whether these levels of performance are a result of mental retardation or of a lack of appropriate physical education opportunities. They find this particularly true when comparing boys and girls with mild mental retardation and their nonretarded counterparts.

Efficient balance, flexibility, running speed, and agility are necessary components of a skilled performer. Most individuals classified as having mental retardation appear to need extra practice if they are to compete favorably with their nonretarded peers. Therefore, direct programming is necessary. Running and balance activities have been described in previous sections in this book.

Agility

Dauer and Pangrazi (1989) define agility as

the ability to change directions swiftly, easily, and under good control. A particularly agile person is one who is hard to catch in a tag game. . . . Agility is necessary for individual safety. Many persons are alive and free from injury because they were agile enough to get out of the way of a moving object. (p. 125)

Specific activities to improve agility are described by Nichols (1990). She refers to the skill of dodging and suggests six activities to practice the skill:

1. Move in general space. Dodge stationary objects placed throughout the room.
2. Move in general space. Dodge anyone you meet.
3. Moving in a reduced general space, dodge anyone you meet.
4. Move with different locomotor movements while dodging individuals or objects.
5. Dodge the balls that half of the class roll toward you.
6. Dribble a ball in general space. Can you dodge others and the balls they are controlling? (p. 175)

Table 10.2   Median Scores for Girls and Boys 9-12 in Stork Stand, 50-Yard Dash, Shuttle Run, and Sit-and-Reach

Age	Level of retardation	Stork stand	50-yard dash	Shuttle run	Sit-and-reach
Girls					
9	Nonretarded	22 s	8.6 s	11.8 s	28 cm
	Mild	17	10.9	15.5	20
	Moderate	13	13.9	18.8	20
	Down	12	15.8	19.8	25
10	Nonretarded	23 s	8.6 s	11.8 s	28 cm
	Mild	23	10.4	16.0	21
	Moderate	16	14.1	20.3	19
	Down	13	20.9	22.4	32
11	Nonretarded	21 s	8.3 s	11.5 s	29 cm
	Mild	24	9.7	13.7	23
	Moderate	17	12.0	19.1	18
	Down	10	16.7	18.3	32
12	Nonretarded	21 s	8.1 s	11.4 s	30 cm
	Mild	19	8.9	15.3	22
	Moderate	16	14.2	17.9	24
	Down	6	14.8	17.1	32
Boys					
9	Nonretarded	22 s	8.2 s	11.2 s	25cm
	Mild	18	10.3	13.6	22
	Moderate	17	13.6	18.7	20
	Down	8	16.1	20.0	28
10	Nonretarded	23 s	8.2 s	11.2 s	25 cm
	Mild	17	10.3	14.8	19
	Moderate	14	13.5	18.6	18
	Down	9	13.1	17.4	32
11	Nonretarded	22 s	8.0 s	10.9 s	25 cm
	Mild	19	9.2	12.3	20
	Moderate	14	12.2	17.4	18
	Down	13	15.2	18.8	26
12	Nonretarded	21 s	7.8 s	10.7 s	26 cm
	Mild	21	9.1	12.4	18
	Moderate	14	14.8	18.1	16
	Down	6	13.3	17.4	28

Note. Scores for nonretarded: stork stand compiled from Arnheim and Sinclair (1979); 50 yd/shuttle run compiled from AAHPERD (1979); sit/reach compiled from AAHPERD (1980). Scores for students with mental retardation compiled from Eichstaedt et al., (1991).

Physical Fitness

Muscular strength, muscular endurance, and cardiorespiratory endurance comprise the general area of physical fitness. They should be in-tegral components of all physical education programs for preteenagers. In most cases, these basic biological concentrations must and can be developed for individuals classified as having mental retardation. Some youngsters may be restricted for medical reasons—for instance, a child with Down syndrome who has a congenital heart defect, or a youngster whose movement is extremely impaired because of cerebral palsy. Instructors must adapt the curriculum for these special girls and boys and always provide exciting and stimulating programs in place of the strenuous overload activities. For a complete review of health-related physical fitness components, see chapter 7.

It is accepted that strength and endurance abilities are subaverage for individuals with mental retardation (Shephard, 1990). Bar-Or (1987) summarized research on aerobic performance of youngsters of ages 5 through 10. He concluded:

Children have been found to respond to conditioning or specific training regimens. There are results of studies, however, that suggest the aerobic trainability in the first decade of life is lower than would be expected from changes in their athletic performance. A case in point is a study in which 91 children, ages 9 to 10 years, underwent various conditioning regimens for 9 weeks. Even strenuous interval runs . . . undertaken four times a week, did not induce any improvement in their $\dot{V}O_2$max, although their running performance markedly improved. . . . Improved performance . . . can be attributed to either a more efficient running style or a better anaerobic capacity. (pp. 54-55)

Dauer and Pangrazi (1989) agree with Bar-Or: "Particularly in children under 10 years of age, aerobic power appears to increase little with training, even though running performance improves" (p. 12). The question arises whether we should continue writing endurance programs for individuals with mental retardation if they cannot develop aerobic power. Of course we should, and these programs should include walking, jogging, running, swimming, and bike riding. Thus, endurance programs are to include both overload workouts *and* improvement of

walking, jogging, running, swimming, and bike-riding techniques.

Basic physical fitness components of strength and endurance become the foundation for other physical activities. Eichstaedt et al. (1991) compared upper body muscular strength and endurance (flexed arm hang), abdominal and hip flexor strength and endurance (sit-ups for 1 minute), and the 6- and 9-minute runs of individuals classified as having mild or moderate mental retardation, Down syndrome, or no retardation between 9- and 12-years-old (see Table 10.3).

There are certain programmatic considerations when developing programs for strength and endurance: alternate-day opportunities, appropriate intensity, and enough duration to show improvement. Specific activities to improve physical fitness are suggested in Highlight 10.14. These components are thoroughly discussed in the physical fitness section of chapter 7.

Muscular strength has a high correlation with motor performance and motor ability. In other words, motor skill is likely to be better in an individual who has at least an average level of muscular strength than in one whose level is below average. Motor ability has been found to be lower in those labeled as having mental retardation than in their nonretarded peers. Thus, if strength were improved, motor skill might also improve.

Additionally, clumsiness and awkwardness are often encountered in individuals with mental retardation. Eichstaedt et al. (1991) report three test items in their research of students labeled as having mild or moderate retardation or Down syndrome. They used the 15-second basketball wall-bounce (eye/hand coordination), the stork stand (static balance), and the standing long jump (body coordination and explosive leg power). The norms are found in Table 10.4. A review of these scores reinforces the general opinion that there is a need to provide appropriate developmental activities for most 9- to 12-year-old youngsters with mental retardation.

Table 10.3   Median Scores for Girls and Boys 9-12 in Flexed Arm Hang, Sit-Ups, and 6- and 9-Minute Runs

Age	Level of retardation	Flexed arm hang	Sit-ups	6-minute run	9-minute run
Girls					
9	Nonretarded	9 s	29	N/A	1425 yd
	Mild	3	18	835 yd	N/A
	Moderate	5	13	528	N/A
	Down	2	9	368	N/A
10	Nonretarded	9 s	32	N/A	1460 yd
	Mild	5	20	1412 yd	N/A
	Moderate	1	11	790	N/A
	Down	0	10	567	N/A
11	Nonretarded	10 s	34	N/A	1480 yd
	Mild	3	23	1614 yd	N/A
	Moderate	1	12	662	N/A
	Down	1	8	668	N/A
12	Nonretarded	9 s	36	N/A	1590 yd
	Mild	4	25	N/A	1145
	Moderate	2	13	N/A	1044
	Down	1	13	N/A	954
Boys					
9	Nonretarded	N/A	32	N/A	1660 yd
	Mild	6 s	20	1141 yd	N/A
	Moderate	2	12	1070	N/A
	Down	5	8	666	N/A
10	Nonretarded	N/A	34	N/A	1690 yd
	Mild	4 s	18	1059 yd	N/A
	Moderate	2	12	889	N/A
	Down	2	7	767	N/A
11	Nonretarded	N/A	37	N/A	1725 yd
	Mild	8 s	25	1704 yd	N/A
	Moderate	4	15	865	N/A
	Down	2	9	833	N/A
12	Nonretarded	N/A	39	N/A	1760 yd
	Mild	8 s	25	N/A	1284
	Moderate	4	11	N/A	1159
	Down	3	13	N/A	903

Note. Scores for nonretarded: flexed arm hang (girls) compiled from AAHPERD (1976); sit-ups and 6- and 9-minute runs compiled from AAHPERD (1980). Scores for students with mental retardation compiled from Eichstaedt et al., (1991).

Team sports are important in the lives of preteenagers. Most youngsters of this age become engrossed in idolizing professional athletes and their teams. This natural attraction gives physical education instructors and Special Olympics coaches an opportunity to motivate boys and girls toward sport and individual athletic events. Nonretarded preteenagers are generally able to take part in organized team play (e.g., Little League baseball), but some lower

HIGHLIGHT 10.14   **IN PRACTICE**

Physical Fitness Test Items

Agility:

Leg thrusts
Shuttle run (30 and 15 ft)
Squat thrusts or burpee
Line jumps
Zigzag run

Balance:

Balance board activities
Beam-rail-bench walks
Object balance activities
Hopping and skipping activities

Cardiorespiratory endurance:

Bench-step cycling
Hiking
Jogging
Rope jumping
300-yard run
600-yard run-walk
6-, 9-, 12-min runs
1/2-, 1-, 1-1/2-mi runs
Swimming activities

Explosive power arms and shoulders:

Medicine ball throw
Softball throw
Volleyball throw

Flexibility:

Back extension activities
Back lifts
Bend, twist, and touch
Floor touch
Head, chest raise (prone position)
Trunk flexion activities
Windmill
Goniometer

General coordination:

Ball bounce
Roll progression
Softball throw
Standing long jump
Running high jump

Leg power:

Mountain climber
Squat jump
Standing long jump
Vertical jump
Wall jump

Muscular endurance abdominal:

Curls
Isometric activities
Sit-ups
V-sit

Physique:

Classification index
Height
Somatotyping
Weight

Speed:

Dashes (25 to 100 yd)
8-second dash

Strength:

Dynamometer
Hand grip
Isometric activities
Isokinetic activities
Tensiometer

Note. From *Testing for Impaired, Disabled, and Handicapped Individuals* (p. 25) by the American Alliance for Health, Physical Education and Dance, 1975. Copyright 1975 by AAHPERD. Adapted by permission.

Table 10.4   Median Scores for Girls and Boys 9-12 in 15-Second Basketball Wall-Bounce, Stork Stand, and Standing Long Jump

Age	Level of retardation	Basketball wall-bounce	Stork stand	Standing long jump
Girls				
9	Nonretarded	14	22 s	51 in.
	Mild	5	17	39
	Moderate	5	13	26
	Down	2	12	26
10	Nonretarded	n/a	23 s	55 in.
	Mild	9	23	41
	Moderate	5	16	27
	Down	3	13	24
11	Nonretarded	n/a	21 s	60 in.
	Mild	12	24	48
	Moderate	5	17	31
	Down	4	10	25
12	Nonretarded	n/a	21 s	63 in.
	Mild	7	19	51
	Moderate	5	16	28
	Down	4	6	26
Boys				
9	Nonretarded	16	22 s	51 in.
	Mild	12	18	45
	Moderate	7	17	28
	Down	5	8	19
10	Nonretarded	n/a	23 s	58 in.
	Mild	10	17	44
	Moderate	6	14	30
	Down	6	9	20
11	Nonretarded	n/a	22 s	62 in.
	Mild	15	19	52
	Moderate	8	14	36
	Down	7	13	27
12	Nonretarded	n/a	21 s	66 in.
	Mild	17	21	55
	Moderate	6	14	33
	Down	7	6	26

Note. Scores for nonretarded: basketball wall-bounce compiled from Latchaw (1962); stork stand/standing long jump compiled from Arnheim et al. (1979). Scores for students with mental retardation compiled from Eichstaedt et al. (1991).

functioning individuals with mental retardation may need more training and will greatly benefit from sport lead-up games. On the other hand, most children labeled as having mild mental retardation should be able to actively take part in community-sponsored sports. There are also many opportunities for all individuals with mental retardation, 8 years or older, in the 22 competitive sport programs provided by Special Olympics. Refer to chapter 12 for an in-depth analysis and description of the Special Olympics and its role in physical and motor development of persons with mental retardation.

Teenagers: 13- to 18-Year-Olds

The teenage years are often called the period of adolescence. This is the time between childhood and adulthood, when individuals are attempting to free themselves from the roles of children but seem not quite ready to assume the responsibilities of adults. Teenagers with mental retardation are either accepted or rejected because of how they act. ''Age-appropriate'' actions are extremely important. Harrison and Blakemore (1989) list typical social and motor characteristics generally found in teenagers (see Table 10.5), and they suggest how physical education activities may apply to improvement of social and motor skills.

In reference to teenagers labeled as having mental retardation, Drew, Logan, and Hardman (1990) describe the teenage period:

> For the individual with mental retardation, the challenges of adolescence are obviously intensified. Many retarded adolescents have the physical attributes of their nonretarded peers but not the capacity to fully cope with the demands of their environment or with their own desires for emancipation from childhood. For the moderately and severely retarded adolescent whose physical and cognitive differences may be readily apparent, the focus is on the level of social and occupational independence that may be possible in our society. (p. 281)

The development of functional behaviors becomes the basis for successful educational programming. A *functional skill or behavior* is one by which an individual learns control over her or his environment in terms of obtaining positive and consistent results. Patton et al. (1990) ask:

Table 10.5　Typical Social and Motor Characteristics in Teenagers

Characteristics and interests	Implications for programs
Affective domain	
Peer-group and dating activities dominate social lives of students.	Provide appropriate social activities with opportunities to learn leadership and social interaction skills.
Continued conflict between youth and adult values; highly critical of adults and peers.	Provide both peer and adult approval. Help students develop a personal value system.
Interest in personal appearance and social skills.	Help students with ways to improve themselves and to impress others.
Interest in new activities, adventure, and excitement.	Help students choose appropriate risk activities; avoid drugs, etc.
Emotional conflicts continue.	Help students learn stress-reduction techniques.
Increased competitiveness in dating, grades, and athletics.	Provide activities that involve a balance between cooperation and competition.
Psychomotor domain	
Physical maturity results in higher levels of motor ability and fitness, with boys ending up bigger, faster, and stronger than girls.	Use different evaluation standards for boys and girls.
Large appetites continue, but some girls restrict intake.	Be aware of incidence of anorexia nervosa and bulimia among girls.
Coordination improves. Interest in personal development continues.	Develop increased specialization in lifetime activities.

Note. From Joyce M. Harrison and Connie L. Blakemore, *Instructional Strategies for Secondary School Physical Education* (2nd ed.) (p. 113). Copyright © 1989 by Wm. C. Brown Publishers, Dubuque, IA. All rights reserved. Reprinted by permission.

Is it functional for junior high students who are moderately retarded who already have good fine motor skills to spend time randomly stringing beads? Teachers must ask if their particular students would benefit in the long run from this type of specialized training. Is the skill likely to be useful in the students' real-life environments? (p. 317)

Therefore, with these questions in mind, teachers, leaders, and therapists find motor and physical fitness programming can be directed toward

1. improving health (strength, endurance, weight control),
2. developing vocational skills (locomotion, manipulation, eye/hand coordination),
3. increasing motor skill to allow for competitive sport, and
4. learning a wide variety of leisure-time pursuits.

Physical Education Programs

The high school physical education curriculum should concentrate on the following styles and formats (Taylor & Chiogioji, 1987):

1. *Disciplinary*. An activity-centered curriculum in which students perform required specific skills.
2. *Social interaction*. This style is based on emphasizing experiences that will promote socialization.
3. *Personalized*. This is a diagnostic-prescriptive format that is student-centered; students have a great deal of choice among the activities.
4. *Social reordering*. This type of curriculum calls for the teacher to be an agent of change by placing students in positive social situations.
5. *Lifetime activities*. The curriculum is based on activities that can be enjoyed through-

out life; frequently recreational activities; usually they are part of an elective system.
6. *Outdoor or adventure*. This curriculum includes "risky" activities that generate high levels of excitement.

To accomplish these instructional guidelines, children's participation in the following physical development groups is suggested:

- Physical fitness programs
- Individual and dual sports
- Team sports
- Dance
- Aquatics
- Combatives and self-defense
- Outdoor education and adventure activities

The percentage of time spent in each group depends on the age and skill of the participants. Younger teenagers should be involved in a wide variety of activities to provide a solid foundation for the development of advanced skills. Short units in many different activities offer opportunities for students to experience new games and sports. It is during this time that many youngsters become fascinated with lifelong leisure-time games and sports. Activity selection depends on student interest, age, and skill level. Not all students will have the necessary skill levels to be successful in competitive games such as softball or volleyball. Therefore, appropriate lead-up games (and in some cases assignment to the individualized special/adapted physical education program) should be used to increase skill to the point where students are able to achieve unrestricted and active participation in the regular physical education program. Mainstreaming of students with mental retardation must always be done cautiously, because careless placement can cause frustration and failure. Therefore, careful assessment is critical before any placement or teaching can begin. For review of assessment practices, see chapter 3.

Health Improvement

Persons with mental retardation often have minor health deficiences. Something as simple as being unable to "keep up" with friends because of being sickly, weak, and constantly tired is often directly related to poor levels of physical fitness. Again, all physical education programs should include ongoing components devoted to the development of physical fitness. Successful experiences in physical education classes and community recreation programs can develop positive attitudes that often lead to participation in leisure- and lifetime pursuits.

Another negative result of inactivity is unsightly overweight or obesity. Physical activity can be a tremendous boon in controlling weight. Excessive fat has become a major health problem in our society. For people without retardation, Cratty (1989) suggests there is an epidemic of childhood obesity in the United States and believes adult obesity will rise in the coming years. For those with mild mental retardation, Kelly, Rimmer, and Ness (1986) found that approximately 50% of their adult sample (N = 553) were in the obese classification. It is well established that individuals with Down syndrome have excessive fatty (adipose) tissue (Eichstaedt et al., 1991; Krebs, 1990; Patton et al., 1990; Pueschel, 1988). The overall negative affects of being overweight or obese are described by Pueschel (1988):

> Increased body weight may reduce the adolescent's level of activity, affecting his or her capacity to participate in recreational or other activities. Being overweight may also limit a child's exposure to experiences that enhance general development, and it reduces the access to opportunities for social interaction with nonhandicapped peers. Moreover, an individual's physical appearance may be an important factor in his or her social acceptability, since in our society, obesity is usually looked upon as a social stigma. (p. 31)

For a more in-depth analysis of overweight and obesity, see chapter 2.

Vocational Skills Development

Regarding career and vocational skills and transitional planning, Patton et al. (1990) observe that

> our society places a great emphasis on each person's ability to support himself or herself and on that person's ability to contribute to society at large. Even people with conditions like mental retardation are not exempted from this social requirement. Yet statistics . . . have shown that many mentally retarded persons in our society are either unemployed, underemployed, or have difficulty retaining jobs. (p. 343)

Vocational opportunities are usually based on an individual's skills. That is, a person should have the necessary skills to perform a specific job. Without this skill, there is little chance of being employed. Most jobs available to workers with retardation tend to be unskilled or semiskilled. For example, Patton et al. (1990) describe the research of Brolin, where it was reported that 50% of their subjects with mild mental retardation held jobs in service occupations (dishwashers, waitress, maid, janitor); 12% in clerical and sales work; 9% in structured occupations like shop work, carpentry, and maintenance. The other workers held positions in machine trades, benchwork jobs, farming, fishing, and so on. The authors observe: "While these are low-level jobs, they do illustrate what a wide variety of jobs adults with retardation can hold" (p. 358).

Meaningful occupations, as described above, all require certain levels of strength and endurance, without which the employees could not perform successfully over an extended period of time. Having better than average levels of strength and endurance would likely improve the chances for individuals with mental retardation to be employed and retain their positions. Obviously, with very low levels of strength and endurance, a person's likelihood of employment and retention are markedly reduced. Too often, high school prevocational programs tend to disregard the importance of the physical education program. If time constraints dictate that something must be cut from the curriculum, it is often physical education. Physical fitness activities, including activities to improve muscular strength and cardiovascular endurance, must become a top priority when planning for transition from school to vocation.

Competitive Sport

The major outlet for competitive sport for individuals with mental retardation has been the Special Olympics. This organization has developed innumerable opportunities at the local, regional, state, national, and international levels. Many competitors have reached heights comparable to the achievements of their nonretarded peers. In fact, it is not uncommon for teenagers with mental retardation to be active members of their high school interscholastic teams. A case in point is a young man labeled as mildly mentally retarded from Deerfield High School, Deerfield, Illinois, who became an "all-state" football player at the defensive line position of middle guard (Adams, 1990).

For most high-school-age boys and girls with mental retardation, competing on the interscholastic teams means long and hard training routines. There is no shortcut to success in competitive sport. Athletic coaches require the maximum effort from all individuals, whether they are labeled retarded or nonretarded. Athletic participation is designed for the highest level of intensity, and competition is structured within the boundaries of individual versus individual or team versus team. Certain sports are more focused on individual effort (e.g., track, cross-country running, swimming), but all are dedicated to the premise of winning. Public Law

94-142 specifically states that no individual can be denied the opportunity to participate on public school athletic teams, but it must be noted that exacting standards for this level of competition must be achieved by the athlete (this would be particularly true if injury or safety were a concern). Although the process of "cutting" lower skilled individuals from a team can be questioned, it is still universally done by most coaches. The answer is to have more coaches to handle more athletes, but in today's extremely tight public school budgets, this is not realistic. Therefore, except for the highly skilled or intensely competitive, opportunities for teenagers with mental retardation to participate in interscholastic athletics is usually limited.

What does this mean? Does it imply that these individuals cannot be members of their high school teams? No, but it does mean they will have to develop their levels of strength, endurance, and motor skill to those of their peers. The challenge is not only to the teenagers themselves but also to physical education teachers and athletic coaches, who understand the process of developing competitive athletes. No youngster should be denied this opportunity, and students having mental retardation should never be reason for not encouraging, guiding, directing, and even pushing them to reach their physical maximums.

Leisure-Time Pursuits

The world of leisure is open to everyone. Kelly (1990) defines leisure as

activity chosen in relative freedom for its qualities of satisfaction. Yet, even with such simplicity, the variety of activity that may be leisure is staggering. There is no list of even a thousand and one activities that encompasses all leisure. It may be that there is no time and place in which leisure is completely impossible. When leisure is defined as a quality of experience and as the meaning of activity, then it may be almost anything, anywhere, and anytime for someone. (p. 2)

There are four general types of leisure programs for individuals with mental retardation.

1. Integrated programs within the community
2. Segregated programs within the community
3. Sheltered programs where segregation is emphasized
4. Institutional programs where individuals are often given recreational activities with little option for selection

There is no question that physically active leisure-time programs are beneficial for everyone. It is common knowledge that individuals are more likely to participate in activities they enjoy and at which they are successful. The major problem arises when individuals are not given the opportunity to experience new games and activities. To increase their options, persons should have at least minimal levels of strength, endurance, and coordination. Without these attributes, they will likely be relegated to nonactive pursuits such as watching TV, bingo, and cards.

Reducing physical restraints can allow individuals to pursue more physically active games and sports. For example, it is not feasible to expect individuals to bowl well who do not possess enough strength to hold a bowling ball or to make the approach with coordination. Pushing a bowling ball down the alley is appropriate for a youngster, but a teenager who did the same would be laughed at. The role of the physical education teacher, therapeutic recreation leader, or Special Olympics coach is to develop in the individual the strength and coordination to bowl properly. Anything less would relegate their students to having a false sense of accomplishment in an artificial world. The final goal is to develop in individuals the ability to achieve

total integration into activities with the nonretarded. The most exciting outcome of any physical education program is that the students *apply* what they have learned in their daily physical education classes. This application of skill should directly affect the lifestyle and leisure-time pursuits of individuals with mental retardation, otherwise the success of the physical education program is questionable.

The concept of "Unified Sports" developed by Special Olympics International provides sport competition where team members must include an equal number of players with and without retardation. "Partner clubs" are offering exciting opportunities for volunteer participation involving junior high, senior high, and college students to coach similar-age peers classified as having mental retardation. Further descriptions of these programs can be found in chapter 12.

Summary

Physical fitness and motor skill development are important for school-age individuals. Children and adolescents with mental retardation and between 6 and 18 years of age face unique challenges as they progress through public school. As for the nonretarded, these times can be difficult as well as very exciting. Peers tend to judge others in very critical ways. Negative and uncomplimentary comments are often made without thinking, and feelings are hurt. Youngsters are excluded from the "in" group for shallow reasons. The awkward child, the fat child, the physically inept child, to name a few, find it difficult to be included. Excellent physical activity programs can have a direct and positive influence and can help to minimize the characteristics that so often lead to rejection.

This chapter reviewed motor development of primary-age youngsters 6 through 8 and discussed this age group's growth and development, along with motor learning patterns. Basic motor skills were identified, and teaching tips and specific activities for the skills of galloping, skipping, throwing, catching, and striking were provided. Rope jumping, parachute play, scooter play, and beanbag play were also included.

For youngsters 9 through 12, specific motor and physical fitness comparisons were made among individuals with mild or moderate mental retardation, Down syndrome, and no retardation. Items included height, weight, static balance, running speed, running agility, cardiovascular endurance, arm strength, abdominal strength, eye/hand coordination, explosive leg strength, and trunk flexibility. These data were designed to provide a new perspective on the existing levels of motor performance for preteenagers with mental retardation. There appears to be a critical need to increase the inten-

sity of existing physical education and recreation programs. Additionally, activities need to be more appropriately designed to meet the needs of girls and boys with mental retardation.

The teenage years have been explored, and the basic goals of a high school physical education curriculum were presented. For those with mental retardation the following areas have been considered:

- Improvement of general health
- Development of vocational skills
- Inclusion in competitive sports
- Leisure-time pursuits

A cooperative approach among physical education, special/adapted physical education, community recreation, and therapeutic recreation was also discussed.

DISCUSSIONS AND NEW DIRECTIONS

1. What height and weight differences are found among primary-age children (6-8) who have mild mental retardation, moderate mental retardation, or Down syndrome?

2. Are there developmental differences in the motor area between children with and children without mental retardation? Also, consider the area of physical fitness—is there recent research to substantiate your conclusions?

3. Is it appropriate to mainstream *all* children with mental retardation into regular physical education classes? What options are available for students who function at significantly lower levels of performance?

4. Can individuals with mental retardation learn basic motor skills? Describe how you will modify your teaching methods for students with moderate mental retardation.

5. Will preteenagers (9-12) with mental retardation be able to improve their levels of physical fitness? Are these same youngsters as clumsy as their nonretarded counterparts?

6. What unique contributions does physical education provide for teenagers with mental retardation? Discuss how participation in a physical education program can improve the likelihood of getting and keeping a job.

7. Explore the possible differences between participation on a Special Olympics team and an interscholastic athletic team? What should a teenager with mental retardation expect when going out for an athletic team? What demands will be placed on the athlete?

References

Adams, P.A. (1990). Personal communication, 12 June, 1990.

American Heart Association (1989). *Jump rope for heart—Special populations guidelines*. Dallas: American Heart Association.

Bar-Or, O. (1987). Importance of differences between children and adults for exercise testing and exercise prescription. In J.S. Skinner (Ed.), *Exercise testing and exercise prescription for special cases* (pp. 49-65). Philadelphia: Lea & Febiger.

Bouffard, M. (1990). Movement problem solutions by educable mentally handicapped individuals. *Adapted Physical Activity Quarterly*, **7**, 183-197.

Cratty, B.J. (1986). *Perceptual and motor development in infants and children* (3rd ed.). Englewood Cliffs, NJ: Prentice Hall.

Cratty, B.J. (1989). *Adapted physical education in the mainstream* (2nd ed.). Denver: Love.

Dauer, V.P., & Pangrazi, R.P. (1989). *Dynamic physical education for elementary school children* (9th ed.). New York: Macmillan.

Del Rey, P., & Stewart, D. (1989). Organizing input for mentally retarded subjects to enhance memory and transfer. *Adapted Physical Activity Quarterly*, **6**, 247-254.

Drew, C.J., Logan, D.R., & Hardman, M.L. (1990). *Mental retardation* (4th ed.). Columbus, OH: Merrill.

Dunn, J.M., & Fait, H. (1989). *Special physical education* (6th ed.). Dubuque, IA: Brown.

Dunn, J.M., Morehouse, J.W., Jr., & Fredericks, H.D.B. (1986). *Physical education for the severely handicapped*. Austin, TX: Pro-Ed.

Du Randt, R. (1985). Ball-catching proficiency among 4-, 6-, and 8-year-old girls. In J.E. Clark & J.H. Humphrey (Eds.), *Motor development: Current selected research* (Vol. 1). Princeton, NJ: Princeton Book.

Eckert, H.M. (1987). *Motor Development* (3rd ed.). Indianapolis: Benchmark.

Eichstaedt, C.B., & Kalakian, L.H. (1987). *Developmental/adapted physical education: Making ability count* (2nd ed.). New York: Macmillan.

Eichstaedt, C.B., Wang, P.Y., Polacek, J.J., & Dohrmann, P.F. (1991). *Physical fitness and motor skill levels of individuals with mental retardation: Mild, moderate, and individuals with Down syndrome: Ages 6-20*. Normal: Illinois State University Printing Services.

Gagnon, J., Tousignant, M., & Martel, D. (1989). Academic learning time in physical education classes for mentally handicapped students. *Adapted Physical Activity Quarterly*, **6**, 280-289.

Harrison, J.M., & Blakemore, C.L. (1989). *Instructional strategies for secondary school physical education* (2nd ed.). Dubuque, IA: Brown.

Horgan, J.S. (1983). Mnemonic strategy instruction in coding, processing, and recall of movement related cues by the mentally retarded. *Perceptual and Motor Skills*, **57**, 547-557.

Horgan, J.S. (1985). Issues in memory for movement with mentally retarded children. In J.E. Clark & J.H. Humphrey (Eds.), *Motor development: Current selected research* (Vol. 1). Princeton, NJ: Brinceton Book.

Horvat, M. (1990). *Physical education and sport for exceptional students*. Dubuque, IA: Brown.

Kelly, L.E. (1989). *Project I CAN—ABC*. Charlottesville: University of Virginia.

Kelly, L.E., Rimmer, J.H., & Ness, R.A. (1986). Obesity levels in institutionalized mentally retarded adults. *Adapted Physical Activity Quarterly*, **3**, 167-176.

Kelly, J.R. (1990). *Leisure* (2nd ed.). Englewood Cliffs, NJ: Prentice Hall.

Kelly, L.E. Personal communication, May 10, 1990.

Kirchner, G. (1988). *Physical education for*

elementary school children (7th ed.). Dubuque, IA: Brown.

Krebs, P.L. (1990). Mental retardation. In J.P. Winnick (Ed.), *Adapted physical education and sport* (pp. 153-176). Champaign, IL: Human Kinetics.

Lavay, B., & Horvat, M. (1989, November). *Jump rope for heart: Special populations guidelines*. Paper presented at the 18th Physical Activity Conference for Exceptional Individuals, Riverside, CA.

McClenaghan, B.A., & Gallahue, D.L. (1978). *Fundamental movement: A developmental approach*. Philadelphia: Saunders.

Nash, J.B. (1963). *Physical education: Its interpretations and objectives*. Dubuque, IA: Brown.

Newell, K.M. (1984). Physical constraints to development of motor skills. In J.R. Thomas (Ed.), *Motor development during childhood and adolescence*. Minneapolis: Burgess.

Nichols, B. (1990). *Moving and learning* (2nd ed.). St. Louis: Times Mirror/Mosby.

Patton, J.R., Payne, J.S., & Beirne-Smith, M. (1990). *Mental retardation* (3rd ed.). Columbus, OH: Merrill.

Payne, V.G., & Isaacs, L.D. (1991). *Human motor development: A lifespan approach* (2nd ed.). Mountain View, CA: Aspen.

Pueschel, S.M. (Ed.) (1988). *The young person with Down syndrome: Transition from adolescence to adulthood*. Baltimore: Brooks.

Shephard, R.J. (1990). *Fitness in special populations*. Champaign, IL: Human Kinetics.

Taylor, J.L., & Chiogioji, E.N. (1987). Implications of educational reform on high school P.E. programs. *Journal of Physical Education, Recreation and Dance*, **58**, 22-23.

Thomas, K.T. (1984). Applying knowledge of motor development to mentally retarded children. In J.R. Thomas (Ed.), *Motor development during childhood and adolescence*. Minneapolis: Burgess.

Titus, J.A., & Watkinson, E.J. (1987). Effects of segregated and integrated programs on the participation and social integration of moderately mentally handicapped children at play. *Adapted Physical Activity Quarterly*, **4**, 204-219.

U.S. Office of Education. Federal Register. The Individuals With Disabilities Education Act, formerly The Education for All Handicapped Children Act of 1975, Section 94-142, 99-457, 89-750, 42 U.S.C., Section 42480-54579, (1977).

Werder, J.K., & Bruininks, R.H. (1990). Motor skills—vital to children's self-esteem, say body skills authors. *Special Education Teacher*, **2**, 1-3.

Wessel, J. (1976). *I CAN*. Northbrook, IL: Hubbard.

CHAPTER 11

Physical Activity for Adults: Leisure and Lifetime Activities

PREVIEW Lisa is now "on her own," and she feels good. Many of her friends have moved away from their parents and are living in apartments or group homes. The feeling is exciting, and her new home is wonderful. She is living with six other friends in an old but nice part of town. She went to school with most of them, except Bob—and that is no problem, because he is a dream. Mr. and Mrs. McGraw, the houseparents, are warm and friendly and seem eager to help whenever needed. The food is okay, but she misses her dad's spaghetti a lot.

Lisa works at Susie's Cafe, only six blocks from her new home, and puts in 30 hours a week. The money she makes helps pay her room and board and still leaves her enough to save $5.00 a week—even with her weekly bowling expenses. Yes, she belongs to a bowling team, which is sponsored by the local park district. Again, most of the teams are made up of old schoolmates and her other Special Olympics friends. She truly looks forward to Wednesday evenings, and her average has gone up to 123, six pins higher than last fall.

Her job is easy enough, cleaning tables, sweeping floors, and carrying dishes and silverware. She is glad she doesn't have to do dishes. She is tired at the end of the day and most of the time likes to take a nap before supper. She wishes she weren't so tired and wonders if everyone feels this way at the end of a workday.

An interesting thing happened about a week ago. Just by chance she began watching a program on TV that shows people in an aerobic dance class. The music is good, and the men and women look like they are having fun. Lisa wonders if she could do these activities. The leader on the TV show says aerobic dance will help her to get stronger and move better and eventually even make her "less tired at the end of her day." She thinks the park district has a class like this one, and tomorrow she will ask Mrs. McGraw to look into it for her. She is anxious about this new opportunity. What night will it be held? How much will it cost? Would any of her friends like to go? Will it really help her be not so tired at the end of the day?

Lisa thinks it is fun being an adult. She likes her town and looks forward to making new friends. There are so many wonderful things to do!

HIGHLIGHT QUESTIONS

- Describe the positive outcomes of participation in physical activities for adults with mental retardation.
- How can improvement in levels of physical fitness affect the job potential for adults with mental retardation?
- Are there minimal levels of physical fitness or motor skill ability to take part in leisure pursuits? If so, how would these minimal levels affect a person who wants to learn to bowl, swim, play volleyball, go outdoor camping, or to go pleasure walking?
- With reference to leisure pursuits and adults with mental retardation, compare and contrast *each* of the following groups and their participation in *all* of the listed activities. Consider entry levels of physical fitness, motor skills, safety, necessity for one-on-one assistance, and potential opportunities for integrated or segregated community programs.

Group	*Activity*
Adults with Mild MR	Jogging
Adults with Down syndrome	Special Olympics basketball
Adults with moderate MR	Recreational swimming
Adults with severe MR	Table tennis
Adults with profound MR	Bowling
	Square dancing

- **Which agencies (local, state, national, international) are available to assist adults with mental retardation in their leisure pursuits? in their desire to be involved in athletic competition?**

One of the most challenging topics facing society today is the integration of adults with mental retardation into the mainstream of everyday life. The transition from the highly structured public school environment, with its Public Law 94-142 emphasis, to the intensely competitive adult world is oftentimes shocking. Will (1984) describes this period:

> Transition is a period that includes high school, the point of graduation, additional postsecondary education or adult services, and the initial years in employment. Transition is a bridge between the security and structure of the school and the opportunities and risks of adult life. Any bridge requires both a solid span and a secure foundation at either end. The transition from school to work and adult life requires sound preparation in the secondary school, adequate support at the point of school leaving, and secure opportunities and services, if needed, in adult situations. (p. 3)

Haring and Field (1990) make special reference to Will's definition of transition: "It is noteworthy that Will's definition includes the importance of providing quality secondary-school and adult services, as well as linkage services, within the scope of transition programming" (p. 523).

Many persons who are mentally retarded are now living in community settings and are dealing with the same problems that everyone must face in adulthood, with its difficulties, pleasures, and complexities. Many find community life not too complicated, but for others, everyday challenges are difficult and are not easily managed. Lack of acceptance and of equal opportunity for persons with mental retardation will always be an obstacle unless these individuals have physi-

cal skills and motor ability to fit into the job market. It must be emphasized that it will be necessary to develop *above average* levels of proficiency, which must include higher standards of strength and endurance than found in the nonretarded population. If they are to compete for jobs, they must offer something special to their future employers.

National estimates of future population trends indicate a tremendous increase in numbers of adults in the United States, particularly in people over 65. It is predicted (MacNeil, 1988) that individuals over 65 will grow from the current 28 million to 35 million by the year 2000, and over 64 million by 2030 (see Figure 11.1). A significant number of these will be people who have been labeled as having mental retardation. Most people with mental retardation (as many

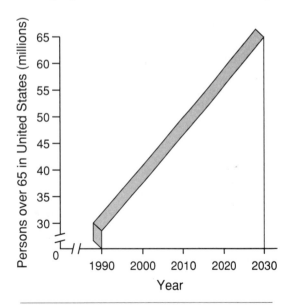

Figure 11.1 Estimated increases in the population size of persons over 65 in the United States, 1990-2030.

as 90%) will possess the intellectual ability to function successfully in the job market, provided they have the basic physical skills. The other side of these statistics is highlighted by the fact that most individuals with mental retardation earn substantially less than $4,500 a year (Wehman & Hill, 1985). Edgar (1987) describes the implications. He has found that any salary under $7,000 per year would not allow an individual to live independently. According to Patton, Payne, and Beirne-Smith (1990), "it has become increasingly clear that the status of adults with disabilities can be described in the following ways: high rates of unemployment, part-time employment, and underemployment; less education; low income levels; lack of mobility; and inadequate preparation for adulthood. These descriptors hold for those with mental retardation as well" (p. 372).

Something seems to be grossly wrong. Why can't persons with lower intellectual functioning be employed in jobs that would pay at least minimal wages? Siegel et al. (1990) believe that present-day vocational special education is primarily concerned with the efficient learning of a large number of job-related skills. The major thrust is to make sure skills learned in a training setting will transfer to a real work setting and be maintained after the student has moved from the school to the workplace. Edgerton (1988) observes:

> It can be said now . . . that although relatively few persons with mental retardation become fully self-reliant, *most* people with mild mental retardation, and a sizable percentage of those with more moderate degrees of handicap, can achieve a semi-independent adjustment to life in community settings *if* 1) they are given enough time to learn coping skills, *and* 2) they have the support of other persons. (p. 311)

Vocational opportunities and employment are possible only if people have the necessary skills to be employed, and health and fitness are as important as actual vocational training. It is clear that healthy individuals who have above-average levels of physical fitness are more likely to be successful in vocational pursuits. When these components (motor skill, health, and physical fitness) are working in unison, then individuals will have reached competitive levels of economic opportunity. The ongoing cycle of adult independence, which includes steady employment with sufficient financial gain, will usually allow individuals free time to engage in leisure and recreational activities. Jansma, Ersing, and McCubbin (1986) summarize the findings of their thorough study of 71 adults labeled as having mental retardation: "Without question, the increases in physical fitness performance demonstrate that with the use of a functionally appropriate curriculum and a systematic approach, these subjects [adults with mental retardation] can improve their level of physical fitness and promote a more healthy lifestyle which assists in preparation for deinstitutionalization" (p. 84).

Leisure and Recreation

Success, happiness, and an exciting quality of life seem to require well-balanced emotional and personal attributes. Edgerton (1988) strongly believes that these psychosocial components are more influential than cognitive ability in successful community adaptation. Thus, there appears to be a definite need for positive social relationships to develop self-esteem and personal satisfaction. Leisure-time activities can be an excellent means for developing social and emotional outlets. Kelly (1990) says that leisure is "a part of the rhythm of life, freedom, and self-development [and] is important to the wholeness of human life. Leisure is good for people" (p. 11). He continues: "In the chosen activities and relationships of leisure, the bonding of intimate groups such as the family and larger groups of the community takes place. In short, a society needs leisure so that people can learn to live together'' (p. 12).

Searle and Iso-Ahola (1988) found an interesting relationship between existing health levels and the intensity and diversity of leisure behavior of elderly people. Recreationally active adults tend to be more healthy than their counterparts who are less active. This indicates a strong need to develop and maintain positive levels of physical fitness in all adults, particularly those with mental retardation. Blair (1985) hypothesized that most individuals with disabilities are at the bottom of the continuum when comparing their cardiovascular fitness and activity levels with nondisabled sedentary individuals, active working people, recreational aerobic participants, and competitive athletes. Figure 11.2 illustrates Blair's theory. There is little doubt that adults with disabilities, including those with mental retardation, are in desperate need of developing a lifestyle that includes regular cardiovascular stimulation.

Community recreation for individuals with mental retardation is potentially one of the most dynamic methods by which these adults can attain an exciting and rewarding quality of life. Schleien and Ray (1988) describe the overall importance of community recreation: ''Participation in leisure and recreation activities is an important aspect of life in our society. When such activities meet the needs of individuals, they promote physical health and conditioning, provide opportunities to develop social relations, and lead to the development of new skills'' (p. 1).

Leisure participation can be expanded from the nearness of the community to include the vastness of all outdoors. Summerfield (1990) observes that ''the leisure experience in the outdoors may include recreation, education, appreciation/spirituality, challenge/adventure, and exploration'' (p. 31). In some cases very little experience is necessary to enjoy outdoor activities. Most community recreation programs offer

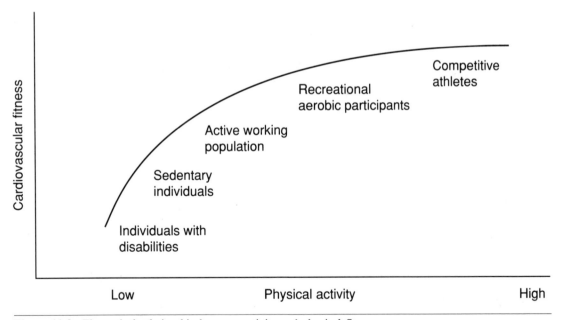

Figure 11.2 Theoretical relationship between activity and physical fitness.
Note. From ''Physical Activity Leads to Fitness and Pays Off'' by S.N. Blair, 1985, *The Physician and Sportsmedicine*, **13**(3), p. 154. Copyright 1985. Reprinted by permission of McGraw-Hill, Inc.

day-long trips to places like forest preserves, where hiking trails are usually found in abundance.

More extensive trips include overnight experiences and can extend from 2 days to several weeks. Camping can be extremely rewarding and promotes development of self-confidence and independence. Partner clubs have proven beneficial when adults with mental retardation are teamed up with nonretarded friends, a form of limited integration that replaces the extensive supervision that was required in the past for most groups with mental retardation. Local community recreation programs usually find this technique a viable option and are likely to endorse and subsidize ventures of this type. When adults with mental retardation have become experienced, that is, can learn to take care of themselves with a minimum of assistance, it is likely they are ready for full integration into traditional activities. Level of functioning and desire on the part of the individual (to be integrated) are key factors when instructors suggest it is time to try programs with persons without disabilities.

An individual's present level of motor skill in a particular activity (e.g., swimming) is an important consideration when determining which activities are most likely to provide success and satisfaction for that person. Swimming instruction, for example, is usually planned with skill progressions in mind. The learning sections, such as beginner, advanced beginner, intermediate, advanced, and competitive, allow for maximum teacher effectiveness and are based on the concept that teaching can be enhanced when students possess similar rather than different abilities. Mainstreaming is much easier if recreation programs offer activities with different entry grouping levels based on ability. In some cases, the therapeutic recreation specialist would be called on to provide instruction for individuals who need special attention.

National Therapeutic Recreation Society

The National Therapeutic Recreation Society,

a branch of the National Recreation and Parks Association, defines its purpose as follows: "The purpose of therapeutic recreation is to facilitate the development, maintenance, and expression of an appropriate leisure lifestyle for individuals with physical, mental, emotional, and social limitations" (Kennedy, Austin, & Smith, 1987, p. 12).

The dimensions of therapeutic recreation services are broad and deep. Peterson and Gunn (1984) aptly describe three areas of service:

1. Treatment
2. Leisure education
3. Recreation participation

It appears that each area would service individuals with different needs.

Treatment is critical for those who cannot function independently due to disease or disability. Permanent impairments cannot necessarily be treated; the individuals will be assisted to overcome these barriers, but little can be done to diminish the impairment. Most assistance comes under the direction of a physician or therapist.

Leisure education is an avenue by which recreation leaders provide exciting learning environments for leisure activities. The instructors are either trained to lead individuals with disabilities (e.g., therapeutic recreation specialist) or are traditional community recreation teachers. Different techniques are employed by the instructors, depending on the learning capabilities of the participants. For lower functioning individuals, more time is necessary to assure that the skills are completely learned and progressions are attained with success and safety.

Recreation participation is the ultimate goal of community recreation and therapeutic recreation. Here participants select the activities they are interested in, and limitations derive from the number and variety of activity offerings, the flexibility and creative abilities of the instructors, and the physical and mental entry levels of the participants. To assure totally effective and appropriate community leisure and recreation programs for all citizens, including those with mental retardation, limitations must be kept to a minimum.

Compton (1989) questions whether these services are being developed in both clinical and community settings:

> It is a fact that public recreation has not fulfilled its responsibility to meet the play, recreation, and leisure needs of those special populations who reside in their communities. Reasons given are varied and quite vague. Over the past decade, public recreation has seemingly lost its sense of responsibility. Programs that are based on high physical skills, are team-oriented, and highly competitive, are the maven of public recreation today. Those who are skilled, affluent, and prefer a particular style engagement are catered to because of growing needs to commercialize the services. This approach excludes many from participating in a functionally integrated manner. (p. 489)

The answer to meeting the recreational needs of individuals with mental retardation is not easy unless the participants are able to take part in regular activities designed for the nondisabled. The lack of special funding for instructors, equipment, and facility accessibility is an ever-present roadblock to providing appropriate programs. However, special recreation programs, which usually employ certified therapeutic recreation specialists, are becoming integral units in a large number of community recreation programs in the United States, and the many communities that have made these commitments should serve as models for others to follow.

Therapeutic Recreation Specialist

The therapeutic recreation specialist (TRS), a key professional in the transdisciplinary team, has been trained to meet the needs of individuals with disabilities. Crawford and Mendell (1987) provide goals for therapeutic recreation specialists to achieve:

> To educate toward quality leisure functioning, and to use leisure and recreation to improve, correct, habilitate, or rehabilitate the physical, social-emotional, and intellectual functional abilities of mentally retarded individuals. Although not a curative itself, therapeutic recreation as a part of treatment can be a catalyst for substantial improvement in a person's overall functional capacities and abilities. (p. 1)

If agencies find that therapeutic recreation specialists are necessary to meet the needs of people with disabilities but lack funds to hire them, neighboring communities could create a working agreement to hire a "traveling" or itinerant TRS consultant. This person would provide assistance in such areas as activity modifications and evaluation (Schleien & Ray, 1988).

Integration or Segregation in Recreation Programs?

Integration and segregation should be viewed not as either/or alternatives but as two options by which professionals can best meet the needs of recreation participants. Ideally, integration is the best choice, but if this is not for the good of some persons, then special segregated programs are viable options. Schleien and Ray (1988) observe: "A continuum of leisure service options for persons with disabilities ranges from segregated, special recreation programs focusing on skill development within homogeneous (i.e., handicapped-specific) groups (e.g., craft activity for persons with developmental disabilities) to integrated programs" (p. 21). The key factor is that all people have the opportunity to do what they want to do. Barriers of omission, that is, the inadvertent exclusion of people because they do not fit into the mainstream of society, are to be avoided at all costs.

Rancourt (1989) provides an interesting solution to the integration/segregation controversy:

The issue is not one of entitlement, but one of ensuring access to the continuum of service settings based on an accurate asssessment of the person's functional ability and the protection of his or her right to be in the least restrictive environment. This mandates a range of age and disability integrated services as well as age and disability segregated services, depending on the functional level of the person. (p. 49)

Exclusion from community recreation programs still happens, but one of the major hurdles is innate apathy and lack of desire on the part of people to do nothing but watch television. Individuals with mental retardation have been known to sit and do nothing unless they were stimulated into activity by others. Mobily (1989) acknowledges this problem: "We can be fairly certain that some patients will refuse to participate in recreation programs we offer. Said differently, if we know recreation is good for people . . . and they still refuse to participate, then what should the TR [therapeutic recreation] practitioner do?" (p. 126). A long-endorsed tenet in physical education is that if individuals are introduced to and taught many different activities, they will desire to pursue the most enjoyable ones in their leisure time. Therefore, involvement in a broad range of individual and team activities should be integral components of all good physical education and recreational programs.

Schloss, Smith, and Kiehl (1986) describe the success found when adults with mental retardation were provided opportunity to take part in an integrated program based on a philosophy of normalization. The basic guidelines included

- progression toward independence,
- development of age-appropriate and functional skills,
- participation in the mainstream of society, and
- taking risks warranted by potential benefits.

The instructors followed six sequential steps in the developmental progression of the program:

1. Identification of recreational opportunities available in the community
2. Development of a checklist and task analysis of various recreational activities
3. Observation of the adults participating in the newly introduced activity
4. Participation in the activity without assistance
5. Development of various intervention strategies for individuals who require assistance
6. Administration of a posttest for adults participating in the activity without assistance

The authors concluded their findings by listing the general benefits of the program. They found that

- activities were conducted in the community, as participation was not limited by the availability of specialized funding or facilities,
- training focuses on skills necessary for successful participation in the community,
- skill training emphasizes the minimal amount of assistance needed for the adult's success, and
- assistance is reduced as the adult's skill level increases.

Persons with mental retardation could be more easily integrated into the mainstream of common recreation activities if they had the fundamental skills necessary to be successful. In many cases, something as simple as improvement of leg strength and endurance could mean the difference between failure and success. Programmatic considerations, including teaching and training, should follow the trends for nonretarded individuals.

Skill learning can be either informal or structured. Structured programs are usually offered in community recreation programs, including outdoor camping environments. Classes can last for a few sessions or for several months. These classes are open to all members of the community, and should be available to those with mental retardation. Minimal levels of strength, endurance, and motor skill are desirable for entrance levels of participation. Most "regular" instructors (e.g., those not trained to teach persons with disabilities) may have apprehensions when faced with an individual needing very special considerations. For example, even something as simple as a jogging program to improve cardiovascular efficiency may cause difficulties for the participant with mental retardation who is in a wheelchair. There should be modifications and adaptations made for this person, but this will demand creative thinking on the part of the instructor. It is hoped that individuals with disabilities will have had the benefit of specially trained instructors while in the public schools. The influence of PL 94-142, and the mandated inclusion of physical education, should have given thousands of individuals with mental retardation an opportunity to develop skill in leisure activities while still in the public school setting. Sherrill (1986) responds to the role of the public school adapted physical education specialist in reference to leisure:

> The adapted physical education specialist should assume the responsibility for helping students acquire the attitude, knowledge, skill, and habits necessary for optimal leisure functioning, both as participants and spectators in various games, sports and dance. Without competences most persons lead entirely passive lives without sufficient vigorous exercise to maintain physical and mental health. (p. 154)

Simmons Market Research Bureau (1985) surveyed participation in the most common sport activities. They sampled 18,000 households and determined at which age individuals were most likely to participate in each of the 11 different activities. The greatest percentage selected swimming, bowling, and jogging as their main areas of participation. Table 11.1 lists these comparisons. This information may assist community recreation program administrators when developing long-range activity plans. People without retardation are likely to select the same age-appropriate activities as people with mental

Table 11.1   Percentage of Sport Participation, by Age

Activity	Age					
	18-24	25-34	35-44	45-54	55-64	65+
Golf	10.3	10.4	9.5	8.5	8.8	4.9
Bowling	28.1	23.4	19.2	15.6	10.4	5.7
Swimming	43.0	43.1	37.8	28.8	19.0	8.8
Downhill skiing	7.4	7.1	5.2	3.8	1.4	0.6
Jogging	23.0	18.6	13.8	10.6	6.0	3.4
Tennis	15.2	11.1	8.8	5.2	2.8	1.5
Racquetball	11.3	8.2	4.7	2.8	1.0	0.7
Softball/baseball	14.9	12.8	8.6	4.5	2.4	0.8
Volleyball	12.8	8.8	6.3	3.3	1.3	0.9
Basketball	12.3	8.0	4.8	2.5	2.0	1.0
Football	11.0	3.0	1.8	1.4	1.2	0.9

Note. From Simmons Market Research Bureau, Inc. (1985). Reprinted with permission.

retardation. If differences are found, then special offerings must be considered.

Outdoor recreation is extremely popular. Bicycling, hiking, backpacking, fishing, and so on are less structured than sport activities. Table 11.2 lists 16 common outdoor activities and indicates which are most often selected by adults.

Activity Selection

People usually choose recreation and leisure activities that they believe will be enjoyable and, in some cases, challenging. Sometimes individuals cannot find any interesting activity on the community program schedule, and the activities they are interested in cannot be scheduled,

Table 11.2 Percentage of the Adult Population Who Engage in Various Outdoor Recreation Activities

Activity	Total (%)	Male (%)	Female (%)
Swimming	31.7	32.1	31.3
Bicycling	14.6	14.2	14.9
Fishing			
Saltwater	4.4	6.4	2.6
Fly casting	2.9	4.5	1.5
Other fresh water	13.0	18.8	7.8
Camping	11.6	12.2	11.0
Hiking/backpacking	8.7	8.9	8.5
Hunting	7.0	12.5	2.1
Boating/powerboating	6.7	8.2	5.4
Downhill skiing	4.5	5.3	3.8
Horseback riding	4.2	3.8	4.5
Sailing	2.9	3.1	2.7
Cross-country skiing	2.5	2.5	2.5
Snowmobiling	2.5	3.2	1.8
Dirt/trail motorcycling	2.3	3.0	1.6
Skin diving/snorkeling	1.9	2.6	1.2

Note. From Simmons Market Research Bureau, Inc. (1985). Reprinted by permission.

because there would be too few participants. In these cases, organized activities can be nicely replaced by informal leisure pursuits, such as walking, jogging, or bike riding. And some people would rather be alone on occasion, and it is not appropriate to force them into group activities.

The *Hope Newsletter* (1986) offers an interesting approach to the selection of leisure activities. Descriptions of activities begin with questions, such as "If you love the outdoors. . . ," or "If you like company . . . ," or "If you're easily bored . . . ." These guides may help an individual make interesting choices. Figure 11.3 lists 16 recreational options and includes guideline statements for possible selections. When one is choosing activities, the level of fitness and skill required by each activity must be taken into consideration.

Sport activities are generally designed for performers with higher skill levels, but certainly all sport activities must originate at the beginner level. Individual and team sports require somewhat different degrees of ability and interest. Lead-up drills and games are usually used by instructors to develop needed skills in an activity. Gallahue (1989) breaks down common sports into the skills needed to learn them, and he notes the areas that he feels need emphasis. For example, specific locomotor, manipulative, and stability skills are listed (see Figure 11.4). These groupings are very helpful when planning programs for individuals with differing motor abilities and cognitive levels.

With regard to leisure and social interaction, Edgerton (1988) notes that "many of these people [with mental retardation] combat their loneliness by absorbing themselves in passive recreational activities such as watching television or listening to music" (p. 313). There is no doubt that many adults without retardation thoroughly enjoy television and music, but it is hoped there might be a positive blending of passive and active leisure-time pursuits. For example, walking and jogging are nicely complemented by the use of cassette music on a portable player.

	Aerobic dance	Aerobicize	Basketball	Cross-country skiing	Cycling (indoor)	Cycling (outdoor)	Handball, racquetball	Jogging	Minitrampoline	Rope skipping	Rowing (indoor)	Skating (ice or roller)	Soccer	Swimming (indoor lap)	Tennis (singles)	Walking
If you're out of shape	●				●	●			●	●	●			●		●
If you're in *great* shape	●	●	●	●	●	●	●	●		●	●	●	●	●	●	
If you want to be alone					●	●		●	●	●	●	●		●		●
If you like company	●	●	●	●		●	●	●				●	●		●	●
If you hate to sweat														●		
If you love the *indoors*	●	●	●		●		●		●	●	●	●		●		
If you love the *outdoors*				●		●		●				●	●		●	●
If you have joint problems					●				●					●		●
If you don't have much time					●			●	●	●	●					
If you're *easily* bored	●	●	●	●		●	●					●	●		●	
If you're competitive		●					●	●				●	●	●	●	
If you can't spend much		●								●			●			●
If you want to be flexible			●	●				●				●			●	
If shorts are "too revealing"				●	●	●			●		●					●

Figure 11.3 Guidelines for selecting leisure-time activities.
Note. From *Hope Newsletter*, April 1986, p. 3. Copyright 1986 by HOPE Publications. Reprinted with permission, HOPE Publications, Kalamazoo, Michigan, (616) 343-0770.

Activities to Improve Physical Fitness

The American way of life for adults is being transformed by concerns for better health. More people are walking, jogging, running, biking, and attending aerobic exercise classes than ever before. These are positive trends, but there are still major problems. Most Americans ride in cars or buses rather than walk, use elevators instead of stairs, and sit at home during free time rather than being physically active. They are also spending millions of dollars a year for weight reduction programs. Today only a few occupations require vigorous physical exertion. These facts are true not only for persons without disabilities but also for those with mental reatrdation. The detailed study by Fernhall and Tymeson (1987) indicates that aerobic fitness of young adults with mental retardation is much lower than would be expected in individuals without retardation. However, one of the most

Sport skill themes	Locomotor skills stressed	Manipulative skills stressed	Stability skills stressed
Basketball sport skills	Running Sliding Leaping Jumping	Passing Tipping Catching Blocking Shooting Dribbling Rebounding	Selected axial movement skills Pivoting Blocking Dodging Cutting Guarding Faking Picking
Combative sport skills	Stepping Sliding Hopping (karate)	Dexterity (fencing) Striking (kendo)	All axial movement skills Dodging and feinting Static balance skills Dynamic balance skills
Dance skills	Running Hopping Leaping Skipping Jumping Sliding Stepping		All axial movement skills Static balance postures Dynamic balance postures
Disc sport skills	Stepping Running Jumping	Tossing Catching	All axial movement skills Static balance postures Dynamic balance postures
Football sport skills	Running Jumping Sliding Leaping	Passing Kicking Catching Punting Carrying Centering	Blocking Pivoting Tackling Dodging
Gymnastic skills	Running Leaping Jumping Hopping Skipping Landing		Inverted supports Rolling, landing All axial movement skills Static balance tricks Dynamic balance tricks
Implement striking sport skills (tennis, squash, racketball, hockey, lacrosse, golf)	Running Sliding Leaping Skating Walking	Forehand Lob Backhand Smash Striking Drop Driving Throwing Putting Catching Chipping Trapping	Dynamic balance skills Turning Twisting Stretching Bending Dodging Pivoting
Skiing sport skills	Stepping Walking Running Sliding	Poling	All axial movement skills Dynamic balance skills Static balance skills

(Cont.)

Figure 11.4 Selected sport skills.

Note. From David L. Gallahue, *Understanding Motor Development: Infants, Children, Adolescents,* 2nd ed. Copyright ©
1989 by Benchmark Press, Inc. Reprinted by permission of Wm. C. Brown Communications, Inc., Dubuque, Iowa. All
Rights Reserved.

Sport skill themes	Locomotor skills stressed	Manipulative skills stressed		Stability skills stressed
Soccer sport skills	Running Jumping Leaping Sliding	Kicking Trapping Juggling Throwing Blocking	Passing Dribbling Catching Rolling	Tackling Feinting Marking Turning Dodging
Softball/baseball skills	Running Jumping Sliding Leaping	Throwing Catching	Pitching Batting Bunting	Selected axial movement skills Dynamic balance skills Dodging
Target sport skills		Aiming Shooting		Static balance skills
Track and field skills	Vertical jumping Horizontal jumping Running Leaping Hopping Starting	Baton passing Shot put Hammer Discus Pole vault Javelin Throwing		All axial movement skills Dynamic balance skills
Volleyball sport skills	Jumping Running Diving Sliding Sprawling Rolling	Serving Dig Volleying Spike Bump Dink Block		Dynamic balance skills Selected axial movements

Figure 11.4   (Continued)

visible and encouraging trends is the growing concern by professionals for the health and physical fitness of all people, including those with mental retardation. If the United States is to prosper and its citizens are to be healthy, more emphasis must be placed on adult fitness. Shephard (1990) describes the importance of health and fitness for individuals with disabilities and instructors and leaders who work with them:

Professional recognition of the social and economic potential of the successfully rehabilitated disabled person has led to the introduction of an increasing number of university courses and programs in adapted physical activity . . . . Graduates from such programs have sought to help the disabled to develop personal fitness (thus countering some of the medical hazards of a sedentary lifestyle), to move with greater efficiency (thus making better use of their restricted physiological potential), and to find pleasure in active recreation (thus addressing some of the adverse psychological effects of disability). (p. viii)

Aerobic Exercise

Aerobic exercise, that is, brisk and sustained activity, contributes to good health in numerous ways. It improves the efficiency of the heart and increases the amount of oxygen that the body can produce in a given amount of time. Individuals with high blood pressure who perform aerobic exercise regularly under a doctor's supervision usually achieve a slower resting heart rate that is a long-term benefit to the cardiovascular system. Exercise also helps people lose pounds of "heart-straining" body fat, which in turn may lower blood pressure.

Adults who exercise regularly are more likely to

- increase strength and endurance,
- burn more calories,
- develop greater resistance to stress and fatigue, and
- improve self-image, which can lead to adoption of other positive health behaviors.

Several researchers have assessed the cardiovascular fitness of individuals with mental retardation, usually using children and adolescents as subjects. Norms need to be developed for adult age groups. Cressler, Lavay, and Giese (1988) determined which test items are most reliable and give the truest indication of cardiovascular fitness in adults. They found the Canadian Step Test to be the best (Reliability [R] factor of .95) and the Balke Ware Treadmill Test to be second best (R = .93). The Cooper 12-Minute Run/Walk was third with an R = .81. Of the three tests, the 12-minute run is most commonly used by practioners because it is easy to administer. Other field tests include distances of 1 mile and 1-1/2 miles, 6- and 9-minute runs, and, for persons with severe retardation, the 300-yard run. For more detailed information regarding assessment of individuals with mental retardation, refer back to chapter 3.

It must be remembered that to improve levels of physical fitness, fitness programs must be constant and ongoing. Commitments to basic physiological principles are necessary, and there are no shortcuts. Workouts must be intense enough to sufficiently raise the resting heart rate. This usually involves a minimum of 20 minutes of continuous exercise. Additionally, there must be *at least* three workouts per week. Progam length must be *at least* 12 weeks. With anything less one could be almost certain that there would be no significant improvement in physical fitness. Pitetti, Jackson, Stubbs, Campbell, and Battar (1989) showed that adults with mild retardation who participated in Special Olympics activities only 2 days a week were unable to improve their physical fitness. For a review

of improving levels of physical fitness in individuals with mental retardation, see chapter 7.

Walking, Jogging, and Running

Walking is an excellent way to begin an exercise program, because it does not require special equipment or facilities, other than good, comfortable shoes and a safe place to walk. Specific suggestions for beginning a walking program are presented in Highlight 11.1.

To improve the efficiency of the heart and lungs and at the same time burn off extra calories, exercise must be brisk. This includes raising the heart and breathing rates. The exercise must be sustained and performed 3 times a week for at least 15 to 30 minutes without interruption. Krosnick (1984) suggests a 12-week progressive walking program, which is considered ideal for adults with mental retardation (see Table 11.3).

When individuals progress to the point of needing to increase their cardiovascular output, a program of walking, jogging, and running can be developed. The President's Council on Physical Fitness and Sports (no date) suggests a developmental workout to meet varied needs. Table 11.4 provides walking, jogging, and running guidelines.

Physical Activity for Adults With Severe or Profound Retardation

Adults with severe or profound retardation bring with them different challenges because of their unique needs. Obviously, people who understand directions and are able to physically participate will appear to benefit more from physical activities than those with lower functioning levels. However, the physical and motor benefits are identical for everyone, even those with minimal levels of understanding. Careproviders must be totally committed to the concept of daily physical activity for those in

Tips on Starting a Walking Program

- Plan to exercise at the same time each day. This will help you establish a routine. The best times are before breakfast or before dinner.
- Most people have better luck sticking to a walking program if they get into the habit of walking *every* day, rather than every other day.
- You'll get more benefit from extending the time, rather than the pace, of your walks.

- To determine the distance of your various neighborhood walks, drive the routes in your car and check the odometer. Or buy a pedometer at a sporting goods store.
- Remember that animals who lead sedentary lifestyles need to increase their activity gradually, too. If you want your dog to accompany you, allow him or her to increase mileage week by week.

their care. Anything less may relegate these individuals to practically useless levels of strength and endurance.

Halvorsen and Sailor (1990) define individuals with severe and profound disabilities as follows:

The field is progressing towards heterogeneous or less categorical groupings of all special education students; here, when we speak of severely and profoundly disabled individuals, we are referring to people who experience the most significant developmental delays. These individuals may have one or more additional disabilities (sensory, physical, or emotional) besides severe functional retardation. No student would be considered so disabled as not to be included in the population, regardless of medical fragility, minimal communication skills, or lack of consistent motor responses. (p. 112)

These authors conclude their definition by stating: "However, some students might acquire a sufficient repertoire of expressive and academic skills to 'graduate out' of the population of interest here" (p. 112). Given these possible improvements in skills, educators, leaders, and

therapists must combine their efforts to bring individuals with severe and profound labels to the maximum of their abilities.

Assessing Leisure Needs

Individual needs are often determined by others and not by the persons themselves. For the lowest functioning individuals, this occurs more often than not. The problem is not easy to solve, and due to a lack of communication, little attempt is made to rectify the situation. When selecting leisure activities—even at the most fundamental levels of sensory pleasure—for people in their care, careproviders should look for signs of enjoyment. As discussed in chapter 4, modification of unwanted behavior and reinforcement of positive behavior often stem from understanding what a person likes and dislikes. Schleien, Light, McAvoy, and Baldwin (1989) observe:

Traditionally, individuals with severe disabilities have not been given the freedom or opportunity to make leisure choices. Even when given opportunities to make these choices, they frequently exhibit skill deficits in communication, facial expression, gross and fine motor movement, attention span and other behaviors commensurate to activity selection. If acquired, these skills become helpful in indicating a preference to participate or terminate an activity, as well as indicating whom he or she wishes to participate. (p. 33)

There is a major hurdle to overcome when attempting to assess individuals with profound disabilities. Schleien et al. (1989) have found an inconsistency of research results because of an inability to determine the arousal levels of individuals at this level of retardation. For example, some individuals were attentive and others were not. In subsequent testings, the individuals' attentiveness changed drastically, and responses became questionable. Sternberg and Richards (1989) developed an extensive observational checklist to determine the arousal state of individuals labeled as having profound retardation. Specific characteristics, with examples, are included to identify sleep, between sleep and awake, awake/active/agitated, awake/reactive/calm, awake/proactive/agitated, and awake/proactive/calm.

Table 11.3   Twelve-Week Progressive Walking Program

Week	Warm-up (slow walking) (min)	Exercise (brisk walking) (min)	Cool-down (slow walking) (min)	Total time (min)
1	5	5	5	15
2	5	7	5	17
3	5	9	5	19
4	5	11	5	21
5	5	13	5	23
6	5	15	5	25
7	5	18	5	28
8	5	20	5	30
9	5	23	5	33
10	5	26	5	36
11	5	28	5	38
12	5	30	5	40

Note. Reprinted with permission from "Walk Your Way to Health," *Diabetes '84*, spring issue. Copyright © 1984 by the American Diabetes Association. For information on joining ADA and receiving a free one-year subscription, call 1-800-232-3472.

Table 11.4   Walk-Jog-Run Pace Chart

Pace	Speed (mph)	Time for various distances (min:sec)					
		55 yd	110 yd	220 yd	440 yd	880 yd	1 mi
Slow walk	3	:38	1:15	2:30	5:00	10:00	20:00
Moderate walk	4	:28	:56	1:52	3:45	7:30	15:00
Fast walk	4.5	:25	:50	1:40	3:20	6:40	13:20
Slow jog	5	:22	:45	1:30	3:00	6:00	12:00
Moderate jog	6	:19	:38	1:15	2:30	5:00	10:00
Fast jog	7	:17	:33	1:05	2:09	4:17	8:34
Slow run	8	:15	:29	:57	1:54	3:47	7:34
Moderate run	9	:13	:25	:50	1:40	3:20	6:40
Fast run	10	:11	:22	:45	1:30	3:00	6:00

Note: Use this card to help anyone follow the basic jogging program provided here or any other exercise program that involves walking, jogging, or running. If the distance is known, timing over the distance will determine speed.

From the President's Council on Physical Fitness and Sports. Jogging/Running Guidelines. GPO number 907-798, (n. d.), p. 6.

Physical fitness assessment has been of questionable accuracy also because it has been difficult to determine whether the individual understands what is supposed to be done. For example, the assessor could not always be certain if the person understood the concept of running 50 yards "as fast as you can." Even if the individual did run, the results were questioned, because there was no assurance the performance was a maximum effort. Jansma, Decker, Ersing, McCubbin, and Combs (1988) took a major step in the right direction to help solve this problem. These researchers developed the Ohio State University's Project Transition, in which they utilized 114 institutionalized adults labeled as having severe mental retardation. They developed and refined a scoresheet to use in the assessment process that included specific reference to the degree of assistance used to motivate and encourage the subjects. The following prompting levels were used:

1 = High physical +: The individual requires constant physical and verbal prompting with modeling.

2 = Minimal physical +: The individual requires physical prompting to initiate the step and verbal prompting and modeling to complete it.

3 = High verbal/modeling: The individual requires constant verbal prompting and modeling throughout the step.

4 = Minimal verbal: The individual requires some verbal prompting (without modeling) throughout the step.

5 = Independent: The individual requires only a verbal prompt to initiate the first step. (p. 226)

The individuals were tested in the areas of sit-ups in 60 seconds, bench press and the number of pounds lifted in eight repetitions, sit-and-reach, grip strength, and a 300-yard run/walk. These researchers conclude: "In sum, the Project Transition assessment system has numerous characteristics that have field-tested merit when assessing individuals with severe retardation, and this system is claimed to be useful for both the practitioner and the researcher" (p. 231).

Teaching and Learning Recreation Skills

Effective teaching techniques to be used with adults with severe retardation are similar to those used with children or beginners. That is, skills should be broken down into small steps and taught progressively. This process is called task analysis (see chapter 4). Wehman, Renzaglia, and Bates (1985) caution: "Often a sequence of steps applicable to a nonhandicapped individual may prove too difficult or impractical for a severely handicapped person to follow" (p. 132). These authors give the following example:

A modified skill sequence applicable to the manipulation of a camera can also be implemented. Typically, an individual will first raise the camera to eye level and then place an index finger over the shutter release button. However, individuals lacking sufficient fine motor coordination could initially be trained to position their finger over the shutter release button prior to lifting the camera. In this way, the individual would merely have to depress the button once the camera was appropriately positioned. (p. 133)

Teaching motor skills to enable participants to enjoy personally selected leisure-time activities requires developing the skills necessary for participating in these activities. Being able to manipulate objects and materials is important. For example, individuals can be taught to operate microswitches that enable them to independently access a variety of leisure activities (i.e., listening to music, watching action videos, activating a blender, viewing a slide show, turning on a fan, activating a hand-held vibrator) (Schleien et al., 1989). See chapter 4.

Age-Appropriate Activities

Today we are obligated to present age-appropriate activities, whereas in the not too distant past, adults labeled as having severe or profound retardation were given activities more suited to young children. Age-appropriate skills and materials should be chosen with typical age-peer interests in mind. For example, Wolery and Haring (1990) suggest "if listening to music is an appropriate skill for a high school student, then listening to music similar to that of the student's peers is more age-appropriate than listening to nursery rhymes" (p. 258). Patton, Payne, and Beirne-Smith (1990) describe age-appropriate activities:

The educational program must focus on teaching *functional, community referenced, and chronologically age-appropriate activities*. Functional activities are those that are needed in everyday home, community, vocational, and recreation and leisure environments. Often teachers of students with severe disabilities answer the question what to teach by teaching students to put pegs in pegboards, match shapes and colors, string beads, complete worksheets, feel different textures, and so forth. These are examples of nonfunctional activities; they are not needed in the real world. Functional activities are practical. A simple test to see if an activity is functional is to ask the question: If (*student*) doesn't do this activity, would someone have to do it for him? If the answer is yes, the activity is probably functional for the student. If the answer is no, the activity is not functional. (p. 245)

With regard to community-referenced teaching Aufsesser (1991) makes an interesting observation:

The two options for CBI [community-based instruction] provide a place for all individuals with disabilities, whether mildly or severely involved. Placement options within CBI include fitness centers, YMCAs, bowling lanes, swimming pools, bike paths, and racquet centers. These placements may be either segregated programs for individuals with disabilities, or may be integrated into existing programs with non-disabled persons. These options offer great promise in the future for individuals with all types and severities of disabilities. (p. 33)

Activities in some cases need only adaptations or modifications to allow for some degree of participation by this population. Schleien et al. (1989, p. 34) list five alternatives for adapting programs or environments:

1. *Material adaptations* (e.g., using a tubular steel bowling ramp to bowl)
2. *Procedural/rule adaptations* (e.g., standing closer to the stake when pitching horseshoes)
3. *Skill sequence adaptations* (e.g., changing into swimming attire before arriving at public swimming pool)
4. *Facility or environmental modifications* (e.g., making the walking path hard surfaced versus graveled)
5. *Lead-up activities* (e.g., learning to play kickball leads to playing softball)

Activities to Improve Flexibility and Stretching

Flexibility and stretching activities are very beneficial, because inactive individuals often become immobile simply because they do not attempt to move and are not moved by someone else. Horvat (1990) observes that "this component [flexibility] of fitness is important for exceptional students to prevent contractures and undue strain upon muscles and joints as well as to provide the suppleness needed for sport- and movement-specific activities" (p. 277). Highlight 11.2 describes the benefits of incorporating a program of flexibility exercises.

| *HIGHLIGHT 11.2* | **IN PRACTICE** |

Flexibility Exercises

Flexibility exercises help in the following ways:

- Assist in preventing injuries, illness, and muscle spasms
- Are essential to good sitting and standing posture
- Prevent premature aging
- Prevent excessive fatigue
- Permit more efficient mobility
- Decrease lower back pain
- Reduce tension

McPherson, Ostrow, and Shaffron (1989) suggest the following exercises to improve flexibility.

Chin Flexion and Extension (5 times)
1. Keep head facing forward.
2. Bend head forward, touching chin on chest.
3. Tilt head backward until forehead is parallel to the ceiling (contraindicated for persons with atlantoaxial instability).

Neck Rotation (5 times)
1. Turn neck to the right as far as possible.
2. Turn neck to the left as far as possible.

Side Bending (5 times)
1. Look straight ahead.
2. Tilt head to the left as if trying to touch ear to shoulder.
3. Tilt head to the right as if trying to touch ear to shoulder.

Chin Tucks (10 times)
1. Nod head slightly forward.
2. Glide neck backward, aligning ears even to shoulders.

Shoulder Back (10 times)
1. Shoulders are straight forward.
2. Bring both shoulders backward as far as possible.

Trunk Rotation (5 times)
1. Twisting from the waist, slowly rotate to the left.
2. Return to the forward position.
3. Twisting from the waist, slowly rotate to the right.

Press Up (10 times)
1. Lie on stomach on a hard surface.
2. Place hands under shoulders with palms facing downward.
3. Push up with arms to extend back.
4. Try to keep waist on the ground when pushing upward.

As with any exercise for nonconditioned or elderly persons, caution is suggested. If the individuals experience dizziness, pain, nausea, or undue fatigue, then the exercise is too demanding, and repetitions should be reduced and the cadence slowed down.

Activities for Recreation Programs

Crawford and Mendell (1987) describe essentials of activity programs for persons with severe retardation:

Training program[s] for the . . . severely mentally retarded should include activities that enhance balance, body-part perception, body-to-object perception, movement with visual control, agility and flexibility, strength and endurance, and integrated physical activities . . . . The functioning level of the learner must always be taken into consideration when beginning a task, rather than her or his chronological age. If a learner cannot perform a task, revert to the performance level at which he or she is successful. (p. 235)

For a list of activities for this population, see Highlight 11.3.

Summary

Physical activity programs (including health, physical fitness, recreation, and leisure programs) are just beginning to be developed for adults with mental retardation. In the past, most of these individuals were relegated to watching television, because there was very little else to do. Programs were not available! Today, numerous opportunities exist. Appropriate leisure-time pursuits for adults with disabilities are now accepted, funded, and implemented. There are new programs, and recreation leaders are also more readily accepting individuals with mental retardation into programs that once were exclusive to the nonretarded. Therapeutic recreation specialists have become invaluable additions to the professional ranks of those who deal with individuals with mental retardation. The specialists become instrumental in providing knowledge and service to adults with special needs. Additionally, they are assisting traditional recreation leaders by providing information for the integration of adults with mental retardation into the mainstream of regular community leisure and recreation programs.

Creative programming and new teaching techniques are surfacing daily. Recreation programs have expanded beyond the simple but delightful concept of "just providing a whole series of different opportunities" to one that allows teaching and learning of new skills and activities. Thus, recreation programs are filling a void that was once filled only by public school physical education programs. Programming for the transition from high school to adulthood promotes an appropriate continuation of physical fitness and motor skill development and includes games and sports.

Due to the importance of obtaining meaningful and lasting jobs, professionals are now realizing the necessity of developing higher levels of strength, endurance, and coordination in adults with mental retardation. By improving health, physical fitness, and locomotor ability, people with mental retardation can more successfully engage in a highly competitive and complicated world. Recreational leaders are assuming the responsibility to provide comprehensive programs that include citizens with mental retardation.

Leisure-time activities, including athletic competition, is being made available to everyone, in both integrated and special programs. Rehabilitation, through physical development, is being provided to meet the special needs of individuals labeled as having severe or profound retardation. These individuals are now being offered meaningful age-appropriate leisure programs, ones that provide necessary stimulation, physical growth and development, enjoyment, and fun.

DISCUSSIONS AND NEW DIRECTIONS

1. List recreation and leisure activities in your community designed for individuals with disabilities. Are accommodations made for individuals with disabilities, such as accessible buildings and special facilities, modified equipment, and therapeutic recreation specialists? Are there special sections for those with mental retardation? Are there specific activities listed for those with severe and profound disabilities?

2. In your community, in regard to recreation and leisure for adults with mental retardation, do professionals communicate with one another? Which professionals are working together (special/adapted physical educators, therapeutic recreation specialists, Special Olympics coaches, physicians, therapists, etc.)?

HIGHLIGHT 11.3   **IN PRACTICE**

Activities for Persons With Severe or Profound Mental Retardation

The following activities are designed to show step-by-step progressions that are useful for individuals with severe or profound mental retardation.

Camera
1. Look through the camera.
2. Press the button on the camera.
3. Wind the camera.

Vending Machine
1. Locate a vending machine.
2. Select an item.
3. Place coins in the machine and pull the lever or push the button.
4. Consume the item.
5. Throw wrapper in the wastebasket.

Books and Magazines
1. Take a book or magazine off the shelf.
2. Turn the pages.
3. Find a seat in the library.
4. Acquire a library card.
5. Check out the book or magazine.

Table/Video Games
1. Place coins in the machine.
2. Operate the machine.

3. Take turns during the game.
4. Demonstrate a knowledge of game completion.
5. Play foozball.
6. Play pinball.
7. Play an electric bowling game.
8. Play pool.

Medicine Ball
1. Roll the medicine ball.
2. Pick up the medicine ball.
3. Throw the medicine ball.
4. Catch the medicine ball.

Bowling
1. Select a bowling ball.
2. Pick up the ball from the ball return.
3. Approach the foul line.
4. Roll the ball down the alley.

Handball
1. Put a glove on dominant hand.
2. Bounce the ball.
3. Serve the ball.
4. Run toward the ball.
5. Hit the ball against the wall.
6. Return the ball that was hit against the wall.

HIGHLIGHT 11.3 CONTINUED

HIGHLIGHT 11.3 CONTINUED

Horseshoes
1. Select horseshoes and walk to the throwing line.
2. Grasp the horseshoe.
3. Throw the horseshoe.
4. Pick up the horseshoe around the stake.

Weight Training
1. Learn to use a spotter.
2. Identify the amount of weight.
3. Put weights on the bar.
4. Learn the underhand grip.
5. Curl the bar.

6. Learn the overhand grip.
7. Lift weight overhead.
8. Bench press.

Fishing
1. Dig for earthworms.
2. Pull a worm out of a pile of dirt.
3. Bait the hook.
4. Cast the baited fishing line.
5. Wait for the fish to bite.
6. Pull in the fish.
7. Take the fish off the hook.

Note. From *Functional Skills for Moderately and Severely Handicapped Individuals* (pp. 151-154) by P. Wehman, A. Renzaglia, and P. Bates, 1985, Austin, TX: PRO-ED. Reprinted by permission of PRO-ED, Inc.

References

Aufsesser, P.M. (1991). Mainstreaming and least restrictive environment: How do they differ? *Palaestra*, **7**, 31-34.

Blair, S.N. (1985). Physical activity leads to fitness and pays off. *The Physician and Sportsmedicine*, **13**, 153-157.

Compton, D.M. (1989). Research initiatives in therapeutic recreation. In D.M. Compton (Ed.), *Issues in therapeutic recreation: A profession in transition*. Champaign, IL: Sagamore.

Crawford, M.E., & Mendell, R. (1987). *Therapeutic recreation and adapted physical activities for mentally retarded individuals*. Englewood Cliffs, NJ: Prentice Hall.

Cressler, M., Lavay, B., & Giese, M. (1988). The reliability of four measures of cardiovascular fitness with mentally retarded adults. *Adapted Physical Activity Quarterly*, **5**, 285-292.

Edgar, E. (1987). Secondary programs in special education: Are many of them justifiable? *Exceptional Children*, **53**, 555-561.

Edgerton, R.B. (1988). Community adaptation of persons with mental retardation. In J.F. Kavanagh (Ed.), *Understanding mental retardation* (pp. 311-318). Baltimore: Brooks.

Fernhall, B., & Tymeson, G. (1987). Graded exercise testing of mentally retarded adults: A study of physiability. *Archives of Physical and Medical Rehabilitaton*, **68**, 363-365.

Gallahue, D.L. (1989). *Understanding motor development*. Indianapolis: Benchmark Press.

Halvorsen, A.T., & Sailor, W. (1990). Integration of students with severe and profound disabilities: A review of research. In R. Gaylord-Ross (Ed.), *Issues in research in special education*, (Vol. 1, pp. 110-172). New York: Teachers College Press.

Haring, N.G., & Field, S. (1990). Transition to work and community living. In N.G. Haring and L. McCormick (Eds.), *Exceptional children and youth* (5th ed., pp. 515-545). Columbus, OH: Merrill.

Hope Newsletter. (1986, April). p. 3.

Horvat, M. (1990). *Physical education and sport for the disabled*. Dubuque, IA: Brown.

Jansma, P., Decker, J., Ersing, W., McCubbin, J., & Combs, S. (1988). An assessment system for individuals with severe mental retardation. *Adapted Physical Activity Quarterly*, **5**, 223-232.

Jansma, P., Ersing, W.F., & McCubbin, J.A. (1986). *The effects of physical fitness and personal hygiene training on the preparation for community placement of institutionalized mentally retarded adults. Project Transition* (Grant Number G008300001). Washington, DC: U.S. Department of Education, Office of Special Education and Rehabilitation Services.

Kelly, J.R. (1990). *Leisure* (2nd ed.). Englewood Cliffs, NJ: Prentice Hall.

Kennedy, D.W., Austin, D.R., & Smith, R.W. (1987). *Special recreation: Opportunities for persons with disabilities*. Philadelphia: Saunders.

Krosnick, A. (Spring, 1984). Walk your way to health. *Diabetes '84*, p. 11.

MacNeil, R.D. (1988). Leisure programs and services for older adults: Past, present, and future research. *Therapeutic Recreation Journal*, **22**, 24-35.

McPherson, K., Ostrow, A., Shaffron, P. (1989). *Physical Fitness and the Aging Driver, Phase II* (Research Report). Morgantown, WV: West Virginia University.

Mobily, K.E. (1989). Other ways of knowing. In D.M. Compton (Ed.), *Issues in therapeutic recreation: A profession in transition* (pp. 125-142). Champaign, IL: Sagamore.

Patton, J.R., Payne, J.S., & Beirne-Smith, M. (1990). *Mental retardation* (3rd ed.). Columbus, OH: Merrill.

Peterson, C.A., & Gunn, S.L. (1984). *Therapeutic recreation program design* (2nd ed.). Englewood Cliffs, NJ: Prentice Hall.

Pitetti, K.H., Jackson, J.A., Stubbs, N.B., Campbell, K.D., & Battar, S.S. (1989). Fitness levels of adult Special Olympic par-

ticipants. *Adapted Physical Activity Quarterly*, **6**, 354-370.

President's Council on Physical Fitness and Sports (no date). *Jogging/running guidelines* (GPO No. 907-798). Reston, VA: AAHPERD Publications.

Rancourt, A.M. (1989). Older adults with developmental disabilities/mental retardation: Implications for professional services. *Therapeutic Recreation Journal*, **23**, 47-57.

Schleien, S.J., Light, C.L., McAvoy, L.H., & Baldwin, C.K. (1989). Best professional practices: Serving persons with severe multiple disabilities. *Therapeutic Recreation Journal*, **23**, 27-40.

Schleien, S.J., & Ray, M.T. (1988). *Community recreation and persons with disabilities*. Baltimore: Brooks.

Schloss, P.J., Smith, M.A., & Kiehl, W. (1986). Rec club: A community centered approach to recreational development for adults with mild to moderate mental retardation. *Education and Training of the Mentally Retarded*. **21**, 282-288.

Searle, M.S., & Iso-Ahola, S.E. (1988). Determinants of leisure behavior among retired adults. *Therapeutic Recreation Journal*, **22**, 38-46.

Shephard, R.J. (1990). *Fitness in special populations*. Champaign, IL: Human Kinetics.

Sherrill, C. (1986). *Adapted physical education and recreation* (3rd ed.). Dubuque, IA: Brown.

Siegel, S., Park, H., Gumpel, T., Ford, J., Tappe, P., & Gaylord-Ross, R. (1990). Research in vocational education. In R. Gaylord-Ross (Ed.), *Issues in research in special education* (Vol. 1, pp. 173-242). New York: Teachers College Press.

Simmons Market Research Bureau, Inc. (1985). Percentage of sport participation, by age. In J. Kelly, *Leisure* (2nd ed., p. 203). Englewood Cliffs, NJ: Prentice Hall.

Sternberg, L., & Richards, S. (1989). Assessing levels of state and arousal in individuals with profound handicaps: A research integration. *Journal of Mental Retardation Research*, **33**, 381-387.

Summerfield, L.M. (1990). Leisure in the outdoors—a brief summary of research. *Journal of Physical Education, Recreation and Dance*, **61**, 31-32.

U.S. Office of Education. Federal Register. The Individuals With Disabilities Education Act, formerly The Education for All Handicapped Children Act of 1975, Section 94-142, 99-457, 89-750, 42 U.S.C., Section 42480-54579, (1977).

Wehman, P., & Hill, J.W. (Eds.) (1985). *Competitive employment for persons with mental retardation: From research to practice* (Vol. 1). Richmond: Virginia Commonwealth University, Rehabilitation Research Training Center.

Wehman, P., Renzaglia, A., & Bates, P. (1985). *Functional skills for moderately and severely handicapped individuals*. Austin, TX: PRO-ED.

Will, M. (1984). *OSERS programming for the transition of youth with disabilities: Bridges from school to working life*. Washington, DC: Office of Special Education and Rehabilitative Services.

Wolery, M., & Haring, T.G. (1990). Moderate, severe, and profound handicaps. In N.G. Haring & L. McCormick (Eds.), *Exceptional children and youth* (5th ed.) (pp. 239-280). Columbus, OH: Merrill.

CHAPTER 12

Special Olympics International: Year-Round Training and Athletic Competition

PREVIEW At a 1989 press conference in Harrisburg, Pennsylvania, Loretta Claiborne, a Special Olympics athlete since 1971 and an experienced marathon runner, wrote and gave this speech to students, school administrators, and media representatives, addressing the importance of Special Olympics. Loretta Claiborne is presently a Board Member of Special Olympics International.

Hello everybody. I would like to tell you a little bit about what sports mean to me. I started out young in elementary school back in the sixties. There I sat behind the windows looking out watching the other kids playing sports . . . something I never had a chance at because, number one, if you were a special education student, you were labeled with the word "retarded."

Back when I was coming up, you were in a special ed school, special classes, and all you were seen as was the retarded kid in Room 8. I've always wanted to participate in sports, but there was no backing in sports unless you were on a regular softball team, basketball team, or whatever. The teachers weren't behind sports then.

I'm going to tell you a little bit about how I got into running. It was through my brother. Back in York [Pennsylvania], he used to run for cross country in school and I followed him around and I started running. He has since quit and I'm still running. But how I got into sports in general was through a program called Special Olympics. Now I play several sports: basketball, I'm learning how to swim, I roller skate—I can just go on down the line to tell about the sports I have been playing.

It's very important for people with disabilities to play in sports. To me, it gives me a chance to think. I used to have what is called behavior problems. I'd sock you in the face as soon as I'd see you. I don't have that problem no more because if I have a problem with somebody, I'll just go out and run 10 miles and know they won't follow me. That's what sports has taught me. It has also taught me to care about myself; self-pride, self-discipline. I've always wanted to keep my weight down and sports was a way to help that problem. People in my family are a little on the heavy side, and I wanted to maintain my good weight, and also with being retarded, I wanted to maintain my self-esteem.

It [sports] is also important for other people with disabilities in the aspect of being there and doing something they would like to enjoy instead of sitting there not doing it. They have the chance to do it. Hey, Unified Sports to me is a dream; a dream come true. It was my dream, now it's your reality. My dream has become reality for students of today. You students out there . . . Unified Sports . . . I hope you get other people into it because I wish I could sit with YH [York High School] on the back of my shirt back in 1965-66-67-68. I didn't have that chance because there was no such thing as Unified Sports. Thank the good Lord for the people who are pushing behind this program. Like the people here . . . your teachers, your administrators, people who are stretching out to have this program grow. It's up to you students to come and participate. Because without you, the sport can't go on.

HIGHLIGHT QUESTIONS

- **What sport organization is the largest and most visible in the world for persons with mental retardation?**
- **What is the origin of Special Olympics?**
- **Who is eligible to participate in Special Olympics?**
- **What types of activities and sport competition are offered through Special Olympics?**
- **Are the various training competitions and opportunities offered based on the unique needs and ability levels of persons with mental retardation?**
- **What is the "10% rule" used in Special Olympics?**

- **What role do such programs as Unified Sports, Partner Clubs, and Sport Partnerships play in Special Olympics?**

Nations with extreme hostility such as Northern/Southern Ireland and Nicaragua/El Salvador have been known to temporarily stop fighting to jointly support Special Olympics. . . . Yet only 20 years ago not one of these athletes received sports training or completed any sport. They were usually locked in institutions, hidden in their homes, and shunned by the community. The most prominent question then is "How did a small group of 100 mentally retarded individuals participating in a day camp, expand in 20 years to an international organization that provides year-round local, regional, and national training and competition to over one million athletes in 1987?" (Cheatum, 1988, p. 22)

This chapter provides an overview of Special Olympics International (SOI), the largest and most visible sport organization in the world for persons with mental retardation (see Figure 12.1). The sport and athletic training opportunities Special Olympics brings to over 1 million athletes with mental retardation is well recognized. However, equally as important is the increased awareness this program provides to the general public regarding the value of physical activity for this population. For example, spectators viewing Special Olympics competition for the first time often remark, "After a while I stopped seeing what the athletes could not do and started observing their accomplishments."

This chapter closely examines the history and structure of this organization and discusses the implementation of SOI's year-round sport training and competitive programming opportunities conducted by certified coaches and officials. This chapter also highlights research studies and future programs that will impact athletes,

coaches, and volunteers of Special Olympics throughout the 1990s and into the 21st century.

History of Special Olympics International

The Kennedy family of Massachusetts, who have always stressed physical fitness in their lives, experienced mental retardation firsthand when one of the daughters of Joseph and Rose Kennedy was born with mental retardation. For a sister, Eunice Kennedy Shriver, who had insight into mental retardation, it seemed only natural to become involved in providing physical fitness and game activities to this population. She believed that if provided the right

Figure 12.1 Special Olympics International is the largest and most visible sport organization in the world for persons with mental retardation. Photo courtesy of Bill Epperidge.

opportunity, persons with mental retardation could achieve success.

The seed for SOI began during the summer of 1963 when Eunice Kennedy Shriver started a 5-week summer camp for persons with mental retardation. The camp program, held on the Shrivers' country estate in Maryland, included 100 youngsters and consisted of activities such as swimming, volleyball, kickball, horseback riding, and bouncing on a trampoline.

Between the years of 1963 and 1968 the Joseph P. Kennedy, Jr. Foundation, with the cooperation of the American Alliance for Health, Physical Education and Recreation (AAHPER), provided financial assistance to interested persons from universities, communities, and private organizations to research and develop programs of physical fitness and sport for this population. For example, a survey by Brace (1968) determined that one third of the children with mental retardation attending elementary schools were not receiving any form of organized physical education. Another study surveyed 335 schools in 21 states and determined that 45% of the students with mild mental retardation were receiving no physical education, and only 25% received an hour or more a week (Rarick, Widdop, & Broadhead, 1970). In addition, studies conducted during this period clearly indicated that with proper training this population could markedly improve in physical fitness. By 1967, the increased number of studies conducted in this area helped to bring a wider acceptance of the need for increased fitness and sport training programs for persons with mental retardation (Haskins, 1976).

In 1968, the Chicago Park District approached the Joseph P. Kennedy, Jr. Foundation with a proposal to host a large-scale track-and-field meet for persons with mental retardation. The foundation approved a $20,000 grant not only to conduct a track-and-field meet, but to include swimming and follow the format of the ''Greek Olympics.'' The games held in July of 1968 on Chicago's Soldier Field would become the first International Summer Special Olympic Games (ISSOG) (see Figure 12.2). The games were represented by 1,000 youths, ages 8 to 17 years, from 26 states, the District of Columbia, and Canada. During the 2-day event there were over two hundred separate competitions and sport clinics. Another significant event during the games was a press conference held by Mrs. Shriver to announce that the foundation was pledging $75,000 to assist any interested communities with the costs of hosting local, state, and regional Special Olympic games the following year.

Following the Chicago games the response from national, state, and local organizations was greater than the foundation ever anticipated. In December of 1968, Senator Edward Kennedy, president of the foundation, announced the formation of Special Olympics International (SOI), a nonprofit organization with Eunice Kennedy Shriver as president (Haskins, 1976). The organization not only would offer sport competition, but would stress physical fitness and sport training for persons with mental retardation 8 years and older. This organization was immediately supported by three nationally recognized associations: the American Association on Men-

Figure 12.2 The first ISSOG were held in Chicago's Soldier Field. Photo courtesy of Special Olympics International.

tal Deficiency, the Council for Exceptional Children, and the National Association for Retarded Citizens (Cheatum, 1988). Since that 2-day event held in the summer of 1968 with 1,000 athletes, SOI has grown to include over 1 million athletes in 25,000 communities in every state and 91 countries. Highlight 12.1 lists historical SOI milestones from 1963 to 1991.

Structure of Special Olympics International

Today Special Olympics is recognized as a worldwide program of year-round training and athletic competition developed in the Olympic tradition. The purpose of the program is to provide persons with mental retardation 8 years and older regardless of their abilities with continued opportunities to develop physical fitness, dis-

play their talents, strengthen their character, and fulfill their human potential.

SOI is granted official recognition by the International Olympic Committee and is a member of the Committee on Sport for the Disabled (COSD) of the United States Olympic Committee. One common public misconception regarding SOI is that it is funded by the Joseph P. Kennedy, Jr. Foundation or the federal government. SOI operates independently by generating funds at the international, national, state, and local levels through corporate and individual donations, special fund-raising events, support from foundations, and grants. The SOI headquarters is located in Washington, DC, and its organizational structure is controlled by an international board of directors (see Figure 12.3).

According to Winnick (1990), "This organization has served as the model sport organization for people with handicapping conditions

---

HIGHLIGHT 12.1	**IN THEORY**

Special Olympics Milestones*

1963   Eunice Kennedy Shriver begins a summer day-camp program for children and adults with mental retardation at her home in Maryland.

1964-1968   Financed by the Kennedy Foundation, hundreds of private organizations establish day-camp programs for children and adults with mental retardation.

1968   The first International Special Olympics Games are held in Chicago's Soldier Field, with 1,000 individuals with mental retardation from 26 states and Canada participating.

1968   Special Olympics International is established as a nonprofit charitable organization.

1970   50,000 Special Olympians are competing in all 50 states and Canada.

1970   The second International Special Olympic Games are held again in Chicago, with 2,000 athletes from all 50 states, Canada, France, and Puerto Rico participating.

1971   The U.S. Olympic Committee gives Special Olympics official approval as one of only two organizations to use the name "Olympics."

*Dates obtained from various SOI sources.

HIGHLIGHT 12.1 CONTINUED

1972   The third International Special Olympics Games are held on the UCLA campus in Los Angeles, with 2,500 athletes participating.

1973   ABC-TV broadcasts a segment of the Third International Games on "Wide World of Sports."

1975   The fourth International Special Olympics Games are held on the Central Michigan campus in Mt. Pleasant, with 3,200 athletes from 10 countries participating. The games are broadcast nationwide as a CBS "Sports Spectacular."

1977   The first International Winter Special Olympics Games are held in Steamboat Springs, Colorado, with 500 athletes participating in skiing and skating.

1979   The fifth International Summer Special Olympics Games are held at the State University of New York at Brockport, with 3,500 athletes from more than 20 countries participating.

1981   The second International Winter Special Olympics Games are held in Stowe, Vermont, with 600 athletes participating in alpine and nordic skiing and skating.

1983   The sixth International Summer Special Olympics Games are held at Louisiana State University in Baton Rouge, with more than 50 countries participating. A crowd of 60,000 people attend opening ceremonies.

1985   The third International Winter Special Olympics Games are held in Park City, Utah, with 800 athletes from 14 nations participating.

1985   The Special Olympics Organization adopts the use of an official logo to identify the program.

1987   The seventh International Summer Special Olympics Games are held at Notre Dame University in South Bend, Indiana, with more than 4,700 athletes from over 70 countries participating. This makes these games the largest sporting event ever held for persons with disabilities. ABC's "Wide World of Sports" broadcasts opening ceremonies. Media coverage reaches 150 million people worldwide.

1989   The fourth International Winter Special Olympics Games are held in Lake Tahoe, Nevada, with 1,400 athletes from 18 nations participating.

1989   Unified Sport programs are launched nationwide, combining athletes with and without mental retardation onto teams to compete against other Unified Sport teams.

1989   The Motor Activity Training Program is started, which emphasizes training and participation for individuals with severe disabilities whose limitations do not allow them to participate in official SOI sports.

1990   More than 750,000 Special Olympics Athletes are competing in 25,000 communities in the United States and over 90 countries worldwide.

1991   The eighth International Summer Special Olympics Games are held at Minneapolis/St. Paul, Minnesota, with nearly 6,000 athletes from around the world participating. This makes these games the largest sporting event of the year.

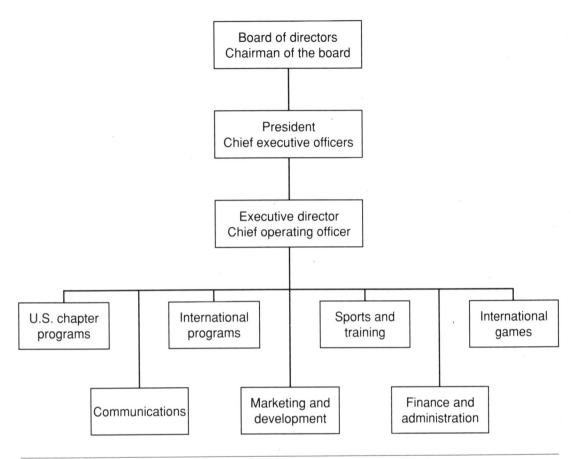

Figure 12.3 Special Olympics International organizational structure.

through its contributions in direct service, research, training, advocacy education and organizational leadership'' (p. 13). In addition, ''It has played a key role in the attention to physical education in federal legislation and the provision of federal funding for professional preparation, research, and other projects through its advocacy activities. The organization has provided a world-wide model for the provision of sport opportunities'' (p. 16).

Philosophy

This statement of the organization's philosophy is taken from the SOI *Philosophy Fact Sheet* (1990a, p. 1):

Special Olympics is founded on the belief that people with mental retardation can, with proper instruction and encouragement, learn, enjoy and benefit from participation in individual and team sports, adapted as necessary to meet the needs of those with special mental and physical limitations.

Special Olympics believes that consistent training is essential to the development of sport skills, and the competition among those of equal abilities is the most appropriate means of testing these skills, measuring progress, and providing incentives for personal growth.

Special Olympics believes that through sport training competition, people with mental retardation benefit physically, mentally, socially and spiritually; families are strengthened;

and the community at large, both through participation and observation, is unified in understanding people with mental retardation in an environment of equality, respect and acceptance.

To provide athletes with mental retardation the most beneficial and challenging activities, SOI

operates in accordance with the 16 principles listed in Highlight 12.2.

Eligibility for Participation

In the past there has been some confusion regarding who is eligible to participate in Special Olympics. For example, not all special

---

HIGHLIGHT 12.2   **IN THEORY**

SOI Principles

To provide the most enjoyable, beneficial and challenging activities for athletes with mental retardation, Special Olympics, world-wide, operates in accordance with the following principles and beliefs.

1. That the Spirit of Special Olympics—skill, courage, sharing and joy—incorporates universal values which transcend all boundaries of geography, nationality, political philosophy, gender, age, race or religion.
2. That the goal of Special Olympics is to help bring all persons with mental retardation into the larger society under conditions whereby they are accepted, respected and given the chance to become useful and productive citizens.
3. That, as a means of achieving this goal, Special Olympics encourages its more capable athletes to move from Special Olympics training and competition into school and community programs where they can train and compete in regular sports activities. The athletes may, at this point, wish to leave Special Olympics or continue to take part in Special Olympics activities. The decision is the athlete's.

4. That all Special Olympics activities—at the local, state, national and international levels—reflect the values, standards, traditions, ceremonies, and events embodied in the modern Olympic movement, broadened and enriched to celebrate the moral and spiritual qualities of persons with mental retardation so as to enhance their dignity and self-esteem.
5. That participation in Special Olympics training programs and competitive events is open to all people with mental retardation who are at least eight years old, regardless of the degree of their disability.
6. That comprehensive, year-round sports training is available to every Special Olympics athlete, conducted by well-qualified coaches in accordance with the standardized Sports Rules formulated and adopted by Special Olympics International; and that every athlete who participates in a Special Olympics sport will have been trained in that sport.
7. That every Special Olympics program includes sports events and activities that are appropriate to the age and ability of each athlete, from motor activities to the most advanced competition.

HIGHLIGHT 12.2 CONTINUED

8. That Special Olympics provides full participation for every athlete regardless of economic circumstance and conducts training and competition under the most favorable conditions possible, including facilities, administration, training, coaching, officiating and events.

9. That Special Olympics gives each participant an equal chance to excel by basing competition in every event on accurate records of previous performance or trial heats and, when relevant, grouping by age and gender.

10. That, at every Awards Ceremony, in addition to the traditional medals for first, second and third places, athletes finishing from fourth to last place are presented a suitable place ribbon with appropriate ceremony.

11. That, to the greatest extent possible, Special Olympics activities will be run by and involve local volunteers, from school and college age to senior citizens, in order to create greater opportunities for public understanding of and participation with people with mental retardation.

12. That, although Special Olympics is primarily and essentially a program of sport training and competition, efforts are made to offer, as an integral part of Special Olympics Games, a full range of artistic, social and cultural experiences such as dances, art exhibits, concerts, visits to historic sites, clinics, theatrical and motion picture performances, and similar activities.

13. That the goal of Special Olympics in every nation is to develop organizations and conduct events at the community level. Countries which, because of specific economic, social or cultural circumstances, may find it difficult to achieve this goal rapidly, may hold National Games on a regular basis to enhance the development of popular understanding and provide increased visibility for their citizens with mental retardation. All participating countries are invited to send a delegation to the International Games held every two years, alternating between Summer and Winter, provided that in all cases, Special Olympics standards are adhered to in the preparation of athletes and coaches for the Games.

14. That the families of Special Olympics athletes are encouraged to play an active role in their community Special Olympics program, to share in the training of their athletes, and to assist in the public education effort needed to create greater understanding of the emotional, physical, social and spiritual needs of people with mental retardation and their families.

15. That Special Olympics encourages community, state and national sports programs, both professional and amateur, to include demonstrations by Special Olympics athletes as part of their major events.

16. That Special Olympics activities take place in public, with full coverage by the media, so that athletes with mental retardation may reveal to the world those special qualities of the human spirit in which they excel—skill, courage, sharing and joy.

education students in schools or developmentally disabled persons living and working independently in the community are eligible to participate. Only persons who have been identified as having mental retardation or cognitive delays (an IQ of 80 or below) are eligible. For example, children and adults with multiple disabilities or severe learning disabilities may participate as long as they meet the eligibility criteria of a cognitive delay requiring special instruction and assistance. Children and adults with learning problems due to an emotional disturbance would not be considered eligible. However, to accommodate unique situations, some flexibility is left to local, area, chapter, or national Special Olympics organizations.

Olympians may participate in other organized sport programs and are encouraged to participate in regular sport programs. In fact, graduating Special Olympians from Special Olympics programs into regular sport programs is a principal objective (Songster, 1984). SOI recommends that athletes participate competitively during each season in only one sport, although they encourage numerous recreational activities. They advise coaches to protect their athletes' eligibility and carefully check the rules and guidelines of other sport governing bodies, athletic associations, leagues, and schools.

Following is part of the definition of eligibility for Special Olympics, taken from the *Definition of Eligibility for Special Olympics Fact Sheet* (1990b):

Persons are eligible for Special Olympics provided that they are 8 years of age or older and

1. have been identified by an agency or professional as having mental retardation; or
2. have a cognitive delay as determined by a standardized measure;* or
3. have significant learning or vocational problems** due to cognitive delay, which require or have required specially designed instruction.***

*IQ 80 or below.
**"Significant learning or vocational problems" refers to learning problems resulting from cognitive delays (intellectual impairment). These do not include physical disability, emotional or behavior difficulties, or specific disabilities such as dyslexia or speech or language impairment. These persons with cognitive delays were formerly classified as educable mentally retarded (EMR) or mildly mentally retarded (MMR).
***Specially designed instruction refers to time when a person is receiving supportive education or remedial instruction directed at the cognitive delay. In the case of adults, specially designed instruction is usually replaced with specially designed programs in the work place or in supported work or at home.

Before participating in Special Olympics an athlete must have a signed and completed parental/guardian/individual release form. Also, a physician must give the participant a medical examination and must sign the medical certification section of the form.

Classification of Sport

There are two classifications of sport in Special Olympics: official sports and demonstration sports. The official sports are further divided into summer and winter Special Olympics sports. Both Summer and Winter Special Olympics Games are held annually as chapter (state), sectional, area or county, and local competitions. In addition, International Summer and Winter Special Olympics Games are held every 4 years. Table 12.1 lists the 22 Olympic-type sports offered through Special Olympics.

In 1984-1985, SOI made a number of policy and rule changes. Since that time the official Special Olympics sports rules, which govern all

Table 12.1   Olympic-Type Sports Offered Through Special Olympics

Official summer sports	Official winter sports	Demonstration sports
Aquatics		
Athletics (track and field)	Alpine skiing	Canoeing
Basketball	Cross-country skiing	Cycling
Bowling	Figure skating	Table tennis
Equestrian	Speed skating	Team handball
Gymnastics	Floor hockey	Tennis
Roller skating	Poly hockey	Power lifting
Football (soccer)		
Softball		
Volleyball		

Special Olympics sports and competitions, have been implemented and are for the most part the same rules and policies that govern the International Sport Federations (ISF) and National Governing Bodies (NGB) for able-bodied athletes. According to Songster (1984), this policy ensures SOI consistency in sport skill training and competition for its athletes. For example, the rules and competitions of SOI basketball are governed by the Federation Internationale de Basketball Amateur (FINA), whereas Special Olympics USA may follow the rules of the National Federation of State High School Associations.

Sport Training Competitions and Opportunities

The rules of the ISF and NGB are closely followed in each sport with only slight modifications. However, SOI recognizes the unique needs and ability levels of each athlete by offering an array of sport training competitions and opportunities, including the following:

- *Motor Activity Training Program (MATP).* Designed to emphasize training and participation for individuals with severe disabilities whose limitations do not allow them to successfully participate in official Special Olympics sports. A MATP guide is available to coaches. this program and its training guide are discussed in greater detail in the MATP section of this chapter.
- *Individual skills.* Designed for athletes who possess the prerequisite fundamental skills and are beginning to acquire the specific sport skills necessary to participate in a particular sport. For example, the team sport of basketball includes such individual skills as field-goal shooting, spot shooting, speed passing, dribbling and rebounding.
- *Team skills.* Designed for members of a team who have acquired the individual sport skills but cannot understand or successfully compete as a member of a team sport. For example, the sport of basketball includes such team skills as team pass, catch, and shooting toward a target.
- *Modified events.* Designed to meet the needs of athletes who cannot follow intricate sport rules and strategies. Examples of modified events include half-court basketball, six-a-side soccer, and tee ball.
- *Team and individual sport.* Designed to meet the needs of the highest ability athletes. Training and competition in the 22 sports are governed by the *Official Special Olympics Sports Rules*.
- *Unified sport.* Combines on a team an equal number of athletes with and without mental retardation in such team sports as basketball and soccer. This program is discussed in more detail in the ''Unified Sports'' section of this chapter.

Competitive Divisions

Competitive divisions include grouping athletes by age, gender, and ability. The age groups are based on those that are most representative of international sport competition. An athlete's age group is determined as age on the day of the actual games or competition. Age-group placement in team events is determined by the age of the oldest athlete on the team. The age-group classifications, taken from *Official Special Olympics Summer Sports Rules* (1988) are listed in Table 12.2.

Special Olympics competitions consist of men's and women's events, with mixed events conducted in pairs figure skating, ice dancing, dance couples' roller skating, table tennis, and tennis. A mixed team may compete when a sufficient number of men or women are not available to form an all-women's or all-men's team and must compete in the men's division.

Perhaps the most unique aspect of Special Olympics competition is the ability grouping of athletes and teams in competitive events so they are "even." Special Olympics recognizes even competitive divisioning as providing all participants, based on past performance, a reasonable opportunity to win. Even competitive divisions are developed by ranking athletes in descending order from previous performance scores, which are entered on the athlete's entry form. Time or performance scores for all athletes entered in a division of an event may not differ by more than 10%. In certain sports, such as diving, equestrian, figure skating, and gymnastics, the "10% rule" is not appropriate and therefore does not apply.

Each competitive division must consist of a minimum of three athletes and no more than eight athletes. Because of the 10% rule, during training it is paramount that coaches correctly assess and secure their athletes' proper performance scores. Burkett (1988), the father of a Special Olympian, shares the following story regarding problems that can occur when volunteers disregard the 10% rule in competitive divisioning. "At the Arizona State Special Olympics Games, Suzy, who has cerebral palsy and mental retardation but is ambulatory, was in the same heat with wheelchair individuals for the frisbee distance throw. . . . Because Suzy is a strong, healthy-looking individual, the volunteers figured she was misplaced and would dominate the heat. Because of this assumption, they had the wheelchair individuals throw first and helped each one. Suzy threw last and threw her usual 2 or 3 feet. The frisbee landed a good 15 feet or more behind the throws of the other competitors" (p. 24).

The 10% rule also applies in team sport competition. Prior to competition, teams perform a classification round, participating in the sport for a short period of time before a panel of judges. In addition, "team skill" performance scores for each team member are submitted upon registering for the team competition.

In summary, Songster (1984) observes that

> competition based on equal ability groups helps to accomplish several goals: it promotes the true spirit of Special Olympics by providing sport training and competition for all mentally retarded people; it provides

Table 12.2 Age-Group Competitive Divisions, SOI Summer Sports

Division	Individual sport (age in years)	Team sport (age in years)
1) Youth	8-11	—
2) Junior	12-15	>15
3) Senior	16-21	16-21
4) Masters	22-29	>22
5) Senior Masters	>30	—
6) Open age group	Reserved for combining age groups to meet the required minimum number of competitors or teams in a division. Efforts are made to combine athletes of similar ability levels.	

Adapted from the Official Special Olympics Summer Sports Rules (1988). 1350 New York Avenue, NW, Suite 500, Washington D.C. 20005.

fair, equitable conditions for competition; it protects the physical well-being of the athlete; and it promotes uniformity so that no competitor can obtain an unfair advantage over another. . . . Through these rules the athletes are organized into fair and equal ability groups, which in turn, allow greater opportunities for the athlete's success. With success comes confidence, and with confidence comes the sense of self-worth and accomplishment. (p. 75) (See Figure 12.4.)

Advancing to Higher Levels of Competition

The rules of SOI dictate that for an athlete to advance to higher levels of competition during a year, the athlete must have participated in an organized training program for a minimum of 8 weeks. The program must be designed for the particular sport or sports in which the athlete is seeking higher-level competition. This is one rule that helps assure that athletes receive proper training. In addition, to successfully advance to a higher level of competition, an athlete must have placed first, second, or third in a lower

Figure 12.4 A unique feature of SOI is competition based on equal ability grouping among athletes. Photo courtesy of Ken Regan.

level of Special Olympics competition in the same sport or sports.

How are athletes selected to advance to higher levels of competition when the number of athletes that qualify exceed the quota? For example, a chapter may have 50 athletes who placed first, second, or third in the 100-meter dash but only a quota of 5 athletes for this event can compete at the next international games. The selection of athletes for higher levels of competition, as stated in *Official Special Olympics Summer Sports Rules* (1988), are based on the following criteria:

a. First priority: Athletes shall be first-place winners in at least the event at the next lower level of competition. If the number of first-place winners exceeds the quota, athletes shall be chosen by random selection from among all division winners.

b. Second priority: Athletes who were second-place finishers in the event shall be chosen next by random selection, then third-place finishers. (p. 19)

Awards

SOI believes that all athletes who start an event should be recognized for their effort in the form of an award. First- through eighth-place official Special Olympics awards are provided in all competitive events recognized by SOI. Because athletes are placed in competitive divisions based on age, gender, and ability, this approach can generate multiple award winners in the various events offered in each sport. For example, in a 100-meter dash a gold medal may be awarded to the first-place finisher in each of the six age groups subdivided into various competitive divisions (Sherrill, 1988).

In keeping with the Olympics tradition, gold, silver, and bronze medals are awarded to individual athletes and team members finishing in the first three places, respectively, while ribbons are provided to individual athletes and team members placing in the remaining five places (see Figure 12.5). Trophies may be provided only in team sport tournaments. All awards are presented to the Special Olympians during an awards ceremony. Celebrities and sport dignitaries are usually responsible for presenting the awards. For example, during the 1988 International Special Olympics Summer Games, sport dignitaries included such U.S.A. Olympians as Mary Lou Retton and Bart Conner.

The Excitement and Pageantry of Special Olympics

The International Summer and Winter Special Olympics Games are held every 4 years, while the chapter (state), sectional, area or county, and local competitions are offered annually at various times of the year. The events provide the athletes with opportunities to showcase their months of training and talents. However, the games are much more than competition, as described by Krebs (1990):

These competitions have the excitement,

Figure 12.5 Special Olympians receiving medals. Photo courtesy of Special Olympics International.

pageantry, fanfare and color associated with Olympic games—including the parade of athletes, the lighting of the torch, the opening declaration, the flag raising, . . . Special Olympians often have the opportunity to meet celebrities and local politicians, experience new sport and recreational activities through a variety of clinics, enjoy an overnight experience away from home with friends, and develop physical and social skills necessary to enter school and community sport programs. (p. 172)

This experience is equally important for family and friends. Sherrill (1988) observes that "families need to feel proud to know their efforts are recognized and appreciated" (p. 39). Although many parents feel sport competition is good for their child, they believe the total Special Olympics experience to be much more important, especially the social part of the games (Burkett, 1988). Parents are an important part of the Special Olympics experience and are encouraged by the organization to get involved in various ways. This involvement can include, for example, supporting their child's efforts, practicing at home, providing transportation, coaching, fund-raising, recruiting new participants, and supporting local efforts in their community.

Volunteers

Today over 500,000 volunteers throughout the world help to make the Special Olympics experience a success (Canabal, 1988). These persons are the lifeblood of the organization; without their assistance these events would be impossible to conduct. Volunteers' duties are quite varied and go beyond training and coaching the athletes. Highlight 12.3 lists many job responsibilities and duties necessary to organize Special Olympics games. Organizing games of this nature is quite an undertaking, requiring many volunteers and a real community effort. This is perhaps one of the most positive outcomes of organizing Special Olympics games,

Volunteer Recruitment

Games management team
   a. Director
   b. Facilities/support service
   c. Special events
   d. Competition

Games committee team
   a. Computer
   b. Finance
   c. Games evaluation
   d. Registration
   e. Schedule

Facilities/support service
   a. Communication
   b. Food service
   c. Game facilities
   d. Housing
   e. Medical services
   f. Security

Public relations
   a. Celebrities/VIPs

   b. Financial development
   c. Licensing/merchandising
   d. Hospitality
   e. Publicity/press

Special events
   a. Awards
   b. Ceremonies, opening and closing
   c. Clinics
   d. Demonstrations
   e. Entertainment
   f. Exhibitions
   g. Families
   h. Olympic Town

Competition
   a. Games rules committee
   b. Officials

Games Evaluation Committee

Reprinted from various sources with permission from Special Olympics International.

as the recruitment of volunteers helps to establish a real genuine community spirit and awareness of persons with mental retardation and their accomplishments.

For the most part volunteers' intentions are good, and these persons perform a meaningful function. However, any organization made up of over 500,000 volunteers will have some problems. For example, in recent years certain practices during SOI events have been questioned —such as the use of "huggers" (people who stand at the finish line of a race to congratulate finishers), referring to all participants as "kids," attaching baggage-style identification cards to

the athletes' uniforms, chaperones being overprotective of participants and not allowing social encounters outside their own group, and the circuslike festive atmosphere for adolescent and adult participants (Brickey, 1984; Hourcade, 1989). To alleviate these problems, volunteers and chaperones who provide services to Special Olympics must be educated regarding the normalization process. Workshops are conducted that train volunteers and chaperones to treat persons with mental retardation with dignity and respect while allowing these persons the opportunity to socially interact in order to make new acquaintances and have a variety of experiences.

In addition, activities and events should never be age-inappropriate (e.g., providing adolescent and adult individuals with activities appropriate only to much younger developmental levels). Additional information regarding the steps SOI is taking to enhance the normalization process with this population is presented later in this chapter.

Special Olympics' Training Program

Proper year-round training of Special Olympians has been and will continue to be the number-one priority of SOI. In recent years, SOI has taken a number of steps to keep pace with this priority. For example, the Special Olympics mission statement reads: "to provide year-round sports training and athletic competition in a variety of Olympic type sports" (*Official Special Olympics Summer Sports Rules*, 1988, p. 1). The rules also clearly point out that it is important for any athlete seeking to advance to a higher level of sport competition to participate in an organized training program for at least 8 weeks in that particular sport. The training program must be a planned regimen of training under the leadership of a volunteer coach, teacher, or parent. In addition, SOI publishes *Coaches Quarterly*, an educational newsletter distributed to all certified Special Olympics coaches. This newsletter contains information of interest to coaches and athletes, such as seasonal training plans and strategies in the various sports SOI offers, interpretation of rules, administrative issues, international perspective, and coaching philosophy. However, according to Roswal (1988), the most dramatic change to help keep pace with offering quality year-round training has been the steady increase and improved quality of coaches' training schools offered by SOI.

Coaches' Training Schools

The Sport Instructional Training Program for both athletes and coaches began in 1980-1981 under the direction of Dr. Tom Songster, director of sport and recreation for SOI. During the first year, SOI sponsored 100 training schools, training 5,595 coaches. Since that time the program has grown dramatically. For example, during the 1986-1987 year, Special Olympics conducted 1,140 training schools in various sports. From 1980 to 1987 over 100,000 Special Olympics coaches have been trained and certified through the SOI sport training schools (Roswal, 1988). By 1991, SOI plans to train and certify an additional 40,000 volunteer coaches. Dr. Songster believes the magnitude of the training schools can only be realized when the number of coaches trained is multiplied by the approximately 10 to 18 Special Olympians each will coach (Cheatum, 1988). Without competent coaches, enhanced training practices and increased competitive levels for Special Olympians cannot be realized. Highlight 12.4 presents a job description for a coaching position in Special Olympics.

Training schools are offered worldwide in all 22 official sports as well as in demonstration sports. Training schools leading to coaching certification include an 8-hour planned program agenda followed by 10 hours of training with a Special Olympics athlete or athletes. An outline of a basketball coaches' training agenda (Roswal, 1988) is presented in Highlight 12.5. This agenda is typical of most coaches' training school programs that lead to certification. The 8-hour training session includes an overview of Special Olympics, the definition and characteristics of persons with mental retardation, information on athletic injury prevention, ability-grouping philosophy, general coaching techniques, and sport skill instruction for the specific sport offered. The afternoon segment of the program usually provides the coaches with

HIGHLIGHT 12.4

Special Olympics Coaching Job Description

Description: The Special Olympics coach is responsible for providing special athletes with comprehensive sport training and preparation for local, area, state, and regional level competition.

Responsibilities

1. To select, assess, and train Special Olympics athletes.

   - **Athlete selection.** The Special Olympics coach will recruit athletes and properly complete and submit all required medical and registration materials by established deadlines.

   - **Assessment**. The Special Olympics coach will assess each athlete to determine the individual and/or team skill level for training and competition in selected sports.

   - **Training**. The Special Olympics coach will develop individualized training programs for each athlete. The program shall include fundamental skill instruction, conditioning, and instruction on competition and rules. The training program should be a minimum of 8 weeks in duration.

2. To know, understand, and abide by the Official Special Olympics Sports Rules.
3. To know and understand the sport being coached.
4. To execute the legal duties of a coach.

   - Provide a safe environment.
   - Properly plan the activity.
   - Evaluate athletes for injury or incapacity.
   - Match or equate athletes.
   - Provide adequate and proper equipment.
   - Warn of inherent risks in the sport.
   - Supervise the activity closely.
   - Know emergency procedures and first aid.
   - Keep adequate records.

Reprinted with permission from Special Olympics International.

hands-on experience training Special Olympians in various fundamental skills. This is followed by a written examination. In addition to coaches' training schools, SOI offers training schools in other areas, such as advanced coaching, for which the training is longer and offers advanced techniques on coaching philosophy, instructional planning, and preparing the Special Olympian for competition; officiating; game directing; and volunteering.

Sport Skills Program Guides

Sport skills program guides play an important part in helping the coach to effectively train Special Olympics athletes. The guides (available by contacting Special Olympics International) are offered in all 22 official and demonstration sports, and each costs about $5. Coaches with a physical education and recreation background will find the guides helpful for introducing a

HIGHLIGHT 12.5   **IN PRACTICE**

Basketball Training School Agenda

8:00 a.m.   Registration (refreshments)

8:30 a.m.   General session
    Introduction, welcome, overview of agenda, etc.
    Role of a Special Olympics coach
    Purpose of training schools
    Story of Special Olympics—philosophy, levels of competition, program
       benefits
    Film
    Impact of Special Olympics
    Motor characteristics of persons with mental retardation
    Athletic injury prevention
    Ability groups—divisioning process

10:15 a.m. Break

10:20 a.m. Working with athletes with mental retardation

10:35 a.m. Effective coaching
    Philosophy of coaching and progression in coaching

10:55 a.m. Styles of coaching
    Specific coaching techniques
    Methods of instructing
    Conducting a training session

11:15 a.m. Overview of Sports Skills Instructional Program
    Assessment—Determining athlete's present level of ability
    Task analysis—Performance of a skill to demonstrate proficiency in the skill
    Teaching suggestions—Methods and materials to help the athlete master
       the skill
    Evaluation

11:30 a.m. Shooting
    Developing the technique
    Importance of balance
    a) Legs and feet
    b) Head
    Concentration
    Eyes on target
    Proper elbow positioning
    Fingertip control of ball placement of hands
    Importance of follow-through

HIGHLIGHT 12.5 CONTINUED

12:00 noon Passing
        Balance
        Fingertip control
        Arm extensions
        Wrist snap
        Importance of techniques involved in different passes

12:30 p.m. Dribbling
        Balance
        Fingertip control
        Importance of keeping head up
        Left and right hand development
        Techniques of different dribbles

1:00 p.m. Rebounding
        Balance
        Footwork
        Reading the defensive man
        Blocking out
        Reaction to the shot—attack it!
        Going up with two hands
        Coming down to a wide base
        Pivot and pitch

1:30 p.m. Lunch

2:15 p.m. Practical session (coach with athletes)
        Station I—Shooting
        Station II—Passing
        Station III—Dribbling
        Station IV—Rebounding
        Rotate stations every 20 minutes.

2:15 p.m. Begin first stations—split clinicians into 4 equal groups

2:35 p.m. Rotation

2:55 p.m. Rotation

3:15 p.m. Rotation

3:35 p.m. Break

3:45 p.m. Discussions with clinicians
        Evaluation of content of training school

4:00 p.m. Overview of certification process

4:15 p.m. Written examination

Note. This table is reprinted with permission from *Palaestra*, 1988, **41**, 36-37. *Palaestra* is a publication of Challenge Publications, Ltd., P.O. Box 508, Macomb, IL 61455.

specific sport to the athletes they train or as a resource guide in teaching a physical education class. However, the strength of the guides is in their ability to assist volunteer coaches, such as parents who for the first time are preparing Special Olympians for sport competition and do not have the knowledge base and coaching experience of a PE professional. The guides are based on the premise that athletes entering the program have mastered the necessary fundamental skills and are fit enough to perform the required sport.

From 1979 to 1981 the sports skills program guides were field-tested at public and private schools, residential centers, activity centers, and recreational facilities by over 100 teachers and 2,000 students in Arizona, California, New Jersey, New York, North Carolina, and Wisconsin. The guides have received positive feedback from professionals in physical education, recreation, and special education as a means to systematically develop and improve sport skills among persons with mental retardation.

Another strength of the sport skills program guides is that they were developed to meet the requirements of PL 94-142 and can assist educators in writing IEP goals and objectives for a particular sport. Each guide addresses a specific sport, but all the guides have similar formats. For an overall description of the sport skills program guide format, see Highlight 12.6.

Sports Medicine and Safety

The rising number of athletes competing in Special Olympics and the increased intensity level of training programs have brought an additional responsibility for coaches to be knowledgeable about sports medicine and safety (Low & Sherrill, 1988). Coaches' training schools include minimal information regarding the care and prevention of athletic injuries, and many coaches feel they are not competent to address the special medical needs of their athletes (see Highlight 12.5). Mangus and French (1985) believe that to more effectively attend to the med-

ical needs of these athletes, it is necessary to recruit more competent medical and paramedical personnel. These authors stress the importance of all coaches' having completed a first aid course and trained athletic trainers' being on site during Special Olympics games and events.

Medical conditions related to mental retardation are discussed in detail in chapter 2. The coach must know which athletes are taking medication. The coach must be familiar with the type of medication and the effect it can have on the athlete's performance (Low & Sherrill, 1988). Although each Special Olympics athlete's required medical form must list the medication dosage and schedule, problems can still occur. For example, athletes may fail to bring their medications for a trip out of town. In addition, because of the excitement of the day's events, Special Olympians may forget to take their medications.

To date, little information has been reported regarding medical problems among Special Olympians at Special Olympics meets. Birrer (1984) reported 58 athletic injuries among the 2,056 Special Olympians participating in the New Jersey State Special Olympics in 1980 and 1981. This 2.8% injury rate comprised primarily injuries environmental in nature and included heat cramps, sunburn, and fatigue. Based on these results, Birrer felt that most of the injuries were comparable to the types of injuries that occur among nondisabled athletes during sporting events and were not due to the condition of mental retardation.

Based on Birrer's findings, Low and Sherrill (1988) believe it is important for coaches to pay special attention to sunburn, dehydration, and heat exhaustion among their athletes. To combat sunburns, coaches must make the use of sunscreen mandatory for all participants. Heat exhaustion can be prevented by being sure athletes replace fluids regularly throughout the competition and when possible are provided with frequent rest periods in shaded areas. Most importantly, coaches and volunteers must recog-

Sport Skills Program Guide

Infusions chart—The use of the sport skills unit in relation to general academic areas such as art, health, home economics, industrial arts, math, physical education, reading/language, science, and social studies. For example, in swimming a reading/language lesson could be reinforced by having Special Olympians read and understand safety rules.

Long-term goal—The individual's expected outcomes.

Modifications and adaptations—Of equipment, rules, and playing area in order to ensure successful participation.

Overview—Explanation of the sport, rules, equipment, instruction, necessary prerequisite skills, warm-up activities, and organization of training sessions.

Short-term objectives—Specific individualized behaviors based on goal statements.

Skill sequence—Sequence of behaviors the learner must demonstrate for acquisition of the skill.

Sport skills assessment—Criterion-referenced testing to determine each individual's present level of performance, which places each participant in the following general ability groups: beginner, rookie, or champ. Pretesting and posttesting are based on the specific skills required to perform the sport.

Student's skills chart—A chart to mark the individual's progress throughout the program.

Task analysis—A further breakdown of the skill into the detailed steps necessary to perform and master the skill.

Teaching skills—Identification of the sport skills to be learned.

Teaching suggestions—Suggestions of methods and materials to assist in the successful mastery of the skill.

Terminology and resources—Glossary of terms, bibliography, and available audiovisual and printed materials.

Reprinted from various sources with permission from Special Olympics International.

---

nize the symptoms of heat exhaustion, which include profuse sweating, chills, throbbing pressure in the head, and nausea. Athletes who exhibit these signs should be immediately removed to a cool place and made to lie down while wet cloths are applied until medical personnel arrive. These authors state that Special Olympians should not be expected to compete at full capacity when temperatures exceed 90 degrees or go below 50 degrees or when the sum of temperature plus humidity exceeds 175. Coaches can help to combat heat exhaustion by paying careful attention to the length, time, and intensity of practice sessions and the type of clothing the athletes wear.

SOI has taken steps to ensure the safety of all Special Olympics participants. Training and competition in certain sports that SOI believes have unnecessarily high risks of injury are prohibited; these sports include javelin, discus, hammer throw, pole vault, boxing, wrestling, all martial arts, contact football, rugby, fencing, shooting, platform diving, nordic jumping, and trampolining (Krebs, 1990). In addition, persons with Down syndrome who are diagnosed as having atlantoaxial instability, a condition that places greater than normal flexion on the neck (see chapters 2 and 7) are restricted from training and competition in certain sports, including artistic gymnastics, diving, equestrian, pentathlon, butterfly stroke and diving starts in swimming, high jump, alpine skiing, soccer, and any warm-up exercise that places undue stress on the head and neck.

Coaching and Training Practices

Though SOI has set up numerous coaching schools across the country, few studies have tested their effectiveness. Among the questions to be answered are these:

- Are coaches who graduate from SOI training schools capable of applying this knowledge to improve Special Olympians' athletic performance?
- Do Special Olympics coaches feel qualified to coach?
- How much training should Special Olympics coaches provide their athletes?

Johnson, Sundheim, and Santos (1989) conducted an investigation to determine whether the application of Special Olympics coaching techniques actually improved the track-and-field event performance of 40 Special Olympians, both males and females, ranging in age from 8 to 26 years (X = 13.5) and classified as having either mild or moderate mental retardation. Thirty-one volunteers including teachers, coaches, and university students attended an SOI coaches' training school and became coaches. The training consisted of information provided in the clinic and the use of the SOI sport skills program guide. The coaches provided training sessions for their athletes which consisted of three 1-hour meetings per week over 8 consecutive weeks. Before training, the athletes were

preassessed to determine baseline data on four track-and-field events. Events were classified as two coached or two noncoached (no training). The Special Olympians were trained for 8 consecutive weeks on only the two coached events. The average performance scores revealed the following: Performance by the athletes in the noncoached events showed little improvement; these same athletes in the coached events demonstrated a significant improvement, maintaining a steady improved performance of 5% per week. In this particular study the use of SOI coaching techniques did improve athletic performance.

Miller (1987) surveyed the coaching characteristics of 170 out of 194 Special Olympics coaches (SOC) in the state of Ohio. Respondents were 46% physical educators and 22% special educators, and 32% served their schools in other capacities. Although 70% had completed some type of coaching training, 30% indicated that they did not feel qualified to coach. Interestingly, only 40% of the respondents felt officials were performing competently during sport competition. All three groups of respondents ranked physical education teachers as their first choice to be a SOC and felt the ideal coach to be a physical education teacher with experience teaching persons with mental retardation.

Roper and Silver (1989), surveyed the training practices of 121 Special Olympians participating in a Connecticut Special Olympics Summer Games who finished in first or second place in various track events (50 meters to 1,500 meters). The Special Olympians were grouped by age (8-11, 11-14, 14-18, and 18+) and by training practices as follows: endurance training, such as run, walk, and aerobics; skill training, such as throwing and jumping; and combination training, which consisted of calisthenics, exercises, and physical education. Next a profile for each athlete was established by developing and combining two separate profiles, a profile of training and a profile of experience. Questions from the survey questionnaire to develop these profiles included these:

How many days a week and hours a day do you train? How many months have you been training for this event? What kind of training are you doing? Results of the survey indicated that most Special Olympians were training less than 5 hours a week. Most importantly, the authors concluded that the extent and specificity of training was insufficient to bring about a noticeable improvement in performance. The investigators believe many Special Olympians are not meeting their athletic potential because training sessions are not highly structured and purposeful. The role of the Special Olympics coach, thus, is vital to motivating athletes into meaningful training endeavors to effectively reach their full athletic performance potential.

Although coaches' training schools have assisted in the development of more competent coaches to train and develop Special Olympians, much work remains. Questions posed earlier in this section as well as additional questions posed by Johnson et al. (1989) that remain unanswered and merit further study include these:

- Will the type of event or particular sport have an effect on performance?
- Are there differences in the training qualifications among coaches who are physical education specialists, classroom teachers, and noneducators?
- How many weeks of training are necessary before improvement occurs?

University courses in physical education should make every effort to provide majors with theory and practical experiences in the area of sport training for persons with special needs. Also, persons studying in such areas as special/adapted physical education and therapeutic recreation should be encouraged to get involved with Special Olympics primarily through coaching. Professionals with expertise and experience in physical education, recreation, and coaching can assist in bettering Special Olympics programs in the following ways: serve as a sports clinician in a coaches' training school or recruit other professionals to assist; be an official; serve as a resource by assisting with rule interpretations and supplying information through books and films; and provide facilities for practice sites or games (see Figure 12.6).

Research on the Benefits of Special Olympics

In the past SOI has focused primarily on developing and expanding program opportunities and perhaps has not given the attention to research that the organization deserves. Songster (1984) believes empirical research in this area has been limited in scope for several reasons:

- Special Olympics is a relatively new program, having been first implemented in 1968.
- The program is based on human principles and human values as opposed to record and data keeping.

Figure 12.6 Proper year-round training of Special Olympians has been and will continue to be the number one priority of SOI. Photo courtesy of Ken Regan.

- Worldwide studies are often logistically impractical.

Most past research has been primarily compilations of reactions to and opinions about the program and its impact on athletes and their parents and their communities (Songster, 1984). Recently, SOI has begun to recognize the importance of conducting data-based research to confirm beliefs that physical, social, and psychological benefits derive from Special Olympics practices. To enhance research efforts, SOI in February 1987 invited a group of renowned researchers and practitioners to Washington, DC, to discuss research topics specific to Special Olympics. SOI has developed a list of the topics that have been under investigation and will continue to be explored in the future (see Highlight 12.7). These include long-term or longitudinal projects such as the Unified Sports program, which was started in 1987 and is discussed later in this chapter.

Research conducted specific to Special Olympics has been limited in recent years, but three distinct areas of investigation have begun to emerge: reactions and opinions, physiological program benefits, and psychosocial program outcomes.

| *HIGHLIGHT 12.7* | **IN THEORY** |

Research Topics

The February 1987 SOI meeting centered around the following 12 questions and issues that were presented to the participants for consideration and discussion.

1. What are the measurable, tangible effects on persons with mental retardation that result from their extended (3 years or more) participation in Special Olympics training and competition? Are they, in fact, more confident socially, more physically coordinated, and more directly involved in home, school, and community activities (e.g., jobs) than their counterparts who do not participate in Special Olympics?

2. What are the specific benefits, if any, that have long-term effects on Special Olympians, particularly in their adult years (i.e., over the age of 25)?

3. What specific sport activities or organizational changes could Special Olympics make that would enhance the opportunities for persons with mental retardation aged 35 and above?

4. Which of the sport-supportive components (family involvement, social and dance activities, travel, extensive involvement of volunteers, etc.) have particularly positive impacts on Special Olympians?

5. Currently, Special Olympics is an active part of physical education in 40% of the school systems in the country. What specific steps should Special Olympics take to expand that number to 80% or 90% of the school districts in the country?

6. Our ultimate goal is to give Special Olympians the opportunity to choose to participate in community sport programs as well as Special Olympics. What data exists that demonstrates that persons with mental retardation can successfully compete in community sport programs against non-mentally-

HIGHLIGHT 12.7 CONTINUED

retarded athletes? What factors made this success possible?

7. What percentage of the current members of Special Olympics has a realistic possibility of competing in community sport programs?

8. For persons with mental retardation who have a realistic possibility of competing in community sport as well as Special Olympics, what social abilities, sport skills, and supportive networks are needed to make this possible?

9. What are the consequences for individuals with mental retardation who have experienced some success in Special Olympics competition and then failed to compete successfully in community sport activities?

10. What do parents of Special Olympians think and feel about the benefits of Special Olympics sport activities for their sons and daughters?

11. What do parents of persons with mental retardation who do not participate in Special Olympics think about sport and recreation opportunities available to their mentally retarded child? What are the reasons they are not involved with Special Olympics?

12. What are the various models of additional steps Special Olympics could take to expand normalized contact and participation between athletes with mental retardation and other persons in their communities?

Note. From *Report on the Special Olympics International Research Committee Meeting* by Special Olympics International, 1987, Washington DC. Reprinted by permission of Special Olympics International.

Reactions to SOI

To date the most extensive reaction or opinion study was conducted by Bell, Kozar, and Martin (1977) and examined the impact of Special Olympics in 224 participants, their parents, and the citizens of their communities. Results of the 3-year investigation funded by SOI revealed the following:

- Special Olympians in the two communities that received a full year of training demonstrated more significant improvement in certain physical fitness scores, such as the softball throw and standing long jump, than athletes from a community that participated in a 1/2-year program or participants from two communities who received no programming in Special Olympics.

- A teacher rating scale demonstrated that the attitudes toward school and physical education activities of individuals who participated in Special Olympics as compared to those individuals who did not was significantly more positive.

- These same teachers rated the progress of certain physical skills such as running, jumping, and throwing as significantly better in individuals who participated in Special Olympics as compared to individuals who did not participate.

- Members living in the communities that had Special Olympics programs had a more positive attitude toward children with mental retardation and their potential when compared to members in communities that did not.

Physiological Benefits

Studies examining the physiological benefits specific to Special Olympics athletes have been extremely limited. Roswal, Roswal, and Dunleavy (1984) conducted an extensive three-phase project to measure the health-related physical fitness (HRPF) of a large sample of Special Olympians 8 to 68 years of age participating in the Alabama Special Olympics State Summer Games. The authors felt that much of the current normative fitness data available was not representative of Special Olympics athletes, and this project was conducted to better assist Special Olympics coaches in making appropriate training decisions for their athletes. Results of the study were used to develop HRPF norm-referenced tables (see chapter 3).

A similar study of physiological benefits conducted by Pitetti, Jackson, Stubbs, Campbell, and Battar (1989) examined the existing fitness levels of 23 Special Olympics adult athletes who qualified for the Kansas Special Olympics State Summer games (age M = 23.6; IQ M = 65). Prior to testing, the athletes had taken part in approximately 13 months of Special Olympics training and sport competition. Training was usually conducted twice a week, with competition on weekends. Results of the study determined that the athletes did not improve their levels of fitness. The researchers attributed low fitness levels to the low intensity of activities offered during training, which did not provide an overload to the cardiovascular system.

The results of the Pitetti et al. (1989) study are similar to the findings of the Roper and Silver (1989) survey, as both studies revealed that Special Olympians will not meet their athletic potential unless coaches develop practice sessions that offer more intense bouts of exercise. Obviously more physiological research, such as the studies mentioned in this section, needs to be continued in order to assist coaches to develop meaningful training sessions that will enhance their athletes' performance.

Psychosocial Outcomes

To date, little research has been conducted regarding psychosocial outcomes for Special Olympians. One major reason for this is a lack of suitable instruments to effectively measure the development of persons with mental retardation in this area (Gibbons & Bushakra, 1989). One of the first studies to systematically investigate Special Olympians' participation and psychosocial dimensions was conducted by Wright and Cowden (1986). The investigators found that athletes (N = 25, 12-18 years of age) who participated in a 10-week, 1-hour, 2-days-a-week Special Olympics swim training program significantly increased their self-concept as measured by "The Way I Feel About Myself" from the Piers and Harris Children's Self-Concept Scale when compared to a control group (N = 25, 12-17 years of age) who followed their daily living activities. In addition, the experimental group significantly improved in cardiovascular endurance as measured by the 9-minute run/walk test from pretest to posttest and obtained higher scores than the control group.

Also exploring the psychosocial outcomes of Special Olympians were Gibbons and Bushakra (1989), who examined the effects of a 1-1/2 day Special Olympics track-and-field event on the perceived competence and perceived social acceptance of two groups of 24 children ages 9 to 13 years (M = 10.6) with mental retardation (IQ M = 58.5). Children who participated in the Special Olympics track-and-field event received significantly higher scores on the physical and peer acceptance subscales of the Pictorial Scale of Perceived Competence and Social Acceptance for Young Children than the nonparticipation control group. The investigators concluded that "this finding also supports the notion that meeting the demands of an optimal challenge will lead to improved perceptions of competence. Thus there is some confirmation of the assumption underlying the goals and structures of Special Olympics events. It appears that the ideal of 'to experience and not to conquer' is upheld'' (p. 47).

Issues To Be Addressed in the Future

We will now highlight new and innovative programs that have been developed recently by SOI. These programs, such as Unified Sports, partners clubs, Sports Partnerships, Outreach, Athletes for Outreach, and the Motor Activity Training Program, are all part of SOI's Expanded Sport Opportunities in Special Olympics. These programs will have a tremendous impact on Special Olympics athletes, coaches, and volunteers in the 1990s and well into the 21st century.

Normalization and Integration of Persons With Mental Retardation

In the past, Special Olympics has been criticized for its segregated grouping of persons with mental retardation. Critics believe participants do not receive opportunities for normalization such as social interaction through training and sport with nondisabled individuals. These critics point out that higher functioning persons with mental retardation, if provided appropriate opportunities, are quite capable of being successfully integrated into sport programs with nondisabled individuals (Brickey, 1984; Hourcade, 1989). SOI has always encouraged the participation of athletes with mental retardation who were capable in regular sport. These mainstreaming opportunities in the past, however, have been too few and far between. To better meet this challenge of enhancing the normalization process and to assist persons with mental retardation to expand their training and sport opportunities while functioning in the mainstream of society, SOI has launched three innovative programs: Unified Sports, partners clubs, and Sports Partnerships. These three programs were developed

to assist schools and communities to successfully integrate Special Olympians into existing afterschool sport programs and community sport programs (Krebs, 1990).

Unified Sports

Very simply, Unified Sports combines an equal number of athletes with and without mental retardation on a team. This is a pioneer program, the first organized effort to combine these two groups of competitors on the same sport team. The program can be implemented through both school and community organizations and currently offers six team sports: basketball, bowling, soccer, softball, volleyball, and long-distance running.

The Unified Sports program officially began in 1989 after a 3-year pilot project and extensive field testing from 1986 to 1988 under the direction of Dr. Milton Budoff, director of the Research Institute for Educational Problems, Inc., in Cambridge, Massachusetts. Results of the field testing revealed that individual and team sport skills improved substantially in the athletes with mental retardation who participated in Unified Sports. The personalized coaching and the modeling by the athletes without mental retardation served to enhance the play of the athletes with mental retardation. In addition, there was an increase in the number of social contacts made among the athletes. Perhaps most important were the increased knowledge base and positive attitudes exhibited by the athletes without mental retardation toward individuals with mental retardation (SOI, 1989a).

The rules for each of the six Unified Sports sports are outlined in the SOI *Unified Sports Handbook* (SOI, 1989a). The key rule to the program is that on each team the number of athletes with mental retardation must be equal to or exceed the number of athletes without mental retardation. Athletes with other disabilities may compete, but they will count as athletes without mental retardation. Team members should be closely matched in age and ability level to play the particular sport. SOI (1989a) suggests that participants 18 years and younger be grouped within 3 to 5 years of age, and that athletes 19 years and older be grouped within 10 years of age. Closely matching teams by ability level can be determined by administering individual skill tests and not allowing team members to exceed a 25% range in ability. In general, coaches should refer to the athletes as a team and not differentiate between athletes with and without mental retardation. Ultimately the casual spectator observing a game should wonder which are the athletes with mental retardation (see Figure 12.7).

Partners Clubs

Another innovative program developed by SOI to foster mainstreaming opportunities is the Partners Clubs program, in which junior high, high school, and college-age volunteers are trained as assistant coaches and provide sport skill train-

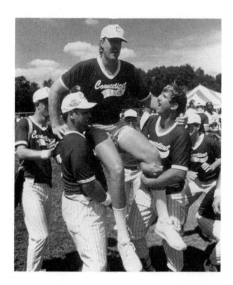

Figure 12.7 Unified Sports combines an equal number of athletes with and without mental retardation on a team. Photo courtesy of Special Olympics International.

ing and competition on a regular basis to Special Olympians. Additional time is spent in other social and recreational endeavors in the school or community. For example, a high school partner and a Special Olympian may go into the community to eat pizza and afterward attend a high school varsity basketball game. The partners club at Burley High School in Idaho has a winter ski club in which the partners and Special Olympians train together and share ski trips to Sun Valley.

To assist interested parties in starting a club, SOI has developed the *Partners Club Leadership Manual*. A partners club should be a sanctioned school club with all the benefits provided other clubs. Being a "partner" is an excellent experience for a young person who desires to pursue a career in education or recreation, such as special education or physical education teacher or coach. Partners attend a Special Olympics training school and learn to utilize the Special Olympics sport skills guides to effectively train their assigned athletes. Each partner is usually assigned to one athlete, working with that athlete for a minimum of 8 weeks prior to the athlete's attending a Special Olympics competition. Partners attend competitions and assist coaches with various duties. By 1990 over 600 partners clubs had been implemented throughout the United States. Feedback from the majority of the partners in the clubs indicates that they gain more from the experience than the Special Olympians.

Sport Partnerships

Perhaps no other program that SOI offers better exemplifies the concept of working toward normalization than School Sports Partnerships. In this program Special Olympians train and compete alongside junior varsity and varsity peers on the interscholastic level. For example, at an interscholastic track-and-field meet, the varsity 100-meter dash is run, followed by the Special Olympics 100-yard dash, or a Special

Olympics soccer game is played prior to a varsity soccer game.

School Sports Partnerships are effective in fostering mainstreaming opportunities, because the athletes with and without mental retardation share the common interest of sport, which helps to open the lines of communication. Many junior varsity and varsity athletes serve as assistant coaches to the Special Olympians, which helps to improve the quality of training these athletes receive. In addition this training and competition time spent together by the athletes helps to build mutual respect and friendships. To date, many high schools are awarding athletic letters to Special Olympians alongside the other athletes at schoolwide assemblies. In this way the entire school can share and take pride in the accomplishments of the Special Olympians. Still another important benefit is that students with mild mental retardation who are often sensitive to participating in programs for persons with disabilities can enjoy and take great pride in being part of a program that is available to the nondisabled and is recognized by the entire school.

Outreach Program

Many persons with mental retardation have not had the opportunity to experience the joy and sense of achievement that participation in Special Olympics can bring (Songster, 1984). In an effort to involve many more eligible persons in Special Olympics, an outreach campaign called "Join the World of the Winners" was launched by SOI in 1987. The program goal is to recruit an additional 1 million athletes by extending training and competitive opportunities into every community, school setting, and workplace where there are potential athletes. Steps to achieve outreach goals include forming a partnership with the public schools, parks and recreation departments, work settings, and athletes and their families who are currently participating in Special Olympics. This effort will include

recruiting an additional 50,000 volunteers as well as 100,000 new coaches to train these athletes!

Athletes for Outreach

A unique aspect of the outreach program is Athletes for Outreach. In this program Special Olympians, in order to effectively recruit new athletes and volunteers, are trained to give formal presentations to peers and potential athletes, to civic, sport, and church groups, to school and community administrators, and to families. Athletes for Outreach are trained in public speaking during a 3-day workshop. At the end of the training each athlete is asked to give a 5-minute presentation, which is critiqued. Athletes for Outreach are expected to give five presentations per year and whenever possible recruit new athletes and volunteers. So far the program has been most successful. Special Olympics Athletes for Outreach have spoken at a number of meetings, including college and university classes, meetings of state directors of special education and superintendents of education, and the National Down Syndrome Congress. Some appeared in a television commercial for Special Olympics and a national television Christmas special. And one was the keynote speaker at a national PTA convention.

Perhaps the most important benefit of the Athletes for Outreach program is the fact that it promotes the concept of normalization. Persons with mental retardation are provided with the opportunity to communicate and become more visible in society. As Eunice Kennedy Shriver (SOI, 1989b) said, "They are speaking for themselves to tell their own story—and telling it far better than any of us could."

Serving the Entire Population

In the past, SOI has come under criticism for not effectively meeting the needs of the entire population it serves, such as persons with severe or profound mental retardation and the physically disabled. To meet this challenge of better serving all persons with mental retardation regardless of ability, SOI in 1989 established the Motor Activity Training Program (MATP).

Motor Activity Training Program

In general, MATP emphasizes training and participation for individuals with severe disabilities whose limitations do not allow them to participate in official SOI sports. Since 1984, this program has undergone numerous revisions and in the past was known as the Developmental Sports Skills Program. With the cooperation of professionals in the fields of physical education, physical therapy, and recreation services, the current format of the MATP is being field-tested, with each of the seven basic motor activities being validated in Maine, Pennsylvania, New Jersey, California, Belgium, the Bahamas, and Norway.

MATP trains participants in the following seven basic motor skills:

1. Mobility (leading to gymnastics)
2. Dexterity (athletics)
3. Striking (softball)
4. Kicking (soccer)
5. Manual wheelchair (athletics)
6. Electric wheelchair (athletics)
7. Aquatics (aquatics)

The skills can be related to a specific official SOI sport or can complement activities of daily living.

The philosophy of the program is to provide persons with severe disabilities a program of skill development that is fun, age and ability appropriate, functional, and school or community based. In addition, the program adheres to the principle of partial participation, with the individual performing whatever part of the skill she or he is capable of and the coach providing assistance as necessary. For example, Figure 12.8 is an example of a task analysis from the MATP guide for mobility training. The prin-

ciple of partial participation allows each individual the opportunity to participate regardless of the severity of the disability. The program is implemented through the MATP guide. This guide follows the same format as the other SOI sport skills program guides discussed earlier in this chapter. The basic difference is that the skills learned are for habilitation and recreation rather than competition. Also included in the guide is information regarding transferring techniques, warm-up activities, strength and conditioning exercises, and sensory motor awareness activities. There are no rules or regulations for competition; instead, a "special training day" is recommended to allow these individuals the opportunity to demonstrate their efforts and accomplishments in front of peers, parents, and volunteers.

To date, little has been written regarding the effectiveness of this program for training persons with severe disabilities. Silliman, Anabelle, and French (1989) describe a community-based SOI program that included training five individuals with profound mental retardation (PMR) while using what at the time of the study was the *Developmental Sports Skills Program Guide*. These five individuals were integrated with 30 other SOI athletes with mild and moderate mental retardation (M & MOMR). All five individuals with PMR received instruction in three events, two developmental events (25-meter walk/run and ball throw for accuracy) and one official SOI track-and-field event, the standing long jump. Training sessions were conducted in circuit fashion, with no more than two individuals with PMR receiving instruction at each station at a time. The coach-to-athlete ratio (4:5) was quite good. Training consisted of providing each participant with short verbal cues, modeling, and/or physical guidance. Pretest and posttest assessments of the five individuals with PMR revealed an increase in performance in all three skills. In addition, social benefits included the opportunity to leave the residential setting and become part of the community, interaction with higher functioning

Given demonstration and practice, the participants will successfully perform mobility activities.

Participant lifts head off mat when placed on abdomen.

Task analysis

a.   Place participant prone on mat or soft surface.

b.   Give participant verbal cue: "Lift your head."

c.   Shake brightly colored object or make sounds to stimulate participant to raise head.

d.   If participant does not lift head, gently stroke the spine area from the neck down the spine several times. Note that this elicits a reflex action that lifts the head. It is not a voluntary action.

e.   As participant lifts head toward stimuli, gradually move stimuli higher and higher.

f.   Encourage participant to maintain head lift for 5 seconds or more.

g.   Repeat three to five times using various objects. Allow participant a 30- to 60-second rest between trials.

Participant rolls to back when placed on abdomen.

Task analysis

a.   Place participant prone on mat or soft surface. Make sure arms are to side of body or above head (not tucked under chest or abdomen).

b.   Give participant verbal cue: "Roll over."

c.   Shake brightly colored object or make a sound to the proper side of the participant to stimulate rolling.

d.   Assist participant by gently turning the head in one direction and pushing with the hand the participant is facing. Then gently turn participant's body over.

e.   Allow participant to, independently or with minimal assistance, perform as much of the activity as possible.

f.   Once participant successfully turns to back, allow him or her time to play with an object. Repeat entire procedure after a 60- to 90-second rest period.

Figure 12.8 Task analysis for mobility training.

Note. From *Motor Activities Training Program Guide* (p. 52) by Special Olympics International, 1989, Washington, DC: Author. Reprinted by permission of Special Olympics International.

athletes with MR, and one individual with PMR competing in an SOI area meet. Self-help skills learned included sitting and waiting in front of the residential center for the van to take them to practice, individuals buckling their seat belts in the residential van, and one individual with PMR being a torchbearer at a local SOI meet. Interestingly, several of the athletes with M & MOMR responded quite favorably when afforded the opportunity to be peer tutors and assist with the training of the individuals with PMR. Perhaps the most significant result was the favorable attitude change by the majority of the SOI coaches toward providing instruction to individuals with PMR.

Summary

In less than 25 years Special Olympics has grown from a backyard summer camp experience to become the largest and most visible sport organization in the world for persons with mental retardation. Today Special Olympics provides training and sport opportunities to over 1 million athletes in 25,000 communities in every state and 91 countries. SOI is granted official recognition by the International Olympic Committee and is a member of the Committee on Sport for the Disabled (COSD) of the United States Olympic Committee. This organization has served as the model sport program in the world for persons with disabilities through its contributions in organizational leadership, direct service, research, training, advocacy, education, and perhaps most importantly, public awareness (Winnick, 1990).

Special Olympics, which offers 22 Olympic-type sports, is an international year-round training and sport skills competitive program for persons with mental retardation ages 8 years and older. Through sport training and competition, persons with mental retardation can benefit physically, cognitively, socially, and spiritually. In addition, participants' families are strengthened, and the community at large,

through both participation and observation, is unified in better understanding persons with mental retardation through experiencing them in an environment of equality, respect, and acceptance (SOI, 1990a).

To ensure consistency in sport skills training and competition for its athletes, the official Special Olympics sports rules, which govern all Special Olympics sports and competition, are implemented. Most are the same as the rules and policies that govern the International Sport Federations (ISF) and National Governing Bodies (NGB) for able-bodied athletes. In addition, SOI recognizes the unique needs and ability levels of each athlete by offering an array of sport training competitions and opportunities, such as the Motor Activities Training Program, individual skills, team skills, modified events, team and individual sports, and Unified Sports. Competitive divisions include grouping athletes by age, gender, and ability. Ability grouping is a unique feature of Special Olympics sports competition, as it is based on even competitive divisioning in which every athlete has a reasonable opportunity to win.

Special Olympics, however, is more than sport training and competition. It is an opportunity for Special Olympians, their parents, their friends, and the community at large to share in the excitement, pageantry, fanfare, and color associated with Olympic-type games offered on the local, county or area, sectional, state, and international levels (Krebs, 1990). The success of these events depends on many factors, the most important being the effective use of volunteers, who are the lifeblood of the organization and today number over 500,000.

The number-one priority of Special Olympics is training. For this reason, as of 1991, SOI has trained and certified through its coaches' training schools over 140,000 coaches worldwide. Even though coaches' training schools have witnessed tremendous growth and have assisted in the development of more competent coaches to train and develop Special Olympians, much work remains. Continued research is one area that will help develop better training practices and more competent coaches and consequently better trained athletes. To date, research conducted specific to Special Olympics has been limited, and three distinct areas of investigation have begun to emerge: reactions and opinions, physiological program benefits, and psychosocial program outcomes.

Recently, certain Special Olympics practices have been questioned (Brickey, 1984; Hourcade, 1989). SOI, being a problem-solving and dynamic organization that is willing to change to better serve the needs of all persons with mental retardation, has taken steps to meet this challenge. SOI has developed new and innovative programs to help schools and communities successfully integrate Special Olympians into existing afterschool programs and sport programs. These programs, which are all part of SOI's Expanded Sport Opportunities in Special Olympics, include Outreach, Unified Sports, partners clubs, and School Sports Partnerships, and the Motor Activities Training Program. These programs will have a tremendous impact on Special Olympic athletes, coaches, and volunteers in the 1990s and well into the 21st century.

DISCUSSIONS AND NEW DIRECTIONS

1. If proper year-round training and athletic competition of Special Olympians is the "number one" priority of SOI, then what future strategies (e.g., training practices) should be taken by this organization to ensure that this priority is properly met? Whose professional responsibility is it to ensure that persons with mental retardation receive year-round training and sport competition?

2. Should Special Olympians participate in both Special Olympics and community-based sport and leisure programs? If so, how can SOI be supportive of this process? What experiences gained from Special Olympics competition will help Special Olympians in their community-based sport and leisure endeavors?

3. In the past SOI has been criticized for its segregated grouping of persons with mental retardation. In response to this criticism, in recent years SOI has developed such innovative programs as Unified Sports, partners clubs, and School Sports Partnerships. Do these programs effectively provide persons with mental retardation opportunities for normalization and integration into the mainstream with their nondisabled peers? If not, what types of programs need to be developed to assure the successful integration of persons with mental retardation into regular school and community programs?

References

Bell, N.J., Kozar, W., & Martin, A.W. (1977). *The impact of Special Olympics on participants, parents, and the community* (Research study funded by Special Olympics International). Lubbock, TX: Texas Technical University.

Birrer, R.B. (1984). The Special Olympics: An injury overview. *The Physician and Sports Medicine*, **12**(4), 95-97.

Brace, D.K. (1968). Physical education and recreation for mentally retarded pupils in publics schools. *Research Quarterly*, **39**, 779-782.

Brickey, M. (1984). Normalizing the Special Olympics. *Journal of Physical Education, Recreation and Dance*, **55**(8), 28-29, 75-76.

Burkett, L.N. (1988). The physically disabled athlete in Special Olympics. *Palaestra, International Special Olympics Games*, **4**, 23-24.

Canabal, M.Y. (1988). Volunteerism—humanity at its best. *Palaestra, International Special Olympics Games*, **4**, 10-11, 27.

Cheatum, B.A. (1988). International Special Olympics—uniting the world. *Palaestra, International Special Olympics Games*, 22-26, 35-40.

Gibbons, S.L., & Bushakra, F.B. (1989). Effects of Special Olympics participation on the perceived competence and social acceptance of mentally retarded children. *Adapted Physical Activity Quarterly*, **6**, 40-51.

Haskins, J. (1976). *A new kind of joy: The story of Special Olympics*. New York: Doubleday.

Hourcade, J.J. (1989). Special Olympics: A review and critical analysis. *Therapeutic Recreation Journal*, **23**, 58-65.

Johnson, R.E., Sundheim, R., & Santos, J. (1989). An outcome study of Special Olympics training techniques on athletes in track and field. *Palaestra*, **5**(2), 9-11, 62.

Krebs, P.L. (1990). Mental retardation. In Winnick, J.P., *Adapted physical education and sport* (pp. 153-176). Champaign, IL: Human Kinetics.

Low, L.J., & Sherrill, C. (1988). Sport medicine concerns in Special Olympics. *Palaestra, International Special Olympics Games*, **4**, 56-57, 60-61.

Mangus, B.C., & French, R. (1985, Fall). Wanted: Athletic trainers for Special Olympics athletes. *Athletic Training*, **20**, 204-205, 259.

Miller, S.E. (1987). Training personnel and procedures for Special Olympics athletes. *Education and Training in Mental Retardation*, **22**, 244-249.

Piteti, K.H., Jackson, J.A., Stubbs, N.B., Campbell, K.D., & Batter, S.S. (1989). Fitness levels of adult Special Olympic participants. *Adapted Physical Activity Quarterly*, **6**, 354-370.

Rarick, G.L., Widdop, J.H., & Broadhead, G.D. (1970). The physical fitness and motor performance of educable mentally retarded children. *Exceptional Children*, **35**, 509-519.

Roper, P.A., & Silver, C. (1989). Regular track competition for athletes with mental retardation. *Palaestra*, **5**(3), 14-16, 42-43, 58-59.

Roswal, G.M. (1988). Coaches' training the Special Olympics way. *Palaestra, International Special Olympics Games*, **4**, 36-37, 41.

Roswal, G.M., Roswal, P.M., & Dunleavy, A.O. (1984). Normative health-related fitness data for Special Olympians. In C. Sherrill (Ed.), *Sport and disabled athletes* (pp. 231-235). Champaign, IL: Human Kinetics.

Sherrill, C. (1988). A time for heroes: International Summer Special Olympics Games. *Palaestra, International Special Olympics Games*, **4**, 16-20, 38-39, 42-48.

Silliman, L.M., Anabelle, M.L., & French, R. (1989). Integrating profoundly mentally retarded children and youth into the community through physical recreation activities. *Palaestra*, **6**(1), 13-15, 36.

Songster, T.B. (1984). The Special Olympics sport program: An international sport program for mentally retarded athletes. In C. Sherrill (Ed.), *Sport and disabled athletes* (pp. 73-79). Champaign, IL: Human Kinetics.

Special Olympics International. (1987, February). *Report on the Special Olympics International research committee meeting*. (Available from 1350 New York Ave., NW, Suite 500, Washington, DC 20005)

Special Olympics International. (1988). *Official Special Olympics summer sports rules*. (Available from 1350 New York Ave., NW, Suite 500, Washington, DC 20005)

Special Olympics International. (1989a). *Special Olympics Unified Sports handbook*. (Available from 1350 New York Ave., NW, Suite 500, Washington, DC 20005)

Special Olympics International. (1989b). *Outreach fact sheet*. (Available from 1350 New York Ave., NW, Suite 500, Washington, DC 20005)

Special Olympics International. (1990a). *Philosophy fact sheet*. (Available from 1350

New York Ave., NW, Suite 500, Washington, DC 20005)

Special Olympics International. (1990b). *Definition of eligibility for Special Olympics fact sheet*. (Available from 1350 New York Ave., NW, Suite 500, Washington, DC 20005)

Winnick, J.P. (1990). History, legislation, and resources. In J.P. Winnick (Ed.), *Adapted physical education and sport* (pp. 3-17). Champaign, IL: Human Kinetics.

Wright, J., & Cowden, J.E. (1986). Changes in self-concept and cardiovascular endurance of mentally retarded youths in a Special Olympics swim training program. *Adapted Physical Activity Quarterly*, **3**, 177-183.

APPENDIX A

Organizations for Individuals With Mental Retardation

American Alliance for Health, Physical Education, Recreation and Dance (AAHPERD)
1990 Association Drive
Reston, VA 22091

American Association on Mental Retardation (AAMR)
1719 Kalorama Road, NW
Washington, DC 20009

American Blind Bowling Association
3500 Terry Drive
Norfolk, VA 23518

American Kinesiotherapy Association, Inc. (AKTA)
259-08 148th Road
Rosedale, NY 11422

American Occupational Therapy Association, Inc. (AOTA)
1383 Pickard Drive
P.O. Box 1725
Rockville, MD 20852

American Physical Therapy Association (APTA)
111 North Fairfax Street
Alexandria, VA 22314

American Therapeutic Recreation Association (ATRA)
P.O. Box 15215
Hattiesburg, MS 39402

The Association for Persons with Severe Handicaps (TASH)
7010 Roosevelt Way, N.E.
Seattle, WA 98119

Association for Retarded Citizens (ARC)
2501 Avenue J
Arlington, TX 76005

Braille Sports Foundation
75-25 North Street
Minneapolis, MN 55426

The Council for Exceptional Children (CEC)
Division of Mental Retardation
1920 Association Drive
Reston, VA 22091

Kirkwood Instruction of Blind Skiers Foundation
P.O. Box 138
Kirkwood, CA 95646

National Association for Down Syndrome (NADS)
P.O. Box 4542
Oak Brook, IL 60522-4542

National Beep Baseball Association
512 8th Avenue
Minneapolis, MN 55413

National Consortium on Physical Education and Recreation for Individuals with Disabilities (NCPERID)
Dr. Jim DePaepe
University of New Mexico
1162 Johnson Center
Albuquerque, NM 87131

National Down Syndrome Congress
1800 Dempster
Park Ridge, IL 60068

National Down Syndrome Society
141 5th Avenue, 7th floor
New York, NY 10010

National Therapeutic Recreation Society
(NTRS)
3101 Park Center Drive
Alexandria, VA 22302

Special Olympics International (SOI)
1350 New York Avenue, NW
Suite 500
Washington, DC 20005

U.S. Association for Blind Athletes
UAF/USC Benson Building
Columbia, SC 29208

U.S. Blind Golfers Association
225 Baronne Street
New Orleans, LA 70112

Very Special Arts
1331 Pennsylvania Avenue NW
Washington, DC 20004

Sign Language for Use in Physical Activity Programs

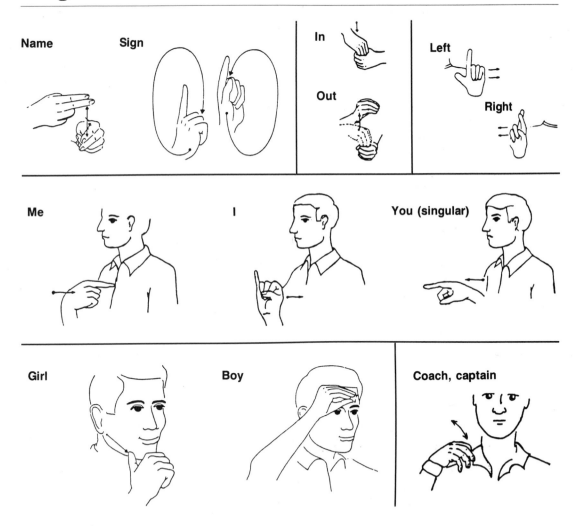

Note. Reprinted with permission from "Communication With Hearing Impaired Individuals in a Physical Education Setting" by C.B. Eichstaedt and P. Seiler, *Journal of Physical Education and Recreation*, **49**(5), 1978, pp. 19-21. The source (now *JOPERD, Journal of Physical Education, Recreation and Dance*) is a publication of the American Alliance for Health, Physical Education, Recreation and Dance, 1900 Association Drive, Reston, VA 22091-1599.

Please

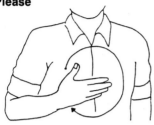

Thank you

Yes

No

Good

Bad

Again

Watch

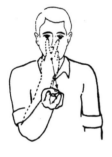

Understand

What

Shower

Under, beneath

Across, over

Stand

Sit, seat, chair

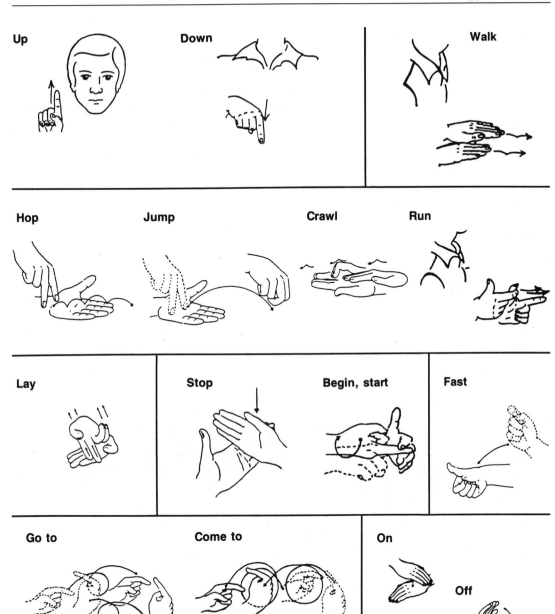

Up

Down

Walk

Hop

Jump

Crawl

Run

Lay

Stop

Begin, start

Fast

Go to

Come to

On

Off

Play

Exercise

Soccer

Basketball

Football

Baseball / softball

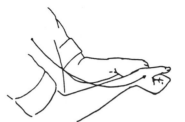

Wrestle

Volleyball

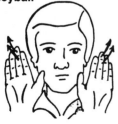

Throw

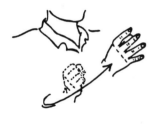

THE ALPHABET NUMBERS

APPENDIX C

Fitness Norms for Males and Females Ages 6 to 20 With Mental Retardation

Key

Ht = height in inches
Wt = weight in pounds
TRISKIN = triceps skinfold millimeters (mm) ("FAT-O-METER")
SUBSCSKIN = subscapular skinfold in mm
CALFSKIN = calf skinfold in mm
SITRCH = sit and reach in centimeters (cm)
SITUPS = situps in 60 seconds with knees bent and arms folded across chest
6M RUN = yards run for subjects 6 through 11 years
9M RUN = yards run for subjects 12 through 20 years
50DASH = time in seconds to run 50 yards
FXARM = holding chinning position in seconds
SHUTRUN = shuttle run; two block exchange; 30 feet × 4
STLJP = standing long jump
STORK = stork stand; hands on hips, toe tucked behind knee. Eyes open, right & left leg; eyes closed R and L legs. Sum of four scores in seconds with maximum of 10 seconds per leg
WLLBN = number of hits against wall with basketball in 15 seconds. From 4 feet away for subjects 6 through 11; 6 feet away for subjects 12 through 20

PCTILE	Ht	Wt	TRISKIN	SUBSC-SKIN	CALF-SKIN	SITRCH	SITUPS	6 or 9M RUN	50 DASH	FXARM	SHUT-RUN	STLJP	STORK	WLLBN
MALE MILD				*6 Years Old (n = ≤16)*										
75	46.0	47.5	15.0	9.8	12.0	29.0	16.0	910	11.1	6.9	16.2	35.5	17.5	3.0
50	45.5	46.5	8.0	6.5	10.0	19.0	15.0	820	11.7	2.0	17.9	27.0	9.0	2.0
25	43.5	42.5	7.0	5.5	9.0	18.0	14.0	790	14.5	1.1	21.5	18.0	6.5	.3
MALE MILD				*7 Years Old (n = ≤29)*										
75	52.0	65.5	22.0	13.0	26.3	25.3	17.5	1100	10.3	5.0	13.5	44.5	18.3	9.3
50	49.0	55.5	14.0	10.0	18.5	20.0	10.5	960	11.2	2.6	14.8	37.0	12.0	7.5
25	45.8	49.0	8.0	5.0	11.3	9.0	6.0	890	13.0	0.0	18.5	28.0	7.0	6.0
MALE MILD				*8 Years Old (n = ≤45)*										
75	51.5	65.0	15.0	11.8	30.0	29.0	31.0	980	9.8	6.8	13.3	49.8	18.5	11.8
50	49.0	59.0	11.0	6.0	13.5	24.5	18.5	900	11.0	3.0	14.6	42.5	10.0	9.0
25	46.0	51.5	7.0	5.0	10.0	16.0	10.3	440	11.9	.3	16.2	35.0	5.5	6.0
MALE MILD				*9 Years Old (n = ≤52)*										
75	55.0	74.5	17.3	11.5	25.0	27.8	26.0	1120	9.0	10.0	12.4	55.0	20.0	15.0
50	53.0	58.0	12.5	8.5	15.0	22.0	20.0	980	9.8	4.2	13.2	49.0	16.5	13.0
25	50.0	54.0	8.8	6.0	9.0	16.3	11.0	847	11.5	2.0	14.7	36.0	12.8	8.0
MALE MILD				*10 Years Old (n = ≤60)*										
75	57.0	94.0	20.5	17.0	23.3	27.0	23.0	845	9.0	6.4	12.1	52.8	26.8	15.3
50	54.0	82.5	15.0	11.5	21.0	19.0	16.0	770	9.9	2.8	13.8	44.5	22.5	9.5
25	52.0	67.3	9.0	6.5	15.0	14.0	10.0	645	10.9	1.0	16.8	33.8	15.0	6.0

MALE MILD														

11Years Old (n = ≤51)

	MILD													
75	58.8	93.0	20.0	15.0	18.0	27.0	38.0	1415	8.3	7.0	11.3	60.0	30.0	20.5
50	56.5	79.5	15.0	9.0	12.5	22.0	34.0	1115	9.1	4.0	12.4	52.0	24.0	15.5
25	54.5	69.5	11.0	6.5	9.0	13.0	23.0	680	10.0	1.3	13.9	44.0	19.5	12.0

12Years Old (n = ≤44)

	MILD													
75	63.0	113.0	19.0	14.0	21.0	23.5	39.5	1660	8.0	12.0	11.0	65.0	32.0	11.5
50	58.0	100.0	15.0	9.0	15.0	17.0	30.5	1300	8.8	5.0	11.9	56.5	26.0	9.0
25	58.0	84.0	11.0	6.0	9.0	12.5	25.5	1110	9.0	3.0	13.3	48.0	17.0	4.5

13Years Old (n = ≤47)

	MILD													
75	65.8	149.8	19.5	20.5	21.0	16.0	34.8	1450	7.6	4.8	11.0	69.0	33.8	10.3
50	63.5	121.0	14.5	12.5	18.0	11.0	32.5	1110	8.6	2.3	12.7	60.0	27.5	7.0
25	59.3	102.3	8.5	8.0	15.8	9.0	29.0	426	9.8	1.0	14.8	40.0	18.0	3.3

14Years Old (n = ≤36)

	MILD													
75	66.0	155.5	24.0	24.3	23.0	25.5	31.3	1333	7.2	15.0	11.1	72.0	34.5	12.0
50	63.0	116.0	18.0	15.0	17.0	18.0	25.0	1155	8.2	5.0	12.9	60.5	30.0	10.0
25	61.0	107.0	10.0	7.0	7.0	13.0	15.5	980	9.4	.8	14.7	48.0	16.8	7.0

15Years Old (n = ≤31)

	MILD													
75	68.5	147.5	15.5	15.5	19.0	30.8	44.0	1635	6.8	20.0	11.0	77.3	35.0	14.0
50	67.0	118.0	12.0	11.0	12.0	20.5	28.0	1317	7.3	9.7	11.9	63.0	31.0	11.0
25	62.5	107.5	7.0	7.3	10.5	13.0	26.0	1003	9.1	1.3	14.0	49.8	14.0	8.8

16Years Old (n = ≤22)

	MILD													
75	69.0	154.0	16.5	16.5	16.0	30.0	36.0	1523	7.1	13.5	10.8	74.3	34.5	19.3
50	68.0	136.0	10.0	10.0	8.0	20.0	32.0	1193	8.3	6.0	12.1	59.0	29.5	12.5
25	64.0	113.0	8.0	7.0	5.3	15.0	23.0	1100	9.1	1.8	14.9	52.0	15.5	10.3

17Years Old (n = ≤22)

	MILD													
75	70.0	151.0	21.0	22.5	27.5	30.5	35.5	1780	7.4	25.5	11.8	76.0	35.3	16.5
50	69.0	143.0	14.0	15.5	12.5	23.0	30.0	1365	7.8	13.0	12.5	60.5	28.0	14.5
25	67.0	132.0	8.5	10.5	7.8	18.0	24.0	958	9.8	3.8	14.1	49.5	16.5	11.3

18Years Old (n = ≤20)

	MILD													
75	69.8	167.5	25.0	24.0	24.0	34.3	40.0	1456	7.6	15.8	11.7	75.5	36.0	15.5
50	67.5	141.0	19.5	18.5	23.0	25.0	26.0	960	8.7	9.0	13.0	65.5	34.0	12.5
25	66.3	134.0	11.8	9.8	21.0	15.5	17.8	487	11.0	1.8	18.5	51.8	10.0	8.3

(Cont.)

Appendix C (Continued)

PCTILE	Ht	Wt	TRISKIN	SUBSC-SKIN	CALF-SKIN	SITRCH	SITUPS	6 or 9M RUN	50 DASH	FXARM	SHUT-RUN	STLJP	STORK	WLLBN
MALE MILD	*19Years Old (n = ≤11)*													
75	71.5	181.0	27.0	26.0	35.5	28.0	29.0	1080	7.5	21.0	11.8	72.0	36.8	19.8
50	69.0	155.0	21.0	18.0	26.0	27.0	25.0	770	8.0	6.0	12.2	62.0	24.5	14.0
25	66.0	112.0	6.0	8.0	7.5	12.0	19.5	534	9.2	1.6	13.6	38.0	13.8	5.3
MALE MILD	*20Years Old* No scores available													
FEMALE MILD	*6Years Old (n = ≤13)*													
75	43.0	49.0	17.0	10.0	21.0	33.5	25.0	930	10.7	7.8	17.3	41.0	20.5	9.0
50	42.0	48.0	14.0	9.0	15.5	30.5	21.0	720	12.3	0.2	20.4	29.0	12.5	6.0
25	41.0	46.0	9.0	5.0	10.0	16.3	14.5	540	14.3	0.1	26.8	19.0	5.0	3.0
FEMALE MILD	*7Years Old (n = ≤26)*													
75	46.5	57.0	19.0	10.0	22.0	25.8	21.8	995	11.0	5.1	15.3	38.5	21.0	7.5
50	45.0	43.0	13.0	7.0	14.0	22.0	18.5	890	11.9	1.1	16.3	34.0	15.0	5.5
25	43.5	37.5	11.0	6.0	6.0	19.0	13.8	562	14.5	0.5	19.9	25.0	12.8	2.8
FEMALE MILD	*8Years Old (n = ≤27)*													
75	50.0	53.5	14.0	11.0	21.0	29.0	31.0	1510	9.5	6.4	13.0	44.3	24.5	13.5
50	48.0	52.0	10.0	6.0	15.0	23.5	21.0	1200	10.3	3.8	14.8	40.0	20.0	12.0
25	45.5	49.0	6.0	4.0	5.0	20.8	12.5	1025	11.9	0.4	18.0	33.0	11.0	5.5
FEMALE MILD	*9Years Old (n = ≤30)*													
75	54.0	80.0	17.0	12.3	27.3	25.5	29.0	900	9.8	5.9	13.4	50.0	27.0	8.5
50	52.0	65.0	13.0	10.0	23.0	22.0	20.0	800	11.0	1.8	14.7	42.0	24.5	7.0
25	50.0	56.0	10.0	6.0	18.8	13.8	10.0	760	11.4	0.5	16.5	35.0	14.5	5.0
FEMALE MILD	*10Years Old (n = ≤27)*													
75	58.0	87.8	24.5	17.8	25.0	26.0	18.5	1675	9.0	9.1	12.7	50.0	27.9	10.5
50	55.5	74.0	12.0	10.0	14.0	19.0	8.0	1200	9.5	3.0	14.5	44.0	24.0	10.0
25	52.8	69.3	8.3	6.0	9.0	13.0	3.2	820	10.6	2.3	15.5	31.0	18.5	6.5

FEMALE MILD

11Years Old (n = ≤ 39)

75	59.0	92.0	24.8	19.8	26.8	27.5	34.0	2218	8.5	5.8	11.8	58.0	29.0	15.0
50	58.0	79.0	15.5	15.5	17.5	21.0	28.0	1305	9.3	3.0	12.7	50.0	26.6	11.0
25	56.0	71.0	12.3	8.3	10.8	18.0	19.5	890	10.2	1.0	14.2	41.0	23.3	10.0

FEMALE MILD

12Years Old (n = ≤ 45)

75	61.0	104.0	22.0	17.0	24.8	28.8	38.8	1343	8.1	6.0	11.6	60.0	29.8	10.5
50	59.6	98.0	15.0	12.0	19.0	23.5	31.0	1173	8.9	2.0	13.1	52.0	24.0	8.0
25	58.0	83.0	12.5	8.0	11.8	14.5	26.0	1005	9.7	1.7	14.6	43.0	21.0	6.5

FEMALE MILD

13Years Old (n = ≤ 32)

75	62.0	115.5	24.0	15.0	35.5	26.8	42.8	1540	8.1	10.0	11.8	57.8	29.8	11.0
50	60.0	107.0	17.0	13.0	32.0	17.5	37.0	1230	9.3	3.0	13.0	52.5	21.3	8.0
25	58.5	92.0	12.0	9.8	18.0	13.0	31.5	780	10.0	1.1	14.2	44.5	13.8	4.0

FEMALE MILD

14Years Old (n = ≤ 25)

75	66.3	122.5	25.5	20.5	32.5	30.5	33.0	1520	8.6	12.0	11.4	59.5	30.0	10.0
50	63.0	111.0	21.0	14.0	27.0	24.0	27.0	1162	9.4	4.0	13.1	50.0	21.0	9.0
25	60.3	96.3	17.0	10.5	20.0	14.0	23.5	950	10.6	1.0	15.0	48.0	9.0	7.0

FEMALE MILD

15Years Old (n = ≤ 23)

75	66.0	138.0	26.0	25.0	25.0	31.3	28.0	880	7.8	5.0	12.4	58.0	34.0	9.5
50	64.0	121.0	20.0	20.0	19.0	19.0	22.0	960	9.0	3.4	14.0	52.0	33.5	8.0
25	62.0	110.0	14.0	10.0	18.0	12.0	13.0	990	10.6	1.6	15.8	43.0	22.5	6.0

FEMALE MILD

16Years Old (n = ≤ 14)

75	66.0	154.8	27.0	27.3	46.0	32.0	28.5	1020	9.0	4.4	12.1	56.5	25.5	11.5
50	64.5	140.5	21.0	18.5	24.0	26.0	25.0	965	9.9	2.0	13.3	47.0	11.0	9.0
25	62.8	120.5	16.5	11.8	5.0	18.0	21.5	889	13.1	0.5	17.2	30.5	6.0	5.5

FEMALE MILD

17Years Old (n = ≤ 13)

75	66.8	160.4	22.8	27.2	27.6	29.3	36.5	1105	8.0	9.5	13.6	55.5	29.7	12.5
50	64.5	147.8	22.2	24.8	24.4	20.0	32.0	940	8.3	4.0	14.0	50.0	27.5	9.5
25	62.0	122.0	21.0	20.0	18.0	15.3	15.5	625	9.6	1.0	14.5	48.0	18.0	7.3

FEMALE MILD

18Years Old (n = ≤ 14)

75	66.8	163.8	22.8	21.8	25.2	27.5	40.8	1130	8.3	8.4	13.0	58.5	32.0	8.8
50	64.9	139.5	22.0	21.8	21.5	20.0	25.0	950	9.5	4.0	14.8	50.0	24.5	7.0
25	63.3	121.0	19.3	18.3	18.8	14.5	22.3	718	10.0	1.0	15.7	47.0	9.0	5.3

(Cont.)

Appendix C   (Continued)

PCTILE	Ht	Wt	TRISKIN	SUBSC-SKIN	CALF-SKIN	SITRCH	SITUPS	6 or 9M RUN	50 DASH	FXARM	SHUT-RUN	STLJP	STORK	WLLBN
FEMALE MILD			19Years Old (n = ≤6)											
75	68.5	139.0	27.0	27.3	26.0	29.0	18.8	945	9.1	6.8	14.0	51.0	35.5	13.5
50	66.0	123.0	22.0	24.0	24.0	26.0	12.5	630	9.7	2.8	15.5	39.0	33.0	8.0
25	62.5	105.0	19.0	17.8	20.0	19.0	2.5	413	13.3	0.5	17.2	30.0	30.0	5.5
FEMALE MILD			20Years Old	No scores available										
MALE MODERATE			6Years Old (n = ≤23)											
75	48.5	55.0	13.5	10.5	19.0	31.5	10.0	1315	16.4	.6	21.0	27.8	11.8	4.0
50	44.0	42.5	9.0	6.0	7.0	27.0	8.0	850	22.0	.4	23.0	17.0	7.0	3.0
25	42.8	40.5	6.5	5.0	5.0	21.5	2.2	492	24.1	.2	30.6	10.5	4.3	2.0
MALE MODERATE			7Years Old (n = ≤45)											
75	50.3	57.5	10.5	7.3	12.5	26.0	17.5	1220	11.4	2.7	16.0	34.0	15.8	8.0
50	48.0	51.0	10.0	5.5	10.0	23.0	8.5	889	14.6	1.8	18.0	24.0	7.5	5.0
25	46.0	44.8	7.0	4.8	7.3	17.5	2.5	567	16.0	.6	24.9	12.0	4.5	3.0
MALE MODERATE			8Years Old (n = ≤52)											
75	52.8	79.0	14.0	11.0	16.0	27.0	26.0	988	10.0	3.0	14.6	39.0	24.0	8.5
50	50.0	67.5	9.0	6.0	11.0	23.0	14.0	768	12.0	1.5	17.5	28.5	9.0	5.0
25	48.5	54.5	6.0	5.0	6.0	20.0	5.3	590	15.1	1.1	22.5	18.8	2.0	4.5
MALE MODERATE			9Years Old (n = ≤62)											
75	54.8	83.3	16.8	12.0	21.0	28.0	21.0	1155	10.9	2.1	13.8	40.3	29.5	10.0
50	53.0	64.5	10.0	6.0	9.0	20.0	15.5	800	13.3	1.0	17.0	30.0	15.0	6.0
25	51.0	56.3	7.0	5.0	7.0	16.0	5.8	580	17.0	.5	23.1	21.8	6.0	4.0
MALE MODERATE			10Years Old (n = ≤59)											
75	57.0	91.5	22.0	17.5	15.8	22.0	21.0	1215	10.5	1.6	13.2	45.0	30.0	9.0
50	55.0	74.5	12.0	10.0	10.0	17.0	13.0	795	13.1	1.0	16.1	32.0	13.0	5.0
25	51.3	64.0	8.8	6.8	7.3	15.0	2.0	663	15.8	.5	20.3	22.0	5.0	3.0

MALE MODERATE 11 Years Old (n = ≤68)

%ile															
75	58.8	94.0	16.0	13.0	12.0	16.0	24.0	21.8	1048	9.6	4.5	13.4	49.8	19.3	11.0
50	54.5	68.0	10.0	7.0	9.0	10.0	19.0	16.0	895	11.1	2.0	15.2	40.0	12.0	8.0
25	52.3	60.5	7.0	5.0	6.0	7.0	14.0	8.5	700	14.1	1.0	18.7	26.3	4.8	5.0

MALE MODERATE 12 Years Old (n = ≤84)

%ile														
75	59.0	112.0	18.1	18.4	18.5	23.0	20.2	1333	9.5	3.6	13.2	45.8	26.0	8.3
50	56.0	80.0	14.5	11.0	13.0	17.0	16.5	1001	12.0	2.3	16.0	37.0	10.0	5.5
25	53.0	74.0	13.0	6.5	7.0	9.8	4.5	810	17.8	.4	21.0	20.3	5.0	3.8

MALE MODERATE 13 Years Old (n = ≤79)

%ile														
75	64.0	116.5	21.0	16.0	20.5	27.0	27.0	1405	9.2	3.5	13.4	47.0	15.0	9.3
50	61.0	99.0	17.0	10.0	12.0	20.5	19.5	1139	10.8	2.9	15.8	37.0	9.0	5.0
25	58.5	88.0	13.0	7.5	9.0	12.5	14.8	1003	13.2	1.3	17.6	24.0	4.0	3.0

MALE MODERATE 14 Years Old (n = ≤111)

%ile														
75	64.7	123.1	19.0	15.0	17.2	26.0	26.0	1380	8.9	5.6	12.6	54.0	30.6	8.3
50	64.0	106.5	11.0	11.0	11.0	18.0	20.0	1197	10.4	3.5	15.0	41.0	17.0	6.0
25	59.5	90.3	6.5	7.0	7.0	10.0	14.0	1030	13.0	2.2	17.8	24.0	7.0	4.8

MALE MODERATE 15 Years Old (n = ≤90)

%ile														
75	69.0	133.0	9.0	10.0	10.0	25.0	26.0	1570	8.4	8.0	12.6	64.0	29.0	11.0
50	66.0	124.0	10.0	9.0	9.8	19.0	21.0	1200	9.9	6.0	14.8	45.0	12.0	9.0
25	63.5	110.5	7.0	8.0	8.0	11.0	15.0	920	12.0	3.0	18.3	31.0	8.0	7.0

MALE MODERATE 16 Years Old (n = ≤95)

%ile														
75	69.8	148.0	16.2	13.0	13.0	27.8	31.3	1535	8.1	7.0	12.4	62.0	30.3	12.0
50	67.0	136.5	13.0	11.0	11.0	18.5	22.0	1260	10.0	2.0	14.0	48.0	12.0	7.5
25	63.3	113.0	8.0	8.0	8.0	11.3	18.3	970	12.9	1.0	18.2	29.0	7.0	5.0

MALE MODERATE 17 Years Old (n = ≤92)

%ile														
75	71.0	163.5	16.5	15.0	14.0	28.3	30.0	1565	7.6	14.2	11.2	72.0	35.3	14.0
50	68.0	143.0	15.0	10.0	10.0	21.5	25.0	1320	9.2	3.0	13.3	54.0	16.5	11.0
25	65.0	122.8	14.0	7.0	7.0	13.0	18.0	985	12.0	1.6	17.8	33.5	10.0	7.0

MALE MODERATE 18 Years Old (n = ≤81)

%ile														
75	70.0	167.0	19.0	19.0	20.3	26.3	31.5	1405	8.0	10.4	12.0	67.0	28.5	12.8
50	68.5	139.0	16.0	16.0	14.0	22.5	23.0	1115	9.0	3.2	14.0	58.0	12.0	9.0
25	66.0	123.8	12.0	10.0	9.0	12.8	18.0	876	10.5	1.4	16.0	40.5	7.0	6.0

(Cont.)

Appendix C (Continued)

PCTILE	Ht	Wt	TRISKIN	SUBSC- SKIN	CALF- SKIN	SITRCH	SITUPS	6 or 9M RUN	50 DASH	FXARM	SHUT- RUN	STLJP	STORK	WLLBN
MALE MODERATE			19Years Old (n = ≤77)											
75	69.0	167.3	21.0	20.3	14.0	29.0	32.0	1515	8.4	9.7	21.3	66.0	33.0	10.5
50	67.5	144.0	11.0	13.0	9.0	21.0	26.0	1290	9.3	2.0	13.7	53.0	9.0	8.0
25	66.0	126.8	6.0	9.0	6.0	12.0	13.3	966	11.4	.6	16.0	36.5	2.5	6.0
MALE MODERATE			20Years Old	No scores available										
FEMALE MODERATE			6Years Old (n = ≤9)											
75	48.0	49.0	14.0	11.0	16.0	28.0	2.0	750	14.1	1.8	18.5	26.0	8.0	8.0
50	46.5	47.5	12.0	9.0	14.0	19.0	1.7	675	18.4	1.2	24.1	20.0	6.5	5.5
25	45.0	46.0	8.0	7.0	11.0	16.0	1.0	550	34.6	.6	26.8	17.0	5.0	2.3
FEMALE MODERATE			7Years Old (n = ≤17)											
75	48.0	53.0	15.0	9.0	12.0	29.5	16.0	990	12.8	1.8	17.0	24.0	19.5	8.3
50	46.0	49.0	11.0	5.0	11.0	25.5	9.0	658	15.3	1.5	19.8	19.0	5.0	5.0
25	43.0	45.0	8.0	4.1	7.0	22.0	3.8	380	20.4	.9	25.1	8.0	1.8	1.8
FEMALE MODERATE			8Years Old (n = ≤29)											
75	50.3	60.8	13.0	7.0	10.0	25.8	20.0	1009	11.9	1.7	16.2	30.0	29.5	8.5
50	49.0	58.8	10.0	6.0	9.0	22.5	11.5	960	14.9	1.0	21.0	22.5	10.0	6.0
25	45.5	53.3	9.0	5.0	6.8	18.0	2.3	942	20.4	.4	23.7	13.0	4.5	3.5
FEMALE MODERATE			9Years Old (n = ≤34)											
75	53.0	81.0	19.4	14.0	17.4	25.0	23.0	944	10.3	7.0	14.8	34.3	22.3	7.0
50	52.0	78.5	17.0	13.0	16.0	21.0	17.0	550	13.3	5.0	17.0	27.0	7.0	5.0
25	51.0	68.5	10.3	7.3	10.0	13.0	10.0	472	16.1	3.2	20.0	21.0	3.8	3.0
FEMALE MODERATE			10Years Old (n = ≤41)											
75	55.0	94.0	14.3	12.4	16.1	23.8	23.0	856	10.5	2.8	14.0	37.0	32.8	8.0
50	53.0	70.0	12.0	10.0	12.5	18.5	16.0	712	13.5	1.3	16.8	25.0	10.5	7.0
25	51.0	59.0	10.0	7.5	8.8	16.3	11.3	605	16.0	.8	21.2	15.5	6.0	2.0

FEMALE   MODERATE

11 Years Old (n = ≤ 40)

75	58.3	107.5	21.5	27.0	22.0	29.0	23.0	825	10.4	2.0	14.0	42.8	34.0	10.0
50	57.0	87.0	13.0	10.0	15.0	22.0	19.0	661	11.7	1.1	16.1	36.0	14.0	7.0
25	55.0	81.3	11.0	6.0	9.3	15.0	11.5	510	13.8	.7	19.1	25.5	5.5	3.5

FEMALE   MODERATE

12 Years Old (n = ≤ 47)

75	61.0	98.8	23.0	20.0	23.0	32.8	27.0	1213	10.4	4.6	13.7	39.3	29.5	7.5
50	55.5	85.0	17.0	16.0	16.0	24.0	19.0	1015	11.5	3.3	15.6	29.0	15.0	5.0
25	54.3	81.3	12.0	7.0	11.5	16.8	13.0	782	15.5	.6	21.0	39.3	6.3	4.0

FEMALE   MODERATE

13 Years Old (n = ≤ 71)

75	61.0	108.0	26.0	21.8	24.0	29.0	23.3	1278	9.8	2.1	13.5	45.0	36.0	8.0
50	57.0	92.0	16.0	14.5	20.5	23.0	15.0	970	12.5	1.1	16.3	34.0	13.0	6.0
25	54.0	79.0	13.0	9.3	11.5	13.0	7.0	802	14.8	.8	20.9	25.0	6.0	4.3

FEMALE   MODERATE

14 Years Old (n = ≤ 67)

75	62.8	115.9	23.3	16.3	21.8	31.0	21.8	1250	9.9	2.8	14.5	45.0	14.0	7.5
50	59.5	98.0	17.0	13.0	20.0	20.5	16.5	1040	11.7	2.1	15.8	33.0	8.0	5.0
25	56.5	73.3	10.0	8.0	14.0	12.0	12.3	782	15.1	1.0	20.9	20.0	5.0	3.5

FEMALE   MODERATE

15 Years Old (n = ≤ 76)

75	63.0	129.0	19.5	16.0	25.0	30.0	23.0	1233	9.4	1.5	13.6	46.0	13.0	9.5
50	61.0	117.6	16.5	12.0	21.2	23.5	16.0	1000	11.6	1.0	16.5	34.0	9.0	7.0
25	60.0	105.0	15.0	10.0	15.0	14.0	9.8	804	14.7	.4	20.0	22.0	6.5	5.5

FEMALE   MODERATE

16 Years Old (n = ≤ 67)

75	64.0	137.0	22.2	20.0	25.0	31.8	25.5	1400	9.5	3.7	13.6	51.0	35.3	11.3
50	62.0	132.0	18.0	17.0	24.5	26.0	19.0	1150	11.9	2.0	15.6	38.0	12.5	7.5
25	60.0	109.5	12.5	11.0	17.0	16.5	14.0	880	14.8	1.0	18.8	25.0	8.3	4.8

FEMALE   MODERATE

17 Years Old (n = ≤ 64)

75	67.0	152.0	26.5	24.4	25.0	29.3	20.5	1275	9.0	1.2	14.0	51.0	36.8	11.3
50	65.0	140.0	20.0	17.0	20.0	22.5	13.5	997	10.9	.8	17.2	38.0	12.5	7.5
25	61.0	126.0	15.0	14.0	18.6	16.8	10.0	797	13.6	.5	20.6	26.0	5.3	6.0

FEMALE   MODERATE

18 Years Old (n = ≤ 72)

75	65.0	141.0	27.0	27.0	22.3	29.0	24.5	1250	9.0	3.7	13.0	52.0	29.0	11.0
50	64.0	118.0	20.0	17.5	19.5	23.0	20.5	1100	11.0	2.1	14.8	42.5	20.0	9.0
25	63.0	115.0	14.8	12.0	13.5	14.0	7.8	880	13.4	1.0	17.4	33.3	14.8	6.0

(Cont.)

Appendix C (Continued)

PCTILE	Ht	Wt	TRISKIN	SUBSC-SKIN	CALF-SKIN	SITRCH	SITUPS	6 or 9M RUN	50 DASH	FXARM	SHUT-RUN	STLJP	STORK	WLLBN
FEMALE MODERATE			*19 Years Old (n = ≤44)*											
75	68.0	155.4	24.1	24.8	34.1	32.8	23.0	1160	9.5	1.8	14.6	47.8	25.0	9.0
50	64.0	135.0	21.0	20.0	22.0	27.5	15.0	933	11.4	.9	17.0	36.0	13.5	7.0
25	62.0	129.0	15.0	11.0	17.5	15.5	10.3	660	15.0	.4	20.0	24.0	6.3	5.0
FEMALE MODERATE			*20 Years Old (n = ≤46)*											
75	65.8	147.5	30.0	28.3	34.0	29.0	30.0	1287	9.7	1.0	14.2	49.5	19.0	9.3
50	64.5	137.5	23.0	18.5	24.0	22.0	19.0	1000	12.4	.7	15.7	39.0	10.0	6.5
25	60.3	126.3	17.0	13.8	11.0	12.0	13.0	790	14.9	.4	17.5	25.5	9.0	3.8
MALE DOWN			*6 Years Old (n = ≤9)*											
75	47.0	47.0	11.0	12.0	15.0	35.0	14.0	800	15.4	.7	19.3	22.8	5.0	2.0
50	46.5	45.5	10.0	8.0	15.0	27.0	5.0	725	18.6	.5	21.8	17.5	3.0	1.5
25	45.1	42.6	7.0	6.0	15.0	21.0	3.0	670	21.3	.2	23.3	15.3	2.1	1.0
MALE DOWN			*7 Years Old (n = ≤16)*											
75	47.5	59.0	18.5	16.5	16.0	35.0	21.0	956	14.8	2.9	16.1	27.0	6.3	9.3
50	44.5	53.0	12.5	9.0	14.0	33.0	12.0	840	16.3	1.3	18.9	20.0	5.0	3.5
25	43.8	49.8	9.5	5.5	12.0	30.3	2.0	750	21.6	1.0	25.6	9.8	2.0	2.3
MALE DOWN			*8 Years Old (n = ≤19)*											
75	47.0	73.5	22.0	19.0	33.5	37.8	14.0	962	14.8	4.6	17.8	27.0	9.8	5.5
50	45.0	56.0	14.0	7.0	14.0	32.5	8.0	819	15.2	2.3	19.7	21.0	5.5	5.0
25	44.0	44.5	9.0	4.0	11.0	28.8	5.0	780	19.9	1.2	21.9	14.0	3.8	3.0
MALE DOWN			*9 Years Old (n = ≤26)*											
75	49.0	73.0	25.8	20.8	35.0	37.5	20.0	890	14.4	4.3	15.8	38.3	13.0	7.0
50	48.0	61.0	16.5	10.5	16.0	29.0	17.0	730	15.7	3.2	17.8	31.0	10.0	5.0
25	45.0	55.0	10.3	8.3	6.0	22.0	7.5	625	18.8	1.5	20.0	23.5	2.0	2.8
MALE DOWN			*10 Years Old (n = ≤31)*											
75	51.0	84.0	21.5	19.8	21.0	37.8	19.0	850	11.6	3.8	14.7	41.0	12.8	7.0
50	50.0	65.0	13.5	14.0	10.0	34.0	18.0	770	13.4	2.8	17.1	35.0	10.0	6.0
25	48.0	60.0	7.5	6.5	8.0	29.3	6.0	680	17.1	1.4	22.3	24.0	6.3	6.0

11 Years Old (n = ≤27)

MALE	DOWN												
75	54.0	98.2	26.7	22.8	23.4	33.0	18.0	1110	12.5	2.3	15.3	39.0	26.0	9.0
50	52.6	84.2	25.3	17.2	21.8	27.0	10.5	700	16.0	1.9	18.0	25.0	16.4	8.0
25	50.0	65.0	17.0	9.0	21.0	19.5	3.0	520	18.0	.6	21.6	19.0	5.0	4.5

12 Years Old (n = ≤24)

MALE	DOWN												
75	58.0	99.0	24.0	28.0	29.3	30.0	25.8	1210	11.8	5.0	15.1	46.0	7.0	8.0
50	56.0	89.0	13.5	18.0	20.0	23.0	16.0	870	12.5	1.8	16.2	37.0	5.0	7.0
25	54.0	80.0	9.8	7.5	15.0	18.0	6.5	700	14.2	1.0	17.1	21.0	4.0	4.6

13 Years Old (n = ≤41)

MALE	DOWN												
75	59.0	122.0	24.3	21.0	26.0	36.0	27.0	931	10.8	4.1	14.2	49.0	8.0	9.0
50	57.0	93.0	13.0	15.0	17.5	30.0	15.5	758	12.0	2.5	15.8	36.0	4.0	4.0
25	54.0	73.5	9.8	8.0	12.3	23.3	7.5	550	17.1	1.4	18.5	23.0	3.0	3.0

14 Years Old (n = ≤39)

MALE	DOWN												
75	61.0	125.0	24.0	22.0	11.0	36.5	27.0	946	10.9	2.9	12.7	50.0	13.0	7.0
50	60.0	101.0	14.0	14.0	10.0	32.0	22.5	880	11.9	1.0	15.7	35.0	7.0	6.0
25	55.0	95.0	10.0	8.0	8.0	29.0	17.0	708	14.0	.4	17.8	24.8	3.0	5.0

15 Years Old (n = ≤39)

MALE	DOWN												
75	62.0	141.0	25.0	25.0	23.0	34.3	27.0	1130	9.3	6.1	12.7	51.0	10.0	7.0
50	61.0	126.0	20.5	20.0	20.0	30.0	24.0	1000	10.0	3.6	14.1	42.0	7.0	6.0
25	57.0	113.0	11.0	14.0	15.0	24.0	14.0	820	11.6	.1	16.6	29.0	6.0	5.0

16 Years Old (n = ≤40)

MALE	DOWN												
75	61.0	160.3	15.0	27.0	15.8	37.0	36.0	960	9.2	8.0	13.9	60.0	12.0	7.3
50	59.5	128.0	12.0	18.0	12.0	32.0	27.0	765	12.9	4.0	17.4	35.5	5.0	6.0
25	57.0	114.0	10.0	8.5	9.8	25.0	17.5	675	18.0	1.8	23.5	11.5	2.0	4.5

17 Years Old (n = ≤48)

MALE	DOWN												
75	62.3	171.8	19.3	25.0	20.0	38.3	30.0	1678	9.1	5.9	13.0	54.0	6.0	9.0
50	60.0	157.5	15.0	18.0	12.0	34.0	21.0	928	10.8	3.1	14.5	46.0	5.0	7.0
25	58.8	117.5	10.5	12.5	9.0	25.0	14.0	626	12.0	1.2	18.0	39.3	2.0	2.0

18 Years Old (n = ≤36)

MALE	DOWN												
75	62.0	180.3	21.3	25.3	23.3	39.0	28.8	920	9.2	4.3	12.8	51.8	14.0	13.0
50	60.0	145.5	17.0	18.5	9.0	36.0	23.0	840	10.4	1.0	14.9	38.5	7.5	10.0
25	59.8	119.3	11.5	10.0	5.3	32.5	15.8	680	12.4	.8	16.6	19.3	4.8	4.0

(Cont.)

Appendix C   (Continued)

PCTILE	Ht	Wt	TRISKIN	SUBSC-SKIN	CALF-SKIN	SITRCH	SITUPS	6 or 9M RUN	50 DASH	FXARM	SHUT-RUN	STLJP	STORK	WLLBN
MALE DOWN	*19Years Old (n = ≤33)*													
75	62.0	155.0	16.0	34.3	17.3	38.0	29.0	1128	8.5	8.7	11.9	59.5	10.0	12.0
50	61.0	137.0	14.0	20.0	12.0	33.0	25.0	891	9.8	5.0	13.4	51.0	7.0	9.0
25	59.0	123.0	10.0	16.5	7.8	25.0	17.0	795	11.4	1.4	16.0	34.5	4.0	7.0
MALE DOWN	*20Years Old (n = ≤37)*													
75	63.0	179.0	20.0	26.5	22.3	37.5	30.3	1258	8.8	6.1	12.7	60.0	10.0	13.3
50	62.0	146.0	14.5	17.5	14.0	29.0	23.5	1100	10.0	1.0	14.0	48.0	8.0	12.0
25	60.3	138.3	8.8	11.0	7.5	24.5	16.5	825	12.0	.5	16.2	40.5	4.0	8.0
FEMALE DOWN	*6Years Old*	No scores available												
FEMALE DOWN	*7Years Old (n = ≤9)*													
75	—	—	19.0	13.5	—	37.5	13.0	606	17.2	5.5	19.1	34.5	—	—
50	—	—	12.0	10.0	—	35.0	6.0	519	21.9	2.1	21.0	25.0	—	—
25	—	—	10.0	6.0	—	27.5	1.0	203	25.1	1.0	24.0	12.5	—	—
FEMALE DOWN	*8Years Old (n = ≤18)*													
75	49.0	77.0	22.3	22.7	25.2	36.0	15.0	655	14.0	.7	18.4	25.5	8.5	4.5
50	46.0	65.0	20.0	17.5	22.0	29.0	10.0	513	16.8	.5	21.2	15.0	4.0	3.0
25	42.0	52.0	14.3	9.0	18.8	26.0	5.3	494	19.6	.2	22.5	11.8	2.5	2.5
FEMALE DOWN	*9Years Old (n = ≤21)*													
75	50.0	82.0	16.8	12.3	20.0	38.0	22.3	768	13.2	2.8	16.6	33.0	28.0	5.0
50	46.0	60.0	15.0	8.5	18.0	31.0	18.5	610	16.0	.9	19.8	26.0	10.4	2.0
25	44.5	58.0	10.5	7.3	10.0	21.6	6.0	490	17.5	.3	18.5	18.5	6.2	1.0
FEMALE DOWN	*10Years Old (n = ≤16)*													
75	53.0	106.9	19.7	18.0	20.2	37.0	20.0	638	13.5	3.5	18.7	32.0	3.0	4.0
50	52.4	99.4	19.2	14.0	17.8	34.0	12.0	540	24.6	2.2	20.5	23.0	1.5	3.0
25	48.5	77.0	13.8	8.3	15.0	26.0	4.0	510	27.0	1.1	26.3	18.0	1.0	2.0

FEMALE	**DOWN**	*11Years Old (n = ≤19)*												
75	54.0	121.0	23.5	28.0	33.0	34.0	21.0	771	12.2	3.0	16.0	31.0	12.5	5.5
50	52.5	79.5	19.0	19.0	25.0	23.0	10.0	726	14.0	2.1	16.7	22.0	9.5	3.5
25	47.0	61.8	16.5	11.5	16.0	10.5	4.0	614	21.0	1.0	16.0	18.0	5.8	2.0
FEMALE	**DOWN**	*12Years Old (n = ≤27)*												
75	54.0	101.8	26.0	25.0	19.0	38.0	22.5	988	13.8	4.4	16.4	32.3	10.0	6.0
50	53.0	78.0	21.0	19.0	17.0	32.0	13.0	900	15.4	2.7	18.1	25.0	3.0	5.0
25	50.8	64.8	16.3	13.0	15.0	27.3	9.3	805	18.0	.6	20.0	20.0	2.0	4.0
FEMALE	**DOWN**	*13Years Old (n = ≤28)*												
75	58.0	137.0	22.0	17.5	25.8	41.0	21.0	976	11.3	3.3	15.4	32.3	6.8	7.0
50	56.0	96.0	18.0	15.0	15.5	38.0	17.0	960	15.0	1.3	16.8	25.0	4.5	6.0
25	51.5	83.5	9.8	11.0	4.0	29.0	9.8	923	16.7	1.0	17.9	22.0	2.3	5.0
FEMALE	**DOWN**	*14Years Old (n = ≤29)*												
75	58.0	156.6	25.2	27.6	26.0	40.0	21.8	1125	10.9	4.1	15.5	39.0	13.0	8.0
50	57.0	99.0	21.6	24.6	23.0	36.0	16.0	890	13.7	3.1	17.1	31.0	9.0	6.0
25	55.8	83.0	14.0	18.0	20.0	31.0	11.5	668	19.0	.5	18.9	22.0	6.3	5.0
FEMALE	**DOWN**	*15Years Old (n = ≤28)*												
75	59.0	123.3	22.5	25.0	27.0	41.8	27.3	1015	10.4	3.8	13.8	39.0	10.0	8.0
50	57.5	101.5	18.0	18.0	21.0	33.0	19.0	790	12.4	1.0	16.9	32.0	6.5	6.5
25	55.3	93.3	14.5	12.5	16.0	26.0	11.8	620	15.0	.2	18.6	28.0	4.3	5.0
FEMALE	**DOWN**	*16Years Old (n = ≤40)*												
75	58.8	148.5	30.0	35.0	38.0	37.0	23.5	943	10.6	3.2	15.7	36.8	9.5	9.8
50	57.0	126.0	20.0	23.0	23.0	31.0	16.0	875	12.6	2.7	17.0	30.0	5.0	8.0
25	55.5	95.8	14.0	16.0	15.5	20.5	12.0	775	14.7	1.3	19.2	18.0	2.3	7.0
FEMALE	**DOWN**	*17Years Old (n = ≤31)*												
75	59.0	152.0	27.0	29.3	33.0	36.0	29.0	1198	11.3	2.8	15.0	44.0	12.5	7.5
50	58.0	133.0	25.0	21.5	21.0	29.5	19.5	985	12.1	1.1	16.2	37.0	8.0	3.5
25	57.0	102.0	16.0	16.8	18.0	15.0	15.0	805	13.8	.6	18.4	27.0	4.5	2.8
FEMALE	**DOWN**	*18Years Old (n = ≤29)*												
75	59.3	130.3	26.3	27.0	19.8	41.0	33.0	1278	10.5	2.0	15.1	49.8	10.5	6.5
50	58.0	110.0	20.0	15.0	13.0	36.0	20.0	800	13.0	1.5	16.8	37.5	4.0	4.0
25	55.0	89.5	12.0	10.5	9.5	26.0	10.0	540	15.4	.5	19.9	25.5	3.5	3.5

(Cont.)

Appendix C (Continued)

PCTILE	Ht	Wt	TRISKIN	SUBSC-SKIN	CALF-SKIN	SITRCH	SITUPS	6 or 9M RUN	50 DASH	FXARM	SHUT-RUN	STLJP	STORK	WLLBN
FEMALE DOWN			*19 Years Old (n = ≤26)*											
75	58.5	159.0	34.0	30.0	35.8	42.0	22.8	1049	11.3	3.7	15.0	41.0	14.3	8.0
50	58.0	142.0	28.5	28.0	26.0	27.0	18.0	858	13.2	1.8	17.8	30.0	9.0	6.0
25	55.5	123.0	19.8	22.0	18.5	24.0	14.3	770	17.9	.9	20.0	23.0	4.5	5.0
FEMALE DOWN			*20 Years Old (n = ≤21)*											
75	59.3	154.0	29.3	31.8	35.8	35.0	22.8	850	10.3	1.5	14.8	40.5	6.8	7.8
50	57.7	146.0	25.2	23.9	35.2	30.5	13.5	790	13.3	1.0	16.5	33.0	5.5	6.5
25	56.0	130.5	17.8	17.5	22.0	23.5	11.0	630	16.2	.6	17.8	18.5	4.3	6.0

Note. From *Physical Fitness and Motor Skill Levels of Individuals With Mental Retardation: Mild, Moderate, and Down Syndrome, ages 6-21* by C.B. Eichstaedt, P.Y. Wang, J.J. Polacek, & P.F. Dohrmann, 1991, Normal, IL: Illinois State University Printing Services. Copyright 1991 by C.B. Eichstaedt et al. Reprinted by permission.

The Kansas Adapted/Special Physical Education Test Manual

Professionals who administer fitness tests to children with special needs are faced with a number of critical issues. Too often, these problems do not allow special-needs children to receive proper fitness testing. The *Kansas Adapted/Special Physical Education Test Manual* was developed in an effort to effectively address the unique needs of children with various resulting disabilities (Johnson & Lavay, 1988). The physical fitness components selected are similar to previous health-related physical fitness components (HRPFT) such as "Physical Best." The primary difference is the adaptations and rationale used to modify the HRPFT items selected in order to allow all students to be tested, regardless of their resulting disabilities.

What follows is a brief description of each test item. A more detailed description of each item including adaptations and rationale are located in the test manual (Johnson & Lavay, 1988) and also appear in an article titled "Fitness Testing for Children with Special Needs: An Alternative Approach" (Johnson & Lavay, 1989). (See Tables 1 and 2 and Figure 1.)

Abdominal Strength/Endurance—Modified Sit-Ups: This item is administered using the same procedures as the "Physical Best" test (AAHPERD, 1989), with one major modification: The exercise is repeated until the individual stops for 4 seconds, quits, or completes 50 correctly executed sit-ups. A 1-minute time limit is excluded to eliminate the motor efficiency factor.

Flexibility—Sit-and-Reach: This item is administered using the same procedures as the "Physical Best" test, with one major modification: The exercise is measured in inches rather than centimeters. Measurement is made to the nearest inch in negative or positive or a zero increment.

Upper Body Strength/Endurance—Isometric Push-ups and Bench Press: Traditionally pull-ups and the flexed arm hang have been used to measure this item of HRPFT. The pull-ups require the students to repeatedly move their entire body weight, while the flexed arm hang requires the students to support their entire body weight in a static position. These two test items will produce many zero scores. For this reason the test committee chose two alternative methods, the isometric push-up (IP) and the 35-pound bench press (BP). In the IP a face-down position is taken with the hands held directly below the shoulders, arms extended, with the whole body in a straight line, and toes touching the floor or mat (the correct up position of a push-up). The test terminates when any bending occurs at the elbows, head, neck, middle of body, or knees. In other words the test is stopped when the correct up position of a push-up is no longer held. The original test item chosen was the 35-pound BP. However, results of the pilot testing revealed the following: (a) Younger students were fearful of the weight and bar, (b) the 35-pound weight was too much for students under 13 years of age to lift, and (c)

Table 1   Health-Related Fitness Test Items—Reliability Scores

Test item

Sit-ups

Intraclass[a]	R = .922	R2 = .85	n = 209
Interclass[b]	r = .964	r2 = .93	n = 209

Sit-and-reach

Intraclass	R = .862	R2 = .74	n = 205
Interclass	r = .952	r2 = .91	n = 205

Isometric push-up position

Intraclass	R = .829	R2 = .69	n = 189
Interclass	r = .875	r2 = .77	n = 189

Aerobic movement

Intraclass	R = .781	R2 = .61	n = 206
Interclass	r = .689	r2 = .47	n = 206

Content Validity

Each test item in the Kansas Adapted/Special Physical Education Test is a modification of similar health-related physical fitness test items deemed valid.

[a]**Intraclass reliability** was determined using the Press Procedure found in *Applied Regression Analysis* (2nd ed.) by N. Draper and H. Smith, 1981. NY: Wiley (pp. 419-420).

[b]**Interclass reliability**: The test-retest reliability of each item was performed 1 week apart and was determined using a Pearson product-moment correlation coefficient.

many of the teachers felt the equipment was inconvenient for those who had to travel between a number of schools in one day. Therefore the testing committee voted to endorse this test item only with students 13 years of age and older.

Aerobic Endurance—Aerobic Movement: Traditionally, runs completed for time or distance, such as the mile run, have been used to measure aerobic endurance. The test item of aerobic movement was chosen because it eliminates motor efficiency bias by using time and pulse rate. In this particular test item the students may

Table 2   Health-Related Fitness Test Items—Means and Number of Subjects for Test and Retest by Age Group

Test item	5-7	8-10	11-13	14-16	17-21
Sit-ups					
Test	3.7	18.8	17.6	22.2	28.2
	(34)	(79)	(54)	(25)	(17)
Retest	4.7	20.2	19.9	25.0	28.8
Sit-and-reach					
Test	−0.5	0.4	0.4	0.7	1.6
	(34)	(75)	(54)	(25)	(17)
Retest	0.3	0.7	0.4	1.4	1.8
Isometric push-up position					
Test	19.3	41.8	29.7	20.6	42.7
	(34)	(75)	(54)	(17)	(9)
Retest	17.5	42.9	32.6	24.8	53.2
Aerobic movement					
Test	8.4	9.4	8.6	7.9	7.9
	(34)	(77)	(53)	(25)	(17)
Retest	9.1	9.6	8.7	9.6	9.4

Note. Number of subjects in parentheses.

run, jog, march, or walk with vigorous arm movement, propel themselves in a wheelchair, ride an exercise bicycle or scooterboard, use a walker, or move in any fashion to get the pulse rate past their resting pulse rate. The major objective for each student is to reach and then maintain a pulse rate between 140-180 beats per minute for 12 minutes after a 6-minute warm-up. The student's pulse rate is monitored by the tester every 3 minutes by taking a pulse rate check at the carotid artery for 6 seconds. If the pulse rate count is above 18 beats, the student is asked to slow down and is closely monitored for stress. If a student's pulse rate is above 20 beats for 2 consecutive checkpoints, the student is stopped and the test is terminated.

Name:_____   **Date of test:**_____

Age (DoB):_____   **Tester:**_____

Items   *Score*

1. **Sit-ups** (number completed, up to 50)   _____

2. **Sit-and-reach** (6 inches considered the zero position)
   *Mark scores as positive or negative values   _____

3. **Isometric push-up** (unlimited time)
   *Test terminates when any bending of the body occurs   _____

   or

3. **Bench press** (13 years or older)
   35-lb free weights
   *Maximum repetitions (50—males; 30—females)   _____

4. **Aerobic movement**
   (Check the appropriate pulse rate during each 3-minute bout)

Pulse rates

	Below 14	14-18	Above 18
6-minute warm-up			
Bout 1 (3 minutes)	_____	_____	_____
Bout 2 (3 minutes)	_____	_____	_____
Bout 3 (3 minutes)	_____	_____	_____
Bout 4 (3 minutes)	_____	_____	_____

Total score = total number of successfully completed minutes: _____

Figure 1. Sample Kansas Adapted/Special Physical Education Fitness Test score sheet.

Located in the manual at the end of each HRPFT item is a section on instructional information prior to testing. This provides the tester with guidelines for general test adaptations.

Certain students may possess impairments so severe as to limit their ability to execute the necessary movements required to successfully perform the health-related fitness test items. Included is information regarding the availability of other alternative standardized tests and references of readings for those students (i.e., severely disabled) who cannot successfully complete the HRPFT items.

The development of the *Kansas Adapted/Special Physical Education Test Manual* was based on the work conducted by a grant from the Kansas State Department of Education, Special Education Section, under title 5 B, Education for the Handicapped. Additional information concerning the manual can be secured by writing: Janet Wilson, Specialist in Physical Education, 120 East 10th Street, Topeka, KS 66612-1103. In addition, the completion and implementation of the material in this manual was the collective effort of many professionals who were concerned that students identified with special needs were not receiving adequate fitness testing. These professionals recognized that fitness testing designed to meet the unique needs of each child will enhance program application, which in turn will lead to healthy lifestyle changes for all children, including those with special needs (Johnson & Lavay, 1989).

References

AAHPERD. (1989). *Physical best test manual*. American Alliance for Health, Physical Education, Recreation and Dance, 1900 Association Dr., Reston, VA.

Johnson, R.E., & Lavay, B. (1988). *Kansas adapted/special physical education test manual*. Kansas State Department of Education, 120 East 10th Street. Topeka, KS 66612.

Johnson, R.E., & Lavay, B. (1989). Fitness testing for children with special needs: An alternative approach. *Journal of Physical Education, Recreation and Dance, **60**(6), 50-53.

Glossary

adapted physical education—Program of physical education modified to meet the unique motor, physical, and behavioral needs of each individual.

adaptive behavior—The effectiveness or degree with which individuals meet standards of personal independence and social responsibility expected of their chronological age and cultural group.

administrative feasibility—The practicality and usefulness of administering a test.

age appropriateness—The development of learning activities that corresponds with the individual's chronological age.

amniocentesis—Process of removing amniotic fluid from a pregnant woman to analyze genes and detect birth defects.

annual goals—General statements of student outcomes projected over the school year.

anoxia—Insufficient availability of oxygen to body tissue.

assessment—The collection and interpretation of relevant student information to aid nondiscriminatory educational decisions. It should be a continuous process and involve a variety of formal and informal strategies.

astigmatism—A curvature defect of the eye where rays from a luminous point are not focused on a single point on the retina but instead spread out as a line.

asymmetrical tonic neck reflex (ATNR)—An infant reflex, which occurs when the head is turned, and causes extension of the arm on the face side and flexion of the arm on the skull side (called "fencer thrust").

ataxia—A type of cerebral palsy characterized by defective muscular coordination, often involving balance difficulties that result from damage to the cerebellum, pons, or medulla.

athetosis (dyskinesia)—A type of cerebral palsy characterized by slow, wormlike movements, and involving a continual change of position of the fingers, toes, hands, arms, and head.

atlantoaxial instability (AAI)—Orthopedic condition found in approximately 12% to 22% of individuals with Down syndrome. There is a misalignment of the 1st and 2nd cervical vertebrae which could cause permanent damage to the spinal cord during hyperflexion or hyperextension of the head and neck.

atonia—Lack of muscle control often found in infants with cerebral palsy and Down syndrome ("floppy baby" syndrome).

backward chaining—The last behavior of a terminal response is presented first. *See* chain.

behavior—Any event by an individual which is observable and measurable, with a beginning and end.

behavioral objectives—Statements of conditions, actions, and criteria that have not been mastered by the student and are directly related to long-term or annual goals.

behavior management—Strategies for developing effective and appropriate behavior in an individual, such as behavior modification, Premack principle, reality therapy, transactional analysis, and relaxation techniques.

behavior modification—Systematic methods designed to alter observable behaviors, including increasing, decreasing, extending, restricting, and maintaining behaviors.

body righting—Primitive infant reflex enabling segmental rotation of the trunk and hips when the head is turned.

borderline mentally retarded—Individuals who possess an IQ of 70 to 85. They are not considered legally disabled.

cardiovascular endurance—Ability to perform numerous repetitions of stress requiring the use of the circulatory and respiratory system, creating muscular endurance specific to the heart, lungs, and vascular system.

cataract—A condition where the normally transparent lens of the eye becomes cloudy or opaque.

catheter—A tube inserted into various body channels, the most common of which is inserted into the bladder through the urethra, allowing urine to drain from the body.

cephalocaudal development—Gross motor development beginning with the head and progressing down the axial skeleton to the feet.

cerebral palsy—A condition characterized by lack of control of voluntary body movement and caused by damage to the brain. The condition is nonprogressive, and occurs prenatally, in infancy, and childhood.

chain—A series of already learned behaviors presented in a fixed order to achieve a more complex terminal response. *See* backward chaining.

chromosomes—Small rod-shaped or v-shaped bodies that appear in the nucleus of a cell during cell division and contain the genes, or hereditary factors, of the cell. Humans normally have 46 chromosomes comprised of 22 pairs of autosomes and 2 sex chromosomes. A common chromosome abnormality is Down syndrome.

chronic—A condition having gradual onset and long duration.

command style teaching—Each student in class conforms to the same instructional level of teaching.

conductive hearing loss—Inability of the outer and middle ear to transmit sound to the inner ear. Most are greatly improved by hearing aids.

congenital—Present at birth.

construct validity—The degree to which a test measures an attribute or trait that cannot be directly measured.

content validity—The degree to which a sample of items on a particular test are representative of the domain or content.

contingency—A relationship between the target behavior to be changed and the events or consequences that follow the particular behavior.

contingent observation timeout—A procedure that combines modeling and timeout, as the individual is removed from the group but is left near enough to observe peers demonstrating appropriate behavior.

continuous reinforcement—A reinforcement schedule where an individual is immediately rewarded each time the target behavior is successfully met.

contracture—Abnormal shortening of a muscle because of extreme lack of use or paralysis; commonly results from spastic cerebral palsy, cerebral vascular accident (stroke), or spinal cord injury (paraplegia/quadriplegia).

contraindication—Any undesirable or improper treatment (e.g., strengthening exercises for flexor muscles of involved limbs of a child with spastic cerebral palsy is contraindicated).

corrective physical education—Appropriate exercises and activities to rehabilitate deficiencies in a person's body alignment and mechanics.

criterion-referenced tests—An individual's performance of a predetermined criterion or standard compared to a specific behavior.

cultural-familial retardation—General classification of mental retardation with no biological brain damage, presumably associated with family history of borderline intelligence or mild retardation and a home environment that is either depriving or inconsistent with the general culture. It is believed to be the major cause of most individuals with mild mental retardation.

curriculum imbedded—The ongoing and continuous process of gathering data as part of the instructional phase of a program.

cytomegalovirus—An infection transmitted to the fetus while the mother is pregnant, causing a devastating generalized infection, including encephalitis. Subsequent damage to the developing brain often causes severe mental retardation.

dance therapy—Movement used as an intervention with individuals who have emotional problems requiring nonverbal therapy. Treatment emphasizes rhythmic, expressive movement as a means of establishing initial contact with persons who have lost the capacity to relate effectively with others.

developmental age—An individual's approximate age in terms of mental development regardless of chronological age.

developmental approach—Matching instruction to ability, as measured by developmental milestones.

developmental milestones—The general age range which a person is expected to perform certain movements such as walking, running, jumping, skipping, throwing, and catching.

developmental period—The time between the beginning and ending of structural growth, from conception to approximately 18 to 20 years.

developmental physical education—The development of fundamental motor patterns and components of physical fitness for students who are below the desired levels of their chronological age group peers.

direct service—Instructional opportunities provided for students with disabilities by certified teachers. Physical education is a direct service. Recreation and physical or occupational therapy are related services.

Down syndrome—A condition resulting from a chromosomal abnormality. Characteristics commonly include mental retardation (IQ generally between 20 and 55); abnormal shortness of hands, feet, trunk, arms, and legs; hyperflexibility; and frequently, congenital heart defects.

dyskinesia—*See* athetosis.

educable mentally retarded (EMR)—*See* mildly mentally retarded.

encephalitis—An acute viral infection causing high body temperature and severe inflammation of the brain. It is a common cause of mental retardation, cerebral palsy, and convulsive disorders.

epilepsy—An involuntary increase in electrical impulses in the brain, which results in seizures. It is caused by damage to the brain or by inherited factors, and is now more appropriately called seizure disorder or convulsive disorder.

equilibrium reactions—The innate ability to maintain an upright position when the center of gravity is moved suddenly out of its base of support.

etiology—The study of the causes and origins of diseases or conditions.

extinction—A behavior management technique involving removal of reinforcers. The technique may also involve removal of the individual from the activity or area.

face validity—A test item that appears to measure the ability or trait in question.

fading—Gradually removing assistance when helping a student perform a task or learn a skill.

feedback—Verbal, gesture, and/or physical consequences given immediately after the individual responds to a cue.

fetal alcohol syndrome—Defects to the developing fetus because of excessive alcohol consumption during pregnancy causing mental retardation, facial anomalies, or heart defects in the child.

flaccid paralysis—Condition characterized by extreme weakness or absence of muscle tone.

flexibility—Action of the joints to move through their full range of motion.

fragile X syndrome (Bell-Martin syndrome)—A chromosome abnormality which accounts for up to 10% of all cases of mental retardation.

functional skills—Skills that possess everyday relevance for an individual.

galactosemia—An abnormal elevation of the concentration of the carbohydrate galactose in the blood. The condition leads to death in infancy or mental retardation.

game intervention—Alternative approaches to a game which will effectively accommodate and include, rather than exclude, all participants.

goal—An annual or long-term observable behavior (e.g., to improve explosive leg power to the 30th percentile).

grand mal—A form of convulsive seizure that includes a tonic phase (stiffening), a clonic phase (violent, whole body contractions), and a recovery phase (postictal). The individual remembers or feels nothing during the seizure.

group contingency—The presentation of a highly desired reinforcer to a group of individuals based on the behavior of one person or the group as a whole. For example, the Good Behavior Game encourages the entire group to earn points toward a predetermined reward.

health related physical fitness (HRPF)—The relationship between health and physical activity as a measure of an individual's current health and potential resistance to disease.

heart murmur—A heart condition involving a backward flow of blood through defective heart valves.

hemiplegia—Paralysis of one side of the body as occurs in a cerebral vascular accident (stroke), or cerebral palsy.

home-based activity—Parents and/or siblings providing physical activity to children outside of the school physical education setting.

hydrocephalus—A condition that develops when spinal fluid accumulates in cerebral ventricles. If not immediately and continuously drained (i.e., shunted), fluid accumulation can produce enlargement of the infant's skull and possible brain damage. *See* spina bifida.

hyperactivity—A condition in children in which they always seem to be in motion. Sitting or standing for any length of time is difficult or impossible.

hyperopia—A condition where individuals have difficulty seeing close objects because the image focuses behind the retina instead of on it, also called farsightedness.

hypertrophy—Increased size or enlargement of body tissue or an organ.

hypotonia—Reduced muscle tone often found in children with Down syndrome. Infants born with this condition are commonly termed floppy babies.

hypoxia—Insufficient availability of oxygen to body tissues also called anoxia.

idiopathic—A disease or condition of unknown cause or origin.

individualized educational program (IEP)—A program specially designed to meet the educational needs (including physical and motor needs) of a specific child with disabilities.

individualized family service plan (IFSP)—A written plan of instruction based on a multidisciplinary assessment of each infant's and toddler's needs and includes an evaluation of family needs.

interrater reliability—The percentage of agreement among observers.

interval reinforcement—Schedule of reinforcement based on the individual being rewarded over a certain period of time for performance of the target behavior.

intrarater reliability—The percentage of agreement within the same observer.

intrinsic—Coming from inside the body.

isometric exercise—Muscle contraction without movement of body parts, often used in rehabilitation when movement is not necessary but muscle strength is desired, also called muscle setting.

isotonic exercise—Muscle contraction with body part movement through a range of motion.

kinesiotherapist (RKT)—In cooperation with a physician, a kinesiotherapist applies principles, tools, techniques, and psychology, of medically oriented physical education to assist individuals with various physical and mental conditions to accomplish prescribed treatment objectives in rehabilitation or habilitation programs.

kinesthesis—Awareness of body position in space as indicated by proprioceptors found in muscles, joints, and tendons.

kyphosis—Increased thoracic curve (also called humpback).

laterality—An internal awareness of both sides of the body.

least restrictive environment—The best possible learning environment for an individual with disabilities, preferably an environment shared with the nondisabled.

locomotor movements—Traversing from one fixed point in space to another such as walking, running, jumping, hopping, sliding, leaping, and skipping.

lordosis—Excessive forward curvature of the lumbar region of the spine (also called swayback), often causing lower back pain.

mainstreaming—Placing students with disabilities in traditional classes with nondisabled students.

manual communication—A communication technique, including finger spelling and sign language, used by individuals with hearing impairments.

meningitis (bacterial)—A highly contagious disease affecting the covering of the brain and spinal cord (meninges), and often leading to permanent brain and spinal cord damage.

mental age—Level of mental development measured by standardized IQ tests.

mental retardation—Significantly below average general intellectual functioning (less than 70 IQ) existing concurrently with deficits in adaptive behavior, all manifested during the developmental period.

microcephaly—A condition in which head size is abnormally small, often resulting in mental retardation.

mildly mentally retarded (EMR)—Individuals with IQ between 50 and 70, who also exhibit maladaptive behavior. Approximately 60 percent of all individuals with mental retardation are in this category.

mosaicism—A rare type of Down syndrome in which some cells have an extra chromosome and others do not, resulting in mental retardation.

model—A person who teaches another, usually through demonstration, how to perform a specific behavior.

modeling—Demonstration of a task, skill, or desirable behavior in order to teach another student.

moderately mentally retarded (TMR)—IQ between 35 and 50. Approximately 29 percent of all mentally disabled individuals are in this category. About 40 percent of individuals labeled TMR have Down syndrome.

monoplegia—Paralysis of one limb, common in cerebral palsy.

moro reflex—Protective opening and closing of an infant's arms and legs when a loud noise is heard. Also called "startle reflex."

motor activities training program (MATP)— Training and participation for individuals with severe disabilities whose limitations restrict them from successfully participating in the Official Special Olympics sports.

movement management—Structuring activities by a teacher, so they move smoothly and maintain momentum from activity to activity.

multidisciplinary model—Separate evaluations and prescriptions by different specialists assigned to identify the individual's specific problem.

muscle testing—A subjective technique used by therapists to evaluate muscle strength and performance.

muscular endurance—Ability to perform work repeatedly against a moderate resistance.

muscular strength—Ability of the body to exert force with usually one maximum effort.

myelomeningocele—The most serious type of spina bifida where the spinal cord protrudes into a sac onto the surface of the back, often causing paralysis or lower extremity impairment. Bowel and bladder control are effected. Mental retardation caused by hydrocephalus is common.

myopia—A condition where individuals have difficulty seeing far objects because the eyeball is too long from front to back and images are brought into focus in front of the retina instead of on it, also called nearsightedness.

negative reinforcement—The removal of an aversive event as a consequence of a behavior in order to increase the frequency of the behavior.

neonatal—Period between birth and 1 month.

normalization—Direct involvement of individuals with disabilities with nondisabled peers by including activities of everyday life that are consistent with the norms and patterns of mainstream society.

norm-referenced tests—The measurement of an individual's performance in relation to the performance of a representative peer group who is composed of individuals with specifically defined characteristics such as age, gender and/or specific disability.

obesity—An increase in body weight (>20%) in excess of skeletal and physical requirements as a result of an excessive accumulation of adipose tissue (fat) in the body.

object control movements—Effective and efficient movements that give and receive force from objects, such as throwing, catching, and striking.

occupational therapy—Assistance in developing the components of performance necessary to maintain an individual's self care, work, and leisure activities. Major components include the following: (a) motor functioning (range of motion, muscle strength, tone, functional use, gross and fine motor skills); (b) sensory integrative functioning (body integration, body scheme, posture, visual-spatial awareness, sensorimotor integration, reflex and sensory development); (c) cognitive functioning (verbal and written communication, concentration, problem solving, time management, conceptualization, integration of learning).

operant conditioning—The use of a consequence to increase the probability that a behavior will be strengthened, maintained, or weakened.

orthopedics—Branch of surgery that includes, but is not limited to, the practice of straightening deformed or injured body parts by use of braces or exoskeletal devices.

otitis media—Chronic inflammation of the middle ear, which can lead to hearing, balance and coordination problems.

parachute reflex—Small children's automatic protective extension of the arms when they fall suddenly forward or to the side. This reflex is often delayed in children with cerebral palsy, and is also called protective extensor thrust.

paraplegia—Loss of motor and/or sensory functions of the legs and lower trunk caused by brain damage or spinal cord injury (commonly in the lumbar region).

partners clubs—A program developed by Special Olympics International to foster mainstreaming opportunities. Junior high, high school, or college-age volunteers are trained to provide social experiences, sports skill training and competition to Special Olympians.

peer tutor—A nondisabled student who serves as an aid or ''buddy'' in order to assist a person with a disability.

percent body fat—An individual's amount of body fat often measured by skinfold thickness.

perception—Receiving sensory input and mentally converting the information to data for use or memory storage.

perseveration—Persistent repetition of a meaningless, irrelevant, or inappropriate word, phrase, or movement.

petit mal—A mild form of seizure characterized by sudden, brief blackouts of consciousness (hardly more than a few seconds long) followed by immediate recovery. Also called absence seizures, this type of seizure occurs mostly in childhood and adolescence.

phenylketonuria (PKU)—A genetic condition in which there is inability to metabolize phenylalanine. If untreated, it results in severe brain damage and mental retardation.

physical activity reinforcement—A systematic procedure where a structured time to choose among various preferred physical activities is contingent on the individual's meeting of a predetermined criterion of behavior.

physical therapy—Process that identifies, prevents, remedies, and rehabilitates acute or prolonged dysfunction in an individual. Therapists evaluate patients and treat through physical measures as opposed to medicines, surgery, or radiation.

positive reinforcer—*See* reinforcement.

positive supporting reaction—Neonatal reflex that causes the legs to extend and the feet to point downward when the young child is bounced on the feet.

Premack principle—A more preferred behavior by the individual is contingent on the successful completion of a less preferred behavior. A high probability behavior can reinforce a low probability behavior.

prematurity—Infants delivered before 36 weeks, and/or weighing 2,500 grams (5-1/2 pounds) or less.

present level of performance—A statement regarding an individual's strengths and needs based on sound assessment practices.

primary reinforcers—A reward that satisfies a biological need, such as food when hungry or a drink when thirsty.

profoundly mentally retarded—IQ between 1 and 20. Approximately 4 percent of all individuals with mental retardation are in this category, most of whom have other serious disabling conditions, including seizures. These individuals usually perform at a developmental age of less than 3 years.

prompt—A cue or stimulus, usually in the form of physical guidance, which occasions a response of a proper behavior.

protective extensor thrust—*See* Parachute reflex.

psychomotor seizures—A seizure classification characterized by inappropriate actions, irrelevant speech, and random ambulation.

Public Law 89-313 Amended Title I of Elementary and Secondary Education Act (1965)—Law providing grants for state-supported schools for students with disabilities.

Public Law 90-538 Handicapped Children's Early Education Assistance Act (1968)—Law establishing experimental preschool programs as demonstration projects of children with disabilities.

Public Law 93-112 Amendments to Vocational Rehabilitation Act (1973)—Law emphasizing provisions for most severely disabled individuals, including Section 504—the Bill of Rights for the disabled. This law assures accessibility to public buildings and programs.

Public Law 94-142 Education of All Handicapped Children Act (EHA) (1975)—Law that increased federal commitment to providing free and appropriate education for all students with disabilities (ages 3-21), in least restrictive environments. The law mandates that all needed supplementary aids and services are provided, the rights of children with disabilities and their parents are protected, and states and localities provide effective education of children with disabilities. Included were protections of due process procedures for parents and children, the individualized educational program (IEP) and evaluation, hearing rights, and appeal. Mandatory physical education is found in this law.

Public Law 98-199 Amendments to Education of the Handicapped Act (1983)—Law extending discretionary grants, established new programs for transition of secondary students into adult life, and provided financial incentives to expand services for infants and toddlers from birth to 3 years of age.

Public Law 99-457 Amendments to Education of the Handicapped Act (1986)—Law requiring that children with disabilities, ages 3 to 5, be served, even in states that do not provide public education for children that young. Part H of the law authorized funds to states to develop statewide interagency programs of early intervention services for infants and toddlers with disabilities and their families.

Public Law 101-476 Individuals With Disabilities Education Act (IDEA) (1990)—Law that changed the name of PL 94-142 and replaced the word "handicapped" with "disabled." The Infants and Toddlers with Disabilities Program, and the Preschool Program which originated as part of PL 99-457 and all other parts of the original PL 94-142 are now incorporated into PL 101-476.

punishment—The presentation of an aversive event or removal of a positive event contingent upon a response, decreasing the probability of that response.

quadriplegia—Impairment of both arms and legs.

ratio reinforcement—An individual is rewarded for performing a certain number of occurrences of the target behavior.

reciprocal style teaching—One student performs a task while another student evaluates and records that student's performance.

referral—A written request for a student to be tested.

reflexes—Involuntary muscular or neurological response to sensory stimulation.

reinforcement—A positive response or reward given by an instructor following a desired behavior, so a behavior is likely to recur.

reinforcement event menu—A list of highly desirable reinforcement items displayed for individuals to observe and attempt to earn by meeting a predetermined criterion of behavior.

related services—Special services that are needed to fulfill students' with disabilities educational, physical, emotional, or social needs. Physical, occupational, and speech therapy are examples of related services.

reliability—The consistency or stability of results that are received under similar conditions.

response cost—The withdrawal of a positive reinforcer, such as money or privileges, as a consequence of an undesirable behavior.

retardation—*See* Mental retardation.

reverse mainstreaming—Placement of nondisabled students into the self-contained setting of students with disabilities.

righting reflexes—Automatic or involuntary reaction of an infant or small child to regain original position when suddenly moved or pushed.

rigidity—Extreme stiffness, as a result of cerebral palsy, when attempting limb movement.

rubella (German measles)—In children, a mild viral infection lasting 3 to 4 days. In pregnant women during the first trimester, the infection is serious and produces fetal abnormalities including defects of the heart, brain, bones, eyes, and ears.

satiation—The elimination of the effectiveness of a reinforcer because of excessive application.

school sports partnership—A program for Special Olympians who jointly train and compete alongside nondisabled junior varsity and varsity peers on the interscholastic level.

scoliosis—Lateral deviation of the spine in the shape of an S, reverse S, C, or reverse C. Deviation can be caused either by functional or structural problems. Functional deviations may be corrected by physician-prescribed exercise. Structural deviations may require braces or surgery to correct.

screening—Initial identification of a child who appears to be displaying movement difficulties.

secondary reinforcers—Reinforcers to which an individual learns or is conditioned to respond.

sensory input—All information received by the body through the following senses: seeing, hearing, kinesthesis, and vestibular and tactual input.

sensory-motor response—A combination of sensory input, brain integration and interpretation, and motor output.

severely mentally retarded—IQ between 20 and 35. Approximately 7 percent of individuals with mental retardation are in this category and are considered dependent. These individuals function at a mental age of 3 to 5 years.

shaping—Reinforcement of small progressions that lead to a desired learner behavior.

short-term objectives—Behavioral terms that explain how individualized educational program (IEP) annual goals will be met: (a) performance/behavior, (b) condition, and (c) criteria.

shunt—A tube inserted into the brain to drain or bypass excess cerebrospinal fluid. Commonly used for treating hydrocephalus.

socially valid—Items selected are specifically important for that particular person as agreed upon by the persons who live and work with the individual.

spastic cerebral palsy—Hard, jerky, uncontrolled movements due to cerebral cortex brain damage. Increased stretch reflex and muscle contractures are common.

special/adapted physical education—An individualized physical education program for children with special needs including the components of adapted, corrective, and developmental physical education.

special education—Specifically designed public instruction that meets the unique needs of children with disabilities.

Special Olympics International (SOI)—The largest and most visible sport organization in the world for people with mental retardation.

spina bifida—A congenital opening in the vertebral column, often with the protrusion of the meninges. *See* myelomeningocele.

status epilepticus—Seizures that last for more than 30 minutes, or when one seizure immediately follows another. Most commonly associated with tonic/clonic (grand mal) seizures.

stereotyped behavior—Complex, repetitive movements that appear to be nonfunctional, especially hand movements, rocking, object twirling, or head banging; "blindisms." It is common among individuals with severe and profound mental retardation or nonverbal infantile autism.

stretch reflex—Muscle contraction as a reflex to sudden muscle movement. It is commonly found in individuals with spastic cerebral palsy.

structured dance—Dance which uses a behavioral, task analysis approach to movement.

symmetrical tonic neck reflex (STNR)—An infant reflex in which the arms flex when the head is hyperflexed, or when the head is hyperextended, the hips and legs will flex. The locomotor process of creeping becomes extremely difficult when this reflex persists beyond the normal time frame of infancy as in children with brain damage.

tactile—Pertaining to touch.

task analysis—Breaking down of a task into smaller parts.

testing—A technique to collect data using specific tools and procedures such as systematic observation.

therapeutic recreation—A helping profession that promotes wellness and improves the quality of life for individuals with disabilities through leisure activities.

time—The speed of a movement such as slow, medium, or fast acceleration and deceleration.

time-out—A behavior modification technique of excluding or removing a child from an activity for a specific period of time.

token economy reinforcement—A reward system that gives tokens, checkmarks, points, or chips for meeting a predetermined criterion of behavior and are later exchanged for items which are reinforcing and or value to an individual.

total communication—A communication technique used by the hearing impaired, which includes signing, finger spelling, speech reading, and speaking.

toxoplasmosis—A congenital infection transmitted from mother to fetus often resulting in cerebral calcification, mental retardation, seizures, hydrocephalus, or microcephaly.

trainable mentally retarded (TMR)—*See* moderately mentally retarded.

transdisciplinary model—Sharing information and cooperation among team members throughout the implementation of services.

translocation—A rare type of Down syndrome where there is an added leg of chromosomal material to the 14th, 15th, or 22nd pair, often resulting in mental retardation.

trisomy 21—The most common type (approximately 95%) of Down syndrome in which the 21st pair of chromosomes has three legs instead of the normal two, resulting in mental retardation and other distinct characteristics. *See* Down syndrome.

tympanic membrane tubes—Tubes which are inserted into the ear drums (tympanostomy) to drain excessive fluid in the middle ear, that is a result of chronic otitis media.

unified sport—A program that integrates equal numbers of athletes with and without mental retardation in such team sports as basketball and soccer.

validity—A test item that effectively measures a researcher's defined topic.

Index

453